A Dictionary of

Buddhism

A Dictionary of

Buddhism

DAMIEN KEOWN

Contributors

Stephen Hodge
Charles Jones
Paola Tinti

OXFORD
UNIVERSITY PRESS

OXFORD
UNIVERSITY PRESS
Great Clarendon Street, Oxford OX2 6DP

Oxford University Press is a department of the University of Oxford.
It furthers the University's objective of excellence in research, scholarship, and education by publishing worldwide in

Oxford New York

Auckland Bangkok Buenos Aires Cape Town Chennai
Dar es Salaam Delhi Hong Kong Istanbul Karachi Kolkata
Kuala Lumpur Madrid Melbourne Mexico City Mumbai Nairobi
São Paulo Shanghai Singapore Taipei Tokyo Toronto

Published in the United States
by Oxford University Press Inc., New York

First published 2003

British Library Cataloguing in Publication Data
Data available

Library of Congress Cataloging in Publication Data
Data available

ISBN 0-19-860560-9

1 3 5 7 9 10 8 6 4 2

Typeset in Pondicherry, India by
Kolam Information Services, Pvt, Ltd
Printed on acid-free paper by
Clays Ltd
Bungay, Suffolk

For my teachers

Preface

Buddhism is a vast subject, and not one that can be compressed into the pages of a volume such as this, even if it is the largest single-volume general dictionary of Buddhism available to date. The richness, diversity, and complexity of the Buddhist tradition escapes simple classification and the present work has no pretensions to being an exhaustive reference source. Such a project would require years of collaboration by experts in the various languages, traditions, and cultures, and would need to be continually updated. It is exciting to note that an initiative of this kind is already under way in Professor Charles Muller's *Digital Dictionary of Buddhism* (www.acmuller.net). This online dictionary for scholars of east Asian Buddhism provides an inspiring model for future digital works of reference. By contrast, the aim of the present volume is modest: it is intended simply as a handy one-volume source of reference for students and the general reader seeking a concise explanation of the various concepts, names, texts, and terms found in the rapidly growing literature on Buddhism. Although the work is not intended as an introduction to Buddhism, it does provide introductory surveys on the development of Buddhism in the main geographical regions of the world, as well as extended entries on the major schools and their teachings. As an aid to general orientation it includes maps and a pronunciation guide, and the end matter contains a guide to Buddhist scriptures and a chronology. Readers seeking a more systematic introduction to Buddhism may wish to consult my *Buddhism: A Very Short Introduction* (1996) also from Oxford University Press.

The choice of what to include and what to omit has not always been easy. With a subject as complex as Buddhism it is unwise to adopt rigid criteria—there are simply too many exceptions to any rule that could be devised. A priority has been to give due weight to all the main traditions of Buddhism, namely those of India, south-east Asia, Tibet, and east Asia. The aim has been to recognize the relative importance of each rather than allowing any one cultural region to predominate. In terms of content, the subjects featured include doctrines, practices, history, art and architecture, mythology, schools and sects, scriptures, biography, and places of interest. These categories are far from exhaustive, and some 20 per cent of the content is given over to an explanation of technical terms that escape simple categorization. In terms of content that is more readily classifiable, biography accounts for some 18 per cent, scriptures 12 per cent, important places 8 per cent, and schools and sects 7 per cent. The selection process is inevitably influenced by personal interests, and the present work includes entries on contemporary ethical issues such as abortion, euthanasia, and cloning, which reflect the author's interest in this field. While contemporary *issues* are featured, however, references to contemporary personalities, whether scholars or teachers, are rare: death is a criteria for admission in most cases. Whether this overall mix of priorities is the right one will be a matter for readers to judge.

The conventions used in the work should be self-explanatory. In each entry the first occurrence of each term for which there is a corresponding headword is indicated by an asterisk. Some of the cross-referenced entries may not always be directly relevant, but since it is not always easy to know precisely what information the user is seeking, and since an element of randomness and serendipity is not altogether undesirable in a work of reference, the system of cross-referencing used is extensive and systematic rather than minimalist. Where a particular term does not occur in the body of the entry the reader's attention is directed to the related topic by '*see*' and '*see also*'. Italicization has been kept to a minimum for ease of reading, and foreign terms are generally not italicized. The names of texts are italicized but collections or groupings of texts are not (thus *Brahmajala Sutta* but Dīgha Nikāya). Diacritics are ignored for the purposes of alphabetization. Where not otherwise indicated, dates shown are CE. The main abbreviations used are shown below.

b.	born
BCE	before the common era
Burm.	Burmese
CE	in the common era
Chin.	Chinese
d.	died
fl.	flourished
Jap.	Japanese
Kor.	Korean
r.	reigned
Skt.	Sanskrit
Tib.	Tibetan

I could not have completed this project on my own, and I must record my thanks to the scholars who collaborated with me on various parts of it. Most of the entries on east Asia were compiled by Professor Charles Jones of The Catholic University of America, and those on Tibet and some aspects of Indian Buddhism by Stephen Hodge. Dr Paola Tinti contributed a smaller number of entries on Theravāda Buddhism and south-east Asia. I am indebted to all three for their erudition and thoroughness. Most of what they contributed found a place in the dictionary at some point, if not always in its original form. I am also indebted to Charles Prebish for permission to adapt my guide to Buddhist scriptures from that in his *Historical Dictionary of Buddhism* (Scarecrow Press, 1993) and to Lance Cousins for his invaluable comments and corrections at the manuscript stage.

Throughout what became a lengthier undertaking than originally envisaged, the editors of Oxford University Press I have worked with have all been supportive and understanding as well as professional and efficient. My thanks go to Angus Phillips and Vicki Rodger, both of whom have since left the press, and to Ruth Langley who finally saw the volume through to publication. I also owe a debt of thanks to my student Katherine Holmes for her help with cross-referencing, proof-reading, and other general matters over the course of the project.

Damien Keown
London, 2002

Contents

The Dictionary 1

Appendix I: Map of India and the region where the Buddha taught and lived 347

Appendix II: Map showing Theravāda Buddhism in Asia 348

Appendix III: Map showing Mahāyāna Buddhism in Asia 349

Appendix IV: Pronunciation Guide 350

Appendix V: Guide to Buddhist Scriptures 352

Appendix VI: Chronology 355

abhabba-ṭṭhāna (Pāli, impossibility). List of nine things of which an *Arhat is said to be morally incapable. These are (1–4) breaking the first four of the Five Precepts (*pañca-śīla), (5) storing up goods, and (6–9) acting wrongly out of attachment, hatred, folly, and fear.

ābhassara (Pāli, radiant). Name of a class of *devas or heavenly beings who reside in the Form Realm (*rūpa-dhātu). Their ethereal natures are said to be suffused with joy (pīti) and love (*maitrī).

Abhayagiri. A major ancient monastic complex in *Anurādhapura, *Sri Lanka, also known as Uttaravihāra. Founded by King *Vaṭṭagāmaṇi Abhaya in the 1st century BCE it consisted of a monastery (*vihāra) and a *stūpa, but the latter alone is now standing. According to tradition, when the king was fleeing from the Tamils, he came upon the Nigaṇṭha Giri, a Jain (*see* JAINISM) *ascetic who made insulting remarks about him. The king vowed that if he were returned to the throne he would build a Buddhist monastery on the spot. He fulfilled his vow, and the name of the monastery was a combination of his own name and that of the Nigaṇṭha. It is unlikely that Abhayagiri was important for a century or two after its foundation. Unlike the *Mahāvihāra, or 'Great Monastery', erected earlier during the reign of King *Devānampiya Tissa (247–207 BCE) in the same city and given to the *Saṃgha, the Abhayagiri was given to an individual *monk. As a result, according to much later sources on which too much reliance should not be placed, a conflict developed between the monks of the Mahāvihāra and the monks of Abhayagiri, allegedly focusing on the issue of whether monks could receive gold or silver, meaning wealth in general, but actually reflecting a struggle for control of *Buddhism on the island. Though for quite a long time the fraternities of the two monasteries seem to have lived side by side in amity, when the Abhayagiri monks openly adopted an alternative canonical literature (the heretical Vaitulya Piṭaka) the animosity between the monks of the two establishments became very bitter and resulted in the heretical books being burnt and the destruction of the Mahāvihāra building. The two communities developed into separate schools, not to be united again for more than a millennium. Mahāvihāra residents were known as the Theriya school (Theriya*Nikāya), while Abhayagiri residents were referred to as the Dhammaruci school (*see* DHAMMARUCI NIKĀYA). In 1165 a council was held at Anurādhapura and reconciliation between rival schools was achieved. In contrast to the above account from the medieval chronicles, there is no actual evidence of any active conflict between the two institutions after the 3rd century CE. When Anurādhapura was abandoned around the 13th century, the history of Abhayagiri essentially ceased.

abhaya-mudrā (Skt., gesture of fearlessness). Iconographic hand gesture (*mudrā) whose purpose is to dispel fear and communicate protection, benevolence, and peace. Commonly found in representations of the *Buddha and *celestial Bodhisattvas, where the figure is usually depicted standing with the right arm bent, the palm raised and facing forwards, and the fingers joined. This gesture is rare among figures of lower status. There are many variations in which the left hand is also used, such as the double abhaya-mudrā

Fig 1 abhaya-mudrā

found in *south-east Asia, or in combination with various left-hand mudrās, although this is more common in east Asia.

abhibhāyatana (Skt.). The 'eight masteries', or eight fields of the mastery or control of perception. These are meditational exercises described in the *Pāli Canon similar to those using coloured objects (*kasiṇa) but in this case based on features or areas of one's own body as the focus of concentration in order to transcend the Desire Realm (*kāma-dhātu). The eight masteries are: (1) perception of forms (colours and shapes) externally on one's body and limited forms beyond it; (2) perception of forms externally on one's body and of unlimited external forms beyond it; (3) the non-perception of forms on one's own body and the perception of small external forms; (4) the non-perception of forms on one's body and the perception of large external forms; (5)–(8) no forms are perceived on one's own body but the colours blue, yellow, white, and red are perceived in that order. Items (5)–(8) are identical with kasiṇa exercises (5)–(8), and with the third stage of the eight liberations (*aṣṭa-vimokṣa).

Abhidhamma-avatāra. 'An Introduction to Abhidhamma', being the title of a treatise on *Abhidharma (Pāli, Abhidhamma) composed in *India by *Buddhadatta. The work is mostly in verse and comparable to the *_Visudhimagga_ of *Buddhaghoṣa, whom Buddhadatta is said to have met. Two sub-commentaries (*ṭīkās) exist, one by Vācissara Mahāsāmi and the other by Sumaṅgala.

Abhidhammattha-saṅgaha. 'A Compendium of Abhidhamma'. A summary of the essential points of *Abhidharma (Pāli, Abhidhamma) philosophy composed sometime in the 11th or 12th century by *Anuruddha, a resident of the Mūlasoma monstery in *Sri Lanka.

Abhidhānappadīpikā. A *Pāli dictionary composed in *Sri Lanka in the 12th century by *Moggallāna Thera. The book consists largely of lists of synonyms for different objects allocated to the three categories of 'heavenly', 'earthly', and 'miscellaneous'.

Abhidharma (Skt.; Pāli, Abhidhamma). Term meaning 'higher doctrine' and denoting the scholastic analysis of religious teachings. The earliest Abhidharma material was composed over several centuries beginning around 300 BCE and formed the substance of the various collections of canonical scholastic treatises (*Abhidharma Piṭaka) of the different early schools. Influential later non-canonical compendia of Abhidharma teachings include the *_Abhidharma-kośa_ of *Vasubandhu and the *_Abhidharma-samuccaya_ of *Asaṅga. The contents of the Abhidharma do not form a systematic philosophy and it is mostly devoted to classifying and analysing material contained in the *Buddha's discourses (*sūtras) using a special analytical framework and technical terminology. The fundamental doctrines discussed are those already presented in other parts of the *canon, which are therefore taken for granted. According to legend the Abhidharma was first preached by the Buddha to his mother during a visit to her in *heaven after her death. The legend also says that after his enlightenment (*bodhi) the Buddha spent a week revolving the complex doctrines of the Abhidharma in all their details in his mind.

Abhidharma-dīpa. 'Lamp of Abhidharma', being a *Sarvāstivādin *Abhidharma text of uncertain authorship, though sometimes thought to have been composed by *Vasumitra in response to *Vasubandhu's *_Abhidharma-kośa_. The text, comprising verse and prose commentary, survives in a unique incomplete *Sanskrit manuscript. The text is important because it confirms the identity of the author of the _Abhidharma-kośa_ with the *Mahāyāna *Yogācāra scholar-*monk Vasubandhu.

Abhidharma-kośa. 'Treasury of Abhidharma', a key *Abhidharma text in verse written by *Vasubandhu and summarizing *Sarvāstivādin tenets in eight chapters with a total of about 600 verses. The verses are then commented on in the accompanying *bhāṣya or 'exposition' (_see_ ABHIDHARMA-KOŚA-BHĀṢYA). The subjects covered include all the main topics of *Abhidharma philosophy, and a refutation of the views of the rival school of the *Vaibhāṣikas is given at many points in the commentary. As well as the original *Sanskrit, translations exist in Tibetan, Chinese, and Mongolian, and also in English and French.

Abhidharma-kośa-bhāṣya. *Vasubandhu's auto-commentary to his *_Abhidharma-_

kośa in which he criticizes the interpretations of the *Vaibhāṣikas and others of the tenets he presented in that work. His critique is made from the *Sautrāntika standpoint. This commentary includes an additional chapter in prose refuting the idea of the 'person' (*pudgala) as held by some Buddhists. The nine chapters in the work deal with what is perceived (*dhātu), the sense-faculties (*indriya), the world (*loka), *karma, the proclivities (*anuśaya), the Noble Ones (*ārya-pudgala), knowledge (*jñāna), meditation (*samādhi), and refutation of the concept of a self (*anātman). A large number of sub-commentaries on this text have been preserved in Tibetan translations.

Abhidharma Piṭaka (Skt., basket of higher doctrine). The last of the three divisions of the corpus of Buddhist canonical literature known as the *Tripiṭaka (Pāli, Tipiṭaka) or 'three baskets'. The fact that the Abhidharma is not mentioned in the *sūtras (where only the first two divisions of *Dharma and *Vinaya are referred to) proves that at one time the Abhidharma Piṭaka did not form a separate section of the *canon. The contents probably had their origin in lists of key terms abstracted from the sūtras known as *mātṛkās. Only two complete Abhidharma collections have survived, those of the *Theravāda and the *Sarvāstivāda schools. The Theravāda Abhidharma (Pāli, Abhidhamma) consists of seven books: **Dhammasaṅgaṇī*, **Vibhaṅga*, **Kathāvatthu*, **Puggalapaññatti*, **Dhātukathā*, *Yamaka*, and **Paṭṭhāna*. Commentaries in *Pāli exist on these seven books, as does an exegetical work on the whole *piṭaka by the title of *Abhidhamma Mūlaṭīkā*, compiled by Ānanda Vanaratanatissa of *Sri Lanka. The seven books of the Sarvāstivāda Abhidharma, which survive mainly in Tibetan and Chinese, are the *Saṃgītiparyāya*, *Dharmaskandha*, *Prajñaptiśāstra*, *Vijñānakāya*, *Dhātukāya*, *Prakaraṇapāda*, and **Jñāna-prasthāna*.

Abhidharma-samuccaya. An *Abhidharma text composed in prose by the *Yogācārin scholar-monk *Asaṅga. Largely *Mahāyāna in orientation, the treatise conforms in structure to the pattern of traditional Abhidharma texts. This work, available in a partial *Sanskrit manuscript as well as Chinese, Tibetan, and Mongolian translations, traditionally functioned as the main Abhidharma text for Mahāyāna Buddhists.

abhijjhā (Pāli, covetousness). One of a range of terms used to denote sensory attachment. It is synonymous with craving (*tṛṣṇā) and *desire (*lobha).

abhijñā (Skt.; Pāli, abhiññā). Supernormal knowledge or supernatural cognition, normally acquired through the development of the power of *samādhi or meditative trance. Up to six forms are recognized: clairvoyance, clairaudience, knowledge of the minds of others, miraculous abilities, knowledge of past lives, and knowledge of the cessation of the 'outflows' (*āśravas).

abhimāna (Skt.). Conceit or arrogance, an aspect of the major *kleśa pride. Abhimāna is characterized by the arrogant posturing that one has achievements which one does not actually possess.

abhimukhī-bhūmi (Skt.). The sixth of the *Bodhisattva Levels (*bhūmi). According to the **Daśabhūmika Sūtra* it means 'the level which is present or turned towards', and is so-called because at this level the Bodhisattva has gained an understanding of the emptiness (*śūnyatā) and sameness of all phenomena through the cultivation of the Perfection of Insight (*prajñā-pāramitā), and has resolutely turned towards enlightenment (*bodhi). *See also* PĀRAMITĀ.

Abhirati. The eastern Buddha-field or *Pure Land associated with the *Buddha *Akṣobhya and described in the *Akṣobhya-tathāgatasya-vyūha Sūtra*. Though the focus of some devotional interest in early *Mahāyāna, Abhirati did not achieve the popularity of the Pure Land of *Sukhāvatī.

abhisamaya (Skt.). Direct and clear understanding or realization of the *Dharma.

Abhisamaya-alaṃkāra. 'The Ornament of Direct Realization', a text in nine chapters with a total of 273 verses ascribed to *Maitreyanātha. The work summarizes the topics covered by the *Pañca-viṃśati-prajñā-pāramitā Sūtra* while arranging them in an ordered sequence corresponding to the *Mahāyāna path. Though highly influential in later Mahāyāna in *India and *Tibet, the text seems to have been unknown in *China.

abhiṣeka (Skt.; Tib., dbang-bskur). Literally 'sprinkling', this is an initiatory ritual of consecration in *tantric *Buddhism based on the classical Indian ceremony of coronation which involved lustration. Typically, a practitioner has the empowerment bestowed at the time of entry into a sacred circle (*maṇḍala) and is cleansed of impurities and thus empowered or authorized to study and practise the tantras. Several kinds of empowerment are known according to the tantric level involved, with an increasing number as one moves higher. Empowerment at the level of the *anuttara-yoga-tantras usually involves four stages: the jar empowerment, the secret empowerment, the insight empowerment, and the so-called 'fourth empowerment'.

abhūta-parikalpa (Skt., the process of imagining or projecting what is unreal). A key *Yogācāra concept describing the function of the 'other-dependent' or 'relative' (*paratantra) nature (*svabhāva) by which the false dichotomy of a perceiving subject (grāhaka) and perceived object (grāhya) is superimposed upon experience and results in the 'imagined' (*parikalpita) nature (*svabhāva). *See also* PARATANTRA, GRĀHYA-GRĀHAKA, PARIKALPITA.

abortion. Abortion as a moral problem is not discussed at length in Buddhist literature. However, there are sufficient references in the *Pāli Canon and other ancient sources to indicate that the practice was regarded as gravely wrong. Buddhist disapproval of abortion is related to its belief in *rebirth and its teachings on embryology. It is widely held that conception marks the moment of rebirth, and that any intentional termination of pregnancy after that time constitutes a breach of the first of the Five Precepts (*see* PAÑCA-ŚĪLA). Broadly speaking, this continues to be the avowed view of most Buddhists, although this position is not always reflected in the abortion statistics in Buddhist countries. In the more conservative countries of *south-east Asia abortion is generally illegal unless there is a threat to the mother's life. Illegal abortions, however, are common, with an annual figure of perhaps 300,000 per annum in *Thailand. In certain east Asian countries abortions are even more numerous, and a figure of one million per annum or greater is sometimes cited for countries such as *Japan and South *Korea. In Japan a memorial service known as *mizuko kuyō has evolved as a response to the large number of abortions carried out in recent decades.

absolute mind. A common English translation of the Chinese *T'ien-t'ai (Jap., *Tendai) term yi hsin, which may be more literally rendered '*One Mind'.

acalā-bhūmi (Skt.). The eighth of the Bodhisattva Levels (*bhūmi), 'the Unshakeable One', according to the **Daśabhūmika Sūtra*. Here the *Bodhisattva engages in the Perfection of Aspiration (*praṇidhāna) through which he aspires to attain what remains to be accomplished. This stage (or sometimes the preceding one) is characterized as 'avaivartika' (Skt., no turning back) since once a Bodhisattva reaches this stage he cannot backslide in his progress and his attainment of perfect enlightenment (*saṃbodhi) is guaranteed. *See also* PĀRAMITĀ.

ācān. *See* AJAHN.

ācariyamuṭṭhi (Pāli, the teacher's fist). Term denoting close-fistedness or secrecy on the part of a teacher who keeps things back and does not reveal all he knows to his students. It is reported in the **Mahāparinibbāna Sutta* that shortly before his death the *Buddha declined a request by *Ānanda that he should make a statement concerning the future regulation of the monastic order. He stated that since he had no 'teacher's fist' and had never made any distinction between 'inner' (secret) and 'outer' (public) teachings there was nothing more for him to reveal before his death.

ācārya (Skt.). A teacher or religious preceptor. In later *Buddhism the term comes to be associated particularly with teachers of tantra. *See also* AJAHN.

access concentration. *See* UPACĀRA-SAMĀDHI.

acinteyyāni (Pāli). Term denoting matters which are incomprehensible or unfathomable. These are commonly divided into four 'spheres' (visaya) concerning matters relating to the nature of (1) the *Buddha; (2) the meditative absorptions (*dhyāna); (3) *karma and karmic retribution; and (4) the world (loka-cintā), particularly concerning whether it had a first beginning. Brooding on these four questions is said to be unproductive and unprofitable.

Aciravatī (Skt.). A river flowing near ancient *Śrāvastī, the present-day Rapti. It is one of the five great rivers flowing from the *Himalayas eastwards into the sea, and there are many references to it in early literature. The *Tevijja Sutta* of the *Pāli Canon was preached on its southern bank in a mango grove where the *Buddha often resided. It also had many bathing places where monks (*bhikṣu) and *brahmins used to bathe. Nuns (*bhikṣunī) were forbidden from bathing in those places on the river where courtesans bathed naked.

acquired enlightenment. A concept which is found in the *Mahāyāna treatise the **Mahāyāna-śraddhotpāda Śāstra* (*The Awakening of Faith in the Mahāyāna*) referring to the enlightenment (*bodhi) that one acquires as the result of religious training. It is paired with the term 'original enlightenment', which is inherent in all things and signifies their subsisting clear and pure nature. Together, these two terms define a soteriology that sees beings as perfected and liberated as they are, and needing religious practice only to realize that this is so.

Adam's Peak. Mountain in *Sri Lanka sacred to many religious traditions. At the top there is a footprint that is variously said to belong to Adam, the Hindu god Śiva, the apostle Thomas, and the *Buddha. In *Pāli sources the mountain is known by various names, such as Samantakūṭa and Samantagiri, and it is said that the Buddha left his footprint there when he descended from the sky on his third visit to the island. The site has been a shrine and an important *pilgrimage centre since ancient times.

adbhuta-dharma (Skt.; Pāli, abbhuta-dhamma). A marvellous or strange phenomenon. The term is used especially to designate one of the nine classes of Buddhist scriptures (nava-aṅga-buddha-śāsana) which comprises, as the term suggests, those *sūtras dealing with various wondrous or miraculous events that occurred during the *Buddha's life.

adhicitta (Pāli, higher mental training). The meditative training undertaken by those following the *Eightfold Path. It relates particularly to the second of the three divisions of the Path, namely meditation (*samādhi). *See also* ADHIŚĪLA; ADHIPRAJÑĀ.

adhigama-dharma (Skt.). The *Dharma as personal realization or as the content of enlightenment (*bodhi). Used in contrast with *Āgama-dharma, or the Dharma as a body of knowledge transmitted through the scriptures.

adhimokṣa (Skt.). Inclination, devoted interest; a mental factor that involves openmindedness and a trusting willingness to become involved in something, especially the *Dharma.

adhiprajñā (Skt.; Pāli, adhipaññā). Literally, 'higher understanding'. The doctrinal training undertaken by those following the *Eightfold Path. It relates particularly to the third of the three divisions of the Path, namely insight (*prajñā). *See also* ADHICITTA; ADHIŚĪLA.

adhiśīla (Skt.; Pāli, adhisīla). Literally, 'higher morality'. The doctrinal training undertaken by those following the *Eightfold Path. It relates particularly to the first of the three divisions of the Path, namely Morality (*śīla). *See also* ADHICITTA; ADHIPRAJÑĀ.

adhiṣṭhāna (Skt.). A transformative power, especially associated with *Buddhas, which is used miraculously to transmute or manifest phenomena. The *Pāli adhiṭṭhāna is the power of will which enables one to control the duration of trance (*samādhi) or (later) manifest a particular result of psychic power.

ādi-Buddha (Skt.). The primordial *Buddha, a term only found in late *Mahāyāna and Tibetan traditions of *tantric *Buddhism, possibly not attested in Indian Buddhism but generated through hyper-Sanskritization (*see* SANSKRIT). The Buddha in question is usually identified as *Samantabhadra in Tibetan Buddhism (*see* TIBET), and it is said that it is from his nature that both *nirvāṇa and *saṃsāra arise.

adveṣa (Skt.). Literally 'non-hatred' but really closer in meaning to love or benevolence. One of the three roots of good (*kuśala-mūla).

Āgama (Skt.). One of the four sections of the *Sanskrit Buddhist *canon that coincide with those of the *Pāli Canon. Thus the Sanskrit *Dīrgha Āgama corresponds to the Pāli

*Dīgha Nikāya; the *Madhyama Āgama to the *Majjhima Nikāya; the *Samyukta Āgama to the *Saṃyutta Nikāya, and the *Ekottara (or Ekottarika) Āgama to the *Aṅguttara Nikāya. The equivalence between these collections is broad but not exact. Note there is no reason to suppose that there was ever a single 'Sanskrit Canon'. The *Sarvāstivādins had a canon in Sanskrit but so did the *Lokottaravādins and presumably other schools. Others again may have had canons in various forms of Middle Indian, such as Gandhārī. It is not known how many of these schools had an equivalent to the fifth *Nikāya of the *Pāli Canon, namely the *Khuddaka Nikāya, but none survives in Sanskrit. The term āgama is used by Buddhaghoṣa in Pāli interchangeably with *Nikāya. Almost certainly the introduction of the term āgama is a later development with the growth of Sanskrit cultural hegemony.

Āgama-dharma (Skt.). The *Dharma as transmitted through the Buddhist scriptures, used in contrast to *adhigama-dharma, or the Dharma as experientially understood.

Aggañña Sutta. The 27th *sutta of the *Dīgha Nikāya. An influential early discourse notable for its narration of a creation myth which explains the stages through which the universe and human society are said to evolve at the start of each new *kalpa or cosmic cycle. The myth describes how beings at this stage are ethereal but, motivated by greed, begin to consume matter and gradually acquire denser bodies. In due course there occurs sexual differentiation and procreation, and human societies organized on *caste lines come into being. Due to greed, wickedness arises and a king is elected to enforce the law. The purpose of the story is to refute the *Brahmin tradition (*see* BRAHMANISM) that their caste enjoys an intrinsically privileged status due to being created from the mouth of *Brahmā. In contrast, moral conduct is declared to be more important than lineage. The first part of the story is also recounted in the **Mahāvastu*.

āgantuka-kleśa (Skt.). Adventitious vices or negative emotions, a concept associated with the notion of the embryonic *Buddha (*tathāgata-garbha) in *Mahāyāna *Buddhism. According to the tathāgata-garbha teachings, the minds of beings are intrinsically pure due to the inherent presence of the potentiality for enlightenment (*bodhi) or *Buddha-nature. This potentiality is temporarily obscured by mental obscuration, such as vices and other negative mental phenomena, which, however, are 'adventitious' since they are temporary obscurations that can be removed.

Aggavaṃsa. A *monk of the region of *Pagān in *Burma who lived in the 12th century. He composed a *Pāli grammar in 1154.

Aggregates. *See* SKANDHA.

Agonshū. Modern Japanese Buddhist sect founded by Seiyū Kiriyama, who claims that the *Bodhisattva *Kannon (Skt., *Avalokiteśvara) appeared to him in 1970 and taught him new techniques to overcome the effects of negative *karma manifesting in the present life. According to Agonshū teachings, many of the misfortunes experiences in daily life are attributable to the actions of *evil spirits, and the karmic ties to the malevolent spirits (normally spirits of the dead) must be cut if the misfortunes are to cease. To this end, followers engage in *ascetic practices such as mass rites of purification, as well as chanting, meditation, and the worship of Kannon, with the aim of cutting off the evil karma (Jap., karuma). The name of the sect derives from the *Sanskrit word *Āgama, being the body of canonical literature containing the *Buddha's teachings.

āhāra (Pāli, nutriment). Four kinds of 'food' in the literal and figurative senses listed in *Pāli sources. These are: (1) solid food that nourishes the body (kabaliṅkārāhāra); (2) sensory and mental impressions (phassa) which are the support of pleasant, unpleasant, and neutral feelings; (3) mental volitions (mano-sañcetanā) which produce *karma; (4) consciousness (viññāṇa, Skt., *vijñāna) as the condition of mind and body (*nāma-rūpa) at conception.

ahiṃsā (Skt., non-harming, non-violence). Moral principle of non-violence and respect for life found in many strands of Indian religion but particularly emphasized in the *śramaṇa schools such as *Jainism and *Buddhism. It was on the basis of ahiṃsā that the heterodox schools opposed the practice of *animal sacrifice central to *Brāhmanism. The principle is pre-Buddhist and probably dates back to the Upaniṣads. It finds expression in Buddhist *ethics in many moral codes, but particularly as the first of the Five Precepts (*pañca-śīla) which prohibits 'onslaught on living creatures' (pāṇātipāta). The principle is not simply a negative one but also enjoins sentiments of benevolence, love, or compassion (*karuṇā) towards living things. In *Mahāyāna Buddhism the principle is widely interpreted as requiring a vegetarian diet (*see* DIET).

ahosi-kamma (Pāli). In *Theravāda *Buddhism, name given to *karma (Pāli, kamma) that is past, expired, or spent and will bear no further *phala or fruit.

ajahn. Also sometimes spelt ācān. Thai term deriving from the *Sanskrit word *ācārya, and meaning a teacher or instructor, often of *meditation.

Ajaṇṭā. The site of a series of 28 artificial cave temples, a number with carvings and murals of great beauty, located along a cliff face in the Indhyadri hills of eastern Mahārāṣṭra. Work on these caves began before 250 BCE but was abandoned until *c.*450 CE when *Mahāyāna-orientated monks (*bhikṣu) resumed settlement and enlargement. The caves were abandoned during the 7th century CE and lay undisturbed until their accidental rediscovery in 1819 by British army officers.

Ajapāla-nigrodha. A banyan tree not far from the *Bodhi Tree, located in *Uruvelā on the banks of the *Nairañjanā river. The *Buddha spent a week meditating under it shortly after his awakening and revisited the spot many times in his life. It is the site where the god *Sahampati interceded with the Buddha to teach the *Dharma, and also where the devil *Māra tried to persuade him not to, and instead to enter *nirvāṇa immediately after his awakening.

ajari (Jap.). Term deriving from the *Sanskrit word *ācārya and meaning a senior *monk who is qualified to take disciples, teach novices, and conduct *ordinations. In *Japan, such monks might also serve as liaisons with the imperial government. The name was also applied to masters in the esoteric lineages of *Tendai and *Shingon who were qualified to take disciples and conduct esoteric rituals.

Ajātaśatru (Skt.; Pali, Ajātasattu). Second encumbent of the throne of *Magadha which he secured by killing his father, *Bimbisāra. Initially a follower of *Devadatta, Ajātaśatru was at first hostile to the *Buddha and conspired with the former to kill him. Subsequently he repented and became a devout follower. An encounter between the two is narrated at length in the **Sāmaññaphala Sutta* of the *Dīgha Nikāya, where the king describes his dissatisfaction with the teachings of the *Six Sectarian Teachers. When the Buddha died in the eighth year of his reign, the king was disconsolate. Ajātaśatru reigned for 32 years and was himself deposed and killed by his son Udāyin (or Udayabhadra).

Ajitakesakambala. One of the *Six Sectarian Teachers who were contemporaries of the *Buddha. His teachings are described in the **Sāmaññaphala Sutta* of the *Dīgha Nikāya as a form of nihilism which holds there is no such thing as good and evil, and that the individual is annihilated at death. Elsewhere, however, he is represented as believing in *rebirth. His name means 'Ajita of the hair blanket' due to his habit of wearing an uncomfortable and evil-smelling blanket of human hair.

Ājivakas (Skt.). A heterodox sect founded by *Makkhali Gosala, a contemporary and rival of the *Buddha. Makkhali was for six years the itinerant companion of the Jain (*see* JAINISM) leader *Mahāvīra, before they parted company after a disagreement. There are similarities in the practices of both sects: initiation (*abhiṣekha) is by tearing out the hair, and the lifestyle is one of extreme austerity involving nakedness, penances, and ordeals. In matters of belief, however, they differ: whereas the Jains, along with the Buddhists, accept the doctrine of *karma, the Ājīvakas denied the existence of free will. Makkhali compared the course of a human life to a ball of string which, when thrown down, rolls along unwinding in a preordained course until it reaches its end. At the time of the Buddha the Ājivakas were an important sect and remained so for several hundred years. After this they declined, and by late medieval or early modern times had disappeared altogether, perhaps reabsorbed into Jainism or the south Indian devotional cults in which Makkhali enjoyed an ephemeral deification.

Akaniṣṭha (Skt.). The highest of the eighteen *heavens in the Form Realm (*rūpa-dhātu), at the very limit of form-bearing existence. At times, Akaniṣṭha is also used in the sense of the entire universe in its pure aspect, comprising all the *Buddha-fields of the ten directions.

ākāra (Skt.). In Buddhist psychology, a perceptual image, constructed by the mind (*manas) from the input of perceptual forms (*nimitta). Through this psychological mechanism a stable and structured view of the world is created.

ākāśa (Skt.). Space. In the *Abhidharma taxonomies it is defined as the container within which the four 'great elements' (*mahābhūta) of earth, water, fire, and air find expression. Generally it is said to be of two kinds: limited by corporeality (in other words the space between objects), and unlimited or infinite. In some Abhidharma systems it is classified as one of the unconditioned (*asaṃskṛta) phenomena (*dharma). Space is often used in *Mahāyāna literature as a simile for the mind in its natural state, since the unlimited expanse of space, which is nothing in itself, is characterized by purity, immutability, and *emptiness, and yet it acts at the same time as the 'container' or support for all phenomena without distinction.

akiriya-vāda (Pāli). The doctrine (vāda) that there are no consequences to moral acts. This doctrine was taught by many of the *Buddha's contempories, including the *Six Sectarian Teachers (with the exception of the *Jain leader *Nigaṇṭha Nātaputta). The teaching of akiriya-vāda is contrary to the belief in *karma, and was condemned by the Buddha for this reason. His own teachings belong in the category of *kiriya-vāda doctrines.

akṣara (Skt.). A syllable, letter, or phoneme, especially of *Sanskrit. In *tantric *Buddhism these syllables often constitute a hidden code with mystical significance known only to initiates.

Akṣobhya (Skt.). The 'Immovable One', one of the five *Jinas, normally depicted iconographically as a blue, or sometimes white, *saṃbhoga-kāya *Buddha associated with the eastern quarter. He is also viewed as the embodiment of Mirror-like Awareness, one of the five awarenesses (*pañca-jñāna), and as the lord of the Vajra Family (*see* FIVE BUDDHA FAMILIES). Early *Mahāyāna devotion to Akṣobhya is associated with a belief in his *Pure Land, known as *Abhirati.

akuśala (Skt.; Pāli, akusala). The opposite of *kuśala. Term of moral disapproval used of wrongful or unwholesome deeds or thoughts. In particular, the term denotes the defilements (*kleśas) and actions which breach the various Buddhist moral codes such as the Five Precepts (*pañca-śīla).

akuśala-mūla (Skt.; Pāli, akusala-mūla). Collective name for the three roots of evil, being the three unwholesome mental states of greed (*raga), hatred (*dveṣa), and delusion (*moha). All negative states of consciousness are seen as ultimately grounded in one or more of these three.

akusō (Jap.). Monks (*bhikṣu) who during the *Heian period abandoned the religious life to become renegades, warriors, and mercenaries.

akusu-kū (Jap, wrong understanding of emptiness). In *Zen *Buddhism, a mistaken notion of emptiness (*śūnyatā) which regards it as nothingness. Correctly understood, however, śūnyatā is not the the mere negation of existence but the true nature of phenomena. According to the **Heart Sūtra*, 'form is not other than emptiness, and emptiness is not other than form'.

ālambana (Skt., foundation, basis). A cognitive object; anything functioning as the objective support or basis of perception, whether in normal states of consciousness (*vijñāna) or during meditation. There are six such objects, corresponding to the traditional Indian classification of the six senses, namely the objects of sight, sound, smell, taste, touch, and ideation. The first five are classified as material in form, while the sixth may be physical or mental, as well as past, present, or future. *See also* ĀYATANA.

Āḷāra Kālāma One of the *Buddha's first two teachers, the other being *Udraka Rāmaputra. After renouncing the world the Buddha became Āḷāra's student. The precise nature of Āḷāra's teachings is unclear, but they involved a meditational practice which enabled one to reach a profound state of trance known as the 'sphere of nothingness' (Pāli, akiñcaññāyatana), later equated with the seventh *dhyāna of classical Buddhist meditation theory. Before long the Buddha surpassed his teacher and took leave of him to continue his religious quest. Āḷāra died shortly before the Buddha achieved enlightenment (*bodhi).

ālaya (Skt.). **1.** Basis, substratum; sometimes used simply as an abbreviation for the *Yogācāra concept of the 'storehouse consciousness' (*ālaya-vijñāna) but also found in Tibetan Buddhist usage as a distinct concept in the sense of the 'ground of being'. These two aspects of the term thus distinguish the ontological and epistemological aspects of the ālaya-vijñāna. **2.** The term also occurs in a non-philosophical sense as a synonym of *tṛṣṇā, meaning attachment, clinging, or *desire.

ālaya-vijñāna (Skt.). The eighth consciousness, being the substratum or 'storehouse' consciousness according to the philosophy of the *Yogācāra school. The ālaya-vijñāna acts as the receptacle in which the impressions (known as *vāsanā or *bīja) of past experience and *karmic actions are stored. From it the remaining seven consciousnesses arise and produce all present and future modes of experience in *saṃsāra. At the moment of enlightenment (*bodhi), the ālaya-vijñāna is transformed into the Mirror-like Awareness or perfect discrimination of a *Buddha.

almsgiving. *See* DĀNA.

alobha (Pāli, non-greed). The absence of craving and attachment. One of the three roots of good (*kuśala-mūla).

amala-vijñāna (Skt.). The 'unsullied consciousness', a term used in *Paramārtha's system of *Yogācāra and equivalent in many repects to *Buddha-nature or the *tathāgata-garbha.

Amarakośa. A *Sanskrit verse dictionary of synonyms arranged by subject matter, composed by *Amarasiṃha.

Amarapura Nikāya. One of the three major *Nikāyas (monastic lineages) of modern *Sri Lanka, taking its name from the city of Amarapura in *Burma with which it is associated. It broke off from the Syāma Nikāya in 1803. Its founder, Ñāṇavimalatissa *Thera, wishing to extend *ordination to *monks other than those of the gogama *caste, originally intended to travel to *Thailand but went instead to Burma where ordination was conferred on him and five others in Amarapura. Within a few years of his return to Sri Lanka, the Amarapura Nikāya subdivided into a number of groups, differing from one another by region and the caste of the monks.

Amarasiṃha. The Indian Buddhist author of the **Amarakośa*. His dates are uncertain but he is unlikely to have flourished before the 5th century CE.

Amarāvatī. An early Buddhist monastic site, associated with the *Mahāsaṃghika school, in eastern Andhra Pradesh near the Kṛṣṇā river with settlements dating from 2nd century BCE. The main *stūpa was built and enlarged over several centuries until the 3rd century CE. The final stūpa is estimated to have been 138 feet in diameter and 100 feet in height. Much of the structure was covered with richly carved bas-reliefs and sculptures. The stūpa is thought have been been intact until the late 18th century CE but was later plundered for building materials. A series of excavations over the past hundred years have yielded many reliefs, inscriptions, and artefacts.

amarāvikkhepika (Pāli). An 'eel-wriggler', or disputant who uses sophistry to avoid stating a definite position on an any issue. An example of such a philosopher is *Sañjaya Belaṭṭhaputta, one of the so-called *Six Sectarian Teachers who were contemporaries of the *Buddha. His views are briefly summarized in the **Sāmaññaphala Sutta* of the *Dīgha Nikāya.

Ambapālī. A beautiful and wealthy courtesan of *Vaiśālī who became a follower of the *Buddha. She was named after the mango fruit (Pāli, amba) because she was reputed to have been found at the foot of a mango tree. It is narrated in the **Mahāparinibbāna Sutta* that Ambapālī invited the Buddha to dine at her house on his last visit to Vaiśāli before his death. He accepted the invitation, declining a similar one from the local princes. Ambapālī donated to the *Saṃgha a residence constructed in her garden. She had a son who became an elder in the Order (*Saṃgha) and she herself eventually renounced the world, gained insight into impermanence (*anitya) through contemplating the ageing of her own body, and became an *Arhat.

Ambedkar, Bhimrao (1891–1956). Charismatic leader of the outcastes or 'untouchables' of *India. Born into the *caste of the Mahar untouchables, Ambedkar converted to *Buddhism on 14 October 1956 at Nagpur. He regarded Buddhism as the religion most capable of resolving the problems of caste that in his view had plagued India down the centuries. Across India thousands of untouchables followed his example as a protest against their social exclusion. Today almost all the Mahars of Maharashtra regard themselves as Buddhist.

America. In Latin America *Buddhism has made little headway. In north America and Canada, however, its impact has been great, particularly in recent decades, and all the major Asian schools and traditions of Buddhism are now represented. The first Buddhist institution in north America was a temple built in San Francisco in 1853 in order to serve the needs of immigrant Chinese labourers. The spread of Buddhism over the next hundred years was largely due to the arrival of immigrant groups from various parts of Asia, culminating in a wave of refugees from Indo-China in the wake of the Vietnam War. Many Tibetan lamas fled to north America following the Chinese invasion of *Tibet in 1959, and Tibetan Buddhism currently enjoys a high profile. Apart from immigrants, many Westerners have converted to Buddhism and influenced the pattern of its development. This group, typically white and middle-class, favours democratic as opposed to hierarchical structures for Buddhist groups and a greater role for *women. It is also more concerned with social and political issues. The number of Buddhists in the United States is currently estimated at around 3–5 million. The situation overall in north America remains fluid as Buddhism continues to adapt itself to Western customs.

Amida. The Japanese pronunciation of the name of the *Buddha *Amitābha or *Amitāyus. This Buddha serves as the primary object of devotion and agent of salvation for the various schools of *Pure Land *Buddhism in *Japan, such as the *Jōdo Shū, the *Jōdo Shinshū, and the *Jishū. *See also* WU-LIANG-SHOU FO.

Amidism. An English term sometimes used to refer to Japanese *Pure Land *Buddhism as a whole, as opposed to individual schools such as the *Jōdo Shū, the *Jōdo Shinshū, and the *Jishū. *See also* CHING-T'U TSUNG.

Amis du bouddhisme. A society for the promotion of *Buddhism founded in Paris in 1929 by the American Buddhist Constant Lounsbery.

Amitābha (Skt.). The *Buddha 'Infinite Light', also known as *Amitāyus (Infinite Life). One of the five *Jinas, he is normally depicted iconographically as a red *saṃbhoga-kāya Buddha associated with the western quarter. He is also viewed as the embodiment of Discriminating Awareness, one of the five awarenesses, and as the lord of the Lotus Family (*see* FIVE BUDDHA FAMILIES). Early *Mahāyāna devotion to Amitābha gave rise to a belief in his *Pure Land, known as *Sukhāvatī.

Amitābha Sūtra. The standard short title for the *Smaller *Sukhāvatī-vyūha Sūtra*, one of the three major scriptures of the *Pure Land school.

Amitāyurdhyāna Sūtra. The putative *Sanskrit title of one of the three major scriptures of the *Pure Land school in east Asia. No Sanskrit text is known to exist, and the text exists only in Chinese and in central Asian languages that are clearly translations from the Chinese. This has led scholars to conclude that the text was not composed in *India, and so the Sanskrit title as given above is a hypothetical reconstruction from the Chinese title *Kuan wu-liang-shou fo ching*. Whether this scripture originated in one of the oasis kingdoms along the *Silk Road or in *China itself is still a subject of speculation among scholars. The Chinese 'translation' is attributed to Kālayaśas between the years 424 and 442 CE.

The principal concern of this *sūtra is to lay out a system of sixteen graded visualizations, the first thirteen of which will enable the practitioner to attain a direct vision of the *Buddha *Amitābha, his *Bodhisattva attendants, and his land. These visualizations include features of the Pure Land such as the setting sun, the western region surrounded by pure undisturbed water, the ground, the jewelled trees, the eight jewelled ponds, and so forth. The text counsels that these visualizations need to be supported by firm faith (*śraddhā) and ethical practices, defined as filiality, respect for and support of teachers, compassion (*karuṇā), and the ten good actions (*daśa-kuśala-karmapatha). Furthermore, they are to be nourished by three mental dispositions: the mind of utmost sincerity, the profound mind, and the aspiration for *rebirth in the Pure Land. With these supporting conditions, the practitioner will have a vision of Amitābha that demonstrates *karmic links to him of sufficient strength to lead to rebirth in the Pure Land.

At the opposite end are the inferior of the inferior, those who have led vicious lives and committed even the so-called 'five heinous deeds' (*ānantarya karma), which would ordinarily disqualify one from attaining Buddhahood. With only the exception of those who have slandered the teachings, these are people who, on their deathbeds, have a premonition of the horrors of *hell awaiting them but, on account of hearing Pure Land teachings in this time of crisis, call upon Amitābha with deep conviction and distress, and are saved by him. These attain the Pure Land, but only make the outer borders of it and spend hundreds of aeons working toward Buddhahood. However, even they are assured of reaching the fruits of non-retrogression and will never return to the evil paths of *saṃsāra again. Thus, although this sūtra is primarily concerned to teach a highly complex meditative discipline as a way to attain *rebirth, it is also the *locus classicus* for the passages that allow for the widest possible access to rebirth for all of humanity.

The last three of the sixteen visualizations are not actually objects of contemplation per se, but rather doctrinal issues relating to the types of beings who can achieve rebirth in the Pure Land and what their accomplishments will be. These include: those of the superior grade, those of the middling grade, and those of the inferior grade. Each of these grades is further subdivided into levels of superior, middling, and inferior, making a total of nine. Those at the highest represent the paragons of Buddhism, practitioners of deep doctrinal understanding, unblemished ethical conduct, unbounded compassionate action, and profound meditative attainments. They will have an immediate vision of Amitābha upon rebirth in the Pure Land and will attain Buddhahood almost instantly.

Amitāyus (Skt.). 'Boundless life', an alternative name for the *Buddha *Amitābha, though perhaps originally used as a epithet for him. He is often depicted with a *begging-bowl containing the elixir of immortality.

Amoghasiddhi (Skt.). 'He of infallible accomplishment', one of the five *Jinas. Normally depicted iconographically as a green *saṃbhoga-kāya *Buddha associated with the northern quarter, he is also viewed as the embodiment of the All-accomplishing Awareness, one of the five awarenesses, and as the lord of the Action Family (*see* FIVE BUDDHA FAMILIES). He is said to have a *Pure Land of his own but this attracted little devotional interest in *India or elsewhere.

Amoghavajra (705–74). A native of south *India, Amoghavajra is considered the sixth *patriarch of *esoteric *Buddhism in *China. He was also a prolific translator. He became a Buddhist novice at the age of 13, arrived in *Lo-yang two years later, in 720, and received full *ordination there in 724. He studied esoteric rituals and texts with *Vajrabodhi until the latter's death in 741, at which time he left China and spent five years travelling in India and *Sri Lanka, collecting new texts which he brought back to China in 746. His skills as a rainmaker and the effectiveness of his amulets in protecting the emperors assured his livelihood in the capital, and he devoted a great deal of time and energy to translating the texts he had brought back to China. In 771 he presented a petition to the throne asking that 77 scriptures in 101 scrolls that he had translated be added to the *canon of scriptures. His disciple Hui-kuo became his successor and the seventh patriarch of esoteric Buddhism, and Hui-kuo in turn recognized *Kūkai, who ultimately transmitted the esoteric teachings to *Japan and founded the *Shingon (or Mantra) school there.

amoha (Pāli). 'Non-delusion.' One of the three roots of good (*kuśala-mūla).

amṛta (Skt., deathlessness). In Indian mythology a drink of the gods conferring immortality, similar to the Greek *ambrosia*. It comes to be used as a synonym of *nirvāṇa as 'the deathless', since one who has attained nirvāṇa has escaped from the cycle of birth and *death (*saṃsāra).

anāgāmin (Skt.; Pāli). Literally 'non-returner, never-returner', the third of the four Noble Persons (*ārya-pudgala). The title designates one who has attained the stage before the last in breaking the bonds which prevent one from becoming an *Arhat. After *death the anāgāmin will be reborn not as a human being but in one of the highest *heavens and there will obtain Arhatship.

anagārika (Pāli). Term meaning 'one who does not inhabit a house'. Before and during the time of the *Buddha the term indicated those who had left home to live a more *ascetic life and therefore became an epithet of a Buddhist monk. The term was adopted by *Anagārika Dharmapāla of *Sri Lanka in the 20th century to denote the intermediate role between layman and monk introduced by him. The term indicates someone without home or family ties who nevertheless lives in the world, as opposed to the isolation of a monastery.

Anagārika Dharmapāla (1864–1933). Also known as Venerable Devamitta Dharmapāla. Born in 1864 as David Hevāvitārana, he was the founder of '*Protestant Buddhism'. Born into a Buddhist family, he was educated at Christian mission schools. In 1880 he came into contact with theosophy and after renouncing his European name, he moved to their Society headquarters, near Madras, where he studied *Buddhism and learned *Pāli. Once he returned to *Sri Lanka he became manager of the Buddhist *Theosophical Society, which he left in 1890. In the following years he travelled extensively, making Buddhists in different Asian countries aware of each other and promoting Buddhism in the West. In 1891 he founded the *Mahabodhi Society, whose primary goal was to regain control of the site of the Buddha's *enlightenment (*Bodhgayā) and to sponsor Sinhala Buddhist monasteries outside Sri Lanka. He was exiled in 1915 for political activities and ended his days as an ordained member of the *Saṃgha. *See also* ANAGĀRIKA.

Ānanda. One of the *Buddha's chief disciples and his first cousin, his father being a brother of *Śuddhodana, the Buddha's father. It appears that he entered the Order (*Saṃgha) in the second year of the Buddha's ministry and was ordained by the Buddha himself. According to the *Pāli accounts, after twenty years in which he did not have the same personal attendant all the time, the Buddha made known his wish for a permanent one. All the great disciples offered their services, but Ānanda, not initially seeking the position, was eventually selected by the Buddha. He agreed to serve the teacher, provided a series of conditions were fulfilled. On one hand Ānanda requested not to receive any extra benefits as a result of his position, such as choice clothes or food, separate lodgings, or the inclusion in the invitations accepted by the Buddha. On the other hand, he asked to be allowed to accept invitations on behalf of the Buddha, to bring to the Buddha those who came to see him from afar, to place before the Buddha all his perplexities, while the Buddha was to repeat to him any doctrine taught in his absence.

Ānanda was highly regarded by his colleagues who often consulted him and it is said that sometimes the monks, having heard a sermon from the Buddha, would ask Ānanda to give them a more detailed exposition since he had a reputation of being able to explain the doctrine clearly. Ānanda's championship of the cause of *women is also well known. In particular, he is especially recognized for his role in the establishment of an order of *nuns. Ānanda was also revered for his powerful memory. For this reason, when the First Council was called in *Rājagṛha (*see* COUNCIL OF RĀJAGṚHA), following the Buddha's *death, he was chosen by *Mahākāśyapa, president of the Council, to recite all of the sermons preached by the Buddha, thus establishing the canonical record known as the *Sūtra Piṭaka, or 'Basket of Discourses'. Ānanda lived to be very old, spending his last years teaching and preaching. The details of his death are not reported in the *Pāli Canon.

Ananda Metteya (1872–1923). British Buddhist, born Charles Henry Allen Bennet, who subsequently adopted the surname McGregor, possibly under the influence of McGregor Mathers or because it was the name of a foster-parent. Bennet was inspired to seek *ordination as a monk (*bhikṣu) after reading Sir Edwin *Arnold's poem *The Light of Asia*. He travelled to *Sri Lanka and *Burma, and received the higher ordination in Burma in 1902 at which point he took the name Ānanda Metteya. The following year he founded the International Buddhist Society (Buddhasāsana Samāgama) in Rangoon, and later opened a branch in England.

Ānanda Temple. A temple in *Pagān, *Burma, constructed by Kyanzittha who ascended the throne of Pagān in 1084. The temple, possibly intended as a funerary monument for its builder, is constructed in the form of a cross with four receding terraces and two receding curved roofs. It is crowned by a śikhara or central spire. In the centre of the interior an enormous cube rises up to the spire and bears on each face a colossal figure of the *Buddha with his hands in the gesture (*mudrā) of teaching. According to *The *Glass Palace Chronicle of the Kings of Burma* the temple is intended to represent the cave of an ascetic in the Himalayas.

ānantarya-karma (Skt.; Pāli, ānantariya-kamma). 'Actions with immediate retribution', the name given to five gravely wrong deeds that are said to result in *rebirth in *hell in the next life. They are parricide, matricide, killing an *Arhat, wounding a *Buddha, and causing a *schism.

ānāpāna-sati (Pāli, mindfulness of the breath). One of the oldest and most basic meditation techniques for attaining *dhyāna or trance. The technique involves merely paying attention to the movement and duration of the breath in the course of inhalation and exhalation. It is the preliminary exercise in establishing the four Foundations of Mindfulness (*smṛti-upasthāna).

Anāthapiṇḍika. A wealthy financier (seṭṭhi) of *Śrāvastī who became a leading lay follower of the *Buddha. He was converted on his first meeting with the Buddha and became a *śrotāpanna. His name means 'feeder of the destitute' and he was renowned for his generosity towards the *Saṃgha. He bought a park near Śrāvastī and constructed a famous *monastery known as the *Jetavana for use by the Buddha and his monks. In the course of time he gave away all his wealth and, predeceasing the Buddha, was said to be reborn in *heaven.

anātman (Skt.; Pāli, anattā). Non-self, the absence of self (*atman); the key Buddhist doctrine that both the individual and objects are devoid of any unchanging, eternal, or autonomous substratum. It is one of the three 'marks' (*lakṣaṇa) or attributes of all compounded phenomena (the other two being *anitya and *duḥkha). Some Buddhist schools, such as the *Vātsīputrīya and the tradition associated with the *Nirvāṇa Sūtra*, did accept the existence of some form of the self, often identified with *Buddha-nature.

Anatta-lakkhana Sutta. A discourse preached five days after the *Buddha gave his *first sermon, the *Dhamma-cakkappavattana Sutta*. The *Anatta-lakkhaṇa Sutta* teaches the doctrine of the five aggregates (*skandha) and explains that no self (*ātman) is to be found in any of them.

Anawrahtā. Also spelt Anorahta, being a Burmese variant of the *Pāli form Aniruddha (or Anuruddha). Name of the king of *Burma who reigned 1040–77 and who played an important role in the promotion of *Buddhism and the consolidation of the country. Following his conversion to *Theravāda Buddhism he sought to turn his capital *Pagān into a centre for the religion, a goal he realized after a series of military victories which in due course served to unite the country.

Anesaki, Masaharu (1873–1949). Professor of Japanese Literature and Life at Harvard University and Professor of the Science of Religion at Tokyo Imperial University, he was *Japan's leading writer on Japanese religious history. His writings on *Shintō and Japanese *Buddhism, especially *Nichiren Buddhism, as well as his general works on Japanese religion, formed some of the earliest scholarly reports on Japanese religious life to become available in the West.

Aṅga. Once a small independent kingdom, located within present-day eastern Bihar, it was absorbed into the *Magadhan Empire by King *Bimbisāra.

aṅgirasa. An occasional epithet of the *Buddha in *Pāli sources. The name derives from an ancient tribe to which, according the Vedic tradition (*see* VEDA), the Buddha's clan (*Gautama) was related.

Angkor Wat. Temple complex in *Cambodia located over 190 miles to the north-west of Phnom Penh and less than 1 mile south of the royal town of Angkor Thom. Founded by Jayavarman VII, the Temple was dedicated to the Hindu god Viṣṇu by king Suryavarman II, who reigned between 1131 and 1150 CE. The name Angkor comes from the *Sanskrit word nagara, meaning 'town'. The temple was constructed over a period of 30 years, and illustrates some of the most beautiful examples of *Khmer and Hindu art. The temple is a huge pyramid structure covering an area of about 200 acres and surrounded by a vast moat. Along the causeway leading to the enormous entrance gate are balustrades shaped as giant serpents, which are believed to represent emblems of cosmic fertility. Angkor Wat consists of a towering complex of terraces and small buildings that are arranged in a series of three diminishing storeys and surmounted by five towers believed to represent the five peaks of Mt. *Meru, the home of the gods and centre of the Hindu universe. The roofed and unroofed structures are covered with bands of finely carved stone sculptures. The walls are covered with carved reliefs that illustrate Hindu mythology, principally scenes relating to the god Viṣṇu. The mass of bas-relief carving is of the highest quality and constitutes the longest continuous bas-relief in the world. At the start of the 13th century, the Angkor and the Khmer empire started to decline and Angkor Wat was turned into a Buddhist temple. Eventually the area, covered in thick jungles, became isolated from the rest of the country. Angkor Wat was then rediscovered by Western scholars in 1860 and a restoration programme begun. Very little damage has been done to the complex as a result of the bloody civil war that terrorized Cambodia in the second half of the 20th century, though many Buddhist monks who lived in the Angkor temples were massacred. Today, archaeologists from all over the world are actively involved in the restoration process of the temples, although theft of artefacts from the extensive site for sale on the black market is a continuing problem.

ango (Jap; Chin., An-chü). In Chinese and Japanese *Buddhism, this is a three-month period of retreat for Buddhist clerics (*see* MONK; NUN). It is usually held during the summer, but can be held in winter as well. In monasteries that observe the retreat, the clergy will not be allowed to venture out of the grounds without permission, and will be expected to spend more time on personal cultivation, *meditation, copying scriptures, attending lectures, and other activities of this kind.

Aṅgulimāla. The son of a Brahmin and a notorious and feared bandit who was converted in a famous encounter with the *Buddha. His name, which means 'garland of fingers', derived from his macabre practice of cutting off a finger from each traveller he killed and stitching them into a garland which he wore around his neck. When only one short of his goal of 1,000 fingers, Aṅgulimāla saw his mother entering the Jālinī forest and prepared to attack her. To prevent this the Buddha intercepted Aṅgulimāla and converted him. Following his conversion Aṅgulimāla became a *monk and was completely rehabilitated. However, at times his presence in the *Saṃgha caused tension with local people and he was subject to assaults and abuse, which the Buddha explained as the effect of bad *karma caused by his earlier evil deeds. On account of these problems the Buddha introduced a rule prohibiting the *ordination of outlaws. In due course Aṅgulimāla became an *Arhat.

Aṅguttara Nikāya. The fourth division of the *Sūtra Piṭaka of the *Pāli Canon, consisting of eleven sections (nipātas) and 9,557 *suttas. It consists of short discourses arranged to a numerical system, probably as an aid to memory. Set out in order are first the units, then the pairs, the triads, and so forth, up to groups of eleven. This method of arrangement has possibly influenced the subject matter as well, as most of the discourses follow a stereotyped formulaic presentation and one seldom finds in it any reasoned arguments. Many of the discourses can be found elsewhere in the *canon. It is said that, when the *Buddha's religion fades away, the first portion of the Sūtra Piṭaka to disappear will be the Aṅguttara Nikāya from the eleventh section to the first, and in that order. The commentary to the Aṅguttara Nikāya, known by the title of **Manorathapūraṇī*, was composed by *Buddhaghoṣa in the 5th century. A subcommentary to the first seven chapters, by the title of *Sāratthamañjūsā*, was composed in the 12th century.

animals. Because of its belief in *rebirth, the Buddhist view of animals is more sympathetic than the traditional Western one. The fact that human and animal forms are seen as interchangeable leads to a greater feeling of kinship between them. For this reason, together with the ethical principle of *ahiṃsā, many Buddhists are vegetarians (*see* DIET). At the same time it is recognized that humans and animals are by no means equal. An animal rebirth is lower on the hierarchical scale (*see* SIX REALMS OF REBIRTH) and to be reborn as an animal is seen as a great misfortune and due to the accumulation of bad *karma.

animitta (Skt.; Pāli). The absence of perceptual attributes (*see also* NIMITTA).

anitya (Skt.; Pāli, anicca). Impermanence, the first of the three marks (*trilakṣaṇa) which characterize all conditioned phenomena. A fundamental tenet of *Buddhism is that all formations (*saṃskāra)—things that come into being dependent on causes and conditions—are impermanent. Impermanence refers to the arising, passing away, changing, and disappearance of things that have arisen, and according to the *Abhidharma is a process that takes place from moment to moment. It is because of the impermanence of the five aggregates (*skandha) that Buddhism teaches there can be no eternal self or soul (*see* ANĀTMAN). For the same reason it is thought that there can be no permanent happiness in *saṃsāra, because situations constantly change and in time all things decay (*see* DUḤKHA).

anjin (Jap.). **1.** In east Asian *Buddhism, a general term for a mind that is settled and unmoving. **2.** In *Jōdo Shinshū thought, the mind that calls upon *Amida *Buddha with complete confidence that he will provide passage to the *Pure Land after death.

Aññāta-Koṇḍañña. One of the eight *Brahmins called upon due to his skill in physiognomy to predict the future career of the infant *Buddha. Aññāta-Koṇḍañña predicted that the child would renounce the world and become an enlightened teacher. When this happened he himself renounced the world with a group of four others and gained enlightenment (*bodhi) on hearing the **Anatta-lakkhaṇa Sutta* preached.

Annen (d. between 889 and 898). Early *Tendai thinker and esoteric practitioner who revised the traditional Chinese *T'ien-t'ai system of doctrinal classification in order to accommodate *esoteric or *tantric practice.

annihilationism. *See* UCCHEDA-VĀDA.

An Shih-kao (d. 170 CE). A Parthian *monk who migrated to *China in 148 and settled in the capital of *Lo-yang. He set himself to the task of translating Buddhist texts into Chinese, according to some accounts producing over 30 translations in the 22 years remaining to his life. Much of his output consisted of *meditation texts.

antara-bhāva (Skt.). The state of intermediate existence between lives, lasting up to 49 days, between *death and an ensuing *rebirth. This concept is not accepted by all schools of *Buddhism: in general, it is accepted by *Mahāyāna schools while is rejected by the *Theravāda. It also forms the core of the Tibetan Book of the Dead (Tib., **Bar-do thos-grol*) teachings where the state is seen as an opportunity for achieving liberation from rebirth.

anukampā (Pāli). Term which literally means 'trembling along with'. It denotes sympathy, or identification with the *suffering of others, and is a sentiment closely related to compassion (*karuṇā).

anumāṇa (Skt.). Inference. In Buddhist logic (*pramāṇa), a term used for the process of inference and proof by means of reasoning and syllogistic logic. Two aspects are distinguished: (1) inference for one's own benefit (svārtha-anumāṇa), which refers to private internal processes of valid reasoning; (2) inference for another's benefit (parārtha-anumāṇa), or the formal process of public proof of a thesis using standard syllogistic logic.

anupādiśeṣa-nirvāṇa (Skt., nirvāṇa without remainder; Pāli, anupādisesa-nibbāna). Final *nirvāṇa, the entry into nirvāṇa that occurs at *death, at which point according to Buddhist teachings *rebirth ceases and personal existence comes to an end. Also known as *parinirvāṇa or skandha-parinirvāṇa, meaning the cessation of the five *skandhas or aggregates. Final nirvāṇa is to be distinguished from 'nirvāṇa in this life' (*sopādhiśeṣa-nirvāṇa), in which the individual continues to live as a normal human being as before.

anupaśyanā (Skt., contemplation; Pāli, anupassanā). A process of investigation or analysis designed to help overcome habitual and erroneous perception. For example, instead of regarding phenomena as stable and permanent one trains the mind to see that their true nature is to be impermanent; instead of regarding them as causing happiness, one comes to see them as a cause of *suffering (*duḥkha), and so forth. The ultimate goal is to see things as they really are (*yathābhūta) rather than how they appear to be. A sevenfold list of such exercises is commonly found.

Anurādhapura. City of *Sri Lanka located in the northern part of the country which, from around the 4th century BCE, was the capital of the island. According to legend the city was founded by King Paṇḍukābhaya. It is the site of important historical monasteries such as the *Mahāvihāra, the *Abhayagiri, and the *Jetavana. It is here that the branch of the original *Bodhi Tree brought to the island by *Sanghamittā was planted to become what now is popularly believed to be the oldest tree in the world. In the 10th century CE, because of repeated attacks from *India, the capital was moved to Polonaruva. Ordinations of south-east Asians were still being carried out in the 13th and 14th centuries, but the city was abandoned as a monastic site after its destruction by the Portuguese. It probably remained a pilgrimage centre for some time but was not reclaimed from the jungle until the 19th century.

Anuruddha. 1. Eminent disciple and cousin of the *Buddha renowned for his loyalty and affection. Anuruddha became an *Arhat and was renowned for his magical powers (*ṛddhi) and ability to forgo sleep. He was present at the Buddha's death and played a leading role in the first council (*see* COUNCIL OF RĀJAGṚHA). **2.** Singhalese *monk of the late medieval period and author of the **Abhidhammattha-saṅgaha*, a famous compendium of *Theravāda *Abhidharma teachings. He also composed the *Paramattha-vinichaya* (Determination of Ultimate Truth) and the *Nāma-rūpa-pariccheda* (Analysis of Name and Form).

anuśaya (Skt.; Pāli, anusaya). 'Outflows', or latent negative tendencies that lie dormant in the mind. Seven are recognized in early Buddhist psychology. In *Pāli they are known as: *desire (kāma-rāga), aversion (paṭigha), speculative views (diṭṭhi), doubt (vicikicchā), pride (*māna), craving for existence (bhava-rāga), and ignorance (avijjā). These factors are the dormant predisposing conditions for corresponding forms of manifest conduct (paryuṭṭhāna) which are symptomatic of mental and emotional turbulence. Until the underlying anuśaya is eradicated, the harmful dispositions will subsist as personality-traits. According to Buddhist psychology these dispositions are carried over to the next life and exist even in the newly born infant. On the path to enlightenment (*bodhi) they are eradicated in a particular sequence with the disappearance of the last two marking the attainment of Arhatship (*see* ARHAT).

anuśrava (Skt., hearsay, tradition; Pāli, anussava). Teachings handed down by word of mouth typically through a lineage of revered masters. The term is used by both Buddhists and *Brahmins, the latter group often being criticized by the *Buddha for their slavish adherence to the authority of tradition and reluctance to think for themselves.

anussati (Pāli, recollection). Group of six or ten objects said to be especially worthy of contemplation. Through meditating on these things the three roots of evil (*akuśala-mūla) can be destroyed. The list of ten is: (1) the *Buddha, (2) the *Dharma, (3) the *Saṃgha, (4) morality (*śīla), (5) generosity (*dāna), (6) the gods (*deva), (7) death, (8) the body, (9) the breath, and (10) peace.

anuttara-yoga-tantra (Skt.; Tib., bla-na-med-pa'i rgyud). A modern Sanskritized form (*see* SANSKRIT), unattested in original Indian texts, of the term commonly used to indicate the highest or 'supreme' form of the four classes of tantras and their associated practices according to the *New School (gsar-ma) of *tantric *Buddhism in *Tibet. Historically, the tantras deemed to be anuttara-yoga in orientation are considered to be the latest to have been developed and compiled in *India, possibly between the early 8th and the 11th century CE, although traditionally they were considered to have been promulgated during the lifetime of *Śākyamuni and then concealed until they later re-emerged in the human world. Three categories of anuttara-yoga-tantras are distinguished by Tibetan exegetes: *Father Tantras, *Mother Tantras, and *Non-dual Tantras. Father Tantras, as typified by the **Guhya-*

samāja Tantra, emphasize the so-called *generation phase (utpatti-krama) of meditative transformation; the Mother Tantras, typified by the **Hevajra Tantra*, the completion phase (saṃpanna-krama); the Non-dual Tantras, typified by the **Kālacakra Tantra*, which combines both the generation and the completion phases. Practices associated with many tantras of this class involve sexual *yoga, fierce rites of destruction, and other antinomian forms of behaviour and hence are treated with great secrecy, to be taught only to those who have received the appropriate initiations (*abhiṣeka).

anuvyañjana (Skt.). A secondary or minor characteristic of a great person or 'superman' (*mahāpuruṣa). There are said to be 80 in all. These include features of the bodily grace and beauty of such a person, for example, perfectly formed and proportioned limbs, elegance of gait, a melodic voice, and auspicious signs on the palms of the hands and soles of the feet. Several versions of the full list occur although the specific attributes and the order of the items vary. On the 32 major marks of a great person, *see* DVĀTRIṂŚADVARA-LAKṢAṆA.

anuyoga (Skt.). The fifth level of *tantric teachings according to the *Nyingma school, equivalent in some respects to the *Mother Tantra class of the *New Schools. The tantric texts that form this category are unique to the Nyingma school.

Apabhraṃśa. An early medieval Indian language of colloquial origins used widely in northern *India after the 5th century CE by some Buddhists, and which later contributed to the development of such languages as Bengali and Oriya. A number of late Buddhist tantras and tantric songs (*doha) have survived in this language.

Apadāna. (Pāli). Literally 'life history, legend'. The thirteenth book of the *Khuddaka Nikāya of the *Sūtra Piṭaka division of the *Pāli Canon. It is a work containing 547 biographies of monks and 40 biographies of *nuns, all mentioned as having lived at the time of the *Buddha. In addition to these, there are two introductory chapters, the Buddhāpadāna and the Paccekabuddhāpadāna, dealing with the Buddha and the Paccekabuddhas (Skt., *Pratyekabuddha) respectively. Despite this, the work contains no account of *Gautama Buddha's life or of any of his previous lives as a *Bodhisattva. In the same way, the Paccekabuddhāpadāna contains no biography of the Paccekabuddhas. The commentary on the *Apadāna* is known as the **Visuddhajanavilāsinī*.

Aparagoyāna. Mythical continent located to the west of Mt. *Meru and said to be populated by human beings who live outdoors and sleep on the ground. Due to the clockwise rotation of the sun over the four mythical continents, sunrise in Aparagoyāna coincides with midday in *Jambudvīpa, the southern continent coinciding with the known world at that time.

Aparānta. The ancient region of western *India, covering much of present-day Gujarat and Mahārāṣṭra. *Buddhism flourished in this region, particularly in the area of the coastal towns of Bharukaccha (Broach) and *Valabhī until Arab military expansion and civil disorders virtually eliminated the Buddhist presence there. It derives its name from a legend that the first settlers came from *Aparagoyāna. *Aśoka is said to have dispatched missionaries to this region after the Third Council (*see* COUNCIL OF PĀṬALIPUTRA II).

apāya (Skt.). Collective name for the four unfortunate realms of *rebirth, namely those of *animals, hungry ghosts (*preta), demons, and hell-beings. *See also* SIX REALMS OF REBIRTH.

apramāda (Skt.; Pāli, appamāda). 'Nonheedlessness'; the virtue of conscientiousness or diligence in all one's activities. It is said to be the foundation of all virtuous qualities.

apratisaṃkhyā-nirodha (Skt.). A state of trance known as 'unconscious cessation' that arises during meditation but which is uninformed by insight (*prajñā). In the *Abhidharmic systems of the *Sarvāstivāda and *Yogacāra schools it is classified as an 'unconditioned' (*asaṃskṛta) dharma.

apratiṣṭha-nirvāṇa (Skt.). Literally, 'unlocalized nirvāṇa'. The *Mahāyāna concept of the ideal state of *nirvāṇa. It is said to be 'unlocalized' because in this state a *Buddha does not dwell exclusively in either *saṃsāra or nirvāṇa. By virtue of his great insight (*prajñā) and awareness (*jñāna) he does not dwell in saṃsāra, and because of his great compassion (*karuṇā) he does not disappear into final nirvāṇa.

apsaras (Skt.). Celestial nymphs who dwell in the *heaven of the god *Indra.

ārāma (Pāli). Site or residence occupied by a monastic community during the rainy season.

araṇya (Skt.). A forest or wilderness. Remote and uninhabited places of this kind are praised in many Buddhist texts as the ideal environment for renunciates to practise the *Dharma.

āraṇya-vāsī (Skt.). A forest-dweller; name given to *monks who choose to emulate the lifestyle of the *Buddha and the early *Saṃgha by dwelling in sparsely populated rural areas. The term especially applies to those who observe the stringent austerities known as *dhutangas. Forest-dwelling monks who practise *meditation as opposed to devoting themselves to the study of texts have always existed and may have played a greater part in the formation of the early *Mahāyāna than has hitherto been appreciated. After having been of minor importance for many centuries, the tradition of living in seclusion has been revived with considerable success in certain *south-east Asian countries such as *Thailand.

arciṣmatī-bhūmi (Skt.). The fourth of the six or ten Bodhisattva Levels (*bhūmi). According to the **Daśabhūmika Sūtra*, its name means 'the Flaming One', because at this level the *Bodhisattva engages in the Perfection of Strenuousness (*vīrya-pāramitā) with the radiant light of awareness. *See also* PĀRAMITĀ.

argha (Skt.). A type of offering used in *tantric rituals, often comprising of water mixed with flowers, leaves, and rice.

Arhat (Skt., worthy one; Pāli, arahant). One who has attained the goal of enlightenment or awakening (*bodhi). Essentially, Arhatship consists in the eradication of the outflows (*āśrava) and the destruction of the defilements (*kleśa). The Arhat is also free of the ten fetters (*samyojana), and on death is not reborn. The difference between an Arhat and a *Buddha is that the Buddha attains enlightenment by himself, whereas the Arhat does it by following the teachings of another. It should be noted, however, that the Buddha is also an Arhat and is frequently addressed as such in invocations such as the *Pāli formula 'Namo tassa Bhagavato Arahato Sammāsambuddhassa' (Homage to the Lord, the Worthy One, the Perfectly Awakened One). As taught in early *Buddhism, the Arhat attains exactly the same goal as the Buddha. *Mahāyāna Buddhism, however, comes to regard Arhatship as an inferior ideal to that of Buddhahood, and portrays the Arhat (somewhat unfairly) as selfishly concerned with the goal of a 'private *nirvāṇa'. In contrast, emphasis is placed on the great compassion (mahākaruṇā) of the Buddhas and *Bodhisattvas who dedicate themselves to leading all beings to salvation.

Ariyapariyesanā Sutta. 'The Discourse of the Noble Quest'. An early *sūtra (Pāli, sutta) that contains biographical information on the early part of the *Buddha's life. In it, the Buddha narrates his search for enlightenment (*bodhi) from the time of his studentship with *Āḷāra Kālāma and *Udraka Rāmaputra down to his preaching of the *first sermon.

Ariyavaṃsa. A *Pāli text, compiled in *Sri Lanka, about the life-histories of eminent members of the Buddhist *Saṃgha. It is read aloud publicly for the edification of the people, a practice that seems to have been a regular feature at gatherings in Buddhist temples on feast days.

Arnold, Sir Edwin (1832–1904). British literary figure who composed the influential poem *The Light of Asia* published in 1879. The poem describes the life and teachings of the *Buddha in a melodramatic style and became very popular with Victorian audiences. Himself a Christian, Arnold saw much in common between Christianity and *Buddhism. He became Principal of Deccan College, Poona, *India, at the age of 25 and as well as composing poetry translated texts from *Sanskrit and authored a Turkish grammar. He visited *Bodhgayā in 1885 and campaigned for funds to restore it from its dilapidated condition.

artha (Skt.). **1.** aim, object, goal, purpose. **2.** an object of perception. **3.** meaning, significance.

artha-kriyā (Skt.). 'Capable of producing effects'; a definition used in Buddhist epistemology (*pramāṇa) to distinguish objects that really exist from illusory ones.

ārūpya (Skt.; Pāli, arūpa). Formless; a term used to qualify various states and divine beings (*deva) that lack any matter or form that may be apprehended by the five senses.

ārūpya-dhātu (Skt.; Pāli, arūpa-dhātu). The Formless Realm; the most subtle of the three levels of existence (*triloka) according to Buddhist *cosmology. This realm is totally devoid of all materiality and *suffering. It comprises four states: boundless space (ākāśa-anantya), boundless consciousness (vijñāna-anantya), nothingness (ākiñcanya), and neither-ideation nor non-ideation (naivasaṃjñā-nāsaṃjñā). Birth in these states is achieved through mastery of one of the four corresponding attainments (*samāpatti) but despite the extremely tenuous nature of existence in this realm, it still forms part of *saṃsāra and beings residing there will eventually return to lower states of existence when the force of their merit (*puṇya) or good *karma is exhausted.

Āryadeva. An early 2nd-century CE *Madhyamaka master, and the foremost disciple of *Nāgārjuna. Born in southern *India or *Sri Lanka, he composed a number of commentaries on the works of Nāgārjuna as well as independent works, the most famous of which is the *Catuḥśataka* (four hundred verses).

ārya-mārga (Skt., noble path; Pāli, ariya-magga). Particularly in early *Buddhism, the fourfold supermundane (*lokottara) level of training leading to *nirvāṇa. Each path has its own fruit (*phala), namely the four attainments of the stream-winner (*śrotāpanna), the once-returner (*sakṛdāgāmin), the non-returner (*anāgāmin), and the *Arhat. Those who have not attained any of these paths are known as 'ordinary folk' (*pṛthagjana). In *Mahāyāna Buddhism, a scheme of five paths is more common. *See* MĀRGA.

Āryans. Collective name of a group of Indo-European tribes that migrated from central and northern *Europe (or possibly Asia Minor or the southern steppes—the precise location is uncertain) around the start of the second millennium BCE, possibly due to ecological or climatic changes and the need to seek new pastures for their animals. Whether the tribes belonged to a single ethnic group is unclear, but even if they did, the Indo-Aryan languages they spoke, of which *Sanskrit is a descendant, may have ceased to be associated with any defined racial type at an early age. Two main routes of migration were followed: one to western Europe, and the other to Iran (which derives its name from the word Āryan), and *India. In India, the Āryans colonized the northern part of the country and according to some accounts subjugated the indigenous Dravidian peoples, who came to comprise the lowest of the four *castes of Āryan society, although this claim is controversial. The religious beliefs of the Āryans are recorded in ancient Hindu scriptures written in Sanskrit known as the *Vedas, and involved the worship (*pūja) of a plurality of divine beings, many of whom are personifications of natural phenomena such as the sun, moon, and atmospheric phenomena like lightning, thunder, and storms. In *Buddhism, the term Ārya is used in the sense of 'noble' or 'venerable', and takes on a specific meaning in connection with the 'noble ones' who have attained various stages of spiritual progress. *See* ĀRYA-MĀRGA; FOUR NOBLE TRUTHS.

ārya-pudgala (Skt.; Pāli, ariya-puggala). A 'noble person', one who is at any stage of the Noble Path (*ārya-mārga). There are four such persons, namely the stream-winner (*śrotāpanna), the once-returner (*sakṛdāgāmin), the non-returner (*anāgāmin) and the *Arhat. According to an alternative sevenfold grouping found in *Pāli sources individuals enter the Noble Path in different ways according to their personal disposition. In terms of this the noble disciples are classified as: (1) one who follows in faith (saddhā-anusārin); (2) one liberated by faith (saddhā-vimutta); (2) one who witnesses with the body (kāya-sakkhi); (4) one liberated both ways (*ubhato-bhāga-vimutta); (5) one who follows in the *Dharma (dhamma-anusārin); (6) one who has attained to vision (diṭṭhippatta); (7) one liberated by insight (paññā-vimutta). Thus the Noble Path may be attained through faith (as with the first), or through an intellectual grasp of the teachings (as with the fifth). One may also enter it and reach fruition on the basis of both (as with the fourth).

ārya-saṃgha (Skt., noble community). The community of the āryas or those 'noble persons' (*ārya-pudgala) who have attained the supermundane path (*ārya-mārga). This is the *Saṃgha referred to in the formula of the three refuges (*triśaraṇa), and is distinct from the broader Buddhist community including laymen and laywomen.

ārya-satya (Skt., noble truth; Pāli, ariya-sacca). *See* FOUR NOBLE TRUTHS.

āryāṣṭaṅga-mārga (Skt.). *See* EIGHTFOLD PATH.

aśaikṣa-mārga (Skt.). The path of 'no more learning', the last of the five paths to Buddhahood (*pañca-mārga), when all defilements (*kleśa) and perverse views about the knowable—such as a belief in an inherent, permanent self (*ātman)—are overcome. It is at this point one becomes enlightened as either an *Arhat or a *Buddha.

Āsāḷha Pūjā. *Festival held in *Theravāda countries to commemorate the *Buddha's *first sermon in the *Deer Park. The festival takes its name from the fact that the sermon was thought to have been delivered on the full moon night of the month of Āsāḷha. In *Sri Lanka the festival is known as the *Esala Perahera.

asaṃskṛta (Skt.). The 'unconditioned', a term referring to anything that transcends conditioned (*saṃskṛta) existence in the state of *saṃsāra. The number of items deemed to be unconditioned varied according to the *Abhidharmas of different schools of *Buddhism. Most commonly, three items were counted: the cessation (or liberation) arising through insight (*pratisaṃkhyā-nirodha), the cessation not arising through insight (*apratisaṃkhyā-nirodha), and space (*ākāśa).

āsana (Skt.). A yogic posture which provides a seat for meditational practice. The most common example is the '*lotus posture' (padmāsana) in which both feet rest on top of the thigh of the opposite leg.

Asaṅga. Along with *Maitreyanātha, the historical co-founder of the *Yogācāra school of *Mahāyāna *Buddhism and half-brother of *Vasubandhu. Born in north-west *India during the 4th century CE, he was originally a member of the *Mahīśāsaka school but was later converted to Mahāyāna. After many years of intense *meditation, he went on to write many of the key Yogācāra treatises such as the **Yogacārabhūmi Śāstra*, the **Mahāyāna-saṃgraha* and the **Abhidharma-samuccaya* as well as other works. There are discrepancies between the Chinese and Tibetan traditions concerning which treatises are attributed to him and which to Maitreyanātha.

asaññasattā (Pāli, unconscious beings). Class of gods (*devas) who exist on a noumenal plane without conscious experience of any kind. These are typically former practitioners of *meditation who, having immersed themselves in the fourth *dhyāna for long periods, now incline to dwell with their minds untroubled by any kind of thought or sensation. Some mistake this condition for *nirvāṇa and become trapped there. As soon as an idea of any kind occurs to these devas, they fall to a lower spiritual abode.

ascetic, asceticism. By the time of the *Buddha asceticism was a well-established feature of the Indian religious tradition, deriving from the ancient Vedic (*see* VEDA) practice of austerities or tapas ('heating' or 'burning'). In several discourses the Buddha describes and criticizes the many and varied practices of contemporary groups. Many went naked while others wore garments of cloth, hemp, rags, or hair. Some imitated the behaviour of *animals and slept on the ground or on beds of thorns. Many restricted the type of food they would eat, the frequency of consumption, and the type of person they would accept it from. These ascetic practices were also being supplemented by the more sophisticated psycho-physical techniques of *yoga. Although the Buddha prohibited extreme practices of this kind he allowed thirteen optional practices (*dhutanga) of a moderately ascetic kind but resisted an attempt to make five of them compulsory for *monks.

In the early stages of his quest for enlightenment (*bodhi) the Buddha experimented with both yogic and ascetic practices and described his experience with two particular methods. The first involved retention of the breath for long periods of time but resulted only in a violent headache. The second was fasting, which he pursued until his body became emaciated and he later describes his appearance in this condition as follows: 'All my limbs became like the joints of withered creepers... my gaunt ribs became like the crazy rafters of a tumble-down shed my scalp became shrivelled and shrunk and the skin of my belly clung to my backbone.' A famous sculpture in the Lahore Museum depicts the Buddha in this wretched state. Renouncing these practices as counterproductive the Buddha took food once again and realized the importance of a harmonious relationship between mind and body in the pursuit of the religious life. He had now experienced both the extremes of a life of ease and comfort (as a prince) and the life of extreme austerity and asceticism. Neither was satisfactory and the Buddha finally chose the 'middle way' (*madhyamā-pratipad) between the two as the only sure path to liberation which he then quickly gained. Thus his own personal experience became central to the formation of Buddhist views regarding extreme attitudes and practices of all kinds, and extreme asceticism thereafter found no real foothold in the tradition.

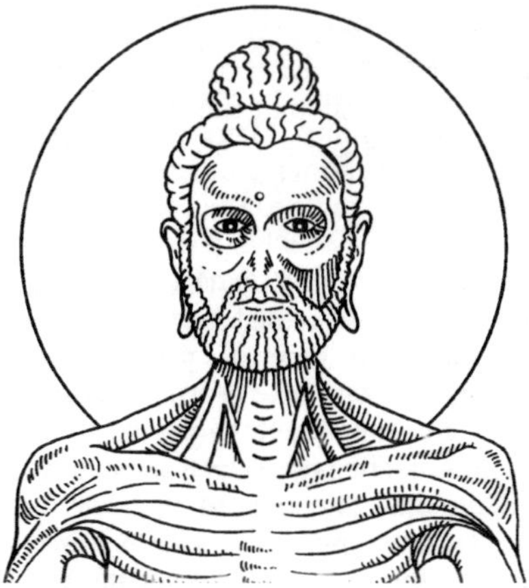

Fig 2 The Buddha Fasting

Asita. Teacher and later chaplain to the *Buddha's father, *Śuddhodana. When the Buddha was born, Asita made a prophesy about the child's destiny based on the auspicious marks on its body (*see* DVĀTRIṂŚADVARA-LAKṢAṆA; ANUVYAÑJANA; MAHĀPURUṢA). He rejoiced in the birth of a future Buddha but was saddened by the realization that he would not be alive to hear his teachings. Because of his great prowess in meditation he was reborn in an immaterial (*ārūpya) dimension after *death.

asmi-māna (Skt.; Pāli, the conceit 'I am'). Inappropriate evaluation of self-worth when drawing comparisons with others. It may take the form of believing oneself to be superior, inferior, or equal. It is the eighth of the ten fetters (*saṃyojana) and should be distinguished from the first of these (*satkāya-dṛṣṭi) which is belief in permanent self or *ātman.

Aśoka (Skt.; Pāli, Asoka). Grandson of *Candragupta Maurya, son of *Bindusāra, and third incumbent of the *Mauryan throne, *c.*272–231 BCE. Aśoka is famous for the edicts he ordered to be carved on rocks and pillars throughout his kingdom. A total of 33 inscriptions have been found which provide invaluable historical and chronological information on early Indian Buddhist history (*see* EDICTS OF AŚOKA). He was a great patron of *Buddhism, and it can be seen from the Edicts that the content of Aśoka's *Dharma is essentially that of a lay Buddhist. Dharma consists, he tells us, of 'Few sins and many good deeds of kindness, liberality, truthfulness and purity' (Pillar Edict 2). In his edicts Aśoka offers fatherlike advice to his subjects, commending moral virtues such as peacefulness, piety, religious tolerance, zeal, respect for parents and teachers, courtesy, charity, sense-control, and equanimity. No reference is made to the technical aspects of Buddhist doctrine as expounded in the *Four Noble Truths. Aśoka relates in Rock Edict XIII that after his bloody conquest of the *Kaliṅga region of north-east *India, he repented of his warlike ways and became a lay Buddhist. From then on he attempted to rule according to Dharma as a 'Dharma-rāja' or righteous king (*see* CAKRAVARTIN). He appointed officers known as 'superintendents of Dharma' (dharma-mahāmātra) to propagate the religion. However, in the best tradition of Indian kingship, Aśoka supported all religions. One of the edicts towards the end of his reign, known as the 'schism edict', condemns *schism in the *Saṃgha and speaks of *monks being expelled. This seems to confirm accounts in Buddhist chronicles of his involvement in a council at *Pāṭaliputra around 250 BCE, reckoned as the 'Third Council' by the *Theravāda tradition (*see* COUNCIL OF PĀṬALIPUTRA II). The edicts also record that Aśoka sent ambassadors to five named kings reigning in the Hellenistic world, which again seems to support the Buddhist tradition that he did much to promote the spread of the religion. He is credited with sending his son *Mahinda, himself a monk, to *Sri Lanka to establish Buddhism there, as well as sending missionaries to other parts of *south-east Asia. After Aśoka's death in 231 BCE Mauryan rule rapidly declined and in the 2nd century BCE the north and north-west were extensively invaded by Greeks from the former Seleucid satrapies of Bactria and Parthia, as well as by central Asian nomadic tribes. Various Aśokan emblems, such as the lion capital found on his pillars, have been adopted for official use by the modern state of India.

Asokārāma (Pāli). A monastery in *Pāṭaliputra, built by and named after the emperor *Aśoka (Pāli, Asoka). The monastery was the site of the Third Council (*see* COUNCIL OF PĀṬALIPUTRA II) and the centre of events leading up to it.

Aśoka-avadāna. *Sanskrit text of the *avadāna genre that narrates a series of legends surrounding the main events in the life of the Emperor *Aśoka.

āśrava (Skt., outflow; Pāli, āsava). A group of basic impurities or defilements which are the cause of repeated *rebirth. There is an original list of three in *Pāli sources, namely sense-desires (kāmāsava), the *desire for continued existence (bhavāsava), and wrong views (diṭṭhāsava). These are sometime supplemented by a fourth, namely ignorance of the truth (avijjāsava). The āśravas summarize the cognitive and affective impediments to the state of full perfection, and their destruction (āsavakkhaya) is equated with the attainment of Arhatship (*see* ARHAT). In Pāli sources the four āsavas are also referred to by the alternative designation of 'floods' (*ogha).

aśraya (Skt.). A basis, support, or foundation. In Buddhist *Sanskrit sources a term used in various contexts as a synonym for the 'storehouse consciousness' (*ālaya-vijñāna) as the basis or support of the other six consciousnesses (*vijñāna) or sense-modalities. It is through the restructuring or transformation (parāvṛtti) of the āśraya that enlightenment (*bodhi) is attained. Less commonly the term is used of the body itself as the substrate or support for conscious experience by means of the sense-organs. *See also* ĀŚRAYA-PARĀVṚTTI.

āśraya-parāvṛtti (Skt.). 'The manifestation of the basis', a term used in *Yogācāra works to describe the manifestation of inherent *Buddha-nature once the mind has been cleared of adventitious impurities (*āgantuka-kleśa).

aṣṭāṅga-śīla (Skt., Pāli aṭṭha-sīla). A list of eight *precepts made up of the Five Precepts (*pañca-śīla) with the addition of abstention from (6) eating at the wrong time; (7) dancing, singing, music, watching shows, wearing garlands, perfumes, cosmetics, and personal adornments; (8) use of high seats or beds.

Aṣṭa-sāhasrikā-prajñā-pāramitā Sūtra. 'The Sūtra of the Perfection of Insight in Eight Thousand Verses'. One of the earliest surviving versions of the Perfection of Insight group of *Mahāyāna *sūtras (*see* PRAJÑĀ-PĀRAMITĀ SŪTRAS). Probably dating from 100 BCE or earlier, this text comprises 32 chapters and covers many key Mahāyāna topics, including the career of a *Bodhisattva, the nature of emptiness (*śūnyatā), and the development and application of the Perfection of Insight. The text survives in *Sanskrit, as well as Tibetan and Chinese translations.

aṣṭa-vimokṣa (Skt.; Pāli, aṭṭha vimokkha). The eight liberations, a meditational practice in which the meditator passes through eight levels of contemplation with the purpose of cultivating detachment. The eight stages are: (1) the contemplation of internal and external forms (i.e. inside and outside the body) as impure; (2) contemplation of external forms as impure (reinforcing and progressing from the first stage); (3) contemplation of the beautiful (śubha). This is in contrast to the impurity contemplated at the first two levels, but no attachment to the beautiful is allowed to develop. It is followed by the contemplation of the four higher or 'formless' *dhyānas, namely (4) the sphere of unlimited space; (5) the sphere of unlimited consciousness; (6) the sphere of nothingness; (7) the sphere of neither-perception-nor-non-perception. The final level (8) is the cessation of perception and feeling (*nirodha-samāpatti). The first two liberations correspond to the first stage of the 'eight masteries' (*abhibhāvayatana) and the third and fourth to the second.

āstika (Skt.). **1.** In *Hinduism, one who is orthodox in belief, accepting the ultimate authority of the *Vedas. **2.** For earlier Buddhists (and Jains), an atthika (Pāli), is one who accepts the doctrine of *karma and the result of deeds. In *Mahāyāna *Buddhism, it refers to one who asserts the real eternal existence of phenomena.

astrology. In *India, *Buddhism adopted the Hindu scheme of astronomy but rejected the latter's preoccupation with astrology. The position and movement of the celestial bodies was of interest to Buddhists only for pragmatic purposes such as calculating the time of day, the length of the lunar month and its holy days, and the period of retreat during the rainy season. Such skills were especially important in the case of forest-dwelling *monks who were cut off from society. Such monks were to learn 'the positions of the constellations, either the whole or one section, and to know the cardinal points'. Astrology as we know it probably did not exist at the time of the Buddha—it is largely a Greek synthesis of Fertile Crescent star-lore, created around the 3rd or 4th centuries BCE. Nevertheless, early sources such as the **Brahmajāla Sutta* of the *Pāli Canon describe numerous techniques of divination including predicting eclipses of the sun, moon, and stars, and forecasting the events they were believed to herald. The Buddha is singled out for praise as one not devoting himself to such 'low arts' (tiracchāna-vijjā). Despite this, in practically all Buddhist cultures, monks officiate as advisers to the laity and employ techniques of divination. In south-east Asia the use of horoscopes is widespread among Buddhists, and they are known in *Burma as *sadā, and as cata in northern *Thailand. In the Buddhism of *Tibet and central Asia, indigenous shamanistic practices were incorporated with only superficial modifications, and in *China a complete system of astrology and divination based on the *Book of Changes (I-ching)* found an accommodation within Buddhism.

aśubha (Skt.; Pāli, asubha). Anything impure or unpleasant. In the context of meditational practice, the term denotes a set of ten meditational subjects designed to eliminate lust or attachment to the physical body by focusing on the ten stages of decay which a corpse passes through.

Asuka period. The period of Japanese history extending from 552 to 646 CE during which *Buddhism was first introduced at the royal court. *See also* JAPAN.

asura (Skt.). Demigods, titans. A group of beings who were considered to be the opponents of the gods according to orthodox *Vedic mythology. Later, they were incorporated into Buddhist *cosmology as occupying one of the six modes of existence shown in the wheel of life (*bhavacakra). They are thought to reside just below the gods who dwell on the slopes of Mt. *Meru.

Aśvaghoṣa. An early *Sarvāstivādin master, born 1st–2nd century CE in *Ayodhyā. A court poet of the *Kusāna king *Kaniṣka (it is not clear whether this was Kaniṣka I or II), he composed poetic and dramatic works on Buddhist themes, such as the **Buddhacarita*, a life of the *Buddha, the *Saundarananda*, an account of the conversion of *Nanda, and the *Śāriputraprakaraṇa* or 'Story of *Śāriputra'. Tradition also ascribes to him the **Māhāyāna-śraddhotpāda Śāstra*. His most famous work is the first of these, a biography of the Buddha in epic mahākāvya style (the style of the great *Sanskrit literary classics). Originally in 28 cantos, only 17 survive in Sanskrit, the remainder being preserved in Tibetan and Chinese translations. The author's deep respect and reverence for the Buddha is unmistakable in all his compositions and he is viewed by many as a follower of the *Mahāyāna.

aśvattha (Skt.). The holy fig tree (*ficus religiosa*) the wood of which is often stipulated for use in rituals.

Atiśa (*c.*980–1055). The short name of Atiśa Dīpaṃkāra Śrījñāna. Born in Bengal into a royal family, he was a renowned Buddhist scholar and *monk who later became one of the leading teachers at the university monastery of *Vikramaśīla. He was invited to *Tibet in 1043, where he stayed until his death, to assist in the re-establishment of *Buddhism. He was especially devoted to systematizing the Buddhist teachings available in Tibet into a structured path, as is reflected in his main work, the *Lamp for the Path to Enlightenment (Bodhi-patha-pradīpa)*. He founded the *Kadampa school with his chief Tibetan disciple, Dromtön, and thus effected a lasting influence upon the nature of Tibetan Buddhism.

atiyoga (Skt.). The sixth level of *tantric teachings according to the *Nyingma school, equivalent in some respects to the *Non-dual Tantra class of the *New Schools. The tantric texts that form this class are unique to the Nyingma school. The term is often used as a synonym for *Dzogchen. The atiyoga class of teachings is further subdivided in the three groups: the *Mind Category, the *Spatial Category and the *Secret Instruction Category.

ātman (Skt., self, soul). In a philosophical context, the concept of an independent, unchanging, and eternal identity at the core of individuals and entities. Normally the existence of such a self is denied in *Buddhism (*see* ANĀTMAN) although a minority of modern scholars have claimed that the *Buddha merely denied a lower ego-self. Additionally, some later *Mahāyāna texts, such as the **Nirvāṇa Sūtra*, speak of a transcendent *Buddha-nature as the true self.

Atthasālinī. Commentary on the **Dhamma-saṅganī*, the first book of the *Abhidharma Piṭaka of the *Pāli Canon. A work of the school of *Buddhaghoṣa (according to its introduction it was written at his request), it was originally composed in *India but revised in *Sri Lanka, as shown by the fact that it bears mention of later works.

Aum Shinrikyō (Jap.). A new religious movement that developed in *Japan during the 1980s under the leadership of its '*guru', Shoko Asahara. A kind of Śaiva-Shinto synthesis, the group also includes Buddhist and Judeo-Christian elements in its beliefs and practices. The cult drew worldwide attention when it released nerve gas in five Tokyo subway lines on 20 March 1995 in accordance with its millennial 'doomsday' beliefs. After several years of decline caused by the subsequent investigations and arrests, the group is reportedly on the rise once again.

avadāna (Skt.). A genre of Buddhist literature that recounts moral stories about the previous lives of various saints. One of the twelve types of literary composition traditionally found in Buddhist *Sanskrit literature, the avādanas are thought to have been compiled for the edification of lay audiences. The stories avoid complex doctrinal matters and depict instead the ways in which good deeds motivated by love and devotion are rewarded, and bad deeds performed out of ill-will and hatred are punished.

The avadāna style of literature seems to have become popular among the schools of early *Buddhism prior to the rise of the *Mahāyāna, which would locate it approximately at the beginning of the Christian era. In the avadānas we see the beginning of a devotional attitude towards the *Buddha which was to become more pronounced in the Mahāyāna. The absence of *Bodhisattva-figures and the down-to-earth flavour and setting of the tales also argues for a pre-Mahāyāna date. There is no reference to a doctrine of salvation through the intercession of the Buddha; instead the avadānas stress the necessity of a long process of moral development in which the individual is personally responsible for his spiritual progress. Modern scholars thus believe that this genre represents a literary transitional phase between *Hīnayāna and Mahāyāna. The most important examples of this type of literature include the **Avadāna-śataka*, the *Aśoka-avadāna*, **Divya-avadāna*, and the later *Avadāna-kalpalatā*.

Avadāna-śataka (Skt., the hundred avadānas). A collection comprising one hundred *avadāna tales. The tales are moral stories and fables from the *Hīnayana Buddhist tradition composed around the start of the first millennium, and the work forms part of an earlier evolving tradition including the *Pāli **Apadāna* and other recently discovered Gandhārī materials. The authorship of the *Avadāna-śataka* is uncertain but its popularity resulted in a Chinese translation being made at a very early date. The work is divided into ten chapters each containing ten stories on a particular theme. The central preoccupation is with the consequences of good and evil deeds and their maturation and effect upon the doer in later lives. The *Buddha himself is the hero of many of the tales in the manner of the *Pāli *Jātaka literature and reverence and devotion to him is undisguised. Other protagonists are *Arhats, gods, and ghosts (*preta), who are reaping the consequences of their moral or immoral deeds.

avadhūti (Skt.). The central channel (*nāḍī) or pathway of psychic energy that runs through the human body, according to the spiritual physiology of *anuttara-yoga-tantra. This channel is visualized as a fine tube, pale blue outside and oily red inside, running up along the spine from the perineum to the point between the eyebrows with four or five *cakras or energy centres situated along it. It is normally sealed at the ends and at the junctures with the cakras but can be opened to allow the entry and free flow of the subtle energy of 'wind' (*vāyu) from the two adjacent channels, the *lalanā and the *rasanā, to actualize the knowledge (*jñāna) of the *dharma-kāya or ultimate reality.

Avalokiteśvara (Skt.; Tib., spyan-ras-gzigs; Chin, Kuan-yin; Jap., *Kannon or Kwannon). One of the eight great *Bodhisattvas, and one whose activities especially involve the active practice of compassion (*karuṇā) in order to save and protect beings. His name means 'the Lord who gazes' (compassionately upon beings). Though well-known from early *Mahāyāna *sūtras, the *worship and cult of Avalokiteśvara in *Tibet derives greatly from later *tantric materials. Recitation of the mantra '*Oṃ maṇi padme hūṃ' is associated with Avalokiteśvara. Several iconographic forms can be distinguished such as that with eleven heads and a thousand arms, the popular four-armed version, as well as several wrathful aspects. Avalokiteśvara is considered to be the main patron Bodhisattva of Tibet, and the *Dalai Lama is viewed as his incarnate manifestation.

Fig 3 Avalokiteśvara

Avanti. Ancient name of a geographical region to the north-east of Bombay. It was a major state in ancient *India, situated on the western borders of *Magadha with its capital located at Ujjayinī on the Sipra river, where three important trade routes converged. In the *Buddha's day it was one of the four principal kingdoms, along with Magadha, *Kosala, and Vaṃsa (or Vatsa), and eventually became incorporated into the first of these. Though the Buddha himself did not visit this kingdom, the *Dharma was promulgated there by *Mahākātyāyana but it did not flourish in this region until it was incorporated into the Magadhan empire by Śiśunāga some time after the Buddha's passing. Subsequently, there was a notable Buddhist presence at places such as *Bhārhut, *Sāñcī, and Vidiśā and many great *stūpas were built in this region, some of which survived or have been excavated in modern times. It would seem from the account of the Chinese pilgrim *Hsüan-tsang that *Buddhism had declined considerably in much of this area by the mid-7th century CE, although this may have simply been a case of monks relocating to new monasteries as political capitals changed. In Avanti there was political fragmentation, but there were large numbers of monks in Mālava and *Valabhī, while the new capitals of Harsa's dynasty at Kanauj and Oudh had very large numbers indeed.

āvaraṇa (Skt., obscuration). The two factors, according to *Mahāyāna, which cause a being to remain unenlightened and enmeshed in *saṃsāra. They are (1) the obscuration of the defilements (kleśa-āvaraṇa) and (2) the obscuration of wrong and perverse views about the nature of reality (jñeya-āvaraṇa). The Mahāyāna teaches that an *Arhat is capable of eliminating the obscuration of negative emotions and thus attains an inferior form of *nirvāṇa, but only *Buddhas and *Bodhisattvas are able to break through the obscuration of false views through a direct realization of the emptiness (*śūnyatā) of all phenomena.

āvāsa (Pāli). A site occupied by monks during the rainy season retreat. The āvāsa marks the geographical boundary within which temporary structures known as *vihāras were constructed to provide shelter from the rains. In the earliest times the sites were abandoned after the rains but in the course of time there was a tendency for them to develop into permanent monastic residences.

Avataṃsaka Sūtra. A *Mahāyāna *sūtra purportedly preached by the *Buddha immediately after his enlightenment (*bodhi) that directly conveys the content of his vision. No complete *Sanskrit text of this sūtra remains extant, although portions of it do exist and *Chih-yen of the *Hua-yen school left an outline of the Sanskrit text from which the translation by Śikṣānanda was produced. There are four translations extant, three in Chinese and one in Tibetan. These are: (1) the translation by *Buddhabhadra in 60 fascicles, completed in 420 CE (*Taishō 278); (2) the translation by Śikṣānanda in 80 fascicles, completed in 699 CE. (Taishō 279); (3) the 40-fascicle translation of the last chapter, called the **Gaṇḍavyūha*, produced by *Prajñā in 798 CE (Taishō 293); and (4) the Tibetan translation in 45 chapters produced by Jinamitra in the 8th century (Peking edition, vols. 25, 26). In addition to the three complete translations (nos. 1, 2, and 4 above), many portions of this sūtra have been translated and disseminated as self-standing works. This fact, plus the existence of autonomous sections in Sanskrit, has led scholars to conclude that this is an encyclopedic work which was augmented over the centuries as other works were added to it.

According to Hua-yen exegesis the sūtra's primary goal is to show the reader how the world appears to a completely enlightened Buddha or advanced *Bodhisattva. It presents a universe conceived as empty of inherent existence and as arising and fading away each moment in response to the activities of mind. The Buddha, realizing that all reality arises in dependence on mind, and having perfect control of his mind through his meditation, is able to produce effects at any distance which may appear to unenlightened beings as magic, but which to him simply manifest reality as it is—mind-made. His transformations are not different in quality from those worked by ordinary beings as they pass from life to life; the crucial difference is that the Buddha is aware of the process and can control it. This places the Buddha in a universe lacking disparate objects with solid boundaries between them. Instead, he sees a constant flow and flux in the basic transformations of mind.

As a result of this fluidity and lack of hard boundaries, all of reality is seen as perfectly interpenetrating. This interpenetration occurs at two levels. First, the ultimate nature of reality, the noumenon, is perfectly expressed in all individual phenomena. More concretely, the single Buddha *Vairocana (of whom the historical Buddha *Śākyamuni is said to be an emanation) is the ground of all reality. Since all individual phenomena emerge from him, he perfectly pervades all things. Second, because of this complete pervasion of noumenon (Vairocana) into all phenomena, all phenomena perfectly interpenetrate each other. Each individual thing arises out of this basic matrix of transformations, and so each implies and influences all of the others. Everything is within everything else, and yet there is no confusion of one phenomenon with another.

The most important sections are the **Daśabhūmika*, which describes the levels (*bhūmi) traversed by a Bodhisattva, and the final chapter, the *Gaṇḍavyūha*, which depicts the journey of a youth named Sudhana as he visits one teacher after another, eventually seeing a total of 53. Each teacher deepens his awareness, and the group represents every level of being, from the prostitute Vasumitrā to the greatest Bodhisattva *Samantabhadra. By the end of his journey, Sudhana experiences the falling of the boundaries that separated his own body and mind from the rest of reality and he sees the ocean of flux that is the *dharma-dhātu, or field of dharmas. His realization renders all former obstacles transparent to him and he wanders unimpeded through the cosmos as he wills. As the sūtra concludes here, the reader is left with a vision and a promise that, upon his or her attainment of perfect enlightenment (saṃbodhi), they will also accomplish what Sudhana accomplished and roam freely in the dharma-dhātu. This text forms the doctrinal basis of the Sino-Japanese *Hua-yen school.

avatāra (Skt., descent). Primarily a Hindu term referring to the manifestation or incarnation of a god in the human realm, typified by the ten incarnations of Viṣṇu. The term may sometimes be used in *Buddhism to describe the manifestation of a *Buddha in the world as an Emanation Body (*nirmāṇa-kāya).

āveṇika-buddha-dharma (Skt.). One of the eighteen 'uncommon qualities of a *Buddha'. Several variant lists are found but typically they are: a Buddha does not make mistakes; he does not shout and so on; he is not forgetful; his mind is ever composed; he treats all beings equally; he is not indifferent to beings; he does not lose his interest, his strenuousness, recollection, *samādhi, insight, and liberation; all his physical, vocal, and mental actions are preceded and accompanied by awareness; his insight and awareness are unattached and unimpeded regarding all things in the past, present, and future.

Avīci. The nethermost of the eight hot *hells, reserved for the most evil beings who must endure excruciating torments there, which though not eternal seem unending as they last for millions of years.

avidyā (Skt.; Pāli, avijjā). Ignorance; in *Buddhism it refers specifically to ignorance about the workings of *karma, the *Four Noble Truths, and the Three Jewels (*triratna). Avidyā is the root cause of continued involvement in *saṃsāra and the experience of *suffering by which one remains confused about the true nature of reality.

avyākṛta-vastu (Skt.). The four avyākṛta-vastu, or 'questions which have not been determined (by the Buddha)' are (1) whether the world is eternal, or not, or both, or neither; (2) whether the world is infinite in space, or not, or both, or neither; (3) whether the *Tathāgata exists after death, or not, or both, or neither; (4) whether the soul (*ātman) is identical with the body or different from it. These four questions were put to the *Buddha on several occasions, including once by *Vacchagotta in the *Aggi-Vacchagotta Sutta* of the *Majjhima Nikāya. The Buddha made no reply because any answer he might have given would have been open to misinterpretation, given the frame of reference that the questions presuppose. In addition, he felt that to discuss speculative questions of this kind is a distraction from the task of overcoming the passions and gaining insight into the true nature of things. In this connection he taught the parable of the poisoned arrow which tells of a man wounded by an arrow who refuses to have it withdrawn until he has the answer to a number of irrelevant questions concerning the archer. Rather than waste time in futile speculation, the urgency is to withdraw the arrow and put an end to *suffering.

Awakening of Faith in the Mahāyāna. *See* MAHĀYĀNA-ŚRADDHOTPĀDA ŚĀSTRA.

āyatana (Skt.). In Buddhist psychology, the twelve āyatanas are the six senses or modes of perception and the six kinds of object they correspond to, namely: (1) sight and colour/form (rūpa-āyatana); (2) hearing and sound (śabda-āyatana); (3) smell and scent (gandha-āyatana); (4) taste and flavours (rasa-āyatana); (5) touch and tangible objects (sparśa-āyatana); and (6) the mind and ideas (mano-āyatana). Each āyatana is thus the sphere or domain of a particular sense, and encompasses everything that can be experienced through that particular 'sense-door'. *See also* ṢAD-ĀYATANA.

Ayodhyā (or Ayojjhā). A city located on the Ganges in Uttar Pradesh, one-time capital of southern *Kośala, visited on two occasions by the *Buddha. It is also thought by Hindus to have been the birthplace of the god Rāma.

B

Bāhira-nidāna (Pāli). The introduction to the **Samantapāsādikā* ('lovely throughout'), a commentary to the *Vinaya Piṭaka attributed to *Buddhaghoṣa in the 5th century. It relates the history of *Buddhism up to the establishment of the Vinaya Piṭaka in *Sri Lanka.

Bahulika (also Bahulikā, Bāhulikā). An early sect, being an offshoot of the *Gokulika. The sect accepted the five theses of *Mahādeva as well as other doctrines regarded as heretical by more conservative groups such as the *Theravāda.

Bahuśrutīya. A subschool of the *Mahāsaṃghikas which emerged in the 2nd century BCE and flourished mainly in south-east *India around *Nāgārjunakoṇḍa. A single inscription suggests they were also present in the north-west of India, but this is almost certainly based on a misreading. Little is known about the distinctive doctrines of this school although it is reported that they stressed the profound implicit meaning of *sūtras in contrast to their parent Mahāsaṃghika school whom they criticized for not going beyond the superficial explicit meaning. It is known that their *canon comprised five elements with the addition of a Saṃyukta Piṭaka and a Bodhisattva Piṭaka alongside the standard three. However, nothing of their literature survives with the exception of the **Satyasiddhi Śāstra* of *Harivarman which has been thought to have a connection with the Bahuśrutīya school.

Ba khin, U (1889–1970). Burmese meditation teacher who developed a technique of insight (*vipaśyanā) meditation for the laity based on intensive retreats. U Ba khin was Accountant General of *Burma from 1948 to 1953, and when about 50 he developed a cancerous growth in the bone and flesh below the right eye. After some years of meditation he cured himself completely. His systematic approach to meditation, which emphasized practice over theory, became popular and has spread to the West. He also founded the International Medical Centre in Rangoon.

bala (Skt.; Pāli, power). Various lists of powers (bala) occur in the sources, but the most common is a group known as the 'five powers'. Each of these eradicates its opposite negative tendency as follows: (1) faith (*śraddhā) overcomes false beliefs; (2) energy (*vīrya) overcomes laziness; (3) mindfulness (*smṛti) overcomes forgetfulness; (4) concentration (*samādhi) overcomes distractedness; (5) insight (*prajñā) overcomes ignorance. The five powers are developed through augmenting the strength of the five spiritual faculties (*indriya). These powers also form part of the 37 'factors of enlightenment' (*bodhipākṣika-dharma).

Bāmiyān. An important early Buddhist site, located in present-day Afghanistan, some 70 miles north-west of Kabul. Its monasteries were associated with the *Lokottara-vāda school which was also responsible for the many artificial caves and the famous colossal figures of the *Buddha carved into the cliff face of a local mountain. The tallest one was 177 feet high, the largest stone statue in the world. The monuments were defaced in 1222 CE by Genghis Khan, and in 2001 the figures were destroyed by the fundamentalist Islamic Taliban regime, who considered them idolatrous. The Buddhist presence in Bāmiyān declined after the 8th century as a result of Arab invasions.

bandha (Skt.) A fetter, bondage, that which ties one to *saṃsāra.

Bangladesh. Modern country on the border region between south and *south-east Asia. Though the majority of the population of Bangladesh is now Muslim, this region was once renowned for its number of Buddhist establishments, including Pāhārpur (*see* PĀHĀRPUR VIHĀRA). It is not known for sure when *Buddhism was introduced in the country but no evidence of Buddhist activities is available before the 2nd century CE. Buddhism reached the highest point of development here under the *Pāla dynasty (765–1175). Following the loss of royal patronage and the arrival of

Muslim invaders, Buddhism almost disappeared from Bangladesh and was preserved by the people living on the border with the Burmese region of Arakan (*see* BURMA), although in a 'corrupted' form not acceptable to Burmese orthodoxy. The reform of these practices and the revival of orthodox *Theravāda Buddhism in Bangladesh took place only in 1856. Today in Bangladesh there are less than one million Buddhists, all living in the district of Chittagong.

Bankei Eitaku (1622–93). Bankei was a *Rinzai *monk who lived during the Tokugawa period in *Japan. During this time, the government required all families to register with a *Zen temple for record-keeping purposes, and Bankei recognized that this increase in the size of his congregation did not mean increased religious aptitude or interest. In response, he worked to make Zen teachings relevant to the dominant *samurai culture and downplayed the need for strict religious practice. His teaching to the masses stressed the inherent Buddha-mind that all possessed, and he frequently spoke of the Unborn that underlay all phenomena and all thought.

bar-do (Tib.). A term associated with Tibetan *Buddhism (*see* TIBET) which denotes a juncture or phase between two states. Six of these are described; the intermediate states of birth, of dream, of meditation, of the moment of *death, of reality, and of becoming. The first three occur periodically during the present lifetime, while the remaining three concern the events that occur during the 49-day period that elapses between death and *rebirth. These latter three form the subject matter of the *Tibetan Book of the Dead* (**Bar-do thos-grol*) since they present an opportunity for liberation from *saṃsāra if correctly understood.

Bar-do thos-grol. A work popularly known in English as the *Tibetan Book of the Dead*, but whose name literally means 'liberation through hearing in the intermediate state'. The text forms part of the large corpus of texts known as the 'Cycle of Peaceful and Wrathful Deities', reputedly revealed by *Padmasambhava and then concealed until its rediscovery by the 14th-century 'treasure revealer' (gter-ston) Karma Lingpa. The *Bar-do thos-grol* gives guidance through hearing its instructions (thos) to enable a person to become liberated (grol) during the experiences encountered during the three intermediate phases (*bar-do) of dying, *death, and *rebirth by recognizing the true nature of the visions encountered as false mental projections which conceal reality itself.

Barlaam and Josaphat. Two Christian saints venerated in both the Greek and Roman churches who were the protagonists of a popular medieval religious tale. Around a century and a half ago it was discovered that the story is based on the legend of the life of the *Buddha. The name Josaphat is a corruption of the *Sanskrit word *Bodhisattva, a term applied to the Buddha before he became enlightened. In the Western version of the tale, Josaphat is the son of a king, and on his birth a prediction is made that he will either become a great king or renounce the world to follow a religious calling. His father does all he can to prevent his son following a religious vocation, but on a visit outside the palace one day Josaphat meets Barlaam, an *ascetic who gives him religious instruction. Guided by his spiritual mentor Josaphat renounces the world and becomes a great saint. The story thus parallels the life of *Siddhartha Gautama at various points, although the theology is adapted for a Christian context and the theme concerns the notion of salvation through faith. There are Greek, Georgian, and Arabic translations of the legend, but it became most widely known in *Europe through a Latin version in the 11th and 12th centuries. From the 13th to the 15th century numerous vernacular versions appeared and new forms of the story were produced in prose, verse, and dramatic form.

Bashō (1644–94). Matsuo Bashō is known mainly as a poet who perfected the art of the *haiku, or short, seventeen-syllable verse, although he also composed linked verses (renga) and travelogues that alternated prose and poetry, including his celebrated *Journey to the Interior*. He studied *Zen with the renowned *Rinzai master Butchō (1643–1715), and appears to have had an enlightenment experience (*satori) at the age of 40, perhaps memorialized by his most famous haiku: 'The old pond; | a frog jumps in. | Splash!'

Bassui Zenji (1327–87). **Also Bassui Tokushō.** Bassui was an itinerant *Zen practitioner of the *Rinzai school, reformer, and popularizer. Fiercely independent by nature, he attached himself to neither school nor teacher, although in later years the enormous number of disciples who gathered around him (over a thousand by some accounts) forced him to settle down. He worked to demystify enlightenment (*bodhi; *satori) and show that it was within reach of any person, whether lay or monastic, male or female. He spoke in simple and direct words, and wrote in Japanese kana script rather than Chinese characters so as to reach a wider audience. He required only that people abide by the moral *precepts and apply themselves energetically to their practice.

Bauddha Pālā Kīrtana. Bengali Buddhist literary genre consisting of a kīrtana, a particular type of religious song, in the form of a pālā, literally meaning ballad, usually having as its theme a *Jātaka, or life-story of the *Buddha. A kīrtana is a song in praise of a god, invoking the name, the qualities, and the deeds of that particular god. It is also a love song that the follower of a god sings to express the pain experienced at being separated from the object of his devotion. The kīrtana was systematized as a regular part of worship (*pūjā) in south *India during the second part of the first millennium and it is closely related to the rise of bhakti, or devotional religion. In Bengal, the kīrtana is linked with the rise in the 16th century of the Vaishnava movement initiated by Caitanya. After Caitanya became a bhakta, a man devoted in heart and life to the service of Krishna, he engaged wholeheartedly in musical worship through the medium of the kīrtana. Caitanya's kīrtana was chorus singing to the accompaniment of drums and cymbals. Beginning in the evening, the kīrtana would increase in volume and emotional intensity as the hours passed: bodily movements and hand-clapping would become more and more intense, sometimes resulting in hysteria. One might think that *Buddhism, based on the principle of mindfulness (*smṛti) and the doctrine of the middle way (*madhyamā-pratipad), could not possibly employ a highly emotional form of worship such as the kīrtana. However, the kīrtana as a form of devotional singing has gained so much popularity in Bengal as to become associated with all religions. While retaining its character as a song of love and devotion, and other characteristics such as the invocation of the name of the divinity the song is dedicated to, the kīrtana has lost its excesses in Buddhism. Very little is known of the history of the Buddhist pālā kīrtana. It is thought that the Bauddha pālā kīrtana is a very recent invention and that the first Bauddha pālā kīrtanas were composed in the 20th century, as a consequence of the flourishing of Buddhism following the revival of 1856. Supposedly, a relatively large collection of Buddhist pālā kīrtanas once existed in Chittagong, but this was lost during the Bangladeshi independence war of 1971. Bauddha pālā kīrtanas are a recent addition to the rich world of Buddhist performing arts in general, and to Buddhist theatre in particular. They contain alternating narrative and song, the latter divided between chorus and solo singing.

Bauddharañjikā. An account of the life of the *Buddha compiled in Bengali in the second half of the 19th century under the patronage of Queen Kālindī of the Chakmas. The queen had ordered her court poet Nīl Kamal Das, who in turn appointed some Buddhist scholars, to prepare a complete biography of the Buddha. We know from the *Bauddharañjikā* itself that Phul Chandra Baruā, a Bengali Buddhist poet of the time, was the pivotal author among them. He translated into Bengali the *Dhātuvaṅ*, written in the Arakano-Burmese language and containing the lives of some previous Buddhas including the Buddha *Dīpaṅkara, as well as relating the career of the present Buddha from birth to *nirvāṇa, and some religious tenets. Nīl Kamal Das gave a literary form to the book. Due to Queen Kālindī's death in 1873, before the printing of the book was completed, only about half of the book was published in 1890.

bDud-'joms rinpoche. *See* DUDJOM RINPOCHE.

begging-bowl (Skt., pātra; Pāli, patta). A bowl used by Buddhist *monks to collect food on their daily almsround. The *Vinaya states that monks may use bowls made of either iron or clay, and they can be either small, medium, or large.

Beluva. A village not far from *Vaiśālī where the *Buddha spent his last rainy season retreat. He suffered a painful illness here but by force of will overcame it and continued his journey.

bhaddavaggiyā (Pāli). A group of 30 young men converted following an encounter with the *Buddha in the forest where they had gone picnicking with their wives. A courtesan stole some of their possessions and while seeking her they met the Buddha. After hearing a sermon by the Buddha they requested *ordination as monks.

Bhadrakalpika Sūtra. A large *Mahāyāna *sūtra which lists the details of the thousand *Buddhas of the Good Aeon (most not known outside of this text) giving their names, places of abode, entourage, and so forth. Due to its length, it is a rather tedious work to read and perhaps functioned more as a kind of devotion or litugical composition.

Bhagavan (Skt.; Pāli, Bhagavant). Reverential title used of the *Buddha in *sūtras, variously translated as 'Lord', 'Master', 'Blessed One', etc.

Bhaggā. Geographical region between *Vaiśālī and *Śrāvastī visited on several occasions by the *Buddha. The region either takes its name from or lends it to a tribe resident in the area.

Bhaiṣajya-guru. The Medicine Buddha, a figure especially venerated in *Tibet, *China, and *Japan. Bhaiṣajya-guru is a *Buddha in the *Mahāyāna who epitomizes the power of healing, both on a physical and a spiritual level. He is the subject of the *Bhaiṣajya-guru Sūtra*, where he is described as being dark blue in colour and holding a jar of medicinal nectar. By virtue of the twelve vows he made prior to becoming a Buddha, beings are guaranteed healing through devotional acts dedicated to him.

bhāṇaka (Skt.; Pāli). One who commits to memory and recites or preaches the scriptures, usually those of the *Sūtra Piṭaka. In *India, such individuals often preached to laypeople and are thought to have been associated with *stūpas and other places of *pilgrimage.

Bhāradvāja. Name of an ancient *Brahmin clan (*gotra), many members of which are mentioned in the *Pāli Canon as residing at *Rājagṛha, *Śrāvastī, and surrounding regions. Many members of the clan visited the *Buddha and were converted, becoming either lay followers or *monks. Several became *Arhats.

Bhārhut. Site in Madhya Pradesh, *India, of one of the earliest *stūpas built on a mound which dates back to the *Mauryan period. It was constructed around 100 BCE, which is before the first images of the *Buddha are found, and is decorated with carvings of trees and *yakṣa figures. Many of the carvings are preserved in the Calcutta Museum.

bhāṣya (Skt.). A type of commentary on a text which quotes and explicates each word or phrase of the source text.

bhava (Skt., Pāli, being, becoming). **1.** The tenth link in the process of Dependent Origination (*pratītya-samutpāda). **2.** The three psycho-cosmological levels of reality or modes of being, namely the Desire Realm (*kāma-dhātu), the Form Realm (*rūpa-dhātu), and the Formless Realm (*ārūpya-dhātu).

bhavacakra (Skt., wheel of becoming). A wheel, commonly known as 'the wheel of life', represented pictorially in the Tibetan Buddhist tradition as a wheel divided into six sections depicting the nature of life in each of the six realms of *rebirth (*gati). The six realms are laid out around a central hub around which a cock (*desire), pig (ignorance), and snake (hatred) chase one another. Around the circumference is a rim divided in twelve sections depicting in symbolic form the twelve links of Dependent Origination (*pratītya-samutpāda). Behind the wheel and grasping it firmly (thus symbolizing that the whole of *saṃsāra is within his power) stands *Yama, the god of death. According to some accounts, the wheel represents a mirror that Yama holds up to a person at the moment of death. The mirror reflects the possible realms of *rebirth, and the dying soul will be drawn to one of them in accordance with its *karma.

bhāvanā (Skt., cultivation). The general term used in *Buddhism for any type of meditational practice involving continuous attention by the mind to any suitable object. The two main kinds of *meditation practised in Buddhism are calming meditation (*śamatha) and insight meditation (*vipaśyanā). *See also* SAMĀDHI; SĀDHANA.

Fig 4 bhavacakra

Bhāvanā-krama. A work by *Kamalaśīla in three parts, partly surviving in *Sanskrit as well as Tibetan and Chinese versions. The work outlines the gradual path to enlightenment (*bodhi) as taught within the Indo-Tibetan tradition in contrast to east Asian teachings of '*sudden enlightenment' found in the *Ch'an and *Zen schools. The *Bhāvanā-krama* is thought to have been written as a summary of orthodox Indian *Mahāyāna Buddhist views to counter the 'sudden path' teachings advocated by *Hvashang Mahāyāna at the *Council of *Lhasa.

bhāvanā-mārga. The 'path of cultivation', the fourth of the five paths to Buddhahood. *See* PAÑCA-MĀRGA.

bhavaṅga (Pāli). Concept evolved primarily in *Pāli *Abhidharma commentarial literature in order to explain the continuity of consciousness and personal identity in the absence of a permanent self (the latter being denied by the *anātman doctrine). The bhavaṅga is the individual's 'life continuum' which flows on like a stream (sota) from one existence to the next. Sometimes known as the bhavaṅga-citta, or 'consciousness continuum', it is the foundation of all experience, both conscious and unconscious. It retains the traces of all impression and sensations, and makes it possible to have recollections of these in the form of memories. At the beginning and end of each individual existence it is known as 'rebirth-linking consciousness' (paṭisandhi) and 'death consciousness' (*cuti-citta) respectively. The concept of the bhavaṅga paved the way for later idealist trends and the evolution of the notion of the *ālāya-vijñāna or 'storehouse consciousness'.

Bhāvaviveka (*c.*490–570). A noted Indian *Madhyamaka philosopher, also known as Bhavya, who wrote a number of important works, including the *Tarka-jvālā*, refuting other contemporary Buddhist and non-Buddhist doctrines. His method of argumentation is characterized by the use of standard syllogisms (svatantra) derived from the Buddhist school of logic in contrast to the *reductio ad absurdum* (prasaṅga) method of argument favoured by the later philosopher *Candrakīrti.

Bhavya. *See* BHĀVAVIVEKA.

bhikṣu (Skt.; Pāli, bhikkhu). A Buddhist *monk, an ordained member of the *Saṃgha. The etymology of the term is uncertain, as is that of its female equivalent, a *nun or *bhikṣunī. During the lifetime of the *Buddha, *ordination was conferred by a simple formula on all individuals who chose to join voluntarily, were of a minimum age and had no disqualifying conditions such as being a criminal or the bearer of a contagious disease. As the community grew, however, additional procedures came to be required. Soon after the Buddha's death two separate ordination ceremonies were adopted: *pravrajyā, literally meaning 'going forth' and *upasaṃpadā, or ordination proper. Candidates cannot be admitted to pravrajyā and become novices (*śrāmaṇera) before the age of 8. A śrāmaṇera acquires two patrons, a preceptor (upādhyāya) and a master (*ācārya), whose companion (sārdhavihārin) and pupil (antevāsin) respectively he becomes. At age 20 (or older), a novice could ask for full ordination, the details of which are fixed by the ritual texts called karmavācanā, and which is conferred by a chapter of at least ten monks. At this point, in order to determine the new monk's rank, the day and hour of his ordination are noted. It should be noted that neither of these ordinations are considered lifelong commitments, and the novice or monk may put off his robes and leave the order at any time.

In order to maintain the highest level of respect among the lay community which supports him and his personal quest for religious attainment, the bhikṣu has to adhere to the moral discipline outlined in the portion of the Buddhist *canon known as the *Vinaya Piṭaka. The regulations for the conduct of the fully ordained monk are set out in the *Prātimokṣa (Pāli, Pāṭimokkha) and consist of more than 200 rules arranged in categories according to the penalty prescribed. Twice a month, bhikṣus in a given area assemble to celebrate the *poṣadha (Pāli, *uposatha) ceremony and recite the Prātimokṣa. There is no difference in principle between *Theravāda and *Mahāyāna monastic observances. Originally, the community of bhikṣus was a mendicant order which travelled extensively, other than during the rainy season, and required only limited necessities. Monks were allowed to possess only their robes, a *begging-bowl, razor, needle, staff, and toothpick. Food was obtained by begging, and no fixed residence was permitted. In time, the eremitical ideal diminished, and wandering gave way to a settled, monastic way of life. While in the Theravāda tradition bhikṣus continue a life that does not permit work or *marriage, monks of the Mahāyāna tradition may include work in their daily activity, and monks in particular Tibetan and Japanese schools are permitted to marry. Given the nature of a bhikṣu's life, monks have always had to rely on the material support of the lay community, and in time, a balance of exchange between lay-people and monks was established (*see* DĀNA), through which both could advance by mutual support. This relationship forms the dynamic base of Theravādin societies. Also, in some Theravāda communities of *south-east Asia it is required (or at least desirable) that a layman should spend a period during the rainy season as a bhikṣu (*see* TEMPORARY ORDINATION).

bhikṣunī (Skt.; Pāli, bhikkhunī). A female member of the Buddhist *Saṃgha, usually translated as '*nun', being a religious professional who has abandoned worldly life to pursue the Buddhist ideal of *nirvāṇa. The *Buddha initially resisted the formation of an order of bhikṣunīs, fearing distraction and moral disorder. This was however introduced at the insistence of *Mahāprajāpatī Gautamī, the Buddha's stepmother, with the support of *Ānanda, one of the Buddha's chief disciples well known for his championship of the cause of *women. Although the transmission lineage of *Theravādin bhikṣunīs died out in 456 CE, that of *Mahāyāna bhikṣunīs has been preserved through the *Dharmagupta Bhikṣuṇī *Vinaya, which has continued as a living lineage in *China and Taiwan.

The career of the nun is closely modelled on that of the *monk. However, before being accepted for *ordination, girls aged under 20 and married women under the age of 12 are subjected to a probationary period which lasts for two years. During that time the female probationer (śikṣamāṇā) must observe six rules which correspond to the first six *precepts. At the time of her ordination the future nun supplied with the necessary requisites (a begging-bowl and the fivefold robe) presents herself, with her preceptress (upādhāyikā) and instructress (ācāriṇī), first before the assembly of nuns and then before that of monks, and receives ordination from this twofold assembly. Eight strict canonical provisions place the nun in complete dependence on the monks. These include that a nun cannot go into retreat where there is no monk; every fortnight she must go to the community of monks and receive instruction, but she herself can neither instruct a monk nor admonish him; the ceremonies of ordination, of the end of the rainy season retreat, and confession (*pāpa-deśanā) must be repeated before the community of monks. The collection of the detailed regulations for the conduct of the fully ordained nun and monk is called the *Prātimokṣa. The discipline to which the nun is subjected is often thought to be stricter than that of the monks. Her regulations consist in principle of 500 articles, double those of the monks, but in practice their number vary between 290 and 355 depending upon the school. Moreover, many of the additional rules concern such items as female garments. More probably, a separate set of female rules is later and therefore incorporates material already given in the exegesis of the rules for monks.

bhrānta (Skt., deluded). Term denoting confusion with regards to the true nature of reality, often used as a general synonym for ignorance (*avidyā).

bhūmi (Skt.). 'Level', a term denoting one of a series of stages of spiritual development. Most schools of *Buddhism recognize a hierarchical scheme of stages which are passed through, beginning with conversion and the taking up of the religious life, and ending in enlightenment (*bodhi). The *Hīnayāna has the four stages of the *ārya-pudgala or 'noble person', and the theory of the bhūmis may be thought of as an outgrowth of this or as an extension of the scheme of progress in the *Eightfold Path through morality (*śīla), meditation (*samādhi), and insight (*prajñā). The most popular sequence involves a list of ten bhūmis, although some texts refer only to six or seven. After the first six stages the devotee achieves the realization of personal selflessness (*anātman), and after the tenth stage the realization of the selflessness of all phenomena (dharma-śūnyatā). Thus personal liberation, the goal of early Buddhism, is supplemented by *Mahāyāna metaphysics with its vision of the 'higher truth' of universal selflessness.

The ten bhūmis are described in detail in the **Daśabhūmika Sūtra*, and become linked to the practice of the Six Perfections (*ṣaḍ-pāramitā) as follows. (1) Joyful (*pramuditā-bhūmi): a *Bodhisattva embarks upon his religious career with the production of the thought of enlightenment (*bodhicitta). (2) Pure (*vimalā-bhūmi): all immoral conduct and dispositions are eradicated. (3) Luminous (*prabhākarī-bhūmi): through *meditation the Bodhisattva strengthens and deepens his insight. (4) Brilliant (*arciṣmatī-bhūmi): all good qualities are vigorously pursued. (5) Hard to conquer (*sudurjayā-bhūmi): the Bodhisattva devotes himself to his own development and to the welfare of others. (6) Facing forward (*abhimukhī-bhūmi): great wisdom is attained and insight into the true nature of all phenomena. (7) Going far (*dūraṃgamā-bhūmi): the power of skilful means (*upāya-kauśalya) is attained. (8) Immoveable (*acalā-bhūmi): the possibility of falling back is gone forever. (9) The Good (*sādhumatī-bhūmi): the Bodhisattva preaches the doctrine and converts beings. (10) Cloud of the Dharma (*dharmamegha-bhūmi): the Bodhisattva reaches full perfection and is consecrated as a fully enlightened *Buddha.

bhūmi-sparśa-mudrā (Skt., earth-touching gesture). A *mudrā, or iconographic posture, in which the *Buddha is depicted seated in the *lotus posture (padmāsana) touching the earth with his right hand. Usually all the fingers are extended and the tips touch the earth while the left hand remains resting in the lap. This posture depicts the moment when the Buddha was seated under the *Bodhi Tree at *Bodhgayā on the night of his enlightenment. He called upon the earth to witness his right to sit upon that seat as a result of the practices of pāramī (*see* PĀRAMITĀ) in many lives. Images of the Buddha *Akṣobhya are also found in this posture.

Fig 5 bhūmi-sparśa-mudrā

bhūta (Skt.) **1.** An element, particularly one of the four material elements, earth, water, fire and wind. **2.** A kind of vampiric spirit or evil ghost.

bhūta-koṭi (Skt.). The limit or boundary of what is. A *Mahāyāna term for what is ultimately real or true, often used as a synonym for the highest reality or ultimate truth (*Paramārtha).

Bhutan. A small kingdom in the eastern *Himalayas, situated between *China and *India, with its capital at Thimphu. The majority of the inhabitants are of Tibetan origin and are staunch Buddhists although some Nepalese *Hindus have settled in the south in the past century. *Buddhism in Bhutan is closely linked to *Tibet and the main schools present belong to the *Nyingma and *Kagyu lineages. The early history of the country is veiled in legends but Buddhism was introduced there in the course of the 7th century CE. The state of Bhutan was founded in the 17th century by Ngawang Namgyel, a Tibetan *monk, who established it along theocratic lines, similar to the system operated in premodern Tibet. Each ruler or 'Dharma-rāja' was believed to be a *reincarnation of his predecessor until the beginning of the 20th century when no reincarnation could be found, thus bringing that system of government to an end. Due to British influence during the colonial period that emerged as a result of a treaty ratified between Bhutan and the East India Company, *Britain took responsibility for Bhutan's external affairs although it never became a colony. This role was taken over by India in 1949, following independence. Since access to the country is strictly controlled to preserve its unique natural and cultural heritage, Bhutan has remained largely untouched by the less desirable aspects of modern development seen in neighbouring countries.

bhūta-tathatā (Skt.). Term used in *Mahāyāna *Buddhism to denote the inherent or true nature of phenomena. The term can mean either 'true suchness' or 'the suchness of things', and is commonly used to contrast the quintessential nature of phenomena with their external appearance. For example, according to the *Madhyamaka school, the 'true suchness' of objects is emptiness (*śūnyatā), whereas they appear to the unenlightened as solid, enduring, and possessed of an individual nature or 'own being' (*svabhāva). Bhūta-tathatā is thus that which is ultimately real as opposed to the changing forms in which phenomena manifest themselves as they arise and pass away.

Bhuvanekabāhu. King of *Sri Lanka from 1237 to 1284 renowned for his piety and for having appointed scribes to copy the whole of the *Pāli Canon, which he then had distributed to the main monasteries of the island. Second of the five sons of Parakkhamabāhu II, he had been entrusted with the defence of the north of the island. Upon King *Vijayabāhu III's death a usurper took the throne which, however, was soon after restored to Bhuvanekabāhu. His son by the same name, who succeeded Parakkamabāhu III, held a great yearly festival to celebrate his coronation and to admit new members into the *Saṃgha.

bīja (Skt., seed). A term used in *Yogācāra *Buddhism to denote the 'packets' of karmic energy produced through habitual actions and stored in the *ālāya-vijñāna. Just as in more conventional understandings of the operation of *karma, it is believed that these 'seeds' will produce their 'fruit' at a future date in the form of pleasant and unpleasant experiences. The term is also used in *Vajrayāna to denote the mantric syllables from which deities and other divine objects are generated.

Bimbisāra. Founder of the *Haryaṅka dynasty and first king of *Magadha, which he ruled for 52 years (*c.*465–413 BCE) from his palace in *Rājagṛha. Bimbisāra was a great patron and admirer of the *Buddha, who was five years his senior, and donated the *Veḷuvana *ārāma for his use. Bimbisāra became a lay follower at the age of 30 and thereafter was zealous in his religious practice. He abdicated in later life in favour of his son, *Ajātaśatru (Pāli, Ajātasattu), who, at the instigation of *Devadatta, had his father imprisoned and tortured to death. Bimbisāra died eight years before the Buddha.

bindu (Skt., spot or drop). A term used in some forms of *anuttara-yoga-tantra to denote the subtle energy whose physical manifestation is identified with male semen. These drops of subtle energy are located in various parts of the body, such as in the heart, and are moved or manipulated around the subtle channels through meditation to generate the bliss associated with enlightenment (*bodhi).

Bindusāra. Second incumbent of the *Mauryan throne which he occupied for 28 years from *c.*297 BCE. Known to the Greeks as Amitrochates, he was the son of *Candragupta and father of *Aśoka.

Biographies of Eminent Monks. *See* KAO-SENG-CHUAN.

birth. *See* JĀTI.

birth-stories *See* JĀTAKA.

Blavatsky, H. P. *See* THEOSOPHICAL SOCIETY.

Blue Cliff Records. A collection of 100 *kōans first collected by *Hsüeh-tou Ch'ung-hsien (980–1052) from previous *Ch'an records. Hsüeh-tou added verses to each kōan. Later, *Yüan-wu K'o-ch'in (1063–1135) added a preface, critique, and biographical note on major characters to each of the kōans, and the work assumed its final shape. Yüan-wu completed the work in 1125, but a few years later his disciple *Ta-hui Tsung-kao (1089–1163) burnt it, citing the Ch'an school's independence of 'words and letters' as his reason. The book was not reprinted and circulated until the Ta-te period of the Yüan dynasty (1297–1307).

Bodhāhārakula (Pāli). Name given to the descendants of the eight families who brought the branch of the original *Bodhi Tree to *Sri Lanka and were entrusted, each having an official function, with the ceremonies in connection with the tree at *Anurādhapura.

Bodhgayā. Modern Indian name for Buddha-gayā, the site of the *Buddha's enlightenment (*bodhi) on the banks of the river *Nairañjanā, a southern tributary of the Ganges, near ancient *Rājagṛha. It was here that the seat of enlightenment (*bodhi-maṇḍa) was located, as well as the *Bodhi Tree under which the Buddha *Śākyamuni had sat. Though the Bodhi Tree was damaged on a number of occasions, the present tree is said to have grown from a cutting of the original tree. The *Mahābodhi Temple at Bodhgayā was begun during *Aśoka's period but repeatedly rebuilt and expanded over the centuries. It still received patronage for its upkeep as late as the 13th century CE, from the rulers of *Burma. By the 16th century, the deserted and ruined building was taken over for a while by Śaivite followers. It was eventually restored as a Buddhist site by the Burmese in the early 19th century CE, though it was later taken over by Hindus. The 1949 Bodhgayā Act ensured that this important site was once again given full recognition as a Buddhist holy place.

bodhi (Skt.; Pāli). Term which literally means 'awakening', but which is commonly translated as '*enlightenment'. It denotes the awakening to supreme knowledge, as experienced by the *Buddha as he sat under the *Bodhi Tree at the age of 35. Technically, the experience of bodhi is said to consists of seven elements known as the 'limbs of enlightenment' (*bodhyaṅga) and is achieved when the *Four Noble Truths are correctly apprehended. According to the earliest sources, *Arhats, *Pratyekabuddhas, and Buddhas all experience the same awakening, but over the course of time the awakening of a Buddha came to be seen as especially profound (see SAṂBODHI). *See also* SATORI; KENSHŌ.

Bodhicaryāvatāra. A classic in the world's religious literature composed by *Śāntideva. (685–763). The *Sanskrit title means 'Entering the Path of Enlightenment', although the original title may have been *Bodhisattvacaryāvatāra*, meaning 'Undertaking the way of the Bodhisattva'. The latter is the title found in Tibetan and Chinese manuscripts, including those discovered at *Tun-huang by Sir Aurel Stein in 1906–8, and on the basis of these texts it seems likely that the extant Sanskrit version is either a compilation or edited version of an earlier composition. The present arrangement of chapters also seems a later arrangement, since in the earlier manuscripts chapters 2 and 3 form one single chapter. This important *Mahāyāna work composed in verse describes the various steps to be taken by one on the *Bodhisattva Path, from the production of the thought of enlightenment (*bodhicitta) through the practice of the Perfections (*pāramitas) to full enlightenment. The text lays special emphasis on placing oneself in the position of others (parātma-parivartana) in order to promote selflessness (*anātman) and compassion (*karuṇā). 'Whoever wishes to quickly rescue himself and another he should practise the supreme mystery—the exchanging of himself and the other' (8. 120). The work culminates in the penultimate chapter (ch. 9) with an explanation of transcendental insight (*prajñā), its realization of emptiness (*śūnyatā), and the doctrine of the '*Two Truths', i.e. reality as seen in its ultimate and relative aspects.

bodhicitta (Skt., thought of awakening). A key term in *Mahāyāna *Buddhism denoting the state of mind of a *Boddhisattva. Two aspects are recognized: the relative aspect (*see* SAṂVṚTI-SATYA), or the mind (*citta) of a Bodhisattva directed towards enlightenment (*bodhi); and the absolute aspect (*see* PARAMĀRTHA-SATYA) or the mind whose intrinsic nature is enlightenment. The former relative aspect is also said to be twofold: the bodhicitta of aspiration (praṇidhāna), when one announces one's intention to pursue the Bodhisattva Path, and the bodhicitta of application, by which one engages in the path.

bodhicittotpāda (Skt., the arising of the thought of awakening). The point at the beginning of the *Bodhisattva path when the aspiration to become a Bodhisattva in order to save sentient beings wells up in the heart. This arising of *bodhicitta is thus a kind of conversion experience that leads to a transformed outlook on the world.

Bodhidharma (3rd-4th c. CE). According to *Ch'an and *Zen legends, Bodhidharma is the Indian *monk and missionary who brought Ch'an to *China. Legend portrays him as a south Indian prince who left the household life and, upon attaining enlightenment (*bodhi), became the 28th in a series of *patriarchs through which the *Buddha's original enlightenment experience had been transmitted directly without the mediation of 'words and scriptures'. Upon bringing Ch'an to China, he became the first Chinese patriarch, and all subsequent Chinese Ch'an and Japanese Zen masters trace their master-disciple lineages back to him.

According to the legend, Bodhidharma arrived in Canton via the sea route in 526, and was invited to the court of Emperor Wu, founder of the Liang dynasty in the south. Expecting the master's praise of his temple-building and lavish support of the *Saṃgha, the emperor received instead enigmatic responses and a brusque discounting of his activities. Bodhidharma then left for the north, reportedly crossing the Yangtze River on a reed, and arrived at the *Shao-lin Temple. Finding the resident clergy weak and prone to the depredations of local bandits, he taught them exercises and self-defence, from which evolved the famous Shao-lin style of *martial arts. He then sequestered himself in a cave for nine years and sat gazing at the wall. Once, enraged at his drowsiness, he ripped off his eyelids and threw them down to the ground, where they sprouted as tea plants. In addition, his legs are said to have withered away because of his constant sitting. (This is the origin of the Daruma doll, a Japanese toy shaped like an egg with a weighted bottom that springs upright again when knocked over. Its wide-open eyes and lack of legs derive from these stories of Bodhidharma.) *Hui-k'o, the man who would become his disciple and the second patriarch, came to him to study during this period, but was unable to get Bodhidharma's attention. The latter looked up and received him only after the former cut off his arm and offered it. When Bodhidharma died at the age of 160, he was buried at the Shao-lin Temple, but the same day one of the temple's *monks who was out travelling met him heading west holding up one of his sandals. When the monk returned, he recounted the story, whereupon the other clergy opened the tomb, and found only a single sandal inside.

Much of the above legend clearly is based on later stories, many of which serve to make polemical points in defence of the Ch'an school as it strove for acceptance and self-definition. However, there is no compelling reason to doubt the historicity of Bodhidharma himself. Numerous early records speak approvingly of him (or someone by that name) as wise and compassionate, and there exists a work purported to be of his composition called *The Two Entrances and Four Practices*. These witnesses confirm that he came from the west, that he was well practised in *meditation, and that he had a disciple named Hui-k'o. *The Two Entrances and Four Practices* gives his teaching on meditation and wisdom in terms that echo later Ch'an practice. However, far from being an iconoclastic and mysterious figure who rejects 'words and letters', these early sources present him as a master of a particular scripture, the **Laṅkāvatāra Sūtra*, and remark on his willingness to speak quite plainly and openly about his understanding of the teachings. All earlier sources report that he himself claimed to be over 150 years old, and one says that the time and circumstances of his death were unknown.

bodhimaṇḍa (Skt., awakening seat). The place where a *Buddha becomes enlightened, such as the site of the Buddha's enlightenment (*bodhi) under the *Bodhi Tree. Sometimes used to refer only to the spot on which the Buddha actually sat and other times to the surrounding area of land with the tree at its centre. Mythologically this spot becomes the site of the enlightenment of all Buddhas, past, present, and future, with the bodhimaṇḍa conceived of as the centre or navel of the world, and the Bodhi Tree as the *axis mundi*. In iconography the Buddha is depicted as seated on the bodhimaṇḍa with his right hand touching the earth to call it to witness his enlightenment (*see* BHŪMI-SPARŚA-MUDRĀ).

bodhi-pākṣika-dharma (Skt., things pertaining to awakening). Thirty-seven 'factors of *enlightenment' or things that are conducive to awakening (*bodhi). These comprise the four foundations of mindfulness (*smṛti-upasthāna), the four efforts or restraints (prahāṇa), the four bases of supernatural power (ṛddhipāda, *see* ṚDDHI), the five spiritual faculties (*indriya), the five powers (*bala), the seven limbs of enlightenment (*bodhyaṅga), and the *Eightfold Path (aṣṭāṅga-mārga).

Bodhiruci (6th c. CE). A north Indian *monk and *esoteric master who came to *China in 508 and became very active as a teacher and translator, producing translations of 39 works in 127 fascicles. Among these, the most important were the *Sūtra on the Ten Grounds* and commentary (Skt., **Daśabhūmika Sūtra*; Chin., *Shih ti ching lun*), and the *Shorter *Sukhāvatī-vyūha Sūtra* and commentary. The former text became the object of study by the *Ti-lun school, of which Bodhiruci is regarded as the *patriarch. This school was the forerunner of the *Hua-yen school. The latter text commented on one of the three foundational scriptures of the *Pure Land school.

Bodhiruci figures prominently in the story of Pure Land master *T'an-luan's conversion to this form of *Buddhism around 530. According to the story, T'an-luan, disturbed by an illness that presented him with the spectre of his own mortality, had travelled to south China to get a *Taoist work on immortality practice. Upon returning north, he encountered Bodhiruci. The latter expressed disdain for Taoist teachings and recommended that T'an-luan concentrate his efforts on attaining the Pure Land instead, handing him copies of Pure Land scriptures. T'an-luan accepted this advice, threw away his Taoist works, and spent the rest of his life in the exclusive practice of Pure Land.

Bodhisattva (Skt.; Pāli, Bodhisatta). The embodiment of the spiritual ideal of *Mahāyāna *Buddhism, in contrast to the earlier *Arhat ideal advocated by the *Hīnayāna. Bodhisattva literally means 'enlightenment being' but the correct *Sanskrit derivation may be 'bodhi-sakta' meaning 'a being who is orientated towards enlightenment'. The ideal is inspired by the lengthy career of the *Buddha before he became enlightened, as described in the *Jātakas. A Bodhisattva begins his career by generating the aspiration (*praṇidhāna) to achieve enlightenment for the sake of all beings, often in the form of a vow, which according to many Mahāyāna texts is often accompanied by a prediction of success (*vyākaraṇa) by a Buddha. He then embarks on the path leading to enlightenment (*bodhi) by cultivating the Six Perfections (*ṣaḍ-pāramitā) and the four means of attracting beings (*saṃgraha-vastu) over the course of three immeasurable *kalpas. The spiritual progress of a Bodhisattva is usually subdivided into ten stages or levels (*bhūmi). Many Mahāyāna *sūtras state that a Bodhisattva forgoes his own final enlightenment until all other beings in *saṃsāra have been liberated, or else describe a special form of *nirvāṇa, the unlocalized nirvāṇa (*apratiṣṭha-nirvāṇa) by virtue of which a Bodhisattva may be 'in the world but not of it'. Earlier Mahāyāna sūtras are specific in their belief that a Bodhisattva can only be male but later texts allow the possibility of female Bodhisattvas.

Bodhisattvabhūmi Śāstra. The sixteenth section of the **Yogācārabhūmi Śāstra*. Attributed to *Asaṅga or *Maitreyanātha, the work deals in detail with the entire career and training of a *Bodhisattva. It comprises four parts; (1) the Adhāra-yoga-sthāna in 29 chapters covering the main features and practices of a Bodhisattva's training; (2) the Adhāra-anuyoga-sthāna in four chapters covering the subsidiary practices; (3) the Adhāra-niṣṭhā-yoga-sthāna in six chapters dealing with the outcome of the training; and (4) the Anukrama which summarizes the stages of the Bodhisattva's path in sequence. The work survives in *Sanskrit as well as Tibetan, Chinese, and Mongolian translations.

Bodhisattva-śīla (Skt.). The rules of moral conduct or discipline prescribed for *Bodhisattvas. Although there is no single universally accepted code of conduct for Bodhisattvas, the various *precepts stipulated througout the *Mahāyāna *sūtras are grouped together and explicated in certain key texts, such as the chapter on morality (śīla-paṭala) of the **Bodhisattvabhūmi Śāstra*. The rules and procedures described there are often adopted by Buddhists as part of the formal ceremony when they accept the Bodhisattva-vow (*pranidhāna).

Bodhisattva-vow. *See* PRAṆIDHĀNA.

Bodhisattvayāna (Skt.). The 'Vehicle of the Bodhisattvas'. An alternative designation for the *Mahāyāna or 'Great Vehicle', it is the way, means, or method by which *Bodhisattvas pursue their religious career. It distinguishes itself from the two methods employed by the *Hīnayāna or 'Small Vehicle', namely the 'Vehicle of the Hearers' (*Śrāvakayāna), and the goal of personal enlightenment (*bodhi) in seclusion of the *Pratyekabuddha (Pratyekabuddha-yāna). Both of these earlier 'vehicles' are thought to be deficient by virtue of their lesser concern for others.

Bodhisena (704–760). Indian *monk who travelled first to *China and then to *Japan in 736 where he played a leading role in the dedication of the great statue to the *Buddha in Nara in 752 CE.

Bodhi Tree. Literally the 'tree of awakening', also known as the Bo Tree, it is the tree under which *Siddhārtha Gautama is believed to have gained enlightenment (*bodhi) after meditating under it for 49 days. In *Pāli it is known as the bodhirukkha, in *Sanskrit as the bodhivṛkṣa, and it is known to botanists as *ficus religiosa*. Given its close association with the occasion of his attaining Buddhahood, the tree has great symbolic significance and according to legend is the centre of the world and the spot at which all *Buddhas past and future gain enlightenment. In the twelfth year of his reign, *Aśoka's daughter *Saṅghamittā took a branch of the Bodhi Tree to *Sri Lanka. When the original Bodhi Tree was destroyed in the 7th century it was replaced with another one from the shoot exported to *Sri Lanka by King *Aśoka in the third century BCE. This was planted in the Mahābodhi temple where it flourishes today. Each *Buddha is associated with a particular Bodhi Tree, but since the earliest accounts of the Buddha's enlightenment fail to mention a tree, it is possible that the cult of the Bodhi Tree is a more recent addition. It has become customary to plant a Bodhi Tree, if possible a cutting, in every monastery (*vihāra) to indicate the presence of the *Dharma. In early Buddhist art the figure of the Buddha was not portrayed, and the image of the tree, along with other symbols, was used to represent him.

bodhyaṅga (Pāli, bojjhaṅga). A list of seven factors that lead to or constitute *bodhi, or awakening. Often referred to as the seven 'limbs of enlightenment', the seven items are listed in *Pāli sources as: (1) mindfulness (sati); (2) investigation of the *Dharma (dharma-vicaya); (3) energy (viriya); (4) joy (pīti); (5) tranquillity (passaddhi); (6) meditation (*samādhi); (7) equanimity (upekkhā). The seven occur as the sixth of the 37 'factors of enlightenment' (*bodhi-pākṣika-dharma).

body, speech, mind. The three vectors of karmic action (*see* KARMA) according to general Buddhist teachings. The three are often used in exegetical systems to link with various other tripartite groups, such as the three 'bodies of the *Buddha' (*trikāya). Here, the body is linked to the Buddha's Emanation Body (*nirmāṇa-kāya), speech with the Enjoyment Body (*saṃbhoga-kāya) and the mind with the absolute or Truth Body (*dharma-kāya). Body, speech, and mind are also important in *Vajrayāna practice where they are to be transformed through mystic gestures (*mudrā), sacred sounds (*mantra) and meditation (*samādhi) into the corresponding body, speech, and mind of a Buddha.

bōkatsu (Jap.). A training technique used by *Zen Buddhist teachers. The master gives a sudden shout (ho) and at the same time strikes the student wth a stick (kyosaku). The aim is to startle the students and help them achieve awakening (*satori).

bokuseki (Jap.). A form of Japanese calligraphy expressing the insights of *Zen masters.

Bön (Tib.). **1.** The ancient pre-Buddhist religion of *Tibet and some neighbouring areas. It was founded by the legendary teacher *Shen-rap Mi-wo (Tib., gshen-rab mi-bo) and comprises two main aspects: the positive White Bön (bon-dkar) and the negative Black Bön (bon-nag). Three historical phases of White Bön are distinguished: the unreformed pre-literate Bön (brdol-bon) of pre-Buddhist times primarily involving rituals for the suppression of evil spirits and the worship (*pūjā) of ancestral deities; imported Bön ('khyar-bon) which was initially widespread in areas to the east of Tibet such as Brusha and Changchung and then propagated in Tibet following the reign of Drigum Tsenpo; and translated Bön (bsgyur-bon), also known as the 'White Water Tradition' (chab-dkar) which was developed during the 8th century CE in reaction to *Buddhism by modifying or recasting Buddhist literature into Bön versions. Black Bön dealt mainly with black magic, malefic rituals, and practices. Supporters of Bön were often hostile to the introduction of Buddhism which they saw as a threat to their role of state religion and several Tibetan kings are known to have been assassinated in the ensuing power struggles. Under Buddhist influence a monastic system was developed which survives to the present day in parts of eastern Tibet and in exile in *India.

bonpu (Jap., ordinary man). Expression used in *Zen to denote the ordinary person or 'man in the street' as opposed to one who is enlightened or advanced on the religious path. The term is equivalent to the *Sanskrit *pṛthagjana.

bonpu no jōshiki (Jap., average man's consciousness). The state of mind of the average person who is deluded as to the true nature of the human condition as set out in Buddhist teachings. Such a person believes in a permanent self (*ātman) and is afflicted by craving (*tṛṣṇā) and ignorance (*avidyā). Such a consciousness is not different in nature from the enlightened consciousness but merely fails to understand its own intrinsic purity.

bonze. Bonzo was an early Portuguese pronunciation of the Japanese word *bussō, meaning 'Buddhist cleric', which then came into English as 'bonze'. It was widely used in English writings on east Asian *Buddhism until the mid-20th century.

Borobudur. Famous Javanese *stūpa and the largest of Buddhist monuments. Built between the 8th and 9th centuries by the rulers of the Śailendra and Sanjaya dynasties, the stūpa was constructed as a giant *maṇḍala or sacred diagram linked with the adventures of Sudhana described in the **Gaṇḍavyūha Sūtra*. Erected around a natural hillside it comprises five terraces, the walls of which are decorated with bas-reliefs, surmounted by three circular platforms on which are positioned 72 miniature stūpas, themselves gathered around a massive central stūpa. On the first four terraces, the traditional *Buddhas of the various directions are represented. On the fifth terrace *Vairocana adorns all sides. Circumambulating the stūpa reveals scenes from *Śākyamuni Buddha's life, *Jātaka tales, and *Mahāyāna *sūtras. The vertical ascent to the top of the stūpa is considered to be a symbolic journey from *saṃsāra to *nirvāṇa. The monument was used until the 10th century and some activity continued to take place here until the 14th century. Now an important *pilgrimage site for Buddhists worldwide, it has become, since its discovery in the 19th century, an important site for Buddhist scholarly research. The meaning of the name Borobudur is unknown.

bosatsu (Jap.). Japanese for *Bodhisattva.

bot (Thai). The main sanctuary of a temple.

Botataung Paya (Burm.). Literally '*Stūpa of the 1,000 leaders'. This stūpa in *Burma was named after the 1000 military leaders who escorted *relics of the *Buddha brought from *India over 2000 years ago. The monument was completely destroyed during the Second World War and the present stūpa, 131 feet high, is a recent structure, built in a very similar style to its predecessor. However, unlike most *zedis, which are solid, this one is hollow and one can walk through it and admire the ancient relics and artefacts, including small silver and gold Buddha images, which were sealed inside the earlier stūpa.

Brahmā. One of the three central Hindu deities, also known in *Buddhism where he is respected but relegated to a lesser position of importance.

brahmacārya (Skt.; Pāli, brahmacariya). General term for a pure or holy life, and in particular the practice of *celibacy.

***Brahmajāla Sūtra*. 1.** The *Sanskrit title of the **Fan wang ching*. **2.** The first *sutta of the *Dīgha Nikāya. The text consists of two sections. The first sets out three lists (short, medium, and long) of moral *precepts. These lists recur in several of the following suttas. The second, longer, section is devoted to the refutation of 62 kinds of wrong view concerning the nature of the soul.

Brahma-loka (Skt.; Pāli, Brahma world). Used in two senses to refer to the *heavens or spiritual realms in Buddhist *cosmology; (1) as a collective name for the two uppermost spiritual realms, namely the Form Realm (*rūpa-dhātu) and the Formless Realm (*ārūpya-dhātu); (2) more specifically, the first three heavens of the Formless Realm. *See also* COSMOLOGY; TRILOKA.

Brahman (Skt.). According to *Hinduism, the impersonal principle of divinity or ultimate reality.

Brāhmaṇa (Skt.; Pāli). **1.** A Brahmin or member of the Hindu priestly *caste against whose abuse of power and deluded ideas of self-importance the *Buddha directed a number of his discourses. **2.** A genre of Hindu religious literature appended to the *Vedas. These sources date to approximately the 8th century BCE and comprise explanatory manuals of instruction relating to the performance of sacrifice, as well as containing a range of cosmological speculations.

Brāhmaṇatissa-cora. Also known as Tissa, a *Brahmin who lived at the time of King *Vaṭṭagāmaṇi Abhaya (1st C.BCE). According to the chronicles of *Sri Lanka, he turned brigand with the intent of acquiring the throne of the island and brought a period of great distress in the country. Because at the same time Tamils from *India were also trying to conquer Sri Lanka, King Vaṭṭagāmaṇi Abhaya sent word to Tissa that the kingdom would be his if he could defeat the foreign invaders. Tissa agreed to this, but was taken captive in a battle. According to the *Pāli commentaries, Brāhmaṇatissa plundered the land for twelve years and his activities were at their height in the period when the king was in hiding. When Brāhmaṇatissa died the king once more came to the throne.

Brahmanism. English word coined from the *Sanskrit term *Brāhmaṇa (from which is also derived the anglicization 'Brahmin') meaning a member of the Indian priestly *caste. The term Brahmanism is best reserved for the early phase in Indian religion (roughly 800 CE to 500 CE) in which ritual sacrifices offered by the priestly caste were the dominant form of orthodox religious practice. The term thus denotes the early form of the religion subsequently known to the West as '*Hinduism'.

Brahma-vihāra (Skt.; Pāli, abode of Brahma). A key set of four meditative practices often translated as the four 'Immeasurables', the four 'Pure Abodes', or the four 'Stations of Brahma'. The four are loving-kindness (*maitrī), compassion (*karuṇā), sympathetic joy (*muditā), and equanimity (*upekṣā). The practice of the four Brahmavihāras involves radiating outwards the postive qualities associated with such states of mind, directing them first towards oneself, then to one's family, the local community, and eventually to all beings in the universe.

Britain. British interest in *Buddhism developed during the colonial period when a stream of officials and administrators were posted to different parts of the British Empire in Asia, and particularly to *India and *Sri Lanka. Sir William Jones (1746–94) founded the Asiatic Society of Bengal (subsequently the *Royal Asiatic Society) in 1784, and the Society began to collect and study oriental manuscripts. The earliest Buddhist texts to be studied were *Mahāyāna *Sanskrit manuscripts collected in *Nepal by the British Resident, B. H. Hodgson. Another British civil servant who made an outstanding contribution to the study of *Theravāda Buddhism was T. W. *Rhys Davids (1843–1922). Rhys Davids became interested in Buddhism during his residence in Sri Lanka and went on to found the *Pali Text Society in 1881. The Society remains to this day the most important outlet for the publication of texts and translations of *Pāli Buddhist literature. Interest in Buddhism was heightened by Sir Edwin *Arnold's famous poem *The Light of Asia*, which inspired Westerners to seek *ordination. Among them was C. A. B. McGregor (1872–1923) who was ordained in 1901 as *Ananda Metteya and who inspired the foundation of the Buddhist Society of Great Britain and Ireland in 1907 with his mission to England in 1908. The Theravāda form of Buddhism was predominant in Britain until the middle of the 20th century when other groups, notably *Zen and Tibetan (*see* TIBET), began to arrive.

Britain has not been affected by mass Buddhist immigration since most of the Asian immigrants to the United Kingdom have been Hindus and Muslims. In contrast to the

USA (*see* AMERICA), there are only around 50,000 refugees from Indo-China in Britain. The majority of British Buddhists are therefore Caucasians who have converted to Buddhism, and most are middle-class. There are something of the order of 200,000 Buddhists in Britain belonging to some 100 Tibetan centres, 90 Theravāda centres, and around 100 or so other groups, including the *Friends of the Western Buddhist Order.

Buddha (Skt.; Pāli). This is not a personal name but an epithet of those who have achieved enlightenment (*bodhi), the goal of the Buddhist religious life. Buddha comes from the *Sanskrit root 'budh', meaning to awaken, and the Buddhas are those who have awakened to the true nature of things as taught in the *Four Noble Truths. By contrast, the mass of humanity is seen as asleep and unaware of the reality of the human condition. Doctrinally, the Buddhas are those who have attained *nirvāṇa by destroying the defilements known as *āśravas. Accordingly they are free of sensual craving (*kāma), becoming (*bhava), and ignorance (*avidyā). Because they have eradicated all craving they have escaped from the round of cyclic existence (*saṃsāra) and will never again be reborn. For *Theravāda *Buddhism, a Buddha is simply a human being who has undergone a profound spiritual transformation. In *Mahāyāna thought, by contrast, the concept of the Buddha developed in various ways, notably in the doctrine of the Buddha's 'three bodies' (*trikāya). In terms of this teaching, the Buddha is seen as a cosmic being who from time to time manifests himself in human form.

An important function of a Buddha is to act as a teacher, leading others to salvation by expounding the *Dharma. The exception to this is the 'private Buddha' (*Pratyekabuddha), who achieves enlightenment but does not teach. Such a Buddha is considered inferior to the 'fully enlightened Buddha' (*samyak-saṃbuddha) who teaches, and, according to Mahāyāna doctrine, is omniscient (sarvajñā) and possesses ten special powers (*daśa-bala). Buddhas are distinguished from other enlightened beings such as *Arhats by virtue of the fact that they discover the truth (Dharma) themselves, rather than hearing it from another. All schools of Buddhism believe there have been many Buddhas in the past and there will be more in the future, for instance *Maitreya. The *Mahāpadāna Sutta* of the *Pāli Canon mentions six previous Buddhas, and the **Buddhavaṃsa* gives a list of 24. In all these cases a similar stereotypical biography is supplied. It is generally believed that there can never be more than one Buddha in any particular era, and the 'historical Buddha' of the present era was *Siddhartha Gautama. Numerous ahistorical Buddhas make an appearance in Mahāyāna literature, notably the five *Jinas who are popular in *tantric schools.

Buddhabhadra (359–429). A north Indian *monk and scholar who joined the monastic order at age 17 and thereafter concentrated on the study of meditation and monastic law (*Vinaya). In 408 he relocated to *China at the invitation of the clergy there, where he set to work as a translator. At first, he settled in the capital city *Ch'ang-an, but because of disagreements with *Kumārajīva, another renowned foreign translator, he left with some 40 disciples and went first to Lu-shan, where he worked closely with the scholar-monk *Lu-shan Hui-yüan (344–416), and then to the southern capital Chien-k'ang (modern Nanking). Working at first in cooperation with Chinese monks, and later on his own, he produced thirteen works in approximately 125 fascicles. Among the most significant of these are the **Nirvāṇa Sūtra* and the *Mahāsaṃghika-vinaya* (both with *Fa-hsien), and the **Avataṃsaka Sūtra* (or *Hua-yen ching).

Buddhacarita (Skt., the acts of the Buddha). A biography of the *Buddha in the style of *Sanskrit epic poetry (mahākāvya) written by *Aśvaghosa about the 2nd century CE. Of the seventeen cantos which survive in the original only the first thirteen are by Aśvaghosa, the remaining four being added in the 19th century and extending the narrative as far as the Buddha's return home to *Lumbinī after his enlightenment (*bodhi). The complete version of the epic is preserved in Tibetan and Chinese translations which both extend to 28 cantos. The *Buddhacarita* is a literary and religious classic, the work of a talented and skilful poet who was also an adherent of the faith. The style is reverent yet restrained and the work is relatively free of the fanciful hagiographic detail found in other sources.

Buddhadāsa (1906–93). Leading Thai Buddhist *monk and reformer named after a former king of *Sri Lanka (r. 362–409). Ordained at the age of 20, Buddhadāsa subsequently founded a centre for *meditation in southern *Thailand in 1932. His general approach, in contrast to the standard Burmese practice of insight meditation (*vipaśyanā) was to teach insight through the attainment of trance (*dhyāna). In his extensive writings he has offered revisionist interpretations of traditional teachings in an effort to make them consistent with scientific discoveries and more applicable to the problems of the modern world. He emphasized ethical conduct over metaphysical beliefs, and even cast doubt on the belief in *rebirth. His views have provoked controversy, as has the manner of his death. After suffering several strokes he went into a coma and against his previously expressed wishes was admitted to Siriraj hospital in May 1993 for treatment. This incident caused a national debate about living wills, euthanasia, and medical intervention at the end of life.

Buddhadatta. Scholar and commentator who lived in Uragapura in *Kāñcī, after having studied at the *Mahāvihāra in *Anurādhapura. Among his works are the *Vinaya-Vinicchaya*, the *Uttara-Vinicchaya*, the **Abhidhamma-avatāra*, and the *Rūpārūpavibhāga*. Tradition has it that he met *Buddhaghoṣa, but this cannot be confirmed.

Buddha-dharma (Skt., Buddha-teachings). The doctrines or teachings of the *Buddha; that which is known in the West as '*Buddhism'.

Buddha-field. *See* BUDDHA-KṢETRA.

Buddha-gāyā. *See* BODHGAYĀ.

Buddhaghoṣa (Skt.; Pāli, Buddhaghosa). A *monk, born at the beginning of the 5th century and considered to be the greatest of commentators on the *Pāli Canon. The hagiographic accounts of his life report that because his speech, like that of the Buddha, was profound and his words spread throughout the world he came to be called Buddhaghoṣa, literally meaning 'Buddha utterance'. Later tradition ascribes to him an exaggerated number of texts. It is said that while living in *India he composed the *Ñāṇodaya* and the **Atthasālinī*, and also began to write a concise commentary (Parittaṭṭhakathā) on the *Tripiṭaka (Pāli, Tipiṭaka). In order to complete his task, he went to *Sri Lanka and studied the Sinhalese commentaries at the *Mahāvihāra. When his studies ended he wrote the **Visuddhimagga*, and having won the approval of the monks of the Mahāvihāra, he rendered the Sinhalese commentaries into *Pāli. According to the *Theravādin tradition the commentaries came to Sri Lanka with the first Buddhist missionaries in the 3rd century BCE. When this task was accomplished, Buddhaghoṣa returned to India. Besides the above-mentioned works Buddhaghoṣa is credited with composing the **Samantapāsādikā* and the **Kaṅkhāvitaraṇī* commentaries on the *Vinaya Piṭaka, and the **Manorathapūraṇī* commentary on the *Sūtra Piṭaka. He is also said to have compiled commentaries on the **Khuddakapāṭha*, the **Sutta Nipāta* and on the **Dhammapada*. Some also ascribe to him the commentary on the *Jātakas (*Jātakaṭṭakathā*). In fact the Vinaya commentary is probably not his work, and the author of the Abhidhamma commentary states that he is writing it at the request of Buddhaghoṣa. It is probably safest to attribute to Buddhaghoṣa only the *Visuddhimagga* and the commentaries on the four *Nikāyas or *āgamas. The rest is best viewed as the work of the 'school of Buddhaghoṣa'. Whatever their exact provenance, these works have exerted a major influence upon the doctrine of the *Theravāda orthodoxy in Sri Lanka, and the teachings of Theravāda Buddhism as we know them today.

Buddha Jayantī. 'Celebration of *Buddhism'. Name given to the celebrations held in 1956–7 to mark the 2,500th year of the Buddhist era. The historical reckoning of this date is probably no more accurate than calculations concerning the date of the second millennium in the West. *See* DATE OF THE BUDDHA.

Buddha-kṣetra (Skt., Buddha-field). The sphere of influence and activity of a *Buddha. In Buddhist cosmology, each world-system (*cakravāla) is the domain of a particular Buddha within which he arises and leads beings to liberation through his teachings. The concept came to prominence in the *Mahāyāna on the basis of early speculations about the range of a Buddha's knowledge and the extent of his sensory powers. With the concept of a plurality of Buddhas came the notion of an infinite number of 'Buddha-fields' extending throughout the reaches of space in many directions or dimensions. These fields vary in their degree of perfection and are divided into two basic categories, pure and impure. The world we inhabit now is an instance of an impure Buddha-field since beings here are still subject to the basic vices of greed, hatred, and delusion. The most famous of the pure Buddha-fields or '*Pure Lands' is the paradise of the Buddha *Amitabha in the west described in the **Sukhāvatī-vyūha Sūtras*, into which all may be reborn by calling upon the name of *Amitābha. The existence of these pure Buddha-fields became immensely important in the development of popular devotional *Buddhism, especially in *China and *Japan.

Buddha-kula (Skt., Buddha family). A term especially associated with *tantric *Buddhism and used to categorize and allocate the various *Buddhas, *Bodhisattvas, other deities and also initiates into groups. Early tantric texts utilize a threefold system, the *three Buddha families, comprising the *Tathāgata Family associated with *Śākyamuni or *Vairocana, the Vajra Family associated with *Vajrapāṇi or *Akṣobhya, and the Lotus Family associated with *Avalokiteśvara or *Amitābha. Later tantric traditions employ a fivefold system, the *five Buddha families or Five *Jinas, correlated to the five awarenesses (*pañca-jñāna) or aspects of enlightenment (*bodhi), comprising the Tathāgata family (Vairocana), the Vajra family (Akṣobhya), the Jewel family (*Ratnasaṃbhava), the Lotus family (Amitābha) and the Action family (*Amoghasiddhi).

Buddha Land *See* Pure Land.

Buddha-nature (Skt., buddhatā, buddha-dhātu; Jap., busshō). In early Buddhist thought, this term referred to the potentiality for becoming a *Buddha through the traditional methods of study and religious practice. Discussion centred on clarifying what kind of beings had this potential and how it was to be developed. After the rise of *Mahāyāna *Buddhism, some thinkers began to question the validity of the distinction between practice and enlightenment (*bodhi), or between potentiality and attainment, and so Buddha-nature gradually came to be seen not as a potential, but as the inherent Buddhahood of every sentient being. In this setting, the task then was not to achieve Buddhahood, but to uncover it. For example, the **Platform Sūtra of the Sixth Patriarch* compares Buddhahood to a full moon covered by clouds. When the clouds blow away, the moon is revealed. It does not gradually come into being nor is it constructed. Similarly, each being is already a Buddha, but this fact is obscured by defilements and impurities. Once these are removed, one's Buddhahood becomes manifest.

Still later, Chinese and Japanese Buddhism came to question the distinction between sentient and non-sentient beings. In this context, some schools came to assert that every phenomenon whatsoever has Buddha-nature, not just sentient beings. One of the goals of practice in this context is to see the unity of all things in the world based on the commonality of Buddha-nature.

Another strain of thought, dating back to Indian Mahāyāna sources, used the term Buddha-nature as a gloss for ultimate reality, or the final nature of all existents. In most Indian and Tibetan forms of Mahāyāna, Buddha-nature is generally understood as a synonym for emptiness (*śūnyatā) and a lack of any abiding core of being (*ātman). For example, *Vasubandhu in his *Treatise on Buddha-nature* equated the term with both emptiness and *nirvāṇa. However, under the influence of the Tathāgata-garbha teachings as developed in the Tibetan concepts of *extrinsic emptiness, and parallel doctrines in Chinese Buddhism, Buddha-nature came to be seen as a more substantial presence endowed with positive attributes, often termed 'ātman' in such *sūtras as the Mahāyāna **Nirvāṇa Sūtra*.

Buddhapālita (470–540). A teacher and commentator of the *Prāsaṅgika branch of the *Madhyamaka school. He is the author of the *Mūla-madhyamaka-vṛtti*, a commentary on the **Mūla-madhyamaka-kārikā* of *Nāgārjuna, the 2nd-century founder of the school. Buddhapālita's commentary, which survives in Tibetan, contains 27 chapters and is divided into ten sections. Buddhapālita's interpretation of Madhyamaka was criticized by the *Svātantrika-Madhyamaka author *Bhāvaviveka who was in turn refuted by *Candrakīrti, the most famous exponent of the Prāsaṅgika interpretation.

Buddha-rūpa (Skt.; Pāli). An image or statue of the *Buddha.

Buddha-śāsana (Skt., The teachings of the Buddha). *See* ŚĀSANA.

Buddhaśānta. A north Indian *monk who went to *China in 511 CE where he cooperated with *Bodhiruci in translating the **Daśabhūmika Sūtra*. Later he worked on a version of the **Mahāyāna-saṃgraha* and other texts.

buddhatā (Skt.). *See* BUDDHA-NATURE.

Buddhatrāta. The putative translator of the *Yuan-chueh-ching* (*Sūtra of Perfect Enlightenment*) but his historicity is doubted since it is generally accepted that this text was composed in *China and his name does not seem to be found in connection with any other works.

Buddhavaṃsa. The fourteenth book of the *Khuddaka Nikāya of the *Pāli Canon. It is a work in verse whose author is not known. In it *Gautama (Pāli, Gotama) *Buddha relates the lives of the 24 Buddhas who preceded him, and his former actions in relation to those Buddhas. His name as a former *Bodhisattva (Pāli, Bodhisatta) under each Buddha is also given. It is said that the *Buddhavaṃsa* was preached, at *Śāriputra's request, after the Buddha had performed the miracle of the ratanacaṅkama (jewelled walk) and the introductory chapter of this work is called the Ratanacaṅkamana-khandha. The last chapter deals with the distribution of Gautama's *relics. The commentary on the *Buddhavaṃsa* is known as the **Madhuratthavilāsinī*.

Buddhism. Western term which became established in popular usage in the 1830s to refer to the teachings of the *Buddha. There is no direct equivalent for this term in *Sanskrit or *Pāli. Instead, indigenous sources use terms like *Dharma ('the Law'), *Buddha-dharma ('Buddhist doctrine'), *Buddha-śāsana ('teachings of the Buddha') and Buddhavacana ('the word of the Buddha').

Buddhist Churches of America. One of the oldest Buddhist groups in north *America established in 1899 in San Francisco. Originally called the Buddhist Mission of North America, the organization adopted its present name after the First World War and membership has since grown rapidly ever since to number over 100,000 today. Japanese in origin, it promotes the teachings of the *Jōdo Shinshū in its numerous centres across the United States.

Buddhist Councils. *See* COUNCIL OF PĀṬALIPUTRA, etc.

Buddhist Hybrid Sanskrit. Name given by scholars to a variant of classical *Sanskrit retaining traces of earlier *Prakrit forms and found in many *Mahāyāna *sūtras.

Buddhist Society. The Buddhist Society of Great Britain and Ireland with its headquarters in London is the oldest Buddhist organisation in *Europe. The Society was founded in 1907 under the presidency of T. W. *Rhys Davids in order to receive the mission of *Ananda Metteyya to England in 1908. The Society was wound up in 1925 and replaced by the Buddhist Lodge, London, in 1926, the Buddhist Society, London, in 1943, and the Buddhist Society in 1952. Its journal *Buddhism in England*, founded in 1926, was renamed *The Middle Way* in 1945. Vice-presidents have included I. B. *Horner and Edward *Conze, and the patron of the Society is the *Dalai Lama. *See also* BRITAIN.

buji-zen (Jap.). Bravado or excessive self-confidence in the practice of *Zen. A tendency attributed to some practitioners, particularly in the *Sōtō school, to convince themselves that since all beings possess the *Buddha-nature they are already enlightened and hence have no need to exert themselves further.

Bun (boun) (Lao, festival). **1.** A religious festival. **2.** The merit (*puṇya) earned through Buddhist religious practices.

buppō (bukkyō) (Jap.). A Japanese rendering of the term '*Buddha-dharma', meaning the teachings of *Buddhism.

Burma. *South-east Asian country now officially known as Myanmar. *Buddhism may have been introduced here by one of *Aśoka's missions, and it has been present among the native *Mons people from the early centuries CE. The Burmese chronicles claim that *Buddhaghoṣa visited the country and established a tradition of *Pāli scholarship. The Pāli name for the Mon country to the south is Rāmañña, and the Sinhalese chronicles relate that when the Sinhalese *ordination lineage died out King *Vijayabāhu I (1059–1114) of *Sri Lanka sent to Rāmañña (Burma) for monks to re-establish the *Saṃgha. From the 5th to the 15th century the dominant power in the region was the *Khmer Empire, in which various forms of *Mahāyāna Buddhism were popular. King *Anawrahtā (1044–77) unified the country by conquering the southern part and gave his allegiance to the *Theravāda, although it is likely the Theravāda was dominant even before then. Anawrahtā's capital, *Pagān, was sacked by the Mongols in 1287 and the city with its many thousand *pagodas and temples was abandoned. The country was not united again until 1752, but soon afterwards was conquered by the British and became part of the British Empire until it was granted independence in 1948 when *U Nu became the first Prime Minister. Attempts to develop a form of 'Buddhist Socialism' with Buddhism as the state religion ultimately failed when General Ne Win led a coup in 1962 from which time onwards the country has been ruled by a military junta (SLORC). The regime is not hostile to Buddhism, which remains strong, and 85 per cent of the population are Theravāda Buddhists. However, Buddhist pro-democracy advocates, such as Aung Suu Kyi, have been placed under house arrest and human rights abuses are commonplace. The country presently remains isolated from the international community.

bushidō (Jap.). A term meaning 'the Way of the Warrior-Gentleman'. More of a general outlook on life than a formal ethic, it was born in the opening years of the Tokugawa Period (1603–1868) (*see* JAPAN), when a prolonged peace made members of the *samurai class nostalgic for former military campaigns and forced them to rethink their role in civil society. This outlook stressed frugality, honour, loyalty, mastery of *martial arts, readiness for combat at a moment's notice, and, above all, a willingess to die at any time. Many samurai found that *Zen training helped to inculcate the austerity, detachment, and presence of mind needed both in combat situations and in daily life. *See also* MARTIAL ARTS.

busshi (Jap.). A Buddhist disciple. This term can be literally rendered as 'Son of the *Buddha'. Occasionally, it is used also to refer to all sentient beings.

busshin (Jap.). Literally 'Buddha-mind', this term can refer either to the (or a) *Buddha's compassionate and enlightened mind, or to the originally clear and pure mind inherent in all beings to which they must awaken.

busshō (Jap.). *See* BUDDHA-NATURE; BUDDHATĀ.

busso (Jap.). A compound meaning either '*Buddhas and *patriarchs' or simply the Buddhas in their capacity as patriarchs.

Bu-stön. *See* BUTÖN RIN-CHEN-GRUP.

Butön rin-chen-grup (1290–1364) (Tib., Bu-ston rin-chen grub). A Tibetan teacher, translator, and historian of *Buddhism. He was born in Tsang in southern *Tibet and trained as a *Kagyü *monk, spending much of his life studying and teaching at the college of Zhalu. He became a novice at 17 and was ordained as a monk at 23. By the age of 30 he had studied under all the great teachers of his day and began to compose treatises in his own name and to translate and edit the canon.

Butön was involved with the redaction and classification of the two parts of the Tibetan Buddhist *canon, the *Kanjur and the *Tenjur. His systematization of these texts became one of the chief bases for the structure of the later printed versions of this corpus of texts. He also composed many texts and commentaries, of which his *Doctrinal History* (chos-'byung) is especially noteworthy as it contains a chronicle of the history of Buddhism in *India, *Nepal, and Tibet as well as an index to all the translations in the Kanjur and the Tenjur. Bu-ston's works number over 200 items, and the impetus he gave to Buddhist scholarship in Tibet was considerable and especially timely in view of the imminent extinction of Buddhism in India.

butsu (butsuda) (Jap.). Renderings in Japanese of the one-and two-character Chinese names for the *Buddha.

butsudan (Jap.). In Japanese *Buddhism, an altar or niche in the wall, found either in the living rooms of private residences or the abbot's apartment in a monastery, where offerings are made to the deceased, who are represented by vertical tablets inscribed with their posthumous names.

Byakue-Kannon (Jap.). *See* PAI-I KUAN-YIN.

C

caitasika (Skt.; Pāli cetasika). Earlier form of the word *caitta. Both forms are found in *Sanskrit commentarial literature. *See also* CETASIKA.

caitta (Skt.). Term in Buddhist psychology (being a later form of *caitasika) denoting derivative mental states or functions of the mind (*citta). Lists of these, derived from the *sūtras and differing in detail, are found in the various *Abhidharma systems. The list found in *Vasubandhu's **Abhidharma-kośa* was regarded as normative by many Buddhists in *India and elsewhere and comprises (1) five universal functions: contact (*sparśa), attention (manasikāra), feeling (*vedanā), ideation (*saṃjñā), and intention (*cetanā); (2) five occasional functions: motivation (*chanda), interest (*adhimokṣa), recollection (*smṛti), concentration (*samādhi), and insight (*prajñā); (3) eleven wholesome functions: trust (*śraddhā), decency (hrī), decorum (apatrapā), non-attachment (*alobha), non-hatred (*adveṣa), non-deludedness (*amoha), effort (*vīrya), lucidity (praśrabhi), carefulness (*apramāda), equanimity (*upekṣā) and non-violence (avihiṃsā); (4) six root negative functions (*kleśa): lust (*rāga), hatred (pratighā), stupidity (*avidyā), arrogance (*māna), doubt (*vicikitsā), and opinionatedness (*dṛṣṭi); (5) 20 subsidiary negative factors (upakleśa): anger (krodha), hostility (upanāha), dissimulation (mrakṣa), malice (pradāsa), jealousy (īrṣyā), avarice (mātsarya), hypocrisy (māyā), dishonesty (śāṭhya), spitefulness (vihiṃsā), pride (mada), contempt (āhrīkya), indecorum (anapatrāpya), overexuberance (auddhatya), inattentiveness (styāna), distrust (āśraddhya), carelessness (pramāda), laziness (kauśīdya), forgetfulness (musitā smṛti), excitability (vikṣepa), and delusion (asaṃprajanya); and (6) four indeterminate functions: regret (kaukṛtya), drowsiness (middha), selection (*vitarka), and discursive examination (*vicāra). *See also* CETASIKA.

caitya (Skt.; Pāli, cetiya). Literally 'tumulus, sepulchral monument'. **1.** An alternative name for a *stūpa, usually one which is empty of *relics. **2.** A Buddhist sanctuary used as an assembly hall, originally referring to rock-cut caves such as those at *Ellorā, which featured a stūpa as a focal point of devotion.

Cakkavattisīhanāda Sutta. 'The lion's roar on the turning of the wheel'. An important early discourse, number 26 in the *Dīgha Nikāya, concerned with the notion of the *cakravartin or Buddhist universal ruler. The discourse narrates a story showing how a society's prosperity or decline depends in large part on the policies adopted by the ruler.

cakra (Skt.; Pāli, cakka). **1.** A wheel, often used symbolically in *Buddhism to signify the various aspects of the *Dharma. With eight spokes it connotes the *Eightfold Path, and with twelve spokes the doctrine of Dependent Origination (*pratītya-samutpāda) or three turnings of the wheel (three times the *Four Noble Truths as mentioned in the *first sermon). **2.** In *anuttara-yoga-tantric practice, the cakras are energy centres in the body, located along the subtle channels (*nāḍī); different numbers of cakras are described according to the specific meditational systems, ranging from three to five or six. It should be noted that the names and descriptions of these energy centres do not correspond to those found in Hindu tantra, and there is no standard set of names and descriptions for the cakras in either Hinduism or Buddhism (standardized versions are all modern inventions). **3.** A religious diagram, or *maṇḍala.

cakraratana (Skt.; Pāli, cakkaratana). The 'wheel treasure' of a *cakravartin or universal ruler. This treasure is a fabulous wheel having a thousand spokes and bedecked with jewels that appears when a cakravartin is born and disappears when he dies. A magical device, it carries the cakravartin and his retinue to each of the four continents where he is received as the rightful ruler, before returning to his palace where it remains as an ornament.

Eventually the wheel begins to slip from its position, announcing the end of the king's reign.

Cakra-saṃvara (Skt.; Tib., bde-mchog 'khor-lo). Literally 'The Wheel of Supreme Bliss', a semi-wrathful *yi-dam or tutelary deity with four heads and twelve arms associated with a particular group of *anuttara-yoga *Mother Tantras. He is also known by the short form of his name, Saṃvara or alternatively Śaṃvara. Normally he is depicted in union with his consort Vajra-Varāhi. *See also* CAKRA-SAṂVARA TANTRA.

Cakra-saṃvara Tantra. The root tantra of the group of *Mother Tantras associated with the *yi-dam *Cakra-saṃvara. Known as the *Śrī-cakra-saṃvara-guhya-cintya Tantra*, the root text describes the deity and main practices that relate to him. It was translated into Tibetan by Gayadhara and Drogmi Śākya Yeshe.

cakravāla (Skt.; Pāli, cakkavāḷa). Term found in late canonical (e.g. the **Buddhavaṃsa* and **Apadāna*) and post-canonical Indian Buddhist *cosmology denoting a 'world system' or inhabited universe. It was thought that the cosmos contained a vast number of these identically structured systems.

cakravartin (Skt.). A 'Wheel-turner', a monarch or emperor whose rule is unbounded as symbolized by the free movement of the wheels of his chariot throughout the land. Four grades of cakravartins are distinguished, the wheels of their chariots being iron, copper, silver, and gold respectively. The term was also used as an epithet for the *Buddha whose teachings also pervaded all lands. The cakravartin represents the Buddhist political ideal of the just ruler or universal monarch who brings peace and prosperity to his subjects, and various kings in history have been seen as embodying this ideal, notably *Aśoka. Representing political authority, the cakravartin may be thought of as the secular counterpart of a Buddha, and both are said to bear the 32 marks (*dvātriṃśadvara-lakṣaṇa) of the superman (*mahāpuruṣa) on their bodies.

Cambodia. *See* KHMER; SOUTH-EAST ASIA; THERAVĀDA; VIETNAM.

Campā. The ancient capital of *Aṅga, located on the confluence of the Campā and Ganges rivers. The town functioned as an important trade-centre. The *Buddha is said to have made a number of visits to Campā and several early sermons (*sutta) are connected with this city.

Candasāra Buddha. One of the most venerated images in *south-east Asia, now in the *Mahāmuni Paya at Mandalay in *Burma. The story of this image is closely connected with the religious and political history of the Arakanese region, since the kings of *Pagān, Prome, and Pegu invaded Arakan from the earliest time, often with no other intention than to obtain possession of this sacred image of the *Buddha. The importance of this statue is indicated by the belief that this is the only exact image of the Buddha. According to tradition, the image was built during the 51st regnal year of Candrasurya, who ascended the throne of Arakan in 146 CE. Despite this date being much later than the Buddha's death, the legend tells that this bronze statue was cast during a visit of the Buddha to Arakan. The 13 feet-high seated image is still much venerated and the countless worshippers who visit it every day have by now covered it with a thick layer of gold leaf. The image is so popular that the curators have installed video monitors around the *Mahāmuni Paya complex so that people can pay their respects to the video image of the Candasāra Buddha.

Candragupta Maurya. Founder of the *Mauryan dynasty and grandfather of *Aśoka, Candragupta seized power with the help of his political adviser Cāṇaka. He established his capital at *Pāṭaliputra and considerably extended the territory of the previous *Nanda dynasty. He defeated the Greek general Seleucus Nikator in 305 BCE and as the result of a treaty concluded between them in 303 territory in the north-west was ceded to the Indians. As part of the same treaty ambassadors were exchanged and the Greek ambassador *Megasthenes took up residence at the Mauryan capital. Candragupta further extended his kingdom to the south down as far as the Narmada river. After reigning for 24 years he was succeeded by his son *Bindusāra, who continued the expansion to the south. According to legend, Candragupta became a Jain (*see* JAINISM) and went to live in south *India where he eventually starved himself to death in accordance with Jain custom.

Candrakīrti. (*c.*7th c. CE) A major *Madhyamaka philosopher and key proponent of the *reductio ad absurdum* (prasaṅga) method of argumentation. This method aims to reduce to absurdity the position of the opponent through a dialectical process that reveals the internal contradictions of his argument. The alternative interpretation of Madhyamaka, that of the *Svātantrika-Madhyamaka subschool led by *Bhāvaviveka, was that the Madhyamaka should seek to establish a positive thesis of its own and that a purely negative dialectic was inadequate. Candrakīrti was the author of a number of important works, including the *Prasannapadā*, a commentary on *Nāgārjuna's **Mūla-madhyamaka-kārikā*, which survives in *Sanskrit and Tibetan, and the **Madhyamakāvatāra*, an outline of the *Bodhisattva Path from the Madhyamaka viewpoint. While his works were much studied in *Tibet, especially by the *Geluk school, he seems to have been unknown to the Chinese.

canon (Gk., kanon, rule). Texts or books that have special authority in a religious tradition. The concept of canonicity derives mainly from Christianity, and in *Buddhism identifies not divinely inspired literature but those writings that are thought to be 'the word of the *Buddha'. This requirement is understood by the *Theravāda school as meaning words actually spoken by the historical Buddha. The canon of this school, known as the *Pāli Canon, was closed according to tradition at the first council (*see* COUNCIL OF RĀJAGṚHA). It is acknowledged, however, that a number of discourses (*sutta) in this collection were in fact uttered not by the Buddha but by senior disciples, and that others postdate him. None the less, they are included in the canon since it is felt they were spoken with the Buddha's authority and faithfully express his teachings. Expanding on this principle, schools of *Mahāyāna Buddhism regard their canons as still open and have accepted as canonical later compositions that are thought to bear the hallmark of inspired teaching. Such texts are designated as *sūtras. In many of these compositions (for example, the **Lotus Sūtra*), the Buddha is depicted as giving the teaching in an atemporal heavenly paradise. Commentaries and treatises which are non-canonical are known as *śāstras. On the composition of the Tibetan canon *see* TENJUR; KANJUR. On the Chinese canon *see* TAISHŌ CANON; CHINESE TRIPIṬAKA.

Cao Dai. A new synchretistic religious movement in *Vietnam established in 1926 by Ngo Van Chieu (1878–1932). Cao Dai literally means 'High Throne', and refers to the highest *God. Based on revelations that Ngo received beginning in 1919, the movement combined Buddhist, *Taoist, and Confucian (*see* CONFUCIANISM) elements, and incorporated political as well as spiritual functions. Its organizational structure was inspired in part by Roman Catholicism, and its religious beliefs and rituals draw heavily on traditional Vietnamese popular beliefs. Followers believe that the Father God, Cao Dai, created the world in concert with the Mother Goddess, Duc Phat Mau, while also revering Jesus Christ and the *Buddha as divine beings. Followers practise morality, of which one aspect is vegetarianism (*see* DIET) and non-violence (*see* AHIṂSĀ) in order to bring about the harmony of the cosmos and the balance of yin and yang forces.

Cariyāpiṭaka. One of the fifteen books of the *Khuddaka Nikāya of the *Pāli Canon. The work contains tales in verse of the *Buddha's previous births which match the corresponding *Jātaka stories in prose, and presupposes an acquaintance with the events of those tales. The *Cariyāpiṭaka* stories, each called a cariyā (a *Pāli term meaning proper conduct), mainly highlight the ten perfections (*pāramī), by means of which the Buddha attained enlightenment (*bodhi). The first two perfections are illustrated by ten stories each, while the remaining ones have only fifteen stories between them. The commentary on the *Cariyāpiṭaka*, ascribed to *Dhammapāla, is part of the **Paramatthadīpanī*. According to the commentary, the *Cariyāpiṭaka* was preached by the Buddha at the request of *Śāriputra after the conclusion of the **Buddhavaṃsa*. It was also preached by *Mahinda in *Anurādhapura soon after his arrival in *Sri Lanka.

caryā-tantra (Skt.). 'Performance tantra', a term used for the second of the four late classificatory categories of tantra in *Buddhism. This category comprises a very small number of texts, the most important of which is the **Mahā-vairocana-abhisaṃbodhi Tantra*. According to Buddhaguhya, who terms this category ubhaya (dual), such tantras share in equal measure the external ritual aspects of *kriyā-tantra with the internal meditative practices of *yoga-tantra.

caste (Portuguese, casta; Latin, castus, pure). Term denoting the hierarchical social structure of south Asian society and the particular social classes or estates which compose it. The indigenous term used is varṇa (Pāli, vaṇṇa) which means 'colour'. Classical Indian sources speak of four castes, namely the Brahmins (Skt., *Brāhmaṇas) or priests, the kṣatriyas or nobles, the vaiśyas or artesans, and the śūdras or servants. In *Pāli these are known as Brāhmaṇa, khattiya, vessa, and sudda, although in early sources the fourth is rarely mentioned and a threefold grouping is more common. The classical framework of the four castes soon gave way to a system of many thousands of castes and subcastes known as jāti (Skt., birth or race). The *Buddha did not condemn the institution of caste as such, but regarded it as irrelevant to the religious life. He was, however, critical of the arrogance of the priestly caste and in numerous early dialogues ridicules the notion that the circumstances of birth can have any bearing on an individual's moral or spiritual status.

Catuḥśataka. The most celebrated work of *Āryadeva. The title of the work means 'the four hundred verses', and it consists of sixteen chapters. The first eight chapters expound the *Madhyamaka philosophy while the remaining eight are a refutation of rival Buddhist and non-Buddhist schools.

Catuḥstava. Four hymns composed by *Nāgārjuna (although his authorship is disputed) entitled *Lokātīta-stava* (Transcending the World), *Niraupamya-stava* (Peerless), *Acintya-stava* (Inconceivable), and *Paramārtha-stava* (Ultimate Truth). The hymns praise various aspects of the *Buddha's enlightenment (*bodhi) and majesty and were widely popular in *India in *Mahāyāna circles. *Sanskrit versions survive of the set and more than four staves (hymns) are known; it is uncertain which are the original four, if any.

caturmahārāja (Skt.; Pāli, catummahārājika). The 'four great kings', being four powerful gods (*devas) who rule over the lowest of the *heavens and thus are close to the human world, which they are said to visit frequently with their retinues. Each king is regent of one of the four cardinal points and they protect the *Buddha and his followers in those regions. *See also* LOKAPĀLA.

catur-nimitta (Skt.). The 'four signs' seen by Prince Siddhartha (*see* SIDDHARTHA GAUTAMA) which caused him to renounce the world and take up the religious life. The four signs were (1) an old man, (2) a sick man, (3) a corpse, and (4) a religious mendicant. It was predicted at the *Buddha's birth that if he saw these four signs he would abandon worldly life, and his father *Śuddhodana therefore tried to shield his son from these unpleasant experiences by distracting him with luxuries inside the palace, but his efforts were unsuccessful. Once confronted with the realities of life and the problem of human suffering (*duḥkha), Siddhartha left the palace and became a religious mendicant (*śramaṇa).

catur yoni (Skt.). The four 'wombs' or modes of birth. According to traditional Buddhist teachings, life arises in one of these four ways: from an egg, from a womb, from heat or exudation (thought to be the case for insects), and 'spontaneous generation' (as in the case of *devas who generate a body through magical power).

Causal Vehicle (Tib., rgyu'i theg-pa). A Tibetan hermeneutical term used to indicate the non-esoteric *Mahāyāna Buddhist path in contrast to the *tantric 'Result Vehicle', so-called because it approaches enlightenment (*bodhi) as something which is to be acquired, and through which the causal basis for Buddhahood is generated. Also known as the Vehicle of Attributes (lakṣaṇayāna), and the Vehicle of Perfections (pāramitāyāna), meaning that it is the vehicle for the cultivation of the perfections (*pāramitā).

causation. *See* PRATĪTYA-SAMUTPĀDA.

Celebrated Chronicle. The oldest extant Burmese chronicle composed by Samantapāsādika Sīlavaṃsa (15th century). Following the pattern of earlier *Theravāda chronicles, the text narrates the history of *Buddhism in *India, the Buddhist conquest of *Sri Lanka, and several purported visits by the *Buddha in the company of 500 *Arhats to Lekaing village in the Tagaung kingdom of *Burma. The same story is repeated in the **Glass Palace Chronicle of the Kings of Burma*. According to this account, the Buddha visited Burma at the request of two brothers, Mahapon and Sulapon, who built a sandalwood monastery for him. The narrative recounts how 500 men and 500 women then became Arhats, marking the establishment of Buddhism in Burma.

celestial Bodhisattvas. English term used to describe the ahistoric great *Bodhisattvas mentioned in *Mahāyāna texts who are highly advanced on the path the enlightenment (*bodhi). The most notable examples of such Bodhisattvas are *Avalokiteśvara and *Mañjuśrī, who may be regarded as symbolic or mythical in nature, in contrast to ordinary human Bodhisattvas at a lower level of development on the Bodhisattva path.

celibacy. Celibacy is obligatory for all members of the *Saṃgha. Sex is regarded as a powerful bond to the mundane (*laukika) world and not appropriate for one who has renounced home and family. Since *Buddhism regards craving (*tṛṣṇā) as the cause of suffering (*duḥkha), the dangers of sexual *desire are obvious, and are frequently pointed out in Buddhist literature. There are strict penalties in the *Vinaya or monastic code for *monks and *nuns who fail to remain celibate. The first of the four *pārājika-dharmas prohibits sexual intercourse, and the penalty for breaking it is lifelong expulsion from the Order. More minor offences, such as masturbation or lewd conduct, reported in the Vinaya, are punished less severely. Married lay-people may also adopt the practice of voluntary celibacy for longer or shorter periods.

cetanā (Skt.; Pāli). Term denoting the conative psychological functions of intention, volition or motivation. It is one of the five ever-present mental functions (*caitta), and is particularly associated with the generation of *karma.

cetasika (Pāli; Skt., caitasika). An early *Abhidharma term denoting psychological phenomena of various kinds that arise in the mind (*citta) as it encounters and processes phenomena. There are 52 according to *Theravādin sources. In Buddhist scholastic psychology the theory of cetasikas is the outcome of the attempt to classify and describe in detail the different states of mind and their various functions in the context of a general account of the modal operations of the psyche (citta). The endeavour is an outgrowth of the canonical classification of the human subject into five categories or 'aggregates' (*skandha) and aims at greater precision in the tabulation of mental elements and faculties in each of the five categories. The different schools tabulate the psychic qualities differently, but all tend to follow a general breakdown into three categories: (1) general psychological functions, e.g cognition or discrimination (saññā), sensation or feeling (*vedanā), volition (*cetana), discursive thought (*vicāra), focused concentration (ekaggatā), etc. (2) Wholesome or virtuous qualities, e.g. goodwill (adosa), non-attachment (*alobha), diligence (appamāda), confidence (saddhā), etc. (3) Unwholesome qualities or vices, e.g. hatred (dosa, Skt. *dveṣa), envy (issā), conceit (*māna), etc. In *Sanskrit sources the cetasikas are known as *caittas, and the classification varies slightly.

cetiya. *Pāli for *caitya.

Cetiyapabbata. 'Shrine Mountain'. Mountain near *Anurādhapura in *Sri Lanka, also known as Missakapabbata and Cetiyagiri. It derives its name from the number of religious sites that came to be built there. It is said to be the point at which *Mahinda descended on the island after travelling through the air from *India to bring *Buddhism to Sri Lanka, and the site of the second *vihāra to be built in the country, which housed Mahinda and his retinue.

Ceylon. Name of the island now home to the modern state of *Sri Lanka.

Chah, Ajahn (1918–92). Thai *monk and *meditation teacher (*ajahn) who founded the Wat Pah Pong forest retreat in Thailand. Later renamed Wat Pah Nanachat, this became a training centre for Westerners, and many of the leading students later established centres in the *Europe, such as the Amaravati Buddhist Monastery in England under the leadership of the American monk Ajahn Sumedho. Affiliated institutions exist in various parts of the world.

chabbaggiyā (Pāli). A group of six *monks mentioned in the *Theravāda *Vinaya Piṭaka who are regarded as exemplifying monastic misconduct. Probably not historical characters, their names are recorded as Assaji, Punabbasu, Panduka, Lohitaka, Mettiya, and Bhummajaka. Despite this, later orthodox historiography elaborates on the historical personae of the group.

chadō (Jap.). *See* TEA CEREMONY.

Ch'an (Chin.). The name of a major movement or school of Chinese *Buddhism that literally means 'the meditation school'. This school generally sees itself as eschewing doctrinal, textual, and ethical studies in favour of the cultivation of a direct realization of the *Buddha's own enlightenment (*bodhi) experience. The word 'ch'an' itself was originally part of a two-character compound written 'ch'an-na', and was an attempt to render the *Sanskrit word *dhyāna (meditation) phonetically. In time, the second character was dropped and it became known simply as 'ch'an'. Its techniques for cultivation include the study of *kōans and 'silent illumination' (Chin., *mo-chao Ch'an). The former involves the contemplation of a short story about past, enlightened masters, or enigmatic phrases that push the practitioner to the limits of rationality in an attempt to break through to a direct realization of reality. The latter, often promoted in opposition to the former, involves simply sitting with no particular mental form or content in order to realize that one's Buddhahood is already complete and perfect as it is. *See also* ZEN; CH'AN-TSUNG.

chanda (Skt.; Pāli; desire, intention, motivation). A psychological faculty that motivates action. Depending on its object, chanda can be good, bad, or neutral (Pāli, dhamma-chanda, kāmacchanda, kattu-kamyatā), unlike craving (*tṛṣṇā), which is invariably bad.

Ch'ang-an. One of the former capital cities in imperial *China, now the modern city of Hsien (or Xi'an). A flourishing trade centre located in the north west of China at the eastern end of the *Silk Road, Ch'ang-an was an important early centre of *Buddhism. *Monks arriving there with trading caravans from *India and central Asia brought scriptures and religious objects with them which attracted the attention of local gentry and stimulated curiosity about Buddhist teachings.

Chan-jan (711–82). The ninth *patriarch of the *T'ien-t'ai school in *China. Chan-jan studied T'ien-t'ai *meditation and doctrine from his teenage years onward, but did not enter the monastic order until the age of 38. During his subsequent career he gained fame as a meditation teacher, and also extended T'ien-t'ai doctrine, most notably in his promotion of the view that even non-sentient objects such as trees and stones have Buddha-nature. His energy, intellect, accomplishments in meditation, and fame sparked a revival in the fortunes of the T'ien-t'ai school in the mid-*T'ang period.

Channa. The charioteer of the *Buddha who accompanied him on the night of the 'great renunciation' when the Buddha renounced the household life to become a homeless mendicant. The Buddha rode out on his horse *Kanthaka, and when they reached the river Anomā he cut off his hair with his sword and gave all his ornaments to Channa to take back to his father's palace along with his horse. Channa later joined the *Saṃgha but was ostracized when he broke the monastic rules and refused to acknowledge his guilt. Shortly before his death, the Buddha charged *Ānanda with ensuring that the appropriate ecclesiastical penalty was inflicted on Channa.

Ch'an-tsung (Chin.). The 'Ch'an school', the Chinese name for the school that preserved and transmitted the methods of *Ch'an from master to disciple. The history of the school in *China is long and complex. By its own account, a lineage of *meditation masters existed in *India from the time of the *Buddha himself. One day, in the middle of an assembly, the Buddha held a flower before the *monks without saying a word. All in the assembly were puzzled by this gesture, except for *Mahākāśyapa, who understood the Buddha's meaning and smiled. The Buddha then confirmed Mahākāśyapa's understanding and publicly 'transmitted his *Dharma' to him. According to later legend, this direct, 'mind-to-mind transmission' passed through 28 generations of *patriarchs in India. The last of these, *Bodhidharma, travelled to

China in 526 and became the first of the Chinese patriarchs, passing the Dharma on to his disciple, *Hui-k'o (487–593).

In time, the Dharma was transmitted from Hui-k'o, the second Chinese patriarch, to the sixth, *Hui-neng (638–713). Historically, this appears to have been a period of transition: while the earlier masters were known as students and teachers of the **Laṅkāvatāra Sūtra*, the school came to define itself in later years as one that eschewed scriptural study and attempted to point directly to the human mind as the fount of enlightenment (*bodhi). In addition to this shift, a controversy broke out over the nature of practice and enlightenment. In Ch'an lore, this was epitomized as the struggle between proponents of '*gradual enlightenment', represented by Hui-neng's fellow disciple Shen-hsiu (606–706), and '*sudden enlightenment', propounded by Hui-neng himself.

At stake was the question: does one have to work towards enlightenment, gaining it step-by-step over a period of time, or does it manifest fully developed in an instant? The former position justified, even required, a long period of study and practice, undergirded by careful observance of moral *precepts. The latter rested on the *Mahāyāna idea that all dualities are ultimately unreal, including such dyads as ignorance–enlightenment, practice–attainment, and *saṃsāra–*nirvāṇa. Under this critique, the position of sudden enlightenment asserted that, since there was nowhere to go and nothing to change, enlightenment could occur instantaneously. This position, enshrined in the foundational work *The *Platform Sūtra of the Sixth Patriarch*, eventually won out. The result was that subsequent Ch'an rhetoric stressed the immediacy of enlightenment, while in actual practice seekers continued to meditate and observe the precepts.

The rejection of written and oral teachings and the acceptance of sudden enlightenment as the orthodox position led to a period of intense experimentation and creativity as teachers sought for ways to directly impart the content of their experience to students. Thus, during the late *T'ang and the Sung dynasties, the school entered into a period sometimes described as 'the golden age of Ch'an', where masters employed 'shock Ch'an' techniques to evoke the students' direct, experiential understanding. These techniques, pioneered by such figures as *Ma-tsu Tao-i (709–88), *Huang-po Hsi-yün (d. 850), and *Lin-chi I-hsüan (founder of the *Lin-chi school, d. 866), included beating with sticks, shouting directly into students' ears, bizarre behaviour, and seemingly nonsensical answers to students' questions. Many stories of such masters were recorded either in a new genre of literature called 'Recorded Sayings', which transmitted the words and deeds of individual masters, or in anthologies such as the **Blue Cliff Records* and the **Gateless Gate*.

Such creativity and spontaneity was difficult to maintain over the long term, and eventually a way was found to appropriate and institutionalize the methods of 'shock Ch'an'. By the late Sung, masters began assigning students to study and contemplate the stories of masters contained in the 'Recorded sayings' literature or in the anthologies, with a view to placing themselves into the stories and attempting to see directly the mind of the master or the student depicted therein. As students had success with this technique, the stories that were found most effective were used again and again, and came to be regarded as kung-an (Jap., *kōan), or 'public cases', and became standardized. This became the favoured practice within the Lin-chi school. Other schools, such as the *Ts'ao-tung school, rejected this method, claiming that its emphasis on a formal, goal-oriented practice violated the basic principle of sudden enlightenment, which, as noted above, held that all beings were already perfectly enlightened and liberated just as they were. This school stressed the practice of 'silent illumination' (Chin., *mo-chao Ch'an) where students simply sat with no goal in mind save to realize their already-perfect Buddhahood. The Lin-chi school, in turn, criticized this practice for its inertness and quietism.

By the Yüan and Ming dynasties, kung-an practice had become overly formalized, and critics of the Ch'an school argued that it mistook witty rejoinders for genuine enlightenment. Practitioners of 'silent illumination' came in for criticism on the account that their practice led to mere laziness and torpor. While a few reformers emerged in the mid-Ming, such as Tz'u-p'o Chen-k'o (1543–1603) and *Han-shan Te'-ch'ing (1546–1623), the

Jesuit missionary Matteo Ricci and his successors found that Buddhist monks, and particularly Ch'an monks, were viewed by the population at large as effete and decadent. These Jesuit reports, however, may not be entirely reliable, and it is likely that many ordinary people remained devout followers of Buddhist teachings.

In the modern period, reformers and accomplished masters such as *Hsü-yun (1840–1959) and Lai-kuo (1881–1953) helped to instil respect for Ch'an once again, and social trends such as modernization, urbanization, and the general rise in educational levels has given the laity increased time and inclination to take up the practice. In the West, the scene has been dominated by Japanese *Zen, but some Chinese Ch'an masters, such as Sheng-yen (1930–) and Hsing-yun (1927–) have developed followings in *Europe and *America.

Chao-chou Ts'ung-shen (778–897). A Chinese *Ch'an *monk of the mid-*T'ang period, famous for his creative and spontaneous teaching methods. Many of his dialogues and sayings have been recorded and anthologized in collections of kung-an (Jap., *kōan). One, in which a student asks whether a dog has *Buddha-nature or not, and Chao-chou answers Not! is frequently given as the first kung-an for beginning practitioners.

Chapata. A *Mon monk who, according to Burmese legend, led a group of five monks from *Burma to *Sri Lanka in about 1180 to study *Theravāda Buddhism as practised at the *Mahāvihāra. The group included a prince of Cambodia (possibly the son of Jayavarman VII, the founder of *Angkor Wat), another originally from Conjeevaram in south *India, and two others from different parts of *south-east Asia. This group, later known as the 'Sinhalese Sect', were ordained in Sri Lanka and spent ten years there, thereby becoming elders (*thera) who could perform ordinations. They returned to *Burma in 1190 to establish the Sinhalese form of Theravāda Buddhism. Whether or not the legend is true, it is certain that, by the beginning of the 13th century, the Sinhalese form of Theravāda Buddhism was spreading in south-east Asia. This form of Buddhism, characterized by strict adherence to the *Vinaya, emphasis on a pure line of succession, and strong links to political authority, has characterized the Buddhism of the region down to modern times.

Ch'eng-kuan (737–820). The fourth *patriarch of the *Hua-yen school in *China. According to legend, he stood over 9 feet tall, his arms extended below his knees, and his eyes glowed in the dark. A member of the monastic order from the age of 11, he travelled extensively around China, studying many *Mahāyāna texts with famous masters, concentrating primarily on the **Hua-yen ching*. In 796, the *T'ang emperor invited him to the capital city of *Ch'ang-an to assist *Prajñā with a new translation of the Sūtra in Forty Fascicles. His own commentaries on the sūtra ran to over 400 fascicles, and he left as his legacy 38 disciples who achieved national prominence. He is credited with extending the influence of the Hua-yen school considerably.

chen jen (Chin.). A term that literally means 'true person'. Originally a *Taoist term meaning an accomplished sage or thaumaturge, Chinese *Buddhism adapted the term as one translation for the *Sanskrit word *Arhat, and also used it occasionally to refer to *Buddhas.

Chenrezi (Tib., spyan-ras-gzigs). The Tibetan name for the *Bodhisattva *Avalokiteśvara.

chen-yen (Chin.). A Chinese Buddhist translation of the *Sanskrit terms *mantra and *dhāraṇī. In the Chinese Buddhist context it refers to oral formulae of any length whose power resides in their sounds rather than their meanings, and which are usually phonetic reproductions of Sanskrit originals. Chinese characters were either adapted or invented in order to represent these sounds and preserve them in writing. These formulae are also referred to as chou, or spells.

Chen-yen tsung (Chin.). A school of Chinese *Buddhism sometimes referred to in English as the '*esoteric school' (*see* ESOTERIC BUDDHISM). It represents an importation of *tantric Buddhism from *India into *China, but once in China, it changed to fit the temperament and mores of Chinese religious culture. Traces of this importation can be detected as far back as the 3rd century, with the first translation of the *Mataṅga Sūtra* with its *mantras at the beginning and end. However, the presence of mantra and *dhāraṇi is common in *Mahāyāna sūtras and does not in itself indicate any kind of esoterism. The real transmission of the school into China may be said to begin with the arrival of the Indian monks *Śubhakarasiṃha (Chin., Shan-wu-wei, 637–735), *Vajrabodhi (Chin., Chin-kang-chih, *c.* 671–741), and *Amoghavajra (Chin., Pu-k'ung, 705–74) at the capital in the 8th century.

Chinese Chen-yen teachings and practice share the following in common with its Indian sources. (1) It is based primarily on practice and action rather than learning and knowledge. The object of the practice is to master the 'three karmas' of '*body, speech, mind' through the practices of (respectively) *mudrā (ritual hand gestures associated with specific deities, *Bodhisattvas, and *Buddhas); mantra or dhāraṇī (spoken formulae transliterated directly from *Sanskrit ritual utterances with no etymological meaning but containing immense power in the sounds); and visualizations of specific deities, Bodhisattvas, or Buddhas. (2) It organizes the cosmos ritually into a series of energies that emanate from the centre and radiate outward, each energy symbolized by a particular deity, Bodhisattva, or Buddha. The primary Buddha is *Vairocana, the Sun Buddha, of whom all other Buddhas and divine beings are emanations. This scheme is represented visually in the *maṇḍala that depicts all divine beings in their proper locations relative to one another. (3) Its transmission depends upon the direct master–disciple link. No one can practise authentically and successfully (or even safely) without having been initiated into the practice by a *guru or teacher who himself stands in a valid succession of masters. (4) The practice also depends upon the protection and support of a specific Buddha, Bodhisattva, or guardian deity. This divine guardian and patron is chosen in the course of the *abhiṣeka, or initiation ceremony, during which the neophyte lets a flower fall upon the maṇḍala, and takes as his patron the being upon whose image it falls. (5) Chen-yen sees its practice as a shortcut that dispenses with the usual gradual cultivation of wisdom on one's own in favour of powerful practices empowered by beings more advanced in the path who lead the practitioner directly to the goal of enlightenment and liberation in one lifetime, or even instantaneously. (6) The power of its practices could also be used for purposes other than religious advancement, such as healing, rainmaking, acquisition of wealth, national protection, and so on.

With these similarities noted, one must also be aware that the Chinese school differed from its Indian counterpart in at least two respects. First, the sexual element in iconography and practice is not as strong as it was in *India and was to become in *Tibet. This element appears to have offended Chinese sensibilities. Second, it did not base itself on a body of literature called tantras, but rather took the *sūtra literature and gave it esoteric interpretations (although some early tantras were called 'sūtra' in China but 'tantra' in Tibet). The three primary transmitters of the school listed above were also responsible for the translation of most of its foundational scriptures and formularies.

Esoteric practices have existed continuously, though at a low level, in Chinese Buddhism since its first transmission. Some groups exist today who devote themselves to esoteric rituals. In addition, esoteric elements pervade almost all corners of the Chinese Buddhist world. For example, every monastery's devotional liturgies contain mantras and make occasional use of mudrās, and many monasteries, whether esoterically based or not, make use of esoteric rituals such as the 'Release of the Burning (*see* fang Yen-K'ou) mouths' or the 'Meng-shan ceremony for feeding the hungry ghosts' (*preta).

The term Chen-yen tsung refers to the esoteric school as it existed in China. It is roughly, but not exactly, synonymous with the term *Mi-tsung, or 'Secret School', a broader term covering esoteric and tantric schools both within and outside of China but which is often used interchangeably with 'Chen-yen tsung'.

Chih-hsü (1599–1655). An eminent *monk and revitalizer of *Pure Land *Buddhism in Ming-dynasty *China. He was a bright Confucian scholar (*see* CONFUCIANISM) in his youth, and wrote anti-Buddhist pamphlets. However, at the age of 17, he read some of the works of *Yün-ch'i Chu-hung (1532–1612), and converted to Buddhism, burning his former writings. He became a monk at 24, and travelled to Mt. Yün-ch'i, where he listened to lectures and practised *Ch'an meditation. He achieved a great enlightenment (*bodhi) there which resolved his doubts about the apparent contradictions between the teachings of various schools of Buddhism. The following year, he took the *Bodhisattva *precepts and entered into *Vinaya study. The experience of grave illness in his late twenties shook his confidence in the efficacy of his Ch'an awakening, and he began to turn towards Pure Land practice. After recovering, he took to the road to broaden his studies again, and journeyed to Mt. T'ien-t'ai to study the doctrines of the *T'ien-t'ai school. He quickly became proficient in this study, and lectured widely on them thereafter. He renewed his devotion to the Pure Land again at the age of 56 after another serious illness, this time composing a volume of poems on the Pure Land. He also edited nine other classic Pure Land texts, and published these together with his book of poems under the title *Ten Essentials of the Pure Land* (Chin., *Ching-t'u shih yao*), which has become a standard of the Pure Land school. He recovered briefly, but fell ill again the following year and died with his hands folded, facing the west, and reciting verses on the Pure Land.

Because of his devotion to Pure Land and his efforts to propagate its practice, Chih-hsü was acclaimed the ninth *patriarch of Chinese Pure Land after his death. However, his interests and activities covered a broad range: he was a reformer who advocated study of and adherence to the Vinaya; he was a wide-ranging scholar who studied the entire scope of Chinese Buddhist thought, and advocated a revival of T'ien-t'ai learning; he was a proponent of the unity of Buddhism, Confucianism, and *Taoism; and he was a popular teacher and lecturer who attracted many disciples. For all this, he is remembered as one of the great revivers of Buddhism in the mid to late Ming period.

Chih-i (538–97). Tradition places Chih-i as the third in the line of *patriarchs in the *T'ien-t'ai school, but in fact he founded the school and furnished most of its distinctive teachings himself, including (1) the T'ien-t'ai method of organizing and classifying scriptures and teachings known as *p'an-chiao which gave the *Lotus Sūtra* the honoured place as the supreme scripture (*see* P'AN-CHIAO); (2) the *Three Truths that overcame the disconnection between the traditional *Two Truths of *Madhyamaka teaching; (3) the idea that the transcendent principle (Chin., li) and phenomenal reality (Chin., shih) mutually interpenetrate without obstruction; (4) and the idea of *One Mind or *absolute mind that underlies all of reality, in both its pure and defiled aspects. He was also renowned as a *meditation master, and wrote a massive treatise on the methods and rationales of meditation, epitomized in the term *chih-kuan, or 'calming and contemplation'.

Chih-i was born into a family in south *China with aristocratic connections, but realized the transitoriness of life at a young age after witnessing troops destroy a library. He became a *monk, and studied with the renowned meditation master from north China *Hui-ssu (515–77), later recognized as the second patriarch of T'ien-t'ai. After a stay in Chin-ling (modern Nanking), he went to Mt. T'ien-t'ai on the eastern seaboard in Chekiang province, and remained there for most of the rest of his life; it is from his residence and work there that the school derived its name. An early visionary experience aroused his faith (*śraddhā) in the supremacy of the *Lotus Sūtra*, and during his career he wrote two commentaries on it, one a general survey of its meaning, the other a line-by-line exegesis. When China was reunited by the Sui dynasty in 581, his family's connections brought him to the attention of the court, where he was invited to preach and was duly honoured. The resulting patronage allowed him to buy the fishing rights along the coastline adjacent to Mt. T'ien-t'ai and to obtain an imperial ban on fishing in the area that remained in effect for at least two centuries.

chih-kuan (Chin.). **1.** A compound consisting of two words meaning 'stop' and 'observe'. The words correspond to the *Sanskrit *śamatha (calming) and *vipaśyanā (insight). These have been interpreted in various ways. Chih can mean either to suppress mental activity in order to focus on a single object of *meditation, to withdraw the mind from sensory engagement with the external world, or (in some *Pure Land texts) to desist from *evil actions. Kuan can mean to observe the natural workings of the mind, to contemplate or observe a mental object closely, or to investigate the nature of reality. **2.** In the *T'ien-t'ai school's system of meditation, as laid out in *Chih-i's manual *Mo-ho chih-kuan* (The Great Calming and Insight), both chih and kuan are glossed in three ways. Chih means (*a*) to calm the mind and suspend its agitated, impure thoughts; (*b*) to fix the mind on the present moment; and (*c*) to realize the non-duality of the agitated mind and the calm mind as equal manifestations of reality. Kuan has the three meanings of: (*a*) to dissipate perturbations of the mind through wisdom that sees through their illusory nature; (*b*) to gain insight into suchness (*tathatā), the fundamental nature of all things; and (*c*) to gain insight into the fundamental equality of non-contemplation and contemplation from the perspective of suchness.

Chih-tun (314–66). A *monk of south *China during the Eastern Chin dynasty. He was primarily a student of Perfection of Insight (prajñā-pāramitā) literature, but interacted with the Neo-*Taoist movement all his life. He used Buddhist ideas to correct what he perceived as mistakes in the Taoist view of the world, and was famous for writing a commentary on a chapter in the Taoist classic *Chuang-tzu*. In it, he argued that people were not prisoners of their own destiny, and that happiness was thus not to be found in simply following one's own inclinations, but in perfecting oneself through active cultivation. He is also said to have made an image of the *Buddha *Amitābha and to have vowed to seek *rebirth in his *Pure Land, but he had no discernible impact on the development of Pure Land *Buddhism in China.

Chih-yen (602–68). The second *patriarch of the Chinese *Hua-yen school, and the teacher of the school's *de facto* founder, *Fa-tsang (643–712).

China. *Buddhism first entered China some time during the 1st century CE, probably with foreign traders who arrived via the *Silk Road or from the maritime route along the south-eastern seaboard. For the first two centuries or so, it existed primarily among immigrant settlements, while slowly making its presence known among the native Chinese population. As interest grew during the 2nd century, a few monks began translating scriptures into Chinese. Notable among these were *An Shih-kao and *Lokakṣema. With the fall of the *Han dynasty in the early 3rd century, interest in Buddhism among the Chinese increased as the unstable political situation inspired people to seek new answers. At the same time, the division of China into kingdoms north and south of the Yangtze River gave Buddhism a different character in these two regions. In the north, greater proximity to *India meant that Buddhism in this region had a greater number of Indian and central Asian *monks and *meditation teachers, and so tended to emphasize religious practice over textual study. In addition, from the early 4th century to the late 6th, the north was under non-Chinese rule. These 'barbarian' rulers favoured Buddhism and many monks served as court advisers, giving Buddhism in the north a more overtly political character. Many of the literati had fled the troubles of the north and migrated to the Southern Kingdoms, bringing with them their emphasis on literary skill. In addition to this, the Northern Kingdoms blocked their access to the living traditions of India and Central Asia, and so the south developed a more literary approach to Buddhist study. During this time, *Tao-an (312–85) produced the first catalogue of Buddhist scripture, and he and his disciples worked to produce critical editions of scriptures and treatises, and to develop principles for their translation into Chinese. It was during this period that *Kumārajīva arrived in 402 and opened his translation bureau in the north, producing some of the finest translations from *Sanskrit, many of which are still considered the standard. His rendering of Indian *Madhyamaka texts led to the foundation of the *San-lun (or 'Three Treatise') school that specialized in Madhyamaka philosophy. Also, the dissemination of Buddhist texts and teachings among the educated élite led to a prolonged exchange of ideas between Buddhism and *Taoism, and Buddhism absorbed and modified many Taoist ideas.

Other significant figures of the Northern and Southern Kingdoms period include *Tao-sheng (360–434) a great textual scholar; *Lu-shan Hui-yüan (344–416) and *T'an-luan (476–542), who helped establish the *Pure

Land teachings; the *San-lun master *Seng-chao (374–414); and the great translator *Paramārtha (499–569), whose translations of Indian Mind-only (*citta-mātra) literature paved the way for the future establishment of the *Fa-hsiang school.

China was reunified by the Sui dynasty in 581 CE, but this was quickly toppled by the *T'ang dynasty in 618. The T'ang dynasty held power for almost 300 years, and this period represents one of China's golden ages. Buddhism flourished during this period, although it also suffered severe setbacks. Increased affluence and patronage enabled many original thinkers and practitioners to establish schools of Buddhism more in keeping with Chinese cultural and intellectual patterns and less dependent upon pre-existing Indian schools of thought. Examples include *Chih-i (538–97), who founded the *T'ien-t'ai school; *Fa-tsang (643–712), who consolidated the *Hua-yen school; and the various meditation masters who established *Ch'an as a separate school that transmitted the Buddha-mind directly 'outside of words and scriptures'. *Tao-ch'o (562–645), *Shan-tao (613–81), and others continued building up the Pure Land movement, extending T'an-luan's teaching further. During this time *Hsüan-tsang (596–664) travelled in India for sixteen years and brought back many texts which he translated into Chinese. After Kumārajīva, he is considered the second of the great translators in Chinese Buddhist history. He concentrated on Indian *Yogacāra thought, and, building on the foundation laid by Paramārtha, founded the Fa-hsiang school.

Prosperity brought its own difficulties. As the numbers of ordained clergy increased, the government became concerned about the revenue and labour pool that would be lost due to the clergy's tax-and labour-exempt status. In addition, ever since Buddhism's inception in China some traditional Confucian scholars had decried it as a foreign religion that violated basic Chinese values, especially the loyalty that all citizens owed to the state and the filial piety that sons and daughters owed their parents. In addition, Taoists sometimes saw in Buddhism an antagonist and competitor rather than a colleague. In the past, the government instituted *ordination examinations and state-issued certificates to control the size of the *Saṃgha, and twice during the Northern and Southern Kingdoms period the state had suppressed Buddhism (in 446 and 574). In the year 845, the T'ang court was incited to suppress Buddhism once again, and for three years it pursued this policy of razing monasteries and temples, forcing clergy back into lay life or even killing them, and burning books, images, and properties. Unlike the previous two persecutions, this suppression happened in a unified China and affected all areas. Scholars are agreed that this event marked the end of Buddhism's intellectual and cultural dominance, as the Saṃgha never recovered its former glory. The T'ien-t'ai and Hua-yen schools experienced some revivals thereafter, but lost most of their vigour. The Pure Land and Ch'an school, being much less dependent upon patronage and scholarship, fared better and became the two dominant schools of Buddhism in China thereafter. After the persecution, Ch'an communities experimented with new teaching methods that circumvented conventional teaching and inculcated a dramatic, instantaneous experience of enlightenment (*bodhi). The leading figures in this movement were *Ma-tsu Tao-i (709–88), *Pai-chang Huai-hai (749–814), *Huang-po Hsi-yün (d. 850), *Lin-chi I-hsüan (founder of the *Lin-chi school, d. 866), *Tung-shan Liang-chieh (807–69), and *Ts'ao-shan Pen-chi (840–901), the two founders of the *Ts'ao-tung school.

After the T'ang, the intellectual vigour of Buddhism was eclipsed by the rise of Neo-*Confucianism in the Sung dynasty. Nevertheless, there were significant figures and movements during this time. Many figures worked to reconcile the very different outlooks and methods of the Ch'an and Pure Land schools, notably Yüng-ming Yen-shou (904–75) and *Yün-ch'i Chu-hung (1532–1612). The latter was part of a revival of Ch'an in the latter half of the Ming dynasty that also included Tz'u-p'o Chen-k'o (1543–1603), *Han-shan Te'-ch'ing (1546–1623), and Ou-i Chih-hsü (1599–1655). All agreed that Pure Land and Ch'an, though differing in method, strove toward the same goal, though Han-shan and Tz'u-p'o still tended to define this goal in Ch'an terms. Chih-hsü, however, emphasized Pure Land teaching almost exclusively and came to be regarded as one of the patriarchs of this school.

From the Ming to the Ch'ing dynasty, Buddhism stagnated (although it remained strong in the central eastern seaboard) until the end of the 19th century, when there was a revival of interest in it as a part of the Chinese heritage that could be brought out to counter Western culture's claims of superiority. During the early years of the 20th century, figures such as Ou-yang Ching-wu (1871–1943) and the monk *T'ai-hsü (1889–1947) sponsored new editions of the scripture and advocated a modernized educational system that would bring Buddhism into alignment with modern currents of thought.

The Communist victory in 1949 cut short the revival of Buddhism, as the new regime tried to undercut all societal support for religion in general. The Cultural Revolution proved a catastrophe for Buddhism during the 1960s and 1970s, as Red Guards destroyed many temples and treasures, and clergy were forced to return to lay status and submit to re-education. However, after the death of Communist leader Mao Tse-tung in 1976 and the passing of many of his allies, the government has grown more tolerant, and many monasteries are back in operation. Currently, the *Chinese Buddhist Association is a thriving organization, and Chinese universities sponsor the academic study of Buddhism. To what extent Buddhism will recover from the setbacks of the Mao era remains to be seen.

Chinese Buddhist Association. The official government organization founded by the People's Republic of *China in 1953 for the regulation of *Buddhism in that country. The Association oversees the activities of both lay and monastic groups, and promotes a revisionist interpretation of Buddhist teachings in line with the thoughts of Marx and Lenin. It calls upon Buddhists to be loyal to the Communist Party and to see their religious practice as contributing towards the class struggle and the overthrow of capitalism.

Chinese Tripiṭaka. This term can refer to any edition of the complete collection of Buddhist literature in Chinese. During the first several centuries of *Buddhism in *China, literature was copied by hand, making the production of complete anthologies impractical. However, the advent of printing made possible the publication and distribution of large collections of literature, and often the Chinese court and nobility, along with large temples, sponsored the collecting, editing, and printing of the entire known corpus of Chinese Buddhist literature.

The first such effort was mounted by the Sung court in the 10th century, and the so-called Shu edition first appeared in 983. This edition involved the carving of 130,000 hardwood printing blocks. This monumental collection contained a total of 1,076 works (according to one catalogue) in 5,586 fascicles. In Northern China the Khitan Mongol rulers of the Liao dynasty had another set of blocks made and printed a new edition of the *Tripiṭaka in 1055 based on the Shu edition. These two editions inspired the Korean court of the *Koryŏ dynasty to print two editions of its own, one during the reign of King Hyeonjong (r. 1009–31), and the other during the reign of King Munjong (r. 1046–82). These two editions together contained some 1,524 works. In 1232, a new set of blocks was ordered, and this was completed between 1236 and 1251. Some 81,000 of these blocks remain stored at the Haein-sa on Mt. Kaya in southern *Korea, and have been used in the 20th century to produce new copies of the Koryŏ edition.

Other editions of the Tripiṭaka based on the Shu edition appeared during the Chin dynasty (1115–1234) and the Yüan dynasty. A completely new edition appeared in southern China in 1176, the product of several decades of work sponsored privately by six successive abbots of the Tung-ch'an temple in Fukien province. This edition contained 50 per cent more content than the Shu edition, was published in an accordion-fold format rather than in hand scrolls, and the arrangement of text on the page mirrored older hand-copied editions, making scholarly comparisons easier. Because of all these factors, this edition became the standard for the remainder of the Yüan dynasty. Subsequent editions followed the Tung-ch'an temple edition closely in content and format, existing alongside other editions derived from the Shu edition.

The wars that brought the Yüan dynasty down and elevated the Ming dynasty to power brought about the destruction of many temple libraries, and the Ming emperor Hung-wu (r. 1368–98) had a new edition printed, based on the Tung-ch'an temple *canon. Editions of the canon generally followed either the northern Shu or the southern Tung-ch'an temple editions until Japanese scholar-monks of the Edo period began conducting detailed comparative studies of both so that each edition could correct the errors and fill in the gaps in the other. These studies eventuated in the publication of three successive composite editions, each of which expanded upon its predecessor: the Dainippon Kōtei Daizōkyō in 1880–5, the Dainippon Kōtei Zōkyō in 1902–5, and the *Taishō Shinshū Daizōkyō in 1924–34. This last edition has become the standard reference for Chinese Buddhist literature for modern scholars. Its 100 volumes contain 3,360 works.

Ching-te ch'uan-teng-lu (Chin.). The title means 'The Transmission of the Lamp [published in the] Ching-te Era', and is a collection of biographies and recorded sayings of past *Buddhas, *patriarchs, and masters of the *Ch'an school in *China. It was composed by the *monk Tao-yüan in the Sung dynasty in 30 fascicles, and was added to the *canon of Buddhist scriptures in the year 1004 during the Ching-te reign period (1004–8). It contains entries on a total of 1,701 figures, and is an invaluable source for early Ch'an history.

ching-t'u (Chin.). *See* JŌDO; PURE LAND; BUDDHA-KṢETRA; SUKHĀVATĪ.

ching-t'u tsung (Chin.). *See* PURE LAND SCHOOL.

Chinnamasta. A goddess described in both Hindu and late Buddhist *tantric works, depicted naked and holding her own severed head with blood spurting from her neck into her mouth.

Chinul (1158–1210). A Korean (*see* KOREA) *Sŏn *monk of the *Koryŏ period (918–1392) who worked to reform the monastic order and provide a rationale for Sŏn practice. Observing that the commercialization of monastic activities (in the form of fortune-telling, services for paying clients, and so on) had brought many into the order for questionable motives, he sought to create a reform group called the 'concentration and wisdom society', which found a home when he established the Sŏngwang Temple on Mt. Chogye. At the same time, he concerned himself with theoretical issues relating to the controversy between *gradual and *sudden enlightenment, and the relationship between meditative experience and doctrinal/textual studies. In the former case, he adopted the typology of the Chinese *Ch'an and *Hua-yen master *Tsung-mi (780–841), which advocated sudden enlightenment followed by a gradual deepening and cultivation as the norm. In order to serve this purpose, he proposed *meditation on *kōans as the best method of practice. As to the latter, he advised that Korean Sŏn not follow the example of the more extreme trends towards rejection of scriptural and doctrinal study exhibited by Chinese Ch'an, but that it keep the two together as an integrated whole. He was particularly interested in incorporating the Hua-yen philosophy of the Chinese lay hermit Li T'ung-hsüan (635–730) into Sŏn practice as its basis and rationale. Chinul produced many eminent and accomplished disciples, and is arguably one of the most influential monks in the history of Korean Buddhism.

Chin-ying Hui-yüan (523–92). An eminent Chinese *monk who lived through the persecution of *Buddhism instigated by the Emperor Wu of the Northern Chou dynasty (r. 561–78). During these difficult times, Hui-yüan was the only monk who dared to debate with the emperor directly and openly on Buddhism's right to exist in Northern *China. Although the emperor was silenced by the cogency of Hui-yüan's arguments at several points, the persecution remained in effect until the emperor's death. Hui-yüan is also known for his literary output, which consisted of commentaries on at least fifteen *Mahāyāna scriptures and treatises. Because the words 'Hui-yüan' are written with the same Chinese characters, and because both men were involved in the early development of *Pure Land thought and practice, he is sometimes confused with *Lu-shan Hui-yüan (334–416).

Chinzei-ha. A school of *Jōdo or *Pure Land *Buddhism founded by Shōkōbo Benchō, a pupil of *Hōnen. Its contemporary descendant is the school of Shirahata-ryū which has its headquarters in Chion-in and another important centre in Zōjōji in Tokyo. *See also* JŌDO-SHŪ.

Chi-tsang (549–623). The greatest systematizer of the *San-lun school in *China, and ironically, its last great master. The son of a Parthian father (who joined the Buddhist order not long after his birth) and a Chinese mother, he became a *monk sometime between the ages of 7 and 13, and began the study of *San-lun (or *Madhyamaka) doctrine immediately under *Fa-lang (507–81). Living through the turbulent period when China was reunited under the Sui dynasty, which then gave way to the *T'ang dynasty, Chi-tsang worked to preserve the corpus of Buddhist literature against the depredations of the times. A prolific commentator and lecturer, he was invited to give talks at the court of the Sui emperor and honoured as a *National Teacher. During his lifetime, *Chih-i of the *T'ien-t'ai school was gaining notice for his doctrinal elaborations that brought the *Two Truths of San-lun, seen as separate from each other, into the greater synthetic vision of his *Three Truths. Perhaps in response to this, Chi-tsang formulated a deeper articulation of the traditional Two Truths in such a way that they interacted through three levels of dialectical critique, and in the final analysis achieved a similar kind of synthesis. However, after Chi-tsang's death no further masters arose to keep the San-lun tradition alive, and its place at the forefront of Buddhist scholarship was taken by the *T'ien-t'ai and *Hua-yen schools.

chöd (Tib., gcod). A Tibetan term literally meaning 'cut off', it refers to a unique system of *meditation introduced into medieval *Tibet by the Indian *ascetic *Phadampa Sangyé, (d. 1117). Its theoretical basis is drawn from the teachings of the *Prajñā-pāramitā Sūtras while its practice seems to include elements derived from Indian shamanic techniques. Its aim is to overcome, in a rapid and dramatic manner, the false belief in and attachent to an abiding ego-self, as well as all fears associated with the dissolution of that belief. Thus, the central feature of the chöd meditation is a ritual in which pratitioners offer their bodies as food to demons, while seated at night-time in a cemetery equipped with the characteristic thigh-bone trumpet and drum. Initially, the demons are treated as truly existent but the meditator subsequently recognizes them as manifestations of the mind lacking any substantial existence. Phadampa Sangyé's most noteworthy disciple was the female saint, *Machig Lapgi Drönma. A few members of all schools of Tibetan *Buddhism still practise chöd, although it is now chiefly associated with the *Kagyü school.

Chogye Order. The largest order of celibate clergy in modern Korean *Buddhism (*see* KOREA), this group traces its origins to the foundation of the Sŏngwang Temple on Mt. Chogye by the eminent master *Chinul (1158–1210). Originally one of the Nine Mountains of Korean *Sŏn, it eventually absorbed all the other schools to become the sole representative of the meditative tradition. During the period of Japanese occupation (1910–45), it opposed the Japanese-sponsored T'aeko order in which clergy married, ate meat, and drank wine according to the Japanese custom. After the end of the Second World War, the Chogye Order fought for many years on the legal and legislative fronts to take control of monastic properties for the exclusive use of celibate clergy, and expel all married monks. It finally succeeded, and today is the most prominent group in Korean Buddhism.

choka (Jap., 'morning section'). Part of the daily round of activities in a *Zen monastery, consisting of the recitation of *sūtras.

chörten (Tib., mchod-rten). A reliquary or *stūpa in *Tibet. These structures proliferate wherever Tibetan *Buddhism has been influential, and are considered to be an object for worship (*pūjā), representing the mind of the *Buddha or absolute reality (*dharma-kāya).

Chosan. *See* CH'OSŎN.

Ch'osŏn (Kor.). A term which can refer either to *Korea as a whole, or to a particular period in Korean history from 1392 to 1909 during which *Buddhism was actively suppressed. This was a period of persecution and declining influence for Buddhism that lasted 518 years. As each ruler ascended the throne, stronger and stronger anti-Buddhist measures went into effect. These included a halt to new temple construction; restrictions on *ordinations; the actual closing of monasteries in urban areas and their gradual restriction to isolated mountain sites; and a proscription on travel by *monks and *nuns.

Fig 6 chörten

Ch'uan-teng Lu (Chin.). A genre of Chinese *Ch'an literature. The term literally means 'the transmission of the lamp', or 'the passing of the torch', and sets out lineages of masters and disciples, usually accompanied by biographies and recorded sayings. *See also* CHING-TE CH'UAN-TENG-LU.

Chu-hung. *See* YÜN-CH'I CHU-HUNG.

Ch'ung-yüan. A Chinese *Ch'an *monk of the *Northern School of unknown date remembered only as Shen-hui's opponent at the Great Dharma-Assembly of Hua-t'ai. Here the latter first proclaimed the *Southern School of *Hui-neng the true successor of the Ch'an of *Bodhidharma, sparking off the *Northern–Southern School controversy.

cintāmaṇi (Skt.). A legendary magical jewel which spontaneously provides its owner with whatever he wishes for. It can create wealth, drive away evil, cure illness, purify water, and perform other marvels. It is often used as a symbolic image for the actvities of *Buddhas and *Bodhisattvas in the *Mahāyāna, or the *Dharma and its marvellous powers.

circumambulation. *See* PRADAKṢINA.

citta (Skt.; Pāli). Mind; in early *Buddhism and present-day *Theravāda, citta is regarded as virtually synonymous with *vijñāna (consciousness) and *manas (intellect) but in later schools of Buddhism it is distinguished from those two. It is defined as the cognitive ground underlying the dynamic system of psychological operations (*caitta). According to many schools, the mind in its natural state is intrinsically luminous (citta-prakṛti-prabhāsvara), free from all attachments and conceptualizing, and thus is empty in nature (śūnya). In this latter sense, some *Mahāyāna and *tantric authorities understand citta as equivalent to *bodhicitta, and hold that when the natural state of mind is obscured by the false split into a perceiving subject and perceived objects, the everyday mind, which is a fragmentation of its natural state, arises.

citta-ekagratā (Skt.; Pāli, citta-ekaggatā). Literally, 'one-pointedness of mind', a meditational state of equipoise in which the mind is focused on a single object. This may be a visual image, a sound, a concept, or other mental representation.

citta-mātra (Skt., mere mind). A term derived from the *Laṅkāvatara Sūtra* used in a loose and somewhat misleading manner in Tibetan Buddhist doxology to denote the *Yogācāra school of *Mahāyāna *Buddhism.

citta-santāna (Skt.). Literally, 'the stream of mind', a general term used to indicate the continuity of the personality of an individual in the absence of the permanently abiding 'self' (*ātman) that *Buddhism denies.

cīvara (Skt.; Pāli). The robes worn by a Buddhist *monk, and the first of a monk's four traditional requirements (*niśraya). The earliest robes were made of rectangular pieces of cotton cloth and typically three were worn: an inner robe, from the waist to the knee; an upper robe around the torso and shoulders; and an outer robe used as an overgarment. Monks are instructed never to enter a village without wearing all three. New robes are traditionally donated by the laity in the *kaṭhina ceremony. In the early Indian orders, and in contemporary *south-east Asia, a reddish-yellow colour is preferred. This is called kasāya or kasāva in the *Pāli sources, or kaṣāya in *Sanskrit, and is often translated into English as saffron or ochre. Elsewhere in Asia there is much variation. In *Tibet the robes are maroon; in *China and *Korea, brown, grey, and blue, and in *Japan, black or grey.

cloning. There is no 'official' Buddhist position on cloning nor is one likely to emerge since there is no central authority qualified to speak for the religion as a whole. Based on traditional teachings, however, the attitude of Buddhists in general towards recent advances in genetic engineering is likely to be one of caution. In particular, there are grounds for serious concern surrounding the technique of nucleus substitution. This is when the nucleus of a fertilized egg cell is extracted and replaced with the nucleus of a cell from another being in order to produce a twin of the mature animal, as in the case of Dolly the sheep in 1997.

Buddhists are unlikely to have the same objections to the technique as Christians or other theistic religions. For Christians, to bring into being a new human or animal life by cloning may be seen as usurping the role of the creator. This is not a problem for *Buddhism, because in Buddhism the creation of new life is not seen as a 'gift from *God'. For this reason the technique *in itself* would not be seen as problematic. Furthermore, although Buddhists understand sexual reproduction to be the overwhelmingly most common means by which humans and animals are reborn, it teaches that life can come into being through one of 'four wombs' (*catur yoni). The last of these refers to the supernatural phenomenon of 'spontaneous generation' by which sages and supernatural beings have the power to materialize a human form. Life can thus legitimately begin in more ways than one.

Although the technique of cloning may be morally neutral in itself, there are concerns surrounding the purposes for which it may be used. These centre on the fact that the nature of the technique leads life to be viewed as a product rather than an end in itself. The clone is produced by technicians in a laboratory, and for most of the purposes envisaged so far is then treated as an expendable resource rather than an individual with its own rights and intrinsic dignity. It is hard to see what purposes—scientific or otherwise—can justify the dehumanization that results when life is created and manipulated for other ends. For example, if the clone is to be used to provide spare organs for the person cloned, it would mean that individual life was being produced to be used as a mere instrument for the benefit of another, and effectively treated as property in the way slaves once were. Such dehumanizing techniques would be repugnant to Buddhism, which teaches that individual beings (both human and animal) are worthy of respect in their own right. Buddhism is more concerned about animals than some other religions, and so is likely to be more cautious about the use of animals in experiments of this kind. It should be remembered that Ian Wilmut, the creator of Dolly, failed 276 times before Dolly was conceived. Naturally, in the case of human beings a failure rate of this kind would be even graver, and when weighed against the benefits to be gained from human cloning identified so far the risks do not appear to be justified. In fact, there appears to be no single compelling reason for cloning human subjects. The benefits identified so far fall into two main groups: as an aid to current IVF techniques, and use for genetic selection or eugenics purposes. The numbers who would benefit from the first are very small, and history has shown the potentially grave consequences of the latter. *See also* STEM CELL RESEARCH; MEDICINE.

compassion. *See* KARUṆĀ.

completion-phase (Skt., saṃpanna-krama). The second phase of meditational practice (*sādhana) associated with the *anuttara-yoga-tantras in general and especially with the so-called *Mother Tantras such as the **Hevajra Tantra*. It involves the use of creative imagination or *visualization but emphasizes the emptiness (*śūnyatā) aspect of reality as a means of personal transformation, characteristically attending to the mystic centres (*cakras) and subtle energy (*vāyu) together with the channels (*nāḍī) through which the energy flows in order to generate the great bliss associated with enlightenment (*bodhi).

confession. *See* PĀPA-DEŚANĀ.

Confucianism (Chin., ju-chia, k'ung chiao). The teachings of the Chinese sage K'ung-tzu (552–479 BCE) or 'master K'ung', known in the West through the Latinized form of his name 'Confucius'. Confucius' teachings have been profoundly influential through east Asia and he has been regarded by countless generations as the great moral teacher of the region. His intellectual legacy has formed the mainstream of Chinese philosophy for most of the past 2,000 years. Little is known for sure about his life, although his teachings are preserved in the *Analects* (*Lun-yü*) in the form of conversations with his disciples. Above all he emphasized the virtue of jen, meaning humanity or benevolence, and sought to inculcate this in a new class of gentlemen-scholars (ju) who would serve and improve society. Such men, also known as shih, would form a class of educated gentry at the top of the social hierarchy. The primary emphasis of Confucian teachings is thus on the *ethics of social relationships, particularly between parents and children, but extending beyond the family to relationships between superiors and inferiors at all levels. His vision was of an orderly hierarchical society animated by the virtues of altruism, humanism, and personal integrity, and while not denying the existence of a transcendent reality he had little to say about the hearafter or the supernatural. In this respect *Buddhism, with its belief in *karma and *rebirth, filled a gap and provided explanations of matters in which Confucianism showed little interest. The two, along with *Taoism, have coexisted down the centuries in an often uneasy relationship involving periods of ascendancy and decline. Confucianism was not always in power, although it enjoyed a renaissance beginning in the 10th century in the form of Neo-Confucianism. This developed in response to the challenge of Buddhist metaphysics and incorporated certain Buddhist ideas in an attempt to explain philosophical and cosmological problems such as the origins of *evil. Confucianism has left an indelible imprint on Chinese civilization which has survived even the Cultural Revolution (1966–76) and repeated Communist attempts to modernize *China by rooting out 'superstition'. The Confucian work ethic and emphasis on family loyalty continue to underpin the daily life and economic prosperity of Chinese ethnic communities throughout the world.

consciousness. *See* VIJÑĀNA.

Conze, Edward (1904–79). A leading Buddhist scholar of German origin who fled the Nazi regime in the 1930s to take up residence in the United Kingdom. He is best known for his pioneering work on the voluminous **Prajñā-pāramitā Sūtras* surviving in *Sanskrit, many of which he edited and translated in English, as well as his *Sanskrit–English Dictionary* based on material from these texts. He also taught at various Buddhist centres in London, such as the *Buddhist Society. His sometimes scurrilous but moving autobiography, *Memoirs of a Modern Gnostic*, has only been partially published.

cosmology. *Buddhism inherited much of its traditional cosmology from common Indian lore, and in certain basic respects is consistent with the concepts of modern science, particularly in conceiving the universe to be vastly greater in space and time than it was envisaged to be in the West. The world (*loka) in its broadest sense includes the whole cosmos, but within this there are smaller units knows as 'world-systems' (lokadhātu), which correspond roughly to solar systems. Such a unit consists of the sun and moon, Mt. *Meru, four continents, four oceans, the four great Kings (*lokapāla, *caturmahārāja), and the sevenfold heavenly spheres. One thousand of these units together forms a 'small world system', and the 'medium' and 'large' systems are each one thousand times greater than the one below. These larger world systems correspond roughly to the modern concept of a galaxy. The cosmos is believed to be infinite in space and also in time, although it passes through immense cycles of evolution and decline. In the post-canonical period of *Pāli literature, the term lokadhātu is replaced by cakkavāḷa (Skt., *cakravāla), and more elaborate details are added to the traditional accounts. Cosmologies among Buddhists outside India tend to be based on the Indian model, although local cultural influences often modify the original blueprint.

Council of Gandhāra. *See* COUNCIL OF KANIṢKA.

Council of Kaniṣka. Council of dubious historicity, sometimes referred to as the 'Fourth Council', and believed to have been held in the 1st–2nd centuries CE during the reign of the *Kuṣāṇa King *Kaniṣka I. The council was said to be supervised by *Vasumitra and attended by 499 *monks. The Chinese pilgrim *Hsüan-tsang records that, according to tradition in *Kashmir, the work of the council involved the composition of extensive commentaries on the *Tripiṭaka. He reports that Kaniṣka had the commentaries inscribed on copper plates, sealed in stone caskets, and hidden inside a specially constructed *stūpa. The texts in question constitute the great treatise entitled the **Mahāvibhāṣā*, an extensive compendium and reference work on *Sarvāstivāda doctrines. In fact it is unlikely that the *Mahāvibhāṣā* itself was compiled before the 2nd century CE.

Council of Lhasa. A name used somewhat misleadingly by certain Western Scholars to refer to a debate held at *Samye (and not the Tibetan capital, Lhasa) in the year 742 CE on the disputed question of whether enlightenment (*bodhi) was a sudden or gradual process. The two main protagonists were the Indian *monk *Kamalaśīla, and the Chinese *Ch'an master *Hvashang Mahāyāna (Chin., Ho-Shang Mo-ho-yen). The latter taught that enlightenment was a spontaneous experience in which all the defilements (*kleśa) are destroyed in a single moment. Kamalaśīla defended the traditional Indian gradualist position in terms of which enlightenment is the natural outcome of a long process of personal transformation accomplished by following a pre-ordained religious path. The Tibetan side won the debate and Indian gradualism became the orthodox form of *Buddhism there from that time. Soon after the council Kamalaśīla was murdered, allegedly by an assassin dispatched by his defeated Chinese opponent. Although some scholars doubt the historicity of this debate, it epitomizes the rejection of Chinese forms of Buddhism by the Tibetans. Some scholars, however, believe that Ch'an Buddhism continued to exert an influence on the *Nyingma and *Kagyu schools even after the council.

Council of Pāṭaliputra I. The 'Third Council' at *Pāṭaliputra *c.*350 BCE is not an historical fact so much as a scholarly hypothesis developed to explain the 'Great *Schism' between the 'Elders' (*Sthaviras) and the 'Great Assembly' (*Mahāsaṃghikas), which was to have a profound effect upon the later tradition. This council is not mentioned in any canonical sources, and is not recognised by the *Theravāda, who identify the Third Council with a later council at the same place held in the reign of *Aśoka (*see* COUNCIL OF PĀṬALIPUTRA II). The circumstances surrounding the 'Third Council' are somewhat unclear, and there are two alternative explanations for why it was called. One concerns five theses put forward by a *monk named *Mahādeva to the effect that the *Buddha was greatly superior in wisdom and compassion to the *Arhat. The Mahāsaṃghikas accepted these five points and emphasized the Buddha's compassion and supernatural qualities, while the Sthaviras rejected them and held to the notion of the Buddha's nature as essentially human. The two groups were unable to reach agreement and went their separate ways. This explanation, however, which comes from sources over 400 years after the event, is almost certainly incorrect. Recent research shows that the 'five theses' have nothing to do with the early Mahāsaṃghikas and therefore can have nothing to do with with the initial schism with the ancestors of the *Theriya tradition.

A second explanation for the split is that the division was caused by an attempt by the Sthaviras to introduce additional rules into the *Vinaya which the Mahāsaṃghikas refused to accept. Most probably the schism was the product of a number of disagreements concerning both doctrine and monastic practice.

Council of Pāṭaliputra II. An early council mentioned only in *Pāli sources and regarded by the *Theravāda school as the 'Third Council'. The council took place around 250 BCE during the reign of *Aśoka, and according to traditional accounts in the **Mahāvaṃsa* and **Dīpavaṃsa* the king played a leading role. The events centred on a monastery (*vihāra) in *Pāṭaliputra where certain residents refused to celebrate the *poṣadha (Pāli, *uposatha) ceremony with colleagues they regarded as lax and unorthodox. Aśoka dispatched an emissary to resolve the matter but he, misunderstanding his orders, had a number of monks executed. Aśoka then intervened and convened a council of 1000 *monks under the presidency of a senior and learned monk named *Moggaliputta Tissa. The orthodox teaching of the *Buddha was identified as *Vibhajyavāda, and one by one the monks were questioned by Aśoka and expelled if their views were non-Buddhist (e.g. if they held the doctrine of *eternalism). The king then departed and the monks held their council (saṅgīti), or communal recitation of the texts. The king was thus not concerned with divergent views among the genuine Buddhist monks. Many of the unorthodox views are recorded in the *Kathā-vatthu. Aśoka's *Edicts contain allusions to dissent in the *Saṃgha, which may support the historicity of the traditional account.

Council of Rājagṛha. The Council of *Rājagṛha, often called the 'First Council', is reported to have been held at Rājagṛha in the year of the *Buddha's death with the objective of establishing the *canon or at least two of its three divisions or 'baskets' (*piṭaka). These include the collection of the Buddha's discourses or sermons (*sūtra/sutta) and the material relating to the organization and history of the order (*Vinaya). A senior *monk, Kaśyapa, was charged with supervising the convocation made up of 500 *Arhats. He called upon *Ānanda (who reportedly gained *enlightenment during the proceedings of the council) to recite the Buddha' discourses, and *Upāli to recite the rules of the Vinaya. Their utterances were accepted as accurate and decreed as constituting the content of the orthodox canon from that time on. It may be noted that the word translated as 'council' in this context is the Pāli word saṅgīti, which in fact means a 'communal recitation' of the kind that took place here. The early Buddhist 'councils', accordingly, should not be thought of as similar to their early Christian counterparts, which were usually convened to settle dogma. Modern research has cast serious doubts on the historicity of the traditional account of the First Council. In particular it is clear from internal evidence that the canon did not receive its final form until many years later, so it could not have been fixed at the early date the report claims. Most probably this claim was a device to retrospectively legitimize certain later literature as canonical.

Council of Rangoon. A council convened in Rangoon, *Burma, to commemorate the 2,500th anniversary of the death of the *Buddha. Sometimes referred to as the 'sixth council', it was held over two years from 1954 to 1956 and was attended by 2,400 monks from *Theravāda countries. The proceedings of the council were dedicated to editing and reciting the texts of the *Pāli Canon.

Council of Vaiśālī. The so-called 'Second Council' took place 100 or 110 years after the *Council of Rājagṛha and was held at *Vaiśālī. It arose out of a dispute concerning monastic practices, and in particular the handling of money by *monks. One faction, the *Vṛjiputrakas (or Vajjians) claimed that this, together with nine other practices, was legitimate. The more orthodox, on the other hand, regarded them as illegal and prohibited by the *Vinaya. The council, consisting of 700 respected monks under the presidency of *Revata, ruled against the Vṛjiputrakas but it is unclear how far their practices were reformed as a result. The need for a council to be convened at this relatively early date shows that serious disagreements were surfacing in the early community, and these soon afterwards led to fragmentation and *schism.

craving. *See* TṚṢṆĀ.

cremation. The standard method for the disposal of the dead in *India where (unlike Christianity, Judaism, and Islam) there is no belief in the resurrection of the body. Since ancient times corpses have been disposed of by burning on pyres in public cremation grounds. The *Buddha himself was cremated and his remains were divided up into eight parts which were distributed among the local kingdoms and clans.

Critical Buddhism (Jap., Hihan Bukkyō). Recent movement among Japanese academics which highlights the doctrinal incompatibility between east Asian and early Indian *Buddhism. The leading scholars in this field, namely Noriaki Hakamaya and Shirō Matsumoto of Komazawa University, have aroused controversy by pointing to the lack of foundation in the early sources for later teachings notably those of *Zen Buddhism, and doctrinal concepts such as that of the 'embryonic *Buddha' (*tathāgata-garbha). They regard such notions as fundamentally incompatible with early doctrines that emphasize the absence of a permanent self (*ātman).

Cūlanāga Thera. Also referred to as Tipiṭaka-Cūlanāga, he was apparently a very well-known commentator since his opinions are quoted in the commentaries of *Buddhaghoṣa. He was a pupil of Summa Thera of the Dīpavihāra, a *Sri Lankan monastery, with whom he does not always seem to have agreed in his interpretations of various matters. Although often cited as an authority, it is not known whether Cūlanāga ever wrote anything himself.

Cūlapanthaka Thera. One of the early *Arhats. His name means 'the junior of the footpath' and derives from the fact that he was the younger of two brothers both born by the side of the road. Both became *monks, and while his clever older brother Mahāpanthaka quickly became an Arhat, Cūlapanthaka was slower at his studies and only reached the goal when the *Buddha gave him a personal teaching. He was famed for his meditational prowess, and in particular his ability to fashion mind-made forms while in a state of trance.

Cūlavaṃsa. Literally meaning 'Short Chronicle', a historiographic work in *Pāli, compiled by several authors over a period of centuries. It is a continuation of the **Mahāvaṃsa* and it covers the history of *Sri Lanka from 302 CE to the 20th century. The name *Cūlavaṃsa* was probably not intended by the author but has been preferred in Sri Lanka since medieval times in order to make clear the distinction from the *Mahāvaṃsa* itself.

Cullavagga (Pāli). The 'minor section' of the *Vinaya, subordinate to the *Mahāvagga or 'major section'.

Cunda. A blacksmith resident at *Pāvā who served the *Buddha his last meal. The nature of the meal, which was the proximate cause of the Buddha's *death, is disputed (*see* SŪKARA-MADDAVA). Before he died, the Buddha instructed *Ānanda to tell Cunda that no blame attached to him for what he had done, and that on the contrary he had acquired great merit (*puṇya) by serving the Buddha his last meal.

cuti-citta (Pāli, *death, consciousness) The final moment of consciousness (*vijñāna) in this life, according to the *Abhidharma classification of consciousness into fourteen functions. *See also* BHAVAṄGA.

D

dāgaba. Sinhalese term often spelt 'dagoba' in European languages. Literally 'relic container', it is a mound or shrine where *relics are kept. *See also* STŪPA.

Fig 7 dāgaba

dai-gedatsu (Jap. great liberation). *Nirvāṇa, or the attainment of Buddhahood.

dai-gidan (Jap.). In *Ch'an and *Zen practice, this represents a highly intense doubt about everything one thinks to be true, including the efficacy of Zen practice itself. It induces a kind of paralysis, described as feeling that one has 'a hot iron ball in one's throat that one can neither swallow nor spit out', and is seen as a necessary precursor to the experience of enlightenment (*bodhi; *satori).

Daikoku. 1. The Hindu god of the Five Grains and of good fortune, who was imported into Japanese *Buddhism as a guardian deity. **2.** A Japanese Buddhist priest's wife.

Daikokuten. Non-wrathful Japanese form of the *tantric deity *Mahākāla.

daimoku. In *Nichiren *Buddhism in *Japan this is the name given to the **Lotus Sūtra*, which the school holds to be the highest revelation of Buddhist teaching. Followers believe that chanting the title of the scripture effects liberation and instils wisdom. In Japanese, the chant is *Namo myōhō renge kyō, which means 'Hail to the Scripture of the Lotus of the Marvellous Dharma!'

Dainichi (or Dainichibō) Nōnin (d. *c.*1194). The founder of the *Daruma school, an early and short-lived school of Japanese *Zen. Nōnin studied Zen texts on his own early in his monastic career, and had a significant *enlightenment experience. Realizing that Zen enlightenment requires authentication by a recognized master, he sent two disciples to *China in 1189 to visit the master Te-kuang (1121–1203) with letters and gifts. The latter sanctioned Nōnin's experience and sent back a certificate and robe. Thereafter, Nōnin's fame spread and he gathered many disciples. An early account says that he was killed by a nephew in either 1194 or 1195, but scholars give little credence to this. After his death, his disciples joined *Dōgen (1200–53).

daiosho (Jap.). A Japanese Buddhist term meaning 'great teacher', used specifically by students to refer to ascendant masters in their lineage.

daishi (Jap.). In Japanese *Buddhism, an honorific, usually granted posthumously, meaning 'great master'.

Daitō Kokushi. *See* SHŪHŌ MYŌCHŌ.

Daitoku-ji. A *Rinzai *Zen temple in *Kyoto, built in 1324 and consecrated in 1327 by *Shūhō Myōchō (1282–1337). It became the home temple of the Daitokuji-ha, one of the major sects within Rinzai.

ḍākinī (Skt.; Tib., mkha'-'gro-ma). In *tantric *Buddhism, a ḍākinī is a type of accomplished *yoginī or else a female deity, depicted iconographically as a naked semi-wrathful figure who acts as a guiding intermediary for practitioners and assists in the actualization of *siddhis. First noted in Indian sources around the 4th century CE, ḍākinīs were probably tribal shamanesses in origin and their name can be linked to cognate terms meaning 'summoning' and 'drumming' rather than 'flying' as suggested by the Tibetan translation which means 'sky- goer'.

Dalada Maligawa. *Kandy's' *Temple of the Tooth' housing *Sri Lanka's most important Buddhist relict: the *tooth relic. The building of the temple was initiated in 1592 and the present building, an imposing pink-painted structure surrounded by a deep moat, was constructed mainly under Kandyan kings from 1687 to 1707 and again from 1747 to 1782. An octagonal tower in the moat was added by Sri Wickrama Rajasinha, the last king of Kandy, and houses an important collection of palm-leaf manuscripts. In the early 1990s President Premadasa added a gilded roof over the relic chamber. The temple is the centre of the *Esala Perahera celebrations.

Dalai Lama. An honorific title derived from Mongolian, the first part of which (dalai) means 'ocean'. Altan Khan, the Mongol ruler of Kokonor, conferred this title on the early *Gelukpa teacher Snam Gyatsho (bsod-nams rgya-mtsho, 1543–88) in 1578. The same title was then applied retrospectively to his two previous incarnations, Gendün Drup (dge-'dun grub) 1391–1474 and Gendün Gyatsho (dge-'dun rgya-mtsho) 1476–1542, who became known respectively as Dalai Lama I and Dalai Lama II. From that time onwards, the successive incarnations through to the current *Dalai Lama XIV have all been given this title. From the time of the *Dalai Lama V in the mid-18th century, the Dalai Lamas were the titular heads of state in *Tibet as well as the spiritual leaders of the Gelukpa. *See also* MONGOLIA.

Dalai Lama V (1617–82). Losang Gyatsho (Tib., blo-bzang rgya-mtsho), often deemed to be the greatest Dalai Lama on account of his political acumen, especially in his dealings with Manchu *China, though he is not renowned as an exceptional scholar. He was largely responsible for the reunification of *Tibet after a period of upheaval and the political dominance of the office of the Dalai Lama and the *Gelukpa school in general, especially through suppression of the *Karma- kagyü and *Jonangpa schools during his time. His reign ushered in a golden age of religious, social, and artistic strength in Tibet. Apart from his overt affiliation to Gelukpa doctrines, he is known to have been favourably disposed to certain *Nyingma teachings and practices.

Dalai Lama XIV (1935–). Tenzin Gyatso (Tib., bstan-'dzin rgya-mtsho). The current Dalai Lama now living in exile. Following the Chinese invasion of *Tibet in 1950, he tried to protect Tibetan interests through cooperation with the Chinese but, after the 1959 uprising, he eventually fled to *India where he is now resident in Dharamsala. Well-known for his tolerence, humility, and tireless efforts to further the Tibetan cause internationally, he received the Nobel Peace Prize in 1989.

ḍamaru (Skt.). A small hourglass-shaped double-headed drum having two hemispheres of wood or human crania with two clappers attached on strings. When twirled, the drum emits a sharp rattling sound, often said to create a sense of urgency in the face of all-pervading impermanency. It is widely used in Tibetan Buddhist *tantric rituals and meditations, with a large ḍāmaru specified for use in *chöd practice.

dāna (Skt.; Pāli). Generosity, a key Buddhist virtue which is both a source of great merit (*puṇya) and also instrumental in overcoming selfishness and attachment. In *Theravādin contexts, it connotes the giving of alms by lay-people to monks, while in *Mahāyāna it usually refers to the Perfection of Generosity (*dāna-pāramitā). A particularly worthy recipient of a gift is known as a 'field of merit' (*puṇya-kṣetra).

Dānapāla. An Indian *monk, originally from Udyāna in north-west *India, he arrived in *China in 980 CE and took up residence in the Northen Sung capital of Kaifeng. There he translated a considerable number of texts, especially those linked to *tantric *Buddhism, including a complete version of the **Sarva-tathāgata-tattva-saṃgraha Sūtra*. Prior to his *death in 1017 CE, he was also involved in preparatory editorial work that was undertaken for the epoch-making printing of the Shu-pen edition of the *Chinese Tripiṭaka, the first time a Buddhist *canon was printed in any language.

dāna-pāramitā (Skt.). The Perfection of Generosity, the first of the Six Perfections (*ṣaḍ-pāramitā) that make up the central element of the *Mahāyāna path; its cultivation involves unselfish giving in three aspects: the giving of material goods to those in need, the giving of security and freedom from fear, and the giving of the *Dharma.

darśana (Skt.; Pāli, dassana). **1**. Literally 'seeing' or 'view', the *Sanskrit word which most closely approximates the Western term 'philosophy', and is used to denote the six classical philosophical schools of ancient India. **2**. In Buddhism it implies insight into reality or certain aspects of Buddhist doctrines such as the *Four Noble Truths, for example, as in the 'path of seeing' (*darśana-mārga), which is the third of the five paths to Buddhahood (*see* PAÑCA-MĀRGA). **3**. Also used in *Hinduism in the sense of an audience with a *guru or holy person, but not found in *Buddhism in this sense.

darśana-mārga (Skt.). The 'path of seeing', the third of the five paths (*pañca-mārga) to Buddhahood. Through the path of seeing, uncertainty (*vicikitsā), false views (*dṛṣṭi), and spiritual defilements (*kleśa) are eliminated.

Daruma. *See* BODHIDHARMA; P'U-T'I-TA-MO.

Daruma-shū. An early Japanese *Zen school founded by *Dainichibō Nōnin (d. *c.*1194). This school received severe criticism from the nascent *Rinzai and *Sōtō traditions, who found it antinomian and lacking in serious practice. However, recent research into texts emanating from the school itself reveal a different picture. The school saw itself as direct *Dharma-descendant of the first Chinese *Ch'an *patriarch *Bodhidharma (Daruma is the Japanese rendering of his name), whom it honoured with esoteric ceremonies. It also based its teachings on three treatises attributed to Bodhidharma, as well as the *Mahāyāna scripture the **Śūraṅgama-samādhi Sūtra*, giving the school its cognomen 'the school of one scripture and three treatises'. It taught the equality of all beings with *Buddhas, universal emptiness (*śūnyatā), and also the magical efficacy of esoteric formulae and rituals in bringing about good fortune. The school flourished briefly, but was overly dependent on Nōnin's personal charisma. Upon his death, members migrated to other Zen schools, primarily the Sōtō-shū.

daśa-bala (Skt., ten powers). The ten powers of a *tathāgata consisting of knowledge relating to: (1) what is and is not possible in any situation; (2) the ripening (*vipāka) of deeds and the maturation of *karma; (3) the superior and inferior qualities of beings; (4) the various tendencies of beings; (5) the manifold constituents of the world; (6) the paths leading to the various realms of existence; (7) pure and impure behaviour; (8) the arising of meditative states (*dhyāna) and related attainments; (9) the *death and *rebirth of beings; (10) liberation through the destruction of the outflows (*āśravas).

Daśabhūmika Sūtra (Skt.). A seminal *Mahāyāna *sūtra which describes the standard set of ten levels (*bhūmi) that are traversed by a *Bodhisattva on the path to enlightenment (*bodhi). Forming a section of the **Avataṃsaka Sūtra*, the work survives in *Sanskrit as well as in translations in Tibetan and Chinese.

daśa-kuśala-karmapatha (Skt.). The 'Ten Good Paths of Action' or 'Ten Good Deeds', a formulation of moral *precepts, especially important in the *Mahāyāna, governing actions by way of the *body, speech, mind. The ten are (1) not to kill; (2) not to steal; (3) to avoid sexual misconduct; (4) not to lie; (5) abstention from slanderous speech; (6) abstention from harsh speech; (7) abstention from idle talk; (8) non-greed; (9) non- hatred; (10) right views. In Mahāyāna sources, this moral code is said to be 'mundane' (*laukika) when adopted by ordinary beings intent on avoiding *rebirth in any of the miserable states of existence, since in that case it does not lead to liberation from *saṃsāra. When accompained by skilful means (*upāya-kauśalya) and insight (*prajñā) and adopted by *Bodhisattvas, however, it is said to be supermundane (*lokottara) as it then leads to liberation.

daśa-śīla (Skt., Pāli, dasa-sīla). The Ten Precepts. These are 1–6 of the Eight Precepts (*aṣṭāṅga-śīla) with additional prohibitions on (7) dancing, singing, music, and watching shows; (8) using garlands, perfumes, and personal adornments; (9) using high seats or beds; (10) accepting gold or silver. The Ten Precepts are observed by novice monks and nuns. *See also* PAÑCA-ŚĪLA; DAŚA-KUŚALA-KARMAPATHA.

dasa silmātā. A body of religious *women in *Sri Lanka whose status lies somewhere between that of laity and *nuns. Their name means 'the ten precept mothers', a reference to the ten *precepts they assume, being the same as the ten precepts for novice nuns (śrāmaṇerī) laid down in the *Vinaya. Although, like nuns, they wear orange robes (*cīvara) and shave their heads, they cannot receive full *ordination because the ordination lineage for nuns has long been extinct in the *Theravāda tradition.

date of the Buddha. The *Pāli Canon records that the *Buddha died at the age of 80, but the dates of his life are not known with certainty. The lack of systematic dating in Indian sources and the problems in correlating Indian and Western calendars pose major obstacles to chronological research in this area. Different dates for his life have become established in different parts of the Buddhist world. In *Sri Lanka and *south-east Asia it is not uncommon to see the life of the Buddha dated from 624–544 BCE. In east Asia, the later dates of 448–368 BCE are accepted. The conventional dates for the Buddha given in most secondary literature based on Western scholarhip are 566–466 BCE, or 563–463 BCE. More recent research, however, suggests that the Buddha lived some 50 years or more closer to our own time, and the current consensus among Western scholars is that he died some time between 410 and 400 BCE.

dāyaka (Skt.). A donor or benefactor, usually a lay-person who gives alms regularly or assumes responsibility for certain costs or expenses incurred by the local monastic community.

death. The point at which life in any of the *six realms of *rebirth ceases. In Buddhist thought, repeated death encapsulates the existential problem of life in *saṃsāra, from which *nirvāṇa is the only release. As such, death is ennumerated as an aspect of suffering (*duḥkha) under the First Noble Truth (*see* FOUR NOBLE TRUTHS). In the *Pāli Canon death is defined in biological terms as the cessation of vitality (āyu), heat (usmā), and consciousness (viññāna, Skt., *vijñāna) (e.g. S. iii. 143). Old age and death is also the twelfth link in the chain of Dependent Origination (*pratītya-samutpāda). In Buddhist scholasticism (*Abhidharma), it is held that death occurs from moment to moment as phenomena arise and perish within the individual life-continuum (*see* BHAVAṄGA). The last of these moments, known as the *cuti-citta, is when existence in any life ceases. Death also has great symbolic significance, and is represented mythologically by the figure of *Māra, the Buddhist devil.

debate. Buddhist traditions of debate have their origins in the early encounters between Buddhists and non-Buddhist philosophers and later within rival Buddhist groups. By the 6th century CE, philosophical sophistication led to a codification of all matters involved in debate such as valid and invalid modes of argument, acceptable sources and means of valid knowledge, as well as logic in general. The rules and traditional Indian techniques and procedures for debate have been preserved in *Tibet and form a key part of the *Gelukpa monastic curriculum, based especially on the works of *Dignāga and *Dharmakīrti. Gelukpa *monks frequently engage one another in debate as part of their monastic training.

Deer Park. The Deer Park (Pāli, migadāya) at Isipatana near present-day *Vārāṇasī was the site of the *first sermon. After gaining enlightenment (*bodhi) the *Buddha came here and preached this sermon to five of his former *ascetic companions, later known as the *pañcavaggiyā *monks.

deity yoga. A key meditational practice associated with *tantric *Buddhism through which the practitioner visualizes a particular deity based on specific tantras or derivative *sādhana texts. The visualized image of the deity can be treated as an object of worship (*pūjā) or as a model for self-identification to actualize the corresponding enlightened attributes within oneself.

de La Vallée Poussin, Louis (1869–1938). Renowned Belgian scholar of *Buddhism and founder of the so-called 'Franco-Belgian' school of Buddhist studies. He made a major contribution to the field notably through the edition and translation of important Buddhist works in *Sanskrit, Tibetan, and Chinese. Born at Liège, he entered the University there before moving to Louvain to study Sanskrit, *Pāli, and Avestan. From there he went to Paris and studied at the Sorbonne and the École des Hautes-Études under the great Indologist Sylvain Levi, before moving to Leiden to work with Hendrik Kern. In 1898 he published a major work entitled *Buddhisme: Études et materiaux*, and in 1907 he published a translation of *Śāntideva's **Bodhicaryāvatāra* in serial form. During the First World War he continued his work in Cambridge and towards the end of his life he was engaged upon two major works, the **Abhidharma-kośa* of *Vasubandhu, and the **Vijñapti-mātratā Siddhi* of *Hsüan-tsang, both of which he completed before his death at the age of 69. The range of his knowledge was extensive and he approached Buddhism as an organic whole rather than restricting his attention to specific topics, schools, or historical periods. His major contributions however were in the fields of *Madhyamaka philosophy and *Abhidharma scholasticism.

Denkō-roku. A Japanese *Sōtō *Zen historical work composed between 1299 and 1301 by the *monk *Keizan Jōkin (1268–1325). This work traces the lineage of masters and disciples of the Sōtō school from the *Buddha through *Dōgen, and is an invaluable source for Zen history. It is number 2585 in the *Taishō collection.

Dependent Origination. *See* PRATĪTYA-SAMUTPĀDA.

Desanā Mahājāti. A ceremony popular in the *Theravāda countries of *south-east Asia such as *Burma, *Thailand, and Laos, involving the ritualized preaching of the **Vessantara Jātaka*. The ceremony takes place around one month after the planting of the rice crop and is regarded as an important opportunity to make merit (*puṇya). It is commonly linked to the festival of *Loi Krathong.

desire. Broad English term for which there is no single *Sanskrit or *Pāli equivalent. Instead, Buddhist psychology classifies the affective impulses according to their various objects. Desire for unwholesome things is generally known as *tṛṣṇā, closer in meaning to the English 'craving'. Other forms of desire, which may be good, bad, or neutral, are analysed into the three forms of *chanda. From this it can be seen that the often-encountered notion that *Buddhism teaches that all desire is wrong is an oversimplification.

deva (Skt.; Pāli, bright, shining). A god or supernatural being, normally resident in one of the numerous heavens and reborn there as the result of good *karma. *Buddhism inherited the *Vedic concept of a pantheon of gods, originally 33, but which rapidly expanded in number. The gods are thought to reside on or over Mt. *Meru, the cosmic mountain, and to be frequent visitors to the human world, especially to hear the *Buddha's teachings. Offerings and sacrifices are made to the gods, and they may be appealed to for help or protection. They enjoy lifespans of hundreds of thousands of years, but are eventually reborn when their good karma is exhausted, and are thus (in contrast to the Buddha) still within the realm of *saṃsāra.

Devadatta. Son of a maternal uncle of the *Buddha, who had been converted by the Buddha himself. After years in which he had become a respected member of the *Saṃgha, Devadatta is said to have started a series of plots including three attempted murders, in order to take control of the Saṃgha from the Buddha. Devadatta confronted the Buddha over a number of *ascetic practices (*dhutanga) which he sought to have made compulsory, but which the Buddha decided should be optional. The enmity between the two was not limited to this life, but each of Devadatta's efforts to overthrow the Buddha resulted in failure.

devala. Sinhalese term for a Buddhist or Hindu temple or shrine where the gods (*deva) are worshipped. Such a place would not normally be found within the precincts of a monastery.

Devānampiya Tissa (247–207 BCE). King of *Sri Lanka. His original name was simply Tissa. Considering the coronation ritual he had undergone not to be sufficient, he sent an embassy to Emperor *Aśoka of *India who sent him all the requisites for a second coronation and invited Tissa to embrace *Buddhism. After the second coronation Tissa added the title Devānampiya, meaning 'dear to the gods'. This was a common royal title that even Aśoka had adopted. In the year of the king's second coronation *Mahinda, son of Emperor Aśoka, arrived in *Sri Lanka at the head of a mission and converted the king and his court to Buddhism, thus officially introducing Buddhism to the island. Following his conversion Tissa donated the Tissārama park, in his capital of *Anurādhapura, to the Buddhist community and had the *Mahāvihāra built on its grounds. He is also known to have sponsored the building of several other Buddhist monuments, including the *stūpa enshrining the *Buddha's collar bone, and the adjacent monastery. When some *women of his court asked to enter the Buddhist Order, Tissa asked again for Aśoka's help. The emperor sent his daughter, the *nun *Saṅghamittā, together with other nuns to the island. With them the women brought a branch of the original *Bodhi Tree to be planted in Anurādhapura.

devatā (Skt.). In *tantric *Buddhism a deity, usually a *Buddha or a *Bodhisattva, who is a transformation or emanation of the qualities and facets of the Truth Body (*dharma-kāya). The devatā may become manifest in various forms, as a sound (*mantra), a gesture (*mudrā), or a physical representation.

devil. *See* MĀRA.

dge-lugs-pa. *See* GELUKPA.

Dhammajarig. Thai term meaning 'travelling *Dharma' and denoting a mission inaugurated in 1963 by the Thai Buddhist *Saṃgha to the non-Buddhist hill tribes of *Thailand. The programme was started by a former *monk who subsequently became chief of the hill-tribes division of the Department of Public Welfare, and the abbot of a large monastery in Bangkok. The aim of the project is to bring *Buddhism to the hill-tribes people and to integrate them politically, socially, and economically into the Thai national community. In a typical year, around 20 teams of five monks visit the tribal areas from March–June. The monks walk to the area and establish a monastic community. No attempt is made to proselytize or disparage the tribal religion. After a month or so a programme of home visits begins, and enquiries are made about the health and general welfare of each family. Elementary teaching and the dispensing of medicines provide the foundation for further development in the relationship. Critics of the programme object that monks are being used as civil servants, but supporters point out that the project is purely Saṃgha-led and that no rules of monastic discipline are broken by those who take part.

Dhammapada. The second book of the *Khuddaka Nikāya of the *Pāli Canon and one of the most popular and best-loved Buddhist texts. It consists of 423 verses divided into 26 sections arranged according to subject matter. In practice it is a sort of anthology of verses from various books of the *canon, though very few are taken from the *Jātaka collection or from the *Sutta-nipāta. It also contains material from other Buddhist schools and non-Buddhist sources. The commentary of the *Dhammapada*, by an anonymous author but attributed to *Buddhaghoṣa, is known as the **Dhammapada-aṭṭhakathā*.

Dhammapada-aṭṭhakathā. The commentary on the **Dhammapada*, a text containing stories similar to those of the *Jātakas and explaining the occasions on which the verses contained in the *Dhammapada* were uttered. A considerable number of these stories are found in various parts of the *Pāli Canon and several are either directly derived from the *Jātaka commentary or are closely parallel to them. The work, by an anonymous author, is usually ascribed to *Buddhaghoṣa. It was apparently compiled in *Sri Lanka, as stated in the book, and its date is unknown.

Dhammapāla. Author of fourteen important commentarial works on *Pāli texts. A native of south *India he lived some time after *Buddhaghoṣa, and composed a subcommentary on Buddhaghoṣa's commentaries on the four *Nikāyas. He resided for a time at the *Mahāvihāra in *Sri Lanka. He is often referred to simply as the 'master' (ācariya).

Dhammaruci Nikāya. One of the heterodox sects of *Sri Lanka which branched off from the *Theravāda. This division supposedly took place 450 years after the *death of the *Buddha. Some sources affirm that Dhammarucika was the name given to the monks of the Abhayagiri when they seceded from the *Mahāvihāra, but the traditional accounts of the origins of the group cannot be relied on. Despite some ups and downs in their fortunes, the Dhammarucikas enjoyed favour in Sri Lanka over a long period, with several kings making provisions and donating monasteries to them.

Dhammasaṅgaṇī. The first book of the *Abhidharma Piṭaka of the *Pāli Canon, which appears to have been also called

Dhammasaṅgaha. Being a compilation from various sources, it deals with more or less the same topics as the *Nikāyas, differing only in methods of treatment. The main subject of the book, which analyses and classifies the phenomena (*dharma) that comprise all mental and material conditions, is that of *ethics. The book enumerates and defines a number of categories of terms occurring in the Nikāyas. The commentary on the *Dhammasaṅgaṇī*, attributed to *Buddhaghoṣa in the 5th century, is known by the title of **Atthasālinī*. King *Vijayabāhu I of *Sri Lanka translated the *Dhammasaṅgaṇī* into Sinhalese, but this translation is now lost.

dhāraṇī (Skt.). The term literally means 'retention' and refers to high levels of mindfulness (*smṛti) and insight (*prajñā) derived from spiritual practice. In early *Mahāyāna *Buddhism, four categories were distinguished: the retention of patience (kṣānti-dhāraṇī), the retention of *mantra (mantra-dhāraṇī), the retention of words (pada-dhāraṇī), and the retention of meaning (artha-dhāraṇī). Mantra-dhāraṇīs were a mnemonic form of mantra designed to facilitate the retention of various teachings, often considered to be a summary version of long *sūtras. Later, with the rise of *tantric Buddhism, dhāraṇīs became indistinguishable from mantras in general though they are generally of greater length than ordinary mantras and can largely be understood as normal speech.

Dharma (Pāli, Dhamma). Dharma is etymologically derived from the *Sanskrit root dhṛ meaning to bear or support. It is a term of great significance with three main meanings. First, it refers to the natural order or universal law that underpins the operation of the universe in both the physical and moral spheres. Secondly, it denotes the totality of Buddhist teachings, since these are thought to accurately describe and explain the underlying universal law so that individuals may live in harmony with it. It is in this sense that it occurs as one of the 'three jewels' (*triratna) and the 'three refuges' (*triśaraṇa), along with the *Buddha and the *Saṃgha. Thirdly, it is used in the *Abhidharma system of taxonomy to refer to the individual elements that collectively constitute the empirical world. Some of these elements (dharmas) are external to the perceiver and others are internal psychological processes and traits of character. It is in this context that the *Madhyamaka school denied the substantial reality of dharmas, claiming that all phenomena were 'empty' (śūnya) of any substantial reality.

Dharma-anusārin (Skt., one who follows in the Dharma; Pāli, Dhamma-anusārī). According to the early teachings, the path to enlightenment (*bodhi) may be entered and its fruit attained in a variety of ways. The Dharma-anusārin is the fifth in a sevenfold list of noble persons (*ārya-pudgala) who enter the Noble Path through a range of dispositions. The Dharma-anusārin is distinguished by the fact that he attains the path through an intellectual grasp of the teachings. This is in contrast to the śraddhā-anusārī (Pāli, saddhā-anusārī), who attains to the state of a noble person on the basis of the faculty of faith (*śraddhā). For the complete list of the seven noble persons *see* ĀRYA-PUDGALA.

Dharma-cakra (Skt., wheel of the law; Pāli, dhamma-cakka). Symbol of the Buddhist teachings represented in the form of a wheel usually with eight spokes which represent the *Eightfold Path. The teachings, like a wheel, are thought to be eternal in having neither a beginning nor end. The symbolism of the wheel derives from the name of the *first sermon given by the *Buddha, known as the *Discourse on Setting in Motion the Wheel of the Law* (*Dharmacakra-pravartana Sutta*) in

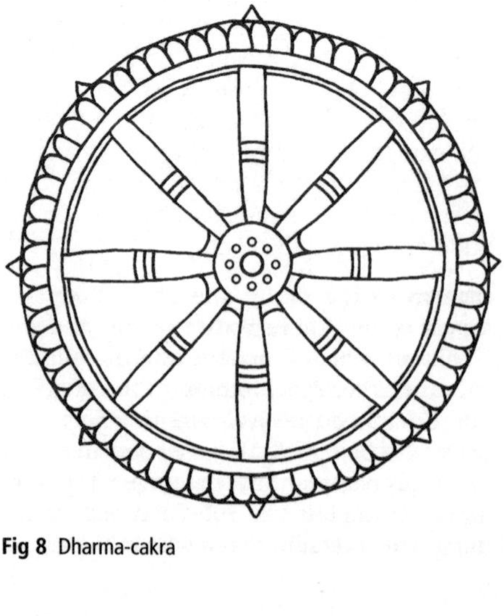

Fig 8 Dharma-cakra

which he sets out the *Four Noble Truths and the 'three turnings of the wheel'. In later *Buddhism a second and third 'turning of the wheel' are recognized: the second is the *Mahāyāna, and the third is the *Vajrayāna. *See also* CAKRA.

Dharma-dharmatā-vibhāga (Skt.). A short *Yogācāra work, attributed to *Maitreyanātha, which discusses the distinction and correlation (vibhāga) between phenomena (*dharma) and reality (*dharmatā). The work exists in both a prose and a verse version and survives only in Tibetan translation although a *Sanskrit original was reported by Rāhula Sāṅkṛtyāyana to exist in *Tibet during the 1930s.

dharma-dhātu (Skt.) **1.** One of the eighteen *dhātus, the objects or contents of the mind. **2.** The universal 'matrix' which is space-like or empty (*śūnya) in nature, from which all phenomena (*dharma) arise. **3.** The universe itself with all its world-systems and societies of beings.

Dharmagupta (d. 619). A south Indian *monk who went to *China during the Sui dynasty and arriving at *Ch'ang-an around 590. He moved to Loyang in 606, where he translated many *Mahāyāna *sutras and treatises.

Dharmaguptaka. One of the *Eighteen schools of early Buddhism patronised by Indo-Scythian rulers and based in north-west India, hence their early importance in central Asia and *China. According to some sources however, they were based in South India. The *Vinaya of this school, which survives in Chinese, is important since its lineage for the *ordination of nuns (*bhikṣuṇī) has survived until the present day. Accordingly, it has been adopted by those attempting to reintroduce the bhikṣuṇī order into Tibetan and south-west Asian Buddhist circles, where the *ordination lineage has died out.

dharma-kāya (Skt.). The Truth Body, one aspect of the 'three bodies of the *Buddha' (*trikāya), which functions as the ground for the other two aspects, namely the Enjoyment Body (*saṃbhoga-kāya) and the Emanation Body (*nirmāṇa-kāya). In earlier forms of *Buddhism it was simply seem as the posthumous presence of the Buddha in the form of his teachings (*Dharma), while in the *Mahāyāna it is considered to be synonymous with perfect enlightenment (saṃbodhi), primordially existent, transcending all perceptual forms (*animitta) and hence not possible to perceive. Among its qualities (guṇa) are freedom from all conceptualization (*nirvikalpa), liberation from all defilements (*kleśa), and the intrinsic ability to perform all activities. In later forms of Indian and Tibetan Buddhism, under the influence of *tantric thought, the dharma-kāya is considered to be equivalent to the mind of the Buddha.

Dharmakīrti (7th c. CE). Born in south *India, Dharmakīrti was a leading representative of the Buddhist school of logic (*pramāṇa) at *Nālandā. Relying on *Yogācāra and *Sautrāntika doctrines, he wrote a number of key works, the most important of which is his **Pramāṇa-vārttika*, in which he extends and develops the thought of his predecessor *Dignāga, dealing with matters of epistemology and logic. The *Pramāṇa-vārttika* contains four chapters dealing with inference, the validity of knowledge, sense-perception, and syllogisms. Few of Dharmakirti's writings survive in the original *Sanskrit but all are preserved in Tibetan translation.

Dharmakṣema (385-433). A *monk from central *India active as a translator in *China during the early 5th century CE. The many works he worked on include versions of the **Bodhisattvabhūmi Śāstra* and the **Nirvāṇa Sūtra*.

dharmameghā-bhūmi (Skt.). The tenth of the Bodhisattva Levels (*bhūmi), 'the Cloud of Dharma', according to the **Daśabhūmika Sūtra*. At this level the *Bodhisattva engages in the Perfection of Awareness (jñāna-pāramitā) which brings him into contact with the *Dharma in the presence of all the *tathāgatas of the ten directions.

dharma-mudrā (Skt.). Seal of *Dharma; one of the four meditational seals (*mudrā) according to the *yoga-tantra. It refers to the process of imaging the *Buddhas in transformational *meditation practice by way of seed-syllables (*bīja) which correlate to their speech aspect (*see* BODY, SPEECH AND MIND).

dharmapāla (Skt., Dharma- protector). Supernatural beings who act as protectors or guardians of the *Dharma and its adherents from all negative forces. In Tibetan *Buddhism (*see* TIBET), they comprise two categories: those who are manifestations of enlightened beings such as *Mahākāla, and the so-called 'oath-bound' unenlightened beings who have been coerced into acting as protectors by magicians like *Padmasambhava and others.

Dharmapāla. One of the leading exponents of the *Yogācāra school in *India, a contemporary of *Bhāvaviveka, active during the early decades of the 7th century CE and dying young at the age of 32. Eventually based at *Nālandā, he initially travelled widely and studied both *Hīnayāna and *Mahāyāna throughout India, with *Dignāga numbered among his teachers. Unlike classical Yogācāra, his interpretation tends towards idealism and it was through the connections his student *Śīlabhadra had with *Hsüan-tsang that this understanding of Yogācāra was eventually transmitted to *China.

Dharmarakṣa. An Indian *monk who who was active as a translator in *China during the 4th century CE at *Lo-yang and *Ch'ang-an. He worked on over 150 key *Hīnayāna and *Mahāyāna texts including the *Lotus Sūtra* and the *Daśabhūmika Sūtra*.

dharmatā (Skt.). The intrinsic nature or reality of phenomena as seen when, according to the *Mahāyāna, they have been freed from a perceiving subject and perceived objects. Equivalent in meaning to suchness (*tathatā) and emptiness (*śūnyatā).

dhātu (Skt.; Pāli). **1.** The perceptual bases or elements, of which there are eighteen in all, consisting of three groups of six. These are the six sense-faculties, their six corresponding objects, and the six perceptual awarenesses, hence: eye, colour-form, sight awareness; ear, sound, aural awareness; nose, fragrance, olfactory awareness; tongue, flavour, gustatory awareness; body, touch, tactile awareness; and mind, phenomena (*dharma), mental awareness. This form of analysis, designed to provide a comprehensive account of the elements present when perception occurs, is used in the Buddhist analysis of perception to show that all the elements involved in the process are impermanent, unsatisfactory, and without autonomous existence. **2.** Term used in compounds such as *dharma-dhātu, Buddha-dhātu, loka-dhātu in the sense of 'source' or 'matrix'.

Dhātukathā. The third volume of the *Abhidharma Piṭaka of the *Pāli Canon. It appears to have been composed as a supplement to the **Dhammasaṅgaṇī*. The book gives a systematic analysis of the elements of physical phenomena and discusses mainly the mental characteristics found in converted and earnest persons. The commentary on the *Dhātukathā*, compiled by *Buddhaghoṣa in the 5th century, is part of the *Pañcappakaraṇa-atthakathā*.

dhutanga (Pāli). A set of thirteen austere voluntary practices which monks (but not nuns) may adopt if they so desire. Probably to be selected one at a time, these practices are not part of the *Vinaya rules and have sometimes been condemned as overly *ascetic. They are: (1) wearing patched-up robes; (2) wearing only the same three robes; (3) eating only alms food; (4) not omitting any house on the almsround; (5) eating at one sitting; (6) eating only from the almsbowl; (7) refusing all further food; (8) living in the forest; (9) living under a tree; (10) living in the open air; (11) living in a cemetery; (12) being satisfied with any dwelling; (13) sleeping only in a sitting position.

dhyāna (Skt., trance, absorption; Pāli, jhāna). A state of deep meditative absorption characterized by lucid awareness and achieved by focusing the mind on a single object (*see* CITTA-EKĀGRATĀ). A prerequisite for its attainment is the elimination of the five hindrances (*nīvaraṇa). A scheme of eight stages of dhyāna was gradually evolved, with four lower assigned to the *rūpa-dhātu and four higher ones assigned to the *ārūpya-dhātu. In dhyāna all sense-activity is suspended, and as the meditator passes from the lower to the higher levels, mental activity becomes progressively more attenuated. Thus, in the first dhyāna, conceptualization (*vitarka) and reflection (*vicāra) occur, but in the second they do not. In the fifth dhyāna various supernormal powers can be attained (*see* ṚDDHI). The names of the *Ch'an and *Zen schools are both derived from the word dhyāna.

dhyāna-pāramitā (Skt.). The Perfection of Meditation, the fifth of the Six Perfections (*ṣaḍ-pāramitā) that make up a central element of the *Mahāyāna path.

dhyāni-Buddhas (Skt.). 'Meditation Buddhas', in the sense of *Buddhas seen in meditation or used as a subject of meditation practice. It is a generally obsolete term invented and formerly used by Western scholars to denote the Five *Jinas or *tathāgatas.

Dhyānottara-paṭala. A key *kriyā-tantra work only surviving in Tibetan translation, puportedly a chapter (paṭala) from the lost *Vajroṣṇīṣa Tantra*, it comprises 74 verses on the basics of tantric *mantra recitation and meditation. A detailed commentary also exists by the early Indian tantric scholar Buddhaguhya.

Diamond Sūtra. *See* VAJRACCHEDIKA SŪTRA.

diet. The *Buddha's advice concerning dietary habits is addressed primarily to those who have embraced the monastic life rather than to lay society. An important principle underlying Buddhist monasticism is that *monks should be dependent upon the laity for alms and should go out daily into the local community to beg for food. It is a familiar sight in the Buddhist countries of south Asia to see a line of saffron-clad monks walking soberly in single file from house to house and pausing with downcast eyes while offerings of food are placed in their bowls by the laity. After completing their round the monks return to the monastery where they must consume their food before midday. Thereafter, except in case of illness, they may take only liquids before the next day. The Buddha commended the practice of eating but once a day for its benefits in terms of overall mental and physical well-being.

As regards the type of food that may be consumed, the general principle is that monks should accept with gratitude whatever they are given and not be selective in preferring or rejecting particular dishes. In *Theravāda *Buddhism there is no prohibition on eating meat providing that the *monk has not 'seen, heard or suspected' that the animal was slaughtered specifically on his behalf, thus avoiding complicity in the breaking of the First Precept (*see* PAÑCA-ŚĪLA) against taking life. To understand this, one must first separate the issues of killing *animals from that of eating meat. While the first is definitely demeritorious and productive of bad *karma, the second may not be. The Buddha himself is said to have died after consuming pork, although the precise nature of this dish has been disputed (*see* SŪKARA-MADDAVA). Since Buddhism is concerned primarily with the effect that moral actions have on the development of mental states and habits, it observes that actually killing an animal requires a state of mind characterized by anger, cruelty, or indifference, while simply eating meat carries no such strong signature. Thus, the Buddha did not categorically prohibit his followers from eating meat, even when it was suggested to him as a way of intensifying the religious practice of the community. Ten specific kinds of flesh, however, were thought to be inappropriate for human consumption, for instance, the flesh of elephants, tigers, and serpents. Monks and lay-people in Theravāda countries still consume meat although they may refrain from it on certain days and they also regard the occupation of butchery as being a form of wrong livelihood. Thus, early Buddhism shows what might be termed a mixed attitude: it recommends that no one make their living as a hunter or butcher, and certainly commends those who undertake a commitment to vegetarianism, but constantly asks that those who do so examine their motives and thoughts for any trace of rigid attachment to views and *precepts, and does not tar those who eat meat with the same brush as those who produce the meat. As well as the *Theravāda countries, this is especially true in *Tibet and *Mongolia, where the harsh and cold climate make the mass adoption of a vegetarian lifestyle impractical. Meat-eating was accepted in Tibetan Buddhist circles on account of the lack of vegetable produce in Tibet, and today even the *Dalai Lama does not follow a wholly vegetarian diet.

The advent of *Mahāyāna in *India saw a movement towards the total abstention from meat-eating as this was felt to contradict a *Bodhisattva's cultivation of compassion. Additionally, a number of Mahāyāna texts such as the **Nirvāṇa Sūtra* and the **Laṅkāvatāra Sūtra* are quite specific in their condemnation of meat-eating, as the *tathāgatagarbha or Buddha-nature doctrines they teach imply that all living beings are embryonic Buddhas. The popularity of these texts in east Asia has resulted in almost universal vegetarianism among members of the *Saṃgha. In east Asian cultures, one of the standard ways of caricaturing wayward clergy and monasteries was to accuse them of 'eating meat and drinking wine'. *China has kept to this practice very strictly, and has thus developed a very sophisticated and tasty repertoire of vegetarian cuisine, all the more surprising since the same scripture also teaches (as does the *Vinaya) the avoidance of the Five Pungent Herbs (onions, garlic, scallions, leeks, and chives). The term 'vegetarian' is not entirely accurate in describing the ideal diet among Buddhists in east Asia, since the term implies only the avoidance of meat. Although the ideal Buddhist diet in China, *Japan, *Korea, and *Vietnam certainly proscribes meat, the term used, chih su ('eat vegetarian') or su shih ('vegetarian diet') also indicates an avoidance of alcohol and the Five Pungent Herbs. The proscriptions on meat and alcohol are explained as fulfilling the requirements of several sets of rules, including the Five Precepts for laymen (pañca-śīla) and the Ten Novice's Precepts against killing and taking intoxicants. The rule against the Five Pungent Herbs is derived from the eighth fascicle of the *Laṅkāvatāra Sūtra*, which explains that these are very 'hot' vegetables that will act as an aphrodisiac and make practice difficult, in addition to which they make the breath foul, which drives away any potential audience one might have for preaching the *Dharma, drives away protective deities, and attracts demons. Japan and Korea, while sharing this concern for vegetarianism early in their history, have in recent centuries been more tolerant of meat-eating among the clergy, while still admiring vegetarianism as an additional discipline that some may choose.

Dīgha-bhāṇaka. Name given to those *monks who specialized in the recitation of the *Dīgha Nikāya, the first section of the *Sūtra Piṭaka of the *Pāli Canon. This tradition ascribed the *Khuddaka Nikāya, minus the last three books, the **Apadāna*, **Buddhavaṃsa*, and **Cariyāpiṭaka*, to the *Abhidharma-piṭaka. They also held the view that the four signs that the *Bodhisattva saw, prior to his renunciation, were seen on one and the same day.

Dīgha Nikāya. The first book of the *Sūtra Piṭaka of the *Pāli Canon. It consists of 34 long (dīgha) discourses (*suttas), divided into three sections known respectively as the Sīlakkhandha, the Mahāvagga, and the Pātheya or Pāṭikavagga. A number of the suttas, such as the *Mahānidāna Sutta* and **Mahāsatipaṭṭhāna Sutta*, expound important doctrines. Also, in many of the suttas, like the *Soṇadaṇḍa Sutta* and the **Sāmaññaphala Sutta*, the *Buddha discusses the views and doctrines of *Brahmanism and various contemporary religious schools and philosophies. The commentary on the Dīgha Nikāya, compiled in the 5th century by *Buddhaghoṣa is known as the **Sumaṅgalavilāsinī*.

Dignāga (*c.*480–540). A south Indian *monk and scholar who was an indirect student of *Vasubandhu. He combined aspects of *Yogācāra and *Sautrāntika theories of perception with his own innovative logical methodology (*pramāṇa). Based in Orissa, he wrote a number of important works on *Abhidharma and pramāṇa, including his highly influential **Pramāṇa-samuccaya*. This combines many of his earlier insights into a complete system of epistemology. The work deals with the problems of sense-perception and its role in knowledge, the reliability of knowledge, and the relationship between sensations, images, concepts, and the external world. After Dignāga the lineage continued through his pupil Īśvarasena to the great *Dharmakīrti in the 7th century.

Dīpaṅkara (Skt.; Pāli, light- maker). Name of the first of a series of 24 mythological *Buddhas mentioned in *Pāli sources. It is said that it was during the time of Dīpaṅkara that the Buddha (then the *ascetic *Sumedha) made a vow to become a *Bodhisattva and seek the enlightenment (*bodhi) which he ultimately attained.

Dīpavaṃsa. Literally 'Island Chronicle', a historiographic work in *Pāli, probably compiled from several loosely edited sources at the beginning of the 4th century CE, and narrating the Buddhist history of *Sri Lanka from its beginnings to the reign of King Mahāsena (334–61). It is the oldest chronicle of the island. Its historical narrative is continued in the **Cūlavaṃsa* and is paralleled by the **Mahāvaṃsa*.

Dīrgha Āgama (Skt.). The Long Discourses; one of the major sections of the *Sūtra Piṭaka corresponding to the *Dīgha Nikāya of the *Pāli tradition. Many of the major *Eighteen Schools of Early Buddhism had their own versions, although for the most part these have not survived. As well as recent discoveries of portions of the *Sarvāstivāda Dīrgha Āgama in *Sanskrit and several *sūtras from that tradition in Tibetan translation, a complete version exists in Chinese. This contains 30 sūtras in contrast to the 34 extant in Pāli, and is thought to be *Dharmagupta in origin. A comparison of the different versions that survive show an overall high degree of consistency of content with little doctrinal innovation.

Divya-avadāna. One of the earliest Buddhist literary compositions in the *avadāna style, being a collection of moral stories relating to how good and evil deeds receive their appropriate retribution in the course of time. The text is divided into 38 sections, varying in literary quality, which were arranged in their present form some time between 200 and 350 CE. The work is in *Sanskrit and most probably belongs to the *Sarvāstivāda school of *Buddhism. It includes many of the stories found in the **Avadāna-śataka*.

Dōgen (1200–53). Also Dōgen Zenji or Dōgen Kigen, founder of the *Sōtō school of Japanese *Zen, and one of *Japan's most profound and original thinkers. He originally joined the *Tendai school on Mt. *Hiei, but became disillusioned and left to study Zen with *Eisai shortly before the latter's death. With questions still unanswered, he decided to study in *China, where he gained insight about the application of the enlightened mind to everyday life from an old monastery cook, and finally attained enlightenment (*bodhi; *satori) in 1225 under the Chinese master Ju-ching (1163–1268) at the Ching-te Temple on Mt. T'ien-t'ung. Ju-ching was a master in the *Ts'ao-tung school, so when Dōgen established his own line of Zen teachings in Japan, he named it after this school, using the Japanese pronunciation Sōtō. Returning to Japan in 1227, Dōgen worked in and around the capital, but the threat of violence from the *sōhei of Mt. Hiei and the competition from another Zen *monk, Enni Ben'en, whose temple next to his offered more of the esoteric services patronized by aristocrats, impelled him to leave the capital and move to the remote mountains of Echizen, where he founded the Eiheiji, or 'Temple of Eternal Peace'. He lived there quietly for the remainder of his days, devoting himself to teaching his disciples and writing the essays that would form his major work, the **Shōbō-genzō*, or 'Treasury of the True Dharma Eye'. After his death, his disciples published a record of his teachings entitled **Shōbō-genzō Zuimonki*.

The problem that vexed Dōgen as a young monk was: if Buddha-nature is perfect and complete in all beings, then why did the *Buddhas and *Bodhisattvas practise so assiduously? The answer that he developed while in China identified practice as a way of manifesting one's Buddhahood rather than a means of attaining it. Based on this, he taught shikan taza, commonly translated as 'just sitting'. This meant that, rather than working on *kōans or engaging in other practices intended to trigger enlightenment, Dōgen simply had his disciples sit with no goal in mind other than to enjoy the enlightenment they had already from the beginning. In the *Shōbō-genzō*, Dōgen also turned his mind to philosophical problems of an extremely speculative nature, such as the relation of time to existence, and the nature of change and stability in the world. In keeping with his discovery that beings already inherently possess the goal of Buddhahood just in being what they are, he postulated a completely immanent transcendent. That is to say, he identified the instability and transience of phenomena as the highest truth and unchanging being; he could find no further transcendent beyond these phenomena themselves. His writings, rediscovered in the 20th century, seem to presage developments in modern Western philosophy, sparking a renewed interest in and study of his work.

doha (Skt.). A particular style of teaching song associated with certain *tantric adepts (*siddha) such as *Saraha, usually composed in *Apabhraṃśa or early Bengali and Oriya. Characteristically these songs use enigmatic language and symbols to describe the realization achieved by their composers.

dokusan (Jap.). In Japanese *Zen *Buddhism, a private audience with one's master in order to allow him or her to evaluate one's progress.

Doṇa. A *Brahmin who presided over the division of the *Buddha's *relics. He avoided a dispute among the local kings who arrived to claim the Buddha's remains by reproaching them for quarrelling and urged them to remain calm out of respect for the recently deceased teacher. He then divided the relics into eight parts and gave one to each king to take away. He retained the vessel used to collect the relics and built a *stūpa over it on the site.

dorje (Tib., rdo je). *See* VAJRA.

dorje-phurba. *See* VAJRAKĪLA.

Dorje Shukden (Tib., rdo rje shugs ldan). A wrathful deity associated with the *Gelukpa school of Tibetan *Buddhism and regarded as its special protector. The cult of Dorje Shukden dates from the 17th century, and the deity is said to be the restless spirit (rgyal po) of Drakpa Gyeltsen, 1618–1655, a rival of *Dalai Lama V who was driven to *suicide by the latter's supporters. Initially only of minor importance, Dorje Shukden was elevated to the position of chief *Dharma protector in the early 20th century, a development which led to sectarian rivalry within the Gelukpa movement in closing decades of the century when the *Dalai Lama XIV urged Tibetans to cease to revere this deity. Most Gelukpas have done so, with the exception of Geshe Kelsang Gyatso and followers of the *New Kadampa Tradition which he founded. The latter have rejected the Dalai Lama's appeal insisting on their right to religious freedom, a position that has caused a bitter sectarian dispute allegedly involving the assassination of Geshe Losang Gyatso, one of the Dalai Lama's leading supporters, and two of his students.

Dōshō 1. (629–700). Japanese *monk and first transmitter of *Hossō (Chin., *Fa-hsiang) teachings to *Japan. He travelled to *T'ang *China where he studied Consciousness-only (*citta-mātra) thought with both *Hsüan-tsang and K'uei-chi, as well as *Ch'an and *Pure Land *Buddhism. He is also remembered for his public engineering projects such as road- and bridge-building, and for being the first Japanese monk to be cremated upon death. **2.** (798–875). An early priest of the Japanese *Shingon school, and one of Shingon-founder *Kūkai's ten major disciples. He is remembered as a skilled lecturer, ritualist, administrator, and restorer of temples.

Drepung (Tib., 'dras-spung). One of the three great *Gelukpa monasteries of central *Tibet, located to the west of *Lhasa and constructed in 1416 by Jamyang Chörje Trashi Palden ('jam-dbyangs chos-rje bkra-shis dpal-ldan). The combined religious and secular government of the Gelukpa school was established initially at the *Ganden Palace in this monastery during the lifetime of *Dalai Lama V and later achieved religio-political domination of the whole of Tibet. At its peak it housed some 20,000 monks. It was largely destroyed in the Cultural Revolution but has since been partly rebuilt.

dṛṣṭi (Skt., sight or view; Pāli, diṭṭi). Views and opinions, especially of a speculative or erroneous nature due to being tainted by the three roots of evil (*akuśala-mūla). Views singled out for special criticism are the belief in a self or *ātman (*satkāya- dṛṣṭi), belief that the self is eternal (śāśvata-dṛṣṭi), and belief that the self is destroyed at *death (uccheda-dṛṣṭi). *See also* ŚĀŚVATA-VĀDA; UCCHEDA-VĀDA.

Drugpa Kunle (Tib., 'drug-pa kun-legs). An iconclastic *yogin of the Drugpa Kagyü school who lived in the 14th century. He is particularly associated with *Bhutan, though he travelled around *Tibet, visiting many of the chief religious centres. The stories of his crazy wisdom and apparently scurrilous conduct preserved in his biography (rnam-thar) are well-loved by all Tibetans.

dry-visioned Arhats (Pāli, sukkha-vipassaka). Term used in *Pāli sources to refer, according to the commentaries, to those who become *Arhats through insight (*vipaśyanā) alone without attaining any of the levels of trance (*dhyāna).

Dudjom Rinpoche (1904–87) (Tib., bdud-'joms rinpoche 'jigs-'bral ye-shes rdo-rje). A renowned modern *tülku and former head of the *Nyingma lineage. He belonged to the Mindroling (smin-drol-ling) lineage but was also well versed in many other lineages as well as being a great *Dzogchen master and revealer of hidden textual treasures (*gter-ston).

duḥkha (Skt.; Pāli, dukkha). The first of the *Four Noble Truths (ārya-satya) and the cornerstone of the *Buddha's teaching. The meaning of duḥkha and of the other Noble Truths is explained in the Buddha's *first sermon, and in many other places in the Buddhist scriptures. There is no word in English covering the same ground as duḥkha in the sense it is used in *Buddhism. The usual translation of '*suffering' is too strong, and gives the impression that life according to Buddhism is nothing but pain. As a consequence, some regard Buddhism as pessimistic. While duḥkha certainly embraces the ordinary meaning of 'suffering' it also includes deeper concepts such as impermanence (*anitya) and unsatisfactoriness, and may be better left untranslated. The Buddha does not deny happiness in life, although this too is seen as part of duḥkha because of its impermanence.

The concept of duḥkha is explained as having three aspects. Ordinary duḥkha (duḥkha-duḥkha) refers to all kinds of suffering in life, such as illness, *death, separation from loved ones, or not getting what one desires. The second aspect of duḥkha, or duḥkha produced by change (vipariṇāma-duḥkha), is the duḥkha resulting from the impermanent nature of all things. The third aspect of duḥkha, or duḥkha as conditioned states (saṃskāra-duḥkha), is the most important philosophical aspect of the First Noble Truth. This teaches that what we call an 'individual' is, according to Buddhism, a combination of ever-changing physical and mental forces known as the 'five aggregates' (pañca-*skandha). This is known as the doctrine of *anātman or no-self. Although some believe this means that according to the Buddha one has no identity, more recent scholarship views the doctrine as a description of how a being functions. Because of their ever-changing nature, the five aggregates are themselves identified with duḥkha. More importantly, like everything else the individual *ego is dependently originated and conditioned (*see* PRATĪYA-SAMUTPĀDA). Holding to the illusion of a independently originated self (*ātman), according to the Buddha, makes one crave for the satisfaction of this self. However, since everything is duḥkha, and impermanent, there cannot be enduring satisfaction. Instead, craving (*tṛṣṇā) only leads to a vicious circle of unfulfilled desires, and therefore more suffering (duḥkha).

Duka-paṭṭhāna (Pāli, groups of two origin). Second part of the *Paṭṭhāna*, the final book of the *Abhidharma Piṭaka of the *Pāli Canon. It is a highly technical text, consisting of a minutely detailed analysis of the doctrine of conditionality. Its commentary was composed by *Buddhaghoṣa in the 5th century.

dukkha. *Pāli for *duḥkha.

dūraṃgamā-bhūmi (Skt.). The seventh of the Bodhisattva Levels (*bhūmi), 'the One which Goes Far', according to the *Daśabhūmika Sūtra*. It is so-called because at this level *Bodhisattvas engage in the perfection of skilful means (upāya-kauśalya-pāramitā) by which they cause beings to be liberated.

durgati (Skt.). The miserable or *evil states of being into which one can be reborn. Specifically, these are the three lower modes of existence: the *hells, the realm of hungry ghosts (*preta), and the *animal world. *See also* BHAVACAKRA.

Duruthu Perahera. Festival held on the full moon day of January at the Kelaniya Temple in Colombo, *Sri Lanka. The festival, the second most important *perahera in the country, celebrates a visit by the *Buddha to Sri Lanka.

Duṭṭhagāmaṇi Abhaya (r. 101–77 BCE). King of *Sri Lanka and the hero of the *Mahāvaṃsa*, in which his battle against the non-Buddhist Damiḷas (Tamils) is celebrated and justified. He was the son of Kākavaṇṇatissa and Vihāradevī, whose antenatal cravings showed that he would be a great warrior. He was called Gāmaṇi-Abhaya and his father gathered at his court the most famous warriors of the land to be his tutors. From an early age he showed signs of audacity and bravery, and resented the confined limits of his father's kingdom, in particular the fact that his father constantly refused him permission to fight the Damiḷas. For this reason he once fled to the hills from where he sent his father a woman's garment, to indicate that he was no man. This earned for him the nickname of Duṭṭha meaning 'wicked, spoilt'. At his father's death he fought his brother Tissa for the possession of the throne and after winning it he prepared himself to march against the Damiḷa king Eḷāra. One after the other, Duṭṭhagāmaṇi defeated all the Damiḷa troops and in a single close battle he slew Eḷāra. After this celebrated victory Duṭṭhagāmaṇi began his great works of piety. He first built the *Lohapāsāda and then began his greatest achievement, the *Mahā-thūpa, erected on a site traditionally said to have been visited by the *Buddha during his third visit to Sri Lanka. Before the Mahā-thūpa was completed Duṭṭhagāmaṇi fell ill and, at the age of 68, he died. It is said that after his death Duṭṭhagāmaṇi was born in the *Tuṣita world where he awaits the appearance of *Maitreya Buddha, of whom he will be the chief disciple.

dvātriṃśadvara-lakṣaṇa (Skt.; Pāli, dvattiṃsa-lakkhaṇa). The '32 marks' or physical characteristics through which as 'great man' (Skt., *mahāpuruṣa; Pāli, mahāpurisa) can be recognized. These marks are found on the body of both a *Buddha and a Universal Ruler (*cakravartin). Listed in the *Lakkhaṇa Sutta* or 'Discourse on Characteristics' of the *Dīgha Nikāya, they include the impression of a wheel on the soles of the feet, webbed fingers and toes, arms that reach to the knees, a penis that is covered by a sheath, 40 teeth with no gaps, a long tongue, and blue eyes. The characteristics are probably pre-Buddhist and drawn from *Brahmin lore and the legendary attributes of gods. Some of the details, such as a tuft of hair between the eyes and a protruberance on the top of the head later feature in statues, paintings, and other iconographic representations of the Buddha.

dveṣa (Skt.; Pāli, dosa). Hatred, one of the three *akuśala-mūla or roots of evil.

Dzogchen (Tib., rdzogs-chen). The central teaching of the *Nyingma school of Tibetan *Buddhism, Dzogchen or the Great Perfection is regarded as the highest and most definitive approach to enlightenment (*bodhi). According to Dzogchen teachings, the intrinsic purity of the mind is ever-present and needs only to be recognized as such. There is a large corpus of texts teaching Dzogchen included in the Nyingma *atiyoga division of the tantras which is subdivided into three groups: the mental class (*sems-sde), the *spatial category (klong-sde), and the instructional class (man-ngag-gi sde). Aspects of Dzogchen were transmitted to *Tibet by *Padmasambhava and *Vimalamitra and later systematized by *Longchenpa and then condensed by *Jigmé Lingpa.

E

Eclectic Movement. (Tib., ris-med). The revolutionary movement that began in eastern *Tibet during the late 18th century which, as its Tibetan name suggests, was 'unbiased' in its approach to all religious schools and saw each as valuable in its own right in contrast to the prevailing sectarianism at that time. Most of the teachers involved were from the *Kagyü and *Nyingma schools, although there was some participation by other schools. The most important figures in this movement were *Jigmé Lingpa (1729–98), Jamyang Khyentse Wangpo (1820–92), *Jamgön Kongtrül (1811–99), and Mipham Gyantsho (1846–1912), all of whom were renowned as polymaths. The ideals of this movement are still alive today in the Tibetan religious community, with the present *Dalai Lama characterizing himself as such in outlook.

ecology. This is a subject of modern concern about which classical Buddhist sources have little to say. Heightened by the interest in *Engaged *Buddhism, efforts are currently being made to develop a Buddhist ecology, with varying degrees of success. The main approaches draw upon traditional values such as compassion, (*karuṇā), and less anthropocentric notions of the relationship between humans and nature than those found in the West. Due to the doctrine of *rebirth, the relationship between man and *animals is seen as closer, and Buddhists do not believe that the world was created for man's use and enjoyment, or that he stands in the position of divinely appointed steward over the rest of creation. Certain *Mahāyāna interpretations of the doctrine of Dependent Origination (*pratītya-samutpāda), particularly of the kind that arose in east Asia which see the universe as a cosmic network within which all phenomena are interrelated, also provide a foundation for ecological concern (*see* INDRA'S NET). On the other hand, Buddhist ecology is hampered by the negative value Buddhism seems to place on the world in the First Noble Truth which teaches that life is suffering (*duḥkha). Rather than a place to be cared for and preserved, the world is depicted in this strand of teaching as a place of woe and sorrow from which one should flee to the only form of durable happiness that exists, namely the transcendent state of *nirvāṇa. Discussion of these issues is still at a rudimentary stage and it remains to be seen if a viable, critical Buddhist ecology can be established.

Edicts of Aśoka. A collection of inscriptions by the Buddhist emperor of *India, *Aśoka (r. 272–231 BCE). A total of 33 have been found to date inscribed upon rocks pillars and caves in various parts of India and surrounding regions such as Afghanistan. The edicts proclaim Aśoka's policy of rule by *Dharma (righteousness) and his belief in the virtues of kindness, toleration, and upright conduct as the means to the happiness and well-being of his subjects both here and in the afterlife. The language of the edicts is *Prakrit, the connecting link between the classical language of *Sanskrit and the modern Indo-European languages of India, and two different forms of script are used for this. Aśoka also uses Greek and Aramaic, giving four forms of script in all. Altogether there are 16 Rock Edicts, 3 Minor Rock Edicts, 7 Pillar Edicts, 3 Minor Pillar Edicts, 2 Pillar Inscriptions, and 2 Cave Inscriptions.

ego. Contrary to what is sometimes believed, *Buddhism does not deny the existence of the ego or seek to obliterate it. However, Buddhist psychology does teach that the sense of self-identity corresponding to the Western concept of the ego is an intellectual construct rather than an eternal self or soul. For further details on Buddhist teachings concerning the nature of personal identity, *see* ANĀTMAN.

eight auspicious symbols. A set of eight symbols of good fortune of Indian provenance but very popular in Tibetan Buddhist circles where they are linked with various aspects of Buddhist teachings. The set comprises the golden fish (good fortune), the parasol (spiritual power), the right-turning conch shell (the same of the *Dharma), the *lotus (spiritual purity), the victory banner (victory of the Dharma), the treasure vase (spiritual and material fulfilment), the wheel (the perfection of the Dharma), and the endless knot (infinite wisdom of a *Buddha).

Fig 9 eight auspicious symbols

Eighteen Schools of Early Buddhism. As *Buddhism spread throughout *India, a diversity of schools developed over the first 400 years, some based on major doctrinal differences and others merely as regional variants. Retrospectively, various *Mahāyāna scholar-monks determined that there were eighteen of these schools, although their accounts of the relationship and differences between them are not consistent. One simple classification, acording to Vinītadeva, has the following four major schools with their offshoots: (1) *Sthavira, and the Jetavanīyas, Abhayagirivāsins, and the Mahāvihāravāsins; (2) *Mahāsaṃghika, and the Pūrvaśailikas, the Aparaśailikas, the *Lokottara-vāda, and the *Prajñaptivāda; (3) *Sarvāstivāda, and the Kāśyapīyas, Mahīśāsakas, *Dharmaguptakas, and the *Mūla-sarvāstivādins; and (4) Saṃmitīya, and the Kaurukullaka, Avantaka, and *Vātsīputrīya. Vinītadeva's list, however, is late and not altogether reliable. For example, the Sthaviras did not exist as a school separately from the three *nikāyas mentioned in group (1), and the same was probably true of the Mahāsaṃghikas and Saṃmitīyas. In group (3), the Sarvāstivādins and Mūla-sarvāstivādins were arguably the same school. The Dharmaguptas and Kāśyapīyas were probably not extant in India in Vinītadeva's day, and the Mahīśāsakas only in a Mahāyāna/Sarvāstivāda influenced form. Mention of these three schools in earlier Sarvāstivādin works led Vinītadeva to classify them in this historically incorrect form. Too much reliance should therefore not be placed on the traditional classifications of the eighteen schools.

Eightfold Path. The Noble Eightfold Path (ārya-aṣṭaṅga-mārga; Pāli, ariya-aṭṭhangika-magga) is the last of the *Four Noble Truths and is the path that leads from *saṃsāra to *nirvāṇa. The Fourth Noble Truth is as follows: 'This, O Monks, is the Truth of the Path that leads to the cessation of *suffering. It is this Noble Eightfold Path, which consists of (i) Right View (samyag-dṛṣṭi), (ii) Right Resolve (samyak-samkalpa), (iii) Right Speech (samyag-vāc), (iv) Right Action (samyak-karmānta), (v) Right Livelihood (samyag-ājīva), (vi) Right Effort (samyak-vyāyāma), (vii) Right Mindfulness (samyak-smṛti), (viii) Right Meditation (samyak-samādhi).' Right View means the acceptance of basic Buddhist teachings such as the *Four Noble Truths; Right Resolve means having a positive outlook and a mind free from lust, ill-will, and cruelty; Right Speech means using speech in positive and productive ways instead of negative ones such as lying or speaking harshly; Right Action means keeping the *precepts, such as the Five Precepts (*pañca-śīla); Right Livelihood means avoiding professions which cause harm to others such as slavery or arms-mongering; Right Effort means directing the mind towards religious goals and the production and fostering of wholesome states of mind; Right Mindfulness means being at all times mindful and aware of what one is doing, thinking, and feeling; Right Meditation means training the mind to achieve the state of focused attention necessary to enter the meditational trances (*dhyāna). The eight factors of the path are often placed in three groups (*skandhas), thus 3–5 relate to morality (*śīla), 6–8 to meditation (*samādhi), and 1–2 to insight (*prajñā). It is important to note that the Eightfold Path is not a linear one in the sense that one passes from one step to the next, but a cumulative programme wherein all the eight factors are practised simultaneously.

eight liberations. *See* AṢṬA-VIMOKṢA.

eight masteries. *See* ABHIBHĀYATANA.

Eiheiji (Jap.). The 'Temple of Eternal Peace', established by *Sōtō *Zen founder *Dōgen in

Echizen Prefecture in 1243, and still one of the head temples of the Sōtō order.

Eisai (1141–1215). The founder of the *Rinzai school of Japanese *Zen. Born into a temple family, Eisai originally entered the *Tendai sect and lived at the Miidera. However, the violent factionalism of the Tendai school at that time repulsed him, and he travelled from place to place seeking teaching. In 1168 he went to *China to visit the famous sites of the *T'ien-t'ai school (Tendai's Chinese root). He arrived at a time when *Ch'an was dominant, and was very excited by its vibrance and novelty. He had no time for formal training, however, since he returned to *Japan after only six months. After his return, he continued to serve the Tendai school. Eighteen years later, he returned to China once again, this time staying for four years and studying Ch'an intensively with masters of the *Lin-chi school in various temples. He had an *enlightenment experience, and returned to Japan in 1191 with the robes and certifications of a Ch'an master. After this, he worked to establish places that would be devoted solely to the study and practice of Ch'an. It is not clear that he wished to found a new school; in fact, he criticized his contemporary *Dainichibō Nōnin for wanting to do just that. He remained a Tendai *monk for the rest of his life and worked at many other projects as well, but it is clear that he at least wanted Zen practice to have a place of its own within the overall framework of Japanese *Buddhism.

Despite the difficulties imposed by the jealousy of the Tendai establishment, Eisai gained increasing patronage among the aristocracy and rising military class, who were attracted by the vigour and action-orientation of his southern Sung-style Zen, as well has by his presentation of Zen as a practice that would help to protect the nation. In 1202 he was granted abbotship of the Kennin-ji, a temple in a government-controlled district of *Kyoto. There he continued to teach Zen even while the court kept him busy overseeing building and restoration projects and performing Tendai-style esoteric rituals. He died in 1215, without having enjoyed any discernible success in establishing a self-standing Zen institution, and it fell to his spiritual descendants to set up *Rinzai as an independent school. Nevertheless, he is honoured as the first transmitter of Rinzai Zen to Japan and the *de jure* founder of the school.

Eizon (1201–90). Esoteric practitioner (*see* ESOTERIC BUDDHISM) and reformer of the *Kamakura period in *Japan. Dissatisfied with the lax moral practices of his times, he studied traditional Buddhist *precepts and ardently worked to reinstitute their transmission and practice. He also established 1,000 wild game preserves where hunting would be prohibited.

Ekavyāvahārika (Skt.). A subschool of the *Mahāsaṃghika that emerged around the 2nd century BCE, also known as the *Lokottara-vādins. The name of the school means 'one utterance' or 'one designation', apparently referring to the notion that the *Buddha taught the whole of the *Dharma in a single utterance.

Ekayāna (Skt.). The One Way or Vehicle; a concept found in certain *Mahāyāna texts such as the **Lotus Sūtra* which teaches that the three Ways (*triyāna)—the *Śrāvakayāna, the *Pratyekabuddhayāna, and the *Bodhisattvayāna—taught by the *Buddha all converge in the single Buddhayāna. This view also teaches that the first two Ways were merely taught as skilful means (*upāya-kauśalya) and that the Bodhisattvayāna is actually identical to the single Buddhayāna. This concept is taught in the **Lotus Sūtra* in the famous parable of the children trapped in a burning house whose father rescues them with promises of various kinds of pleasing carts but then rewards them all with the same magnificant cart once they are safe.

Ekottara Āgama (Skt.). The 'Increased by One' Discourses. One of the major sections of the *Sūtra Piṭaka, corresponding to the *Aṅguttara Nikāya in the *Pāli tradition, and in which the *sūtras are arranged in increasing order of their topics from one to eleven. Many of the major *Eighteen Schools of Early Buddhism would have had their own versions, although for the most part these have not survived. As well as recent discoveries of small portions of the *Sarvāstivāda version in *Sanskrit, a complete version exists in Chinese which is thought to be Sarvāstivādin in origin, although this is controversial. There is considerable disparity between the Pāli and the Sarvāstivādin versions, with more than two-thirds of the sūtras found in one but not the other compilation, which suggests that much of this portion of the Sūtra Piṭaka was not formed until a fairly late date.

Ellorā. The site of 34 artificial caves carved into a cliff-face, 19 miles north of present-day Auraṅgabad, constructed during the 8th to 9th centuries CE. Twelve of the caves are Buddhist in orgin, while the remaining are Hindu and Jain (*see* HINDUISM; JAINISM). The Buddhist caves are thought to have been constructed by workers from *Ajaṇṭā and exhibit similar sculpted features and bas-reliefs.

Emerald Buddha. Buddha image dating to the 1st century BCE made of green malachite. The image was discovered in 1436 when a monument was struck by lightning and the image was found inside. It was taken to Chiang-mai, Laos, and finally to Bangkok in 1779, where it resides today in the Grand Palace. It is regarded as a symbol of the *Buddha's protection of the king and people of *Thailand. *See also* WAT PHRA KEO.

Empō Dentō-roku. A record of masters and disciples of the *Zen school of Japanese *Buddhism, compiled over a 30-year period by the *monk Shiban (1626–1710) and published in 1678. It includes over 1,000 biographical sketches of Zen masters, beginning with the first *patriarch of Chinese *Ch'an, *Bodhidharma, and including *monks, *nuns, lay men and women, emperors and aristocrats. It gives their Dharma-lineages, and often includes records of their talks, writings, and poetry.

empowerment. *See* ABHIṢEKHA.

emptiness. *See* ŚŪNYATĀ.

Enchin (814–91) Japanese *Tendai *monk, scholar, and esoteric practitioner, and fifth abbot of the *Enryakuji on Mt. *Hiei. Enchin travelled to *China in 857 and studied both *T'ien-t'ai doctrine on Mt. T'ien-t'ai and *esoteric *Buddhism in the capital of *Ch'ang-an. Upon returning to *Japan he began actively promoting Tendai esoteric practice, and became head of the Miidera in 866. Two years later, he was named chief monk of the Tendai school, from which position he petitioned for the Miidera to be made an official temple for esoteric transmissions. This aroused the anger of the Mt. Hiei monks, which led to the split between the Sanmon sect (based on Mt. Hiei) and the Jimon sect (based in the Miidera).

Engaged Buddhism. A contemporary movement formerly but now less commonly referred to as 'Socially Engaged Buddhism', concerned with developing Buddhist solutions to social, political, and ecological problems. The engaged movement cuts across the lay–monastic divide and includes Buddhists from traditional Buddhist countries as well as Western converts. It originated in the latter half of the 20th century and has increasingly become part of mainstream Buddhist thought and practice. The term 'Engaged Buddhism' was coined in 1963 by the Vietnamese (*see* VIETNAM) *Zen *monk Thich *Nhat Hanh at a time when his country was ravaged by war. Nhat Hanh began to seek solutions to this and other problems by applying Buddhist teachings in a more activist way than had hitherto been the case. He has remained one of the leading protagonists of the movement and, now resident in France, has founded the 'Order of Interbeing' to promote worthy social causes. The aim of this and other 'engaged' groups is to reduce *suffering and oppression through the reform of unjust and repressive social and political structures, while not losing sight of the traditional Buddhist emphasis on inward spiritual growth. In part, this development is a response to the charge that Buddhism has been too passive and aloof, emphasizing meditation and withdrawal rather than reaching out to the mass of humankind. Accordingly, the *Mahāyāna *Bodhisattva is seen as the ideal or icon for the activist. Some commentators trace the origins of the movement to the encounter between Buddhism and Christianity during the colonial period, and in the challenge to Buddhism to develop a 'social gospel' that speaks to the needs of the poor and oppressed along Christian lines.

Engakuji. A *Rinzai *Zen temple founded in 1282 by the Chinese *monk Wu-hsüeh Tsu-yüan (Jap., Mugaku Sōgen) in the city of Kamakura. It is the head temple of the Engakuji sect of Rinzai, and was one of the original '*Five Mountains' temples established by the Ashikaga government at the end of the 13th century in an effort to gain some control over the Zen movement.

enlightenment. Common English translation of the *Sanskrit term *bodhi, which strictly means 'awakening' rather than 'enlightenment'. Some scholars have criticized the translation 'enlightenment' as possibly misleading in view of its Western cultural and historical associations, although it has become widely established in the secondary literature. Enlightenment is the state that marks the culmination of the Buddhist religious path. The archetypal enlightenment was that of the *Buddha when he attained *nirvāṇa under the *Bodhi Tree at the age of 35, although many disciples subsequently achieved the same goal. In Japanese *Buddhism (*see* JAPAN) the experience of awakening is known as *satori or *kenshō.

Enni Ben'en (1202–80). Early Japanese *Rinzai *Zen *monk. He entered the *Tendai order at the age of 5, and while growing up received a broad education in Buddhist and Confucian studies (*see* CONFUCIANISM), and after receiving full *ordination as an adult, was introduced to Tendai esoteric rituals. He travelled in *China from 1235 to 1241, and studied with the eminent *Ch'an master Wu-chun Shi-fan (1177–1249) of the Yang-ch'i branch of *Lin-chi (Jap., *Rinzai). He transmitted this lineage back to *Japan upon his return, and became the fountainhead of this branch there. Because of him, and because his own Japanese Zen masters failed to propagate the *Dharma of their own lineage (the Huang-lung branch of Lin-chi), Yang-ch'i (Jap., Yōgi) became the dominant branch in Rinzai. Also, when he returned to Japan, he was given charge of a temple very near to *Dōgen's (1200–53). Because he was more broadly trained and more willing and able to provide the services that the aristocracy demanded, he soon diverted much of Dōgen's support, which precipitated the latter's move to Echizen province and his founding there of the *Eiheiji.

Ennin (794–864). Early *Tendai *monk and third abbot of the *Enryakuji, the main temple and headquarters of the school on Mt. *Hiei. He began training with Tendai founder *Saichō at age 15. In 838 he travelled to *China, and remained there until 847, studying all aspects of *Buddhism including *Sanskrit language, esoteric rites, *Ch'an and *T'ien-t'ai meditation techniques among others. His sojourn spanned the *Hui-ch'ang persecution of 845, and the diary he kept during this time provides an invaluable historical source for that period. His promotion of the T'ien-t'ai 'constantly walking' meditation, which centres upon chanting the name of the *Buddha *Amitābha and seeking a vision of him, helped establish *Pure Land practice as a part of the Tendai repertoire and laid the groundwork for the later development of the Pure Land schools.

Enryakuji. The main temple and headquarters of the *Tendai school of Japanese *Buddhism, located on Mt. *Hiei outside of *Kyoto.

Epic of Gesar. *See* GESAR.

Esala Perahera. Sinhalese term meaning the 'procession of the full moon of Esala' and being the Sri Lankan version of the *Āsāḷha Pūjā. The procession takes place in the course of a festival held in July or August in *Kandy, one of the ancient capitals of *Sri Lanka, to honour the relic of the *Buddha's tooth (*see* TOOTH RELIC) preserved in the *Dalada Maligawa or *Temple of the Tooth. The celebrations, including processions of decorated elephants, drummers, and dancers, last for the ten days ending on the full moon of July/August. The celebrations of the first six nights are relatively minor but from the seventh the parade's route lengthens and the procession becomes more and more splendid. The procession is actually a combination of five separate *peraheras. Four come from the four Kandy *devalas, the shrines to the deities who protect the island. These are Natha (a *deva) and the gods Viṣṇu, Skanda, and Pattinī. The fifth and most splendid procession comes from the Dalada Maligawa. A replica of the golden case in which the Buddha's tooth is preserved is carried on the back of a heavily decorated elephant specially trained for the task.

esoteric Buddhism. A general term for certain Buddhist schools and practices originally developing in parallel with Hindu (*see* HINDUISM) *tantra with mutual influence at a later stage. It is distinguished from exoteric *Buddhism by its secrecy; rather than being given openly these teachings are available only to students who have received a proper initiation (*abhiṣekha) from a *guru who stands in a valid lineage of masters and disciples. Practice will then make use of a number of techniques in which the student visualizes a guardian *Buddha, *Bodhisattva, or deity with whom he or she has a special relationship established at their initiation, and then realizes his or her non-duality with that being. This appropriation of the divine guardian's role involves the establishment and spiritual fortification of a special place of practice and the use of ritual formulae (*mantras), gestures (*mudras), and *visualization techniques. Occasionally, this also makes use of sexual imagery or actual ritualized sexual practices as a way of harnessing the physical energy and the feeling that one has transcended personal boundaries and merged with another that come with orgasm. Esoteric Buddhist schools, including many Tibetan lineages, *Chen-yen in *China, and *Shingon and *Tendai in *Japan, claim that these techniques represent a short-cut to *enlightenment and enable one to attain Buddhahood in this lifetime. Many of the techniques are also used for other this-worldly purposes such as weather control and healing.

eternalism. *See* ŚĀŚVATAVĀDA.

ethics. There is no Buddhist term which exactly corresponds to 'ethics' as a branch of philosophy concerned with the analysis and evaluation of conduct in the way the subject is classified in the West. Instead, the various rules of moral conduct are subsumed under the rubric of *śīla, which denotes internalized moral virtue and its expression in practice as abstention from immoral conduct. As far as monks are concerned, the *Vinaya provides an externally enforced code for the regulation of communal life.

Europe. European interest in *Buddhism first began to develop during the colonial period. The earliest Buddhist texts to be studied in Europe were *Mahāyāna *Sanskrit manuscripts collected in *Nepal by the British Resident, B. H. Hodgson. Another British civil servant who made an outstanding contribution to the study of *Theravāda Buddhism was T. W. *Rhys Davids (1843–1922). Rhys Davids became interested in Buddhism during his residence in *Sri Lanka and went on to found the *Pali Text Society in 1881. The Society, based in Oxford, England, remains to this day the most important outlet for the publication of texts and translations of *Pāli Buddhist literature. Professional scholars from many European countries played an important role in the transmission of Buddhism to the West. In 1845 the Frenchman Eugène Burnouf published his *Introduction to the History of Indian Buddhism* and followed this seven years later with a translation of the **Lotus Sūtra*. Interest in Buddhism in Germany was stimulated by the publication of Herman Oldenberg's *The Buddha, his Life, his Doctrine, his Community* in 1881. The great Belgian scholars Louis *de la Vallée Poussin and (later) Étienne *Lamotte also made an enormous contribution through their work with Sanskrit, Tibetan, and Chinese sources. The German philosopher Arthur Schopenhauer (1788–1860) was the first major Western thinker to take an interest in Buddhism. Due to the absence of reliable sources, Schopenhauer had only an imperfect knowledge of Buddhism, and saw it as confirming his own somewhat pessimistic philosophy. Of all the world religions Buddhism seemed to him the most rational and ethically evolved, and the frequent references to Buddhism in his writings brought it to the attention of Western intellectuals in the latter part of the 19th century. In England, Sir Edwin *Arnold (1832–1904) published his famous poem *The Light of Asia* in 1879. The poem describes the life and teachings of the *Buddha in a melodramatic style. The German novelist Herman Hesse often alluded to Buddhist themes in his writings, notably in his 1922 novel *Siddhartha* which has been translated into many languages (the eponymous protagonist of the novel is *not* *Siddhartha Gautama, the *Buddha).

In more recent times, immigration has influenced the situation of Buddhism in Europe, although not to the degree it has done in the USA. Although the United Kingdom has received large numbers of Asian immigrants these have come mainly from the Indian subcontinent and are mostly Hindus or Muslims. There are some 19,000 refugees from Indochina in *Britain, 22,000 in Germany, and 97,000 in France. The majority of Buddhists in Europe are Caucasians who have converted to Buddhism rather than immigrants who brought their beliefs with them. Although accurate numbers are difficult to come by, in the UK there are around 100 Tibetan centres, about 90 *Theravāda centres, and some 40 *Zen centres, together with a further 100 or so other groups including the *Friends of the Western Buddhist Order. As in north *America, converts to Buddhism come predominantly from the middle classes. The increase in the popularity of Buddhism has been notable although less spectacular than in north America. Estimates suggest there are over a million Buddhists in Europe, with about 200,000 in the UK and an equivalent number in France.

euthanasia. As a practice that involves the intentional taking of life, euthanasia is contrary to basic Buddhist ethical teachings because it violates the first of the Five Precepts (*pañca-śīla). It is also contrary to the more general moral principle of *ahiṃsā. This conclusion applies to both the active and passive forms of the practice, even when accompanied by a compassionate motivation with the end of avoiding *suffering. The term 'euthanasia' has no direct equivalent in canonical Buddhist languages. Euthanasia as an ethical issue is not explicitly discussed in canonical or commentarial sources, and no clear cases of euthanasia are reported. However, there are canonical cases of *suicide and attempted suicide which have a bearing on the issue. One concerns the monastic precept against taking life, the third of the four *pārājika-dharmas, which was introduced by the *Buddha when a group of monks became disenchanted with life and began to kill themselves, some dying by their own hand and others with the aid of an intermediary. The Buddha intervened to prevent this, thus apparently introducing a prohibition on voluntary euthanasia. In other situations where monks in great pain contemplated suicide they are encouraged to turn their thoughts away from this and to use their experience as a means to developing insight into the nature of suffering and impermanence (*anitya).

evaṃ mayā śrūtam (Skt.; Pāli, evaṃ me sutam). 'Thus have I heard'. Form of words which introduces the discourses (*sūtra; Pāli, *sutta) of the *Buddha as preserved in their canonical form. Tradition has it that the speaker is *Ānanda, the Buddha's attendant, who was present when the discourse was delivered, and who recited them at the first council (*see* COUNCIL OF RĀJAGṚHA). This opening is usually followed by a statement specifying the place where the discourse was delivered and the names and number of those present. After this preamble, known as the *nidāna, the discourse itself is narrated.

Evans-Wentz, Walter Yeeling (1878–1965). A scholar of Celtic mythology who later became involved in the publication of several works of Tibetan *Buddhism (*see* TIBET), including the famous *Tibetan Book of the Dead* (**Bar-do thos-grol*), even though he himself could not read Tibetan or *Sanskrit. These works were initially translated by a Tibetan, Kazi Dawa Samdup, and Evans-Wentz took it upon himself to revise the text and preface it with lengthy but often misleading introductions giving his views about the significance of the work in question. Though highly influential in their day, these translations have been strongly criticized by modern scholars and should now generally be regarded as historical curiosities.

evil. *Buddhism has no concept of evil as a cosmic force or objective reality. The nearest it comes to this is the mythological figure of *Māra, the Buddhist 'devil'. However, it has much to say about evil in the sense of human suffering (*duḥkha), and these teachings are set out in the First Noble Truth (*see* FOUR NOBLE TRUTHS). Buddhism recognized that human experience inevitably contains much that is painful, such as sickness and *death, and that human beings are exposed to many natural evils such as floods, fires, earthquakes, and the like. Alongside these there is also the category of moral evil, which is analysed into various vices known as defilements (*kleśa). The most fundamental of these are the three roots of evil (*akuśala-mūla), namely greed (*rāga), hatred *(dveṣa), and delusion (*moha). The so-called 'problem of evil' which afflicts theistic religions is not so acute in Buddhism since many (but not all) of life's misfortunes can be explained by the doctrine of *karma.

extrinsic emptiness (Tib., gzhan-stong). A theory developed in *Tibet by Dolpopa Sherap Gyeltshan (Tib., Dol-po-pa shes-rab rgyal-mtshan, 1292–1361) and others based on the embryonic *Buddha (*tathāgata-garbha) concept expounded in the **Ratna-*

gotra-vibhāga and other related texts which contrast with the standard *Madhyamaka view of *intrinsic emptiness. According to this theory, ultimate reality (*paramārtha) is not empty of its own intrinsic nature (*svabhāva) but is inherently endowed with all the qualities of enlightenment (*bodhi) and Buddhahood, though it is empty of all aspects of delusive conventional phenomena.

F

Fa-chao (8th–early 9th c. CE). A Chinese *Pure Land *monk of the *T'ang dynasty period. During his early career he cultivated the trance (*samādhi) of Buddha contemplation (Chin., nien-fo san-mei), and while in *meditation at Lu-shan, he attained a vision of the *Buddha *Amitābha, who directly expounded Pure Land doctrines and practices to him. After this, he moved to the capital city and began teaching the literati to recite the name using five different chant tunes that Amitābha had taught him. Besides his ardent devotion to the practice of invoking the Buddha's name as a means to gain *rebirth in the Pure Land, he also made use of his training in *T'ien-t'ai thought in order to explain the practice, using arguments that were at the forefront of Buddhist intellectual activity during that time. Due to his success in spreading Pure Land teachings amidst competition from other schools of practice, such as *Ch'an and *esoteric *Buddhism, he became known popularly as the 'latter-day *Shan-tao', and was honoured by the emperor with the title '*National Teacher'.

Fa-hsiang. A school of Chinese *Buddhism that teaches that all of reality is an evolution of a fundamental level of consciousness. Because of this, it is often refered to as the *wei-shih, or 'consciousness-only' (Skt., *vijñapti-mātra) school. This school derives from pre-existing streams of Indian *Mahāyāna thought based on the writings of *Asaṅga and *Vasubandhu which crystallized into the Indian *Yogācāra (also known as the *Vijñānavāda) school. This school taught that there are within each individual's mind eight levels of consciousness: the five senses, the mind that gathers and processes their sensory data, a seventh mind that is the centre of analytical thought called *manas, and finally, an eighth level called the *ālaya-vijñāna or 'storehouse consciousness'. This last contains all of the 'seeds' implanted by *karmic acts which will in the future give rise to all perceptions and actions when conditions for them become right. In unenlightened beings, these seeds come to maturity as mistaken perceptions of reality, and give rise to its artificial division into 'self' and 'other', obscuring the realization that all things are equally projections of the ālaya-vijñāna. Enlightenment (*bodhi) comes about when beings realize that all things are merely evolutions of the ālaya-vijñāna, that is, are 'consciousness-only', thus eradicating any remaining notion of a separation of self and other, or that phenomena enjoy any kind of independent existence.

Another feature of Fa-hsiang thought was the analysis of the world into three levels of perception and existence, called the 'three natures' (san hsing). The first, representing objects of perception, was called the 'other-powered nature' (Skt., *paratantra-*svabhāva; Chin., ta ch'i hsing) since they arose only in dependence upon causes and conditions external to themselves. The second was the 'imaginary nature' (Skt., *parikalpita-svabhāva; Chin., suo chih hsing), and represented things as mistakenly perceived by the unenlightened, that is, as independently existing things that are separate and distinct from the consciousness that perceives them. The third was called the 'consummate nature' (Skt., *pariniṣpanna-svabhāva; Chin., ch'eng shih hsing), and represented things perceived correctly by an enlightened consciousness, that is, as evolutions of that consciousness with no distinction between subject and object. An aspect of this school's teaching that was to have decisive consequence for its fortunes in *China was the idea that there were certain beings, called *icchantikas, who lacked any seeds of Buddhahood in their makeup, and thus would never attain this goal.

The school in China traces its origin to the Indian *monk-translator *Paramārtha (499–569), who arrived in China in 546. Among the many texts that he brought and translated, he was best known for his teaching of *Asaṅga's **Mahāyānasaṃgraha* (Compendium of the Mahāyāna). Known in China by its short title *She-lun*, it became the basis for the She-lun school that studied it intensively. Later, the great Chinese pilgrim and translator *Hsüan-tsang (596–664) brought back and translated many more Indian Yogācāra texts, and a new school consolidated around him, superseding the older She-lun school. However, the teaching of icchantikas did not suit the atmosphere of Chinese Buddhism, which took universal salvation as an object of faith, and so the school did not survive past the first generation of Hsüan-tsang's disciples, the best-known of whom was K'uei-chi (632–82). The system of doctrinal classification put forward by the *Hua-yen school shortly thereafter placed Fa-hsiang at the level of 'elementary Mahāyāna', just one step above *Hīnayāna.

Interestingly, when Buddhism experienced a revival of interest among intellectual circles in the late 19th and early 20th centuries, Fa-hsiang studies came to the forefront once again. The revivers saw in Fa-hsiang thought the best chance for harmonizing traditional Buddhist philosophy with the modern scientific viewpoint. *See also* HOSSŌ; WEI-SHIH.

Fa-hsien (4th–5th c. CE). The first Chinese *monk to travel to *India, stay for an extended period of time, and successfully return home. Spurred by a desire to obtain a complete copy of the *Vinaya, or monastic rule, he set out in 399 through the oasis kingdoms of central Asia and across the Taklamakan desert. Once in India, he spent several years studying languages, collecting texts, and visiting famous sites. He returned via the southern sea route, staying in *Sri Lanka for two years. He returned to *China in 414, bringing numerous texts and artefacts, and spent the remainder of his days translating the texts into Chinese. He also composed a travelogue, called *The Record of Buddhist Lands* or alternatively *Biography of the Eminent Monk Fa-hsien* (2085 in the *Taishō collection), that is a valuable source for Indian history.

faith. *See* ŚRADDHĀ.

Fa-jung (594–657). The founder of the *Oxhead school of Chinese *Ch'an *Buddhism, named after its headquarters on Oxhead Mountain (Chin., Niu-t'ou shan). During the time when the controversy between the Northern and Southern Schools (*see* NORTHERN–SOUTHERN SCHOOL CONTROVERSY) was at its height, he attempted to chart a new path that would reconcile the two. He stressed the need to develop both meditative concentration and wisdom in tandem, the first through *meditation, the second through doctrinal and scriptural study. He also accepted the *T'ien-t'ai doctrine that all phenomena whatsoever have the Buddha-nature (as opposed to the Southern School's insistence that only sentient beings enjoyed this).

Fa-lang (507–81). Chinese master of the *San-lun school ordained in 528 CE. His exposition of the San-lun teachings met with great success and his work was continued by his student *Chi-tsang.

Falun Gong. A new syncretistic religious movement founded in *China in 1992 by Li Hung-chih, which blends together elements of *Buddhism and *Taoism in order to generate a spiritual awakening similar to the Buddhist experience of *bodhi. Followers seek to cultivate moral values such as honesty, truthfulness, patience, and goodwill, which they believe will free them from *rebirth as well as cumulatively transforming society. The movement, which has some 15 million members, has been persecuted by the Chinese government and many of its leading members are in prison. Li Hung-chih fled the country and now lives in New York.

fang yen-k'ou (Chin.). An esoteric ritual performed in Chinese *Buddhism. This ceremony makes use of elements of esoteric practice (*mantras, *mudras, and *visualizations) in order to open the doors of *hell and summon the hell-denizens and hungry ghosts (*preta), who are then fed and given an opportunity to hear the *Dharma preached. This ceremony dates to the translation of the *Sūtra of the Dhāraṇī for the Rescue of the Hungry Ghost Burning Mouth* (*Taishō 1313) by *Amoghavajra (705–74) during the *T'ang dynasty. A highly complex ritual, it takes several hours to perform, but the sense of drama generated by its various parts, its variations in colour and sound, and occasional flourishes such as tossing handfuls of sweets and small coins into the audience, make it a popular rite among lay sponsors. *See also* ESOTERIC BUDDHISM.

Fan wang ching (Chin.). The *Brahmajāla Sūtra* or 'Sūtra of Brahma's Net', 1484 in the *Taishō *canon, translated by *Kumārajīva in the early 5th century. The text describes the practices in which a *Bodhisattva (in this case meaning the ordinary practitioner of the *Mahāyāna path) ought to engage. The scripture is most significant for its list of ten 'grave' and 48 'light' Bodhisattva *precepts which are now normally taken as the third set of precepts by Chinese *monks and *nuns. Lay Buddhists in *China also take a set of so-called Bodhisattva precepts, but these are derived from the *Sūtra on Upāsaka Precepts*, 1488 in the Taishō canon. The precepts of the *Fan wang ching* came to be the sole precepts taken by certain Japanese Buddhist clerics following a petition by *Saichō (767–822) that his *Tendai monks not be required to take the '*Hīnayāna' precepts.

Father Tantra. One of the three main classes of *anuttara-yoga-tantras, typified by the *Guhyasamāja Tantra*. Meditative practice (*sādhana) based on the Father Tantras emphasizes the so-called '*generation phase' of *visualization as a means of personal transformation.

Fa-tsang (643–712). Although tradition lists him as the third *patriarch of the *Hua-yen school in *China (after *Tu-shun (557–640) and *Chih-yen (602–68)), Fa-tsang is in fact the real founder and consolidator of this school. Although his family was of Sogdian ancestry, by the time he was born in the capital of *Ch'ang-an, it had become completely sinicized. He joined the monastic order as a novice, and studied the **Hua-yen ching* with Chih-yen. Apparently his ethnic background gave him some facility with *Sanskrit and central Asian languages, and he went to work with *I-ching's translation bureau after the death of Chih-yen. Later, in the capital, he brought his previous training in the teachings of the *Hua-yen ching* to bear as he assisted with the retranslation of the scripture being carried on by Śikṣānanda. He also worked with the great translator and *Fa-hsiang master *Hsüan-tsang (596–664), but broke with him over the Fa-hsiang teaching of *icchantikas, beings with no potential at all to achieve Buddhahood (*see* FA-HSIANG). Despite this extensive experience working on translations, he is primarily remembered for his original writings expounding Hua-yen philosophy and his efforts to organize the Hua-yen school and set it on an enduring foundation. Some of his works, such as the *Essay on the Golden Lion*, remain classics of clear exposition and the imaginative use of metaphor to convey the subtleties of Hua-yen philosphy in accessible language. He also followed the example of *Chih-i (538–97) of the *T'ien-t'ai school in setting up a system for organizing all of the disparate teachings of *Buddhism then known in China into a single hierarchical scheme, based on the extent to which they conveyed the entire truth of the nature of reality. *See also* P'AN-CHIAO.

Fa-yen wen-i (885–958). Founder of one of the so-called '*Five Houses' of Chinese *Ch'an. It was, in fact, he who first coined the term 'Five Houses' to refer to the major schools of Ch'an in his day. Ironically, the 'House of Fa-yen', based in the Ch'in-liang Temple near modern Nanking, did not last beyond the next generation, in which Fa-yen's own predilection for doctrinal studies led his most eminent followers to allow the line to be absorbed by *T'ien-t'ai.

festivals. Early sources can give the impression that a somewhat puritanical view of festivals was held in the early monastic community. For example, dancing, singing, music, and watching shows are all prohibited by the seventh of the Eight Precepts (*aṣṭāṅga-śīla). The general attitude towards festivals, however, is unlikely to have been quite so severe. For lay-people especially it is likely that pre-Buddhist festivals, such as the full-moon festival, operated with little change. More specifically Buddhist ceremonies were also developed, such as the *uposatha (Skt., *poṣadha) and the *kaṭhina ceremony, and as lay involvement grew religious events of this kind provided the occasion for popular festivals. Notable events in the life of the *Buddha such as his birth, enlightenment (*bodhi) and *parinirvāṇa, are commemorated on the day of the full moon in May. In *Sri Lanka this is known as Vesak (or *Wesak) and in *Thailand, Visākhā Pūjā. His *first sermon is commemorated in the *Āsāḷha Pūjā (*see also* ESALA PERAHERA). In *Japan the Buddha's birth is celebrated on 8 April in the Hana Matsuri festival, his enlightenment on 15 February (Nehan) and his *death on 8

December (Rōhatsu). Many Buddhist festivals coincide with new year festivities, such as the Tibetan 'Great Prayer Festival' (Tib., smon lam chen mo), or with events in the agricultural cycle such as sowing and harvesting. The *Poson ceremony commemorates the arrival of *Buddhism in Sri Lanka. In *China, the festival of the 'hungry ghosts' (Skt., *preta) is very popular (*see* FANG YEN-K'OU). Where Buddhism coexists with other religions, as in east Asia, Buddhist festivals often become fused with those of local traditions such as *Confucianism, *Taoism, and *Shintō.

fetters. *See* SAMYOJANA.

First Propagation (Tib., snga-dar). The initial period of dissemination of Buddhist teachings in *Tibet which came to an end during the suppression of *Buddhism by *Lang Darma in the mid-9th century CE.

first sermon. The *Buddha's first sermon delivered at the *Deer Park, known in the commentaries as the *Dhamma-cakkappavattana Sutta* (Pāli) or *Dharma-cakra-pravartana Sūtra* (Skt.), meaning 'The Discourse of Setting in Motion the Wheel of the Law'. In this discourse the Buddha sets out the basis principle of the middle way (*madhyamā-pratipad), and the teaching of the *Four Noble Truths. It was said to be delivered on the full-moon night of the month of Āsāḷha.

five awarenesses. *See* PAÑCA-JÑĀNA.

five Buddha families. The fivefold classificatory system for *Buddhas, *Bodhisattvas, and other divine beings derived from the middle period *Mahāyāna *sūtra tradition and adopted by the later *tantras. Each family is headed by a particular Buddha endowed with specific qualities. The families are the *Tathāgata Family (*Vairocana), the Vajra Family (*Akṣobhya), the Jewel Family (*Ratnasaṃbhava), the Lotus Family (*Amitābha), and the Action Family (*Amoghasiddhi). The five Buddha family system replaced the earlier *three Buddha family scheme.

five degrees of enlightenment. Scheme adopted within the *Ch'an and *Zen schools of *Buddhism which classifies the nature of *bodhi, or religious awakening, into five increasingly profound levels, the fifth being the highest. The gradations are based on the doctrine of '*Two Truths', namely relative and absolute truth, as expounded by the *Madhyamaka school, and concern the manner in which each level of truth, and the relation between them, is perceived. The five degrees of enlightenment are termed: (1) Sho-chu-hen, or the absolute within the relative; (2) Hen-chu-sho, or the relative within the absolute; (3) Sho-chu-rai, or the absolute alone; (4) Ken-chu-shi, or the relative alone; (5) Ken-chu-to, or the absolute and the relative together.

Five Houses. The designation given to five early important lineages of Chinese *Ch'an *Buddhism, of which only two, the *Ts'ao-tung and *Lin-chi, survived more than a few generations. The term 'Five Houses' was first coined by *Fa-yen Wen-i (885–958), founder of the latest of the 'houses' to appear. The five were as follows: (1) Kuei-yang was named after the two mountains (Kuei and Yang) where its headquarter temples were located. The founder was *Kuei-shan Ling-yu (771–853). (2) Lin-chi, founded by *Lin-chi I-hsüan (d. 866). (3) Ts'ao-tung, named after two mountains, Mt. Tung, home of the founder *Tung-shan Liang-chieh (807–69), and Mt. Ts'ao, home of his disciple *Ts'ao-shan Pen-chi (840–901). (4) Yün-men, founded by *Yün-men Wen-yen (864–949). (5) Fa-yen, founded by Fa-yen Wen-i (885–958).

Five Mountains and Ten Temples. 1. The name given to a cluster of *Ch'an temples, all of the Yang-ch'i line of the *Lin-chi school. All were located in either Hang-chou or Ning-chou and enjoyed imperial patronage beginning in the Southern Sung dynasty (1127–1278). While these temples benefited from such patronage, they also suffered from the control that the state demanded as an unspoken condition of its support. While formally the Five Mountains constituted a first ranking, and the Ten Temples a second, with a third tier below them, the system was very vague in practice. Nevertheless, it served as an inspiration and model for a later Japanese attempt to institute a set of official temples under a system that also used the name 'Five Mountains and Ten Temples'. **2.** The name given to a system of official temple ranking that began in the late 13th and early 14th centuries in *Japan, based on the 'Five Mountains and Ten Temples' system of Sung-dynasty *China. The gozan, or 'five mountains', were *Rinzai *Zen temples of the first rank, that is, temples that received the official patronage of the Ashikaga government. In the next rank below them were the 'ten distinguished temples' (Jap., jissetsu), and in the third rank were the 'miscellaneous temples' (Jap., shozan). The temples that actually occupied these ranks varied with the rulers' favours, and often included more than five temples within the first rank or ten within the second. While the system was in effect it helped the government to organize *Zen temples into a bureaucratic hierarchy and provided it with outposts in the provinces from which it could counteract the rising influence of local warlords. This system embraced over 300 temples at its zenith (along with thousands of affiliated subtemples), but went into a decline in the 15th century due to the rise of rival Zen schools.

Five Periods and Eight Teachings. A name given to the *p'an-chiao, or doctrinal classification system devised by *Chih-i (538–97), the founder of the *T'ien-t'ai school in *China.

five powers. *See* BALA.

Five Precepts. *See* PAÑCA-ŚĪLA.

Five Pungent Herbs. *see* DIET.

Five Ranks (of Ts'ao-tung). This is a classic statement of the nature of reality first formulated by the founder of the *Ts'ao-tung school of Chinese *Ch'an, *Tung-shan Liang-chieh (807–69), and passed down through the Ts'ao-tung school to its Japanese successor, the *Sōtō school as the central understanding of this line of Ch'an. Using a series of five verses composed by Tung-shan, it presents five different ways of viewing the nature of ultimate reality as it manifests in particular phenomena. (1) The Absolute is seen in the identity of all differentiated phenomena in so far as they all share in the ultimate nature of emptiness, (2) The Absolute is seen in each and every individual phenomenon considered separately, since the nature of all things is complete and sufficient in itself, (3) The Absolute contains within itself the potential to manifest all particular phenomena, even those that are opposite or contrary to one another, (4) Despite their identity in terms of their ultimate nature, all phenomena are distinct and unconfused. In fact, it is only in their real differentiation that their relationality to each other and to the Absolute can be seen—for example, both fire and ice arise from the Absolute and share the same fundamental nature, but fire is not ice and ice is not fire, (5) The enlightened mind directly perceives the active and dynamic interplay between the Absolute and individual phenomena, and between one phenomenon and another.

fo. The Chinese word for '*Buddha', the full form of which is fo-t'o.

forest renunciates. *See* ĀRAṆYA-VĀSĪ.

Fo T'u-teng (4th c. CE). A central Asian *monk and thaumaturge who arrived in north *China in the early 4th century, during the period when the area north of the Yangtze River was ruled by non-Chinese tribes of Turkic or Tibetan origin. He ingratiated himself at court by his abilities at rainmaking and prognostication, and exerted some civilizing influence over the ruling houses by counselling compassion (*karuṇā) and justice in carrying out affairs of state. He is thought to be one of the first Buddhist monks to have become involved in government in Chinese history, and is also emblematic of the practical rather than theoretical bent of *Buddhism in the north, which contrasted with the more speculative and textual orientation of Buddhism in the southern kingdoms.

Foundation for the Preservation of the Mahāyāna Tradition. An international organization founded in 1975 for the promotion of *Mahāyāna teachings. The founders were two Tibetan lamas, Tupten Yeshe and Tupten Zopa Rinpoche, and the FPMT now has over 100 centres all over the world with its headquarters at Kopan monastery in Kathmandu, *Nepal.

four certainties. *See* VAIŚĀRADYA.

four exertions. *See* SAMYAK-PRAHĀṆA.

four famous mountains. Four sacred mountain sites that serve as major centres of *pilgrimage in Chinese *Buddhism. The four are: Mt. Wu-t'ai in Shansi province (identified with the *Bodhisattva *Mañjuśrī); Mt. O-mei in Szechuan (*Samantabhadra); Mt. P'u-t'o, an island off the coast of Chekiang (*Avalokiteśvara); and Mt. Chiu-hua in Anhui

(*Kṣitigarbha). These four formed a pilgrimage circuit, and their symbolism expanded as time went on. For example, they became emblematic of the four cardinal points, the four fundamental elements, and so forth.

Four Noble Truths. The four foundational propositions of Buddhist doctrine ennunciated by the *Buddha in his *first sermon (*Dharma-cakra-pravartana sūtra*). The first Noble Truth (Skt., ārya-satya; Pāli, ariya-sacca) is *duḥkha (Pāli, dukkha), usually translated as 'suffering' but often closer in meaning to 'flawed' or 'unsatisfactory'. This states that all existence is painful and frustrating. The second Noble Truth is samudāya or 'arising', and explains that suffering arises due to craving (*tṛṣṇā; Pāli, taṇhā) for pleasurable sensations and experiences. The third Noble Truth is that of 'cessation' (*nirodha), which states that suffering can have an end (this is *nirvāṇa), and the fourth Noble Truth is the Noble *Eightfold Path, which consists of eight factors collectively leading to nirvāṇa.

The stereotyped text which often recurs in the *Pāli Canon is as follows: **I.** But what, O Monks, is the Noble Truth of Suffering? Birth is suffering, sickness is suffering, old age is suffering, death is suffering; pain, grief, sorrow, lamentation, and despair are suffering. Association with what is unpleasant is suffering, disassociation from what is pleasant is suffering. In short, the five factors of individuality (*skandha) are suffering. **II.** This, O Monks, is the Truth of the Arising of Suffering. It is this thirst or craving (tṛṣṇā) which gives rise to *rebirth, which is bound up with passionate delight and which seeks fresh pleasure now here and now there in the form of thirst for sensual pleasure, thirst for existence, and thirst for non-existence. **III.** This, O Monks, is the Truth of the Cessation of Suffering. It is the utter cessation of that craving (tṛṣṇā), the withdrawal from it, the renouncing of it, the rejection of it, liberation from it, non-attachment to it. **IV.** This, O Monks, is the Truth of the Path that leads to the cessation of suffering. It is this Noble Eightfold Path, which consists of (1) Right View, (2) Right Resolve, (3) Right Speech, (4) Right Action, (5) Right Livelihood, (6) Right Effort, (7) Right Mindfulness, (8) Right Meditation. In the **Visuddhimagga* (XVI) *Buddhaghoṣa uses an analogy with medical treatment to explain the four truths: 'The truth of Suffering is to be compared with a disease, the truth of the Origin of suffering with the cause of the disease, the truth of Cessation with the cure of the disease, the truth of the Path with the *medicine.'

Fourth Council. *See* COUNCIL OF KANIṢKA.

Friends of the Western Buddhist Order. Western-orientated Buddhist group founded in 1967 by the British Buddhist Sangharakshita, who became a *monk in 1950 after working for nearly 20 years in *India much of the time among *Ambedkar Buddhists. The group is in principle non-sectarian but tends to emphasize *Mahāyāna teachings. A form of *ordination is provided which bestows the title 'follower of the *Dharma' (Dharmacari) on those admitted to it. This does not correspond to the conventional monastic ordination, and straddles the traditional distinction between laity and monks. Within the group emphasis is placed on *meditation, study, and observance of traditional moral teachings. The FWBO runs co-operatives in urban centres where members live and work in communities and it has branches throughout the West and in India.

front generation. A form of meditative *visualization used in *tantric *Buddhism in which the deity is visualized as being present in the sky facing the practitioner as opposed to the self-identification that occurs in *self-generation. This approach is considered less advanced, hence safer for the practioner, and is used more for propitiatory forms of worship.

Fudō Myō-ō (Jap.). One of the four 'wisdom kings' adopted into *Japanese *Buddhism from the Indian tradition, whose *Sanskrit name is Acalanātha. These kings appear as guardians of temples and esoteric ritual sites (*see* ESOTERIC BUDDHISM), and manifest extremely fierce and angry countenances and attitudes. Despite their frightening appearance, their primary motivation is compassion (*karuṇā): they protect the Buddhist teachings in order to dispel ignorance (avidyā) and bondage and allow beings to find liberation.

fugyō-nigyō. A Japanese phrase meaning 'to not practise and thus practise' (Chin., bu hsing erh hsing). This means to carry out one's religious cultivation naturally and spontaneously, without any calculation or forced, artificial effort.

fuju-fuse (Jap.) A phrase that means 'not receiving, not giving'. This phrase became the motto of certain lines of *Nichiren *monks who, vowing to adhere to the pure doctrine of their master Nichiren (1222–82) to the exclusion of all other teachings, refused to have anything to do with other schools of Japanese *Buddhism. *See also* NICHIREN-SHŪ.

fukasetsu (Jap., ineffable). Term used in the *Zen tradition to denote the inexpressible nature of ultimate truth. It is held that words alone cannot encompass or communicate its nature, which can only be known through the direct personal experience of awakening (*bodhi).

Fuke school. An independent *Zen school in *Japan that traces its lineage to the *T'ang dynasty Chinese *monk P'u-hua (whose name in Japanese pronunciation, Fuke, gives the school its name). However, the connection with this Chinese master is unclear. The founder of the school in Japan is Shinchi *Kakushin (1207–98), who trained in *Rinzai and *Sōtō Zen as well as *Shingon, and later went to *China where he attained enlightenment (*bodhi) under the master *Wu-men Hui-k'ai (1183–1260). He returned to Japan, bringing the famous *kōan collection the *Mumonkan*, or **Gateless Gate*, with him, thus introducing Japanese Zen to this important text. Later, the Fuke school came to be composed primarily of wandering, non-ordained *ascetics who specialized in playing the shakuhachi flute. Their informal status and lack of official residence made them attractive to social outcastes and the rōnin, or masterless *samurai of the late Tokugawa. The same factors also made them highly suspect in the eyes of the government, and some attempts were made to regulate them. In 1677 the government arbitrarily assigned three temples to serve as the school's 'headquarters', and 1847 it was placed under the jurisdiction of the Rinzai school. Finally, in 1871 it was banned as part of the Meiji government's proscription of *Buddhism (*see* MEIJI RESTORATION).

G

gaing. Burmese term meaning a sect or monastic group. Some scholars argue that 'sect' is not the best translation of the term, since the various Burmese gaings have not developed separate doctrines and distinguish themselves largely in terms of their different practices. The chief characteristics of a gaing are: a distinctive monastic lineage, some form of hierarchical organizational structure, separate rules, rituals, and behavioural practices, affiliation across local boundaries, and some recognition by the secular authorities. In historical terms, after the mission of *Chapata to *Sri Lanka, the Burmese *Saṃgha at *Pagān split into two divisions known as the purimagana (earlier going) and paccagana (later going). After the fall of the Pagān dynasty six gaing were known to have flourished in the early 14th century in the land of the Mons (*see* MON) in lower *Burma. After a period of reunification, however, the Saṃgha in lower Burma declined. Town-dwelling monks began to adopt a distinctive headgear and became influential in the closing decades of the 17th century, sparking off a conflict with their forest-dwelling counterparts. A dispute also arose between the so-called Ton Gaing and Yon Gaing, which centred on the manner of wearing the robe in public, namely whether it should be worn over one shoulder or both. Successive monarchs were drawn into the dispute, which was only resolved in 1782 when King Bodawpaya intervened and restored the orthodox practice favoured by the Yon Gaing of covering both shoulders. After this the Saṃgha remained united for some seven decades until the advent of the *Shwegyin Gaing. There were nine officially acknowledged gaing when the state-sponsored 'Congregation of the Saṃgha of All Orders' was convened in May 1980 in a successful attempt to form a unified Saṃgha with a national character.

Gal Vihāra. Group of rock carved *Buddha images. The complex, which is part of *Parakkamabāhu's *Uttarārāma, consists of four separate images: a standing Buddha, a 14m long reclining Buddha, and two seated Buddhas. The images are all cut from one long slab of granite and originally were surrounded by their own image houses.

Gampopa (1079–1153) (Tib., sgam-po-pa). Epithet of the Tibetan teacher Dakpo Lharje Sönam Rinchen (Dvags-po dha-rje bsod-nams rin-chen). The name Gampopa, meaning 'man of Gampo', comes from the fact that he spent several years in meditation in the Gamp po region. Born in the district of Nyel in 1079, he initially worked as a skilled physician (lha-rje), and is also known as 'The Doctor of Takpo' (Dwags po lha-rje). In 1110, he received the *Kagyü lineage from *Milarepa. After some years of private practice, he founded Daklha Gampo in 1121 and resided there. He combined together the gradual path of the *Kadampa school and the Great Seal (*mahāmudra) instructions of Milarepa, and consequently composed the **Jewel Ornament of Liberation*. He died in 1153 at the age of 75. Thereafter, his teaching lineage became known as the Dakpo Kagyü. *See also* TIBET.

gaṇa (Skt.). A circle or group, especially in *anuttara-yoga-tantra where it denotes a secret coven-like group of initiates and devotees who engage in ritual practices in deserted places such as charnel grounds.

Gaṇḍavyūha Sūtra. The 'Array of Flowers Sūtra'. Included in the **Avataṃsaka Sūtra*, this text outlines the path of a *Bodhisattva in the form of the story of Sudhana's quest for teachings that will lead him to enlightenment (*bodhi). In the course of his travels, he encounters 53 teachers, many of them male or female lay-persons, until his eventual encounter with the Bodhisattva *Samantabhadra when he finally attains enlightenment. The text, impressive in its own right as a piece of literature, survives in *Sanskrit as well as one Tibetan and several Chinese translations.

Ganden. Founded in 1409 by *Tsongkhapa, Ganden ('Blissful') was the foremost of

*Gelukpa teaching monasteries. It is located on the ridge of Mt. Wangkur on the south bank of the Kyichu river to the east of *Lhasa. It was destroyed during the Cultural Revolution and its population of 3,000 monks was reduced to only a few hundred. In recent years significant restoration work has been carried out.

Gandhāra. A Buddhist kingdom situated between the lower Kabul Valley in present-day Afghanistan and the Indus river in Pakistan, which particularly flourished first under the rule of the Bactrian Greeks from the 2nd century BCE and later under the *Kuṣāṇas, a Scythian tribe from central Asia. Gandhāra forms the background to the famous *Pāli work *Milinda's Questions* (**Milindapañha*), and the so-called 'Fourth Council' was convened here in the 1st–2nd century CE during the reign of *Kaniṣka I or II (*see* COUNCIL OF KANIṢKA). This council was dominated by the *Sarvāstivādin school and resulted in the compilation of the major *Abhidharma treatise, the **Mahāvibhāṣā*. Gandhāra is also noted as a centre of Buddhist art, especially sculpture, intially strongly influenced by Hellenic styles. Some of the earliest representations of the *Buddha were produced in the region. Gandhāra ceased to exist as an independent kingdom by the 7th century CE and a Buddhist presence in the area continued on a small scale thereafter.

gandharva (Skt.; Pāli, gandhabba). **1.** A class of heavenly beings, famed particularly for their musical skills. Their name, meaning 'fragrance-eater', derives from the belief that they feed only on fragrances. **2.** A term for the non-material form a being is believed to take after *death, according to some schools of *Buddhism. In this ethereal form the spirit of the deceased person passes through the intermediate state or *bar-do prior to a new birth, entering the mother's body at the moment of conception.

Gandhavaṃsa. A late *Pāli work written in *Burma possibly in the 17th century. It relates, in brief, the history of the *Pāli Canon and gives accounts of post-canonical Burmese and *Sri Lankan Pāli texts. The colophon states that the work was composed by a forest-dwelling elder (*Thera) named Nandapañña. The sources used by the author are not known.

Gaṅgā. Indian name for the river Ganges.

Ganjin (688–763). A Chinese *monk who journeyed to *Japan in 753 in response to an embassy sent by the court in order to find a qualified *Vinaya master to come to Japan and institute orthodox monastic *ordinations. Ganjin received the invitation in 742 and consented to go, but various factors, ranging from adverse conditions, shipwreck, and the machinations of his disciples who desired to keep him in *China, delayed his arrival by eleven years, during which time he lost his eyesight. In 755, he supervised the construction of an *ordination platform at the *Tōdaiji in Nara, and administered both monastic and lay *precepts to several hundred devotees, including the retired emperor. After this initial success, however, he found himself in conflict with the already established *Ritsu (Vinaya) school, which had already staked out the study and administration of precepts as its territory, and the Ritsuryō government, which disapproved of Ganjin's assertions regarding the independence of the clergy from the government. His blindness and advanced age left him little inclined to conflict, so he quickly resigned his post on the Bureau of Priests (sōgō), and retired to his own temple, the Tōshōdaiji, where he passed his remaining days quietly in study and teaching.

garuḍa. In Indian mythology, a class of large bird-like beings, ever in a state of enmity with the *nāga serpents whom they eat.

garu-dhamma (Pāli; Skt., guru-dharma). The eight additional 'weighty rules' that the *Buddha imposed as a condition of allowing *women to be ordained as *nuns. The intention behind the rules is commonly said to be to place nuns in an inferior position to monks, but a recent alternative explanation suggests they are intended more as a safeguard for women living in vulnerable situations. The additional rules are listed in the *Cullavagga as follows. (1) A nun must always show deference to monks, for example by bowing even to the most junior monk. (2) A nun should not spend the rain-retreat (*vassa) in a place where there are no monks. (3) The monthly *poṣadha ceremony should be led by a monk. (4) At the end of the rain-retreat a nun must appear before the assemblies of monks and nuns to report on any actual or suspected breaches of the disciplinary rules. (5) If a nun commits a serious offence she must undergo expiation before both assemblies. (6) After her two-year period of training as a novice (*śrāmaṇerī) is complete, a nun must be ordained by both assemblies. (7) A nun must never offend or insult a monk. (8) Nuns must never admonish a monk, but monks may admonish a nun.

gasshō. A Japanese term meaning 'to bring the palms together' as in the Indian gesture of respectful salutation known as 'añjali'. This is a gesture of respect between clerics and also a ritual gesture of worship. The term is also found in Chinese *Buddhism under the Chinese pronunciation 'ho-chang'.

Gateless Gate (Chin., *Wu-men kuan; Jap., Mumonkan*). A collection of *kōans compiled by the Chinese *Ch'an master *Wu-men Hui-k'ai (1183–1260) and published in 1229. It contains 48 stories of *Ch'an encounters between various well-known Chinese Ch'an figures that shows a decisive moment in their teaching. These stories, given in a very condensed form, are accompanied by Wu-men's own comments and a short poem. It gained wide currency in *China, *Japan, *Korea, and more recently, in *Europe and *America.

gāthā. A *Sanskrit term for a religious verse or stanza, especially, but not only, of praise. Many *Mahāyāna *sūtras are composed entirely in such verses or else incorporate lengthy verse portions repeating and summarizing teachings previously given in prose.

gati (Skt.; Pāli, course or destination). Name for the various destinies or realms of *rebirth, of which there are generally held to be six: (1) the gods (*deva); (2) humans; (3) demons (*asura); (4) *animals; (5) hungry ghosts (*pretas); (6) *hell (naraka). The first three are regarded as good destinies (sugati) and the last three as woeful (*durgati). Early Buddhist sources usually speak of five realms, omitting the third. *See* ALSO BHAVACAKRA.

Gautama (Pāli, Gotama). Name of the clan to which the *Buddha belonged. Sometimes he is referred to simply by this name, particularly in *Pāli sources and also in some of the Dīrgha *Āgama sūtras. *See also* SIDDHARTHA GAUTAMA.

Geluk (Tib., dge-lugs). The largest of the four main orders of Tibetan *Buddhism, and that to which the *Dalai Lamas belong. Founded by *Tsongkhapa in the 14th century, the school became dominant in the 17th century under *Dalai Lama V and has remained the most influential down to modern times. This tradition integrates the methodical study and practice of the *sūtras and *mantras developed by Tsongkhapa and his successors, based in part upon the older *Kadampa lineage which derived from the teachings of *Atiśa. In addition to an emphasis on textual study, the school also stresses the importance of compliance with the monastic code (*Vinaya). The *monks of the Geluk school have also been known traditionally as the 'Yellow Hats' because their ceremonial hats are yellow, as opposed to the red hats of other schools. *See also* TIBET.

Gelukpa (Tib., dge-lugs-pa). Any person or thing connected with the *Geluk school.

Gendun (Tib., dge-'dun). The Tibetan term for the monastic community or *Saṃgha.

generation phase (Skt., utpatti-krama). The first phase of meditational practice (*sādhana) associated with the *anuttara-yoga-tantras in general and especially with the so-called '*Father Tantras' such as the **Guhyasamāja Tantra*. The generation phase involves the use of creative imagination or *visualization as a means of personal transformation through which the practitioners either visualize a divine being before them (*front generation) or as themselves (*self-generation) in order to alter their perception and experience of the appearance aspect of reality.

Genshin (942–1017). A Japanese *Tendai priest and scholar who produced a significant corpus of works on a wide variety of Buddhist topics. He is known primarily as the author of the **Ōjōyōshū*, or 'Essentials of Rebirth (in the Pure Land)', a systematic survey of Chinese *Pure Land literature that helped pave the way for the development of Pure Land as an independent school a century later. This work was also one of the few original Japanese works that travelled back to *China and influenced the development of *Buddhism there.

Gesar (Tib., Ge-sar). A mythical hero king whose wondrous exploits inspired the *Epic of Gesar* which achieved great popularity in *Tibet and *Mongolia. The events of Gesar's life probably draw on many different central Asian sources and traditions, and the name 'Gesar' itself is thought to derive ultimately from the title 'caesar'. The epic comprises several cycles of stories and is composed in verse and prose. It was formerly handed down by an oral bardic tradition though now the diverse oral traditions have been largely collected together in written form.

geshé (Tib., dge-bshes). A Tibetan title given to *Gelukpa scholars, especially those in the tradition of the three great *Gelukpa monasteries around *Lhasa. The term is an abbreviation of dge-ba'i bshes-gyen, meaning a spiritual benefactor.

ghaṇṭā (Skt.). A ritual bell used in Buddhist *tantric practice, often in conjunction with the *vajra. The half-vajra which surmounts the bell as a handle normally has the usual five prongs but examples with one, three, or nine prongs are also found, the latter especially associated with the Tibetan *Nyingma lineage. In Tibetan *Buddhism, the bell has a range of meanings from a simple reminder of impermanence (*anitya) to a symbolic representation of the female principle of insight (*prajñā). In Japanese *Shingon it is associated with the Matrix of Compassion Realm (karuṇā-garbha-dhātu).

Fig 10 ghaṇṭā

Ghositārāma. A monastery in *Kosambī named after its donor Ghosita (or Ghosaka) and given over for use by the *Buddha and the *monks. The Buddha stayed here frequently and the location is mentioned numerous times in *Pāli sources. It was the site of the first *schism which arose when two monks resident at the monastery provoked a dispute, causing the Buddha to turn his back on them and seek solitude in the nearby Pārileyyaka forest.

Gilgit. A region in northern *Kashmir above the central valley of the Jhelum river, known to the neighbouring Tibetans as Bru-zha. The location of Gilgit upon one of the main routes from *India into central Asia resulted in considerable Buddhist influence, both *Hīnayāna and *Mahāyāna. It also became a refuge for many *monks from Kashmir during the 10th century CE fleeing Muslim persecution. Gilgit is also famed as the site of a *stūpa which when excavated in 1931 yielded over 200 priceless Buddhist manuscripts in *Sanskrit, many of which are the sole extant copies.

Glass Palace Chronicle of the Kings of Burma. Burmese chronicle compiled in 1829 by a committee of scholars appointed by King Bagyiday. The name of the chronicle was taken from the Palace of Glass, the chamber of which the compilation was made. The work relates the history of the kings of *Burma, who are said to be descendants of the *Buddha's own people, the *Śākyans, and among other topics, goes on to report on the establishment of *Buddhism in the country and the acquisition of sacred *relics.

go butsu (Jap.). In Japanese *esoteric *Buddhism, these are the 'five *Buddhas' who occupy the centre of the *maṇḍala. Although the contents of the two fundamental maṇḍalas—the Womb-treasury maṇḍala and the Diamond World maṇḍala—differ, they both place the Buddha Mahāvairocana (*see* VAIROCANA) at the centre, and then place a subsidiary Buddha at each of the four cardinal points around the centre.

God. Buddhism is atheistic and does not believe in the existence of a Supreme Being or Creator God. However, it acknowledges the existence of a wide range of supernatural beings known as *devas, many of whom were incorporated into Buddhist mythology from *Hinduism.

go-i. *See* FIVE RANKS.

Godenshō. A classic biography of *Jōdo Shinshū founder *Shinran (1173–1262) composed by his great-grandson *Kakunyo (1270–1351) and published in 1294 as part of a plan to consolidate the new school around the cult of its founder.

gohonzon (Jap., object of worship). Tablet on which the Japanese *monk *Nichiren (1222–82) inscribed the Chinese characters of the *daimoku or sacred chant '*Namo myōhō renge kyō', meaning 'Homage to the **Lotus Sūtra*'. He believed these words to contain the essence of all Buddhist teaching and practice. The chant has remained central to the daily practice and liturgy of the schools that trace their origins to Nichiren, especially the *Nichiren Shōshū and the *Sōka Gakkai.

Gokulika. A *Mahāsaṃghika sect which gave birth to two later schools, the *Prajñaptivāda and the *Bāhulikas (or Bahuśrūtikas). They based their teachings primarily on the *Abhidharma Piṭaka rather than on the *Sūtra Piṭaka.

Golden Pali Text. *See* ŚRI KṢETRA PYU GOLDEN PĀLI TEXT.

gompa (Tib., dgon-pa). A monastery or hermitage, traditionally isolated from the nearest village by the distance of a single reach of hearing.

gopura. Thai term for the entrance pavilion to a temple precinct, especially *Khmer.

Gosan. *See* FIVE MOUNTAINS AND TEN TEMPLES.

gotra (Skt.). A clan or family; often used in *Mahāyāna in the sense of a religious group or spiritual communion, either innate or acquired. According to *Yogācāra, there are five such spiritual groups: three corresponding to the three *yānas (Śrāvaka, *Pratyekabuddha, and *Bodhisattva), to which are added an indeterminate group (aniyata) and a group totally lacking any spiritual potentiality (agotra).

Govinda, Lama Anagarika (1898–1985). Western student of *Buddhism who was drawn first of all to *Theravāda and later to Tibetan Buddhism. Born E. L. Hoffman of Bolivian and German parents, he was an artist by profession and became interested in Buddhism on a visit to *Sri Lanka in 1928. This motivated him to become an *anāgārika. Later he went to *Tibet where he met his *guru, Tomo Geshe Rinpoche. He describes his experiences in Tibet in his autobiography *The Way of the White Clouds* (1966). Other of his works include *The Psychological Attitude of Early Buddhism* (1937) and *Foundations of Tibetan Mysticism* (1960).

gozan. *See* FIVE MOUNTAINS AND TEN TEMPLES.

gradual enlightenment. In Chinese *Ch'an history, this represents the view, traditionally imputed to the '*Northern School', that enlightenment (*bodhi) is acquired gradually through long practice. A famous verse that appears in *The *Platform Sūtra of the Sixth Patriarch* attributed to *Shen-hsiu (606–706) compares the mind to a clear mirror upon which dust has accumulated. By wiping away the dust, the mirror gradually emerges in its clarity. Subsequent Ch'an thought came to reject this conception of religious practice, claiming that it was based on a false duality between delusion and enlightenment, practice and attainment, and prior and subsequent moments in time. In its place, Ch'an came to embrace the view of '*sudden enlightenment', which held that the mind was always inherently clear and enlightened, and that beings had only to realize this fact, a feat that could be accomplished instantaneously.

grāhya-grāhaka (Skt.). The 'grasped' and the 'grasper'; a *Yogācāra term for the duality of a perceiving subject and perceived objects. The school attributes the perception of duality to a false imagining (*abhūta-parikalpa) which fabricates and superimposes upon reality the idea of a conscious self which perceives, and the objects which are perceived by it, thus generating *saṃsāra.

Gṛdhrakūṭa. *See* VULTURE'S PEAK.

great ball of doubt. *See* DAI-GIDAN.

Great Perfection. *See* DZOGCHEN.

Great Renunciation. Name given to the important event in the *Buddha's life at the age of 29 when he left his father's palace and abandoned the world to become a homeless mendicant. A popular theme in art and literature, the Buddha is depicted riding out on his white horse, *Kanthaka, accompanied by his charioteer, *Channa.

Great Seal. *See* MAHĀMUDRĀ.

Great Vehicle. *See* MAHĀYĀNA.

gter-ston (Tib., treasure discoverer). One who discovers or reveals *terma (Tib., gter-ma), which according to the *Nyingma lineage of Tibetan *Buddhism are hidden textual 'treasures' concealed by *Padmasambhava in the 8th century. The location of the treasures is communicated by female spirits (*ḍākinīs) to advanced practitioners of *anuttara-yoga-tantra.

Guhyasamāja Tantra (Skt.). The 'Tantra of the Secret Assembly', an important early *anuttara-yoga-tantra in eighteen chapters deriving in part from earlier material such as that found in the **Sarva-tathāgata-tattva-saṃgraha* but with important innovations such as the use of overt sexual symbolism and practices. This text gave rise to a rich exegetical tradition and paved the way for further developments in *tantric literature. As well as surviving in *Sanskrit manuscripts, it was also translated into Tibetan and Chinese.

Guṇabhadra (394–468). An important translator of central Indian origin who travelled to *Sri Lanka and later arrived by sea in *China during the Liu Song period. He carried out most of his translation of *Mahāyāna and *Hīnayāna texts, including such texts as the **Śrīmālā-devī Sūtra* and the **Laṅkāvatāra Sūtra*, while residing in southern *China.

Gupta dynasty. An Indian dynasty that governed northern and central *India from 350 CE to 650 CE, during which period all aspects of Indian artistic, architectural, and religious life flourished. Many great *Mahāyāna masters lived and wrote at this time while various Buddhist establishments such as *Nālandā attracted many pilgrim-monks from *China and elsewhere.

guru (Skt., heavy). General Indian term for a teacher, particularly a religious preceptor. The term is more commonly found in *Hinduism than *Buddhism. It is very rare in early Buddhism, which prefers the term *ācārya (Pāli, acariya), but more common in the *Vajrayāna particularly among those schools of *tantra that emphasize personal transmission of mystical knowledge from teacher to disciple, such as the Tibetan *Kagyupa.

guru pūjā (Skt.; Tib., bla-ma mchod-pa). A Tibetan ceremony in which ritual offerings are made to the past spiritual teachers of one's lineage.

Guru Rinpoche. A title of respect and devotion for *Padmasambhava.

guru yoga (Skt.). A devotional meditative practice associated with Tibetan *Buddhism (*see* TIBET) in which one's root teacher or *guru is identified as the quintessence of all *Buddhas. The student then forms an identification with the guru by meditating on his own and the guru's emptiness (*śūnyatā) and visualizes himself as of the same fundamental nature. Through this practice it is believed that all the virtuous qualities of a Buddha can rapidly be transmitted to the adept.

Gyel-tshap (1364–1431). The short name of Gyel-tshab Darma Rinchen (rgyal-tshab dar-ma rin-chen), one of *Tsongkhapa's two main disciples. His short name (meaning 'regent') was given in view of his acting as Tsongkhapa's trusted representative, later becoming abbot of *Ganden Monastery from 1419 until his death.

Gyōgi (668–749). An influential Japanese *monk of the *Nara period. Unlike other more conventional Nara monks, Gyōgi did not remain in residence at an official temple in the capital, but took to the road preaching to the people and pursuing public works. The court and aristocracy, wishing to keep *Buddhism under control and strictly in the service of the state, held him in suspicion for a while on account of his influence among the masses, but eventually brought him into government service as the head of the Bureau of Monks in 745. Emperor *Shōmu Tennō (r. 724–49) held him in high regard, and when he erected the Great *Buddha, a massive image of *Vairocana to be housed at the *Tōdaiji in Nara, he dispatched Gyōgi to the Ise shrine to obtain the consent of the deity (*kami) Amaterasu.

gzhan-stong. *See* EXTRINSIC EMPTINESS.

H

Haein Temple. A temple at the southern tip of *Korea built in 892 that houses the 81,000 woodblocks preserved from a 13th-century printing of the Korean *canon of scriptures. It is still active as a *Sŏn temple. *See also* TRIPIṬAKA KOREANA.

haiku (Jap.). A Japanese poetic form consisting of three lines of five, seven, and five syllables. Although not originally connected with *Buddhism, its simplicity, directness, and spontaneity were congenial to the *Zen spirit, and it became associated with Zen in some quarters. The most famous exponent of haiku as a vehicle for expressing direct realization was Matsuo *Bashō (1644–94).

Hakuin Zenji (or Hakuin Ekaku) (1685–1768). Tokugawa-era reformer and restorer of the *Rinzai school of Japanese *Zen. He is known for his efforts at popularizing Zen among the common people, his systematization of *kōan practice into a graded curriculum, his works on secular *ethics, his ink drawings, and his invention of the famous kōan: 'What is the sound of one hand clapping?'

hakushi (Jap., white paper). In *Zen *Buddhism, a term describing the state of mind brought about through the practice of *meditation or *zazen. The achievement of this state, in which the mind is emptied of all thoughts, is regarded by many as a precondition for the experience of *bodhi or awakening.

Hakuun Yasutani (1885–1973). A *Sōtō Zen *monk who received early training under *Harada Daiun Sōgaku (1871–1961). Like his master, he sought to correct what he felt were the overly quietistic propensities of Sōtō by bringing in *Rinzai elements, in particular use of the *kōan and a new emphasis on the active search for enlightenment (*bodhi). Feeling that Zen was best practised in everyday life, he founded the Sambōkyōdan in 1954, a fellowship in which he trained laypeople in and around Tokyo. At this time he also broke formal ties with the Sōtō school. In 1962, already 71 years of age, he came to the United States and lived an active peripatetic life thereafter, travelling extensively across the country and holding *sesshin often. His students included many figures that would later become influential in the establishment of Zen in *America, notably Roshi Philip Kapleau.

Han dynasty. A period of Chinese history extending from 206 BCE to 220 CE during which *China was united, prosperous, and (excepting a short period at the middle of the dynasty) stable. It was during this time that *Buddhism entered China.

hannya (Jap.). The Japanese pronunciation of the Chinese term 'pan-jo', a translation of the *Sanskrit *prajñā (insight).

Han-shan (7th or 8th c.). A Chinese *Ch'an recluse and mountain *ascetic famous for a collection of poems that were found written on trees and walls scattered around the *T'ien-t'ai mountain in south-east *China where he lived. Very little is known about him, but stories abound of his relationship with Shih-te, a kitchen *monk at a nearby temple where Han-shan sometimes came for food. The two of them engaged in extremely eccentric conversation and behaviour, much of which has survived in the memory of the 'wild Ch'an' tradition. Over 300 poems attributed to him are gathered in the collection.

Han-shan Te-ch'ing (1546–1623). One of the four great reformers of Chinese *Buddhism in the mid-Ming dynasty period. He was primarily a *Ch'an *monk, but like many masters of the period, he advocated the dual practice of Ch'an and *Pure Land, emphasizing the use of the Nien-fo technique as a means of purifying the mind and realizing its non-duality with the enlightened mind of the *Buddha *Amitābha. He was also renowned as a lecturer and commentator, and admired for his strict adherence to ethical *precepts.

hara (Jap.). In Japanese esoteric (*see* ESOTERIC BUDDHISM) and *martial arts practice, this refers to a spot in the human body about 3 inches below the navel in the middle of the abdomen. This place serves as the centre of gravity in martial arts and a place where the subtle energy of the body (ch'i) is collected and transformed in a manner metaphorically described as an alchemical process whereby cinnabar is heated and made into an elixir of immortality. For this reason, it is also called the 'tanden', or 'cinnabar field'.

Harada, Daiun Sōgaku (1871–1961). An influential *Sōtō *Zen master of the modern period. He was born in Obama city (Fukui prefecture) on 13 October 1871, and ordained as a *Sōtō *monk in 1883. From 1911 till 1923, he was a professor of Sōtō-shū Daigakurin (later to become Komazawa University) after completing his own course of studies there. He became the abbot in the Hosshin-ji temple in 1924, and also served as the abbot of a number of other temples. Harada was eclectic and modernizing, and sought to transcend traditional Sōtō–*Rinzai sectarian rivalries in order to utilise the strong points of both schools. Thus, unlike most Sōtō monks, he made use of *kōans and encouraged students to work actively towards enlightenment (*bodhi). His disciple *Hakuun Yasutani was instrumental in transmitting the Zen tradition to *America after his arrival there in 1962.

hara-kiri (Jap.). A vulgar term meaning 'to slice the abdomen', which refers to a ritualized form of *suicide carried out by Japanese *samurai beginning in the Tokugawa period. More properly called seppuku, it involved making two small cross-wise slices across the gut while in a kneeling position, after which a second would behead the samurai with a sword. In practice, the first step was rarely carried out.

Haribhadra (8th c. CE). A leading *Mahāyāna scholar-*monk active during the late 8th century CE in northern *India, he was famed as a commentator on *Prajñā-pāramitā Sūtras and the *Abhisamaya-alaṃkāra* of *Asaṅga or *Maitreyanātha. With the support and patronage of king Dharmapāla he founded the Buddhist university-monastery of *Vikramaśīla in eastern India. He is noteworthy for having controversially interpreted the concept of the 'intrinsic body' (*svābhāvika-kāya) as a separate fourth element underlying the standard *Mahāyāna doctrine of the *Buddha's 'three bodies' (*trikāya).

Harivarman (c.4th c. CE). A Buddhist *monk from central *India, sometimes thought to be a member of the *Bahuśrutīya subschool of the *Mahāsaṃghikas, although his writings seem straightforwardly *Sautrāntika. Reputedly a native of *Kashmir he studied under the Sautrāntika master Kumāralāta before becoming dissatisfied with the conflicting views of the schools and desiring to reconcile their positions in a manner consonant with the original teachings of the *Buddha. To this end he composed a treatise called the *Tattvasiddhi Śāstra* (also known as the **Satyasiddhi Śāstra*). His only surviving work, it is extant only in Chinese. It attained some popularity due to a mistaken belief that it taught orthodox *Mahāyāna doctrines, such as emptiness (*śūnyatā). In this work, which is divided in accordance with the *Four Noble Truths, the author discusses a multitude of technical problems in Buddhist doctrine, and rejects those opinions which are not sanctioned by scripture. He follows the interpretation of no single school and states that he wishes to establish his own conclusions independently. He argues strongly for the recognition of the role played by the mind in the construction of reality through the medium of concepts and intellectual constructions (prajñapti). The present value of the treatise to scholars is as a compendium of proto-Mahāyāna teachings.

Haryaṅkas. A royal dynasty that ruled the state of *Magadha from 546–414 BCE. The dynasty had six kings in all, and the first two, Śreṇika *Bimbisāra and Kūṇika *Ajātaśatru, were contemporaries of the *Buddha.

hassō (Jap.; Chin., pa hsiang). In east Asian *Buddhism, this term refers to the 'eight acts' of the *Buddha through which he revealed the teachings and saved other beings. Although lists vary from source to source, the following is representative: (1) descent from the *Tuṣita *heaven; (2) entry into the womb; (3) gestation; (4) *birth; (5) renunciation of the householder life; (6) enlightenment (*bodhi); (7) setting the Wheel of *Dharma in motion; (8) final *nirvāṇa. Other lists omit gestation and substitute the Buddha's suppression of *Māra after the renunciation.

hassu (Jap., transmitted). Term used in *Zen *Buddhism to denote the successor of a Zen master. The student chosen by the master receives the 'seal of authentication' (*inka) from him and thereby becomes his legitimate religious heir, empowered to continue his teachings.

haw tai. Lao term for a monastery (*vihāra) building dedicated to the storage of the *Tripiṭaka.

Hayagrīva. A *tantric *yi-dam or tutelary deity considered to be a wrathful form of the *Bodhisattva *Avalokiteśvara. His name means 'horse neck', and he is generally depicted with a horse's head. The cult of Hayagrīva may have its origins in *Hindu mythology where he is regarded as a minor incarnation (Skt., *avatāra) of Viṣṇu who was half man, half horse.

Heart Sūtra. A highly influential and popular *Mahāyāna scripture used in both Tibetan and east Asian *Buddhism; the full title is 'The Sūtra of the Heart of the Perfection of Insight'. This scripture, only one paragraph in length, is a terse summary of Perfection of Insight (*prajñā-pāramitā) teaching, and describes the truth realized in *meditation by the *Bodhisattva *Avalokiteśvara. This truth is that form (one of the five *skandhas and here standing in for all individual, differentiated phenomena) is emptiness (*śūnyatā, the transcendent and undifferentiated absolute) and vice versa. In this way, it affirms that the transcendent is found only in its manifestation in the immanent and nowhere else. It ends with a *mantra to be recited, the effect of which is to induce understanding of ultimate truth in the reciter. Because of its extreme brevity, it has been used both as a summary statement of Mahāyāna truth, and as a liturgical and ritual text. Recent research has shown that the *Heart Sūtra* is almost certainly a Chinese composition back-translated into *Sanskrit.

heaven. *Buddhism has no concept of heaven as an eternal realm, but it recognizes a hierarchy of spiritual levels above and beyond this world into which one may be reborn as a god (*deva). Later scholastics list 26 such heavenly worlds, although the number varies slightly in different schools. All the Buddhist heavens, however, are impermanent states, and in due course one will be reborn in a lower realm when the good *karma which caused the heavenly birth runs out. The ultimate goal of the Buddhist is therefore not heaven, but *nirvāṇa. *See also* COSMOLOGY; GATI; HELL.

Heian period. A period of Japanese history (*see* JAPAN) that takes its name from the time when the capital was located in the city of Heian (modern *Kyoto) from 794 to 1185. This period saw the foundation of the *Tendai and *Shingon schools of Japanese *Buddhism.

heikan (Chin., pi-kuan). In *Zen practice, a period of sealed confinement, where the practitioner remains within a single room for an extended period of study and practice, usually three years.

hell. *Buddhism has no concept of hell as a place of eternal punishment, and its notion of post-mortem retribution is closer to the Western notion of purgatory. The accumulation of bad *karma can lead to *rebirth in one of a number of hells (Skt., naraka; Pāli, niraya), often vividly depicted in popular art and folklore. There are said to be both hot hells and cold hells, each with numerous subdivisions where evil-doers are tormented by demons until their bad karma has run its course and they are reborn in a better state. The deepest of all the hells is *Avīci. *See also* COSMOLOGY; HEAVEN; GATI.

Heruka. A 'blood-drinker'; a term for the wrathful deities, such as Hevajra or *Cakra-saṃvara, associated with *anuttara-yoga-tantra and often adopted by a practitioner as a tutelary deity (*yi-dam).

hetu (Skt., Pāli, causal ground). Technical term often found in a scholastic context in *Abhidharma literature meaning cause, condition, or reason, in the sense of an originating or motivating ground. It is the first of 24 causal conditions listed in the **Paṭṭhāna*. The six most basic hetus are the three roots of evil (*akuśala-mūla) namely greed (*rāga), hatred (*dveṣa), and delusion (*moha), and their opposites.

Hevajra Tantra (Skt.). One of the key *anuttara-yoga *Mother Tantras associated with the *yi-dam Hevajra and his consort Nairātmya. The text describes the deity and main meditational practices that relate to him. The work survives in *Sanskrit and was also translated into Tibetan and Chinese. In *Tibet, the *Hevajra Tantra* is especially popular with the *Sakya school.

Hiei, Mt. A mountain to the north-east of *Kyoto that rises to a level of 2,600 feet above sea level at its peak. It is the site of the *Enryakuji, the headquarters temple of the *Tendai school.

Higashi-honganji. *See* HONGANJI.

Hihan Bukkyō. *See* CRITICAL BUDDHISM.

hijiri (Jap.). A wandering holy man or saint. The term has been applied to Buddhist clergy, some only self-ordained, who live in the mountains or wander on the roads as itinerant preachers, healers, thaumaturges, diviners, or engineers of public works.

Himalayas (Skt., hima-ālaya, abode of snow). The Himalayan region is known in Buddhist sources by various names such as Himavā, Himācakam, and Himavanta. As one of the seven mountain ranges known to classical Indian sources it is described in largely mythological terms. It is said to be 300,000 leagues (yojana) in extent, with 84,000 peaks, the highest one being 500 yojanas in altitude. The region is said to encompass seven great lakes from which flow 500 rivers. The area also serves as a kind of retirement zone for sages who withdraw there to end their days in solitude and *meditation.

Hīnayāna (Skt., lesser vehicle). A collective name used disparagingly by *Mahāyāna Buddhists for the schools of early *Buddhism which preceded the Mahāyāna or 'great vehicle'. In the eyes of the Mahāyāna, these schools were inferior because their followers were preoccupied selfishly with their own salvation and the advancement towards the goal of becoming an *Arhat, as opposed to that of *Bodhisattva who strives for the salvation of all beings. A more accurate but less familiar name for forms of early Buddhism is Śrāvakayāna, or the 'Vehicle of the Hearers'.

hindrances. *See* NĪVARAṆA.

Hindu. *See* HINDUISM.

Hinduism. English term denoting the mainstream religious tradition of *India which regards the ancient scriptures known as the *Vedas as ultimately authoritative. Recent scholarly usage tends to reserve the term Hinduism for the post-classical or more popular phase of the tradition, commencing around 400 BCE, and characterizes the preceding phases as the Brāhmanical (*see* BRĀHMANISM) or Vedic periods. The word Hindu is derived from the Persian term for the river Indus and its surrounding region. About 80 per cent of the approximately one billion population of India are Hindus, and there are around another 30 million living abroad. Hinduism is not a unified system of belief and practice, and should at best be regarded as a convenient shorthand for a complex social and cultural phenomenon. Those identified as Hindus do not use this term to refer to themselves or their religion, and instead speak of their beliefs as the 'eternal truth' (Skt., sanātana *dharma). Since *Buddhism originated as an offshoot of Hinduism the two share many basic beliefs about *cosmology, *karma, and *rebirth, as well as identifying the basic soteriological problem as the need to escape from the cycle of *saṃsāra. They differ in that Buddhism rejects the Hindu belief in a supreme being or cosmic power (*Brahman), a personal soul (*atman), sacrifice, and the *caste system. *See also* BRAHMANISM.

hōben. *See* UPĀYA-KASUŚALYA.

hōgen (Jap., Dharma eye). 'Enlightened vision'. Japanese term for an advanced *Ch'an or *Zen practitioner's capacity to see all phenomena for what they are in reality.

Hōgen school. The Japanese pronunciation for the Fa-yen school of Chinese *Ch'an (*see* FA-YEN WEN-I). *See also* FIVE HOUSES.

Hōjō (Jap.; Chin, fang-sheng). **1.** The practice of buying live *animals at the market and then releasing them as an act of compassion. (*karuṇā). Sometimes this is done in a ritual in which large quantities of birds and fish are bought for the purpose. The practice is widespread throughout the Buddhist world. **2.** A *samurai family that ruled *Japan as regents from 1199 to 1333, which saw the formative years of the *Zen, *Pure Land, and *Nichiren movements.

hōkyōin-darani (Jap.). One of three *dhāraṇī or formulae recited daily by esoteric practitioners (*see* ESOTERIC BUDDHISM) of the *Shingon and *Tendai schools in *Japan. It consists of 40 sentences, and is drawn from the *I-ch'ieh ju-lai-hsin mi-mi ch'üan-shen she-li pao-ch'ieh-yin t'o-lo-ni ching* (1022 in the *Taishō *canon) translated by *Amoghavajra in 746. This formula is said to have the power to release beings caught in *hell, heal the sick, and give fortune to the destitute.

homa (Skt.). The ancient Vedic (*see* VEDA) fire ritual in which offerings are burnt for the gods. The ritual was adapted in Buddhist tantra for the elimination of internal and external obstacles. Various categories of homa ritual are delineated in texts according to the chosen aim—pacifying, enriching, subduing, or destroying—and this determines the shape of the hearth to be used, the fire-wood, and the types of offerings to be burnt.

homosexuality. Buddhist sources from the earliest period contain references to homosexuality and homosexual practices. The matter is not discussed as a moral issue, however, and the subject of sexual *ethics in general receives little attention. This is largely because *Buddhism regards monastic life as the ideal and enjoins strict *celibacy upon those who follow it. Any kind of sexual activity, whether of a heterosexual or homosexual nature, is prohibited by the monastic code (*Vinaya), and there are severe penalties for those who break the rules. Sexual intercourse is the the first of the four most serious monastic offences (*pārājika-dharma), and any *monk or *nun found guilty of it faces the penalty of lifelong expulsion from the community. Rather than an ethical issue, homosexuality is treated instead as a practical matter that arises in connection with admission to the order. Certain classes of individuals were not allowed to be ordained as monks. Among these were hermaphrodites and a class of individuals known in the *Pāli *Vinaya texts as paṇḍakas, who appear to have been sexually dysfunctional passive homosexuals who were also transvestites. These were excluded on the grounds that their admission into a celibate community would be inappropriate. The question of whether homosexual acts are in some sense worse than heterosexual ones and perhaps intrinsically immoral is not pursued in the literature. However, Buddhism is generally conservative in matters of sex, and references in certain texts suggest it was regarded with disapproval by some ancient authorities. Contemporary Buddhist groups concerned with gay rights, on the other hand, argue that such comments reflect the taboos of pre-modern society and need to be reassessed in the light of more tolerant contemporary attitudes. To a large extent the arguments in Buddhism mirror the debate taking place on the issue of homosexuality within other religious traditions.

Hōnen (1133–1212). Founder of the *Jōdo Shū, or *Pure Land school, in medieval *Japan. Hōnen was born into a locally prominent family, and lost his father at an early age when a manager of nearby imperial estates raided his family lands. He was sent to the local *Tendai school temple, where his maternal uncle was the priest, for safekeeping, but he took to monastic life and spent many years practising and studying in various places, finally receiving full *ordination in 1147 on Mt. *Hiei. He eventually became quite well-known for his scholarship, sincerity, and strict morality. Dissatisfied with the corruptions of life on Mt. Hiei, he retired to Mt. Kurodani, long known as a centre of *nembutsu practice. He remained there for 20 years. During this time, he remained doubtful that his own accomplishments were enough to guarantee liberation, and he searched the scriptures for other ways of practice more suited to his capacities. In 1175 he found the inspiration he sought in *Shan-tao's *Commentary on the Meditation Sūtra*, which advised keeping the name of the *Buddha *Amitābha in mind at all times to guarantee *rebirth in the Pure Land.

From then on, Hōnen advocated this practice of reciting the *Buddha's name aloud for extended periods and keeping it fixed in one's mind at all times. He took the further step of proclaiming this practice the only one that could be effective in the troubled times of *mappō, or the declining period of *Buddhism. He himself was very discreet in his teaching, but some of his disciples began causing trouble by either proclaiming loudly that all other practices were ineffective, arousing the ire of the established schools, or proclaiming that Amitābha Buddha's compassion (*karuṇā) and 'other-power' (*tariki) were effective in themselves for salvation, thus rendering morality nugatory. Accusations of troublemaking and antinomian behaviour ensued, and Hōnen found himself under attack. His own irreproachable conduct and willingness to engage in other practices, such as monastic ordinations and esoteric rituals (*see* ESOTERIC BUDDHISM), protected him for a time, but in 1206 two of his disciples passed the night in the ladies' quarters of the emperor's palace, giving rise to rumours of sexual improprieties against the emperor himself. Four of Hōnen's disciples were executed, and Hōnen himself was banished to Shikoku and forced to return to lay life. Even though he was pardoned soon thereafter, he was prevented from re-entering the capital until just before his death in 1212. After his death, clerics outside his immediate circle of disciples discovered that he had compiled an anthology of scriptural passages defending the exclusive use of the oral nembutsu as the only practice suited to the times, and they moved to have copies confiscated and the wood printing blocks burnt. As the nascent Jōdo Shū gained strength his reputation was rehabilitated, and he is today honoured as the founder of the first independent Pure Land school.

hongaku (Jap.). A term meaning 'original' or 'innate *enlightenment'. The concept originated in *The Awakening of Faith (see* MAHĀYĀNA-ŚRADDHOTPĀDA-ŚĀSTRA), where it referred to the inherently enlightened and *luminous mind that all beings possessed, and was opposed to '*acquired enlightenment', or the practices that led to the gradual realization of the endowment that the practitioner had all along. In the Japanese *Tendai school and the schools that branched off from it in the *Kamakura period (*Zen, *Pure Land, and *Nichiren), this basic idea was developed in a number of ways that allowed for many ways of understanding the relationship between the absolute and the contingent.

Honganji. The headquarters temple of the *Jōdo Shinshū in *Japan, located in the Kyoto area. This establishment was originally not a temple at all, but the mausoleum containing the ashes of the founder of Jōdo Shinshū, *Shinran (1173–1262), constructed in 1272 by his daughter *Kakushinni in the Ōtani area outside Kyoto. During the two centuries following his death, many branches of the highly decentralized Jōdo Shinshū rose to prominence, often in competition with one another. Shinran's descendants, seeking to consolidate their influence over the school, played on the mausoleum's potential as a *pilgrimage site and focal point of a cult of the founder. During this time, they rechristened the building as a temple, and installed an image of *Amitābha *Buddha, later erecting a separate building to house it. At the same time, they sponsored the publication and distribution of Shinran's works, and made the temple a centre of Jōdo Shinshū study. Under Shinran's eighth-generation descendant, *Rennyo (1415–99), the temple reached a position of prominence, but this led monk-soldiers (*sōhei) from Mt. *Hiei to attack the buildings and level them in 1465. Ten years later, the temple was rebuilt on another site in the Yamashina area of Kyoto, where it resumed its growth. This structure was destroyed in another attack in 1532, and the tenth-generation caretaker, Shōnyo, moved to an Osaka branch of the Honganji built earlier by Rennyo and established it as the Honganji proper. In 1559, Kennyo was granted the title 'abbot' by the emperor. However, the warrior Oda Nobunaga, in his drive to quell the political power of the larger temples, attacked the Osaka temple, subduing it in 1580. Oda's successor, Toyotomi Hideyoshi, granted Kennyo land back in the Horikawa suburb of Kyoto, and another Honganji was erected and remains to this day. However, Kennyo's son Kyōnyo had refused to submit to Oda when the Osaka Honganji surrendered, and he made separate arrangements with Toyotomi's successors to construct a rival Honganji within the Kyoto city limits with himself as abbot. This came to be known as the Higashi-, or Eastern Honganji, while the Horikawa temple came to be known as the Nishi-, or Western Honganji. The split was finalized in 1619 when the government recognized both temples as independent entities.

honji-suijaku (Jap.). Term meaning 'original nature and provisional manifestation', and denoting a way of relating the *Buddhas and *Bodhisattvas of *Buddhism to the *kami, or divinities, of the native *Shintō religion. This theory, which held sway from the earliest period of Buddhism in *Japan until the *Meiji Restoration of 1868, maintained that

Buddhas and Bodhisattvas were the 'true' image or nature of the spiritual beings to whom the people prayed, while the kami were localized, provisional manifestations of these same beings. The intent may have been to valorize the kami within a Buddhist framework, but this theory ultimately derogated the kami as mere expedients, and thus caused dissatisfaction among Shintō priestly families and intellectuals.

honshi (Jap.). A Japanese Buddhist honorific meaning 'original teacher', it is used to refer either to *Śākyamuni *Buddha or to the founder of a particular school or lineage.

Horner, Isaline Blew (1896–1981). British scholar of *Pāli *Buddhism and President of the *Pali Text Society from 1949 until her death. She was also vice-president of the *Buddhist Society. A Fellow and Librarian of Newnham College, Cambridge, she edited and translated many Buddhist texts, including the *Vinaya Piṭaka, the *Majjhima Nikāya, and **Milindapañha*.

ho-shang. A Chinese term of respect for a senior *monk.

ho-shang Mo-ho-yen. *See* HVASHANG MAHĀYĀNA.

hossen (Jap.). Term used in *Zen *Buddhism to describe an encounter or exchange between two practitioners as a means of expressing and deepening their understanding of the nature of reality. The exchange may be verbal or involve gestures or movements, or a combination of all three. The exchange is not a philosophical *debate so much as a manifestation or disclosure of each individual's intuitive apprehension of religious truth. The activity shares certain similarities with the practice of *mondo.

Hossō. One of the *Six Schools of *Nara *Buddhism in *Japan, this school consisted of scholar-monks whose primary concern was the texts and doctrines of the *Fa-hsiang school of *China (of which Hossō is the Japanese pronunciation). Their philosophy was also known as yuishiki, or 'consciousness-only', because of its fundamental belief that all of reality, including both the objective world and the subjective mind that regards it, are but evolutions of consciousness according to *karma. The school was transmitted to Japan by Japanese clerics who studied in China with Fa-hsiang masters such as *Hsüan-tsang and K'uei-chi, and became one of the most powerful of the six Nara schools. *See also* CITTA-MĀTRA; YOGĀCĀRA; VIJÑAPTI-MĀTRA.

Hōtei (Jap.). Japanese pronunciation of Chinese *Pu-tai, the name of the *Buddha *Maitreya.

ho trai. Thai term for a scripture library.

Ho-tse Shen-hui (670–762 CE). A Chinese *Ch'an *monk who is historically credited with instigating the *Northern–Southern School controversy. He had been a disciple of the fifth *patriarch *Hung-jen (601–74) towards the end of the latter's life, and may have later studied with Hung-jen's most successful disciple *Shen-hsiu (605–706). However, in 732, concerned with a trend toward the position of *gradual enlightenment in the 'northern' Ch'an movement, he ascended a platform at the Ta-yun Temple near *Lo-yang in 732 and delivered a scathing critique of Shen-hsiu (by that time long dead) and his followers, whom Shen-hui called the '*Northern School'. He advocated the adoption of the position of *sudden enlightenment, which he claimed had been carried on in the south by another of Hung-jen's disciples, *Hui-neng (638–713), with whom he had studied after leaving Shen-hsiu. At first, Ho-tse Shen-hui attracted scant attention, but he kept up his attacks from his base at the Ho-tse Temple. By 745 he achieved more fame and followers, but in 753 he aroused the wrath of powerful government officials, and was banished. Later, however, the An Lu-shan rebellion broke out along the northern tier of provinces, and the *T'ang dynasty government needed to raise revenue very quickly to finance the military campaigns needed to quell it. At this time, Shen-hui demonstrated a great talent for inducing people to seek *ordination, for which they needed *ordination certificates from the government. By charging a fee for these certificates, which carried with them an exemption from further taxation and military service, the government was able, with Shen-hui's help, to raise the capital needed to defend the dynasty and retake the fallen capital. He was rewarded with a temple of his own near the capital and imperial patronage; ironically, he had criticized Shen-hsiu for receiving these very things, claiming that the master had sold out the true *Dharma for 30 pieces of silver. During the more settled and prosperous final years of his life, he took in many students and perpetuated what came to be called the 'Ho-tse School' or '*Southern School', but backed away from the extreme, non-dualistic position of sudden enlightenment and taught instead a more nuanced approach that acknowledged the need for some preparation and practice leading up to the enlightenment experience.

Hsiang-lin Ch'en-yüan (908–87). A *Ch'an *monk of the House of Yün-men (*see* FIVE HOUSES) who appears in the *kōan, case number 17, in the **Blue Cliff Records* (Chin., *Pi-yen lu*). According to this case, a student asked Hsiang-lin 'Why did *Bodhidharma come from the west?' to which Hsiang-lin replied, 'To exhaust himself with long sitting.'

Hsiang-yen Chih-hsien (d. 898). A famous *Ch'an master of the House of Kuei-yang (*see* FIVE HOUSES) to whom the following story is attributed. A man, hanging high in a tree by only his teeth, is asked why *Bodhidharma came from the west. What should the man say? This story, and the question it poses to the listener, became a *kōan in the collection known as the **Gateless Gate*.

Hsi-hsia. *See* TANGUT.

Hsin-hsing (540–94). A Chinese *monk who established the School of the Three Stages (Chin., *San-chieh-chiao).

Hsüan-sha Shih-pei (835–908). An influential *Ch'an *monk of the *T'ang dynasty period, whose fellow disciple under *Hsüeh-feng I-ts'un (822–908), *Yün-men Wen-yen (864–949), established the Yün-men House of Ch'an, and whose second-generation disciple, *Fa-yen Wen-i (885–958) founded the Fa-yen House (*See* FIVE HOUSES). A record of his *Dharma-talks in three fascicles was published in 1080, and a re-edited version was published again in 1626.

Hsüan-tsang (596–664). A Chinese *monk who travelled in *India for seventeen years collecting scriptures and studying languages. The second of the great translators after *Kumārajīva, Hsüan-tsang left for India without government leave in 629, primarily to pursue an interest in *Vijñānavāda or 'consciousness-only' philosophy. He returned in 645, bringing many texts and gifts from famous Indian monasteries and kings. The emperor questioned him for many days about his travels, and offered him an official post, which Hsüan-tsang refused. He dedicated the remainder of his life to translating the texts he brought back. Because his output was so extensive (73 items in all) and of such high quality, and because he retranslated many texts that already existed in Chinese using new vocabulary of his own devising as translation equivalents, his activity is held to mark the transition from the 'old translation' period (dominated by Kumārajīva's work) to the 'new translation period'. In addition to his translations, Hsüan-tsang also published a travelogue called *The Record of Western Lands of the Great T'ang* [Dynasty] (*Ta T'ang hsi-yü chi*, 2087 in the *Taishō *canon), which has proved an invaluable source for Indian history. This work also became the basis for the Chinese literary classic, *The Journey to the West*.

Hsüeh-feng I-ts'un (822–908). A prominent *Ch'an master of the *T'ang dynasty period, who was a student of the illustrious master *Te-shan Hsüan-chien (782–865). His *Dharma-lineage was later to include both *Yün-men Wen-yen (864–949), who established the Yün-men House of Ch'an, and *Fa-yen Wen-i (885–958), who founded the Fa-yen House (*See* FIVE HOUSES). His name derives from the temple he himself established on Elephant Bone Mountain in Fu-chou, where the snows came early each year, giving it the name 'Snowy Peak' (Chin., hsüeh feng). Beginning as a simple thatched hermitage in 870, under his charismatic leadership it eventually evolved into a large temple, and Hsüeh-feng is said to have accumulated over 1,500 lay and monastic disciples.

Hsüeh-tou Ch'ung-hsien (980–1052). A prominent *Ch'an *monk of the Sung dynasty period who belonged to the House of Yün-men (*see* FIVE HOUSES) and authored the 100 short verses of the **Blue Cliff Records* along with other collections of poetry.

Hsü-yün (1840–1959). *Ch'an *monk and modern revitalizer of Chinese *Buddhism. Hsu-yün ('empty cloud') was known for his rigorous practice, his warm preaching, his encounters with the *Bodhisattva *Mañjuśrī while on *pilgrimage, his austere and simple lifestyle, his uncompromising adherence to Buddhist morality, and his remarkable longevity. Many Buddhists in *China rank him as one of the 'four great reformers' of the modern period, along with the modernizer *T'ai-hsü (1890–1947), the *Vinaya master Hung-yi (1880–1942), and the *Pure Land revitalizer *Yin-kuang (1861–1940).

htī. Burmese term for the umbrella-like decorated top of a *stūpa.

Huai-kan (7th c. CE). A Chinese *Pure Land *monk who was active during the *T'ang dynasty (618–907). He resided in the capital city of *Ch'ang-an, and early in his career specialized in 'consciousness-only' (*citta-mātra) thought and monastic disciplinary studies. He became quite proud of his attainments, and disdained the faith (*śraddhā)-based practice of *Nien-fo, or invocation of the name of the *Buddha *Amitābha. However, when he met the monk *Shan-tao (613–81), the latter impressed him with his combination of both learning and piety, and he converted to the school Pure Land. At first he attempted practising austerities in order to gain a vision of Amitābha, but after three weeks with no success, he lamented that his past guilt was simply too great, and resolved to fast to death. Shan-tao dissuaded him, and after three more years of effort, Huai-kan finally attained a vision of Amitābha with golden skin and jade hair, and after further efforts achieved the Nien-fo *samādhi (trance). He is best remembered for the highly influential apologetic work *Shih ching-t'u ch'ün-yi lun* (Treatise Explaining the Mass of Doubts about the Pure Land), even though he died before its completion.

Huang-lung Hui-nan (1002–69). A *Ch'an master of the *Lin-chi school in the early Sung dynasty period. His line, along with the line of Yang-ch'i Fang-hui (992–1049) constituted the two major lineages of Lin-chi Ch'an during the Sung; however, Huang-lung's line died out before the end of the Sung. It was Huang-lung's Ch'an that Japanese *Rinzai founder *Eisai (1141–1215) brought to *Japan.

Huang-po Hsi-yün (d. 850). A well-known *Ch'an figure of the late *T'ang dynasty period, and the teacher of *Lin-chi I-hsüan (d. 866), the founder of the *Lin-chi line of Ch'an.

Hua-yen. One of the major schools of Chinese *Buddhism, whose highly abstract philosophy is generally accepted as the highest expression of Buddhist thought in *China. Two aspects of this school's teachings are notable: doctrinal classification and the theory of unobstructed interpenetration of all phenomena.

History

The school derives its name from the scripture that forms its primary object of study, the **Avataṃsaka Sūtra* (Chin., **Hua-yen ching*), a text notable for its effort to describe the way the world appears to an enlightened *Buddha. Indeed, the *sūtra was said to have been preached by *Śākyamuni directly after his attainment of enlightenment (*bodhi). The scripture had been known and studied in China at least since the year 420, when *Buddhabhadra completed the first translation in 60 fascicles. A group of scholars around *Tu-shun (557–640) were attracted to the 'Chapter on the Bodhisattva Grounds' in the eighth fascicle of this translation. Consequently, they were called the **Ti-lun* ('discourse on the grounds') school, and this is commonly taken as a forerunner of the Hua-yen school itself. Tu-shun's disciple *Chih-yen (602–68) also specialized in study and preaching the sūtra. However, credit for the foundation of the Hua-yen school proper goes to Chih-yen's disciple *Fa-tsang (643–712; also called Hsien-shou), although, in deference to his illustrious predecessors, he is listed as the school's third *patriarch. Fa-tsang, perhaps because of his central Asian ancestry, had some facility with Indian languages, and so was called to the capital *Ch'ang-an to work in *Hsüan-tsang's translation bureau. He broke with the latter, and later was asked by Empress Wu Tse-t'ien to assist the Indian *monk Śikṣānanda with a new translation of the *Avataṃsaka*, which came out in 704 and consisted of 80 fascicles. However, it was not Fa-tsang's skill as a translator, but his facility in expounding the abstruse philosophy of the sūtra in accessible language and appealing metaphors that helped attract imperial patronage and consolidated the school's position.

After Fa-tsang, the line of patriarchs continued with *Ch'eng-kuan (738–820 or 838).

Also versed in Indian languages, Ch'eng-kuan assisted the monk *Prajñā to produce a 40-fascicle version of the last section of the sūtra, the **Gaṇḍavyūha*, which added new material to the end and helped bring the sūtra to a more satisfying conclusion. In addition, Ch'eng-kuan's teaching activities and his prolific commentaries on the sūtra further established the school on a secure basis.

The fifth and last patriarch was *Tsung-mi (780–841), who was also acknowledged as a master in the *Ch'an school. Like his two predecessors, he achieved great eminence for his learning and teaching, and served in the imperial court, assuring continued patronage. However, four years after his death, the next emperor instigated the most wide-ranging persecution of Buddhism in China prior to the Cultural Revolution in the 20th century, and this school, dependent as it was on royal patronage for maintenance of its academic facilities and the upkeep of its masters, perished at that time.

Doctrine

Before the foundation of the *Hua-yen school, *Chih-i (538–97), founder of the *T'ien-t'ai school, had already established criteria for taking the highly varied corpus of Buddhist texts and teachings and placing them into an overall structure that brought order and explained discrepancies (*see* P'AN-CHIAO). However, his system had developed some deficiencies: it used three different criteria to generate three different schemes, and it failed to take into account the teachings of the *Fa-hsiang school, which had not been established until after Chih-i's death.

Fa-tsang therefore constructed a Hua-yen scheme of doctrinal classification, or p'an-chiao, in order to correct these problems. He established a single hierarchy of teachings that included Fa-hsiang in the following list. (1) The doctrine of the *Hīnayāna, which was lowest because it recognized only the lack of selfhood in living beings, but not in other phenomena, and also because it lacked compassion for others and set as its goal only the liberation of the individual. (2) The elementary *Mahāyāna recognized the lack of selfhood in both beings and phenomena, but it still lacked compassion because it failed to discern *Buddha-nature in all beings, and thus taught that some beings could never attain Buddhahood. This was the level in which Fa-tsang placed the Fa-hsiang school, because of its teaching on the eternal entrapment of the *icchantikas due to their lack of the seeds of Buddhahood. (3) The advanced Mahāyāna covered the doctrines of the T'ien-t'ai school, which recognized the *emptiness of both beings and phenomena, acknowledged the universality of *Buddha-nature and thus the potential of all beings to become Buddhas, and its teachings of the *Three Truths reaffirmed the provisional existence of things even as it taught their ultimate emptiness. (4) The Sudden Teaching covered texts and schools that inculcated the experience of *sudden enlightenment, which appeared at once without prior doctrinal or scriptural study. This included the **Vimalakīrti-nirdeśa Sūtra* and the Ch'an school. (5) The Perfect (or Round) Teaching, as found in the *Avataṃsaka Sūtra* affirmed the perfect interfusion of all phenomena within the *One Mind and within each other, and the simultaneity of past, present, and future. This doctrine revealed completely the content of the enlightened mind.

The Hua-yen school considered its great advance over the achievements of the T'ien-t'ai school to be found in its teaching of perfect interpenetration. This school had already shown that all particular phenomena subsist completely in the unity of the absolute or One Mind, and that the latter was not to be found apart from or transcending particular phenomena. Thus it taught the perfect interpenetration of the absolute, called 'principle', and phenomena. Fa-tsang went further and, following the sūtra, asserted the perfect interpenetration of all phenomena with each other. To illustrate this, he resorted to many images and metaphors to make his meaning clear. One was the parable of Indra's net, which described the world in terms of the fishing net of the Hindu god *Indra. At each node of the net was a jewel, and each jewel reflected the light of every other jewel perfectly, thus causing its own light to be part of their light and accepting their light as part of its own. He also used the example of a house and one of its rafters as metaphors for the whole and the parts, or principle and phenomena. The rafter is part of the house, and since a house is nothing other than its parts, and the parts cannot be parts unless they are integrated into the whole, the house and the rafter create each other. This would be the T'ien-t'ai view of the interpenetration of principle and phenomena. However, since the house does not exist apart from its parts, the rafter then depends upon all the other parts of the house being in place for the house to exist and give it its meaning as a rafter. Furthermore, based on the axiom that any change in a thing makes it an unrelatedly different thing, Fa-tsang asserted that if the rafter were removed and another one put in its place, the house would then be a different house, and all its other parts would then undergo a complete change of state from being part of one house to being part of another. Thus, the rafter (or any individual part) totally determines the being of all other parts. In this way, Fa-tsang demonstrated that every particular phenomenon in the cosmos exercises a complete and determinative role in the being of all other particular phenomena, and in turn has its own being completely determined by all other particular phenomena. In such a manner, it was thought, all phenomena interfuse without obstruction. *See also* KEGON.

Hua-yen ching **(also *Hua-yen Sūtra*).** The Chinese name for the **Avataṃsaka Sūtra*.

***Hua-yen Sūtra*.** *See* HUA-YEN CHING.

Hui-ch'ang persecution. Initiated in 845 by Emperor *Wu-tsung of the *T'ang dynasty, this was the third and, prior to the Cultural Revolution, the most catastrophic persecution of *Buddhism in Chinese history. After many years of anti-Buddhist policies, the emperor decreed an unconditional proscription on Buddhism in the fourth month of 845, with the result that most temples and monasteries were destroyed, *monks and *nuns forcibly returned to lay life, foreign monks expelled, metal Buddha images recast as coins, and monastic properties confiscated. These measures remained in effect until the following year, when Wu-tsung died and was succeeded by a new emperor who was much more sympathetic to Buddhism. Many scholars think this event marked the end of Buddhism's golden age in *China: the loss of so many academic, material, and human resources sounded the death knell for such intellectual traditions as *T'ien-t'ai, *Hua-yen, and *Fa-hsiang, and left the field solely to the *Ch'an and *Pure Land traditions. These two, not needing the same kind of infrastructure and support as the others, were able to carry on and became the predominant forms of Buddhism in China thereafter.

Hui-k'o (487–593). A disciple of the Indian *Ch'an *monk *Bodhidharma and the one traditionally recognized as the second *patriarch of the Ch'an tradition in *China. He is renowned for his dedication and perseverance: when he first approached Bodhidharma for teaching, the latter ignored him and carried on with his own meditation. After standing patiently in the snow for several days, Hui-k'o finally cut off his own arm and offered it to Bodhidharma as a token of his earnestness (although other sources say his arm was cut off by bandits earlier).

Hui-neng (638–713). An early *Ch'an *monk who, while historically obscure, is honoured as the sixth *patriarch, the fountainhead of the so-called '*Southern School' of Ch'an, and the main character in the classic *The *Platform Sūtra of the Sixth Patriarch* (Chin., *Liu-tsu t'an ching*, 2007, 2008, in the *Taishō *canon). From a historical perspective, not much is known about Hui-neng. His name appears on lists of the '*ten great disciples' of the fifth Ch'an patriarch *Hung-jen (601–74). Other than this, sources vary widely as to the details of his life and teaching, rendering a true biography difficult to construct. Whatever the bare facts of his life may have been, he is more important within the tradition as the figure who carried on the true teaching and practice of '*sudden enlightenment'. In the *Platform Sūtra*, there is a famous episode where Hui-neng, represented as an illiterate, unordained temple worker, bests *Hung-jen's senior disciple *Shen-hsiu (606–706) in a poetry contest that Hung-jen had arranged in order to see whose *enlightenment was most profound and would thus merit designation as his own successor and sixth patriarch. Shen-hsiu's verse, which speaks of the need to wipe away the dust (representing defilements) that accumulates on the mirror (the mind), is taken as a statement of the '*gradual enlightenment' position, while Hui-neng's, dictated to a monk and written on a wall, speaks of the ultimate non-existence of both mind and defilements, a view more compatible with the position of '*sudden enlightenment'. In the end, due largely to the efforts of his disciple *Shen-hui (670–762) championing his cause, the 'sudden enlightenment' position came to dominate Ch'an, and the stories of Hui-neng transmitted through the *Platform Sūtra* and other sources attained quasi-scriptural status. In time, every Ch'an monk came to trace his or her *Dharma-lineage back to Hui-neng, giving him the status of *paterfamilias* or common ancestor within all subsequent Ch'an schools. Hui-neng himself is said to have returned to south *China after his training with Hung-jen at his East Mountain Monastery, was finally ordained a monk, and eventually settled in the Ts'ao-hsi Temple in his hometown of Hsin-chou. To this day a body coated in red lacquer is kept there that is said to be Hui-neng's.

Hui-ssu (515–77). The second *patriarch of the *T'ien-t'ai school of *Buddhism in *China, known mainly for his devotion to the **Lotus Sūtra* and for being the master of *Chih-i (538–97) the *de facto* founder of the school,

Hui-wen (fl. 550). The first *patriarch of the *T'ien-t'ai school of *Buddhism in *China. Almost nothing is known of him, except that he was the teacher of *Hui-ssu (515–77), who in turn was the master of the *de facto* founder of the school, *Chih-i (538–97).

human rights. In recent times Buddhism has had to face a range of human rights problems in different parts of the world, notably in *Tibet, *Sri Lanka, and *Burma. In common with most Asian traditions, however, *Buddhism has never formulated an explicit doctrine of human rights. The concept of human rights is Western in nature and has its intellectual origins in the Enlightenment, and it is unclear to what extent the concept is compatible with traditional Buddhist teachings. Some Buddhists feel that a strong emphasis on individual rights runs counter to the doctrine of no self (*anātman), and that rather than mimic the West Buddhism should evolve a distinctive approach grounded in compassion (*karuṇā) and interrelatedness (*see* PRATĪTYA-SAMUTPĀDA) rather than in a belief in the inviolable status of the individual. Others, such as the present *Dalai Lama, seem to feel that the discourse of human rights is in harmony with the moral values of traditional Buddhism and provides a useful vocabulary for expressing Buddhist views on contemporary political and social issues.

Humphreys, Travers Christmas (1901–83). A pioneer of *Buddhism in England, Humphreys converted to the religion in his late teens and later became a barrister and High Court judge. He founded the Buddhist Lodge of the *Theosophical Society in 1924, which later changed its name to the *Buddhist Society in 1943. *See also* BRITAIN.

Hung-chih Cheng-chüeh (1091–1157). A *monk of the Ts'ao-tung (Jap., Sōtō) line of *Ch'an, known as the author of a collection of poetry and *kōans, and the founder of the 'Hung-chih' line within the *Ts'ao-tung school, and as an avid proponent of the 'silent illumination' (Chin., *mo-chao Ch'an) style of meditation.

Hung-chou school. A line of Chinese *Ch'an established by *Ma-tsu Tao-i (709–88) named after Hung-chou, the site of Ma-tsu's home temple in what is now southern Kiang-hsi province. This school laid emphasis on seeing *Buddha-nature (ultimate reality and the potential to achieve Buddhahood) in everyday activities and objects. In this way it sought to steer a middle course between the teachings of its two main contemporary rivals, the *Northern School (which emphasized the delusiveness of everyday activities and things) and the *Oxhead school (which taught that all things were like a dream). Later, this line came to be seen as the main trunk of the Ch'an school, and the others as collateral lines.

Hung-jen (601–74). An early *Ch'an *monk revered as the fifth Chinese *patriarch of the line established by the first patriarch *Bodhidharma. He was the head of a large monastic community on Tung Shan (East Mountain) first established by the fourth patriarch *Tao-hsin (580–651). Little is known of his life, his teachings, or his style of practice, although a manuscript found at *Tun-huang is attributed to him. If this attribution is correct, then it shows a man devoted to the teachings of the **Laṅkāvatāra Sūtra* whose practice concentrated on preserving the original purity and clarity of the mind using methods derived from the *Pure Land-oriented *Meditation Sūtra*. He is also traditionally remembered as the last patriarch of a unified school of Ch'an, since in the next generation his disciples *Shen-hsiu (606–706) and *Hui-neng (638–713), based on the positions of *gradual and *sudden enlightenment, established the *Northern School and *Southern School respectively (whether this account is historically accurate is highly disputed).

hungry ghosts. *See* PRETA.

Hvashang Mahāyāna. Tibetan version of the name of the the leading Chinese teacher of a form of *Ch'an, Ho-shang Mo-ho-yen, who was active in *Tibet during the reign of Trisong Detsen. He was an advocate of the '*sudden enlightenment' position, which brought him into conflict with the predominant Indian '*gradual enlightenment' perspective. His views were defeated at the *Council of Lhasa by *Kamalaśīla and thereafter the influence of Ch'an in Tibet was eclipsed.

Hyujŏng. *See* SŌSAN TAESA.

I

icchantika (Skt.). A being who, according to some *Mahāyāna texts, is lacking in *Buddha-nature or the potential for enlightenment (*bodhi). This view was controversial since it implied that some beings would never become free from *saṃsāra and was generally reinterpreted in later Mahāyāna traditions when it was thought that even such beings would eventually be redeemed through the intervention of *Buddhas or *Bodhisattvas. *See also* FA-HSIANG; FA-TSANG; HUA-YEN; TAO-SHENG; NIRVĀṆA SCHOOL; *NIRVĀṆA SŪTRA*.

ichiji-fusetsu (Jap.; Chin., yi tzu pu shuo). A Japanese phrase meaning 'not a word is preached'. This indicates the ineffable quality of a *Buddha's awakening, which ultimately cannot be put into words, and indicates that, for many schools of *Buddhism in east Asia, the words into which the teachings are put ought not to be confused with the experience of awakening or enlightenment (*bodhi) itself. Buddhas can communicate the full extent of their realization without resorting to words only to other Buddhas.

ichimi-Zen. A Japanese term meaning 'one-flavour *Zen', referring to pure Zen practice, unmixed with other practices.

ichinengi (Jap.). The 'doctrine of single recitation (of the *nembutsu)', as opposed to the 'doctrine of multiple recitations' (tanengi). After *Hōnen's *death, a dispute broke out among his disciples regarding the way in which the practice of the nembutsu effected *rebirth in the *Pure Land. Those advocating ichinengi held that one calling of *Amitābha's name was sufficient, because the *Buddha would honour every request for salvation and rebirth out of his compassion (*karuṇā). Those who held the tanengi position claimed that repeated chanting of Amitābha's name would purify the mind and make it more fit for rebirth. Thus, the issue related closely with the problem of 'self-power' (*jiriki) versus 'other-power' (*tariki), that is, whether the devotee had any part to play in the attainment of rebirth in the Pure Land, or whether the matter rested entirely with the power of the Buddha.

I-ching (635–713). Chinese Buddhist *monk, pilgrim to *India, and translator of the *T'ang dynasty period. An admirer of earlier pilgrims such as *Fa-hsien and *Hsüan-tsang, he took the southern maritime route to India in the year 671, and remained there until 695 (with the exception of one return trip to Canton in 689 to recruit assistants). He came back with approximately 400 Buddhist scriptures and treatises, was honoured and given support by Empress Wu Tse-t'ien for his translation activities, and by the time of his death, had produced translations of 56 works in 230 fascicles. He also wrote of his experiences travelling among the archipelagos of *south-east Asia, where he had visited more than 30 kingdoms. Together with Hsüan-tsang (596–664), *Kumārajīva (343–413), and *Paramārtha (499–569), he is considered one of the 'four great translators' of Chinese *Buddhism.

ignorance. *See* AVIDYĀ.

Igyō school. Japanese pronunciation of the Kuei-yang House of Chinese *Ch'an that flourished in the late *T'ang dynasty period.

Ikeda, Daisaku (1928–). The third president (since 1960) of *Sōka Gakkai International, an organization that originally was the lay auxiliary of the *Nichiren Shōshū. Ikeda presided over the group's split from the parent organization in 1992 and oversaw its second great period of expansion following the Second World War.

ikkō ikki (Jap.). A series of peasant uprisings against the landowning classes (Jap., daimyō) in *Japan that began in the 1470s in Kaga province and spread to other regions. The religious underpinnings of these rebellions arose from *Jōdo Shinshū beliefs, in particular from its faith in the absolute power of the *Buddha *Amitābha to effect the salvation of all people regardless of their own lifestyles or abilities. This belief fostered a democratic spirit among the population by negating all differences arising from economic or social class and stressing the equality of all people. In Kaga province itself, the ikkō ikki leagues were so successful that they ousted the landed aristocrats in 1475 and ruled the province themselves for 92 years. Their allegiance to the Jōdo Shinshū organization, as well as the skilful management of the peasants and minor *samurai that participated in the movement by Jōdo Shinshū head *Rennyo (1415–99), bolstered the political power of the school's headquarters temple, the *Honganji, which effectively gained the province as its feudal domain.

Ikkyū Sōjun (1394–1481). A Japanese *Zen *monk of the *Rinzai lineage known primarily for his uncompromising rigour in Zen training and practice, balanced by his often eccentric behaviour and his ardent love late in his life for a blind female entertainer named Mori. He left no disciples to carry on his own teachings, but did leave behind some collections of verse, notably the *Crazy Cloud Anthology*.

I-kuan Tao. A syncretic folk Buddhist organization in *China whose name translates roughly as 'the Way of Unity'. Formally founded in 1928 by Chang T'ien-jan (1889–1947), it is an offshoot of the older Lo-chiao tradition that believed in a deity called the Unborn Venerable Mother (Wu-sheng Laomu), and divided human history into three epochs, during each of which the Mother sent an emissary to call an errant humankind home (in the case of I-kuan Tao, these are three successive *Buddhas, the last of whom, *Maitreya, has yet to come and effect final salvation). Thus, while incorporating elements of *Buddhism, *Taoism, *Confucianism, Christianity, and Islam, the religion has its own distinctive worldview under which these other religions are subsumed and understood.

i-k'ung (Chin.). A Chinese Buddhist term meaning 'single-emptiness'. This signifies that, despite the apparent multiplicity and diversity of individual phenomena, they still share a single, underlying nature.

impermanence. *See* ANITYA.

India. Although *Buddhism originated in India it now flourishes predominantly in other parts of Asia. Pockets of Buddhism have always existed in the northern extremities of the subcontinent in the Tibetan-influenced regions of Ladakh, *Sikkim, and *Bhutan. There has also been a limited revival of Buddhism in India in the 20th century, due partly to an influx of refugees from *Tibet, and the conversion of the so-called '*Ambedkar Buddhists' who became Buddhists in an attempt to improve their former low status as members of the untouchable *caste.

Leaving modern developments to one side, the history of Buddhism in India (used here as a geographical term for the whole of the subcontinent rather than simply the territory of the present republic) extends from the 5th century BCE to the 15th century CE, and perhaps somewhat later. Buddhism originates with the teachings of the *Buddha, who lived at the beginning of the Magadhan period (546–324 BCE) when the kingdom of *Magadha was undergoing rapid expansion. In the year of the Buddha's death the *Council of Rājagṛja compiled a *canon, and some hundred years later the *Council of Vaiśālī resolved a dispute over monastic practice, indicating the beginning of sectarianism among the originally unified community. Towards the end of the period north-west India had been colonized by Alexander the Great, and by this time Buddhist monks had established the foundations of their canonical writings and organized themselves into monastic communities. The *Mauryan period (324–187 BCE) is dominated by the figure of *Aśoka and witnessed the expansion of Buddhism throughout India under his patronage. The *Edicts of Aśoka carved on rock provide the first tangible historical evidence of Buddhism, and record that the emperor dispatched missions abroad to promote Buddhism. This period was marked by dissension among the monks, and the *schism of the *Mahāsaṃghikas split the early community into two rival parties (*see* COUNCIL OF PĀṬALIPUTRA I). The period of the Śuṅgas and Yavanas (187–30 BCE) brought mixed fortunes: in the region of the Ganges Basin Buddhism encountered hostility and persecution under Puṣyamitra Śuṅga, but this period also sees the construction of great *stūpa complexes such as those at *Sāñcī, *Bhārhut, and *Amarāvatī. In the north-west Buddhism flourished under Indo-Greek monarchs such as Menander (*see* MILINDAPAÑHA). The Śakas and Pahlavas (100 BCE–75 CE) who succeeded the Greeks in the north-west also favoured Buddhism, as did the ruler of the later *Kuṣāṇa dynasty, *Kaniṣka I, who is said to have supported Buddhism and convened the 'fourth council' in *Gandhāra (*see* COUNCIL OF KANIṢKA).

The early centuries of the Christian era saw the rise of the *Mahāyāna, a broad-based movement emphasizing inclusivity and an expanded role for the laity. The early understanding of the Buddha was reworked in the new doctrine of his 'three bodies' (*trikāya), and the figure of the *Bodhisattva came to prominence, replacing the early ideal of the *Arhat. New *sūtras, purportedly also the word of the Buddha, began to appear, notably in the Perfection of Insight literature (*see* PRAJÑĀ-PĀRAMITĀ SŪTRAS) and other profoundly influential texts such as the **Lotus Sūtra*. New philosophical schools, notably the *Madhyamaka and the *Yogācāra, arose to interpret this material, and in doing so they offered radical reinterpretations of the early teachings. A final wave of new literature known as tantras appeared around the 7th century promoting radical forms of practice, including rituals and meditation techniques for accelerating spiritual progress. This form of *tantric Buddhism became known as the 'diamond vehicle' or *Vajrayāna.

The intellectual vigour of Buddhism during this period attracted large numbers of students to monastic centres of learning. The most famous of these (at least among Mahāyānists) was *Nālandā, founded in the second century and later patronised by Kumāra Gupta I, 414–455 CE (*see* GUPTA DYNASTY). It was reputed to have been home to 10,000 students, with admission being gained through an oral exam at the main gateway. Through continuing royal patronage, such as that of King Harṣa and the rulers of the *Pāla dynasty (650–950 CE), other major centres of learning such as *Vikramaśīla and *Odantapurī also flourished. It was these institutions that produced the great generation of Indian Buddhist scholars like *Śāntarakṣita and *Kamalaśīla, who would play a vital role in the transmission of Buddhism to *Tibet.

A less fortunate consequence of the growth of monastic centres was that monks became increasingly specialized in abstruse doctrines and began to lose touch with the world outside the cloister. Although little is known about popular Buddhism in ancient India, it can be conjectured that unlike *Hinduism, which has always had roots at the village level, Buddhism became concentrated in a few key institutions of higher learning. This proved to be its undoing when Muslim raiding parties began to enter India from the 11th century. Undefended Buddhist monasteries, often containing valuable treasures, proved irresistible targets to raiders bent on booty in the name of holy war. The Turkic general Mahmud Shabuddin Ghorī sacked Nālandā in 1197 and Vikramaśīla in 1203, burning their libraries and destroying priceless literary and artistic treasures. These traumatic events effectively marked the end of the history of Buddhism in India until modern times although some limited activity continued in the south: there were Buddhist monasteries in Orissa and south India in the 15th century, and Buddhist teachers went from India to Tibet even later.

Indra (Skt.; Pāli, Inda). Indo-aryan storm god revered in the *Vedas and referred to in *Pāli sources as 'devānaṃ indo', or 'king of the gods'. He is also known as *Śākya (Pāli. Sakka).

Indrabhūti. Up to three legendary kings of this name are known from Indic and Tibetan *tantric sources. They are associated with the development or revelation of certain *anuttara-yoga-tantras and may have lived during the late 7th and early to mid-8th centuries CE in the regions of *Oḍḍiyāna or *Sahor. No independent epigraphical corroboration for their existence has been found anywhere in *India.

Indra's net. 1. Title of the first *sutta of the *Dīgha Nikāya of the *Pāli Canon (*See* BRAHMAJĀLA SUTTA). **2.** An image used by *Fa-tsang to illustrate the *Hua-yen 'teaching of totality' according to which all phenomena in the universe are interrelated. He compared the universe to a cosmic net strung with jewels such that in each jewel can be seen the reflection of all the others. To illustrate this notion he placed a statue of the *Buddha in the centre of eight mirrors located according to the major and minor cardinal points, with two additional ones above and below. When the statue was illuminated by a candle the mirrors reflected the image and each other in an infinite series. This demonstrated the Hua-yen tenet that the nature of the entire universe is contained in each particle.

indriya (Skt.; Pāli, sense-organ). The sense-organs, powers or faculties of the human individual, commonly grouped into a list of 22. These consist of (1–6) the six sense bases (*āyatana), namely the eye, ear, nose, tongue, body, mind; (7–9) three factors concerning gender, namely femininity, masculinity, and vitality; (10–14) five feelings, namely pleasant bodily feelings, painful bodily feelings, happiness, sadness, indifference; (15–19) five spiritual faculties, namely faith (*śraddhā), energy (*vīrya), mindfulness (*smṛti), meditation (*samādhi), insight (*prajñā); three *supermundane faculties, namely (20) knowing what is not yet known, which marks the attainment of the supermundane path (*ārya-mārga); (21) the highest knowledge, which marks the attainment of stream-entry (*see* ŚROTĀPANNA); (22) perfect knowledge, which marks the stage of the *Arhat.

initiation. *See* ABHIṢEKHA.

inka. Japanese term meaning the 'seal of enlightenment' or certification by a *Ch'an or *Zen master of the authenticity and depth of a student's experience of enlightenment.

intermediate state. *See* BAR-DO.

International Association of Buddhist Studies. An international organization of professional academic scholars of *Buddhism founded in 1976. The association hosts a major international conference every few years and publishes the premier journal, the *Journal of the International Association of Buddhist Studies*.

International Network of Engaged Buddhists. An international organisation founded in 1989 by the Thai activist Sulak *Sivaraksa for the promotion of world peace, the protection of the environment, and an end to economic exploitation, particularly in the developing world. The organization has an informal structure and aims to foster contacts and facilitate cooperation among interested parties. The emphasis is on a 'back to basics' approach which emphasizes the early Buddhist teachings on right livelihood as the best way to resolve the problems of the modern world.

intrinsic emptiness (Tib., rang-stong). The standard *Madhyamaka view of emptiness in contrast to the doctrine of '*extrinsic emptiness'. According to the theory of intrinsic emptiness all conventional phenomena are empty and devoid of inherent existence (*svabhāva). Accordingly, conventional phenomena and experiences are regarded as delusive fabrications of the unenlightened mind which falsely imputes existence to them.

Ippen (Yugyō Shōnin) (1239–89). Founder of the *Jishū (literally, 'time school') of Japanese *Pure Land *Buddhism. His sobriquet, Yugyō Shōnin, means 'wandering holy man', and accurately reflects his homeless lifestyle. He made it his primary practice to chant the name of *Amitābha *Buddha constantly, and to try to convert others to the practice by handing out amulets inscribed with the *nembutsu which he would encourage people to chant. Once a *monk declined this gift, saying that he had no faith in Amitābha, and that it would be hypocritical for him to chant the name. This caused a crisis in Ippen's thinking: if Amitābha were powerful enough to bring all beings to the Pure Land after their death, then could he not bring even those who had no faith? This doubt was resolved during a trip to Kumano, where a manifestation of Amitābha assured him that faith was immaterial; the Buddha's power was indeed enough to bring beings to *rebirth. After that, he continued to distribute his amulets and encourage people to recite the name even if they did not believe. Ippen travelled with a group of disciples, both male and female, and they became known for their performance of the odori nembutsu, or 'dancing nembutsu', in which he and his followers would dance while chanting Amitābha's name. Spectators frequently reported miraculous occurrences during these performances, such as the appearance of purple flower-like clouds in the sky. Because he travelled with a mixed group, Ippen was very concerned with issues of morality, and he had his followers carry a set of blocks wherever they went, with which they would construct a wall between the men and the *women at night when they slept. The Jishū remained strong for a time after Ippen's death, but by the 15th century it was eclipsed by the *Jōdo Shinshū.

Iryŏn (1206–89). A Korean *monk and writer of the *Koryŏ period known chiefly as the author of the *Samguk Yusa* (Affairs of the Three Kingdoms), a historical work that serves as one of the major primary sources on the history of Korean *Buddhism. *See also* KOREA.

I-shan I-ning (1247–1317). A Chinese *Ch'an *monk whom the Yüan dynasty government sent to *Japan as a missionary. After an initial misunderstanding in which he was imprisoned by the Japanese court as a spy, he was later recognized as a great teacher and attracted many of the brightest Buddhist clerics as his students.

ishin-denshin (Jap.; Chin., yi hsin ch'uan hsin). Term meaning 'to transmit the mind by means of the mind'. This *Zen phrase indicates the direct transmission of enlightenment (*bodhi) from one mind to another, without resorting to verbal or written teachings. Through this transmission the student directly intuits the master's meaning.

Isigili. One of the five hills around *Rājagṛha (*see also* *GṚDHRAKŪṬA) in the modern state of Bihar in *India. Famed for its natural beauty, Isigili was a favourite residence of the *Buddha and his *monks as well as other *ascetic groups like the Jains (*see* JAINISM).

Isipatana. An open area near *Vārāṇasī on the Ganges and site of the *Deer Park where the *Buddha delivered his *first sermon.

isshi injō (Jap.). Within Japanese *Sōtō *Zen this indicates the custom of receiving certification of one's enlightenment (*bodhi) from only one master, whose lineage one then inherits. One may not subsequently seek authentication from other masters.

isshin. *See* ONE MIND.

Itivuttaka (Pāli, 'so it has been said'). Fourth book of the *Khuddaka Nikāya of the *Sūtra Piṭaka of the *Pāli Canon. It consists of 112 short discourses written in a mixture of prose and verse. It has been argued that the *Itivuttaka* was compiled as a result of a critical study of the authentic teachings of the *Buddha, considered in a certain light and made for a specific purpose. Each one of the discourses begins with the same words meaning 'So spoke the Buddha'. The discourses were preached by the Buddha to Khujjutarā, a woman lay disciple, who then repeated them and prefaced each of them with the above sentence in order to emphasize that she was reporting the Buddha's words. The commentary to the *Itivuttaka*, compiled by *Dhammapāla, possibly in the 6th century, is part of the **Paramatthadīpanī*.

I-tsing. *See* I-CHING.

J

Jainism. A non-orthodox Indian religious movement similar in some respects to *Buddhism but differing on important matters of doctrine, of which the belief in an eternal soul (jīva) is one of the most fundamental. The movement takes its name from the title of its leaders known as *Jinas (Skt., victors) or 'ford makers' (Skt., tīrthaṅkaras), of whom there are said to be 24. The last of these, *Mahāvīra, was a contemporary of the *Buddha and is mentioned in early sources as one of the *Six Sectarian Teachers. Jain monks follow a strict moral code and apply the principle of non-violence (*ahiṃsā) scrupulously, even respecting the lives of insects.

Jakumetsu (fl. *c.*1235). A Japanese *monk who was involved in the opening of the tomb of the renowned *Nara period monk *Gyōgi (668–749) and the discovery of the latter's epitaph. This was subsequently sent on to the capital and has become an important documentary source for the study of Nara *Buddhism.

Jakushitsu Genkō (1290–1367). An influential *Rinzai *Zen *monk of the medieval period in *Japan. After a period of initial study with famous Chinese masters in Japan, he travelled in *China from 1320 to 1326 and studied with other eminent monks, most notably with Chung-feng Ming-pen (1263–1323) of the Yüan-wu lineage of *Lin-chi. Returning to Japan, he then lived an itinerant lifestyle until his last five years, when he settled in the Eigenji in Ōmi, a temple constructed especially for him by a local landlord. He is noted for his warmth, his detachment from all worldly enticements, his flute-playing, and his poems, which are held to be some of the finest examples of Zen poetry.

Jambudvīpa (Pāli, Jambudīpa). 'The island of the Jambu tree'. Name of the southernmost of the four great continents of traditional Buddhist mythology, corresponding to the known world at the time and most probably to be identified with the Indian subcontinent and south-east Asia (especially when contrasted with *Tambapaṇṇi-dīpa, or the island of *Sri Lanka). The Jambu tree, from which the continent takes its name, is a vast tree thought to be located in the *Himalayan region. *Buddhas and Universal Rulers (*cakravartin) are said to arise only on this continent.

Jamgön Kongtrül (1813–99) (Tib., 'Jam-mgon kong-sprul). One of the great scholar-monks from eastern *Tibet associated with the so-called *Eclectic Movement which ushered in a period of religious and intellectual revival in 19th-century Tibet. He received *ordination in both the *Nyingma and *Kagyü schools and also many transmissions and instructions from the other schools. He was a prolific writer and compiler of texts who believed that all the religious schools of Tibet including *Bön were equal in value.

japa (Skt., recitation). Recitation or recital, particularly of *mantras, for which a rosary (*mālā) of 108 beads in traditionally used.

Japan. The earliest official account of *Buddhism in Japan states that it arrived at the imperial court in 552 (or 538 according to some authorities), when a delegation from the kingdom of Paekche on the Korean peninsula brought a *Buddha image and some scriptures as gifts for the emperor. It is likely, however, that Buddhism was already known in Japan through other non-official channels. After this initial contact, the court had to decide whether allowing the practice and study of this new religion would anger the local deities or *kami, whose protection the imperial family needed in consolidating their rule over the newly centralized kingdom. During this earliest period, Buddhist texts and clergy came to Japan along with a wave of Chinese cultural imports that also included writing, political thought, urban planning, and other innovative ideas. It seems clear that the court and aristocrats understood Buddhism as a variant of their native religion, and used it primarily as a way to cure illnesses and gain supernatural support for their political and military efforts. Prince *Shōtoku (572–621), who ruled Japan as regent after the death of his father, is credited with being among the first to see Buddhist teachings as distinct from the native cults. He is thought to have composed commentaries to several scriptures, and he fostered a programme of rapid temple construction.

Scholars generally divide the subsequent history of Japanese Buddhism into periods defined by the location of the capital city. The Nara (710–94), Heian (794–1185), and Kamakura (1185–1392) periods are the most important, since these are the periods in which the main schools of Buddhism were established and took shape.

The Nara Period

During the *Nara period, Buddhist activity went in two primary directions: the clergy were busy trying to understand the doctrines found in newly imported texts, and the government put Buddhist rituals and organizations to work for the welfare of the state. As to the first of these tasks, the so-called '*Six Schools of *Nara Buddhism' comprised groups of clergy who concentrated on the texts and thought of six different Chinese schools. Almost all of the scholar-monks who engaged in these studies lived in the capital under government auspices and were housed in the main temple there, the *Tōji. Outside of this government-sponsored establishment, a few self-ordained practitioners left society and lived in the mountains performing austeries and magical services for ordinary citizens. In addition to the scholarly activity in the capital, the primary activity of clergy was to perform rituals on behalf of a paid clientele that came almost entirely from the imperial family and the aristocracy.

The Heian Period

This saw a movement of Buddhism away from government centres and out among the people, although this movement fell far short of a full-scale popularization of the religion. During this time both *Saichō (767–822) and *Kūkai (774–835) journeyed to *China to deepen their knowledge of Buddhism. Saichō went to Mt. T'ien-t'ai to study *T'ien-t'ai doctrines, but while waiting for a ship to take him home, he encountered a *monk who practised esoteric rituals. After a short period of training and the conferral of the proper initiation, he returned to Japan and settled on Mt. *Hiei, where he established the *Tendai school to be a successor to the Chinese T'ien-t'ai school. However, because the real patronage came from the performance of esoteric rituals (*see* ESOTERIC BUDDHISM), he divided this new school's focus between the exoteric doctrines of T'ien-t'ai and esoteric ritual performance. In addition, he made a crucial move to establish the Tendai school independently from the government-controlled monastic establishment in Nara when he asked for permission to ordain his own monks on Mt. Hiei using only the *Mahāyāna *precepts of the **Brahmajāla Sūtra* (Jap., *Bonmōkyō*). Permission was granted after his death, and the Tendai school was thus freed from the necessity of submitting its monks to the *Ritsu school in the capital for *ordination. Meanwhile, Kūkai went to China exclusively to receive training in esoteric texts and rituals, and the *Shingon school that he established on Mt. *Kōya upon his return concentrated solely on esoteric Buddhism, and for a time outshone the Tendai school in patronage and popularity.

The relationship between Buddhism and its assembly of *Buddhas and *Bodhisattvas, and the *Shintō pantheon, continued to concern many in Japan, and during the Heian period the theory known as *honji-suijaku, or 'original nature and provisional manifestation', came to dominate. According to this theory, the local kami of Shintō were manifestations of various Buddhas and Bodhisattvas that appeared in Japan to teach the people and protect the nation. Thus, for example, the Sun goddess Amaterasu was in fact a local manifestation of the great Sun Buddha *Vairocana. In this way, both religions could be accommodated in a single institution that incorporated both Buddhist and Shintō personnel and practices (known as the jingūji, or 'shrine-temple').

The Kamakura Period

By the opening years of the Kamakura period the Tendai school was the largest and most powerful of the eight schools in existence at that time, and its broad focus on both doctrinal and esoteric study and practice, as well as its laxity, corruption, and militance (as seen in its infamous 'monk-soldiers', or *sōhei), made it the breeding ground for subsequent reform movements and schools. Out of the Tendai matrix, the following figures emerged to establish new schools under the following broad categories: (1) *Pure Land: *Hōnen (1133–1212) founded the *Jōdo Shū; *Shinran (1173–1262) the *Jōdo Shinshū; and *Ippen (1239–89) the Jishū. (2) Zen: *Eisai (or Yōsai, 1141–1215) founded the *Rinzai school, which took its lineage of *Dharma-transmission from the Chinese *Lin-chi school; and *Dōgen (1200–53) the *Sōtō school, derived from the Chinese *Ts'ao-tung lineage. (3) *Nichiren (1222–82) founded the *Nichiren school, which proclaimed the superiority of the **Lotus Sūtra* (*Myōhō renge kyō*) over all other scriptures and recommended the constant repetition and praise of its title as the sole means of salvation. In addition to the formal establishment of these schools and their institutions, the tradition of mountain *asceticism continued under the name *shugendō, or 'the way of experiential cultivation'. Drawn primarily from the ranks of Tendai and Shingon esoteric clergy, practitioners lived in the mountains and practised by fasting, repentance, esoteric rituals, and long, arduous journeys through the mountains that covered as much as 50 miles in a single day.

Ashikaga and Tokugawa Periods (1392–1868)

By the end of the Kamakura period, Buddhism was a significant presence at all levels of Japanese society. At times, this was a source of concern for the feudal government. In the 15th century, Jōdo Shinshū adherents formed popular leagues called *ikkō ikki, which rose up in rebellion against local aristocratic rule in Kaga and in 1488 took control of the province themselves. In 1571 the shōgun Oda Nobunaga, distrustful of the enormous landholdings and secular power of Buddhist monasteries, attacked and razed the *Enryakuji on Mt. Hiei, dispersing its sōhei once and for all, and he suppressed many other Buddhist establishments. On the other hand, the pervasive presence of Buddhist institutions could be a source of strength for the government. For instance, after the ban on Christianity in 1612 and the subsequent expulsion of Christian missionaries, the government required all citizens to register with local Buddhist temples beginning in 1640, effectively co-opting these institutions as a census bureau. Buddhism's close cooperation with and support by the government in this way led to an inevitable decline, although a few notable figures stand out as exemplars: *Takuan Sōhō (1573–1645), *Bankei Eitaku (1622–93), and *Hakuin Zenji (1685–1768) in the *Zen school, and *Rennyo (1415–99) and Shimaji Mokurai (1838–1911) of the Pure Land school, to name a few. However, as the Tokugawa period drew to a close in the early 19th century, the real locus of religious vitality was in *Confucianism and various intellectual and spiritual renewal movements within Shintō. In addition, the first appearance of the so-called 'New Religions' such as Tenrikyō offered real competition for the loyalty of the peasants and the middle classes.

The Meiji and Modern Periods

When the Meiji emperor succeeded in restoring real political and executive power to the imperial family in 1868, one of his first acts was to abrogate the honji-suijaku understanding of the relationship between Buddhism and Shintō, and declared the two put asunder in a move called shimbutsu bunri, or 'separation of kami and Buddhas'. Buddhism itself came under persecution during the first decade or so of the Meiji period, but the attack galvanized Buddhists into action, and they successfully demanded recognition and toleration under the new constitution. At the same time, Buddhist chaplains who accompanied Japanese troops on military adventures in China, *Korea, Taiwan, and *south-east Asia, as well as missionaries who travelled to *America and *Europe to participate in the 1893 World's Parliament of Religions and to settle abroad, gave Japanese Buddhism an international presence. While all schools of Japanese Buddhism came to Hawaii and the American mainland with the large numbers of immigrants at that period, Zen had the most success in making an impression on Euro-American culture. The westward expansion of Japanese Buddhism accelerated after the Second World War. At the same time, social changes taking place in modern Japan have fostered the development of many Buddhist-derived 'New Religions', most of which sprang from offshoots of the Nichiren school and its devotion to the *Lotus Sūtra*. Prominent among these are the *Nichiren Shōshū and its lay branch, the *Sōka Gakkai (which broke away from its parent organization in 1992), and *Risshō Kōseikai. Today, Japanese Buddhism is a combination of the old and the new: even the most ancient of the Nara schools continues to coexist alongside the newest of the 'New Religions'. The Sōtō and Jōdo Shinshū schools are the largest of the traditional schools, and Buddhism remains completely integrated as a vital part of Japanese life and culture.

jarā-maraṇa (Skt.; Pāli). Old age and *death, the last of the twelve links in the chain of Dependent Origination (*pratītya-samutpāda).

Jātaka (Pāli). A genre of early literature describing the former lives of *Gautama *Buddha, and title of the tenth book of the *Khuddaka Nikāya of the *Sūtra Piṭaka of the *Pāli Canon. Since Jātaka legends occur in the *canon these must have been always recognized in Buddhist literature and constitute an old and widespread tradition, as shown by the fact that Jātaka scenes are found depicted in early sculptures. The Pāli Jātaka contains 550 birth-stories arranged in 22 books. Each story opens with a preface which relates the particular circumstances in the Buddha's life which led him to tell the birth-story, while at the end there is always a short summary where the Buddha identifies the different actors in the story in their present birth. In addition, every story is illustrated by one or more verses. According to the tradition of *Sri Lanka, the original Jātaka book consisted only of these verses and a commentary on these containing the stories which they were intended to illustrate was written in very early times in Sinhalese. This was translated into *Pāli about 430 CE by *Buddhaghoṣa as the **Jātaka-aṭṭhakathā*, and after this the original was lost. It is not known when the Jātakas were put together in a systematic form, but it is assumed that they were first handed down orally. In *India, the recollection of previous lives is a common feature in the histories of the saints and heroes of a sacred tradition, and it is considered a result of a pious life of self-mortification. The Jātakas are interesting as examples of Buddhist literature, but they are particularly interesting as a portrait of social life and customs of ancient India.

Jātaka-aṭṭhakathā. A commentary on the *Jātaka, the tenth book of the *Khuddaka Nikāya of the *Pāli Canon. The *Jātaka-aṭṭhakathā* is a translation into *Pāli of a Sinhalese work handed down in *Sri Lanka and controversially attributed to *Buddhaghoṣa (5th c. CE). This work comprises all the verses of the Jātaka and gives also, in prose, the stories connected with the verses. Each such story is preceded by an introduction, determining the circumstances in which it was told, and each story has at the end the identification of the main characters mentioned with the *Buddha and his contemporaries in some previous *birth. The collection is also prefaced by a long introduction separately known by the title of **Nidānakathā* giving the story of the Buddha before his birth as *Siddhartha, and also during his last life, up to the time of the enlightenment (*bodhi).

Jātaka-mālā. A compilation in verse of 34 birth-stories (*jātaka) concerning past lives of the *Buddha composed by Āryaśūra in the 4th century CE. This version of the birth-stories was very influential in *India and is said to have provided inspiration for depictions of the Buddha's previous lives in the murals of the *Ajaṇṭā caves and elsewhere. The text survives in *Sanskrit and a Tibetan translation.

jāti (Skt.; Pāli; birth). **1.** The interuterine period from conception to parturition, with particular emphasis on the moment of conception and the early stages of embryonic development as the beginning of a new existence. In this sense jāti forms the tenth link in the series of Dependent Origination (*pratītya-samutpāda). **2.** In Buddhist theories of causation, the moment when anything comes into being. In the *Abhidharma this moment was thought to be succeeded by a moment of duration (sthiti) and then one of *death or dissolution (bhaṅga).

jedi. Lao term for a *caitya.

Jetavana. 1. A park in *Śrāvastī in which the lay disciple *Anāthapiṇḍika constructed a residence for the *Buddha and the *monks. It was a favourite place of the Buddha's, and he spent nineteen rain-retreats (*vassa) there.

2. Temple complex in *Anurādhapura (*Sri Lanka) founded by Mahāsena. Originally the Jetavanārāma comprised a *vihāra (monastery), a large *stūpa, and other buildings. The complex was given to the *monks of the *Mahāvihāra after a protest against a monk named *Tissa who had instigated its building.

Jewel Ornament of Liberation (Tib., *Thar pa rin po ch'ei rgyan*). A celebrated guidebook (lam-rim) to the *Mahāyāna Buddhist path written by *Gampopa. The work deals with every aspect of a practitioner's progress from his or her intial contact with the *Dharma up to enlightenment (*bodhi).

Jigmé Lingpa (1729–98) (Tib., 'Jigs-med gling-pa). One of the great *Nyingmapa masters associated with the *Eclectic Movement in eastern *Tibet. He became a disciple of *Longchenpa as a result of a series of visions and was responsible for systematizing aspects of Longchenpa's teachings as well as redacting the Nyingma *tantra collection into its present form.

jikkai. Japanese term meaning: **1.** The ten *precepts taken by novices in Buddhist monasteries and convents. **2.** As different Japanese characters but with the same transliteration, the 'ten realms' of *Mahāyāna thought: *hell, hungry ghost (*preta), *animal, human, *asura, *heaven, Śrāvaka, *Pratyekabuddha, *Bodhisattva, and *Buddha.

Jina (Skt.). A title used of the Buddhas, meaning 'victor'. The term refers to the fact that through his enlightenment (*bodhi) a *Buddha conquers all the negative forces which hold beings captive in *saṃsāra. These are often symbolized collectively in the figure of the devil, *Māra, and the Buddha's victory over Māra is a popular theme in Buddhist art. A scheme of five Jinas is common in *Mahāyāna and tantric sources (*see* FIVE BUDDHA FAMILIES).

Jinakālamālīpakaraṇa. Literally, 'The Sheaf of Garlands of the Epochs of the Conqueror'. A *Pāli Buddhist chronicle compiled by Ratanapañña *Thera of *Thailand in 1516, with updates by the same author bringing the series up to 1528. The work is a study of the epochs of *Buddhism from its origin in *India and its spread to *Sri Lanka to the establishment of *Theravāda Buddhism in *south-east Asia. Besides containing abundant information on the religious intercourse between Sri Lanka and south-east Asia, the work contains accounts of several south-east Asian kingdoms. However, it is of particular value as a chronicle of the religious history of Lampoon and Chieng Mai (both in modern Thailand).

jiriki (Jap.; Chin., tzu-li, self-power). A term found in *Pure Land thought indicating the individual's own effort in religious cultivation leading toward liberation, *enlightenment, and *nirvāṇa. Within Pure Land thought, this is contrasted with 'other-power' (Jap., *tariki; Chin., t'a-li), or the power of *Amitābha *Buddha to effect the *rebirth of the individual in his Pure Land after death. Within Chinese Pure Land thought, rebirth in the Pure Land and eventual liberation are brought about by a combination of self-power and other power working together, while in the Japanese tradition after *Hōnen (1133–1212), Amitābha's 'other-power' becomes the sole effective source of salvation, eliminating 'self-power' altogether.

Jishū. A school of *Pure Land *Buddhism that developed during the *Kamakura period in *Japan under the leadership of *Ippen (1239–89). This school teaches that the sole power to effect an individual's salvation lies with the vows of *Amitābha (Jap., *Amida) *Buddha, and that all of an individual's own efforts count for nothing. Thus, not even faith is necessary for liberation; all one need do is call upon the *Buddha's name once, and liberation is assured. It also teaches that, as a result of this single calling, one is already in the Pure Land, something that other Pure Land schools believed would happen only after death. The Jishū (whose name means 'the time school') predominated over other Pure Land schools during the early Kamakura, but was eclipsed by the *Jōdo Shinshū in the early 16th century.

Jiun (1718–1804). *Shingon priest and Buddhist reformer of the late Tokugawa period in *Japan. His chief interests were in Buddhist education and internal moral reform. With regard to the former, he is known for his erudition in all aspects of Buddhist studies, and in particular for composing one of the first extensive textbooks on *Sanskrit in Japan. As to the latter, he revived the *precepts, and was especially active in promoting the traditional ten good actions (*see*

DAŚA-KUŚALA-KARMAPATHA), speaking and publishing widely on the subject. He established *Vinaya studies within Shingon, and set up a separate sub-school devoted to the study of Buddhist precepts that he called the Shōbōritsu (Vinaya of the True *Dharma), which received government recognition in 1786.

Jīvaka-komārabhacca. Personal physician to the *Buddha and to the kings *Bimbisāra and *Ajātaśatru. He studied *medicine for seven years in *Taxila, and on his return became wealthy by curing several influential patients. After he became a stream-winner (*śrotāpanna) he donated a mango grove in *Rājagṛha known as the Jīvakambavana to the *Saṃgha and built a monastery (*vihāra) there.

Jizō bosatsu. Japanese form of the *Bodhisattva *Kṣitigarbha. His legendary vow to travel into the underworld to rescue beings in torment made him an immensely popular figure in east Asia, where he became known as the chief of the *ten kings who judge the dead and as the patron of longevity. Scriptures promoting his cult were composed in *Japan and ceremonies directed to him carried out from an early date. Offerings are traditionally made to him on the 24th of each month. He is also regarded in Japan as the patron of travellers, and of infants who die before birth. *See also* TI-TSANG; ABORTION.

jñāna (Skt.; Pāli, ñāṇa). General term meaning knowledge, particularly in the context of the understanding of doctrines. In terms of Buddhist epistemology, tradition (*anuśrava) is not by itself a valid form of knowledge, nor are sense-perception or reason reliable means of knowledge until the distorting influence of unwholesome mental factors such as the three roots of evil (*akuśala-mūla) have been eliminated. Once this has been achieved, one who reflects with right attention (yoniśo manasikāra) will perceive with the proper mode of cognitive awareness and see things 'as they really are' (yathābhūta). In later *Mahāyāna sources jñāna comes to mean 'non-conceptualizing' or 'non-dual' awareness, and is sometimes used synonymously for enlightenment (*bodhi) itself. Based on the *Buddhabhūmi Sūtra* and *Yogācāra doctrines, the basic *Buddha awareness of enlightenment is subdivided according to the function into the five awarenesses (*pañca-jñāna).

jñāna-darśana (Skt., knowledge and insight; Pāli, ñāṇa-dassana). Insight arising from knowledge, particularly relating to the central truths of *Buddhism (including *nirvāṇa) which are said to be 'seen' by intuitive insight (*prajñā). This insight arises when the five hindrances (*nīvaraṇa) are removed and a state of mental concentration (*samādhi) is attained corresponding to the fourth level of trance (*dhyāna). At this point the *yogin turns his mind to jñāna-darśana and gains 'insight into the real nature of things' (yathābhūta-jñāna-darśana) (*see* YATHĀ-BHŪTA). In this way it is held a person gains direct personal corroboration of the truth of Buddhist doctrines.

Jñāna-prasthāna. The basic *Abhidharma text of the *Sarvāstivāda school, comprising eight sections that cover all the basic topics of *Buddhism such as the nature of the individual, the types of awareness, practice, *samādhi, and refutations of rival views. This work only survives in two Chinese translations and a handful of *Sanskrit fragments. The voluminous **Mahāvibhāṣa* forms a commentary on this work.

jñāna-sattva (Skt.). 'Awareness-being', a term used in later *tantric *Buddhism to denote the true form of a deity (*devatā) as an aspect of enlightenment (*bodhi). The awareness being was often summoned to merge with the samaya-sattva, or visualized image of the deity, as a part of the process of worship (*pūjā) or self-transformation.

jōbutsu. Japanese term meaning 'to become a *Buddha' or 'to attain Buddhahood'.

Jōdo. The Japanese pronunciation of the Chinese term *Pure Land (Chin., ching-t'u). *See also* BUDDHA-KṢETRA; CHIANG-T'U.

Jōdo Shinshū. The 'True Pure Land School' founded by *Shinran (1173–1262) in the early *Kamakura period. Shinran had been a disciple of *Hōnen (1133–1212), but was exiled and forcibly defrocked in 1207 along with Hōnen himself and other disciples when the group suffered the wrath of the imperial court after two of Hōnen's disciples spent the night in the ladies' chambers of the palace. No longer a priest, but unable to accept lay status completely, Shinran began working among the common people, married, and had children. He took an even more extreme view about the inability of beings in this world to effect their own salvation than his master, and taught that believers could do nothing for themselves, but had to rely exlusively upon the grace of *Amitābha (Jap., Amida) *Buddha, even for the awakening of the faith (*śraddhā) that impelled them to call upon him to take them to *rebirth in the *Pure Land after *death. Consequently, in the debates about 'once-calling' (Jap., *ichinengi) versus 'many-calling' that ensued among Hōnen's disciples after Hōnen's death, Shinran took the 'once-calling' position, claiming that to call Amitābha's name repeatedly as a means of religious cultivation was useless and a sign of hubris. When true faith had arisen, one calling of the name sufficed, since the Buddha had all the power necessary to save the individual.

After Shinran's death, the local congregations that had grown up under his leadership in the Kantō region in eastern *Japan became increasingly fragmented. The doctrine of absolute reliance on the 'other power' (*tariki) of Amitābha and the elimination of a monastic elite gave the groups a sense of autonomy and complete equality, while the lack of basic education in Buddhist teachings gave rise to diverse interpretations of Shinran's teaching. Eventually, Shinran's grandson *Kakunyo (1270–1351) and great-grandson Zonkaku (1290–1373) managed to consolidate leadership by appealing to a cult of Shinran centred on the mausoleum where his remains were enshrined, which came to be known as the *Honganji (Temple of the Original Vow). While the principle of hisō hizoku ('neither *monk nor lay') still held, the Shinshū did acquire a kind of clerical establishment over time, although their functions within locally autonomous meeting-halls (Jap., dōjō), centring as they do on preaching and pastoral care, resemble those of Protestant ministers rather than those of traditional celibate *monks. These local meeting-halls also supported themselves through the direct contributions of the faithful, rather than depending upon revenues and grants from aristocratic patrons, which gave believers a new sense of independence from traditional, hereditary rulers. Leadership at the Honganji devolved upon blood-descendants of Shinran, while entrance into clerical ranks at the local and regional levels came about as a result of education and aptitude rather than the conferral of a new status perceived as soteriologically superior to that of the laity. All of these ideas—equality of all people (including *women and men) before the grace of Amitābha, the autonomy of the local congregation, support of local halls through the contributions of the faithful, and leadership based on competence rather than status—gave the Shinshū a very modern outlook.

The Honganji organization expanded rapidly under the leadership of Shinran's eighth-generation grandson *Rennyo (1415–99). He launched several new initiatives: recruitment drives in areas not previously penetrated by the Shinshū message, preaching tours, and pastoral letters (Jap., ofumi). His efforts blended well with social changes that were gathering momentum at that time, which saw the erosion of older aristocratic and imperial power and the rise of a new middle class and increased autonomy for local peasants. Oppressive taxation had driven many of these local groups into a posture of self-defence, and the Shinshū message of complete equality before the highest Buddha provided an ideological impetus for their self-assertion (in contrast to the hierarchy of Buddhas and *Bodhisattvas espoused by older, imperial-sponsored *Buddhism in order to justify centralized power). During Rennyo's tenure, local rebellions known as *ikkō ikki broke out under the Shinshū banner. In Kaga province, the ikkō ikki leagues were so successful that they ousted the landed aristocrats in 1475 and ruled the province themselves for 92 years. (It is perhaps significant that Christianity, espousing similar teachings, also provided the basis for rebellion against the old, entrenched aristocracy in other provinces.) Rennyo also had 27 children with five wives, and his placement of all of them, sons and daughters alike, in top administrative positions helped give women greater prominence at the uppermost circles of the Shinshū.

After Rennyo, the Shinshū became a prominent economic force in Japanese society. It combined multiple circles of membership, including local congregations, ikkō ikki leagues, and commercial ventures called jinaichō in the larger towns, all of which provided avenues for the exchange of wealth outside of the old aristocratic and warlord-dominated domains. In this way, Shinshū gained great significance in providing avenues for the expansion of the middle and lower classes' economic power. On the religious front, it also aided modernization by actively suppressing aspects of older *kami faith that tended to elevate the aristocracy, esoterism in any form, belief in magic and curses, belief in demonic possession, and any other practice it considered 'superstitious'. Shinshū's increasing encroachments into the civil sphere were cut off by the reunification of Japan under the Tokugawa regime in the second decade of the 17th century. After a forcible repression of its activities by Oda Nobunaga, the Shinshū organization came to an accommodation with the government. At the same time, a lineage dispute in the *Honganji resulted in a rift that saw the establishment of two Honganji temples, the Nishi (west) and Higashi (east). After these disruptions, however, the two Shinshū groups grew rapidly, especially after the government issued orders that all citizens register with some Buddhist temple. By 1850 the two Honganjis claimed about 25 per cent of the population. Shinshū continues to the present to be the largest Buddhist group in Japan.

Shinshū beliefs, following Shinran's teachings, emphasize the complete depravity of human beings and their total dependence upon the vow of Amitābha Buddha to bring those who call his name with faith during their lives to *rebirth in the Pure Land after death. In contrast to the *Jōdo Shū, which holds that one can lose the assurance of rebirth during one's lifetime, Shinshū teaches that rebirth is certain after one calls Amitābha's name once with faith (although this faith is itself Amitābha's gift). Because of this certainty, a believer's first calling of the name with faith marks their entrance into the stage of non-retrogression, since rebirth in the Pure Land assures one of the eventual attainment of Buddhahood. In this, Shinshū contrasts with the teachings of the *Jishū, which holds that when one calls Amitābha's name, with or without faith, one is at that moment reborn into the Pure Land. Shinshū religious practice centres around meetings of local self-supporting congregations, consisting primarily of preaching and singing hymns of praise. At the upper levels, the primary ritual of the Honganji is the hō-onkō, held each year on the anniversary of Shinran's death to express the gratitude of the faithful for his vision and ministry.

Jōdo Shū The 'Pure Land school' founded by *Hōnen (1133–1212), which was the first new school of *Buddhism to be founded in *Japan outside of and without the sanction of imperial authority. Hōnen was a *Tendai *monk who grew despondent over the failure of his religious practices to provide him with the assurance of liberation. After 30 years of practice, he reached a crisis point during which he came upon a passage in *Shan-tao's commentary to the *Meditation Sūtra* stating that even the most unworthy will achieve *rebirth in the *Pure Land of *Amitābha (Jap., Amida) by relying on the power of Amitābha's vow to save all beings who call upon his name. Convinced by Shan-tao's assertions of the superiority of the practice of calling Amitābha's name (as opposed to other practices aimed at the attainment of rebirth in the Pure Land such as *visualization and esoteric rituals), Hōnen began preaching to lay and monastics alike the wisdom of choosing this practice to the exclusion of others. While Hōnen's own conduct was irreproachable, this teaching led to problems among his followers. The exclusion of traditional Buddhist *precepts led some to advocate an antinomian position, claiming that since Amitābha saved even the worst sinners, then conduct did not matter as long as one relied on his grace. This led to scandals, and in 1207 two of his disciples passed a night in the ladies chambers of the retired emperor's palace. In his anger, the retired emperor executed four followers, and banished Hōnen himself along with his other disciples. Many, including *Shinran, were forced to revert to lay status.

Hōnen's own views on the practice of reciting the *nembutsu (name of the Buddha Amitābha), its relation to other practices, and the relation of self-power (*jiriki) to other-power (*tariki) were vague. He advocated the recitation of the nembutsu as the only practice conducive to rebirth and the eventual attainment of Buddhahood, but in his own religious life he engaged in many other practices and advocated the maintenance of traditional Buddhist morality. He denigrated self-power, saying that in the age of the decline of the teachings (Jap., *mappō), people did not have any ability to effect their own liberation. Instead, he urged reliance on the 'other-power' of Amitābha to bring this about. However, he himself recited the nembutsu 60,000 to 70,000 times daily, saying that it was a powerful tool for purifying the mind. Thus, after his death, disputes broke out among his disciples over the nature of proper teaching and practice. The largest and most successful branch, the *Chinzei-ha, owed its existence to Hōnen's disciple Shōkōbo Benchō (1162–1238). In his works, he stressed the compatibility of the single practice of reciting the nembutsu with other methods of attaining rebirth in the Pure Land that had been preserved in the *Tendai school. He established several temples around the capital, and his willingness to accommodate other practices within the framework of Jōdo Shū teachings facilitated good relations with other temples and schools. The Chinzei-ha continues to advocate nembutsu recitation as a continuous practice, stressing the need to recite as many times as possible in order to maximize the purification of one's mind and the chance of attaining rebirth at the moment of death.

The Seizan-ha grew out of the activities of Zennebō Shōkō (1177–1247). Like Shōkōbo Benchō, he advocated multiple recitations of the nembutsu (he himself recited it 60,000 times daily), and cooperated closely with the Tendai school in advocating other practices alongside the nembutsu. He was of an aristocratic family, and his political connections and willingness to accommodate other practices gained his group court recognition as the official *Jōdo school. Both of these subschools advocated the position of 'many recitations' (Jap., tanengi). Their reasoning was that rebirth in the Pure Land could not be assured until the moment of death. At that critical moment, the mind needed to be set on Amitābha and the desire for rebirth. The practice of multiple recitations of the nembutsu, sometimes running as high as 84,000 times per day among the more avid practitioners, helped to clear the mind of other thoughts that distracted it away from the Pure Land, and made it more likely that the mind would be properly focused at the moment of death. They denied that this smacked of 'other-power' (Jap., tariki), because it still depended upon Amitābha's vows to be effective. Other disciples, however, held that, if Amitābha has vowed to save all those who call his name, then one recitation ought to be enough to achieve rebirth. Multiple recitations done with the intention of purifying the mind struck them as instances of 'self-power', which was a betrayal of Hōnen's basic vision. Thus, they took the 'one recitation' position (Jap., *ichinengi). This position was defended by Jōkakubō Kōsai (1163–1247) and *Shinran (1173–1262). The advantage of the 'one recitation' position was that it alleviated the anxiety of not knowing whether one's rebirth in the Pure Land was assured by stressing complete reliance on Amitābha's power to bring it about. After one recitation of the nembutsu, one could trust Amitābha to bring one to the Pure Land after death; in the 'many recitation' framework, one could not be sure until one died. However, the position had the disadvantage of being more conducive to antinomian heresy; the belief that one can do nothing that is good enough to effect one's salvation carries with it the contrapositive position that one can do nothing *evil enough to impede one's salvation. Many of Kōsai's and Shinran's disciples were accused of antisocial and sinful behaviour on just this basis. Kōsai's group eventually dwindled and died out; Shinran's consolidated itself as a separate school called the *Jōdo Shinshū.

After Hōnen's death, the full content of his teaching became known, and the Tendai establishment around the capital incited the court to a persecution in 1227. At that time, Hōnen's tomb was razed and the wooden printing blocks of his books burnt, although advance notice of the attack did give his disciples time to remove his body. While in the keeping of one of Hōnen's disciples, the body was cremated; however, the final disposition of the ashes cannot be verified, since possession of them came to be seen as a tool for legitimation among contenders for recognition as his legitimate successors, and many made up stories to show that they had them in their keeping. Another consequence of the persecution was that the Jōdo Shū lost its independence for a time, and was forced to become part of the Tendai school until the early 15th century. At first, the Seizan-ha dominated the *Chinzei-ha, since Benchō's willingness to compromise Hōnen's exclusive nembutsu practice made it more acceptable to the monastic establishment, and because it was located in the capital, while the Chinzei-ha was more active in the countryside. However, the Chinzei-ha overcame many obstacles put in its way and established its presence in the capital by gaining control of the Chion-in, a temple built on the site of Hōnen's original tomb, which they turned into a centre for a cult of Hōnen. Unlike the other main Pure Land movement of the *Kamakura period, the Jōdo Shinshū, the Jōdo Shū maintained a central tradition of ordained clergy, and sought support among the imperial family, aristocratic classes, and major *samurai families. Thus, their fortunes tended to rise or fall along with those of their supporters. Both of the dominant subschools derived from founders who subscribed to the 'many recitations' view of practice. While ascribing the efficacy of the practice to the 'other-power' of Amitābha Buddha, thus affirming the inability of people to gain liberation through their own efforts, they still practise the nembutsu as much as possible in order to purify the mind, believing that rebirth is not assured until the moment of death. It stressed the outward recitation of the nembutsu rather than the inward disposition of faith, and also affirmed the usefulness of 'auxiliary' practices such as *meditation, scripture-chanting, worship, and offerings. Thus, it was not as radical as the Shinshū in its re-envisioning of Buddhist practice.

Jōjitsu school. One of the *Six Schools of *Nara *Buddhism that flourished under government patronage during the early period of Japanese Buddhism. This school took as its focus the **Satyasiddhi Śāstra* written by the Indian sage *Harivarman during the 3rd century. This text's teachings were *Sautrantika in form and very similar to those of the *Madhyamaka school, which was represented in *Japan at the time by the *Sanron school, and the Jōjitsu school later became identified with it. Harivarman had sought to establish the emptiness of both persons and phenomena by analysing both into smaller and smaller building blocks, until at the end nothing could be found.

Jokhang. An important temple in *Lhasa dating from the 7th century CE, containing an image of *Śākyamuni in the guise of a *Bodhisattva.

Jonangpa (Tib., jo nang pa). The Tibetan Buddhist school expounding the view of *extrinsic emptiness, which was founded by Yumo Mikyo Dorje (Tib., Yu-mo mi-bskyod rdo-rje) in the 11th century, named after the location of its chief monastery. Subsequent lineages developed through Dolpopa Sherap Gyeltshen (Tib., Dol-po-pa shes-rab rgyal-mtshan), *Tāranātha, and others. The Jonangpa were often viewed with suspicion by adherents of the other schools for their controversial theories, such as their interpretation of the embryonic tathāgata (*tathāgata-garbha) as a real essence enjoying a form of self-established being like a permanent self (*atman). Remnants of the Jonangpa school still survive in *Tibet today although they were severely suppressed during the reign of *Dalai Lama V.

jōriki (Jap.; Chin., ting-li). A Sino-Japanese term meaning 'power of concentration'. This refers to a meditator's ability to enter into and maintain a deep trance state for long periods of time. It also sometimes means 'powers gained through concentration', and can indicate such attainments as divine vision or other supernatural powers, or the miraculous preservation of one's body for a long time after *death.

Jōshin 1. (d. 1157). A *Tendai *monk who specialized in esoteric studies and ritual, and was one of *Eisai's (1141–1215) first teachers. **2.** A Sino-Japanese Buddhist term meaning 'pure mind', which indicates the inherently pure mind with which all beings are endowed (Chin., ching hsin). **3.** A Sino-Japanese Buddhist term meaning 'eternal body', or the body of a perfectly enlightened *Buddha, which is opposed to the impermanent body of beings still trapped in *saṃsāra (Chin., ch'ang-shen).

Jōshu Jūshin. *See* CHAO-CHOU TS'UNG-SHEN.

Journal of Buddhist Ethics. An online journal founded by Damien Keown and Charles Prebish in 1994. The journal publishes scholarly articles on a range of subjects connected with Buddhist *ethics, such as *human rights, *ecology, and medical ethics. It periodically hosts online 'virtual' conferences, such as one on human rights in 1995 and another on *Engaged Buddhism in 2000.

jū gyū (no) zu. *See* OXHERDING PICTURES.

jūjūkai (Jap.; Chin., shih chung chieh). A Sino-Japanese Buddhist term meaning 'ten heavy *precepts'. The term occurs in both exoteric and esoteric contexts. **1.** Within exoteric teachings, this refers to the first ten of the so-called '*Bodhisattva precepts' contained in the **Brahmajāla Sūtra* (Chin., *Fan wang ching*, *Taishō 1484), which were intended to parallel the four *pārājika-dharma offences (or 'offences entailing defeat') of the monastic *Vinaya. These were opposed to the 48 'light offences' that followed. The ten are: (1) not to kill; (2) not to steal; (3) not to engage in illicit sex; (4) not to lie; (5) not to trade in intoxicants; (6) not to make accusations against other Buddhists; (7) not to boast of oneself while slandering others; (8) not to withhold donations from the *Saṃgha or slander others who make donations; (9) not to harbour anger without confessing it; and (10) not to slander the three jewels. **2.** Within the esoteric tradition, masters drew the 'ten heavy precepts' from the ninth and seventeenth fascicles of the *Commentary on the Mahāvairocana Sūtra*. (*Taishō 1796). These are: (1) not to abandon the jewel of the *Buddha; (2) not to abandon the jewel of the *Dharma; (3) not to abandon the jewel of the *Saṃgha; (4) not to abandon the thought of enlightenment (*bodhicitta); (5) not to slander the teachings and scriptures of the three vehicles; (6) not to be stingy in conferring all teachings; (7) not to give rise to false views; (8) not to obstruct others from developing the mind of enlightenment; (9) not to give teachings inappropriate to the recipient's capacities; and (10) not to give out things unbeneficial to all beings. Sometimes, masters might confer a similar set of esoteric precepts, drawn from the *Wu-wei san-tsang ch'an-yao* (Taishō 917), instead.

jukai. A Sino-Japanese term. Depending upon the character used to write the first syllable, this can mean either **1.** to receive the *precepts; or **2.** to confer the precepts.

K

Kaccāyana-vyākaraṇa. The oldest extant treatise on *Pāli grammar, composed by Kaccāyana (5th/6th c. CE). The author is identified by tradition with the *Arhat Mahākaccāyana (Skt., *Mahākatyāyana).

Kadampa (Tib., bka'-gdams-pa). A philosophical system founded by *Atiśa in the 11th century CE, based on oral teachings (gdams-pa) derived from the transmitted teachings (bka') of the *Buddha. Though it became defunct as an independent school by medieval times, the Kadampa approach was preserved by other schools and especially formed the basis of the later *Geluk school.

Kagyü (Tib., bka' brgyud). One of the four main schools of Tibetan *Buddhism (*see* TIBET). Its name means 'oral transmission lineage', and its teachings were brought from *India in the 11th century CE by *Marpa. *Gampopa, a student of *Milarepa, organized the teachings and practices into the Kagyü school. The core doctrines of this school concern the Great Seal (*mahāmudrā) and the *Six Yogas of *Nāropa. The orginal school later became subdivided into the Shangpa (Shangs-pa) and the Dakpo (Dwags-po) lineages, the latter being further subdivided into four major branches: the Karma (Karma), Tshal-pa (Tshal-pa), Ba-rom ('Ba'-rom), and Phakdru (Phag-gru). Further subdivions of the above are also known, such as the Drugpa ('brug-pa) associated with *Bhutan.

Kagyüpa (Tib., bka' brgyud-pa). Any person or thing connected with the *Kagyü school.

kaidan (Jap.; Chin., chieh-t'an). A Sino-Japanese term meaning 'precepts platform', which refers to the raised dais upon which new *monks and *nuns receive the monastic *precepts and *ordination. As a synecdoche, it also refers to the ordaining monastery (*vihāra) wherein the platform is located.

kaigen (Jap.; Chin., k'ai yen). **1.** A term meaning 'to open the eye', used in *China and *Japan as a synonym for enlightenment (*bodhi). **2.** The 'eye-opening' ceremony during which the pupils of the eyes are painted onto an image of a *Buddha, *Bodhisattva, or guardian deity to complete it. This act is thought to awaken and empower the image. There are several other terms for this ceremony: 'open the light of the eyes' (Chin., k'ai yen kuang; Jap., kaigenkō), 'open the brightness of the light' (Chin., k'ai kuang ming; Jap., kai kō myō), 'open the light' (Chin., k'ai kuang; Jap., kaikō), and 'open the brightness' (Chin., k'ai ming; Jap., kai myō).

kaimyō (Jap.; Chin., chich ming). **1.** A 'precept-name' conferred on postulants when they undergo the novice's *ordination in *China or *Japan, replacing their secular name. Also called a 'Dharma-name' (Chin., fa-ming or fa-hao; Jap., hōmyō or hōgō). **2.** Written with a different set of characters meaning 'open the brightness', an alternative term for the ceremony of 'opening the eyes' of an image (*see* KAIGEN).

Kakacūpama Sutta. 'The Discourse of the Saw'. The 21st *sutta of the *Majjhima Nikāya wherein occurs the memorable image of limbs being amputated by a saw. It is said that a *monk should not give way to anger even if he is sawn limb from limb by a two-handed saw (Pāli, kakaca). The text claims that the *Buddha himself gave the discourse this title.

Kaku-a (b. 1143). Japanese *monk who travelled to *China in 1175. He studied *Ch'an with a qualified master, received *inka (his master's verification of the authenticity of his *enlightenment), and returned to *Japan. However, after his return he failed to evoke any interest in Ch'an (Jap., *Zen) and finally retired to solitary practice. In one story, he appeared before the Emperor Takakura upon his return, and when the emperor asked about the essence of Ch'an, he took up a flute and blew a single note, an act which the court found unimpressive.

Kakuban (1095–1143). A Japanese *Shingon priest and the founder of the Shingi (or New

Doctrine) subschool of Shingon. Ordained at the age of 13, he rose to prominence rapidly and by 1134 had gained the abbotship of two temples on Mt. *Kōya, the headquarters of the Shingon school. However, fierce and sometimes violent opposition to his teachings forced him to escape to Mt. Negoro, where he founded the Emmyōji. He remained there, immersed in esoteric meditation (*see* ESOTERIC BUDDHISM) and the composition of texts, until his death.

Kakue (1238–1307). A grandson of *Shinran (1173–1262), the founder of the *Jōdo Shinshū, through his daughter *Kakushinni (1224–83), and, after her, the second caretaker of the mausoleum in which Shinran's remains resided. His right to the position was disputed by one of Kakushinni's other sons by her second husband, the actual donor of the land in which the mausoleum stood. This succession dispute lasted into the tenure of Kakue's son *Kakunyo (1270–1351), when it was settled in Kakunyo's favour through imperial intervention. The dispute itself gave the mausoleum added visibility, and helped it become the centre of a cult of Shinran during which it evolved into the *Honganji, the head temple of the Jōdo Shinshū, giving the caretaker the high status as leader of the school.

Kakunyo (1270–1351). A great-grandson of *Shinran (1173–1262), the founder of the *Jōdo Shinshū, and the third caretaker of Shinran's mausoleum. At the time of his accession to the post at the age of 41, the right of the heirs of *Kakushinni (1224–83), Shinran's daughter, through her first husband was disputed by the heirs of her second husband, who had donated the land for the mausoleum. Before his death, the imperial court intervened and settled the matter in Kakunyo's favour, thus establishing a blood succession from Shinran for the position. At this time, the mausoleum itself had begun to take on more importance as the focal point of a cult of Shinran among Shinshū believers, which eventually led to its transformation into the *Honganji, and the caretaker into the *de facto* head of the school.

Kakushin (1207–98). A Japanese *monk of the *Kamakura period who blended *Zen and *esoteric *Buddhism. Trained in the *Shingon school, he later studied with Zen masters, including *Dōgen (1200–53), and also in *China, where he received certification from *Wu-men Hui-k'ai. After his return to *Japan in 1254, he founded the Saihōji near Wakayama (later called the Kōkokuji), and enjoyed great success and prestige for his abilities in conducting esoteric rituals. He was honoured posthumously as *National Teacher Hottō Emmyō. His lineage subsequently became known as the Hottō-ha.

Kakushinni (1224–83). The daughter of *Shinran (1173–1262), founder of the *Jōdo Shinshū. The line of abbots of the *Honganji trace their descent from her rather than through one of his sons. *See also* KAKUE; KAKUNYO.

Kālacakra Tantra. Possibly the last great tantra to be compiled in *India around the 10th century CE, the *Kālacakra* (Wheel of Time) *Tantra* is said to have been written down by the mythical King Suchandra of *Shambhala. Exegetically, it is said to comprise three sections dealing with outer, inner, and secret levels of teachings covering respectively the workings of the outer macrocosm, the inner spiritual microcosm, and the integration of these two aspects. As its title suggests, special calendrical and astronomical teachings are stressed in the *Kālacakra*, and it is believed that those who receive the *Kālacakra* *initiation (performed each year by the *Dalai Lama) will be reborn in the mythical land of Shambhala. The *Kālacakra Tantra* also includes a set of six *yogas similar in some respects to the *Six Yogas of *Nāropa.

Kālāma Sutta. An important discourse in the *Aṅguttara Nikāya of the *Pāli Canon preached by the *Buddha to the Kālāmas, a family or clan of nobles (khattiyas; Skt., kṣatriyas) resident in *Kosala (Skt., Kośala). In it, the Buddha warns against blindly accepting hearsay or tradition and emphasizes the importance of knowing for oneself through intuitive insight (*prajñā).

Kālī. A popular Indian goddess of Assamese origin, mentioned but hardly ever revered in *Buddhism although elements of her iconography and worship may have been borrowed by practitioners of late *anuttara-yoga-tantra.

Kaliṅga. An ancient Indian kingdom located in the region of present-day Orissa and northern Āndhra Pradesh. Its inhabitants are thought to have been non-Indo-Aryan as is still the case today. Kaliṅga was conquered by *Aśoka in the mid 3rd century BCE but the excessive bloodshed and destruction which resulted was one of the main reasons that Aśoka adopted *Buddhism and implemented pacifist policies in his empire. Later the region fragmented into a number of smaller kingdoms such as Utkala, Oḍra, and Tosali, which were largely independent of their nominal overlords of northern *India. Buddhism flourished in this region after Aśoka's invasion and survived there until at least the 15th century in a haven from Muslim raiders. A number of important Buddhist monastic universities were located in this region such as Ratnagiri and Udayagiri.

kalpa (Skt.; Pāli, kappa). An aeon; a measurement of time widely used in ancient *India. Several accounts exist of the precise number of years involved, and there are also small, medium, great, and 'uncountable' kalpas. The most common values given for an 'uncountable' (asaṃkhyeya) kalpa are 10^{51}, 10^{59}, or 10^{63} years. A *Bodhisattva is said to become a *Buddha after three of these 'uncountable' kalpas.

kalyaṇa-mitra (Skt.). A 'good friend'; any person who can act as a reliable spiritual friend or adviser. In some forms of *Buddhism such persons are normally one's teachers and preceptors, but more widely, and especially in the *Mahāyāna, it can be anyone who is sufficiently mature and experienced in the practice of the *Dharma. Early sources in particular, for example the **Sigālovāda Sutta*, emphasize the importance of keeping the right company and avoiding the fellowship of those who are drunkards and gamblers.

kāma (Skt, Pāli). Love or *desire, particularly of a sexual nature. In the hierarchical cosmological scheme of the 'three realms' (dhātu), it is the quality that characterizes the lowest of the three, known as the Desire Realm (*kāma-dhātu). Kāma is a great obstacle on the path to enlightenment (*bodhi); it comes first among the five hindrances (*nīvaraṇa) and the three outflows (*āśravas).

kāma-dhātu (Skt.; Pāli). The Desire Realm; the lowest of the Three Realms (*dhātu), and the one which forms a large part of *saṃsāra as it contains the first five of the six modes of existence, namely the *hells, hungry ghosts (*preta), *animals, humans, and *asuras, together with the lower gods who form part of the sixth mode of existence. *See also* COSMOLOGY; BHAVACAKRA.

Kamakura period. A period of Japanese history, running roughly from 1185 to 1392, during which several new schools of *Buddhism arose, including *Zen, *Pure Land, and *Nichiren-derived sects. In response to sweeping social changes then taking place, such as the fall of the aristocracy and the rise of local landholding families, these new schools marked Buddhism's shift further away from the interests of the ruling classes and towards increased engagement with the masses. *See also* JAPAN.

Kamalaśīla. The 8th century CE Indian scholar-*monk and student of *Śāntarakṣita, who continued his teacher's work of disseminating *Buddhism in *Tibet during the period known as the 'first diffusion' (snga dar). During this period the influence of *Ch'an Buddhism was strong, and a disagreement arose as to whether enlightenment (*bodhi) was a sudden or gradual experience (*see* SUDDEN ENLIGHTENMENT; GRADUAL ENLIGHTENMENT). A *debate took place at *Samyé (*see* COUNCIL OF LHASA) in 792–4 CE in which Kamalaśīla represented the gradualist position and emerged victorious over his opponent the Ch'an master *Hvashang Mahāyāna. In accordance with the conditions of the debate the views of the victor became the orthodox form of Buddhism in Tibet. Shortly after this in 795 CE Kamalaśīla was murdered, apparently by Chinese assassins. Kamalaśīla left a rich legacy of scholarship, mainly on *Madhyamaka philosophy. His most important work is the *Madhyamakāloka* (Light on the Middle Way), and he also composed commentaries on two works by Śāntarakṣita, the *Madhyamakālaṃkāra* (Ornament of the Middle Way), and the *Tattvasaṃgraha* (Compendium of Reality). His own views are expressed in a trilogy on meditation known as the **Bhāvanākrama* (Stages of Mental Cultivation).

Kāmarūpa. An ancient region which largely corresponds to present-day Assam and eastern *Bangladesh, especially associated with the cult of *Kālī. In Buddhist times, it was generally considered to lie beyond the sphere of Indian political and cultural control. Though some Buddhist missionary efforts were directed towards this region, *Buddhism never truly flourished here except in the northern area which bordered on *Tibet.

Kamboja. One of the sixteen *mahājanapadas or north Indian states that existed at the time of the *Buddha. According to *Aśoka's Rock Edict No. XIII, Kamboja was among the countries visited by Aśoka's missionaries and later identified with an area on the banks of the Kabul river. However, in later literature Kamboja is the name given to the western region of *Thailand.

kami (Jap.). Objects of prayers and offerings and the subjects of mythology in the Japanese *Shintō religion. In some senses they are analogous to the gods of ancient Greco-Roman or Nordic mythology, although the range of the term covers not only beings who have names and life-stories but also dimly perceived entities that manifest as the awe inspired by particular objects or landscapes. When *Buddhism came to *Japan, one of the leading questions that caused concern was: how would the native kami respond to the importation of foreign deities? One answer that allowed Buddhism and Shintō to coexist for a time was the theory of *honji-suijaku, which held that the kami were local manifestations in Japan of the universal forms of the *Buddhas and *Bodhisattvas of Buddhism. Another was to see them as converting to Buddhism themselves and taking on the role of protector deities for particular shrines and temples.

kammaṭṭhāna. *Pāli term meaning 'working ground' and denoting a meditation subject used as a means of entering the trances (*jhānas; Skt., *dhyāna). A list of 40 such topics is found in the **Visuddhimagga*. These include 10 *kasiṇas, 10 repulsive (asubha) objects, 10 recollections (*anussati), 4 *Brahma-vihāras, 4 immaterial spheres (arūpāyatana), perception of the repulsive nature of food, and analysis of the four elements. Topics from this list are allocated to the student by the meditation teacher depending on the student's personality, paying particular attention to any negative tendencies that need correction.

Kāñcī. An important south-eastern Indian city (present-day Kachipuram), the capital of the ancient Dravidian state of Drāviḍa. *Buddhism is thought to have reached this area by the 3rd century BCE due to its close connections with *Sri Lanka, and over the following centuries flourished in this renowned centre of learning. Several great Buddhist scholars are associated with Kāñcī, including *Buddhaghoṣa and *Buddhadatta. At a later date, Kāñcī seems to have had a degree of importance in the development of *tantric Buddhism, with some scholars suggesting that it is the true identity of the legendary land of *Oḍḍiyāna. Buddhism maintained a presence in this area and Sri Lankan sponsored temples were built here as late as the 14th century CE.

Kandy. Former capital of *Sri Lanka from 1592 to 1815 and site of the *Temple of the Tooth housing a tooth believed to belong to the *Buddha. Every August in the *Perahera festival the *relic is carried on the back of an elephant around the city in a torchlight procession.

k'an-hua Ch'an. A Chinese term meaning 'the *Ch'an that looks at the words/phrases'. This refers to the practice of meditating on Ch'an stories and riddles (Chin., kung-an; Jap., *kōan) in the search for enlightenment (*bodhi). Normally, after studying the story for a time, students would identify a sentence, phrase, or word as the 'critical phrase' (Chin., hua-t'ou) and would concentrate all of their efforts on penetrating the meaning of that one phrase. Thus, their practice was referred to as 'k'an-hua Ch'an'.

Kaniṣka I. The third king of the north-west and central Indian *Kuṣāṇa dynasty who ruled *c.*128–51 CE. He was renowned as a patron of *Buddhism, sometimes even regarded as a 'second *Aśoka', and was particulary associated with the *Sarvāstivāda school. A council was held under his patronage at *Gandhārā, which led to the compilation of the **Mahāvibhāṣā* (*see* COUNCIL OF KANIṢKA).

Kanjur (Tib., bka'-gyur). The Tibetan *canon of the translated (gyur) instructions (bka') of the *Buddha, it comprises around 100 volumes containing over 1,000 *sūtras and *tantras, mainly translated from *Sanskrit and other Indic languages with a few texts from Chinese. This collection is of great value to scholars since it preserves faithful translations of many Indic texts lost in the original Sanskrit. *See also* Tenjur

Kaṅkhāvitaraṇī (Pāli, the dispeller of doubts). A commentary composed by *Buddhaghoṣa on the code of disciplinary rules for *monks (*Prātimokṣa).

kanna Zen. The Japanese pronunciation of *k'an-hua Ch'an.

kannen-nembutsu (Jap.). A *Pure Land practice wherein the devotee keeps the image of *Amitābha *Buddha in mind. This term is opposed to *kushō-nembutsu, or orally invoking the Buddha's name.

Kannon. The Japanese form of the name of the *Bodhisattva *Avalokiteśvara. Within Japanese *Buddhism (*see* JAPAN), the historical Prince *Shōtoku (572–621) has often been regarded as a manifestation of Kannon, and a vision of the Bodhisattva also figured prominently in the biography of *Shinran (1173–1262), founder of the *Jōdo Shinshū. *See also* KUAN-YIN; KWANNON.

Kanthaka. Name of the *Buddha's horse, said to have been pure white in colour and born on the same day as the Buddha. Kanthaka features prominently in the story of the *Great Renunciation where Prince *Siddhārtha renounces the world and leaves his father's palace. The horse carries him 30 leagues away from the city, with *Channa the charioteer holding onto its tail. When the Buddha crosses the river Anomā, the horse remains on the other side where it dies of grief but is reborn in *heaven.

Kanzan Egen (1277–1360). A disciple of the *Zen *monk *Shūhō Myōchō (1282–1337), whose lineage was known for its strict adherence to a Chinese style of Zen practice and its resistance to the Japanization of Zen or its accommodation to the agenda of the imperial authorities. Kanzan was the first abbot of the Myōshin-ji upon its founding in 1335, a temple that became the centre of the Myōshinji-ha, an independent subschool of *Rinzai Zen.

Kao-Seng-Chuan. A Chinese term that both refers to a genre of Buddhist literature and is the title of the earliest example of that genre. The term means 'Biographies of Eminent Monks'. Works in this genre consist of biographical accounts of various notable monks during a certain period, and the title generally follows from the period. The earliest is the 'Liang Dynasty Biographies of Eminent Monks' (Chin., *Liang-ch'ao kao seng chuan*), composed by Hui-chiao (497–554) in fourteen fascicles (*Taishō 2059), followed by *Tao-hsüan's (596–667) 'Continued Biographies of Eminent Monks' in 30 fascicles (Taishō 2060). The *monk Tsan-ning (919–1001) composed the 'Sung Dynasty Biographies of Eminent Monks' (Chin., *Sung kao seng chuan*) during that period (Taishō 2061), and during the Ming dynasty Ju-hsing (date unknown) wrote the 'Great Ming Dynasty Biographies of Eminent Monks' (Chin., *Ta Ming tai kao seng chuan*) in eight fascicles (Taishō 2062). The Chinese tradition refers to these four as the 'Biographies of Eminent Monks of the Four Dynasties'. Other collections appeared later in *China, and the form was also used in *Japan and *Korea. Some editions were limited by school (such as those dedicated to masters of the *Pure Land, *T'ien-t'ai, or *Vinaya schools, while others were limited by geographical area.

kapala (Skt.). A skull bowl, made from either a human cranium or brass, and used in Tibetan Buddhist *tantric rituals as a container for the elixir of immortality.

Kapila. The legendary founder of the influential non-Buddhist Sāṃkhya school. No reliable details of his life or works have survived.

Kapilavastu. The capital of the *Śākya polity located in present-day *Nepal, and childhood home of the *Buddha *Śākyamuni. Despite its importance for *Buddhism, it was not a great cultic centre for later Buddhists and was virtually abandoned by the time the Chinese pilgrim-*monk *Hsüan-tsang, visited it. The location of Kapilavastu has proven elusive, though many archaeologists believe the remains found in the 20th century at Tilaurakot can be identified as the site, though others favour the nearby town of Piprahwa.

karma (Skt.; Pāli, kamma, action). The doctrine of karma states the implications for *ethics of the basic universal law of *Dharma, one aspect of which is that freely chosen and intended moral acts inevitably entail consequences (Pāli, kamma-niyama). It is impossible to escape these consequences and no one, not even the *Buddha, has the power to forgive *evil deeds and short-circuit the consequences which inevitably follow. A wrongful thought, word, or deed is one which is committed under the influence of the three roots of evil (*akuśala-mūla), while good deeds stem from the opposites of these, namely the three 'virtuous roots' (*kuśala-mūla). These good or evil roots nourished over the course of many lives become ingrained dispositions which predispose the individual towards virtue or vice. Wrongful actions are designated in various ways as evil (*pāpa), unwholesome (*akuśala), demeritorious (apuṇya), or corrupt (saṃkliṣṭa), and such deeds lead inevitably to a deeper entanglement in the process of *suffering and *rebirth (*saṃsāra). Karma determines in which of the *six realms of rebirth one is reborn, and affects the nature and quality of individual circumstances (for example, physical appearance, health, and prosperity). According to Buddhist thought the involvement of the individual in saṃsāra is not the result of a 'Fall', or due to 'original *sin' through which human nature became flawed. Each person, accordingly, has the final responsibility for his own salvation and the power of free will with which to choose good or evil.

Karma-kagyü (Tib., Karma bka'-brgyud). One of the main subdivisions of the *Kagyü lineage, descended from Düsum Khyenpa (Dus-gsum mkhyen-pa), the student of *Gampopa.

karma-mudrā (Skt.) **1**. Action Seal; one of the four meditational seals (*mudrā) according to the *yoga-tantra. It refers to the process of imaging the *Buddhas in transformational *meditation practice by way of hand-gestures and so forth, which correlate to their 'action' aspect. *See* ANUTTARA-YOGA-TANTRA. **2**. In *anuttara-yoga-tantra, a female partner used in sexual yoga.

Karmapa. The title of the reincarnating head of the *Karma-kagyü lineage, the first of whom was Düsum Khyenpa (Dus-gsum mkhyen-pa, 1110–93), who was suceeded by sixteen further incarnations down to the present day. The Karmapa's main role in the lineage is to ensure that the transmission of the school's *tantric teachings is passed intact down through the generations. A key element of the installation of a new Karmapa is the use of a black hat said to be woven from the hair of a *ḍākinī.

karuṇā (Skt.). Compassion, a virtue which is of importance in all schools of *Buddhism but which is particularly emphasized by the *Mahāyāna. In early Buddhism, karuṇā figures as the second of the four *Brahma-vihāras or 'Divine Abidings'. These qualities are cultivated especially through the practice of *meditation and are directed towards other beings without restriction. In the Mahāyāna, karuṇā is emphasized as the necessary complement to insight (*prajñā) and as an essential ingredient in the perfection of the fully enlightened. In Mahāyāna sources, insight and compassion are compared to two wings with which one flies to the island of *enlightenment. The followers of the *Hīnayāna are criticized for their lack of karuṇā and for seeking a purely personal enlightenment regardless of the needs of others. The *Bodhisattva of the Mahāyāna, on the other hand, seeks to attain *nirvāṇa for the benefit of all, and vows that he will not cease from his efforts until all being have attained liberation. Some sources go so far as to allow karuṇā to override all other considerations, and enjoin the commission of immoral actions if the Bodhisattva sees that the use of skilful means (*upāya-kauśalya) would reduce *suffering. In Mahāyāna iconography and art the symbolic embodiment of compassion is the great Bodhisattva *Avalokiteśvara, 'the one who looks down from on high'. He is portrayed as having a thousand arms extended in all directions to minister to those in need. He is constantly appealed to for aid and intercession by those in difficult circumstances. In the course of time there appeared a doctrine of salvation by faith according to which the mere invocation of the name of a *Buddha was sufficient, given the extent of the Buddha's compassion, to ensure *rebirth in a '*Pure Land' or *heaven.

Kashmir. The ancient Indian state of Kaśmīra, corresponding to present-day Kashmir in north-west *India. According to legend, *Buddhism reached Kashmir soon after the *Buddha's passing but the conquest of the area by *Candragupta, *Aśoka's grandfather, would seem to be a more reliable date. Under *Mauryan patronage, many monasteries and *stūpas were established in this region which soon became a stronghold of the *Sarvāstivāda school with whom such masters as *Kātyāyaniputra, *Vasumitra, and *Saṃghabhadra are associated. Buddhism in Kashmir flourished under the later *Kuṣāṇas and continued to do so during the lengthy period of virtual independence that followed the demise of the Kuṣāṇas, though there were brief periods of violent persecution including the devastation caused by the White Hun (Hephthalite) leader, Mihirakula. The so-called 'Fourth Council' is thought to have been convened under the auspices of *Kaniṣka in this region (*see* COUNCIL OF KANIṢKA). Kashmir's location made it an important staging-post for the transmission of Buddhism into central Asia and western *Tibet, with many famous scholar-monks such as *Kumārajīva and *Buddhabhadra who travelled to *China, or Śīlendrabodhi and Vidyākaraprabha who went to Tibet. A dwindling Buddhist presence continued in Kashmir from the 12th century CE onwards, although retaining important religious ties with Tibet, but Buddhism seems to have all but disappeared by the time of the Moghul invasion in the 16th century.

Kāśī. A kingdom of ancient *India, bordering the River Ganges to the north and centred on its capital *Vārāṇasī. During the lifetime of the *Buddha, its independence was extinguished when it was incorporated into the Magadhan empire (*see* MAGADHA).

kasiṇa. *Pāli term of uncertain etymology denoting a device used as a meditation object, mainly in the *Theravāda tradition. The object functions as a support for concentration and the mind and the object become one. The *Pāli Canon provides a list of ten kasiṇa: earth, water, fire, wind, blue, yellow, red, white, space (*ākāsa), and consciousness (viññāṇa; Skt., *vijñāna). As an example of kasiṇa practice, the meditator may set up a coloured disk a few feet away. This object is known as the preparatory image (parikamma-nimitta). He concentrates his attention on this until a mental image of it, known as the acquired image (uggaha-nimitta), arises. By directing attention further towards this a perfectly clear and stable counter-image (paṭibhāga-nimitta) is produced, and at this point the meditator will have reached the threshold of the trances (*dhyāna).

Kāvśyapa-parivarta. *The Kāśyapa Chapter*, title of an early *Mahāyāna text, written in prose and verse, forming part of the **Ratnakūṭa* collection of *sūtras. The text uses many similes and parables to elucidate the qualities of a *Bodhisattva and the nature of emptiness (*śūnyatā).

Kāśyapīya. A school that originated some three to four centuries after the *death of the *Buddha and flourished in north-west *India. The school owes its origins to the *Arhat Suvarṣaka Kāśyapa, a contemporary of the Buddha, and is also known by the name Sauvarṣaka.

Kathāvatthu. 'The Book of Disputed Points', being a canonical book belonging to the *Abhidharma Piṭaka of the *Pāli Canon. The fifth of the seven books in the collection, it is traditionally regarded as having been compiled by *Moggaliputta Tissa after the council at *Pāṭaliputra which was held in the reign of *Aśoka (*see* COUNCIL OF PĀṬALIPUTRA II). The work contains 23 chapters and is a digest of disputed points of doctrine.

kaṭhina. Cotton cloth supplied to *monks by the laity for the purpose of making robes. The offering of the cloth, which should be new or in good condition, is made after the annual retreat during the rainy season in countries where *Theravāda *Buddhism is practised. A ceremony has developed around the offering, which goes back to ancient times, and is one of the few ceremonies that follows an almost identical form throughout *south-east Asia. It is one of many ceremonies in Theravāda Buddhism in which the laity plays a part. *See also* CĪVARA; FESTIVALS.

katsu (Jap.). In Japanese *Zen, an expletive uttered by one who has had a breakthrough experience, such as solving a *kōan or realizing enlightenment (*bodhi; *satori). In ordinary usage, it is a verb meaning 'to win' or 'to gain dominance over'. There is also another word pronounced 'katsu' that occurs in Zen literature represented by a different Chinese character which means simply 'to shout'.

kaṭvaṅga (Skt.) A staff of the kind carried by deities associated with the *anuttara-yoga *Mother Tantras. The staff has three human heads at the upper end—one freshly cut, one shrivelled, and a skull—and is surmounted by a *vajra or a trident. The three heads symbolize the overcoming of the three roots of evil (*akuśala-mūla), namely greed (*rāga), hatred (*dveṣa), and delusion (*moha).

Katyāyana-abhidharma. Title of an early *Abhidharma text attributed to the *Arhat *Mahākatyāyana.

Katyāyanīputra. An important *Sarvāstivādin scholar-*monk, active during the late 2nd century BCE in *Kashmir. He compiled the **Jñāna-prasthāna*, the basic summary of *Abhidharma according to Sarvāstivādin tenets.

Kauśāmbī (Pāli, Kosambī). The capital of the ancient Indian kingdom of Vatsa, located on the Yamunā river near to its confluence with the Ganges. Like many major early Indian cities, it was located at the juncture of important trade routes. The *Buddha *Śākyamuni made several visits there and several early monastic precincts were established there during his lifetime.

Kegon (or Kegon-shū). As one of the '*Six Schools of Nara Buddhism', Kegon is one of the oldest schools of *Buddhism in *Japan. The name represents the Japanese pronunciation of the Chinese words *Hua-yen, and this school saw itself as the inheritor of the Chinese Hua-yen tradition and its transmitter to future generations of Japanese Buddhists. The Hua-yen teachings were first transmitted to Japan by the Korean *monk Shinjō (d. 742), and gained currency in the Japanese court because of the lectures given by his disciple Ryōben (or Rōben, 689–773). Based on the Indian *Mahāyāna scripture, the **Avataṃsaka Sūtra*, this school taught that the *Buddha Mahāvairocana (*see* VAIROCANA) was himself the centre and ground of the universe, and all phenomena emanated from his own being. The imperial court appreciated the imagery of a central power to which all subsidiary things owed their being, because the emperor saw in this an image that could be used to inculcate an analogous political culture in which the emperor would occupy the place of the Buddha, while all subsidiary political units in the nation would trace the source of their authority back to him. Consequently, the emperor *Shōmu Tennō granted the school a headquarters temple called the *Tōdaiji in the capital of Nara, in which he installed a monumental statue of Mahāvairocana, completed in 749. Shōmu himself took on the name Roshana, a partial transliteration of the Buddha's name. The Kegon school, never more than a small group of scholar-monks devoted to the study of this very abstruse scripture, found itself in danger of being absorbed into the politically powerful *Tendai school during the *Heian period (794–1185). Even though it resisted complete assimilation, it never thrived as an independent institution or congregation, but as an area of concentration and study into which those with motivation and aptitude could enter as need and inclination dictated. As in *China, Kegon philosophy was regarded by all as the highest and most profound statement of the way in which the enlightened mind sees the world. *See also* HUA-YEN.

Keizan Jōkin (1268–1325). A Japanese *Sōtō *Zen *monk who authored the **Denkō-roku* (*Taishō 2585), an authoritative Sōtō Zen historical work composed between 1299 and 1301. He was a fourth-generation successor to Sōtō founder *Dōgen (1200–53), and considered the second great *patriarch of the school. Strongly spiritual, he had frequent visions of the *Bodhisattva *Kannon (*Avalokiteśvara) in his youth, and entered the monastic order very early in his childhood at the behest of his mother. He trained at the Sōtō headquarters temple, *Eiheiji, and from 1285–88 went on a *pilgrimage to many temples and masters around *Japan, broadening his knowledge of *Buddhism. Following the transmission of the *Dharma from his master, Tettsu Gikai (1219–1309), he was sent to be founding abbot of the Jōman Temple in Awa, and later succeeded his master as abbot of the Daijō Temple. He founded other temples and posted his disciples as abbots, but his greatest achievement in this regard came when he was given charge of a former *Shingon temple which he renamed the *Sōjiji. Under his direction it became the main temple of the Sōtō school, rivalling the Eiheiji in importance and gaining imperial patronage. By the time of his death, his spiritual achievements, charisma, diplomatic skills, and administrative ability had helped heal the *schisms that the Sōtō school had undergone during his master's lifetime, and Keizan's branch of Sōtō became predominant.

Keizan Oshō Denkō Roku. *See* DENKŌ ROKU.

kendō. (Jap.) Japanese term meaning 'The way (dō) of the sword (ken)'. One of the Japanese *martial arts that came to be associated with *Zen from the Muromachi (1392–1603) period to the present.

kenshō (Jap.). A *Ch'an and *Zen term (jienhsing in Chinese) that literally means 'to see (one's true) nature'. This is another term for awakening (*satori, *bodhi), defined as seeing oneself for what one really is: impermanent, ever-changing, and one with the truth that underlies all of reality.

kesa (Jap.). Japanese Buddhist monastic robe. The two characters with which this is written (Chin., chia-sha) were chosen to represent the *Sanskrit word kaṣāya, or 'soiled rags'.

Khaḍga dynasty. Buddhist dynasty ruling over East Bengal between 660 and 750 CE.

Khaggavisāna Sutta. 'The Discourse of the Rhinoceros Horn'. Popular discourse from the **Sutta-nipāta* made up of 41 verses. The *sutta takes its name from the refrain 'fare alone like the horn of the rhinoceros', which occurs at the end of each verse.

Khemā Therī. *Nun regarded by the *Buddha as chief among his female followers because of her great insight (mahāprajñā). In her earlier life she was famous for her beauty and became the chief consort of King *Bimbisāra. She subsequently met the Buddha who conjured up a vision showing how a woman's beauty fades, and explained to her the dangers of infatuation with physical things. At that moment she became an *Arhat.

Khenpo (Tib., mkhan-po; Skt., paṇḍita). A Tibetan title for a high-ranking teacher or the head of a monastery or monastic college.

Khmer. Ancient kingdom roughly corresponding to present-day *Cambodia. Though in contact with both *India and *China, the Khmers favoured various forms of *Hinduism rather than *Buddhism, which did not make any significant headway until the reign of Jayavarman VII, the founder of *Angkor Wat in the early 12th century CE. There was a presence of *Theravāda Buddhism thereafter, though the monastic population was decimated under the Khmer Rouge government during the late 1970s and early 1980s.

Khotan. A small early medieval oasis state on the southen route of the *Silk Road which became an important centre and staging-post for *Buddhism by the 2nd century CE. As Buddhism became established here, both *Hīnayāna and *Mahāyāna monastic establishments were founded. The dry climate of the area has resulted in the preservation of fragments of Buddhist manuscripts and some important early paintings and murals.

Khuddaka Nikāya (Pāli, The Minor Collection). The fifth and last division (*Nikāya) of the *Sūtra Piṭaka, containing a miscellaneous collection of both early and later canonical works. The texts are predominantly in verse and include some of the most popular and uplifting material in the *Pāli Canon. There are fifteen works in all: (1) **Khuddakapāṭha* (Collection of Little Readings); (2) **Dhammapada* (Verses on Dhamma); (3) *Udāna* (Uplifting Verses); (4) **Itivuttaka* (Thus it was Said); (5) **Sutta-nipāta* (Group of Discourses); (6) **Vimānavatthu* (Stories of Heavenly Abodes); (7) **Petavatthu* (Stories of Hungry Ghosts); (8) **Theragāthā* (Verses of the Male Elders); (9) **Therīgāthā* (Verses of the Female Elders); (10) **Jātaka* (Birth Stories); (11) **Niddesa* (Exposition); (12) **Paṭisambhidāmagga* (Way of Analysis); (13) **Apadāna* (Legends); (14) **Buddhavaṃsa* (Lineage of the Buddhas); (15) **Cariyāpiṭaka* (Basket of Conduct).

Khuddakapāṭha. The first book of the *Khuddaka Nikāya of the *Sūtra Piṭaka of the *Pāli Canon. It is thought that this book was the last one to be added to the Khuddaka Nikāya collection and its rightful claim to be included as part of the *canon was disputed both by the *Dīgha-*bhāṇakas and the Majjhima-bhāṇakas. It appears to be a later composition, possibly compiled as a handbook for novices. The *Khuddakapāṭha* consists of nine short texts, probably compiled in *Sri Lanka, only one of which is not found elsewhere in the canon. The commentary to the *Khuddakapāṭha*, traditionally attributed to *Buddhaghoṣa (5th century CE), is part of the **Paramatthajotikā*. According to the commentary, the book derives its name from the first four texts, which are shorter than the remaining five.

khwan (or khuan). Term found in various of the Thai languages denoting the 'vital essence' of a human being, rice plant, or certain animals (such as buffaloes and elephants). Known in Burmese as leikpya, and in Khmer as pralu'n, this 'vital essence' is thought to exist in 32 parts of the human body according to the Thai belief, and in nineteen parts according to the Khmer. In practice, however, it is thought of as a unity, and as the spirit that must be within the body of the human being, the rice plant, or the animal if it is not to wither and die, or suffer misfortune. Periodic rituals are performed to secure the khwan to the body, especially following any sudden change in status or place of residence. At death the khwan ceases to exist and a new khwan is formed at conception. Since the khwan is impermanent, and is not understood as an *ātman or eternal soul, it poses no direct conflict to the Buddhist teachings of not self (*anātman).

kihō ittai (Jap.). A Japanese *Pure Land doctrinal concept that the *Buddha *Amitābha and the believer who recites the *nembutsu are of one substance. This idea accounts for the efficacy of the practice by identifying the very Buddhahood of Amitābha with the assurance of the believer's *rebirth in the Pure Land; without this direct link, the Buddha would not be a Buddha because his vow (that all believers who call upon him would achieve rebirth or else he would not accept Buddhahood) would not be fulfilled, and without the fulfilment of this vow, the believer could not attain rebirth in the Pure Land of *Sukhāvatī. This idea originated in the literature of the *Jōdo Shū, but later became common in the *Jōdo Shinshū and the *Jishū as well.

kill the Buddha. A teaching ascribed to the Chinese *Ch'an master *Lin-chi I-hsüan (d. 866). In full, his teaching reads, 'If you meet the *Buddha, kill the Buddha; if you meet the *patriarchs, kill the patriarchs; if you meet an *Arhat, kill the Arhat; if you meet your parents, kill your parents... in this way, you attain liberation.' (*Taishō, vol. 47, p. 500b). According to the Ch'an tradition, his intention was to shock students into realizing that they themselves were Buddhas, patriarchs, Arhats, and so on, and that they had no need to depend upon, mistakenly objectify, or inordinately revere figures external to themselves.

kiṃnara (Skt.; Pāli, kinnara). A class of heavenly beings who in early sources resemble a bird with a man's head and according to later texts are similar to centaurs. They act as musicians in *Śakra's *heaven.

kinhin (Jap.; Chin., ching-hsing). In *Ch'an and *Zen practice, to walk slowly and mindfully between sessions of meditation in order to restore circulation and feeling to the legs and clear the mind of drowsiness.

kiriya-vāda (Pāli). The doctrine (vāda) that there are consequences to moral acts. This doctrine, which involves a belief in *karma, was taught by *Buddha along with many other orthodox and sectarian teachers. Certain of his contemporaries, however, rejected the notion of karma and denied the reality and efficacy of moral choice (*see* six SECTARIAN TEACHERS), holding instead to the rival theory of *akiriya-vāda. Such teachings were condemned by the Buddha as erroneous and leading to immorality.

Kisagotami Therī. 'Thin Gotamī', a poor woman from the town of *Śrāvasti mentioned in the *Pāli Canon who bore a child who died when a toddler. Distraught, she carried the dead child about with her until she met the *Buddha, who asked her to bring him a mustard seed from the houses in the village where no one had died. She soon realized the quest was impossible and understood the ubiquity of *death. Laying her dead child on its funeral pyre she sought *ordination and in due course became an *Arhat.

Kitthiwutthō Phikkhu (1936–). Thai monk, also known by his *Pāli name Kittivuḍḍho Bhikkhu. Ordained in 1957 he began to speak out on political issues when *Thailand was rocked by large student demonstrations between 1973 and 1976. In his speeches and writings he supported the current regime and criticized the Communists and other radical groups behind the demonstrations. He became linked to a right-wing political movement known as the Navaphala (New Power Movement) and founded a college for the study and propagation of *Buddhism where he developed and promoted his ideas. He became notorious for a controversial speech delivered to government and religious leaders entitled 'Killing Communists is Not Demeritorious' in which he argued that killing Communists would not produce bad *karma since they were opposed to the *Buddha, the nation, and the king. He defended this unusual claim by arguing that, so long as the intention was to protect the nation, the act of killing was more akin to destroying moral impurities (*kleśa) and like killing *Māra, the devil. Kitthiwutthō's more liberal opponents accuse him of distorting Buddhist teachings and subverting the *Dharma for political purposes.

Kiyozawa Manshi (1863–1903). A Japanese Buddhist reformer and educator of the Meiji period (1868–1912). A member of the *Jōdo Shinshū Higashi-Honganji school (*see* HONGANJI), he was ordained at an early age and educated at the school's expense. A brilliant student, he specialized in philosophy and concentrated his own thought on elucidating the relationship between the contingent and the absolute. He credited three sources as having decisive influence in the formation of his thought: *Shinran (1173–1262), Epictetus, and the early Buddhist *Āgamas. Based on this combination of influences, he followed Shinshū teaching in entrusting himself entirely to the compassion (*karuṇā) and the vows of the *Buddha *Amitābha, but still led a rigorously *ascetic life of reflection and study.

In the early 1890s, he established a reform movement within the Higashi-Honganji school sometimes referred to as the Shirakawa Party, which tried to turn the school's administration away from its focus on financial matters to those of more spiritual import. For this, he and his companions were expelled from the school, although they were later reinstated. Despite contracting tuberculosis, he accepted an invitation to act as the founding dean of a new Shinshū University in Tokyo, but was forced to resign because of conflicts with the authorities. His highly intellectual approach often created misunderstanding among Shinshū authorities and was not appreciated by the average believer, but it gave a new respectability to sectarian doctrine and practice among the educated classes and the younger generation of Shinshū priests. One of his works, the *Skeletal Outline of a Philosophy of Religion*, was presented in English translation at the 1893 World's Parliament of Religions in Chicago. In these ways, he was an important contributor to the modernization and globalization of Shinshū teachings.

kleśa (Skt.; Pāli, kilesa). General term for defilements, vices, or negative psychological tendencies. The term means something like 'affliction', in the sense of disturbances of the mind. The three most basic are greed (*rāga), hatred (*dveṣa), and delusion (*moha), although many different lists and variant terms are found. Thus, according to *Vasubandhu in the *Abhidharma-kośa* the six basic defilements are greed (rāga), hatred (pratigha), ignorance (*avidyā), arrogance (*māna), doubt (*vicikitsā), and false views or opinionatedness (*dṛṣṭi). Sometimes the list is extended to ten to include delusion (moha), laxity (styāna), exciteability (auddhatya), shamelessness (ahrīka), and recklessness (anapatrāpya). Under the influence of these defilements individuals perform unwholesome (*akuśala) acts which produce bad *karma leading to an inferior rebirth. They can be eliminated by the cultivation of their corresponding virtues and through *meditation.

kōan (Jap.; Chin., kung-an). Sometimes referred to as '*Zen riddles', kōans are brief stories or dialogues from the *Ch'an/Zen tradition upon which Zen students focus during their *meditation in order to penetrate their meaning. During the late *T'ang and early Sung dynasties in *China, the Ch'an community experimented with many new teaching methods that would allow masters to directly elicit an experience of awakening (*Satori) on the part of their students. These 'shock Ch'an' or 'crazy Ch'an' techniques included beating, shouting directly into the student's ear, or giving paradoxical or nonsensical responses to their questions. Later, during the mid- to late Sung period, stories of master–student encounters that had succeeded, or simple tales of a master's strange behaviour, circulated within Ch'an circles in the form of 'sayings of the master' or 'transmission of the lamp' (Chin., *ch'uan teng lu*) literature. Examples included the *Record of Lin-chi* (Chin., *Lin-chi lu*) and the *Patriarchs' Hall Anthology*

(Chin, *Tsu t'ang chi*). As students reflected upon these stories, they found that they could use them as helpful devices in their own meditation. In reading the story of a master whose teaching methods had led a student to enlightenment (*bodhi), they could ask themselves: what was the master's mind at that moment? What did the student experience? In other cases not involving the recounting of an enlightenment experience but simply giving an instance of a master's teaching or even a casual dialogue, the student could try to break through the obstructions in their own mind that kept them from directly experiencing their own nature and seeing their own inherent enlightenment. The formal use of such stories as a teaching device for students is first mentioned in connection with Nan-yüan Hui-yung (d. 930).

Fen-yang Shan-chao (942–1024) of the *Lin-chi school was the first to compile an anthology of kōans, many of which he composed himself. These appear in the middle volume of the *Record of Fen-yang* (Chin, *Fen-yang lu*). Subsequently, many Sung-period masters of the Lin-chi school excelled in the use of kōans and in the contrivance of situations later enshrined in kōans. However, two anthologies of kōans stand out in the Ch'an tradition. The first is the **Blue Cliff Records* (Chin., *Pi-yen lu*; Jap., *Hekigan-roku*), first compiled by *Hsüeh-tou Ch'ung-hsien (980–1052) and later expanded by *Yüan-wu K'o-ch'in (1063–1135). Hsüeh-tou had compiled the hundred cases comprising the work and added his own verse to them, while Yüan-wu added an introduction and commentaries to the case and Hsüeh-tou's verse to each case. The second is the *Wu-men kuan* (Jap., *Mumonkan; see* GATELESS GATE), a collection of 48 cases compiled by the *monk *Wu-men Hui-k'ai (1183–1260) that appeared in 1229. The title could mean 'Wu-men's Pass' or 'Wu-men's Barrier', but a play on the meaning of the characters of Wu-men's name also make it possible to give it the more paradoxical translation the 'Gateless Gate' or 'The Pass with No Door'. The kōans included in this text are stripped of all but the most essential elements in order to confront the student with the pith of each story. While other kōan collections have appeared through the years, these two have enjoyed the greatest status, serving as textbooks in kōan training. Use of kōans has been mostly been the province of the Lin-chi school (and its Japanese successor, the *Rinzai school), while the *Ts'ao-tung (Jap., *Sōtō) has tended to downplay their use, seeing kōan practice as an artificial effort to attain Buddhahood, to which they oppose simply sitting in meditation as a more direct experience of Buddhahood. Even within circles that made use of them, kōan practice has received criticism for encouraging mere cleverness and wordplay rather than genuine *enlightenment, and periodically answer-books have appeared purporting to give students an easy way to pass through the 'curriculum' and gain credentials.

However, when used properly, kōans are credited with helping students break down the barriers to enlightenment that the rational habits of the mind erect, and with instilling a profound understanding of *Buddhism and its goals at a direct, experiential level. An example is the following, which is number 43 in the *Wu-men kuan*: 'Shou-shan held out his short staff and said, If you call this a short staff, you oppose its reality; if you do not call it a short staff, you ignore the fact. Now quickly, say what it is!' Students of Buddhist doctrine might recognize in this the teaching of the *Two Truths of the *Madhyamaka: the ultimate truth (its 'reality'), and the conventional truth ('the fact'). However much a student understands this doctrine intellectually, the kōan confronts him or her with the need to synthesize the two into a concise understanding of the application of the doctrine to an actual thing. To do so, the student must break through to a new level of understanding. While the two anthologies mentioned earlier represent the core of the kōan tradition, it remains a living tradition, with new kōans being proposed to fit new times and places.

Kōbō Daishi. *See* KŪKAI.

ko-i (Chin, 'matching meanings'). A way of coining a necessary technical vocabulary in Chinese for Buddhist texts and translations. This technique, which involved looking for terms within pre-existing Chinese religious thought (primarily *Taoist), as opposed to using Chinese characters strictly for their sound value as a way of representing *Sanskrit words, carried with it the danger that readers unfamiliar with the Sanskrit originals would read the words in their ordinary native meaning, thus distorting the Chinese understanding of the texts.

Koliya (also Koḷiya). Name of a republican clan in *India at the time of the *Buddha. Their territory was adjacent to the *Śākyas, the clan to which the Buddha belonged, and the clans intermarried. Their lands were separated by the river Rohiṇī, and the Buddha once intervened to settle a quarrel between them concerning rights to the waters. After the Buddha's *death the Koliyans were given a one-eighth share of his *relics, over which they erected a *stūpa.

komusō (Jap.). In *Japan, wandering *monks belonging to the *Fuke school who traverse the countryside playing the bamboo flute. They can be recognized by their distinctive bamboo hats in the form of a beehive, which conceal their identities.

Korea. The history of *Buddhism in Korea can conveniently be divided into six periods.

The Three Kingdoms Period (*c.*1–668)
Buddhism was introduced into the Korean peninsula at a time when the local tribes were first consolidating into three large kingdoms (Koguryŏ, Paekche, and Silla), and when Chinese religion, writing, calendrics, and so forth were making inroads into Korean culture. Official histories give the date of Buddhism's introduction as 372 CE, when a Chinese *monk arrived in Koguryŏ as an emissary of the Chinese court bringing scriptures and images. Buddhism reached Silla by the 5th century CE, but the fact that the local élites already knew something of its teachings leads scholars to believe that it had already penetrated the peninsula through more informal channels prior to its official reception.

The Unified Silla Period (668–918)
Silla, originally the smallest and most isolated of the three kingdoms, came to prominence in the sixth century. During this time, Buddhism became the official religion of the court under King Pŏphung (r. 514–39), who used it as part of an ideological campaign to justify the newly established institution of kingship. This factor, plus the absorption of the more fully sinicized populations of Paekche and Koguryŏ, led to increased ties with *China, and delegations of young men went there to study Buddhism. The Unified Silla period also marked one of the high points of Korean Buddhist art. The early part of this period, extending to the year 780, was marked by a peace and stability that enabled intellectuals to travel, practise, and explore Buddhist doctrines. During this time, scholar-monks such as *Wŏnhyo (617–86), Ŭisang (625–702), and *Wonch'uk (631–96) travelled to China and worked with eminent masters and translators, returning to Korea to share their accomplishments and learning. Through their efforts, Korean Buddhism absorbed scholastic forms of Buddhist thought such as *Hua-yen (Kor., Hwaŏm), consciousness-only (Skt., *vijñapti-mātra; Chin., Wei-shih; Kor., Yusik), and *tathāgata-garbha thought, and also took in more popular forms, most notably *Pure Land (Kor., Chŏngt'o). Wŏnhyo in particular contributed to the systematization of scholastic Buddhism into an overarching structure called 't'ong pulgyo' or 'unified Buddhism', and disseminated Pure Land practice widely among the commoners after his return to lay life. During this period in China, the *Ch'an, or meditation, school began its ascent to prominence, and its methods and teachings began filtering into Korea during the 7th century. However, it was during the period of instability and upheaval at the end of the Silla period beginning about 780 that the Ch'an school, known in Korea as *Sŏn, came into its own. During this period many students of Hwaŏm and other intellectual schools began travelling to China to study Sŏn meditation, and they established the so-called 'nine mountains' (Kor., kusan), or nine prominent monastic centres of Sŏn recognized by the government. These institutions, along with the five officially sanctioned schools of doctrinal study, gave Korean Buddhism its designation as the 'five schools and nine mountains' (ojong kusan), or 'five doctrinal and two meditation schools' (ogyo yangjong).

The Koryŏ Period (918–1392)
Buddhism continued to dominate national religious life during the early *Koryŏ period. T'aejo, the dynasty's founder, even left instructions to his heirs stating that the success of the nation depended upon the vitality of Buddhism. With government backing, the

monasteries acquired extensive tracts of agricultural land, engaged in banking, and even retained private militias to protect their interests. Such extensive material resources allowed the publication of the entire known Buddhist *canon between 1210 and 1231. When the woodblocks from this first printing were destroyed by Mongol invasions in 1232, a new set of blocks was ordered, which were completed between 1236 and 1251. Some 81,000 of these blocks remain stored at the Haein-sa on Mt. Kaya in southern Korea, and represent a cultural and religious legacy unique in the world. Buddhism's political and economic power led many people into the ranks of the clergy for very worldly reasons, leading to increasing corruption. In addition, the schools of doctrinal study and meditation had difficulty defining their unity, and often quarrelled loudly and publicly. This situation called forth efforts at reform and definition, led in the early Koryŏ by Ŭich'ŏn (1055–1101) and later by *Chinul (1158–1210). The former, a prince of the royal court, remained too hostile to Sŏn to have much success, but the latter, through both scholarship and meditative attainment, did bring some degree of unity to the scene. He drew upon the Chinese master *Tsung-mi's (780–841) pioneering work to effect his synthesis, and promulgated the latter's formula '*sudden enlightenment followed by gradual practice' as the norm. He also spread the method of *kōan practice among Sŏn adherents. Later figures such as T'aego Pou (1301–82) built upon Chinul's work and, after travelling in China, brought the *Lin-chi school of Ch'an (Kor., Imje) into Korea. However, despite the efforts of these figures, Buddhism in the latter part of the Koryŏ went into a decline as corruption and decadence worsened, and these prepared the scene for Buddhism's formal suppression under the Yi dynasty.

The Ch'osŏn Period (1392–1910)

The fall of Koryŏ in 1392 and its replacement by the heavily pro-Confucian Yi dynasty spelt the end of Korean Buddhism's golden age and the beginning of a period of persecution and declining influence that lasted 518 years. As each ruler ascended the throne, stronger and stronger anti-Buddhist measures went into effect. These included a halt to new temple construction; restrictions on *ordinations; the actual closing of monasteries in urban areas and their gradual restriction to isolated mountain sites; and a proscription on travel by *monks and *nuns, which eventuated in their being forbidden from entering cities altogether. On the intellectual and institutional front, the panoply of doctrinal and meditative schools in existence at the end of the Koryō was reduced to only two: doctrine and Sŏn. By the end of the period, only the latter remained.

The Japanese Annexation (1910–45)

In August 1910, the Japanese government officially annexed Korea and made it part of a wider sphere of colonial influence outside of the constitutional protections it offered its own citizens. Ironically perhaps, this development helped bring to an end Buddhism's long exile from the mainstream of Korean life. Since the Japanese saw Buddhism as a point of contact with Korean culture, they demanded, and received, the lifting of many of the restrictions imposed on the clergy during the long Ch'osŏn period. Monks and nuns could freely travel and enter cities once again, and new temples could be constructed closer to population centres. At the same time, however, the Japanese exerted pressure on Korean monks and nuns to abandon their distinct ways of life and practice in order to adopt Japanese Buddhist practices, and to give up their institutional independence in order to submit themselves to Japanese Buddhist schools and lineages. The most contentious issues concerned clerical *marriage and the addition of wine and meat to the *diet, trends that had marked Japanese Buddhist life for some time. Some monks (though no nuns) adopted the new style, while others resisted, thus setting the stage for the conflicts that ensued when the Japanese withdrew in 1945.

1945–Present

In 1945 the country was divided in two at the 38th parallel and in 1948 the communist Democratic People's Republic of North Korea was declared in the north and the pro-USA Republic of Korea was founded in the south. Since that time Buddhism has been completely suppressed in the north. In the south, with the restoration of native rule in 1945, an intense conflict broke out between monks who had taken wives and abandoned many of the normal monastic *precepts, and those who had not. These latter insisted upon the full restoration of *celibacy and the strict enforcement of traditional Korean rules, and they further insisted that the former group be ejected from monastic properties, which would then be turned over to their control. The latter group, consolidated under the now-dominant *Chogye Order, eventually won out after several court battles, legislative victories, and open hostilities. Thus, after a painful transition period, married monks left the monasteries, and monastic life returned to pre-Japanese practices. Since then, the Chogye Order has overseen the revival and revitalization of Korean Buddhism. Some bitterness broke out in the late 1980s and early 1990s between Buddhists and Christians (the latter group having grown dramatically over the last century), leading to the burning of some Buddhist temples, but overall, Buddhism has once again taken its place as an integral part of Korean society.

Körösi, Csoma (1784–1842). Hungarian scholar who travelled to western *Tibet and parts of central Asia in a quest to find the origins of the Hungarian people. During a two-year stay in Ladakh, he was the first Western scholar to study Tibetan and produced a translation of the **Mahāvyutpatti*, a Tibetan grammar, a survey of the Tibetan *canon, and articles on Tibetan culture.

Koryŏ Period (918–1392). A period of political unity in *Korea during which *Buddhism flourished under state support. This period saw the publication of the Korean Buddhist *canon in the early 13th century, and also the intellectual and ecumenical activities of influential figures such as Ŭich'ŏn (1055–1101) *Chinul (1158–1210), and *T'aego Pou (1301–82). However, prosperity also brought laxity and corruption, and by the end of the period, the Buddhist monastic establishment had fallen into much disrepute, paving the way for the repression of Buddhism in the subsequent *Ch'osŏn Period (1392–1909).

Kośa school. A minor school of *Buddhism during its early period in *China, which focused on the study of the **Abhidharmakośa* by the Indian sage *Vasubandhu, translated into Chinese by *Paramārtha between 563 and 567. This text, usually seen by the Chinese as a *Hīnayāna work, was Vasubandhu's attempt to synthesize the *Abhidharma thought of the *Sarvāstivāda school of north *India, and deals with all aspects of Buddhist psychology and metaphysics. The school always had a tenuous existence, and by 703 the imperial court registered specialists in this text as belonging to the *Fa-hsiang school. However, it did flourish during a time when *Japan actively sought Buddhist teachings and texts, and it was transmitted to that country as the '*Kusha school', one of the *Six Schools of *Nara Buddhism.

Kośala (Pāli., Kosala). One of the major Indian states at the time of the *Buddha *Śākyamuni which was situated to the north-west of its great rival, *Magadha. The capital was located at *Śrāvastī, an important junction of three major trade routes in northern *India from which it derived its wealth. The Buddha spent much of his time in this region and was on especially good terms with its king, *Prasenajit, who was an early patron of *Buddhism. Within a few decades, Kośala was conquered by *Ajātaśatru and absorbed into the growing Magadhan Empire.

Kosambī. Important city in the time of the *Buddha located some 30 leagues west of *Vārāṇasī (Benares) by river. There were four residences (*ārāma) for use by the *monks, and the *Buddha stayed in them on several occasions. Kosambī was the site of the only *schism to occur during the Buddha's life when a monk was excommunicated as a result of an alleged monastic offence. The monk disputed his guilt and a bitter quarrel broke out between his supporters and opponents. The Buddha intervened but the parties refused to heed him and even came to blows. A second intervention by the Buddha failed to secure results and disgusted he withdrew to the forest for a solitary retreat. Under pressure from the laity the monks repented, resolved their dispute, and sought the Buddha's pardon.

kotsu. A kind of ornamental mace or baton held by the abbot of a Japanese temple or a senior teacher as a symbol of authority.

Kōya, Mt. Mountain located south of Kyoto, this mountain serves as the headquarters of the *Shingon school. The founder of Shingon, *Kūkai (774–835) received imperial permission in 816 to establish a centre of esoteric practice there, but was unable to complete the temple complex before his death. At first, Mt. Kōya shared leadership with the *Tōji, which had been the other primary centre of Kūkai's activities, which led to a struggle for supremacy. However, Kūkai's body had been entombed on the mountain, and legends of the master's 'eternal *samādhi' on the mountain made it a popular *pilgrimage site. Based on this and other factors, the mountain did eventually achieve clear leadership.

Koyasan (also Kōyasan). *See* MT. KŌYA.

kriyā-tantra (Skt.). 'Action tantra', a term used for the first of the four late classificatory categories of tantra in *Buddhism. This group of tantras largely represent the earliest developmental phase of *tantric Buddhism and comprises key works such as the **Susiddhikāra Tantra*, the **Subāhu-paripṛcchā*, the **Sarva-maṇḍala-sāmānya-vidhi-guhya Tantra* and the **Dhyānottara-paṭala*. According to later Indo-Tibetan exegesis, this class of tantras primarily teach external, object-based practices and rituals.

kṣānti (Skt.; Pāli, khanti). Patient acceptance, endurance, or tolerance, an important Buddhist virtue aimed at overcoming anger.

kṣānti-pāramitā (Skt.). The Perfection of Patience, the third of the Six Perfections (*ṣaḍ-pāramitā) that make up the central element of the *Mahāyāna path. The cultivation of this virtue involves two aspects: to be patient without anger in the face of harm done by others and to endure various afflictions and *suffering; and to be unafraid of the implications of such *Mahāyāna teachings as emptiness (*śūnyatā).

kṣatriya (Skt.; Pāli, khattiya). The noble or warrior *caste, the second of the four castes.

Kṣitigarbha. A mythical *Bodhisattva in *Mahāyāna *Buddhism, especially associated with the underworld. Kṣitigarbha is popular in *Japan where he is known as *Jizō bosatsu and associated with the care of young children who have died an untimely death. Statues of Kṣitigarbha are common in Japanese cemeteries which depict him as a smiling *monk with a staff and jewels in his hands; these statues usually have votive bibs of red cloth tied around his neck. *See also* ABORTION.

Kuan-yin (Jap., *Kannon). One form of the Chinese name assigned to the *Bodhisattva of compassion (*karuṇā), *Avalokiteśvara. This Chinese form means 'to hear or regard the sounds', and is a contraction of Kuan Shih Yin 'to hear or regard the sounds of the world', indicating the Bodhisattva's ability to hear the cries of all beings in need or trouble. In the **Heart Sūtra*, he is given the name Kuan Tzu Tsai. He is one of the most popular objects of devotion and reverence in east Asian *Buddhism. The *locus classicus* for Kuan-yin's major attributes and functions is the seventh fascicle of the **Lotus Sūtra*, in which the Bodhisattva proclaims his all-embracing compassion and willingness to act on behalf of all *suffering beings. He tells the assembly that if anyone is in any need or trouble, whether shipwreck, threat of bandits, storms, or other perils, all they need do is call upon his name single-mindedly and he will deliver them. In addition, he will grant the requests of all who pray to him. In particular, he promises to grant a child to any woman who prays to him for one, and the image of the 'child-granting Kuan-yin' has become especially popular. Finally, he says that he will assume any form in order to conform to the expectations and inclinations of anyone in order to teach them the *Dharma and convert them: he might manifest as a *Buddha, a high *celestial Bodhisattva, a *monk, a *nun, a layman or laywoman, or even a prostitute if required. In addition to these characteristics found in the *Lotus Sūtra*, the *Pure Land traditions in *China and *Japan revere Kuan-yin as one of the Three Holy Ones of *Sukhāvatī. As described in the *Meditation Sūtra*, the *Larger *Sukhāvatī-vyūha Sūtra*, and the *Smaller Sukhāvatī-vyūha Sūtra*, the Buddha *Amitābha presides over this Pure Land, and is assisted by the two Bodhisattvas Avalokiteśvara and *Mahāsthāmaprāpta.

Kuan-yin's ability to appear in any form needed has led to a profusion of iconographic representations. The Bodhisattva can be represented as both male and female as need and occasion demand. The greatest number of variations appear within esoteric scriptures, *maṇḍalas, and images, in which he can appear in normal human shape, or with any number of heads, eyes, and arms, and also in independent guises with different names such as Chun-t'i. In one common practice, the devotee recites the Great Compassion

Mantra (Chin., Ta pei chou) while visualizing 108 separate forms of the Bodhisattva in sequence. The Bodhisattva's broad compassion (*karuṇā), all-embracing vows, ability to manifest in various forms, and easy accessibility have all served to make him the most widely called-upon source of help not only in east Asian Buddhism, but in the folk beliefs of all regions as well.

Kucha. A small early medieval oasis state situated on the northern route of the *Silk Road. *Buddhism was established here at an early date under the influence of the *Kuṣāṇa dynasty and Kucha soon became an important centre for *Hīnayāna forms of Buddhism. Apart from a number of manuscript fragments found in the region, Kucha is especially important to the art historian for the volume and quality of paintings that have been found in the area. Kucha was also famous as the birthplace of the great translator, *Kumārajīva.

Kuei-shan Ling-yu (771–853). A Chinese *Ch'an *monk and the founder of the Kuei-Yang lineage, one of the '*Five Houses' of Ch'an.

Kūkai (774–835). *Heian period Japanese *monk and the founder of the *Shingon ('Mantra' or 'True Word') school of *Buddhism. Born into a prominent family in Shikoku, he was sent to study *Confucianism, poetry, and culture in Nagaoka and later at the imperial university, with hopes for attaining a high governmental position. However, he abruptly abandoned his studies midway and entered the Buddhist order. From the beginning Kūkai was attracted to esoteric practice, and devoted himself to chanting *mantras and studying esoteric scriptures. After a period of living in the mountains as a self-ordained monk, he decided to go to *China to further his knowledge. Sailing with a diplomatic delegation in 804, he went to the capital *Ch'ang-an and met the esoteric master Hui-kuo (746–805), a man widely recognized as the seventh *patriarch of the esoteric school (*see* ESOTERIC BUDDHISM) of China. According to legend, Hui-kuo, upon seeing Kūkai enter the temple, immediately saw in him the disciple for whom he had been waiting all his life. He personally took Kūkai through many stages of esoteric initiation (*abhiṣekha) and training in the brief time remaining in his life, and Kūkai returned to *Japan in 806 wearing the mantle of the eighth patriarch. At first, Kūkai had difficulty establishing himself. *Saichō (767–822), who had sailed to China in the same fleet and later was to found the *Tendai school, had returned to Japan first bringing his own training in esoteric rituals to the court, and so Kūkai appeared redundant at first. However, it became apparent that his training had been far more extensive and specialized than Saichō's, and after three years he began to rise to prominence and ultimately overshadowed Saichō as Japan's premier esoteric master.

Kūkai is remembered as one of Japan's greatest calligraphers, and it was this that finally brought him to the attention of the court, since Emperor Saga valued this art and is himself considered a master of it. After he gave Kūkai many commissions to inscribe court documents, the two became friendly and Kūkai successfully petitioned him for permission to construct a monastery complex (*vihāra) on Mt. *Kōya to serve as an exclusive centre for esoteric training. Construction on this site began in 819. Although much work was done during his lifetime, the imperial court kept Kūkai very busy making inscriptions, performing rituals for the protection and peace of the nation, and renovating other temples. This, combined with the remoteness of Mt. Kōya, prevented Kūkai from seeing the completion of this project. The next emperor Junna gave Kūkai the task of completing the *Tōji, or Eastern Temple, in the capital city, in return for which he promised to make it an exclusive venue for esoteric practice in which Kūkai would have charge of 50 monks. Perhaps reflecting on the benefits of his own early education, Kūkai made this temple the site of a 'School of Arts and Sciences', which accepted students from all walks of life regardless of ability to pay and offered a complete curriculum in both Buddhist and secular subjects. In 847, however, the burden of maintaining the school became too great, and the Tōji sold it off. Esoteric Buddhism was still new, even in China, during Kūkai's lifetime, and his many writings, as well as his work in cataloguing scriptures and ritual texts, put the school on a firm intellectual footing by the time of his death.

kuladuhitṛ. *Sanskrit term meaning 'a nobly born daughter', a term used in *Mahāyāna *sūtras to denote lay female devotees of the Mahāyāna.

kulaputra. *Sanskrit term meaning 'a nobly born son' or 'member of a clan', a term used frequently in *Mahāyāna *sūtras to denote lay male devotees, often with the added implication that they are *Bodhisattvas. The *Pāli equivalent, 'kulaputta', is equally common in Pāli sūtras.

Kumārajīva (343–413). A central Asian Buddhist *monk who travelled to *China and became one of the 'four great translators' of Chinese Buddhist texts. Born in *Kucha, he entered the monastic order at the age of 7 and distinguished himself in both *Sarvāstivādin and *Mahāyāna studies. In 379 his fame had reached even into China, and the Emperor Fu Chien of the Eastern Ch'in dynasty sent a delegation to invite him to court. Kumārajīva accepted, but on the way back the general sent to fetch him, Lü Kuang, rebelled and held out against the court in north-western China for seventeen years, during which time he held Kumārajīva captive. While this delay frustrated the court, it gave Kumārajīva a chance to become very fluent in Chinese prior to undertaking his translation activities. After Lü Kuang's rebellion was suppressed, Kumārajīva arrived in *Ch'ang-an in 401 and immediately began producing translations. The combination of his mastery of Indian Buddhist thought and his proficiency in Chinese not only enabled him to produce translations that are still the standard (as, for example, his translation of the **Lotus Sūtra*), but also to provide instruction that cleared up many misapprehensions of Buddhist doctrine, in particular the teaching of emptiness (Skt., *śūnyatā).

Kumāra Kassapa. An elder (*thera), famous for his eloquent preaching. His mother became a *nun unaware that she was pregnant with him. He received the lower *ordination (*pravrajya) as a young boy and was dubbed 'the boy' (kumāra) Kassapa as a result. At the age of 20 he was given the higher ordination (*upasampadā), and when it was pointed out that the rules require a minimum age of 21, the *Buddha allowed the time spent in the mother's womb to be included in the reckoning.

Kum-bum (Tib., sku-'bum). An important monastery (*vihāra) of the *Gelukpa school situated in the district of Tsongkha in present-day Ch'ing hai province. It was founded in 1588 at the birthplace of *Tsongkhapa, in accordance with the decree of *Dalai Lama III, Sonam Gyatso (bsod-nams rsya-mtsho), and later underwent considerable enlargement. Its name, literally 'a hundred thousand *Buddha images', derives from its extensive iconographical features.

Kün Dün (Tib., Kun 'dun). Name by which the Tibetans commonly refer to the *Dalai Lama. It means 'the presence.' An alternative appellation is Gyelwa *Rinpoche (Tib., rgyal ba rin po che), meaning 'precious lord'.

k'ung. The Chinese word for emptiness (Skt., *śūnyatā).

kung-an (Chin.). *See* KŌAN.

kung-fu (Chin.). In Chinese, a general term for spiritual discipline. While many in the West use the term to refer to a particular form of *martial arts, the word actually means any discipline that one undertakes as a vehicle for spiritual development. Thus, besides martial arts, other arts such as dancing, flower arranging, calligraphy, or painting can be considered one's 'kung-fu'.

Kuru. One of the sixteen polities of ancient *India lying to the north-west near modern Delhi, between the Yamunā and the Ganges, north of *Mathurā. Though relatively unimportant during his lifetime, the country is said to have been visited on a few occasions by the *Buddha *Śākyamuni and a few discourses were given there.

Kurundī-aṭṭhakathā. Body of early commentarial literature on the texts of the *Pāli Canon, and in particular on the *Vinaya Piṭaka. This material, written in Sinhalese and now lost, was used by *Buddhaghoṣa in the composition of his exegetical works. Its name derives from the site where it was compiled, the Kurundavelu monastery (*vihāra) in *Sri Lanka.

kuśala (Skt.; Pāli, kusala). Term of moral approbation denoting that which is good, virtuous, or wholesome, such as the 'ten good actions' (*daśa-kuśala-karmapatha). Deeds which are kuśala produce good *karma or merit (*puṇya). They are thus conducive to happiness in general, prevent *rebirth in negative modes of existence, and weaken ties to *saṃsāra.

kuśala-mūla (Skt.; Pāli, kusaka-mūla). Collective name for the three roots of good, being non-greed (arāga), non-hatred (adveṣa), and non-delusion (amoha). Expressed in a positive form they correspond to unselfishness, benevolence, and understanding. All good or virtuous states of consciousness are seen as ultimately grounded in one or more of these three. They are the opposite of the three roots of evil (*akuśala-mūla) or unwholesome mental states of greed (*raga), hatred (*dveṣa), and delusion (*moha).

Kuṣāṇa. A dynasty established in north-west and central *India by people of Turkic origin who had earlier migrated from the Chinese borders of central Asia. At its peak under *Kaniṣka I, the Kuṣāṇa territory extended from present-day Afghanistan as far east as *Magadha, but the empire was short-lived and disintegrated by the end of the 3rd century CE. The Kuṣāṇas were devout adherents of *Buddhism and were instrumental in supporting its growth throughout India and its transmission to many parts of central Asia.

Kusha school. One of the so-called '*Six Schools of *Nara *Buddhism' that appeared in *Japan during the early period of *Buddhism's development. More an area of specialized study than a school as such, this group of scholarly *monks concentrated on the study and teaching of the Indian Buddhist master *Vasubandhu's **Abhidharma-kośa*, a compendium of *Sarvāstivādin teachings. These scholars saw themselves as successors to the *Kośa school in *China.

kushō(-nembutsu) (Jap.). The *Pure Land practice of orally invoking the name of *Amitābha *Buddha in order to gain *rebirth in the Pure Land of *Sukhāvatī. This term is opposed to *kannen-nembutsu, wherein the devotee attempts to keep a visualized image of the Buddha constantly in mind.

Kuśinagara (Pāli, Kusinārā). The capital of the *Malla state at the time of the *Buddha, located on one of the tributaries of the river Gogrā. It was here that the Buddha passed into *parinirvāṇa under a pair of śāla trees and was cremated outside this town. Shortly after the Buddha's death, the land of the Mallas was absorbed into the growing *Magadhan empire. The town of Kuśinagara flourished for many centuries after as an important *pilgrimage place for Buddhists, though it was all but forgotten by the 13th century CE. The ruins of the great Parinirvāṇa *Stūpa were discovered and excavated by archaeologists in 1878, and the stūpa was later restored in 1927 and 1956 with donations from *Burma.

Kūṭāgārasālā. Pāli term meaning 'The Hall of the Gabled Roof', being the name of a residence near *Vaiśālī where the *Buddha often stayed and received visitors. Several noteworthy incidents took place here. It was here that the Buddha finally agreed to allow *women to be ordained as *nuns, and where a number of *monks committed *suicide as a result of misinterpreting a sermon by the Buddha on the foulness of the body. Also here the Buddha made the prediction that his death would take place in three months' time.

Kūya (903–72). The earliest Japanese *monk to spread the practice of the *nembutsu, or oral invocation of the name of *Amitābha *Buddha, among the common people. Widely admired for his devotion to the practice and his willingness to live outside the élite circles within Buddhist temples, he became the precursor of an entire class of religious wanderers called nembutsu *hijiri, or 'wandering sages of the nembutsu'.

Kwannon. Japanese name of the *Bodhisattva *Avalokiteśvara in an older form of orthography, now obsolete. Also known as *Kannon.

kyabdro (Tib., skyabs-'gro). Tibetan term for the act of taking refuge in the three jewels (the *Buddha, the *Dharma, and the *Saṃgha) as a verbal or mental declaration of adherence to *Buddhism. The taking of refuge in Tibetan Buddhism begins with a fourth jewel, the *guru, through whom knowledge of the other three is imparted. *See also* TRIŚARAṆA.

kyaung. Burmese term for a monastery or *vihāra, similar to the Thai and Khmer term '*wat'.

kyōsaku (Jap.). Literally meaning 'warning stick', this refers to a long, thin, flat stick used during sessions of formal seated *meditation in *Zen monasteries. The godō, or head trainer, in a Zen monastery uses it to give a series of sharp blows on the shoulders of any practitioners whom he sees dozing or slackening in their efforts. At times, practitioners themselves signal the godō to administer blows in order to sharpen their concentration.

Kyoto. A city in *Japan known for the quantity of famous old Buddhist temples and monuments. During the *Heian period, it was the capital city (called Heian at the time), and remained the centre of the imperial court even after the military rulers of the *Kamakura and later periods established the bakufu government elsewhere. Thus, it attracted the founders of many of the schools of *Buddhism that came into existence during the Heian and Kamakura periods as a suitable place for their temples.

Kyoto school. A school of *Zen Buddhist studies in 20th-century *Japan that combines traditional Zen learning with influences from European, primarily German, philosophy. The founder of this school is generally acknowledged to be *Nishida Kitarō (1870–1945), whose writings, such as *An Inquiry into the Good* (1911), *Intuition and Reflection in Self-Consciousness* (1917), and his major work *Fundamental Problems of Philosophy* (1933), enunciated an experiential understanding of 'nothingness' and 'the identity of contradictories' based in his own early Zen training and enlightenment (*satori), but here expressed in conversation with European mystics and German idealism. After Nishida, the inquiries of the school were carried forward by Tanabe Hajime (1885–1962), Hisamatsu Shin'ichi (1889–1980), and *Nishitani Keiji (1900–90).

kyūdō (Jap., way of the bow). In *Zen *Buddhism, the art of archery when used as a technique of concentration and spiritual discipline.

L

lakṣaṇa (Skt., mark). Term used mainly in Buddhist scholasticism (*Abhidharma) to denote the specific identifying attribute or defining characteristic of an entity. As an example, all phemomena (*dharma) are said to bear the three 'marks' of impermanence (*anitya), suffering (*duḥkha), and no-self (*anātman). In *Abhidharma tabulations, various defining characteristics were identified for different phenomena, such as heat as the defining characteristic of fire, or hardness as that of earth. In some *Mahāyāna sources the lakṣana of a thing came to be defined as that mental concept (*vikalpa) by which one knows, defines, and understands an object which has a particular perceptual form (*nimitta), such as being of a particular colour, and so forth.

lalanā. In *tantric mystical physiology, the channel (*nāḍī) to the right of the *avadhūti which starts in the right-hand nostril and terminates at the anal orifice. It is visualized as a fine red tube and the energy or 'wind' (*vāyu) flowing through it is thought to generate the subjective aspect of cognition. Like the *rasanā channel, it is thought to coil around the avadhūti and form knots at the *cakras of the the navel, heart, throat, and the crown of the head.

Lalitavistara (Skt., graceful description). An early *sūtra, probably 1st century CE, surviving in *Sanskrit and Tibetan, primarily concerned with a biography of the *Buddha *Śākyamuni up to the start of his teaching mission. This text is thought to have been based on *Sarvāstivādin material which was subsequently developed into its present form of 27 chapters in mixed prose and verse. Originally it was probably a non-*Mahāyāna work to which Mahāyāna elements were subsequently added. Its depiction of the Buddha in supernatural terms may have been influential in the development of Mahāyāna Buddhology such as the concept of the 'three bodies' (*trikāya), although this may equally be the result of the influence of *Yogācāra Buddhology.

lama (Tib., bla-ma). A Tibetan title of respect used to translate the term '*guru', originally denoting a teacher but now used more widely for any *monk.

lama dancing (Tib., 'chams). Tibetan Buddhist religious dance, performed to ritual music by masked dancers enacting various religious dramas depicting subjects such as the subjugation of demons.

lamaism. An obsolete term formerly used by Western scholars to denote the specifically Tibetan form of *Buddhism due to the prominence of the *lamas in the religious culture. The term should be avoided as it is misleading as well as disliked by Tibetans.

lam-dre (Tib., lam-'bras). The cycle of 'path and result' teachings transmitted to *Tibet by the great Indian *siddha Virūpa (*c.* 11th century CE), especially associated with the *Sakya school. The teachings are based on a short root text, the *Vajra Verses*, and aim to actualize an experience of the indivisible nature of *saṃsāra and *nirvāṇa through a combination of *sūtra and *tantric teachings and practices. These are believed to lead to an insight into the true nature of mind, identified as its luminosity, its *emptiness, and the union of these two aspects.

Lamotte, Étienne (1903–1983). A renowned Belgian scholar of *Buddhism, Mgr Étienne Lamotte was an ordained priest and Prelate of the Pope's Household. As a young man, his studies included classical philology and theology and later oriental languages at Rome, Paris, and Louvain. He studied under his great compatriot Louis *de La Vallée Poussin, and specialized in the translation of Buddhist texts from Tibetan and Chinese where the *Sanskrit original was no longer extant. His contributions in this field include translations of the **Mahāyāna-saṃgraha*, the **Vimalakīrti-nirdeśa Sūtra*, and the **Śūraṅgama-samādhi*

Sūtra. His greatest works were his *Histoire du Bouddhisme Indien* and his five-volume translation of the *Mahāprajñā-pāramitā Śāstra*. In the course of his life he received many honours, among them honorary fellowships of the *Royal Asiatic Society and the British Academy.

lam-rim (Tib., path stages). A class of Tibetan religious literature which, as its name 'stages of the path' suggests, chiefly deals with practical matters to guide the Buddhist practitioner from his or her first contact with *Buddhism up to enlightenment (*bodhi). The teachings include a hierarchical set of levels through which the adept proceeds, while progressively cultivating the virtues and qualities of a *Bodhisattva. This class of literature has Indian antecedents such as the *Bodhi-patha-pradīpa* (Lamp for the Path to Enlightenment) by *Atiśa, but masters of Tibetan Buddhism have produced such works suitable for their own school, such as *Gampopa's **Jewel Ornament of Liberation* or *Tsongkhapa's *Lam-rim chenmo* (Great Stages of the Path).

Lang Darma (803–42) (Tib., glang dar-ma). The brother and successor of Ralpachen, he became ruler of *Tibet in 836 when he began a persecution and suppression of *Buddhism at the instigation of several powerful *Bön families who were hostile to Buddhism. He was assassinated by a Buddhist *monk, Belgi Dorje (Tib., dpal gyi rdo je), an event commemorated in the so-called 'Black Hat Dance'. After his assassination, the Tibetan royal dynasty of Yar lung ended and Tibet entered a period of civil and cultural chaos.

Laṅkāvatāra Sūtra. A Buddhist scripture that has exercised a great deal of influence in the development of east Asian *Buddhism. Three translations appear in the Chinese *canon of scriptures: (1) a translation in four fascicles done by *Guṇabhadra while residing in Yang-chou in 443 (*Taishō 670); (2) a translation in ten fascicles by *Bodhiruci completed in 513 (Taishō 671); (3) a translation in seven fascicles by Śikṣānanda completed between 700 and 704 (Taishō 672). As the wide variation in the lengths of the completed translations shows, the text of the *sūtra was not stable, but varied over time, and it is likely that the translators worked with different *Sanskrit recensions from different times or different geographical areas. The text itself lacks systematicity, and is more of a compilation or miscellany of *Mahāyāna teachings recorded in no particular order. This led the Japanese scholar D. T. *Suzuki to speculate that it represented nothing more than a notebook containing the jottings of a Mahāyāna master who recorded various teachings, doctrines, and stories as he (or she) came across them (D. T. Suzuki, *The Laṅkāvatāra Sūtra: A Mahāyāna Text* (London, 1932), p. xi).

The disorderliness of the text notwithstanding, this scripture has exercised an enormous influence in the development of east Asian Buddhist thought. It united the teaching of the *tathāgata-garbha (embryonic Buddha) with that of the *ālaya-vijñāna, or 'storehouse consciousness', into a single entity that lay at the base of both human consciousness and the external world. It expounded the doctrine of 'mind-only' (*citta-mātra), that is, that the world and all its contents are but manifestations of the mind, and that because of this, the division of the world into perceiving subject and perceived objects is false and the source of ignorance. Because of this teaching, the *Laṅkāvatāra Sūtra* was an important text for the *Fa-hsiang school in *China and the *Hossō school in *Japan. It is also a pivotal work in the history of *Ch'an Buddhism in China. The first *patriarch of Ch'an, *Bodhidharma (3rd–4th centuries), was revered as a master of the *Laṅkāvatāra Sūtra*, and indeed an early history of the Ch'an school is the text, *Record of the Masters and Disciples of the Laṅkāvatāra Sūtra* (Chin., *Leng-ch'ieh shih-tzu chi*). This focus on the *Laṅkāvatāra Sūtra* remained a feature of the school until the 7th century, and a dispute over whether or not to continue its emphasis may have been a factor in the controversy between the so-called '*Northern' and '*Southern' Schools. This is symbolically narrated in the **Platform Sūtra of the Sixth Patriarch* in a scene in which *Hui-neng (638–713) has his enlightenment (*bodhi) verse inscribed on a wall that had recently been prepared for a painter to paint scenes from the *Laṅkāvatāra Sūtra*. After the fifth patriarch, *Hung-jen, sees the verse, he cancels the artist's commission, a gesture compatible with the Ch'an school's later self-characterization as a school that eschewed words and scriptures. One other area in which the *Laṅkāvatāra Sūtra* influenced Chinese Buddhism in particular is in its chapter on eating meat, which has become the standard proof-text for Chinese Buddhism's staunch adherence to vegetarianism (*see also* DIET).

Lao-tsu. *See* TAOISM.

Laughing Buddha. *See* PU-TAI.

laukika (Skt., mundane). Any activity or practice associated with the profane world of unenlightened beings (*pṛthagjana) and which is regarded as not conducive to liberation.

left-hand tantra. A term derived from Hindu tantrism, used erroneously by some scholars in a Buddhist context to indicate those tantras which teach sexual *yoga, fierce rites of destruction, and other forms of antinomian behaviour.

Lhasa. The capital of *Tibet, sited on a tributary of the Brahmaputra river, possibly founded during the 7th century CE reign of *Songtsen Gampo (Tib., Srong-btsan sgampo) who is credited with constructing a fortress there as well as the famous *Jokhang. Its importance declined somewhat during the period after the last Tibetan king in the 9th century but regained its importance under the *Dalai Lama V who established it as the secular and religious headquarters of his hegemony. The construction of the *Potala, the residence of the *Dalai Lamas until 1959, was completed during his reign. A number of important *Gelukpa monasteries such as *Sera and *Ganden are located in the region surrounding Lhasa.

Licchavi. One of the powerful tribes of northern *India at the time of the *Buddha *Śākyamuni who formed part of the Vṛji (Pāli, *Vajji) confederacy with the *Mallas and the *Videhas (*see also* VṚJIPUTRAKA). The capital was located at *Vaiśālī. Unlike many of the contemporary states in ancient India, the Licchavis had adopted a republican form of government which was praised by the Buddha and may have partly inspired the structure and organization of the *Saṃgha.

Light of Asia. *See* ARNOLD, SIR EDWIN.

Lin-chi I-hsüan (d. 866). *T'ang dynasty Chinese *Ch'an *monk and founder of the *Lin-chi school. He originally came from a family named Hsing in Ts'ao-chou, but left home while still quite young and studied Buddhist teaching and practice in many places with many teachers. He achieved his enlightenment (*satori) experience and received *inka from *Huang-po Hsi-yün (d. 850), and thereafter made free use of Huang-po's methods of beating students and shouting directly into their ears. Aside from these 'shock' techniques, Lin-chi also gained renown for his mastery of the most complex Buddhist thought as contained in the **Hua-yen ching*, and his ability to teach and illustrate it in plain and straightforward language. In 851 he moved into the Lin-chi Temple in Hopei, from which he took the name by which he is mainly known and which lent its name to the lineage that followed after him. The Lin-chi school thereafter became the most successful and widespread of the '*Five Houses' of Ch'an, and became the ascendant line of the *Rinzai school of *Zen in *Japan. He is perhaps best known for his dictum, 'If you meet the *Buddha on the road, *kill the Buddha', through which he attempted to turn students' attention away from external images and teachers so that they could discover the truth about themselves.

Lin-chi school. The school of *Ch'an *Buddhism that acknowledged the *T'ang-dynasty *monk *Lin-chi I-hsüan (d. 866) as its *patriarch. During the later *T'ang dynasty this school was relatively minor and was counted as one of the '*Five Houses' of Ch'an at the time. However, by the early years of the Sung dynasty (960–1279), it had risen to great prominence and became, along with the *Ts'ao-tung school, one of the two major schools of Ch'an in *China. During this period of its ascendancy, several monks from *Japan, most notably *Eisai (1141–1215), travelled to China and attained enlightenment (*satori) under the tutelage of masters in the Lin-chi school, and transmitted the lineage back to Japan where it became known as *Rinzai. The lineage of Lin-chi I-hsüan was carried forward by a centralized lineage from master to chief disciple for six generations, but during the seventh two masters came to prominence and established parallel lineages: Yang-ch'i Fang-hui (992–1049) and *Huang-lung Hui-nan (1002–69). Both men were forceful and charismatic teachers, described respectively as the 'tiger and dragon' of Ch'an. The strength of these two lineages was recognized in the designation of the 'Five Houses and Seven Schools' of Ch'an at the time. However, by the end of the Sung period, the Huang-lung school declined while the Yang-ch'i school gained in strength.

Taking its major teaching methods from the example of Lin-chi himself and his teacher, *Huang-po Hsi-yün (d. 850), the Lin-chi school emphasized the use of 'crazy Ch'an' or 'shock Ch'an' techniques during its early period. These methods included shouting directly into a student's ear, beating him, or giving seemingly nonsensical responses to questions. However, as the school gained in popularity and established new temples throughout China, the number of teachers who understood and could skilfully employ these techniques declined, and by the time of Yang-ch'i and Huang-lung, the school shifted its emphasis from the actual use of these methods to the recounting of stories depicting occasions when a teacher had used such a method and successfully prodded a student into enlightenment. These stories, or at least the critical portions of them, came to be collected into anthologies of 'public cases', or kung-an (Jap., *kōan), and their use created a viable alternative to actual beating and shouting. A student could now meditate on the story under the guidance of a master and try to penetrate the sayings and actions of past masters and understand the enlightenment experience for themselves.

The use of 'shock' techniques and kōans stood in contrast to the methods of the other most popular school of Ch'an, Ts'ao-tung, which tended to emphasize 'silent illumination' (Chin., *mo-chao Ch'an). This meant that the student did not use any particular method such as kōan study, because there was nothing to be gained: they were already fully enlightened *Buddhas just as they were, and the point of meditation was simply to realize that fact. The controversy reached its height in the exchange between the Lin-chi school's *Ta-hui Tsung-kao (1089–1163) and the Ts'ao-tung school's *Hung-chih Cheng-chüeh (1091–1157) in which both argued for the superiority of their chosen practices. The literature that emanated from their argument helped to define and harden each school's position. Ironically, the terms 'silent illumination Ch'an' (Chin., mo chao ch'an) and 'kōan-contemplation Ch'an' (Chin., k'an hua ch'an) were first used in this *debate as derogatory terms that each used to caricature his opponent's position, but later entered the vocabulary as standard designations for two equally valid modes of practice. However, in the real world beyond the literary remains of these two great minds, the goal-oriented activity of kōan contemplation appealed more to the artistic and military communities, who saw that the methods of the Lin-chi school produced tangible results, whereas Ts'ao-tung's 'silent illumination' simply rested on the platitude that there was no goal to attain. Therefore, Lin-chi outstripped Ts'ao-tung in its ability to draw support from the lay community. By the end of the Sung, Lin-chi had absorbed all of the other of the 'Five Houses' of Ch'an with the exception of Ts'ao-tung, but at the same time the ascendancy of Neo-*Confucianism drew the interest of the Chinese intelligentsia away from Buddhism and into Confucian studies, and so during the post-Sung period, Lin-chi became marginalized along with the rest of Buddhism.

Liu-tsu Ta Shih (Chin.). Title meaning 'Sixth *Patriarch, Great Master', an honorary title given to *Hui-neng, the sixth patriarch of the *Ch'an school.

lobha (Skt.). Greed, craving (*tṛṣṇā), or *desire. A synonym for *rāga, the first of the the three roots of evil (*akuśala-mūla).

logic. *See* PRAMĀṆA.

lo-han (Chin.). A contraction of the Chinese term a-lo-han, which was used as a phonetic transcription of the *Sanskrit *Arhat.

Lohapāsāda (Pāli). Literally 'copper building'. Name of the building serving as uposatha-hall (*see* UPOSATHA, Skt., poṣadha) for the *Mahāvihāra. Originally built by *Devānampiya Tissa, it was pulled down and rebuilt by *Duṭṭhagāmaṇi Abhaya as a nine-storey building roofed with copper plates, hence its name. The building underwent major repairs and reconstruction through the years and its name was changed to Maṇipāsāda, meaning 'jewel building', after Jeṭṭhatissa, who had offered to the building a very valuable jewel, had it rebuilt. As a result of the rivalry between the monks of the *Abhayagiri and Mahāvihāra monasteries the building was destroyed, but was later rebuilt and subsequently underwent further renovations. Many famous sermons are said to have been preached in the Lohapāsāda.

Loi Krathong. Thai name for The Festival of Lights or The Festival of the Floating Boats, a popular celebration held in *Burma, *Thailand, and Laos on the full-moon day of November. The event takes place approximately one month after the planting of the rice crop, which is also one month after the end of the monastic rainy-season retreat (*vassa). The festival also traditionally coincides with the preaching of the story of Prince Vessantara from the **Vessantara Jātaka* (*see* DESANĀ MAHĀJĀTI) but otherwise has no specific connection with *Buddhism and appears to be agricultural in origin. The festivities involve the floating of small boats on which are placed lighted candles, incense, and small coins. Children may swim out to retrieve the most attractive boats and their cargoes of coins. The celebration is accompanied by picnics and fireworks, and may have some connection with the Hindu (*see* HINDUISM) festival of Dīvālī which is also celebrated in October–November.

loka (Skt.; Pāli, world). The world or universe, in both a cosmological and psychological sense. In the former it is the habitat of gods and human beings, and in the latter all that can be known or experienced through the senses. In general, *Buddhism reserves judgement on the ontological status of the external world: early Buddhism assumes the world is more or less as we experience it, while some later schools move in the direction of idealism (*see* YOGĀCĀRA). However, in Buddhist terms, the objective status of the world is of less importance than how one responds to it and whether one becomes enmeshed in its vanities. Loka is also used to refer to the three *dhātus or cosmological realms (as *kāmadhātu, etc). *See also* COSMOLOGY.

loka-dhamma (Pāli). 'Worldly matters' or concerns that arise in connection with secular life. A list of eight, consisting of four contrasting pairs, is found in *Pāli sources: namely profit and loss, fame and dishonour, praise and blame, and happiness and unhappiness.

Lokakṣema (b. 147 CE). A Han-dynasty Buddhist *monk and one of the earliest translators of Buddhist literature into Chinese. Originally from Scythia, he arrived in the capital *Lo-yang and worked there between 178 and 189, producing about 20 translations, including the important **Pratyutpanna Sūtra* (containing the first mention of *meditation upon *Amitābha *Buddha and his *Pure Land) as well as the first translations of Perfection of Insight literature (*see* Prajñā-pāramitā Sūtras). Thus, his work paved the way for the earliest practice of Pure Land meditation and the discussions of Buddhist philosophy that made possible the 'Profound Learning' (Chin., hsüan hsueh) conversations between Buddhists and *Taoists.

lokapāla (Skt.; Pāli; world protector). In Buddhist mythology the four guardians of the world who stand at the four cardinal points and protect the world and Buddhist teachings. Often known as 'the regents of the four directions' or the 'four great kings' (*caturmahārāja) they are gods who inhabit the lowest *heaven above the human world. Statues of the four lokapālas are often found guarding religious sites.

lokottara (Skt.; Pāli, lokuttara, supermundane). Things related to salvation and the quest for *nirvāṇa as opposed to the mundane world (*see* LAUKIKA). The term is used especially of the 'four paths and four fruits' associated with the Noble Path (*ārya-mārga). In *Mahāyāna *Buddhism, the *Buddha is thought to be supermundane and is regarded as a transcendent being of limitless wisdom and power. *See also* LOKOTTARA-VĀDA.

Lokottara-vāda (Skt.). 'The Supermundane School', also known as 'The One-utterance School' (*Ekavyavahāra), being a subdivision of the *Mahāsaṃghika which taught that a *Buddha in reality is endowed with a supermundane (*lokottara) nature, omniscience, limitless power, and eternal life. It also taught the docetic doctrine that any physical manifestations or actions on earth undertaken by a Buddha are merely appearances or illusory projections performed to save beings. Little literature remains of this school with the exception of the **Mahāvastu* and the *Bhikṣunī*

**Vinaya*, or monastic rule for nuns. The Buddhological ideas of this school seem to have influenced the development of similar *Mahāyāna concepts.

Longchenpa (1308–64) (Tib., klong-chen-pa). The great *Nyingma master and scholar who synthesized the *Dzogchen traditions of *Padmasambhava and *Vimalamitra, and who also wrote prolifically on all aspects of *Buddhism from the Nyingma viewpoint. He also received instructions from outstanding masters of the *Sakya and the *Karma-kagyü schools. He resided as the abbot of *Samyé monastery (*gompa) for a while but also spent much of his life in retreat or travelling as a political refugee. He wrote over 270 works, among which the most noted include the so-called *Seven Treasuries*, a set of seven interrelated treatises, and the cycle of *Easing the Mind*.

long-dé. *See* SPATIAL CATEGORY.

losar (Tib., lo-gsar). The Tibetan New Year, celebrated around February, the precise annual date being calculated according to the traditional Tibetan calendar.

lotus (Skt, padma; Pāli, paduma). The lotus flower (*nelumbium speciosum*), a member of the water-lily family. The plant is used throughout Buddhist literature as a symbol of purity, since it grows with its roots in the mud but its blossom above the water. The mud symbolizes the roots of evil (*akuśala-mūla), namely greed (*rāga), hatred (*dveṣa), and delusion (*moha), while the blossom stands for enlightenment (*bodhi). In iconography, holy figures are often depicted seated on a lotus blossom. Red and white are the colours most commonly associated with the lotus, although a blue lotus (Skt., *utpala) is also known.

lotus posture. Classic *yoga posture known in *Sanskrit as the 'padmāsana' or 'lotus seat'. Seated in this posture the lower legs are drawn in and both feet placed on top of the thighs. Where only one foot is placed on the thigh the posture is known as the 'half lotus'. In both cases the hands rest in the lap and the head is slightly inclined. This position is recommended for *meditation as it provides physical stability for long periods and keeps the spine straight.

Lotus Sūtra. The standard short English title for the highly influential text of which the full title is *The Sūtra of the Lotus Blossom of the Marvellous Dharma* (Skt., *Saddharmapuṇḍarīka Sūtra*; Chin., *Miao-fa lien-hua ching*; Jap., *Myōhō renge kyō*). It is one of the earliest *Mahāyāna scriptures extant, possibly dating from the 1st century BCE, and versions exist today in *Sanskrit, Chinese, and Tibetan. The *Lotus Sūtra* makes two main points to its readers. First, there is only one goal for practitioners of the Buddhist path, that is, Buddhahood. This replaces an older typology that divided the Buddhist path into three distinct streams: (1) that of the *Buddha's disciples (*Śrāvakas, or 'hearers', a term synonymous with *Hīnayānists); (2) that of the *Pratyekabuddhas, or those who find the path to Buddhahood on their own and are fully enlightened, but lack compassion (*karuṇā) and so do not go forth to preach; and (3) *Bodhisattvas, those who vow to achieve perfect wisdom and compassion for the sake of others instead of solely for their own liberation from *suffering. In the *Lotus Sūtra*, the Buddha affirms that he did in the past teach the three paths, but that this teaching was a simple expedient to accommodate those who would be frightened, discouraged, or fatigued by the prospect of working towards full Buddhahood. Second, the *sūtra teaches that a Buddha, upon attaining *nirvāṇa, does not go into extinction, but abides in the world for aeons out of compassion for those still in need of teaching. He reveals to his audience that he himself has been active for many millennia since his attainment of Buddhahood, and that his present, apparently limited life as *Śākyamuni was only an illusion conjured for those unable to cope with receiving teaching from an apparently immortal being. As a confirmation of this teaching, in the midst of the preaching of the sūtra a giant, jewelled *stūpa appears suspended in the air, and as its door opens, the audience sees a Buddha from a previous era named Prabhūtaratna inside, not extinct at all but still quite alive and active, who appears at this time in accordance with a vow to be present whenever the *Lotus Sūtra* is preached. In addition, chapter 25, 'The Universal Gate of the Bodhisattva *Avalokiteśvara', which describes the efficacy of calling upon the Bodhisattva's name in times of distress, contributed greatly to the popularization of his cult, under his Chinese name *Kuan-yin (Jap., *Kannon or *Kwannon).

This sūtra has had a long history in east Asia. Old catalogues of Buddhist literature list at least six Chinese translations dating from 255, 286, 290, 335, 406, and 601 CE, of which only the third, fifth, and sixth remain extant. The third, by *Dharmarakṣa, was superseded by *Kumārajīva's translation of 406. The sixth 'translation' is but a re-editing of the fifth, and so the translation of Kumārajīva remains the standard text. In structure the text alternates between prose and poetry, where the verse reiterates what was said in the prose portions. The verse appears to be the earlier stratum of the text, which points to its possible origin in oral preaching, where metre and rhyme would aid the preacher's memory.

The popularity of the scripture in east Asia is no doubt due to its doctrinal simplicity; it makes only the two primary points listed above, and eschews discussions of abstruse philosophical matters. In addition, it makes copious use of vivid imagery and appealing parables in order to reinforce its points. Finally, many commentators and scholars have noted its lengthy and vigorous defence of its own sacrality, expressed in frequent interruptions of the narrative to assert its own veracity, and to recommend to readers that they venerate and propagate the text, and condemning those who slander it to dire *rebirths in *hell.

The high esteem in which the sūtra was held gained official status with *Chih-i (538–97), whose system of 'doctrinal classification' (Chin., *p'an-chiao) placed it at the apex of all Buddhist scriptures as the perfect expression of the Buddha's teaching, a position that remained official dogma for the *T'ien-t'ai school that he founded. After this school and its teachings were transmitted to *Japan where they took root as the *Tendai school, and as it became the dominant school of the late *Heian period, the assertion of this scripture's supremacy became widespread in Japan. During the *Kamakura period, *Nichiren (1222–82), founder of the *Nichiren-shū, came to teach that one could be saved simply by chanting homage to the sūtra in the formula, 'I pay homage to the Lotus Blossom of the Marvellous Dharma' (Jap., *Namo myōhō renge kyō). During the 19th and 20th centuries, many of the 'New Religions' of Japan arose out of the Nichiren-shū, and these have also carried on devotion to the *Lotus Sūtra* as their primary practice. Examples include *Sōka Gakkai and *Risshō Kōseikai.

Lo-yang. A city located on the south bank of the Yellow river in Honan Province that served as one of the imperial capitals in ancient times. It is traditionally regarded as the site where *Buddhism was first propagated into *China during the later *Han dynasty by Indian diplomats in the court of Emperor Ming. While this may be dubious from a strictly historical point of view, we can be sure that the city served as the site of the earliest translations of Buddhist texts, and currently houses many significant sites for the history of Buddhism in *China, such as the famous White Horse Temple and the *Lung-men caves.

Lumbinī. The place of the *Buddha's *birth, being a park located near to *Kapilavastu in present-day *Nepal near the *Himalayan foothills. Though initially an important place of *pilgrimage, it seems to have declined in importance by the 7th century CE and eventually fell into total obscurity until its discovery in 1896. Subsequent excavations have revealed extensive foundations of *stūpas, monasteries, and other features; it has also regained its importance as a place of pilgrimage, particularly associated with Buddhist initiatives for world peace and harmony.

luminous mind. The 'intrinsically luminous mind' or 'brightly shining mind' (Skt., prakṛti-prabhāsvara-citta) is a concept first noted in certain early discourses and later adopted by the *Mahāyāna. It refers to the underlying radiant or luminous intrinsic nature of the mind (*citta), especially when freed from the enveloping overlay of defilements (*kleśa). Identified in *Theravādin *Abhidharma teachings with the *bhavaṅga, the concept was later understood in Mahāyāna as an alternative designation for the inherent *Buddha-nature or *tathāgata-garbha.

lung-gom (Tib., rlung-gom). A meditative technique transmitted in *Tibet aimed at achieving mastery (gom) of the breathing processes and the flow of subtle energies (lung) within the body. Adepts who master this technique are said to be able to walk at great speed over long distances without tiring.

Lung-men. A valley along the Yi river about 8 miles from the ancient capital city of *Lo-yang in which patrons of *Buddhism began carving out caves during the reign of Emperor Hsüan-wu of the Northern Wei dynasty (r. 500–16). These caves, intended as hermitages for Buddhist *monks, are notable for the abundance of Buddha images and other statuary cut into their walls that are valuable not only for their artistic merit, but which also provide a window into the rise and fall of cults of particular *Buddhas and *Bodhisattvas.

Lü school. *See* LÜ-TSUNG.

Lu-shan. Also known as Mt. Lu, a large mountain encompassing many peaks and scenic views, located along the Chiu river near its juncture with the Yangtze river in Kiangsi Province. Although its fame as a centre for spiritual practice was established from ancient times, it became particularly significant as a Buddhist site through the career of *Lu-shan Hui-yüan (334–416). His two major contributions to the fame of the mountain consist in his convening of the first recorded society of devotees to contemplate the *Buddha *Amitābha for the purpose of gaining *rebirth in the *Pure Land, accounted by tradition as the inception of the Pure Land school in *China; and his invitation to many famous translators to come and pursue their activities in his Tung-lin Temple on the mountain. Over the years, hundreds of temples, *pagodas, pavilions, and grottoes were built on the mountain. In the 20th century, over 80 still remained, along with numerous large and small pagodas (including Hui-yüan's memorial pagoda), and other sites.

Lu-shan Hui-yüan (334–416 CE). An early Buddhist *monk who is known for his contributions to textual and translation theory, and is also popularly accounted the first *patriarch of the *Pure Land school. A student and disciple of *Tao-an (312–85), Hui-yüan was the only person Tao-an allowed to use the method of *ko-i or 'matching meanings'. Because of the risk of misunderstanding, Tao-an had forbidden his own students to use this method in their preaching and teaching. However, he thought Hui-yüan's depth of understanding of both the native terms and their Buddhist meanings would allow him to use them without distortion. Later in his life, Hui-yüan carried on a correspondence with the great central Asian translator *Kumārajīva to further clarify his understanding, and he sponsored the work of other translators. In addition, in the year 402 he gathered a group of disciples, both clerical and lay, to make a statue of the *Buddha *Amitābha and to vow to take *rebirth in the *Pure Land. Although the details of their meeting and their understanding of the nature of Pure Land practice show it to be very different from later expositions, it still represents one of the earliest organized efforts at Pure Land practice and, on this basis, Hui-yüan appears first on the list of Pure Land patriarchs.

Lü-tsung. In *China, this was the *Vinaya school, or the school of scholar-monks who specialized in studying and commenting upon the monastic regulations and procedures, as well as the study and administration of both lay and clerical *precepts. *Tao-hsüan (596–667) is commonly recognized as the founder, and it was under his influence that Chinese Buddhists adopted, from among the four canonical Vinayas available in translation, that of the Indian *Dharmaguptaka school (known in China as the 'Vinaya in Four Parts' (Chin., Ssu-fen lü)) as the official precepts for the clergy. The school has always been very small in terms of numbers, but has gained influence and respect for its work in systematizing and providing high-quality guidance for monastic and lay life. The texts of this school were transmitted to *Japan, where they became the basis for the *Risshū, one of the *Six Schools of *Nara *Buddhism.

M

Machig Lapgi Drönma (1055–1145). (Tib., Ma gcig lab kyi sgron ma). Great Tibetan female saint and celebrated *tantric exponent of the Tibetan *chöd (gcod) practice. The practice involves visualizing one's body being progressively dismembered by demons in order to weaken attachment to it. According to the traditional accounts, Ma gcig was born in *India as a male and received the chöd teachings from the Indian master *Phadampa Sangyé. Threatened by hostile *Brahmins, he subsequently fled to *Tibet where he projected his consciousness (*vijñāna) into a female body, that of Machig Lapgi Drönma, and subsequently lived as a woman to the age of 95.

Madhurā. *See* MATHURĀ.

Madhuratthavilāsinī. 'The Clarifier of the Sweet Meaning', being the *Pāli commentary on the **Buddhavaṃsa*.

Madhyama Āgama (Skt., middle collection). *Sanskrit equivalent of the *Pāli *Majjhima Nikāya or 'Middle-length Discourses', being one of the main sections of the *Sūtra Piṭaka (Pāli, Sutta Piṭaka). Many of the major *Eighteen Schools of Early *Buddhism had their own versions but for the most part these have not survived. As well as recent discoveries of small portions of the *Sarvāstivāda Madyama Āgama in Sanskrit, and several sūtras from that tradition in Tibetan translation, a complete Sarvāstivādin version exists in Chinese. This contains 222 sūtras, in contrast to the 152 extant in Pāli.

Madhyamaka (Skt.). The 'Middle School', a system of Buddhist philosophy founded by *Nāgārjuna in the 2nd century CE which has been extremely influential within the *Mahāyāna tradition of *Buddhism (a follower of the school is known as a Madhyamika). The school claims to be faithful to the spirit of the *Buddha's original teachings, which advocate a middle course between extreme practices and theories of all kinds (*see* MADHYAMĀ-PRATIPAD). It applies this principle to philosophical theories concerning the nature of phenomena. Thus the assertions that 'things exist' or that 'things do not exist' would be extreme views and should be rejected. The truth, it is thought, lies somewhere in between and is to be arrived at through a process of dialectic in the course of which opposing positions are revealed as self-negating. The adoption of any one position, it was argued, could immediately be challenged by taking up its opposite. The Madhyamaka therefore adopted a strategy of attacking opponent's views rather than advancing claims of its own (which is not to deny that they might none the less hold their own philosophical views). Chief among the views they attacked was the theory of *dharmas. This had been evolved in the *Abhidharma tradition as a solution to philosophical difficulties arising out of problems concerning causation, temporality, and personal identity. The scholastic solution was to posit a theory of instantaneous serial continuity according to which phenomena (dharmas) constantly replicate themselves in a momentary sequence of change (dharma-kṣanikatvā). Thus reality was conceived of as cinematic, like a filmstrip in which one frame constantly gives way to the next: each moment is substantially existent in its own right, and collectively they produce the illusion of stability and continuity. The Madhyamaka challenged this notion of the substantial reality of dharmas, arguing that if things truly existed in this way, and were possessed of a real nature or 'self-essence' (*svabhāva), it would contradict the Buddha's teaching on selflessness (*anātman) and, moreover, render change impossible. What already substantially exists, they argued, would not need to be produced; and what does not substantially exist already could never come into being from a state of non-existence. Thus real existence cannot be predicated of dharmas, but neither can non-existence since they clearly enjoy a mode of being of some kind. The conclusion of the Madhyamaka was that the true nature of phenomena can only be described as an 'emptiness' or 'voidness' (dharma-śūnyatā), and that this emptiness of self-nature is synonymous with the doctrine of Dependent Origination (*pratītya-samutpāda) taught by the Buddha. This reasoning is set out in Nāgārjuna's terse **Mūla-madhyamaka-kārikā*, the root text of the system.

There were important implications in Madhyamaka metaphysics for Buddhist soteriology. Since emptiness is the true nature of what exists, there can be no ontological basis for the differentiation between *nirvāṇa and *saṃsāra. Any difference which exists, it was argued, must be an epistemological one resulting from ignorance (*avidyā) and misconception. Accordingly, the Madhyamaka posits 'two levels of truth', the level of Ultimate Truth (*paramārtha-satya), i.e. the perception of emptiness of the true nature of phenomena (in other words, the view of the enlightened,) and the level of 'relative or veiled truth' (*saṃvṛti-satya), i.e. the misconception of dharmas as possessing a substantial self-existent nature (in other words, the view of the unenlightened).

After Nāgārjuna the work of the school was carried forward by his disciple *Āryadeva. After the time of Āryadeva, in middle period Mādhyamaka (6th–7th century CE), a division arose leading to the formation of two branches of the Madhyamaka; the *Svātantrika, led by *Bhāvaviveka, and the *Prāsaṅgika, championed by *Candrakīrti, which adhered to the negative dialectic of Nāgārjuna. The Madhyamaka system was transmitted from *India to *Tibet and east Asia, where it flourished as arguably the most influential school of Mahāyāna philosophy. In *China it is known as *San-lun (the 'three treatises' school). Due to certain potentially nihilistic trends implicit in Madhyamaka doctrines the school was criticized vehemently, both within the Buddhist fold by the *Yogācāra school as well as by many non-Buddhists. Late period Madhyamaka is marked by a convergence with and synthesis of concepts drawn from the Yogācāra and Buddhist *pramāṇa schools as can be seen in the work of scholars such as *Śāntarakṣita.

Madhyamakāvatāra. The 'Entrance to the Middle Way', being a work of *Candrakīrti which relates the *Madhyamaka doctrine of emptiness (*śūnyatā) to the religious practice of a *Bodhisattva. The text contains ten chapters, each devoted to one of the ten perfections (*pāramitā) practised by the Bodhisattva as he advances through the ten stages (*bhūmi) to Buddhahood. The sixth perfection, the Perfection of Insight (*prajñā-pāramitā), receives the most extensive treatment and accounts for over half the text. In the course of the work the main tenets of Madhyamaka thought are expounded, such as emptiness (śūnyatā), the *Two Truths, and the selflessness of persons and all phenomena. The work survives only in Tibetan along with a commentary (*bhāṣya) also by Candrakīrti. These works are considered essential for understanding Madhyamaka thought and are studied intensively in Tibetan monastic institutions, particularly among the *Gelukpa.

Madhyamaka-kārikā. *See* MŪLA-MADHYAMAKA-KĀRIKĀ.

madhyamā-pratipad (Skt.; Pāli, majjhimā-paṭipadā). The 'middle way' or 'middle path' a term which resonates at many levels in *Buddhism. In the first place it stands as a synonym for the totality of Buddhist doctrine and practice. Second, it emphasizes the nature of Buddhist practice as a *via media*, that is to say, a spiritual path that lays emphasis on moderation, and endeavours always to steer a middle course in the face of conflicting extremes. The emphasis on moderation stems from the *Buddha's personal experience of a life of ease and comfort as a prince followed by six years of hardship and austerities as an *ascetic in the forest. Realizing that neither of these extremes was profitable he abandoned them in favour of a moderate lifestyle, and from that moment made rapid spiritual progress culminating in his enlightenment (*bodhi). This sense of the term is not dissimilar to Aristotle's notion of the 'golden mean'. Third, it is used to validate Buddhist doctrines on the assumption that the truth always lies between extremes. The teaching of no-self (*anātman), for example, is said to be the middle way between belief in a permanent soul (*ātman) that is eternal (the so-called doctrine of 'eternalism' or *śāśvatavāda); and the view that the individual is wholly annihilated at *death (the doctrine of annihilationism or *uccheda-vāda). As Buddhism developed, various attempts were made to use the principle of the Middle Way as the touchstone for the authentication of doctrine. *Nāgārjuna, for example, the founder of the 'Middle School' (*Madhyamaka), claimed that his radical doctrine of emptiness (*śūnyatā) was the authentic interpretation of the Buddha's teachings on causation or Dependent Origination (*pratītya-samutpāda) because it steered a middle course through dialectictically opposed positions.

Madhyānta-vibhāga-kārikā. A key *Yogācāra work by *Maitreyanātha in 112 verses which delineates the distinctions and relationship (vibhāga) between the middle view (madya) and extremes (anta). It comprises five chapters: Attributes (*lakṣaṇa), Obscurations (*āvaraṇa), Reality (*tattva), Cultivation of Antidotes (pratipakṣa-bhāvanā), and the Supreme Way (yānānuttarya). As well as Chinese, Tibetan, and Mongolian translations, the text survives in a single *Sanskrit manuscript discovered in *Tibet by Sāṅkṛtyāyana which also included the commentary (*bhāṣya) by *Vasubandhu. An important subcommentary (*ṭīkā) by *Sthiramati also survives in Sanskrit as well as a Tibetan version.

Magadha. One of the major kingdoms of ancient *India at the time of the *Buddha *Śākyamuni, it was located south of the Ganges and included much of present-day Bihar in its core territory, with its capital first at *Rājagṛha and later *Pāṭaliputra. Magadha was ruled by King *Bimbisāra during most of the Buddha's lifetime but the king died from mistreatment at the hands of his son and successor, *Ajātaśatru. Bimbisāra himself was a devoted follower of the Buddha and Magadha can perhaps be considered the heartland of the early Buddhist movement. Later, especially under Ajātaśatru, many of the smaller neighbouring states were conquered and assimilated into what became the Magadhan Empire. The area continued to be at the centre of political and religious life in India even after the demise of the empire itself.

Mahabodhi Society. Organization founded in 1891 by Anagārika *Dharmapāla (1864–1933) with the immediate aim of restoring *Bodhgayā from Hindu to Buddhist control. A branch was established in *Britain in 1925 and today there is a network of centres all over the world.

Mahābodhivaṃsa. *Pāli translation of a Sinhalese original text, being the account of the arrival of the *Bodhi Tree in *Sri Lanka. It is ascribed to Upatissa who compiled it in the 10th century at the request of Dāṭhānāga.

mahā-bhūta. *Sanskrit term meaning the 'great elements'. These are the four forces which constitute materiality, namely solidity, fluidity, heat, and movement, and which are commonly referred to as earth, water, fire, and wind. To these a fifth element, space (*ākāśa) is often added and consciousness (*vijñāna) is sometimes mentioned as a sixth item.

Mahādeva. A *monk who put forward five theses which were debated at the conjectured Third Council (*see* COUNCIL OF PĀṬALIPUTRA I). The five points as formulated by later commentators were as follows: (1) Arhats can still be led astray by others; (2) Arhats are still subject to ignorance—not 'defiled ignorance' (*avidyā) but of the lesser kind known as 'undefiled ignorance' (akliṣṭa ajñāna); (3) Arhats are still subject to doubt (kāṅkṣā) and (4) can be instructed and informed by others; (5) entry into the Noble Path (*ārya-marga) by an Arhat can be accompanied by a vocal utterance (vacībheda), an artifice meant to generate the appearance of the Path.

mahājanapadas (Pāli). The sixteen states or political entities that according to tradition existed at the time of the *Buddha. They were *Kāsī, *Kosala, *Aṅga, *Magadha, *Vajji, *Malla, Cetiya, Vaṃsa, *Kuru, *Pañcāla, Maccha, Sūrasena, Assaka, *Avanti, *Gandhāra, and *Kamboja. The first fourteen are included in the 'central region' (Pāli, *majjhimadesa), while the last two are part of the 'northern territory' (*Uttarāpatha).

Mahākāla. *Sanskrit name meaning 'The Great Black One'. Originally a non-Buddhist deity, sometimes seen as a form of the Hindu god Śiva (*see* HINDUISM), he is a wrathful tutelary deity (*yi-dam) and protector of the faith (*dharmapāla). In *tantric *Buddhism he is considered to be a manifestation of the *Bodhisattva *Avalokiteśvara, and his worship (*pūjā) and related practices are described in detail in the *Mahākāla Tantra*. Various iconographic forms exist of Mahākāla in Indian and Tibetan tantric Buddhism with between four and sixteen arms. A non-wrathful form exists in *Japan where he is associated with good fortune and is known as *Daikokuten.

Mahākāśyapa (Skt.; Pāli, Mahākassapa). Also known as Kāśyapa, an *Arhat and senior disciple of the *Buddha famed for his saintly and austere lifestyle and exceptional accomplishments. The Buddha regarded him as his equal in exhorting the monks, and in entering and abiding in the trances (*dhyāna). Mahākāśyapa is said to have borne seven of the 32 marks of a superman (*dvātriṃśadvara-lakṣaṇa) on his body and was renowned for his supernatural powers (*ṛddhi). He was not present at the Buddha's death and it is said that the funeral pyre refused to light until he arrived a week later. As the most senior *monk present he was nominated to act as president at the *Council of Rājagṛha that followed shortly after the Buddha's demise. At the council he personally questioned *Ānanda and *Upāli in order to establish which were the orthodox *sūtra and *Vinaya teachings. He also brought certain charges against Ānanda, including having interceded with the Buddha to allow the *ordination of *women, and of failing to request the Buddha to extend his life. Mahākāśyapa is regarded by the *Ch'an school as its first *patriarch because he was the only one to grasp the meaning of a wordless sermon in which the Buddha simply held up a flower and smiled. The meaning of this gesture is that the truth is beyond all verbal explanation, and as such needs to be taught not through doctrines but by direct transmission from teacher to student.

Mahākatyāyana (Skt.; Pāli, Mahākaccana, Mahākaccāyana). An eminent disciple of the *Buddha, skilled in explaining at length what had been stated only concisely by the master. He was born at Ujjain and received a classical *Brahminical education studying the *Vedas. With a group of seven friends he invited the Buddha to visit, and gained enlightenment (*bodhi) while listening to him preach. He was ordained, and made numerous converts in the state of *Avantī. Tradition attributes the authorship of the *Nettipakaraṇa* (a work of grammar) and the *Peṭakopadesa* (a treatise on exegetical methodology) to Mahākatyāyana, although these were most probably composed by a school descended from him.

Mahāmaudgalyāyana (Skt.; Pāli, Mahāmoggallāna). The second of the *Buddha's senior disciples after *Śāriputra. The two were born on the same day and were lifelong friends. Second in wisdom only to Śāriputra, Mahamaudgalyāyana was pre-eminent in miraculous powers (*ṛddhi). He could conjure up innumerable living shapes and change himself into any form at will. He was beaten to *death by brigands who were said to have been in the pay of the Jains (*see* JAINISM). The Buddha explained his death as due to a wicked deed committed in a previous life when he had beaten his own blind parents to death.

mahāmudrā (Skt.) **1.** Great Seal; one of the four meditational seals (*mudrā) according to *yoga-tantra. It refers to the process of imaging the *Buddhas in transformational *meditation practice by way of their body-images (bimba) which correlate to their body aspect (*see* BODY, SPEECH, MIND). **2.** A category of practices and their associated goal, especially linked with *anuttara-yoga-tantra, although there are two aspects to the practice: the *sūtra-based 'ordinary' form and the tantra-based 'extra-ordinary' form. In both cases, the aim of the practice is to realize the emptiness (*śūnyatā) of all phenomena, their intrinsic luminosity and the inseparable union of these two aspects. A major form of *tantric Buddhist teaching and practice, mahāmudrā was transmitted to *Tibet by *Marpa who received it from the *mahā-siddha ('great adept') *Nāropa. From Marpa, the teachings went to *Milarepa, and from him to *Gampopa. Through the efforts of the latter, mahāmudrā became one of the core elements of the *Kagyü school. The central element of mahāmudrā teaching involves a recognition of the inseparable nature of *compassion (*karuṇā) and insight (*prajñā) or the identity of emptiness (*śūnyatā) and *saṃsāra.

Mahāmuni Paya. Literally '*Stūpa of the great sage', this Mandalay stūpa is also known as Rakhine/Arakan *Paya. It was originally built by King Bodawpaya in 1784, but the shrine was destroyed by fire in 1884 and the current one is relatively recent. The centrepiece of this shrine is the highly venerated *Candasāra *Buddha image which was transported here from Arakan. The complex also contains other artefacts also looted from

Arakan but originally from *Angkor Wat from which they were taken in 1431. The temple courtyard also contains several inscriptions. The Mahāmuni Paya Festival, attracting thousands of people is held here every year in early February.

Mahāmuni Temple. 'Temple of the Great Sage' in the Burmese region of Arakan where the *Candasāra *Buddha image was preserved until 1784. Until then the temple was one of the most sacred in *south-east Asia. The religious history of Arakan centres around this temple and the Candasāra Buddha image.

Mahāparinibbāna Sutta. 'The Discourse on the Great Decease', being the sixteenth and longest discourse in the Collection of Long Discourses (*Dīgha Nikāya) of the *Pāli Canon. The text describes the events leading up to the *Buddha's *death and his travels during the last few months of his life. The discourse makes reference to an impending war between *Magadha and *Vajjī, and begins with King *Ajātaśatru (Pāli, Ajātasattu) dispatching a minister to seek the Buddha's advice. Most of the rest of the text consists of a sustained conversation between the Buddha and *Ānanda, and it reiterates much material that occurs in other canonical sources. In the course of the narrative the Buddha predicts the end of his life three months hence, and partakes of the meal which causes a grave illness shortly before his death (*see* SŪKARA-MADDAVA). He also states that if he had been requested to do so it was within his power to prolong his life until the end of the aeon. The narrative ends with the Buddha's *cremation and the distribution of his *relics.

Mahāparinirvāṇa Sūtra. *See* *NIRVĀṆA SŪTRA*.

Maha Pasan Guha. Burmese term meaning 'the great cave' and denoting an artificial cave built in the north of Rangoon, *Burma. It was here that the Sixth Buddhist Council was held in 1956, to coincide with the 2,500th anniversary of the *Buddha's enlightenment (*bodhi).

Mahāprajāpatī (Pāli, Mahāpajāpatī). The *Buddha's stepmother. Co-wife of *Śuddhodana and sister of *Māyā, she raised the infant Buddha following the death of his mother one week after giving birth. On the death of Śuddhodana, Mahāprajāpatī, along with 500 other *women, sought the Buddha's permission to be ordained as *nuns. When he refused, the women cut off their hair, donned yellow robes (*cīvara), and followed him on foot. The Buddha refused the request a second time but acceded to the third request following the intervention of *Ānanda. Mahāprajāpatī became an *Arhat shortly after *ordination and reputedly lived to the age of 120.

mahāpuruṣa (Skt., great man; Pāli, mahāpurisa). In traditional Indian and Buddhist lore, a great man, hero, or superman. One born to greatness and destined to be either a Universal Ruler (*cakravartin) or a *Buddha. One such destined by fate bears the 32 major marks (*dvātriṃśadvara-lakṣaṇa) and 80 minor marks (*anuvyañjana) on his body, by which people may recognize and prophesy his greatness.

Mahāsaṃghika (Skt.). The adherents of the self-styled 'Majority Community' or 'Universal Assembly', a school of *Buddhism which originated in the *schism with the *Sthaviras that occured after the Second Council (*see* COUNCIL OF VAIŚĀLĪ) and possibly just prior to the Third Council (*see* COUNCIL OF PĀṬALIPUTRA I). The dispute that led to this schism seems to have largely concerned with interpretation of the *Vinaya, in respect of which one side took a more liberal approach. A degree of doctrinal difference also seems to have been involved concerning disagreements over the nature of an *Arhat (*see* MAHĀDEVA). This school went on to become one of the most sucessful and influential forms of Buddhism in *India, giving rise to several subschools in later years such as the *Ekavyāvahārika, the *Lokottara-vāda, and the *Bahuśrutīya. Some of the teachings of this school concerning the nature of *Buddhas and *Bodhisattvas have features in common with *Mahāyāna concepts, but since there is no evidence of innovation by the Mahāsaṃghikas in this respect before the rise of the Mahāyāna, in the view of some scholars, such elements should be ascribed to Mahāyāna influence. According to this view there is thus not much likelihood that the Mahāsaṃghika school played a part in the formation of the Mahāyāna before the latter emerged as a distinct entity. Other scholars see evidence for the converse in the formation of certain Mahāyāna sūtras, such as the **Nirvāna Sūtra*.

Mahāsaṃnipāta Sūtra. A compilation of seventeen *Mahāyāna *sūtras. A complete version of this collection only exists in Chinese translation although there is clear evidence that it also existed in a similar form in *India and many individual sūtras were also translated into Tibetan. It includes such important works as the *Dhāraṇīśvara-rāja Sūtra* and the *Akṣayamati-nirdeśa Sūtra*.

mahāsattva (Skt., great being). Honorific title used of advanced *Bodhisattvas.

mahā-siddha (Skt, great adept). A great accomplished master, especially connected with *Vajrayāna practices, who displays magical powers (*siddhi) as an outward sign of his or her attainment. The 84 Indian mahāsiddhas, whose number includes several *women adepts, are well-known as representatives of antinomian forms of *tantric *Buddhism, who flourished between the 8th and 12th centuries CE. Short accounts of their careers and activities are contained in the *Biographies of the Eighty-Four Mahāsiddhas*, surviving in *Tibet translation.

Mahāsthāmaprāpta. 'He who has obtained Great Power', the name of an important mythical *Bodhisattva. He is especially popular in east Asian *Buddhism and is believed to open people's eyes to the need to strive for awakening (*bodhi). Mahāsthāmaprāpta is mentioned at an early date in *Mahāyāna works such as the **Lotus Sūtra*, and is often paired with *Avalokiteśvara and depicted together with the latter flanking *Śākyamuni or *Amitābha in the form of a trinity. Iconographically, he is white in colour and is depicted holding an unopened *lotus bud in his hand; sometimes he is also shown in east Asian art with a *pagoda in his hair.

Mahā-thūpa (Pāli). The Great *Stūpa at *Anurādhapura in *Sri Lanka which has been a centre for *pilgrimage down the centuries. It was constructed by King *Duṭṭhagāmaṇi Abhaya after his victory of the Tamils, although he did not live to see the work fully completed. Tradition asserts that *relics of the *Buddha were miraculously obtained and enshrined in the relic chamber. The structure itself has been the object of continous pilgrimage and devotion over the last 2,000 years, undergoing periodic works of reconstruction and restoration.

Mahāvagga. The 'major section' of the *Vinaya. *See also* CULLAVAGGA.

Mahā-vairocana-abhisaṃbodhi Tantra. The 'Tantra of the Awakening of Mahā-vairocana', a highly influential *caryā-tantra probably composed in the mid-7th century CE. It is possibly the earliest such work to systematically present the entire range of tantric practices with the exception of sexual *yoga. It teaches the manner in which the enlightenment (*saṃbodhi) of *Mahā-vairocana is expressed in the world through various *maṇḍalas, *mantras, and *mudrās so that practitioners may also achieve that state through the ritual cultivation of the practices assocated with them. Though this work was soon overshadowed in *India by later tantric developments, it became extremely important in the east Asian transmission of esoteric *Buddhism and is still highly revered in the Japanese *Shingon school. Apart from a few *Sanskrit fragments, the text has survived in Tibetan and Chinese translations together with several important commentaries that provide much information about early tantric practices and doctrines.

Mahāvaṃsa. Literally 'Great Chronicle'. A *Pāli Buddhist chronicle, attributed to Mahānāma, reporting the history of *Sri Lanka from the time of the *Buddha to the reign of King Mahāsena (334–61). Its account is continued in the **Cūlavaṃsa* and is paralleled by the **Dīpavaṃsa*.

Mahāvastu. A lengthy composite work, the earliest sections of which go back to the 2nd century BCE. The text incorporates many early short *sūtras and *jātakas, structured around a core biography of the *Buddha said to have been a work attached to the *Vinaya of the *Lokottara-vāda school. The text also appears to contain later material, including substantial intrusions from *Mahāyāna. The work only survives in a manuscript written in a form of *Sanskrit known as *Buddhist Hybrid Sanskrit, and no translations are available in either Tibetan or Chinese.

Mahāvibhāṣā. A great treatise whose name means the 'Great Book of Alternatives' or 'Great Book of Options', compiled probably during the 3rd century CE in *Gandhāra under the patronage of King *Kaniṣka II. It is traditionally believed to have been composed at the *Council of Kaniṣka, held in the reign of Kaniṣka I, but this is unlikely since the text contains a specific reference to the 'former king Kaniṣka'. Moreover, inscriptions and recent finds in Afghanistan suggest that it is unlikely that *Sanskrit was used by any Buddhists before the 2nd century CE. The treatise is a commentary on a fundamental work of *Abhidharma, the *Jñānaprasthāna* (Basis of Knowledge) of Katyāyanaputra, a *Sarvāstivādin philosopher. Also known as the *Vibhāṣā*, the text is an encyclopedia of the views of the *Vaibhāṣika school and records the views of distinguished teachers of different schools on technical points of doctrine. The *Mahāvibhāṣā* survives only in three Chinese translations, and a partial translation made into Tibetan is now no longer extant. The Chinese translation contains additional material not found in the *Sanskrit fragments that have been recovered. The *Mahāvibhāṣā* formed the basis of *debate between the schools of the *Hīnayāna (Small Vehicle) for many centuries, and many shorter treatises such as *Vasubandhu's **Abhidharma-kośa* were composed to criticize and supplement it.

Mahāvihāra (Pāli). Literally 'Great monastery'. For many centuries a monastery (*vihāra) that was the main seat of the ancestral branch for present-day *Theravāda *Buddhism in *Sri Lanka. It was founded by King *Devānampiya Tissa (247–207 BCE) in his capital of *Anurādhapura on the site of the Tissārama, given to visiting missionaries from *Aśoka's court, and it included many buildings and shrines. Its residents, claiming to represent the orthodox tradition of Sri Lankan Buddhism, referred to themselves as the Theriya Nikāya (or *Theravāda) in contrast to the monks of the rival monasteries of *Abhayagiri, known as the *Dhammaruci Nikāya and *Jetavana (in fact all three schools laid claim to the name Theriya Nikāya or Theravāda while seeking to deny it to their opponents). Though they managed to live side by side without major conflicts for long periods, the fraternities of the Mahāvihāra and of the Abhayagiri had earlier come into conflict in a struggle for control of the Buddhist tradition in the island. When the Abhayagiri monks then openly adopted the heretical Vaitulya Piṭaka the animosity between the monks of the two establishments became very bitter and resulted in the heretical books being burnt and the destruction of the Mahāvihāra. The two communities remained separate until 1165 when a council was held at Anurādhapura and reconciliation was achieved. When Anurādhapura was abandoned around the 13th century, the history of the Mahāvihāra came to an end.

Mahāvīra (Skt., great hero). Honorific title given to the Jain teacher Vardhamāna, known in Buddhist sources as *Nigaṇṭha Nātaputta. He died near Patna at the age of 73. Ranked as one of the *Six Sectarian Teachers by the Buddhists, he is regarded by Jains as the greatest of all their teachers. *See also* JAINISM.

Mahāvyutpatti. An early 9th-century CE Tibetan dictionary of *Sanskrit Buddhist terminology containing 9,565 lexical items arranged thematically into 277 chapters. The work was devised partly as a means of standardizing translations from Sanskrit into Tibetan. Later versions of this text were produced in the 17th century with Chinese, Mongolian, and Manchurian equivalents added.

Maha Wizaya (Vijaya) Paya. A *zedi built in 1980 in Rangoon to commemorate the unification of *Theravāda *Buddhism in the country. The king of *Nepal contributed sacred *relics for its relic chamber while the Burmese people, through donations, paid for its construction. Also, the Burmese leader Ne Win had it topped with an eleven-level spire (*htī), two levels higher than the one of the nearby *Shwedagon *pagoda. *See also* PAYA

Mahāyāna (Skt., the great vehicle). A major movement in the history of *Buddhism embracing many schools in a sweeping reinterpretation of fundamental religious ideals, beliefs and values. Although there is no evidence for the existence of Mahāyāna prior to the 2nd century CE, it can be assumed that the movement began to crystallise earlier, incorporating teachings of existing schools. Great emphasis is placed on the twin values of compassion (*karuṇā) and insight (*prajñā). The *Bodhisattva who devotes himself to the service of others becomes the new paradigm for religious practice, as opposed to the *Arhat who is criticised for leading a cloistered life devoted to the self-interested pursuit of liberation. Schools which embraced the earlier ideal are henceforth referred to disparagingly as the *Hīnayāna (Small Vehicle), or the *Śrāvakayāna (Vehicle of the Hearers).

The philosophical teachings of the Mahāyāna are adumbrated in a new body of literature known as the *Prajñā-pāramitā Sūtras or 'Perfection of Insight' texts. Here the doctrine of emptiness (*śūnyatā) comes to prominence, and the *Buddha is seen in a new light as a supernatural being who is worthy of loving devotion. This new conception of his nature is later formalized in the doctrine of the *trikāya (three bodies). In due course new teachings and schools arose under the umbrella of the Mahāyāna such as the *Mādhyamaka, the *Yogācāra, the *Pure Land tradition, and the *Vajrayāna. The Mahāyāna form of Buddhism is predominant in north Asia. It spread from *India to *Nepal, *Tibet, and central Asia, *China, *Korea, and *Japan. Under the influence of these cultures it has taken many forms: the Buddhism of Nepal and Tibet has been influenced by *tantric practices and the shamanism of central Asia, while in China the influence of *Taoism and *Confucianism have left their mark. The interaction between Buddhism and Taoism gave rise to the *Ch'an school of contemplative quietism which developed into Japanese *Zen.

Mahāyāna-saṃgraha. 'The Mahāyāna Compendium', a key work of the *Yogācāra school in eleven chapters attributed to *Asaṅga. It introduces various Yogācāra concepts such as the storehouse consciousness (*ālaya-vijñāna), the three natures (*trisvabhāva), the fivefold path (*pañca-mārga), and the fruits of enlightenment (*bodhi). Although no *Sanskrit original has been found, the work survives in Tibetan and Chinese translations together with several important commentaries.

Mahāyāna-śraddhotpāda Śāstra. 'The Awakening of Faith in the Mahāyāna', a short *summa* of *Mahāyāna thought attributed to the Indian Buddhist thinker and poet *Aśvaghoṣa and translated into Chinese in the year 550 CE by *Paramārtha. A second translation, by Śikṣānanda, was produced in the *T'ang dynasty. In spite of these two 'translations', no Indian original has ever been discovered, and it is now certain that the text is an apocryphal work of Chinese origin. Despite its brevity and terseness, the work displays its author's brilliance at synthesizing many of the major ideas of Mahāyāna *Buddhism, and so this treatise has exercised an enormous influence on east Asian Buddhist thought.

The text's major theme is the relationship between the noumenon (the absolute, enlightenment (*bodhi), the universal, and the eternal) and phenomena (the relative, the unenlightened, the particular, and the temporal), and it poses the following questions. How are limited, ignorant beings to attain the bliss of wisdom? How shall the particular attain to the universal, the temporal to the eternal? To answer these questions, the treatise postulates a transcendent that pervades the immanent. The noumenon, called suchness (*tathatā) or *absolute mind, does not exist in a pristine realm above and beyond phenomena, but expresses itself precisely as phenomena. The conjunction of the noumenal and the phenomenal occurs in the concept of the *tathāgata-garbha, or 'embryonic *Buddha'. The term 'garbha', meaning both embryo and womb, denotes the simultaneous appearance of the goal sought (the embryo) and the conditions that make it possible (the womb). Suffering beings, in so far as they are suffering, remain deluded and in bondage. However, insofar as they are beings, they display their suchness and are aspects of the activity of absolute mind, and in this sense they already contain the goal of transcendence and liberation within themselves.

These ideas are worked out in more detail through the use of the concepts of 'original enlightenment' and '*acquired enlightenment'. The first symbolizes the perfect and complete presence within all beings of ultimate reality and the absolute mind. The second serves as a recognition that, on the level of phenomena, suffering and ignorance (*avidyā) are real, and beings must still work to overcome them. However, because noumenon and phenomena do not exist separately, but only in and through each other, there is no unbridgeable gap between them; quite the contrary, they coincide completely. Because this is true, beings can gain enlightenment (*bodhi) and liberation from suffering. The second half of the text presents practical suggestions for religious cultivation so that readers may develop faith (*śraddhā) and ultimately attain liberation. These exercises serve to correct flawed or biased views, and to increase the practitioner's faith and devotion.

Mahāyāna-sūtrālaṃkāra. A major work in verse attributed to *Maitreyanātha presenting the *Mahāyāna path from the *Yogācāra perspective. The work, whose name means 'The Adornment of Mahāyāna Sūtras', comprises 22 chapters with a total of 800 verses. It shows considerable similarity in arrangement and content to the **Bodhisattvabhūmi Śāstra*, although the interesting first chapter proving the validity and authenticity of Mahāyāna is unique to this work. Associated with it is a prose commentary (bhāṣya) by *Vasubandhu and several subcommentaries by *Sthiramati and others. The portions by Maitreyanātha and Vasubandhu both survive in *Sanskrit as well as Tibetan, Chinese, and Mongolian translations.

mahāyoga (Skt.). The fourth level of *tantric teachings according to the *Nyingma school, equivalent in some respects to the *Father Tantra class of the *New Schools. Many of the tantric texts that form this category are considered to be canonical and thus are included in the *Kanjur, although they may be alternative translations.

Mahinda (c.282–222 BCE). *Monk son of Emperor *Aśoka of *Magadha and brother of the *nun *Saṅghamittā. He was ordained at the age of 20 and on the same day is said to have become an *Arhat. After some years spent in the study of the *Dharma he took over the duties of his retiring preceptor who had left 1,000 disciples. At the 'Third Council' (*see* COUNCIL OF PĀṬALIPUTRA II) held in 250 BC under Emperor Aśoka, Mahinda was charged with the mission of bringing the Buddha's teachings to *Sri Lanka. Once he reached the island he began his mission by first converting King *Devānampiya Tissa, to whom he preached the *Cūlahatthipadopama Sutta*. Later, he sent an embassy to his father requesting some *relics of the *Buddha. At Mahinda's suggestion, Devānampiya Tissa sent another embassy to Aśoka, asking for Saṅghamittā to come to Sri Lanka with other nuns so that female converts could be ordained in the *Saṃgha, and requesting a branch of the *Bodhi Tree. The request was granted, and Saṅghamittā and other nuns arrived in Sri Lanka with the branch. During the last part of Devānampiya Tissa's reign, Mahinda is said to have advised the king to build several monasteries (*vihāras). He is also said to have taught the commentaries to the *Tripiṭaka in the Sinhalese language, after translating them from *Pāli. Mahinda continued to live in Sri Lanka after the death of Devānampiya Tissa and he died there at the age of 60. His body was cremated and a *cetiya was erected on the *cremation spot over half of his remains, the other half being distributed in *stūpas elsewhere.

Mahinda festival. *Sri Lankan festival, better known as *Poson, commemorating the arrival of *Mahinda and the establishment of *Buddhism on the island.

Mahīśāsaka. One of the major *Eighteen Schools of Early *Buddhism, thought to have been a 2nd century BCE offshoot of the *Vibhajyavādins. Based on present knowledge of its *Abhidharma doctrines, it is sometimes considered to be a mainland Indian parent school linked to *Sri Lankan *Theravāda.

Mahmud of Ghazni. A Muslim Turkic adventurer who seized control of Afghanistan and neighbouring areas and established the short-lived Ghaznavid Empire (997–1030 CE). He led several extremely destructive forays into *India as far as the heartland of *Buddhism on the plains of the Ganges. Although his advance was repulsed, he was soon followed by other Muslim armies who systematically looted and destroyed most of the great Buddhist establishments in that region, such as *Nālandā.

Maināmati-Lalmai range. Hill range and vast Buddhist archaeological site lying between the villages of Maināmati and Lalmai, in *Bangladesh. The site comprises over 50 buildings, most not yet excavated. The earliest of the ruins date to the 6th century CE, and the building of a new monastery (*vihāra) was still sponsored here in the 13th century. Among the sites in the Maināmati-Lalami range Salban Vihāra is perhaps the best known. The complex's name derives from a nearby Sal tree forest. This monastery is in the form of a square and was quite large in size, comprising 115 cells. In the middle of its central courtyard rises a large *stūpa, which once contained large Buddhist images. Another major site within the Mainamati range is known as Kutila Mura. Here, a massive wall encloses a large area on which stand the remains of three main stūpas together with nine subsidiary stupas. Other sites in the Mainamati-Lalmai range include the so-called Ānanda Vihāra.

Maitreya. (Skt.; Pāli, Metteya). One of the great mythical *Bodhisattvas whose cult was introduced into *Buddhism at a fairly early date, and who is venerated in both *Mahāyāna and non-Mahāyāna forms of *Buddhism. Though his name signifies 'loving-kindness', some scholars suggest he was orginally linked to the Iranian saviour-figure Mitra and that his later importance for Buddhists as the future *Buddha currently residing in the *Tuṣita *heaven who will follow on from *Śākyamuni Buddha derives from this source.

Maitreyanātha (270–350 CE). One of the three founders of *Yogācāra, along with *Asaṅga and *Vasubandhu. His dates are uncertain, and scholars are divided as to whether the name denotes a historical human teacher or the *Bodhisattva *Maitreya, used pseudo-epigraphically. The number of works attributed to him vary in the Tibetan and Chinese traditions but variously include the **Yogācārabhūmi Śāstra*, the **Mahāyāna-sūtrālaṃkāra*, the **Dharmadharmatā-vibhāga*, the **Madhyānta-vibhāga-kārikā*, the **Abhisamaya-alaṃkāra*, and the **Ratna-gotra-vibhāga*.

maitrī (Skt.; Pāli, metta). Kindness, benevolence, or goodwill, as in the disposition of a friend (Skt., mitra). An important Buddhist virtue, maitrī is to be cultivated towards all in a spirit of generosity which is free of attachment or thoughts of self-interest. As the first of the four Divine Abidings (*Brahma-vihāra), maitrī is practised as a meditational exercise by being directed first of all to oneself, then those close to one (such as friends and family), and then extended by stages to embrace all living beings. The *Pāli **Metta Sutta*, which expresses the wish that all beings may be well and happy, is a very popular text recited daily by many *monks and lay-people.

majjhimadesa (Pāli, central region; Skt., madhyamadeśa). The birthplace of *Buddhism in north-east *India comprising, according to early sources, a territory 300 leagues in length, 250 in breadth, and 900 in circumference. Within it were fourteen of the sixteen states or political units (*mahājanapadas) mentioned in classical Indian sources.

Majjhima Nikāya. The second collection of the *Sūtra Piṭaka of the *Pāli Canon. It contains 152 *suttas including some of the best known ones in the *canon such as the *Alagaddūpama Sutta* (*see* RAFT PARABLE), *Aṅgulimāla Sutta* (*see* AṄGULIMĀLA) and *Mahāsīhanāda Sutta*. At the First Council (*see* COUNCIL OF RĀJAGṚHA), held shortly after the *Buddha's death, the duty of learning and preserving the Majjhima Nikāya was entrusted to *Śāriputra's disciples. A commentary to the Majjhima Nikāya by the title of **Papañcasūdanī* was composed by *Buddhaghoṣa in the 5th century CE, and Sāriputta of *Sri Lanka later compiled its subcommentary.

Makiguchi Tsunesaburō (1871–1944). Founder of the Japanese religious group *Sōka Gakkai (Value Creation Society). A teacher by profession, Makiguchi believed that values had to be created through education in order to build a good society, and he also was deeply committed to the truth of *Nichiren *Buddhism. The Sōka Gakkai was originally established as a lay auxiliary of the *Nichiren Shōshū, although it broke away in 1992. During Makiguchi's lifetime the membership of the Sōka Gakkai never exceeded a few thousand, and during the Second World War he was imprisoned for his refusal to comply with government directives that all religious groups give their support to the war effort. Within his exclusivistic religious outlook, this entailed a level of compromise and cooperation with other religious groups that he found unacceptable. He died in prison. *See also* JAPAN.

Makkhali Gosāla. An elder contemporary of the *Buddha and founder of the *Ājīvaka sect. Little is known for certain about his life, but he is disparaged on several occasions by the Buddha for holding perverse beliefs. As one of the *Six Sectarian Teachers his doctrines are preserved in Buddhist sources, from which the following is an extract: 'There is no cause either proximate or remote for the depravity of beings, they become depraved without reason and without cause. There is no cause either proximate or remote for the rectitude of beings, they become pure without reason and without cause ... There is no such thing as power, or energy, or human strength or human vigour. All *animals ... are without force and power of their own. They are bent this way and that by their fate' (*Dialogues of the Buddha*, i. 7, tr. T. W. and C. A. F. Rhys Davids 1899, Pali Text Society, Oxford). Makkhali thus appears to have been a determinist who held that fate or destiny (niyati) controlled everything and that moral choice was an illusion. According to him, all living beings belong to one of six classes and purification is ultimately obtained after a long course of evolutionary transmigration, the course of which could not be changed. It was for his denial of the doctrine of *karma and the efficacy of the religious effort that the Buddha castigated him so severely.

makyō (Jap.) **1.** The 'realm of devils' in Japanese *Buddhism. In *Zen, this can be used to mean hallucinations that arise while in *meditation. **2.** With a different Chinese character for the second syllable, this means the 'country of *Māra', as opposed to the *Pure Land of the *Buddha *Amitābha.

mālā (Skt.) A rosary, used for reciting *mantras or other prayers mainly by *Mahāyāna Buddhists. The beads on a mālā, normally 108, can be made of wood, hard nut kernels, bone, crystal, or other materials. Shorter, half or quarter mālās are also used by some Japanese lay Buddhists.

Mallā. One of the small republican states at the time of the *Buddha that formed part of the Vṛjian confederacy (*see* VAJJĪ), including the *Licchavis and the *Videhas. At that time, the country was divided into two parts with their respective capitals at *Pāvā and *Kuśinagara. The Buddha took his last meal at the house of the metal-worker *Cunda in Pāvā from whence he travelled on to Kuśinagara where he died. Soon after the Buddha's passing, the entire Vṛjian confederacy was assimilated into the expanding *Magadhan Empire.

Mallikā. Senior wife of King *Pasenadi of *Kosala. A devotee of the *Buddha she was instructed in the *Dharma by *Ānanda and was renowned for her wisdom.

Mālunkyāputta. Son of the king of *Kosala. He joined the Order (*Saṃgha) on hearing the *Buddha preach, and later became an *Arhat.

māna (Skt.; Pāli, conceit). The eighth of the ten fetters (*samyojana) which bind one to the cycle of *rebirth (*saṃsāra). Māna consists of an egocentric preoccupation with one's status vis-à-vis others, and is said to be threefold depending on whether the concern is that one is equal, better, or worse than them. It arises from the belief in a permanent self (*ātman) and only disappears completely when this belief is destroyed on the attainment of enlightenment (*bodhi). Māna is also the fifth of the seven negative mental tendencies known as *anuśayas, as well as being one of the defilements (*kleśa).

manas (Skt.). The intellect or thinking mind. In early *Buddhism and present-day *Theravāda, manas is regarded as virtually synonymous with *citta (psyche) and *vijñāna (consciousness), although it was included among the twelve *āyātanas (sense-spheres) and eighteen *dhātus (realms). In later schools of Buddhism, however, it is distinguished from those two. It came to be understood as that aspect of the mind which synthesizes perceptual forms derived from the six modes of perceptual awareness (sight, hearing, taste, smell, touch, and mental awareness) into conceptual images. In *Yogācāra Buddhism, it is counted as the seventh of the eight consciousnesses (vijñāna). It perceives the *ālaya-vijñāna (store consciousness) which underlies it, but mistakenly apprehends this as a personal self (*ātman) and hence is the location of that false belief.

maṇḍala (Skt.). A sacred circle or circular diagram (also occasionally oblong as in Japan) having mystical significance. Maṇḍalas are most commonly found in *tantric *Buddhism, where they are believed to represent the *body, speech, and mind of a *Buddha, and are used for initiatory, meditational, and other purposes. Maṇḍalas are said to exist in several planes of reality: the intrinsically existent maṇḍala (svabhāva-maṇḍala), not accessible to ordinary beings, which is the actual configuration of the qualities of enlightenment (*bodhi); the meditational maṇḍala (samādhi-maṇḍala) as visualized by a tantric practitioner, and the representational maṇḍala which is the maṇḍala as depicted with colours and so forth. Maṇḍalas are also subdivided according to whether they are Body Maṇḍalas which embody the body-form of the deities or aspects of enlightenment, Speech Maṇḍalas which represent the speech aspect with seed-syllables (bīja-mantra), or Mind Maṇḍalas which represent the mind aspect with symbols such as lotuses, *vajras, or wheels.

Fig 11 maṇḍala

Mandāravā. The daughter of the king of *Sahor who became the consort of *Padmasambhava with whom she later travelled to *Nepal and Bengal. Legend tells that an attempt was made to burn her and Padmasambhava alive but this failed due to their spiritual accomplishments.

Mañjughoṣa (Skt.). 'Sweet Voice'; an alternative name for the *Bodhisattva *Mañjuśrī.

Mañjuśrī. One of the great mythical or celestial *Bodhisattvas in *Mahāyāna *Buddhism, also known by the fuller name of Mañjuśrī-kumāra-bhūta. He is first mentioned in some of the early Mahāyāna texts such as the *Prajñā-pāramitā Sūtras and through this connection soon came to symbolize the embodiment of insight (*prajña). He later figures widely in many texts associated with *tantric Buddhism such as the important *Mañjuśrī-mūla-kalpa*. Iconographically, he is depicted in a peaceful form holding a raised sword—symbolizing the power of insight—in his right hand and a book of the *Prajñā-pāramitā Sūtra* in his left. According to the tantras, he has a wrathful aspect, known as *Yamāntaka.

Fig 12 Mañjuśrī.

Mañjuśrī-mūla-kalpa. A *kriyā-tantra associated with the cult of the *Bodhisattva *Mañjuśrī. Often cited as the earliest extant example of a Buddhist tantra, it is more likely to represent the product of a lengthy process of compilation and addition beginning with a core element that was written no earlier than the late 6th century CE. The text survives in a *Sankrit version which is comparatively more lengthy than its corresponding Tibetan and Chinese translations.

mano-jalpa (Skt., mental chatter). A term especially used in *Yogācāra to denote the process of mental designation that precedes verbal designation. Used synonymously with *vikalpa or *vicāra.

Manorathapūraṇī (Pāli, fulfiller of wishes). *Buddhaghoṣa's commentary on the *Aṅguttara Nikāya of the *Pāli Canon.

mantra (Skt.). Sacred sounds, thought to be imbued with supernatural powers. These range from single syllables (bīja-mantra) to lengthy combinations that, according to *tantric *Buddhism, are manifestations of the speech aspect of enlightenment (*bodhi) both in the form of various deities and also as the sounds and letters which reveal the qualities embodied by them. Traditionally the word is understood as that which 'protects' (tra) the 'mind' (man), although scholars analyse it as a 'device for thinking' (man). Through using mantras in creative imagination and *meditation, one is able to access and develop the power of the various qualities they represent, whether for self-transformation or to accomplish various aims.

Mantrayāna (Skt., mantra vehicle). A general term for the path of *tantric *Buddhism which highlights the importance of *mantras in that practice. The term seems to have evolved from the earlier 'mantra method' (mantra-naya) in contrast to the 'perfection method' (pāramitā-naya), used when the tantric path was seen as an alternative approach within *Mahāyāna as a whole. The term 'Mantrayāna' is more widely used in traditional literature than the synonymous *Vajrayāna.

mappō. A Japanese term meaning 'the end of the *Dharma'. During the medieval period in Chinese *Buddhism (*see* CHINA), the Buddhist community came to accept that the history of Buddhism would be divided into three periods: that of the True Dharma, that of the Counterfeit Dharma, and that of the End of the Dharma. During the first, which would last 500 years, the teachings of the *Buddha would be transmitted with minimal distortion, and beings had a good chance of understanding and practising them, and of achieving enlightenment (*bodhi). During the second period, also 500 years, the substance would be gone and only the outer forms of practice would remain. Fewer beings would attain the goal at this time. During the third period, even the semblance of genuine practice would disappear, and beings would be left to their own devices. According to most calculations of the time of the Buddha's death, the world was already in the period of mappō. While this may appear to be cause for despair, many in east Asia actually responded to this analysis not by giving up, but by advocating new and creative doctrines. In response to mappō, new schools arose, such as the *Pure Land and *Nichiren schools, asserting that the Buddha had foreseen and provided for the advent of this final age by preparing texts and teachings suited for beings born in this time. These teachings had been discovered and propagated to counter the adverse conditions of mappō and give beings hope for liberation. This assertion validated texts, teachings, and practices that obviously conflicted with what was known of early Buddhism by arguing that the difference between the first period of the True Dharma and the present period made it necessary that the teachings be significantly different. It was felt that the degenerate conditions of the present age demanded it. *See also* SHŌ-ZŌ-MATSU; THREE PERIODS OF THE TEACHINGS.

Māra. The Buddhist 'devil'. Technically a god (*deva), Māra is the enemy of the *Buddha and constantly tries to disrupt his teaching in order to prevent beings reaching *nirvāṇa where they would be beyond his grasp. He makes two main appearances in the Buddha's life, one just before he gains enlightenment (*bodhi) and the other shortly before his *death. On the first occasion, accompanied by his daughters (*see* MĀRA'S DAUGHTERS) he tries alternately to tempt and frighten the Buddha, but to no avail. On the second occasion he tries to persuade the Buddha to pass away into *parinirvāṇa, but the Buddha delays his passing for a time. More abstractly, Māra, whose name literally means 'death', symbolizes all that is connected with the realm of *rebirth (*saṃsāra) and opposed to nirvāṇa. There are said to be four forms of Māra: (1) Māra of the *aggregates (skandha-māra), or Māra as a symbol of human mortality; (2) Māra as the Lord of Death (mṛtyu-māra); (3) Māra as the vices and moral defilements (kleśa-māra); and (4) the gods in the retinue of Māra (devaputra-māra).

maraṇa (Skt.; Pali, death). General term meaning *death. In Buddhist thought this has two senses. (1) Physical death as it occurs at the end of life: in this sense maraṇa is the twelfth link in the chain of Dependent Origination (*pratītya-samutpāda). (2) Death as the dying process: in this sense, particularly common in the *Abhidharma, death occurs continuously as each moment perishes to be replaced by the next. Death in both senses is a product of the universal principle of *anitya, or impermanence.

maraṇānussati (Pāli, mindfulness of death). The seventh of the ten recollections (*anussati), being a meditational exercise on *death (*maraṇa) seen as an inevitable and possibly imminent eventuality. The exercise is undertaken in order to stimulate effort and zeal in religious practice. The meditator reflects on the brevity and fragility of life and the numerous directions from which death can come, e.g. from snakebite, accident, illness, and assault.

Māra's daughters. Māra has three daughters knows as Ratī (delight), Aratī (discontent), and *Tṛṣṇā (craving). According to legend, when their father failed to prevent the *Buddha gaining enlightenment (*bodhi) the three daughters approached the Buddha five weeks later and attempted, also without success, to seduce him with their wiles.

mārga (Skt., path; Pāli, magga). Path or way, particularly in the sense of a system of religious practice leading to *nirvāṇa. Various formulations are found, the most common of which is the Noble *Eightfold Path. In early *Buddhism, the scheme of the four *ārya-mārga (noble paths) is common, and in *Mahāyāna Buddhism a formula of five paths takes precedence. These are: (1) the path of accumulation (*saṃbhāra-mārga); (2) the path of preparation (*prayoga-mārga); (3) the path of seeing (*darśaṇa-mārga); (4) the path of cultivation (*bhāvanā-mārga); and (5) the path of no further learning (*aśaikṣa-mārga).

marks of a superman. *See* DVĀTRIṂŚADVARA-LAKṢAṆA.

Marpa (1012–97). A celebrated Tibetan *yogin, Marpa initially trained as a translator. He visited *India on three occasions and *Nepal on four occasions where he attended upon such spiritual masters as *Nāropa and Maitripa, who introduced him to doctrines and practices of *tantric *Buddhism, especially those connected with Hevajra, Guhyasamāja, and *mahāmudrā. An important account of his encounters with Nāropa survives. Following his return to *Tibet, he resided in the Lhodrak area and taught many students, including the great *Milarepa. He introduced the set of six special tantric practices known as the *Six Yogas of *Nāropa and established the teaching tradition of the *Kagyü school.

marriage. While *Buddhism regards the celibate monastic life as the higher ideal (*see* CELIBACY), it also recognizes the importance of marriage as a social institution. However, in Buddhism marriage is essentially a secular contract of partnership in which the partners assume obligations towards one another. Unlike in Christianity, marriage is not a sacrament, and *monks do not officiate at wedding ceremonies. They are also prohibited by the *Vinaya from playing the role of matchmaker or go-between in bringing couples together. Nevertheless, it is customary for newlyweds to attend the local monastery (*vihāra) later for a blessing and a simple ceremony in which texts are chanted. An early text from the *Pāli Canon, the **Sigālovāda Sutta*, summarizes the obligations of husband and wife as follows. 'In five ways should a wife ... be ministered to by her husband: by respect, by courtesy, by faithfulness, by giving her authority (in the home), by providing her with adornments'. The wife reciprocates by ensuring that 'her duties are well performed, she shows hospitality to the kin of both, is faithful, watches over the goods he (her husband) brings, and shows skill and artistry in discharging all her business.' While monogamy is the preferred and predominant model, there is much local variation in marriage patterns across the Buddhist world. Early documents mention a variety of temporary and permanent arrangements entered into for both emotional and economic reasons, and in different parts of Buddhist Asia both polygamy and polyandry have been tolerated. Buddhism has no religious objection to divorce, but due to social pressures in traditional societies it is much less common than in the West. Western Buddhist groups, like the *Friends of the Western Buddhist Order, have experimented with new models of community life without marriage, in order to overcome the perceived exclusiveness of the nuclear Western family unit.

martial arts. Martial arts is a broad term that covers a variety of schools and forms whose unity derives only from their origins in the arts of war and single combat. Thus, it covers the 'empty-hand' fighting style of karate as well as forms that concentrate on the use of various weapons, from swords and bows and arrows to farming implements such as sickles and threshers. Within Buddhist history, the martial arts have been closely identified with the teachings and practices of *Ch'an and *Zen from an early period, a situation that arose when the military classes discovered that Zen practice enhanced fighting techniques by eliminating the fear of defeat and *death and by enabling the combatant to keep his mind and energy focused in the present moment, thus shutting out distraction and enhancing concentration and reflexes.

In *China, the origin of this connection is traced to the putative founder of Ch'an himself, *Bodhidharma (3rd–4th centuries). It is said that when he arrived at the *Shao-lin monastery (*vihāra) in Honan Province, he found the resident *monks in poor physical condition and subject to the depredations of local bandits, and so he taught them fighting techniques to improve their health and security. To this day, the monks of the Shao-lin monastery are famed for their fighting skills. A similar school of Buddhist Martial Arts (as opposed to 'Royal Court Martial Arts') arose in *Korea. In *Japan, the association of Zen and fighting led the *samurai class to associate primarily with the *Rinzai school from the mid-*Kamakura period onward. They found in the Rinzai school an active, goal-oriented programme of self-cultivation that accorded with their own drive to self-discipline and achievement, and so a symbiotic relationship developed. Rinzai saw in the practice of martial arts a way to self-realization and expression of one's *Buddha-nature of much the same sort that other arts (such as painting, calligraphy, and poetry) provided. The samurai found in Zen practice a way to further their own goals in becoming more skilled warriors. Some figures even straddled both worlds, such as *Suzuki Shōsan (1579–1655), who as a young man was a warrior who made use of Zen in his combat, and later in life became a Zen *monk whose teachings were filled with martial images.

Mathurā (also Madhurā). The ancient capital of the state of Surasena, situated on the river Yamunā, to the west of *Kuru, located a few miles from present-day Mathurā in Uttar Pradesh. Though visited by the *Buddha at least once, he does not seem to have stayed there long nor had any particular liking for the place, though he seems to have had a few followers there, notably his disciple *Mahākatyāyana. In later centuries, the Chinese pilgrims *Fa-hsien and *Hsüan-tsang reported that there was a flourishing *Saṃgha there. Mathurā was also important as a centre of Buddhist art, producing some of the earliest sculpted images of the Buddha. Not to be confused with a city of the same name near Madras in south *India.

mātṛkā (Skt.; Pāli, mātikā). A rubric or tabulated summary of contents used in the philosophical sections of the books of the *Abhidharma Piṭaka. Originally a *Vinaya term, used in the singular (Pāli, mātikā), it meant a keyword. Used in the plural (also mātikā), it means the keywords for a topic, and hence a list.

Ma-tsu Tao-i (709–88). A Chinese *Ch'an *monk of the third generation after the Sixth *Patriarch *Hui-neng (638–713) known for his iconoclastic language and energetic teaching. His teaching style was rough, and he is counted as one of the early pioneers of the 'shock Ch'an' or 'crazy Ch'an' method of imparting enlightenment (*satori) directly to his disciples. His methods included shouting directly into a student's ear, beating him, or giving nonsensical replies to questions in order to force the student to rely on his own resources. Tales of Ma-tsu, both as a student under *Nan-yueh Huai-jang (677–744) and as a teacher in his own right, have been preserved in the great *kōan collections of the Ch'an and *Zen traditions. Perhaps the best known is the following: 'Ma-tsu was residing in the Chuan-fa Temple and sat constantly in *meditation. The master (Huai-jang), aware that he was a vessel of the *Dharma, went to him and asked, Virtuous One, why are you sitting in meditation? Tao-i answered, I wish to become a *Buddha. Then the master picked up a tile and began to rub it with a stone in front of the hermitage. Tao-i asked, What is the master doing? The master replied, I am polishing a mirror. Tao-i exclaimed, How can one make a mirror by polishing a tile? The master retorted, How can you become a Buddha by sitting in meditation?'

Mauryan dynasty. Early Indian dynasty

centred on the state of *Magadha which ruled from 324 to 184 BCE, although these dates and the chronology of the period as a whole are uncertain: the date of 184 is simply one of a number of guesses, and some authorities date the start of the dynasty to 313. The dynasty was founded by *Candragupta who overthrew the preceding *Nanda dynasty and founded a capital at *Pāṭaliputra. He defeated the Greek king Seleucus Nikator in 305 and as part of the terms of a marriage treaty in 303 a Greek ambassador known as *Megasthenes came to reside at his court. Megasthenes composed a detailed account of contemporary life in *India which has not survived. According to Buddhist accounts, Candragupta converted to *Jainism late in life and went to south India where he starved himself to death according to Jain custom (*see* JAINISM). Candragupta was succeeded by his son *Bindusāra in 297. He extended the empire to include Mysore, and by this time much of the subcontinent was under Mauryan control with the exception of *Kaliṅga (present-day Orissa). Bindusāra died in 272 and was succeeded by his son *Aśoka, who was consecrated in 268 (some modern authorities say 277) and who conquered Kaliṅga and consolidated the greatest Indian empire down to the time of the Moghuls and the British Raj. The name Maurya (Pāli, Moriya) derives from the word for a peacock. *See also* INDIA.

Māyā. Also known as Mahāmāyā, the mother of the *Buddha. When the Buddha was conceived she dreamt that a white elephant entered her womb, a very auspicious omen. She died seven days after giving birth and was reborn in the *Tuṣita *heaven. Her husband, *Śuddhodhana, then married her sister *Mahāprajāpatī.

meat-eating *See* DIET.

medicine. For over 2,000 years the Buddhist monastic order (*Saṃgha) has been closely involved with the treatment of the sick. Several centuries before Christ, Buddhist *monks were developing treatments for many kinds of medical conditions and played a significant role in the development of traditional Indian medicine (Āyurveda). Medical expertise was required as a means to securing the healthy physical constitution necessary to withstand the rigours of the monastic life. Treatments were given in the monasteries, and the medical practices that were institutionalized as part of the monastic rules (*Vinaya) provide some of the earliest codifications of Indian medical knowledge. In the Vinaya, the *Buddha counsels monks to care for one another in the following terms: 'You, O monks, have neither a father nor a mother who could nurse you. If, O monks, you do not nurse one another, who, then, will nurse you? Whoever, O monks, would nurse me, he should nurse the sick.' As monasteries grew, hospices and infirmaries supported by the laity increasingly formed part of the structure, and medicine became integrated into the curricula of the major monastic universities. The great Buddhist monarch *Aśoka states in his second Rock *Edict that he has made medical provision for both men and *animals, and that he has imported and planted medicinal herbs, along with roots and fruits. In modern times Buddhist monks continue to practise traditional medicine from a range of cultures as well as Western medicine.

Medicine Buddha. *See* BHAIṢYAJA-GURU.

meditation. English word often used to translate a range of more specific indigenous terms denoting techniques and practices designed to concentrate and focus the mind. *See* BHĀVANĀ; SAMĀDHI; SĀDHANA; VIPAŚYANĀ; ŚAMATHA.

Megasthenes. Greek ambassador of Seleucus Nikator who came to reside at the court of *Candragupta Maurya in 303 BCE. Megasthenes composed a detailed account of contemporary life in *India which has not survived, although fragments are quoted in classical Western sources. *See also* MAURYAN DYNASTY.

Meiji Restoration. The restoration of the Japanese emperor to power in 1868 after several centuries during which real political power resided in the hands of shōguns or military commanders while the imperial family played only a ceremonial role in national life. The restoration of power to the Meiji emperor had serious repercussions for *Buddhism. The Tokugawa shōguns had made much use of Buddhist ideology in their *martial arts and had co-opted Buddhist temples as *de facto* government bureaux, while the emperor returned to power with the aid of *Shintō intellectuals. Since his sympathy lay with the latter, after his accession he ordered the separation of Buddhist temples from Shintō shrines, bringing to an end the existence of hybrid institutions and the dominance of Buddhism over Shintō. For a short period, Buddhism was even officially proscribed and persecuted, although the emperor found he was unable to sustain this policy for long. *See also* JAPAN.

Men-ngak-dé. *See* SECRET INSTRUCTION CATEGORY.

merit. *See* PUṆYA.

Meru. Also known as Sumeru or Sineru. According to ancient Indian cosmological beliefs, the *axis mundi* or world mountain that stands at the centre of the world, surrounded by oceans and continents. It was generally thought to be surrounded by four continents, with the continent known as *Jambudvīpa (which included the then-known world) located to the south. Various *heavens were said to be located on top of and above Meru while the hell realms lie beneath it. Some scholars believe the orgin of the concept lies in the Mesopotamian ziggurats of ancient Sumer, a possibility given the early trade links between ancient *India and the Euphrates region.

metta. *Pāli form of *maitrī, a *Sanskrit word meaning love, goodwill, or benevolence.

Metta Sutta. A popular discourse from the **Sutta Nipāta* of the *Pāli Canon, also known as the *Karaṇīyametta Sutta*. The *sutta is a discourse on goodwill preached by the *Buddha. It states that one should be upright, gentle, modest, and straightforward, and commends the practice of goodwill towards all beings, modelled on the attitude of a mother to her only son. The text is recited daily by *monks and often lay-people.

Mettiyabhummajakā (Pāli). Name given to a group of *monks, said to be followers of Mettiya and Bhummajaka, forming part of the *chabbaggiyā monks.

Middle Way. *See* MADHYAMĀ-PRATIPAD.

Migāramātupāsāda (Pāli). Name given to the monastery (*vihāra) erected by *Visākhā in the *Pubbārāma, to the east of *Śrāvastī, *India. According to tradition it was the *Buddha who suggested the erection of this monastery which is said to have consisted of a two-storey building with 500 rooms on each floor, all richly equipped. During the last 20 years of his life, when the Buddha was living at Śrāvastī, he divided his time between the residence (*ārāma) donated by *Anāthapiṇḍika and this monastery. For this reason it is assumed that numerous *suttas were preached there. Also, it was here that the Buddha gave permission for the *Prātimokṣa to be recited in his absence.

Mihintale. Town 7 Miles north-east of *Anurādhapura, *Sri Lanka. Its great spiritual importance to the Buddhists of the island is due to the fact that it is here that *Mahinda, son of Emperor *Aśoka, met King *Devānampiya Tissa and converted him to *Buddhism, thus officially introducing the religion to the country.

Mikkyō. *See* MI-TSUNG.

mi-lam (Tib., rmi-lam, dream). A dream or illusion, a term often used as a metaphor for the nature of mundane (*laukika) experience. The concept of the unreality of the external world also forms the basis for certain forms of *tantric *yoga such as found in the *Six Yogas of *Nāropa.

Milarepa (1040–1123) (Tib., Milaraspa). One of the most revered and loved of Tibetan *yogins, whose name literally means 'cotton clad Mila'. Milarepa initially first studied sorcery to slay many family enemies, but later, overcome with remorse, went to train with *Marpa who made him undergo many hardships in expiation for his evil deeds. After six years had elapsed, Marpa finally conferred the desired initiations and teachings upon Milarepa. From the age of 45, Milarepa meditated alone and performed great austerities for nine years, such as wearing just a single cotton garment and eating only cooked nettles. After his full realization, he travelled widely, giving teachings on *mahāmudrā and other aspects of *tantric *Buddhism, often by means of his famous songs. Though he did not leave any personal writings, his biography and the famous collection of his songs, the *Hundred Thousand Songs*, survive to the present day. His main disciples were Rechungpa and *Gampopa.

Milindapañha. 'Milinda's Questions', being

the title of an important *Pāli work that records the conversations between the 1st century CE Bactrian King Milinda (or Menander), and the *monk *Nāgasena. Milinda is probably a Bactrian king of Śākala in the east Punjab who ruled in the 2nd to 1st centuries BCE (*see also* INDIA). The initial part of the text (also in Chinese translation) probably dates from the 1st century CE, although most of the work was written in *Sri Lanka at a later date. The work is often quoted by *Buddhaghoṣa. Nāgasena makes use of illustrations, similes, and metaphors in a lively conversational style to resolve problems and dilemmas in Buddhist doctrine pointed out by the king. The discussions concern questions such as how there can be *rebirth in the absence of a self (*ātman), how there can be moral responsibility without an enduring *ego, why the *evil prosper and the innocent suffer, and why the scriptures often seem to be in contradiction. The most famous simile is that of a chariot used to illustrate the doctrine of no-self (*anātman). Just as a chariot is simply the sum of its constituent parts, namely the wheels, yoke, axles, etc., so a human being is said to be simply the sum of the five aggregates (*skandha). Although individuals bear a name (e.g. Nāgasena), in the ultimate sense there is no self or essence corresponding to it. At the conclusion of the *debate Milinda becomes a Buddhist lay disciple.

Milinda's Questions. *See* MILINDAPAÑHA.

Mind Category (Tib., sems-sde). The first of three subdivisons of the *Nyingma *atiyoga class of teachings in which all appearances are perceived as the play of the mind.

mindfulness. *See* SMṚTI.

mindfulness of death. *See* MARAṆĀNUSSATI.

mindfulness of the body. A meditational practice devoted to contemplation of the body (kāya) in an attitude of detached awareness. It is the first of the four 'Foundations of Mindfulness' (*smṛti-upasthāna).

mind-only. *See* CITTA-MĀTRA.

Ming-ti (r. 58–76 CE). An emperor of the Later *Han dynasty. According to one traditional account of *Buddhism's inception in *China, this emperor had a dream of a flying golden man one night in the year 67. The next day, he asked his ministers about it, and one of them said it must have been a vision of the *Buddha, and advised the emperor to send envoys to the western regions to find out more. He did this, and the envoys returned with some Buddhist *monks who helped translate a few texts into Chinese. Historically, this legend is untenable, as there is good evidence that Buddhism had already entered China as much as 50 years prior to this event (as witnessed by the minister's ability to identify the figure in Emperor Ming's dream).

miracles. The display of a wide range of miracles is described throughout Buddhist scriptures. The ability to perform such miracles is said to derive from the attainment of supernatural knowledge (*abhijñā) and psychic powers (*ṛddhi) as a culmination of lengthy practice of meditation (*samādhi). In the earliest Buddhist sources, the display of one's miraculous abilities is discouraged or even forbidden by the *Buddha. Later textual sources, however, especially those emanating from *Mahāyāna circles, take a different view and regularly commend such miracles, particularly when said to be performed by the Buddha, as an appropriate means of demonstrating his unlimited powers and bringing beings to salvation. Many accounts of miracles are also mentioned in connection with the lives of the *tantric adepts (*siddhas). *See also* PĀṬIHĀRIYA; ṚDDHI.

Miroku. Japanese name for the *Buddha *Maitreya.

Mithilā. The capital of the ancient Indian state of *Videha, one of the members of the Vṛjian confederacy (*see* VAJJĪ). The town was visited several times by the *Buddha who taught a number of discourses there.

Mi-tsung. Chinese term for *esoteric *Buddhism, denoting practices such as those found in the *Vajrayāna tradition. The equivalent term in Japanese is mikkyō.

mizuko kuyō (Jap.). A practice in modern Japanese *Buddhism of making offerings to the spirits of aborted foetuses. The practice takes the form of a memorial service held at a Buddhist temple in which a statue resembling a young child in the form of a Buddhist *monk is set up and prayers are recited. Given the high rate of *abortion in contemporary

*Japan (in recent years over 1 million per annum) it is not uncommon to find row upon row of these statues, to which offerings are made and prayers recited by relatives each year on the anniversary of the abortion. *Women who have had abortions find the memorial service comforting, and it is also believed to avert misfortune for the family caused by the angry spirit of the aborted child.

mo-chao Ch'an. A Chinese term meaning 'silent illumination *Ch'an'. This term refers to a style and orientation of Ch'an practice as having no goal beyond itself. In seated *meditation, one simply realizes that one was a fully enlightened *Buddha all along, and that there is no goal to attain and nothing into which one need transform oneself. This was the dominant style of the *Ts'ao-tung school of Ch'an, and was opposed to the '*k'an-hua Ch'an' ('Ch'an that contemplates the words') of the *Lin-chi school, in which the latter phrase refers to the use of *kōans in practice with a view to attaining the goal of enlightenment (*bodhi). This distinction was carried forward by the Japanese inheritors of these traditions: the *Sōtō school continued the practice of silent illumination (Jap., *mokushō zen), while the *Rinzai school continued to practise kōan contemplation (Jap., *kanna zen).

Moggaliputta Tissa. Senior *monk who presided over the council held during the reign of *Aśoka (*see* COUNCIL OF PĀṬALIPUTRA II). Due to prosperity enjoyed by the Order (*Saṃgha) as a result of Aśoka's patronage, a number of corrupt *monks were admitted. In protest, Moggaliputta withdrew to live in solitary retreat for seven years, and on his return Aśoka assembled all the monks to be questioned by himself with Moggaliputta in attendance. The heretical monks were expelled and Moggaliputta later celebrated the third council (*see* COUNCIL OF PĀṬALIPUTRA II) with 1,000 *Arhats in attendance. Moggaliputta died at the age of 80 in the 26th year of Aśoka's reign.

Moggallāna. *Pāli name of *Mahamaudgalyāyana.

moha (Pāli). 'Delusion', one of the three roots of evil (*akuśala-mūla), which, together with craving (*lobha) and hatred (*dveṣa), leads to *rebirth and *suffering in cyclic existence (*saṃsāra). Moha is synonymous with ignorance (*avidyā), which is the first link in the series of Dependent Origination (*pratītya-samutpāda) and which must be removed if suffering (*duḥkha) is to cease. Most fundamentally, moha and avidyā relate to ignorance about the true nature of things as summarized in the *Four Noble Truths. This includes ignorance of one's own nature and that of the world at large and manifests itself in the belief that phenomena are permanent and stable, and that a self or soul (*ātman) underlies personal identity. The way to cleanse the mind of these misconceptions is through the practice of the *Eightfold Path, which destroys delusion and replaces it with insight (*prajñā).

mokushō Zen. The Japanese pronunciation of the Chinese term *mo-chao Ch'an, or 'silent illumination'. As this was the favoured practice of the *Ts'ao-tung school of Chinese *Ch'an, so it was carried on by its successor, the *Sōtō school in *Japan.

Mon. A people indigenous to *south east Asia, also formerly referred to as the Talaing, who established some of the earliest urban centres in the region of lower *Burma, the Chao Phraya delta and north-eastern plateau of Siam (now Thailand). The Mons were one of the earliest literate peoples in the region and the Mon language is one of the earliest recorded vernaculars along with Pyu (now extinct), Cham, and Khmer. The language was written in the Indian Pallava script, and *Sanskrit and *Pāli were also in use. The *Theravāda form of Buddhism was present among the Mon and Pyu people from the 5th century, and perhaps earlier. The first datable archaeological finds of the Mon civilisation stem from the Mon kingdom of Dvāravatī in the south of *Thailand. They consist of a Roman oil lamp and a bronze statue of the *Buddha which are believed to be no later than the 1st or 2nd century CE. The Chinese Buddhist pilgrim, *Hsüan-tsang, who travelled to India in about 630 AD, describes a single Mon country stretching from Prome to Chenla in the east and including the Irrawaddy and Sittang deltas. The Mons were influential in Siam until the 13th century when they were eclipsed by the rise of Chiang Mai and other Tai states, although they remained a political force in Burma until the 18th century. Today the Mons have no independent political status and the Mon language is dying out.

monastery. *See* VIHĀRA.

mondo (Jap.). 'Question and answer', a term used in Japanese *Zen practice to refer to a discussion or interview between master and student in which a religious theme is addressed obliquely rather than in the form of a *debate or lecture. Normally the student raises a problem in connection with doctrine or practice and the master attempts to provide an answer without recourse to theoretical or analytical explanations. The records of these exchanges are often preserved as *kōans for use by subsequent students.

mondop. Thai term derived from *Sanskrit maṇḍapa meaning a pavilion and denoting a small square temple building used to house minor images or religious texts.

Mongkut. Former *monk and, as Rāma IV, ruler of *Thailand 1851–68. During his period of 27 years as a monk, 1824–51, he studied the *Pāli scriptures intensively, and as a result of his research founded the *Thammayut (Pāli, Dhammayuttika) sect in about 1833. This group, whose name means 'those holding to the Law', was a reform movement advocating stricter compliance with the *Vinaya, in contrast to the mainstream Mahānikai (Pāli, Mahānikāya) order. As abbot of Wat Bovoranives, which became the centre of the Thammayut sect, he laid down strict rules governing ordination, wearing of the monastic robe (over both shoulders instead of just one), and for the conduct of the *kaṭhina or robe-giving ceremony. Mongkut was keen to learn from the West and invited Christian missionaries, scientists, and intellectuals to discuss their ideas with him. A sense of his desire to modernize his country comes across in the depiction of his character in the popular novel, play, and film, *The King and I*. Mongkut's reforms emphasized scripture, intellectualism, and rationalism, and laid the foundations for modern Thai Buddhism which became established under his son Chulalongkorn (Rāma V, 1886–1910).

Mongolia. Despite traditions of early contacts with Buddhist teachers, the historical transmission of *Buddhism to Mongolia occurred at a late date, primarily through the efforts of the Tibetans and to a lesser extent the *Uighurs. Prior to the foundation of the Mongolian state by Jenghis Khan in the 12th century CE, the earliest Mongolian contacts with Buddhism probably occurred through contact with Chinese Buddhist missionaries and the flow of travellers along the *Silk Road. During the 13th century, under Jenghis Khan, the *Uighur script was adopted for Mongolian use and some Buddhist texts are thought to have been translated at that time. However, Buddhism did not make great inroads among the population until the Tibetan leader *Sakya Paṇḍita visited the court of Godan Khan in 1244 and made some conversions. This process was accelerated by cordial contacts between *Phags pa blo dro (1235–89) and Kublai Khan. In contrast to this interest in Buddhism among Mongolian aristocrats, it was not until the *Dalai Lama III (1543–88) made contact with the court of Altan Khan and gained his support that large-scale missionary efforts were undertaken among the populace in general and the construction of the first monastery took place. This was further promoted by the efforts of Jaya Paṇḍita in the 17th century who was active among the western and northern Mongols. The translation and printing of the entire Buddhist *canon into Mongolian from the Tibetan *Kanjur and *Tenjur was undertaken in the 18th century with the patronage of the Ch'ing emperors Kang-hsi (1661–1722) and Ch'ien-lung (1736–95). This generated an enormous impetus in the growth of Tibetan-style Buddhism in Mongolia and led to the establishment of almost 2,000 temples and monasteries in all areas of the country. The Mongolian Communist revolution in 1920 heralded a period of wholesale decline and persecution of Buddhism and resulted in the destruction of virtually all of the previously existing monasteries and temples, estimated to have exceeded 1,200 in the 19th century, as well as the execution or forcible laicization of the *Saṃgha. The return to a democratic form of government in the 1990s has allowed a considerable revival of interest in Buddhism.

monk. Usual English translation of the *Sanskrit word *bhikṣu (Pāli, bhikkhu). Buddhist monks are referred to in different ways throughout the Buddhist world. For example, in *Tibet they are known as *lamas, in Burma as *phongyi, and in *Korea as *pigu.

Monkey or The Monkey King. (Chin., *hsi-yu chi*). One of the titles of a work also known as *The Journey to the West*. The work is a supernatural novel about a world of fantastic invention, in which gods and demons loom large and vie for supremacy. The novel began with a series of oral and written versions until the Ming-dynasty scholar-official Wu Ch'eng-en (1500–82) gave it its definitive form and it was published in 1592. The story is based on the journey of the *T'ang-dynasty *monk *Hsüan-tsang (596–664) across the desert into *India in search of Buddhist scriptures. Along the way, he meets the title character, the monkey 'king' *Sun Wu-k'ung, and rescues him from his prison under a mountain. This monkey is an extraordinary character: born from a rock, and having studied with famous *Taoist masters, he possesses magical powers, extreme prowess in *martial arts, and wonderful weapons. Prior to his imprisonment, the readers are told, he spent many years in rebellion against the Jade Emperor (a heavenly analogue to the rebellion of local warlords against the Chinese emperor, according to critics), before being imprisoned by the *Buddha himself. Now, the Buddha has arranged for Hsüan-tsang to find him so that he can do penance by serving the monk as escort, bodyguard, and guide through a series of 81 dangers. The story of *Journey to the West* is divided into three parts: (1) an early history of the Monkey spirit; (2) a pseudo-historical account of Hsüan-tsang's family and life before his trip to fetch the *sūtras in India; (3) the main narrative, which recounts the dangers and calamities faced by Hsüan-tsang, Sun Wu-k'ung, and two other animal companions: Piggsy (a former heavenly general who assaulted a fairy and was punished by transformation into porcine form), and Sandy (a reformed sea-monster). While loosely based on historical fact, the novel is a treasure-trove of Chinese folklore and legend, as well as being a literary masterpiece in its style, construction, vivid imagery, and pacing.

Moriya. *Pāli form of *Maurya.

mosshōryō. Japanese term for the loss of a sense of separation between two discutants in a conversation or dialogue.

Mother Tantra. One of the three main classes of *anuttara-yoga-tantras according to the New Transmission lineage in *Tibet, typified by the **Hevajra* and **Cakra-saṃvara Tantras*. Meditative practice (**sādhana*) based on the Mother Tantras emphasizes the so-called '*completion-phase' of *visualization as a means of personal transformation.

Movement of the Wondrous Law of the Lotus. *See* NIPPONZAN MYŌHOJI.

moxa (Jap., mokusa, burning herbs). Moxa or moxibustion is the practice of placing a small cone of incense on the head and allowing it to burn down to the scalp where it leaves a mark. This practice is found as part of the monastic *ordination procedure in both *China and *Japan, but is unknown in *India and *south-east Asia. Enduring the pain demonstrates courage and commitment, and can be repeated at later times in the monastic career. Burning marks on other parts of the body, such as the chest or arms, or setting fire to limbs, also sometimes occurs in east Asian *Buddhism as a token of devotion or as the result of a vow.

mu. This is the Japanese pronunciation of the Chinese character 'wu', which means 'to lack' or 'there is not'. In ordinary usage it negates the presence of something. It is famous in *Ch'an and *Zen circles as the 'critical phrase' (Chin., hua-t'ou) of the *kōan 'Chao-chou's dog', the first case in the *Mumonkan* collection (*see Gateless Gate*). When asked whether or not a dog has *Buddha-nature, Chao-chou replied, 'It does not' (wu/mu). Practitioners working with this kōan try to penetrate the meaning of this answer.

Mucalinda. Name of a tree which was the abode of serpent-king of the same name. The tree was located in the *Ajapāla-nigrodha in *Uruvelā. According to the commentarial accounts, in the sixth week after his enlightenment (*bodhi), the serpent-king (*nāga) sheltered the *Buddha during a rainstorm by winding his coils seven times around the Buddha's body and covering his head with its hood. The motif is a common theme in Buddhist art.

muditā (Pāli, gladness). Sympathetic joy or rejoicing in the good fortune of another. It is the third of the four Divine Abidings (*Brahma-vihāra).

mudrā (Skt. a seal) **1.** A symbolic gesture of the hands or bodily posture communicating a specific meaning. From the earliest artistic representations onwards, *Buddhas are always depicted with their hands in certain standard mudrās, the most important being the 'wheel of the *Dharma' (*dharma-cakra-mudrā), the first finger and thumb of each hand forming a circle; the earth-touching mudrā (*bhumi-sparśa-mudrā), the right hand touching the earth calling it to witness the Buddha's enlightenment (*bodhi); and the gesture of protection or fearlessness (*abhaya-mudrā), the right arm extended with palm facing forwards. The repertoire of hand mudrās in Buddhist iconography is extensive, and is a key to identifying the figures depicted. Mudrās become increasingly important in *Mahāyāna and particularly in *Vajrayāna *Buddhism, where they are associated with a dense symbolism of signs and mystical sounds (*mantras). **2.** In Vajrayāna Buddhism, mudrā also denotes the imagery used in any meditation or visualization practice to imprint certain qualities upon or to modify the practitioner, just as a seal leaves an identical impression on clay or paper. In this sense, four kinds of mudrā are mentioned in connection with *yoga-tantra—*mahāmudrā, *dharma-mudrā, *samaya-mudrā and *karma-mudrā.

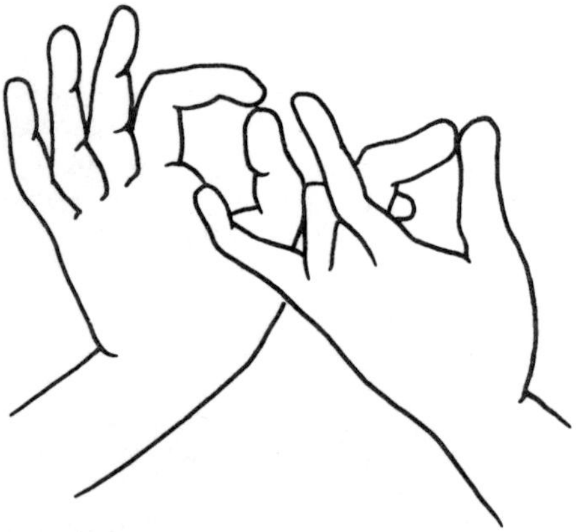

Fig 13 dharma-cakra-mudrā

mujō. 1. The Japanese pronunciation of the Chinese wu-ch'ang, which means 'impermanence' (*anitya). **2.** The Japanese pronunciation of the Chinese wu-cheng, which means 'no dispute' or 'no striving'. This word cheng is a synonym for fan-nao, meaning vexations or defilements, and thus the term mujō can indicate attainment of the end of all defilements. Because of this, the term can also be used as a synonym for an *Arhat.

Mukan Fumon (1212–91). A Japanese *Rinzai *Zen *monk and the first abbot of the Nanzen Monastery. This monastery had been established when the Emperor Kameyama converted an imperial palace on the outskirts of *Kyoto into a Zen hall. However, when he tried to meditate there, he was frightened away by ghosts. After many attempts to exorcise the spirits failed, the emperor called upon Mukan, a disciple of *Enni Ben'en (1202–80), to resolve the problem. Mukan arrived with several disciples, and after one night of group Zen *meditation, the spirits appeared to be gone, and the precincts were quiet thereafter. The emperor gratefully appointed him the founding abbot of the monastery, but Mukan died within the year.

Mūla-madhyamaka-kārikā. 'The Root Verses on the Madhyamaka System', being the title of the most important work by *Nāgārjuna which laid the foundations for the *Madhyamaka school of *Mahāyāna *Buddhism. It comprises 448 verses arranged in 27 chapters. Its overall aim is to highlight the inconsistencies that arise through reifying Buddhist and non-Buddhist philosophical concepts and theories, including causation (*pratītya-samutpāda), existence, impermanence (*anitya), bondage, and liberation. Nāgarjuna's intention is to establish the absence of any substantial or autonomous reality (*svabhāva) underlying these concepts and to replace such wrong views with a true understanding of emptiness (*śūnyatā) which is a corollary of Dependent Origination (*pratītya-samutpāda). Many major commentaries were written on this work by later Indian scholar-monks such as *Buddhapālita, *Bhāvaviveka, *Candrakīrti, and *Sthiramati.

Mūla-sarvāstivāda. As explained by later commentators, an appellation adopted by the Buddhist *Sarvāstivāda school some time in the 7th century to distinguish it from three subschools that had detached themselves from it by that time. The term mūla (Skt., root) indicates that the Sarvāstivāda was the parent school from which the others were descended, although it is thought by some to have been an alternative name for the *Sautrāntikas, a group within the Sarvāstivāda which did not accept the centrality accorded to the *Mahāvibhāṣā and its privileging of *Abhidharma. Some scholars believe that the term Mūla-sarvāstivāda is simply an alternative designation for the Sarvāstivāda school, although their *Āgamas are different. Others suggest that 19 Gandhāri Sārvastivādins called themselves Mūla-Sarvāstivāda or Sautrāntika in contrast to the Kashmiri Sārvāstivādins who were Vaibhāṣikas. The *Vinaya of this school, which substantially survives in *Sanskrit, was later adopted as the standard monastic code in *Tibet.

mūla-vijñāna (Skt., root consciousness). The basis or root consciousness, a concept associated with the *Mahāsaṃghikas. This form of consciousness was said to act as the support for the sensory consciousnesses and may be seen as a forerunner of the *Yogācāra concept of the 'storehouse consciousness' (*ālaya-vijñāna).

Müller, Friedrich Max (1823–1900). German historian of religion and pioneering scholar of the comparative study of religion. After completing a doctorate in Leipzig in 1843 he studied *Sanskrit and philosophy in Berlin before moving to Paris and finally Oxford. He edited the series Sacred Books of the East and began the series *Sacred Books of the Buddhists in 1895. He made a translation of the *Dhammapada* from *Pāli, but regarded *Buddhism as negative and pessimistic. He was a strong supporter of the 'solar myth' school, according to which gods and heroes were understood as personifications of natural phenomena. This and others of his theories, such that *India was the original home of humanity, have since been discredited. His legacy as a promoter of the study of Indian religion, however, has been great.

Mumonkan. *See* GATELESS GATE.

Muṇḍa. 1. A king of *Magadha, the grandson of *Ajātaśatru, who followed family tradition and murdered his father to seize the throne, only to be killed by his own son later. **2.** A large group of tribal people in *India belonging to the Austro-asiatic ethnic group and, as such, their languages and culture owed little to the dominant Brahmanical culture of India. Although they may have been more widely spread throughout India in very early times, they are now concentrated in the hill tracts of Orissa, southern Bihar, and west Bengal. There seems to have been some input from these people in the development of *tantric *Buddhism but this connection has not yet been fully explored by scholars.

mundane. *See* LAUKIKA.

muni (Skt.; Pāli, a sage). General term in Indian religion for a holy man or sage. The term occurs mainly in the older verse portions of the *Pāli Canon (such as the *Sutta Nipāta*) as an epithet of *Buddhas and *Pratyekabuddhas, but rarely of *Arhats. The *Buddha is referred to as *Śākyamuni (Pāli, Sākyamuni), or the 'sage of the Śākyas'. In the *Mahāyāna, with its expanded pantheon of Buddhas, the name Śākyamuni becomes the principal designation for the historical Buddha *Siddhartha Gautama (Pāli, Siddhatha Gotama).

Musō Soseki (1275–1351). An influential Japanese *Rinzai *Zen *monk of the *Kamakura period. He came from a minor aristocratic family in Ise, and entered the monastic order at a young age, at first joining the esoteric *Shingon school but later transferring his allegiance to Rinzai Zen after the painful, lingering death of his Shingon master left him shaken, and after two famous Chinese *Ch'an masters appeared to him in a dream during a period of solitary practice. From that point, even as he looked for a teacher to guide him, Musō practised Zen in several places, and eventually reached enlightenment (*satori) on his own in 1305, although the experience was confirmed and authenticated by Kōhō Kennichi (1241–1316), which technically made him the latter's disciple. After that, he found himself called by a succession of seven emperors to engage in a project or to take charge of a large temple, despite his own wish to retire from the world and live quietly in the country. For the first twenty years after his enlightenment, he lived in a succession of small hermitages, most of which he himself founded, but after a time was forced to move on because so many clergy and laity were attracted to his teachings that the hermitages grew into temples through his own charisma. Finally, in 1325, the Emperor Go-Daigo called him to take over one of the major temples of *Kyoto, the Nanzen-ji. Leaving this post after only one year, he spent time in Ise where he built the Zennō-ji, and then in Kamakura in the Jōchi-ji. In 1329 he was called to the *Engakuji, a once-prominent temple that had fallen to corruption and decay. After a year reforming this temple, he moved on again. The remainder of his life conformed to this pattern: official appointment to a large temple followed by retreat to smaller temples away from the centres of power. Some authorities credit him with a keen eye for the political instabilities of the time and his ability to know when to draw near to the court or the shōgun and when to withdraw.

Musō's style mixed academic learning (carried forward from his early years in the Shingon school) and the *kōan method of the Rinzai school. While officially, Zen has represented itself as a 'special teaching outside of the scriptures' that 'does not rely on words and letters', Musō saw no contradiction: he once said when questioned on this, 'to explain the *sūtras is to speak of Zen'. For him, the point of all practice and learning was to direct the student to a realization of reality as it is; if kōan practice can accomplish this, then one makes use of the kōan; if doctrinal study proves effective, then one instructs the student in doctrine. Biased clinging to one method and rejection of the other only betray the master's own lack of enlightenment and insight. Musō's involvement in so many different temples, particularly those that had fallen into corruption and needed reform, led him to compose books of monastic rules (particularly the shingi or '*Pure Rules' variety, which sets forth the 'house rules' for a Zen temple) as well as admonitions for strict practice. He was also well known for his artistic accomplishments. He is credited with the establishment of a 'Musō line' of Rinzai Zen, which has sustained itself to the present day.

Myōchō. *See* SHŪHŌ MYŌCHŌ.

Myōe Kōben (1173–1232). A member of the *Kegon school, one of the *Six Schools of *Nara *Buddhism in *Japan. During the time when new schools were arising in Japan (such as *Pure Land, *Zen, and *Nichiren), he tried to defend the older schools and spoke out against the new ones. His works include a piece entitled *Smashing the Wheel of Heresy*, which was directed against *Hōnen (1133–1212) and his new Pure Land school (Jap., Jōdo Shū). Renowned for his purity and obedience to the monastic *precepts, he attracted many disciples and patrons, and also contributed to a revival in Kegon studies.

myōkōnin. In the *Jōdo Shinshū school of Japanese *Pure Land *Buddhism, this term refers to a Pure Land practitioner who is particularly devoted to the practice of *nembutsu out of a sense of gratitude for *Amitābha's compassion (*karuṇā). A Jōdo Shinshū text, the *Myōkōninten*, contains many biographies of such figures.

N

nāḍī (Skt.). In *tantric mystical physiology, the channels or pathways of psychic energy (*vāyu) visualized as part of *completion-stage *meditation in *anuttara-yoga-tantra. Three main channels are mentioned—the *avadhūti, *rasanā, and *lalanā—although there are many subsidiary channels that branch out and bifurcate from the *cakras located along the avadhūti so that all parts of the body are pervaded by psychic energy. A similar system of nāḍīs is envisaged in Tibetan medicine but this structure differs in many aspects from that used in tantric meditation.

nāga (Skt.). A class of serpent-like beings in Hindu and Buddhist mythology. They are said to live in the underworld and inhabit a watery environment. Frequently considered to be benevolent, they also believed to act as guardians of hidden *Mahāyāna texts. The philosopher *Nāgārjuna is said to have been given many scriptures by them, such as the *Prajñā-pāramitā Sūtras.

Nāgadīpa. Ancient name for the Jaffna Peninsula in *Sri Lanka. Formerly an important centre of *Buddhism with many *pilgrimage sites, it was reputed to be the site of the *Buddha's second visit to the island, according to the legends of the **Mahāvaṃsa*.

Nāgārjuna. A major figure in the rise of philosophical *Māhāyana, deemed to be the founder of the *Madhyamaka school. Little is known of his life although it is generally accepted that he lived during the late 2nd century CE and was active primarily in south *India. The accounts of his life agree that he was born as a *Brahmin in south India and entered the Buddhist Order (*Saṃgha) as a young man. It is reported that he was presented with the texts of the **Prajñā-pāramitā Sūtras* by the king of the *Nāgas, a mythical race of serpents with magic powers. Nāgārjuna is reputed to have been friendly with a Śātavāhana ruler who built a monastery (*vihāra) for him in Śrīparvata. This was probably King Gautamīputra, for whom Nāgārjuna composed his 'Friendly Epistle' (**Suhṛllekha*). The details of his death are obscure: he is reported to have either ended his own life or allowed himself to meet death at the hands of another. He is regarded by many Buddhists of the Mahāyāna tradition as a 'Second *Buddha,' and his philosophy of emptiness (*śūnyatā) was of enduring significance for later Buddhist thought. Although over a hundred works are attributed to him, many of these are pseudo-epigraphical, but included among his authentic works are the **Mūla-madhyamaka-kārikā*, the **Śūnyatā-saptati*, the **Vigraha-vyāvartanī*, the **Yukti-ṣaṣṭikā*, the **Catuḥstava*, the **Ratnāvalī*, and the *Suhṛllekha*.

Nāgārjunakoṇḍa. The ancient site of a major Buddhist centre near *Amarāvatī, associated with *Nāgārjuna. The site was most noted for its great *stūpa which was constructed prior to the 3rd century CE by the south Indian Śātavāhana kings. By medieval times, the site was abandoned and fell into obscurity until its discovery and partial excavation in 1927. The site was fully excavated in the 1950s prior to the flooding by the Nāgārjunasagar Dam of the entire valley in which it is situated. Much of the site was preserved by relocation of the remains while the Nāgārjunakoṇḍa stūpa survives on an island in the middle of the reservoir.

Nāgasena. An *Arhat, famous for his *debate with king Milinda. *See* MILINDAPAÑHA.

Nairañjanā (Skt.; Pāli, Nerañjarā). A small tributary of the Ganges alongside which the *Buddha became enlightened at the site now known as *Bodhgayā.

Nakagawa Soen (1907–84). *Rinzai *Zen *monk in *Japan who was active in the period leading up to and following the Second World War in transmitting Zen to the United States (*see* AMERICA). He travelled to the USA several times and, while still in Japan, kept up a close correspondence with Nyogen Senzaki during the latter's missionary sojourn on the west coast of America. He was also noted as an artist, poet, and calligrapher.

Nālagiri. A fierce elephant of king *Ajātaśatru that was sent by *Devadatta to attack the *Buddha on his almsround through the streets of *Rājagṛha. A woman fleeing in terror dropped her child at the feet of the Buddha, and as the elephant was about to trample it the Buddha spoke to Nālagiri, suffused the beast with loving kindness, and stroked its forehead. At this the elephant sank to its knees, subdued.

Nālandā. One of the greatest Buddhist monastic universities in *India, located between *Pāṭaliputra and *Rājagṛha in present-day Bihar. It is believed to have been founded by King Śakrāditya of *Magadha in the 2nd century CE and went on to receive continued royal support from the *Gupta and *Pāla dynasties. Its enormous size and the quality of its resident teachers attracted students and other visitors from all over the Buddhist world, including the notable Chinese pilgrim monks *Hsüan-tsang and *I-ching in the 7th century CE who both describe it in their travelogues. Ties were also formed with the nascent Buddhist movement in *Tibet, resulting in a number of leading Tibetan monks visiting Nālandā and reciprocal visits to Tibet by Indian Buddhist masters. Nālandā was destroyed in one of the greatest acts of cultural vandalism by Muslim invaders in the 12th century CE—the great library is said to have smouldered for six months afterwards. The site was fully excavated in the 20th century and now attracts many visitors.

nāma-rūpa (Skt.; Pāli, name and form). Mind and body, or the totality of physical and mental processes that constitute an individual. It occurs as the fourth link in the chain of Dependent Origination (*pratītya-samutpāda), where it is preceded by consciousness (*vijñāna) and followed by the six sense fields (*ṣad-āyatana). In this context nāma-rūpa stands for conception, the moment at which the mind and body of the new individual come into being. In the doctrine of the five aggregates (*skandha), the first four aggregates are allocated to the category of 'body' (rūpa), and the fifth (consciousness or vijñāna) to 'mind' (nāma). In *Buddhism, the relation between mind and body is not a dualistic one, rather the two function together in mutual dependency as different aspects of the same whole. Thus they are compared to two sheaves of reeds that lean on one another for support, or to a strong blind man who carries a keen-sighted cripple on his shoulders.

Namo myōhō renge kyō (Jap.) A phrase meaning 'Hail to the Scripture of the Lotus of the Wonderful Dharma!' Chanting this phrase as an expression of devotion to the **Lotus Sūtra* is the primary religious practice of the *Nichiren school of Japanese *Buddhism. *See also* DAIMOKU; JAPAN.

nam-thar (Tib., rnam-thar). A Tibetan hagiography or biography of a saint. Literally meaning 'liberation', the stories recount the manner in which the subject achieved enlightenment (*bodhi).

Namu Amida Butsu. The Japanese pronunciation of the 'six-character form' of the *nembutsu, or oral invocation of the *Buddha *Amitābha. The phrase means 'Hail to Amitābha Buddha', and is chanted or recited by Japanese *Pure Land Buddhists in order to gain *rebirth into the Pure Land after death. *See also* NIEN-FO.

Namuci (Pāli, the non-releaser). A name for the devil *Māra, so called because as the personification of *death he allows none to escape from his clutches.

Nan-ch'uan P'u-yüan (748–834). A Chinese *Ch'an *monk of the *T'ang dynasty who studied with *Ma-tsu Tao-i (709–88), and was the master of another well-known figure, *Chao-chou Ts'ung-shen (778–897). He was in most respects a very conventional *monk: he had mastered the regulations of the monastic *Vinaya with teachers of the *Lü-tsung after *ordination, studied various *sūtras and the literature of the *San-lun school, and had an awakening (*satori) while staying with Ma-tsu. However, he is best known for one strange incident memorialized in the *Transmission of the Lamp of the Ching-te [reign-period]* and as case number 14 in the collection of *kōans known as the **Gateless Gate*. It is recorded that one day he heard the monks of the eastern and western halls arguing over a cat, whereupon he took up the cat and a knife and challenged the monks to say a single true word about it. If they could not, he would cut the cat in two.

The monks were speechless, and Nan-ch'uan killed the cat. Later, he related the incident to his student Chao-chou, who said nothing, but put his sandals on his head and left the room, which caused Nan-ch'uan to say, 'If you had only been there, you could have saved the cat!'

Nanda. Half-brother of the *Buddha, being the son of *Śuddhodana and *Mahāprajāpatī. Renowned for his good looks, Nanda was married to the beautiful Janapadakalyāṇī, and on the day of the wedding the Buddha asked him to become a *monk. Nanda reluctantly agreed but was later tormented by longing for his wife and became depressed and unwell. The Buddha then took him to the *heaven of the 33 gods where they were attended by heavenly nymphs from the retinue of *Śakra, king of the gods. The Buddha promised him one of the nymphs if he devoted himself to the monastic life, and Nanda agreed. Exerting himself he soon became an *Arhat and abandoned all thoughts of lust and *desire.

Nanjio. A Japanese *Zen *monk who became friendly with the Jesuit missionary Francis Xavier after the latter's arrival in *Japan in 1549 and who provided him with assistance and information on Zen thought and practice. The dates of his life are unknown.

Nanjio Bunyū (1849–1927). One of the first Asian Buddhists to travel to the West to pursue Buddhist studies. He arrived in England in 1876 according to the instructions of his Higashi-honganji superiors (*see* Honganji), and studied languages at Oxford with Friedrich Max *Müller. After several years of *Sanskrit study, Nanjio returned to *Japan and became one of the pioneers of modern Buddhist studies there.

Nan-yang Hui-chung (675–775). An early *T'ang dynasty Chinese *Ch'an *monk, and a direct disciple of the sixth *patriarch of the Ch'an school, *Hui-neng (638–713). After attaining enlightenment (*bodhi) under his master, Nan-yang spent 40 years in solitary practice, but was finally called out by an invitation from the emperor to minister and teach at the court. Case number 18 of the *kōan collection called the **Blue Cliff Records* recounts his final conversation with the Emperor Su-tsung in which the latter asks him what he can do to commemorate the master's 100th year. To this Nan-yang gives the enigmatic answer that he should build him a 'seamless *pagoda'. After his death, the emperor named him a *National Teacher (Chin., kuo shih).

Nan-yueh Huai-jang (677–744). A Chinese *Ch'an master and direct disciple of the Sixth *Patriarch *Hui-neng (638–713), and founder of one of the main lines of Ch'an during the *T'ang dynasty. He came from a family in Shaan-hsi surnamed Tu, and is sometimes referred to as Ch'an master Ta-hui. He functions in Ch'an literature chiefly as a transitional figure linking his famous disciple *Ma-tsu Tao-i (709–88) back to the Sixth Patriarch.

nāraka. *See* HELL.

Nara period (710–94). One of the earlier periods of Japanese *Buddhism, which derives its name from the fact that the capital of the empire was located in the city of Nara at that time. Nara Buddhism is characterized by the scholastic and disciplinary endeavours of the *Six Schools of *Nara Buddhism. These concentrated on studying and coming to terms with the volumes of Buddhist literature that found their way across the sea from *China at this time. The Buddhism of this period was characterized by an almost complete devotion of its energy to the needs of the aristocracy, as well as to courtly religious practices aimed at the protection and welfare of the nation.

Nāro chos drug. *See* *SIX YOGAS OF *NĀROPA.

Nāropa (1016–1100). Born in *Kashmir, Nāropa was one of the chief Indian *mahāsiddhas or 'great adepts'. A disciple of *Tilopa, Nāropa was famed during his early years as an outstanding scholar of non-*tantric *Mahāyāna *Buddhism when he held the office of abbot at *Nālandā. After he had achieved realization and established himself as a tantric teacher, he transmitted to *Marpa the lineages of *mahāmudrā and the **Cakra-saṃvara Tantra* that became the central teaching of the Tibetan *Kagyü school. He also passed on to his student the set of practices he systematized, known as the *Six Yogas of *Nāropa.

Naropa University. A Buddhist university in Boulder, Colorado, USA founded by Chogyam *Trungpa in 1974. The institution takes its name from *Nāropa, the 11th-century abbot of the ancient university of *Nālandā in *India. Nāropa was renowned for bringing together scholarly wisdom with meditative insight, and this has become the ongoing inspiration for the development of Naropa University. The mission of Naropa University is to: (1) offer educational programmes that cultivate awareness of the present moment through intellectual, artistic, and meditative disciplines; (2) foster a learning community (composed of students, faculty, staff, trustees, and alumni) that uncovers wisdom and heart; (3) cultivate openness and communication, sharpen critical intellect, enhance resourcefulness, and develop effective action in all disciplines; (4) exemplify the principles grounded in Naropa University's Buddhist educational heritage; (5) encourage the integration of world wisdom traditions with modern culture; (6) be non-sectarian and open to all.

nāstika (Skt, nihilist). **1.** According to *Hinduism, one who is heterodox in belief and does not accept the ultimate authority of the *Vedas. **2.** In *Buddhism, one who denies any real existence to phenomena or denies the the doctrine of *karma.

national protection Buddhism. Name given to the belief, widely held in east Asia, that the primary purpose of religious practice and the rituals performed by religious specialists is to enlist the assistance of spiritual powers in order to protect the interests of the nation. For example, the esoteric traditions of Chinese and Japanese *Buddhism (*see* ESOTERIC BUDDHISM) received lavish state support for their often extravagant and expensive rituals because the national government believed that such rituals would bring rain to end droughts, avert plagues, and help to fend off invasions. *See also* CHINA; JAPAN.

National Teacher (Chin., kuo-shih; Jap., kokushi). An honorific title bestowed by the emperor on eminent Buddhist clergy throughout the history of east Asian *Buddhism. The honour was usually accomanied by a certificate and a purple robe.

nats. In *Burma, a class of spirits with supernatural powers who are venerated and invoked for mundane (*laukika) benefits. They occupy a realm just below the *heavens of the gods (*deva). In former times images of 37 famous nats adorned the terrace of the *Shwedagon Pagoda, but are now located in a nearby shrine. Some of the most powerful nats who are regarded as guardian deities (mahāgiri nats) have their home on Mt. Popa, some 30 miles from Pagān.

Nechung Chöje (Tib., gnas chung chos rje). A deity who guides the government and political leaders of *Tibet by providing advice through the medium of an oracle. He is consulted on important matters of state and gives his replies through taking possession of a human oracle who communicates in high-pitched tones. The answers are noted down carefully and deciphered by attendants. The present *Dalai Lama (*Dalai Lama XIV) regularly consults the Nechung oracle before taking decisions on sensitive religious and diplomatic issues.

nembutsu. The term 'nembutsu' (Chin., nien-fo) refers to several practices oriented toward *Amitābha, the *Buddha of the western *Pure Land. The ambiguity of the first of the two Chinese characters ('nem') has served to provide for several modes of practice. First, the term means 'to contemplate', and originally meant to meditate on the image (either an actual image or a visualized one) of the Buddha, contemplating all of his excellent qualities. For example, the *T'ien-t'ai school's 'constantly walking *samādhi' involved circumambulating (*see* PRADAKṢINA) an image of Amitābha for 90 days, keeping an eidetic image of the Buddha in the mind at all times until he actually appeared. Later Chinese Pure Land masters, such as Chi-hsing Ch'o-wu (1741–1810) dispensed with the image and taught disciples to contemplate the name of the Buddha as itself containing all the Buddha's qualities. Second, the term also means 'to recite aloud', and this reading gave rise to the practice of calling the Buddha's name, either orally or mentally. This is the sense in which the practice is understood by the Pure Land traditions of *China (with some exceptions), *Japan, and *Korea.

Within the meaning of nembutsu as mental or oral invocation, there are two more subdivisions related to the purpose of one's practice. In the first, one recites the name of the Buddha to purify and concentrate one's mind, and to create links to the Buddha and his Pure Land in order to ensure *rebirth there after one dies. When this is the purpose, one practises constantly and vigorously. This is the dominant conception of nembutsu practice in Chinese Pure Land *Buddhism. This practice was based on the notion of 'self-power' (Chin., tzu-li; Jap., *jiriki), in which the practitioner works to achieve certain results, although no results are expected without the Buddha also contributing his own virtue and power to the process. The second way of looking at oral and mental invocation is in terms of 'other-power' (Chin., t'a-li; Jap., *tariki). This idea is based on a set of vows undertaken by the Buddha Amitābha prior to his attaining Buddhahood. A passage from the *Longer Sukhāvatī-vyūha Sūtra* reads: 'If, when I attain Buddhahood, sentient beings in the lands of the ten directions who desire to be born in my land, and call my name even ten times should not be born there, may I not attain perfect enlightenment.' Since he did indeed become a Buddha, then this vow must have been fulfilled, which means that practitioners, having little confidence in their own abilities, can call on the Buddha's name and attain rebirth in the Pure Land. While the Chinese tradition acknowledges this understanding of nembutsu as necessary for some, it still maintains that the practitioner should work towards rebirth in the Pure Land to the best of their abilities. The Japanese tradition, by contrast, emphasizes the believer's powerlessness to effect his or her own liberation, and sees practice entirely in terms of invoking Amitābha's name in dependence upon 'other-power'. This constitutes the chief difference between the Chinese and Japanese traditions. *See also* NIEN-FO; NAMU AMIDA BUTSU.

nenju (Chin., nien-chü). A Japanese term denoting a rosary, or string of beads, used for counting the number of times one has recited the name of *Amitābha *Buddha.

Nepal. The ancient history of Nepal has still not been fully researched but it seems that the Katmandu Valley was in early contact with *Buddhism through its proximity to *India. The Licchavi dynasty was founded around 300 CE and ruled until the 9th century. Buddhism was likely to have been systematically introduced into Nepal during the reign of King *Aśoka and has continued to flourish there to the present day alongside *Hinduism. The location of Nepal between the Buddhist heartland of India and *Tibet meant that it was frequently visited by travelling Tibetan and Indian monks, with the Nepalese at times acting as interpreters. Present-day Nepal has a strong Tibetan Buddhist presence alongside the traditional supporters of Buddhism among the native population. As it was never subjected to the devastating destruction wrought on Buddhist establishments by early Muslim invaders in India, large quantities of Buddhist manuscripts have survived there which have received careful attention from scholars.

New Kadampa Tradition. A contemporary Tibetan Buddhist organization founded by Geshe Kelsang Gyatso which has its headquarters in *Britain. As the name implies, the group sees itself as the heir to the early *Kadampa tradition and as faithful to its tenets. By contrast, it alleges that the present *Gelukpa school under the leadership of *Dalai Lama XIV has departed from the teachings of the founders of the movement. In recent years there has been intense sectarian rivalry between the two groups centring on the propitiation of the protector-deity *Dorje Shukden.

New School (Tib., gsar-ma). The schools of Tibetan *Buddhism that rely on the translation and teaching transmission of *tantric texts during the period of the '*Second Propagation', inaugurated by *Rinchen Sangpo, as opposed to those transmitted during the '*First Propagation' (Tib., snga dar) of Buddhism in *Tibet. Those designated as the New Schools are the *Gelukpa, *Sakyapa, and *Kagyüpa.

ngak-pa (Tib., sngags-pa; Skt., mantrin). A full-time practitioner of the *mantra path, similar in many respects to a *yogin.

Nhat Hanh, Thich (1926–). A Vietnamese *Zen monk and founding father of the *Engaged Buddhism movement. Nhat Hanh became active in the peace movement in his country in the wake of the *Vietnam War and in 1964 founded a volunteer organization known as the School of Youth for Social Service to help rebuild the rural infrastructure. However, his anti-war activism made him unpopular with the authorities and he was forced into exile and now resides in France. He has taught widely in *America and *Europe and is the author of many books on Engaged Buddhist themes.

nibbāna. *Pāli for *nirvāṇa.

nibbuta (Pāli, extinguished). The state of one who has attained *nirvāṇa. Such a person is said to have cooled or quenched the 'three fires' of greed, hatred, and delusion (*see* AKUŚALA-MŪLA).

Nichiren (1222–82). Founder of the *Nichiren-shū school during the *Kamakura period in *Japan. Born in 1222 in the seaside town of Kominato in Awa province to a family of fishermen, he is the only founder of one of the new sects of Kamakura *Buddhism not to come from the central provinces around the capital and not to be from an aristocratic family, a factor that some scholars believe accounts for his hard-hitting and uncompromising style of religion. At the age of 12, he entered religious life at the Kiyosumi-dera, a *Tendai temple near his family home, and studied Tendai *nembutsu practice there with his master. Fully ordained at 16, he went to the capital in 1239 to study at the eminent temples in Kamakura and *Kyoto, where he no doubt encountered discrimination and derision due to his rustic speech and manner. Perplexed by the complexity and lack of consistency in the doctrines of various schools, he determined during this period of study that the Tendai school needed to return to its teachings, given by Chinese *T'ien-t'ai founder *Chih-i (538–97) and Japanese Tendai founder *Saichō (767–822), promulgating the **Lotus Sūtra* as the *Buddha's definitive teaching, and relegating all other teachings to a provisional status. However, unlike his predecessors and others in the history of east Asian Buddhism who assigned some value to these provisional teachings as expedient devices designed to reach those not prepared to accept a full revelation of the truth, Nichiren decided that these other teachings were of no account whatsoever and were to be abandoned as heretical. Returning to his home district in 1253, he took the new religious name Nichiren (Lotus of the Sun) and began promoting his views and attacking the teachings of the other schools openly. He went so far as to blame a series of calamities such as earthquakes, epidemics, and typhoons in the eastern provinced between 1257 and 1260 on the popularity of other sects, notably *Zen and *Pure Land, and promised the shōgunate that such disasters could be averted by returning to the true faith of the *Lotus Sūtra*. He set forth his recommendations to the government in a tract composed in 1260 and presented to the regent, Hōjō Tokiyori, entitled *Risshō ankoku ron* (Treatise on Establishing the Right for the Protection of the Nation). He experienced exile and persecution for his efforts, but accepted it as fulfilment of a passage in the *Lotus Sūtra* itself that said proponents of the true teaching would be persecuted in the Age of the Final *Dharma (Jap., *mappō).

In terms of religious practice, Nichiren wanted people to place their faith in the power of the *Lotus Sūtra*, expressing this faith by reciting the *daimoku, or 'great title': *Namo myōhō renge kyō, 'I take refuge in the Sūtra of the Lotus of the Wonderful Dharma'. For those lacking in time or ability to read the scripture, this simple declaration of faith in the *sūtra's efficacy and truth gained salvation, and this simple means to liberation itself was provided by the *Buddha *Śākyamuni himself as a means for those living in the time of mappō. His unrelenting practice of shakubuku, or direct confrontation with heretical teachings, continued to earn him persecution and attack. In 1268, an envoy arrived in Japan with a message from the Mongol leader Kublai Khan (*see* MONGOLIA) demanding tribute and vowing to attack Japan if it were not forthcoming, and Nichiren heightened his call for national conversion to faith in the *Lotus Sūtra*. However, the attack did not materialize immediately, and Nichiren was sent into exile on Sado Island in 1271, where he remained for three years. These were productive years, and mark a turning point in Nichiren's thought in several ways. First, he wrote several more treatises there, in which he made a break with the Tendai school and began styling himself simply as 'a priest of Japan'. Second, he created the Daimandara, or 'great *maṇḍala' there, in which he created a map of the cosmos with the words of the daimoku springing out of the earth and connecting it with the *heavens, surrounded by the Buddhas Śākyamuni and Prabhūtaratna (both prominent in the sūtra) and four *Bodhisattvas. Third, he began to identify himself as an incarnation of the Bodhisattva Jōgyō, or 'Eminent Conduct', who appears in the *Lotus Sūtra* as the protector of the scripture. Significantly, this Bodhisattva leads all the others in Nichiren's maṇḍala. Fourth, he began turning his energy from the conversion of the nation as a whole to be effected by direct appeal to the government to conversion of individuals one at a time.

After his release from exile in 1274, Nichiren returned briefly to Kamakura. Many in government felt that the threatened Mongol invasion was then imminent, and requested him to perform rituals for the protection of the nation. However, they balked at his demand that only he be engaged to perform these rituals and that all other schools of Buddhism be barred, and the success of another group's rituals in producing rain damaged his case to exclusive efficacy. Discouraged, he finally retired from the world and repaired to Mt. Minobu in Kai province, a high and almost inaccessible peak, where he built a small hermitage in which he and his followers would await the coming of the Mongols. They fully expected the utter destruction of Japan for its failure to place its faith exclusively in the *Lotus Sūtra*. The invasion did indeed arrive late in 1274, but both this first wave and the much larger second wave that arrived in 1281 were destroyed in Hakata Bay by typhoons, and ritual specialists of the *Shingon school claimed credit for having produced these storms through their rites. Nichiren spent his last years on Mt. Minobu, tending to the flock of residents whose swelling numbers gradually transformed his residence from a crude hermitage to a temple, and in the composition of further works detailing his theology, notably the *Hokke-shuyō-shō* (Treatise Selecting the Essentials of the Lotus School). The disappointments of life and hardships of the mountain proved severe, and he died in 1282 at the age of 60.

Some scholars have pointed out that both the simplicity of the practice that Nichiren advocated and the vehemence with which he set his views forth stemmed from his humble beginnings and the discrimination he experienced as a young rustic *monk thrust into the company of aristocratic scions. However, Nichiren was also a subtle thinker and the originality of his reshaping of Tendai theology deserves attention. From the beginning of the school in Sui-dynasty *China, the T'ien-t'ai and Tendai schools have always asserted that the *Lotus Sūtra* is the highest Buddhist scripture and the one in which the Buddha states his teachings most directly, and that the essence of the scripture is contained in its title. Furthermore, the Tendai school had always understood enlightenment (*bodhi) to be both a goal and an immanent part of human nature. It was precisely because of innate original enlightenment (Jap., *hongaku) that one had any real hope of working toward the attainment of *acquired enlightenment (Jap., shikaku). Nichiren, unlike other thinkers in Buddhist history who were willing to grant a place to expedient or indirect teachings as a means of reaching beings unable to assimilate a full and direct exposition of the truth, sought to eliminate all expedient or gradual approaches altogether, and make available to common followers a direct access to the absolute. The *Lotus Sūtra*, as the scripture that directly revealed the totality of Buddhist truth, provided a door, and since its essence was contained within its title, the chanting of this title could, by itself, unlock the enlightenment that was always already part of the makeup of the human being. With this practice in place, all other expedient means and theoretical speculations could be nothing more than distractions from the path, and so Nichiren sheared away everything in his Tendai heritage that represented idle philosophizing and compromise with other paths in order to provide his followers and the nation with the most direct means of liberation.

Nichiren Shōshū. An offshoot of *Nichiren *Buddhism that split from the Honmonshū in 1900, taking the name Nichiren-shū Fuji-ha. In 1913, the group changed its name to Nichiren Shōshū and developed rapidly, even though most accounts of the Nichiren school omit it and some count it as one of *Japan's New Religions. It is the parent organization of the *Sōka Gakkai (Value-Creation

Society), which began as a lay auxiliary, but became independent in 1992.

Nichiren-shū. A general designation for the Nichiren school, that is, all of the schools and sects that derive from the original teachings and vision of *Nichiren (1222–82), even though it never existed as a unified school. All groups agreed with the main outlines of Nichiren's teachings. (1) The **Lotus Sūtra* stands at the summit of all Buddhist scriptures. It represents the culmination of all of the *Buddha *Śākyamuni's preaching and sets forth his complete vision in a straightforward fashion without resort to skillful means (*upāya-kauśalya). One achieves liberation in this age of the Decline of the *Dharma (Jap., *mappō) by simply chanting its title (Jap., *daimoku). (2) The teachings of the *Lotus Sūtra* have five principal aspects leading to its implementation: (*a*) Teaching: the contents of the *sūtra itself; (*b*) Object: that the proper object to whom the teachings are directed is to be those who damage the true teachings; (*c*) Time: that the age of mappō is the appropriate time for beings to be saved by the sūtra; (*d*) Master: that Nichiren himself had been the most appropriate master to expound this teaching, as evidenced by the persecutions he had received as a result of his preaching; and (*e*) Country: that *Japan was the right country where all the above four elements existed. (3) All other forms of *Buddhism and all other religious practices whatsoever were distractions and impediments in the Way, to be discarded in favour of the chanting of the daimoku.

In spite of the agreement on the above three points, some controversy and *schism occurred as certain groups adapted to current religious conditions more than others. Thus Nichiren's disciples experienced discord within the first generation after his passing. Nichiren had left no provisions for any kind of centralized control over the teachings and activities of his disciples, and so no unified school came into being. Each of his major disciples staked out their own territories and doctrines, and set up their own institutions. There were three major areas of disagreement. (1) The issue of *fuju-fuse: this term, meaning 'no receiving and no giving', indicated a complete break with all other schools of Buddhism. Those who espoused this view held that only exclusive faith in the saving power of the *Lotus Sūtra* could bring peace and security, and put this view into practical action by eschewing all contact with other groups. Other leaders, while accepting the superiority of Nichiren's teachings, felt that some degree of cooperation and contact with other Buddhist schools did not endanger or vitiate the true teachings, and so they were more willing to make overtures to other institutions and engage in cooperative ventures and ceremonies. Proponents of the fuju-fuse position at first suffered punishment and exile for their unwillingness to work with others, and persecution induced them to band together as a school based on this principle. Finally, in 1876 the government granted permission for the establishment of the Fuju-fuse-ha. A second group, the Fuju-fuse Kōmon-ha, gained government recognition in 1882. (2) Shakubuku: this term means 'to bend and shake', and is used to describe an extremely confrontational style of proselytization. Some Nichiren groups adopted it and would harangue people on the streets and disrupt other religious gatherings, while other groups preferred other, less abusive forms of evangelization. (3) The status of the two major divisions of the *Lotus Sūtra*. The scripture is commonly divided into two sections, the 'manifestation gate' (Jap., shakumon) and the 'origin gate' (Jap., honmon). The first demonstrates that Buddhas and *Bodhisattvas deploy expedient teachings as manifestations of the truth in order to assist beings to enlightenment (*bodhi), while the second reveals the truth manifested in a more direct manner. Some Nichiren groups held that the sūtra was equally holy in all its parts, while others held that the 'origin gate', since it states the truth directly, is superior to the 'manifestation gate'.

During the *Meiji era (1868–1912), the various streams of Nichiren teaching coalesced into definite schools. Aside from the two Fuju-fuse schools listed above, the others are as follows. The *Nichiren-shū, which advocated the equality of both sections of the *Lotus Sūtra*, formed in 1874. In the same year, five other branches gained recognition, all maintaining the superiority of the honmon section: Myōmanji, Happon, Honjōji, Honryūji, and Fuji-ha. These five all changed their names in 1891 to, respectively: Kempon

Hokkeshū, Honmon Hokkeshū, Hokkeshū, Honmyō Hokkeshū, and Honmonshū. In 1900 the Daisekiji in Shizuoka broke from the Honmonshū to form the Nichiren-shū fuji-ha, changing its name in 1913 to the *Nichiren Shōshū. It gained a wide following, and spawned a lay auxiliary group called the *Sōka Gakkai (Value Creation Society) founded in 1937 by *Makiguchi Tsunesaburō (1871–1944). This group broke from the Nichiren Shōshū and became independent in 1992.

nidāna (Skt.; Pali, link). A contributory cause or condition. It is the term used for each of the twelve links that constitute the chain of Dependent Origination (*pratītya-samutpāda).

Nidānakathā (Pāli, introductory tale). The Introduction to the *Jātaka commentary. It narrates the biography of the *Buddha in three sections: the first concerns his previous lives from the time he was the *Bodhisattva *Sumeda until his *birth in the *Tuṣita *heaven; the second concerns his birth as *Siddhartha and recounts his life up unto his enlightenment (*bodhi); the third describes his life as the Buddha up to the donation of the *Jetavana *monastery by *Anāthapiṇḍika.

Niddesa. A commentarial work forming part of the *Khuddaka Nikāya of the *Pāli Canon. It is divided into two subsections: the Culla-Niddesa (shorter exposition) and the Mahā-Niddesa (longer exposition). Authorship of the work is attributed to *Śāriputra.

Nien-fo. *See* NEMBUTSU; NAMU AMIDA BUTSU.

nigaṇṭha (Pāli, without bonds). Name used in early Buddhist sources to refer to the Jains, and to their leader *Nigaṇṭha Nātaputta (*see* MAHĀVĪRA). The Jains were referred to as nigaṇṭha because they claimed that their practices freed them from all bonds. *See also* JAINISM.

Nigaṇṭha Nātaputta. Name by which the Jain leader *Mahāvīra is referred to in *Pāli sources. *See also* JAINISM.

Nigrodhārāma. A grove near the town of the *Buddha's *birth, *Kapilavastu. The grove was donated by Nigrodha, a member of the *Śākya clan. The Buddha stayed here on many occasions, including his first visit to the town in the year after his enlightenment (*bodhi). It was here that the Buddha performed the 'twin miracle', when flames and water issued forth from his body (*yamaka-pāṭihāriya), and that *Mahāprajāpatī first requested him to admit *women to the Order (*Saṃgha).

Nihon reiiki. *See* NIHON RYŌIKI.

Nihon ryōiki. A collection of stories, the full title of which is *Nihonkoku genpō zen'aku ryōiki* (Miraculous stories of the retribution of good and evil in the country of *Japan). The work was first published in Japan in the year 822 by the *monk Keikai (or Kyōkai), and its purpose is to present a series of illustrations of the workings of *karma and cause and effect in the lives of living beings.

nijushi-ryū. This Japanese phrase, which literally means 'the 24 streams', is a conventional idiom referring to the 24 schools and sects of *Zen.

nikai. Thai word for *Nikāya.

Nikāya (Skt.; Pāli, assembly). **1.** The five collections of texts that constitute the *Sūtra Piṭaka of the *Pāli Canon, namely: (i) *Dīgha Nikāya (Collection of Long Discourses); (ii) *Majjhima Nikāya (Collection of Medium Discourses); (iii) *Saṃyutta Nikāya (Collection of Connected Discourses); (iv) *Aṅguttara Nikāya (Collection of Incremental Discourses); (v) *Khuddaka Nikāya (Collection of Lesser Discourses). *See also* ĀGAMA. **2.** A group of *monks or a monastic order.

nimitta (Skt., sign). Technical term in Buddhist psychology and philosophy denoting the cognition or apprehension of forms. The term denotes the basic data of perception such as colours, shapes, sounds, and so forth which are then processed by ideation (*saṃjñā).

nine vehicles. The *Nyingma school's special classificatory system of Buddhist teachings. The nine vehicles comprise the three 'outer vehicles' of the *Śrāvakayāna, *Pratyekabuddhayāna, and *Bodhisattvayāna; the three 'outer' *tantric vehicles of *kriyā-tantra, ubhaya-tantra, and *yoga-tantra; and the three 'inner' tantric vehicles of *mahāyoga, *anuyoga, and *atiyoga.

nine yānas. *See* NINE VEHICLES.

Nippon reiiki. *See NIHON RYŌIKI.*

Nipponzan Myōhoji. A *Nichiren-based Buddhist organization founded by Nichidatsu Fujii (1885–1985), often referred to as Guruji within the movement. Fujii, disturbed deeply by the nuclear bombing of Hiroshima and Nagasaki in 1945, began conducting a series of peace marches around the world in various places, during which he and his followers chanted the *daimoku, or title of the **Lotus Sūtra*. He also devoted himself to the construction of large, white 'peace *pagodas', of which there are currently over 70 around the world.

Fig 14 Peace Pagoda.

niraya. *See* HELL.

nirmāṇa-kāya (Skt.). The Emanation Body or physical embodiment of a *Buddha, according to the *Mahāyāna doctrine of the 'three bodies' (*trikāya). The concept may have originated in *Mahāsaṃghika circles (although the link is unproven), where it was maintained that the Buddha was essentially eternal and primordially enlightened in his cosmic or *dharma-kāya aspect, but had the ability to manifest in various forms appropriate to different beings in *saṃsāra in order to demonstrate to them the manner in which enlightenment (*bodhi) may be attained. This docetic concept was largely adopted unchanged by later Mahāyāna followers. Some authorities, however, hold that docetism was a Mahāyāna development which then influenced certain later Mahāsaṃghika sources. In *tantric *Buddhism, the nirmāṇa-kāya is considered to be equivalent to the body vector of a Buddha's activities. *See also* BODY, SPEECH, MIND.

nirodha (Pāli, cessation). Name given to the third noble truth concerned with the cessation of suffering (*duḥkha). This states that, by putting an end to greed, hatred, and delusion, an end to suffering can be found. Nirodha is synonymous with *nirvāṇa, but the word nirvāṇa does not itself occur in the formulation of the *Four Noble Truths.

nirodha-samāpatti (Pāli, attainment of cessation). Ninth level of trance which was added to the scheme of the eight trances (*dhyāna). In this ninth stage, all mental activity is suspended and bodily functions are greatly attenuated. The subject remains in a state of suspended animation in which it is difficult to detect any vital signs. In due course the meditator emerges spontaneously from this condition. Stories are told of *monks who remained in this state while there was great tumult around them, even to the extent of being absorbed in trance in the middle of a village that was on fire. The state is also known as 'the cessation of ideation and feeling' (Pāli, saññā-vedayita-nirodha). *See also* PRATISAṂKHYĀ-NIRODHA; APRATISAṂKHYĀ-NIRODHA.

nirupādhiśeṣa-nirvāṇa (Skt.; Pāli, nirupādhisesa-nibbāna). 'Nirvāṇa without remainder', an alternative designation for the *nirvāṇa that is attained at *death. Also known as 'final' nirvāṇa or *parinirvāṇa. The remainder or residue referred to (upādhi) is the five aggregates (*skandha) that consitute individuality, and which cease at the point when nirupādhiśeṣa-nirvāṇa is attained. For this reason the state is also known in *Pāli sources as 'the nirvāṇa of the aggregates' (khandha-parinibbāna). One who attains this nirvāṇa is not reborn. This condition is accordingly to be distinguished from *sopādhiśeṣa-nirvāṇa or 'nirvāṇa with remainder', where the embodied individual continues to exist.

nirvāṇa (Pāli, nibbāna). The *summum bonum* of *Buddhism and goal of the *Eightfold Path. The attainment of nirvāṇa marks the end of cyclic existence in *saṃsāra, the condition to which it forms the antithesis, and in the context of which nirvāṇa has to be understood. Saṃsāra is thus the problem to which nirvāṇa is the solution. The word nirvāṇa is formed from the negative suffix nir and a *Sanskrit root which may be either vā, meaning to blow, or vṛ, meaning to cover. Both connote images of extinguishing a flame, in the first case by blowing it out and in the second by smothering it or starving it of fuel. Of these two etymologies, early sources generally prefer the latter, suggesting that they understood nirvāṇa as a gradual process, like cutting off the fuel to a fire and letting the embers die down, rather than as a sudden or dramatic event. The popular notion that nirvana is the 'blowing out of a flame' is thus not widely supported in the canonical literature. In general, nirvāṇa is described in negative terms as the end or absence of undesirable things, such as suffering (*duḥkha), although positive epithets also occur, notably the famous description of nirvāṇa as the 'Unborn, Unoriginated, Uncreated, Unformed' found at *Udāna* 8. 3.

It is important to distinguish two kinds of nirvāṇa: the first is the moral and spiritual transformation that takes place in life, and the second is the condition that subsists in the post-mortem state. The former is known as 'nirvāṇa with remainder' (*sopādiśeṣa-nirvāṇa) and the latter as 'nirvāṇa without remainder' (*anupādiśeṣa-nirvāṇa) or 'final nirvāṇa' (*parinirvāṇa) although in the earliest sources nirvāṇa and parinirvāṇa are used interchangeably. The former is attained through the destruction of the defilements known as the outflows (*āśrava), and the latter is characterized by bringing to a halt for all time the dynamic activity of the psycho-physical factors (*saṃskāra) that compose the human individual. One in the latter condition is free from the effects of *karma, but one in the former is not, although no new karma will be produced.

In *Mahāyāna Buddhism, the *Bodhisattva ideal diminishes the importance of nirvāṇa as a religious goal. This is because the Bodhisattva makes a vow not to enter nirvāṇa until all other beings have entered before him. Nirvāṇa thus becomes a collective endeavour rather than a personal one. As new doctrinal positions emerge, moreover, the concept of nirvāṇa undergoes development and is understood differently according to the philosophical perspective of the main schools. The *Madhyamaka, for example, famously conclude that one who perceives emptiness (*śūnyatā) as the true nature of phenomena will see nirvāṇa and saṃsāra as co-terminous. The *Yogācāra school also teaches that the cessation of dualistic mental discrimination will lead to the realization that the opposition between nirvāṇa and saṃsāra is merely conceptual. Schools such as *Zen Buddhism also emphasize that for those who are awakened and perceive with insight (*prajñā), nirvāṇa saturates every aspect of saṃsāra. Certain texts also elaborate a distinction between two types of nirvāṇa, mirroring the one made in the early sources between nirvāṇa in this life and final nirvāṇa. In the Mahāyāna these are known as localized (*pratiṣṭhita) and unlocalized (*apratiṣṭhita) nirvāṇa. The latter corresponds to the state of *parinirvāṇa, but in the former a Buddha remains 'in the world but not of it', free of any attachment to saṃsāra but accessible to help suffering beings.

Nirvāṇa school. An early school of Chinese *Buddhism that focused its attention and study on the **Nirvāṇa Sūtra*, translated into Chinese in the early 5th century (earlier versions are now all lost). Three translations of this *sūtra exist in the Chinese canon, and controversies surrounding the first and second of these played an integral role in the establishment of this school. The first, translated by *Fa-hsien (4th–5th centuries CE) and *Buddhabhadra (359–429) in 418, consisted of six fascicles, and included material that appeared to indicate support for the view that a class of beings called *icchantikas lack *Buddha-nature, or the potential to achieve Buddhahood, and thus were eternally doomed to course through *saṃsāra. A prominent *monk named *Tao-sheng (360–434), who had been working with the great translator *Kumārajīva (343–413) in the capital *Ch'ang-an, felt strongly that such a teaching violated the basic spirit of *Mahāyāna *Buddhism and publicly declared that the Fa-hsien/Buddhabhadra translation must be incomplete. For daring to contradict scripture, he was denounced and left the capital, convinced that he would be vindicated. In

422, another translation by *Dharmakṣema (385–433) appeared in 40 fascicles that showed the earlier translation to be incomplete and provided clear statements of the universality of *Buddha-nature. Tao-sheng returned to his teaching post with renewed prestige.

The Nirvāṇa school that centred on this text stressed what it took to be the scripture's central teachings: (1) that (final) nirvāṇa is not annihilation but an eternal and joyous state; (2) that all beings have Buddha-nature and are capable of attaining salvation; (3) that this Buddha-nature is not only the potential for Buddhahood, but identical with the final nature of reality, or emptiness (*śūnyatā), thus removing some of the negative connotations of the latter term and making more of a positive vision of the truth of things; (4) that, since the ultimate nature of things is undivided and without characteristics that one could grasp, then the wisdom that realizes the ultimate nature of things must arise and comprehend it all at once; and (5) that even though living beings have no self (*ātman) that travels through saṃsāra and is the subject of suffering, this does not mean that there is no self that realizes wisdom and nirvāṇa; rather, wisdom reveals Buddha-nature as the true self beyond all the transitoriness and delusion of the present world. These teachings gave a positive cast to doctrines that had previously seemed pessimistic and nihilistic by asserting that the removal of illusion reveals the real state of things, such that the discovery of transcendent reality lay at the end of the process of denying falsehoods. Aside from this fact, this text became more and more a popular subject of study and lecture because of the controversy surrounding Tao-sheng and the issues it raised, and because of Dharmarakṣa's own efforts in promoting his translation. His student Tao-lang composed a commentary explaining further the identity between Buddha-nature and the Middle Way (*madhyamā-pratipad) that realizes emptiness, thus helping spread the notion of truth as an active force at work in the world as it is expressed in the nature of living beings, as opposed to prior notions of emptiness which saw the nature of reality as static. Because of this interest, a *monk named Tao-p'u attempted a journey to *India to recover other *Sanskrit versions of the scripture, but failed in the attempt. Another group of monks and laymen, acting under orders of King Wen of the Liu-Sung dynasty (r. 424–453) took the previous two translations and collated their contents, adding polish to the text and rationalizing its section headings to produce the so-called Southern Text in 36 fascicles.

While one may speak of the 'Nirvāṇa school' as an area of interest and study centred upon the **Nirvāṇa Sūtra*, it never had an institutional structure or identity. Rather, it existed as a lineage of masters and students devoted to the text and its propagation. Even these lineages came to an effective end with the reunification of *China by the Sui dynasty in 581 and the founding of the *T'ien-t'ai school, which subsumed study of the *Nirvāṇa Sūtra* by placing this text alongside the **Lotus Sūtra* as the highest expressions of the truth of Buddhism.

Nirvāṇa Sūtra. The standard English short title for the **Mahāparinirvāṇa Sūtra*, a Buddhist scripture that enjoyed a period of intense interest and study in the early period of Chinese *Buddhism and was for a time at the centre of the so-called *Nirvāṇa school. The text has its apparent origin in the *Pāli **Mahāparinibbāna Sūtta*, but *Mahāyāna versions appeared later incorporating many new ideas such as *tathāgata-garbha ('embryonic Buddha') thought, teachings on emptiness (*śūnyatā), *Buddha-nature, and the eternally abiding nature of the *Buddhas. This Mahāyāna version of the text was translated twice in *Tibet and at least three times in *China. The discrepancies between the Tibetan and Chinese versions, and between the first two Chinese versions, show that the contents of the *Sanskrit originals were quite disparate, indicating a text still undergoing active redaction and augmentation well into the 5th century. The three surviving translations in the Chinese canon are: (1) the six-fascicle version produced in 418 by *Fa-hsien and *Buddhabhadra (*Taishō 376); (2) a 40-fascicle translation produced in 422 by *Dharmarakṣa (Taishō 374); (3) a new edition (rather than a new translation) produced between 424 and 453 in south China in 36 fascicles (Taishō 375). This last edition was produced by collating the contents of the previous two translations, polishing the language, and adding new section headings.

This *sūtra was highly influential in the development of Chinese *Buddhism in several ways. It provided a scriptural basis for asserting that all living beings have Buddha-nature, and thus even *icchantikas, beings previously thought to have no potential for enlightenment (*bodhi) and liberation, may eventually attain nirvāṇa. It further identifies this Buddha-nature with the final nature of reality, which profoundly changed the way Buddhism in China presented its vision of the truth. Whereas before the final nature of reality, expressed as the truth of emptiness, consisted simply in clearing away delusions about reality and presenting a static statement of the nature of things, the identification of emptiness and the Middle Way (*madhyamā-pratipad) with Buddha-nature made the truth of things an active force working in the world by expressing itself in living beings themselves. The text is also noteworthy for its strictures against meat-eating (*see* DIET). Finally, it taught (in concert with the even more influential **Lotus Sūtra*) that Buddhas do not simply enter extinction upon the attainment of nirvāṇa, but instead are eternally abiding and remain active in the world on behalf of suffering beings. These ideas gained currency through the work of the Nirvāṇa school and the numerous lectures and commentaries that expounded and promoted the text's teachings throughout China. As a result, these teachings became part of the fundamental currency of Chinese Buddhism, and played an active role in the formation of the *T'ien-t'ai school (into which the Nirvāṇa school was eventually subsumed), and the *Ch'an school

nirvikalpa (Skt.). The absence of the false dualistic division that is, according to *Yogācāra, imposed upon reality, involving a belief in the existence of a perceiving subject and perceived objects (*see* ALSO grāhya-grāhaka).

nirvikalpa-jñāna (Skt.). The awareness associated with enlightenment (*bodhi) which is free from the overlay of dualistic concepts (*vikalpa) found in ordinary unenlightened beings. This term is associated with, but not unique to, the *Yogācāra school.

Nishida Kitarō (1870–1945). 20th-century Japanese *Zen philosopher and founder of the *Kyoto school. During his early life he immersed himself in German language studies and, through that, the study of European philosophy. In particular, he studied the phenomenology of Brentano and Husserl, but had a broad familiarity with the entire tradition of German philosophy from Kant to Heidegger. In addition, he spent time studying European mystical writings from Pseudo-Dionysius to Eckhart and Nicholas of Cusa. Kitarō first made a name for himself while teaching at Imperial University, when he published his path-breaking book, *An Inquiry Into the Good* (1911). In this work, he drew together ideas from both Zen and German phenomenology. Beginning from 'pure experience', contingent, finite human beings discover within themselves a bottomless reality that connects to the absolute and infinite, which is both *God and emptiness (*śūnyatā), both speaking and silent. This connection of the human with the divine, the finite with the infinite, does not eventuate in one subsuming the other or in the indiscriminate mixture of the two or in the relativization of the one to the other; rather both aspects of human life stand in both differentiated contradiction and undifferentiated unity. This 'identity of contradictories' is both inconceivable and the basis for all human aspiration. All contradictories meet in the point of absolute 'nothingness' (a concept related to the Buddhist idea of emptiness), which is nothing in itself but is the font from which all things arise in their multiplicity and contrariety. Nishida extended these ideas and linked them more explicitly to religious themes in later works such as *Intuition and Reflection in Self-Consciousness* (1917), *Art and Morality* (1923), and *Fundamental Problems of Philosophy* (1933).

Nishi-honganji. *See* HONGANJI.

Nishitani Keiji (1900–90). A student of *Nishida Kitarō (1870–1945), the founder of the *Kyoto school that combined German philosophy and Christian mystical thought with *Zen experience to present a new synthesis of modern thought in *Japan. Like his teacher, he was concerned to synthesize elements of all three streams of thought in order to address more fully fundamental human philosophical problems. Unlike Nishida, he took as his point of departure the challenge of Nietzsche and nihilism, and sought throughout his work a resolution to the problem of the self. The Western formulation of the problem was flawed, he argued, because the search for self remained strictly within the realm of the cognitive, the logocentric, and the rational. Zen could enrich the search because the breakthrough sought through Zen *meditation was one that involved the total person and yielded truths about the nature of the self that went beyond the cognitive to produce a total experiential realization of the self.

The self thus realized is the self seen through the Buddhist concept of emptiness (*śūnyatā). The problem with Western attempts to address Nietzsche's nihilism was that they attempted to limit it, to find a place to establish the self in reality, when in fact all such attempts ultimately serve only to bind human thought in conceptual chains of its own making. Emptiness allows nihilism free play and follows it to the end, wherein nihilism discovers even itself to be nothing but a reification imposed upon the world. At that point, when, in Buddhist terms, even emptiness is emptied, the east Asian Buddhist tradition asserts that all false conceptualizations are cleared away, leaving, not nothing whatsoever, but the luminous truth of things-as-they-are. The self thus finds itself as itself, unbound by any fabricated conceptions and too-easy harmonizations of contradictions, but in open, space-like reality. In both Zen masters and Christian mystics, Nishitani found the via negativa that follows negation to its end-point in the affirmation of all and the clear vision of that-which-is, or, in Buddhist terms, 'suchness' (*tathatā).

niśraya (Skt.; Pāli, nissaya). A support or basis. The term is used in various contexts, such as the five supports for eliminating evil and cultivating good, namely *faith, shame, decency, effort, and insight. It also refers to the four requisites of a *monk, namely: the root of a tree for abode (vṛkṣa-mūla), almsfood for nourishment (piṇḍapāta), refuse rags for garments (pāṃsukūla), and cow's urine for *medicine (pūtimukta-bhaiṣajya).

nīvaraṇa (Skt.; Pāli). The five nīvaraṇas or 'hindrances' are vices that disturb the mind and obscure one's vision of the truth. In *Pāli sources they are: (1) sensuous *desire (kāmacchanda), (2) hatred (vyāpāda), (3) sloth (thīnamiddha), (4) anxiety (uddhaccakukkucca), and (5) doubt (vicikicchā). It is impossible to enter the trances (*dhyānas) while these hindrances are present.

Niwano Nikkyō (1906–99). Co-founder of *Risshō Kōseikai, one of the 'New Religions' of *Japan belonging to the *Nichiren family. Niwano was born in 1906 in Niigata Prefecture, in northern Japan. Several years after leaving school, he went to Tokyo to work and there began studying and practising various spiritual disciplines. Eventually, in 1938, as a member of the new religion Reiyūkai (*see* REIYŪKAI KYODAN), he attended a series of lectures on the **Lotus Sūtra* given by Mr Sukenobu Arai. That year, together with Mrs Myōkō Naganuma, Niwano founded a new lay Buddhist organization that they called Risshō Kōseikai (Society for Success in Establishing the Right). After her death in 1957, he became the sole president of the organization. Believing that all religions spring from the same source, Niwano has met with people of religion the world over in order to further the cause of world peace through interreligious cooperation. He dedicated himself to the establishment of the World Conference on Religion and Peace (WCRP) and the Asian Conference on Religion and Peace (ACRP). In 1994 he attended the sixth assembly of the WCRP in Italy and presided at its opening session with Pope John Paul II in the Vatican's Synod Hall. He also appeared repeatedly before the United Nations to call for the abolition of nuclear weapons.

True to the *Nichiren tradition, Niwano remained devoted to the study of the *Lotus Sūtra* as the final and most direct revelation of the *Buddha's teaching, and to the chanting of its title, called the *daimoku in Japanese, as a simple means of salvation for all people. As a personal act of devotion he wrote out a copy of the *sūtra by hand, using his own blood. His efforts in interreligious cooperation have been widely recognized. In 1979 he was awarded the Templeton Foundation Prize for Progress in Religion. In 1992 he was made Knight Commander with the Silver Star of the Order of St Gregory the Great by the Vatican. In 1993 he received the Interfaith Medallion from the International Council of Christians and Jews.

niyama (Skt.; Pāli, constraint). The laws, conditions, or constraints that govern processes or phenomena. The *Pāli commentaries recognize five areas that are subject to law-like principles: (1) natural science and *ecology (utu-niyama); (2) botany (bīja-niyama); (3) morality (*karma-niyama) (4) psychology (citta-niyama); (5) certain religious phenomena (dhamma-niyama).

Nō (Jap.). A form of traditional Japanese drama that emerged in the late 14th and early 15th centuries, and whose dialogues, story lines, and aesthetic qualities have been influenced by *Buddhism. The form was introduced by the actor Kan'ami, but brought to its theoretical and practical maturity in the work and writings of his son, Zeami (1363–1443). Zeami brought many aspects of the Buddhism of his day to bear. From *Zen, he imported the sense of theatre as an ongoing practice, as the actors work from day to day and performance to performance to perfect their craft and, through it, themselves. Many themes and elements entered in from those facets of Buddhist life and practice with which audiences would have been aware in their daily lives as well: the character of the wandering *monk (frequently portrayed as one of the *yamabushi of *shugendō), tastes and aesthetic sensibilities stemming from Zen, a sense of impermanence (*anitya) and loss, portrayal of humans and other phenomena as both finite beings as well as expressions of the absolute, esoteric ritualism (*see* ESOTERIC BUDDHISM), and so on. Thus, Nō represents the osmosis of Buddhist thought and sensibility into a popular art form.

noble persons. *See* ĀRYA-PUDGALA.

Non-dual Tantras. The numerically smallest group of the three main classes of *anuttara-yoga-tantras according to some adherents of the New Transmission lineage in *Tibet. These comprise the **Kālacakra Tantra* and the *Mañjuśrī-nāma-saṅgīti*. Meditative practice (*sādhana) based on the Non-dual Tantras emphasizes an integration of the *generation and *completion-phases of *visualization as a means of personal transformation.

non-injury. *See* AHIṂSĀ.

non-returner. *See* ANĀGĀMIN.

Northern School. A conventional name assigned to a faction of *Ch'an *Buddhism that flourished during the early *T'ang dynasty (618–907) consisting of the distinguished *monk *Shen-hsiu (606–706) and his disciples P'u-chi (651–739) and I-fu (658–736). In Ch'an lore, this was the school that took the position of '*gradual enlightenment' against the so-called '*Southern School's' position of '*sudden enlightenment' as espoused by *Hui-neng (638–713). Whether the controversy happened as recorded in Ch'an literature is a problem for scholars, but the school of Shen-hsiu did exist and put forward a position on Ch'an methods and enlightenment that is open to historical research. (*See* NORTHERN-SOUTHERN SCHOOL CONTROVERSY for an account of this debate.)

Shen-hsiu's extant writings reveal that he taught a method of looking at or contemplating the mind (Chin., k'an-hsin or kuan-hsin) that assumed its inherent purity. In other words, to contemplate one's own mind was in itself to contemplate the pure Buddha-mind. Later Northern School texts equated this mind with 'the unlocalized', emphasizing that the mind, seen in its inherent purity, could not be positively identified in this or that place, but pervaded and underlay all reality. This means that their term 'to gaze at the mind' indicated an objectless contemplation, since its object was both everywhere and nowhere. The development of this vision might take some practice, and hence the Southern School's later accusation of gradualism may apply, but *Ho-tse Shen-hui (670–762), the chief polemicist of the Southern School, also conceded that such practice was necessary for the attainment of 'sudden' enlightenment. Thus, the traditional characterization of the Northern School as 'gradualist' and the Southern School as 'subitist' (*see* SUBITISM) seems to disappear under historical and textual scrutiny. Shen-hsiu, like other Ch'an masters of the various schools of the time, was also concerned to simplify Buddhist *meditation. Perhaps in reaction to the profusion of methods catalogued in the *Great Calming and Insight* (Chin., *Mo-ho-chih-kuan*) of *T'ien-t'ai master *Chih-i (538–97), Shen-hsiu adapted the phrase 'one-practice *samādhi' from earlier scriptures and interpreted it to mean that only one practice, that of seated meditation focused on the contemplation of the mind, was necessary.

The Northern School tradition suffered a gradual decline following the Northern-Southern School controversy. The An Lu-shan rebellion of 755 left the central government greatly weakened, and put more power into the hands of provincial military governors. Because of this, the imperial favour that the Northern School enjoyed counted for less and less. In addition, court officials who had entered government service via the examination system generally put their support behind the 'Ho-tse School' of Shen-hui rather than the Northern School. Nevertheless, disciples of Shen-hsiu and his two chief successors continued to distinguish themselves, and they managed to found communities away from the capital, many of which attained significant followings. The Northern School finally fell, along with the rest of pre-classical Ch'an, in the persecution of 845. The Northern School's influence extended beyond the borders of *China. A monk of the school named *Hvashang Mahāyāna represented the Ch'an tradition at the *Council of *Lhasa which took place in 792 in *Tibet but lost the debate according to the official records.

Northern–Southern School controversy. A controversy that arose between two factions of pre-classical *Ch'an during the early 8th century whose polemics centred on the positions of '*sudden enlightenment' (the 'subitist' position) (*see* SUBITISM) and '*gradual enlightenment' (the 'gradualist' position). The traditional account of the controversy is found in the **Platform Sūtra of the Sixth Patriarch*. According to this Chinese text, both *Shen-hsiu and *Hui-neng were disciples of the fifth *patriarch *Hung-jen (601–74). As Hung-jen was preparing to pass the title of sixth *patriarch to his successor, he asked his disciples to compose a poem that would demonstrate their level of enlightenment (*bodhi). All the other monks deferred to Shen-hsiu, the senior disciple. Shen-hsiu composed a verse which Hung-jen publicly praised while telling Shen-hsiu in private that it fell short of the mark. When Hui-neng heard about the contest, he instantly knew what to write and, being illiterate, had a temple page inscribe his verse on a wall. Hung-jen, hearing of this, said publicly that this verse was lacking, but late that night called Hui-neng to his room and 'transmitted his *Dharma' to him, naming him as his successor and sixth patriarch, and giving him the robe and bowl of *Bodhidharma as tokens. In traditional Ch'an literature, Shen-hsiu's verse puts forward the gradualist position while Hui-neng's expresses the subitist position, and Hung-jen's approbation of the latter's verse is meant to demonstrate that the subitist position is the true teaching of the patriarchs.

Thus, in Ch'an documents, the *Northern School (the name given to the line of disciples coming from Shen-hsiu) is represented as teaching the position of 'gradual enlightenment'. From a philosophical viewpoint, 'gradual' here does not necessarily mean taking an extended period of time to achieve enlightenment, but indicates the dualistic view that differentiates enlightenment from ignorance or practice from attainment. No matter what length of time one specifies from the beginning of practice to the attainment of enlightenment, it becomes 'gradual' only because the two are separated. According to teachings of *Buddha-nature that had been current in *China from the 4th century onwards, all sentient beings have the capacity to be *Buddhas. Teachings of 'sudden enlightenment', which became standard doctrine within Ch'an after the controversy, posit Buddha-nature as an already fully endowed Buddhahood inherent in all beings, in light of which enlightenment takes literally no time at all, since practice and attainment are collapsed. Thus, on this reading, the Northern School adhered to a position of untenable dualism, and so fell out of the mainstream.

A historical examination of the controversy reveals many problems with the traditional account of both the events themselves and the views ascribed to each side. There is good reason to think that the two protagonists in the poetry contest, Shen-hsiu and Hui-neng, never resided at Hung-jen's monastery on Tung Shan at the same time. Furthermore, the Northern School's views on practice and enlightenment reveal a subitist position, while *Southern School literature written during less heated moments frankly acknowledges the need to spend time preparing oneself for the moment of 'sudden' enlightenment. Ironically, during the *Council of *Lhasa held in *Tibet in 792 to debate the subitist and gradualist positions, Indian monks argued the gradualist position, and a Northern School monk represented the subitist position.

In China, the controversy appears to have been politically motivated. Both Shen-hsiu and Hui-neng lived out their days peacefully enjoying great success in their own spheres. Shen-hsiu in particular had been highly prominent at the court of the infamous Empress Wu of the *T'ang dynasty, and is one of only three Buddhist monks to have a biography in official court records. However, in the year 732, some 24 years after Shen-hsiu's death, a disciple of Hui-neng named *Ho-tse Shen-hui (670–762) denounced Shen-hsiu's lineage for espousing a gradualist position and claimed that his own master had received and maintained the true position of sudden enlightenment. While he received a sympathetic hearing from some court officials, the Northern School had some powerful allies in court who convinced the throne to have Shen-hui exiled. He and his school might well have come to nothing but for the outbreak of the An Lu-shan Rebellion in 755. This rebellion lasted for many years and put a severe strain on the imperial treasury, and so Shen-hui was called back to the capital and put to work selling *ordination certificates, a task at which he succeeded brilliantly. The court, in gratitude, granted him his own temple in the capital, providing him a base from which to recruit his own disciples in competition with the Northern School, which also remained active. His lineage was known at the time as the 'Ho-tse School', after the monastery in which he resided, but was also called the Southern School because of the southern provenance of his master Hui-neng. While neither the Northern nor the Southern School survived the persecution of *Buddhism in 845, Shen-hui's rhetoric of sudden enlightenment became the norm for all subsequent Ch'an schools and literature, such that no master could espouse what appeared to be a gradualist position without fear of being accused of holding to a false dualism. In addition, the lineage of Shen-hui succeeded in having the mantle of 'sixth patriarch' transferred from Shen-hsiu to their own progenitor Hui-neng, so that all Ch'an monks from that time to the present trace their enlightenment lineage back to the latter.

no self. *See* ANĀTMAN.

nun. Usual English translation of the *Sanskrit word *bhikṣunī (Pāli, bhikkhunī). In this sense the term refers only to fully ordained member of the *Saṃgha. In various parts of the Buddhist world there are orders of *women who devote themselves to the religious life but are not fully ordained. These usually follow a lesser number of *precepts, such as the *dasa-sīlmātā of *Sri Lanka.

Nyanatiloka (1878–1957). Name taken on *ordination by the German, Anton Walter Florus Gueth. Originally a Catholic and student of the violin, he became attracted to *Buddhism while studying in Frankfurt. He travelled to *India and *Sri Lanka, and was ordained in *Burma in 1903. He returned to Sri Lanka and in 1911 founded a hermitage where many Europeans later became *monks. His extensive writings include a *Buddhist Dictionary* and *Guide through the Abhidhamma Piṭaka*.

Nyingma (Tib., rnying-ma). The oldest of the four main schools of Tibetan *Buddhism. Its doctrines and practices derive from teachings brought to *Tibet during the period of the '*First Propagation' in the 8th century CE by the scholar-monks *Śāntarakṣita and *Kamalaśīla, the *tantric *yogin *Padmasambhava, as well as the monks *Vimalamitra and Vairocana, who were all based at *Samyé, the first Tibetan monastic centre. The characteristic Nyingma teachings focus on *Dzogchen and a separate collection of tantras not included in the later standard compilation of the *Kanjur by *Butön rin-chen-grup. The Nyingma school gained its name retrospectively during the 11th century CE to distinguish it from teaching lineages transmitted during the '*Second Propagation' period. As well as its unique classificatory system of Buddhism, the *nine vehicles, the Nyingma school also has a tradition of continuous revelation of hidden teachings known as *terma, which include such works as the 'Tibetan Book of the Dead' (*Bar-do thos-grol*). Many Nyingma teachings were systematized by *Longchenpa (1308–64) and *Jigmé Lingpa (1730–98). Although many Nyingma adherents were either lay-persons or *yogins, there has also been a continuous monastic tradition. Nyingma *monks use red ceremonial hats from whence they derive their popular name, the 'Red Hat' school.

Nyingmapa (Tib., rnying-ma-pa). Any person or thing associated with the *Nyingma school of Tibetan *Buddhism. *See also* TIBET.

O

Ōbaku school. A school of Japanese *Zen *Buddhism that entered *Japan from *China with the arrival of the master Yin-yüan (1592–1673) in the year 1654 at the invitation of the government. Known in Japanese as Ingen, this master took up residence in the Genjū-ha Zen temple in Uji, which he refashioned as a replica of a Chinese *Ch'an temple of the Huang-po line ('Ōbaku' is the Japanese pronunciation of 'Huang-po'). For the first thirteen generations, masters of this temple were all native Chinese, and even after that the abbacy alternated between Japanese and Chinese masters. Consequently, this lineage retained a very Chinese flavour: in opposition to the typically Japanese concern for sectarian purity in lineage and practice, this line incorporated practices other than pure Ch'an *meditation into its programme, including *Pure Land meditation and *tantric practices. In addition, the head temple has retained Chinese as its official language and emphasized Chinese cultural arts as well as Buddhist practice, to the extent that visitors have been known to comment that a trip to the Genjū-ha Zen temple is like a tour of China. Recognized as an official Zen school in 1876, it now includes over 500 subsidiary temples.

Obon. A festival in *Japan that takes place on the fifteenth day of the seventh lunar month (July–August) in which offerings are made to the spirits of the deceased. The ceremony originated in *China around the 6th century CE and over the centuries has absorbed elements of non-Buddhist beliefs and practices.

Odantapurī. One of the great Indian monastic universities. It was founded during the 8th century CE and was later supported by the *Pāla dynasty. Little is known about this place beyond what is recorded in Tibetan sources although its layout provided a model for the construction of *Samyé (Tib., bsam-yas), the first Tibetan monastery. It was destroyed by Muslim invaders around 1198 who converted it into a fortress after having slaughtered the resident monks. The location of Odantapurī has only recently been identified with the ruins at Bihārsharif, some 7 miles north-east of *Nālandā. *See also* TIBET.

Oḍḍiyāna. A small country in early medieval *India associated with the rise of *tantric *Buddhism. Its actual location is open to dispute. Many scholars conventionally place it in the Swāt Valley region of present-day Pakistan although a case on literary, archaeological, and iconographical grounds may be made for locating it in the east of India in present-day Orissa. On this understanding the name derives from the Dravidian Oṭṭiyan, meaning a native of Oḍra (Orissa) or from Oṭṭiyam, Telegu for Oḍra. However, Oḍḍiyāna is also the Middle Indic form of Udyāna, the name by which *Hsüan Tsang knew the region (he translates it as 'garden'). It was said to be a kingdom ruled by several kings each of whom bore the name Indrabhūti, and was visited by several key figures in the later history of tantric Buddhism, among them *Padmasambhava. In later Tibetan traditions, the country tends to be viewed more as a mythical divine land, akin to *Shambhala, inhabited by *ḍākinīs and inaccessible to ordinary mortals. *See also* KĀÑCĪ; SAHOR.

ogha (Skt.; Pāli, a flood). Term denoting negative moral and mental qualities, such as ignorance and vain *desires, that impede a person on the path to enlightenment (*bodhi). Various such qualities are identified and grouped into lists, originally of five and later of four. The later designation, that of the 'four floods', is identical with that of the four 'outflows' (*āśrava) namely sense-desires (kāmāśrava), the *desire for continued existence (bhavāśrava), wrong views (dṛṣṭāśrava), and ignorance (avidyāśrava)

ōjō (Jap.; Chin., wang-sheng). A term meaning to attain *rebirth in the *Pure Land of *Amitābha.

ōjōden (Jap.). A genre of Japanese *Pure Land literature consisting of biographical sketches of believers who have attained *rebirth in the Pure Land of *Amitābha.

Ōjōyōshū. A classic text of Japanese *Pure Land *Buddhism composed in the year 985 by the *Tendai *monk *Genshin (942–1017). This work lays out 25 different methods of visualizing the *Buddha *Amitābha, and was primarily aimed at *meditation masters within the ranks of Tendai clergy rather than at the population at large. In this work, Genshin took 617 extracts from 112 scriptures and treatises having to do with Pure Land practice and arranged them topically, fashioning a comprehensive compendium of Pure Land thought. This systematic arrangement of Pure Land literature proved very influential not only in *Japan, but also in *China where it became a widely used reference work.

Olcott, Henry Steele (1832–1907). American army colonel and psychic investigator who became first president of the *Theosophical Society.

Oldenberg, Hermann (1854–1920). Pioneering German scholar of *Pāli Buddhist literature. Oldenberg edited and translated the **Dīpavaṃsa* (1879), and produced a five-volume edition of the *Vinaya Piṭaka (1879–83). He is also the author of the classic early work *The Buddha, his Life, his Doctrine, his Community* (1881).

Oṃ (Skt.). An ancient Indian sacred syllable. Various complex explanations of its meaning are found in exegetical literature and it characteristically prefixes most *mantras used in *Buddhism. It becomes a symbol of spiritual knowledge, especially of emptiness (*śūnyatā), in *Mahāyāna and *tantric Buddhism.

Oṃ maṇi padme hūṃ (Skt.). The chief *mantra associated with the salvific *compassion of the *Bodhisattva *Avalokiteśvara, who is especially venerated in *Tibet. The literal meaning of the mantra is often given as 'Praise (Oṃ) to the jewel in the *lotus, hail (hūṃ)!', the lotus symbolizing the ordinary human mind with its inherent jewel-like potentiality for enlightenment (*bodhi). However, such a reading presents grammatical problems. An alternative reading is to take the mantra as an invocation to a female deity by the name of Maṇipadmi ('Praise to the goddess Maṇipadmi, hail!'), but no such deity is known. Many further speculative explanations of the significance of the mantra are found in Tibetan *Buddhism. Most commonly, each of the six syllables of the mantra is associated with one of the *six realms of *rebirth in *saṃsāra.

Fig 15 Oṃ maṇi padme hūṃ in Tibetan Script

one hand clapping. A short name for the *Zen riddle (*kōan) 'What is the sound of one hand clapping?' This kōan, unlike others in Zen, did not originate from stories of Chinese *Ch'an masters, but was composed by the Japanese master *Hakuin Zenji (1685–1768) and presented, along with his comments, in a work entitled *Yabukōji* composed in 1752.

One Mind (Chin., yi hsin; Jap., isshin). **1.** A general term in east Asian *Buddhism for a focused, undisturbed mind, or for the process of concentrating the mind on a single object. **2.** In the Consciousness-only (Chin., *wei-shih) school, a term designating the most fundamental level of mind or consciousness, the evolutions of which in accordance with *karma give rise to all the myriad individual phenomena. **3.** In Chinese *T'ien-t'ai thought, the single mind that serves as the underlying ground of all being, in both its pure and its defiled aspects. Although this idea can be found in previous sources such as the **Hua-yen ching* and *The Awakening of Faith* (**Mahāyāna-śraddhotpāda Śāstra*), the T'ien-t'ai school developed its range of applications further. According to this school, since the very defilements that kept beings imprisoned in *saṃsāra were manifestations of the ultimate reality, they could become proper objects of *meditation and instruments of liberation. In one T'ien-t'ai formulation, this was like being able to enter and exit one's prison at will, whereas the traditional concept of liberation through the eradication of defilements was like simply destroying the prison. In addition, the idea that ultimate reality could be characterized as Mind represented an advance over traditional *Madhyamaka thought and its categories of the '*Two Truths'. In this scheme, ultimate truth was static, a simple realization about the nature of reality. By characterizing the final nature of things with the term 'Mind', the T'ien-t'ai school re-envisioned truth as living and active, and could visualize it as working within the world through the ordinary things in the world to effect the liberation of sentient beings.

one-pointedness of mind. *See* CITTA-EKĀGRATĀ.

one vehicle. *See* EKAYĀNA.

ordination. Buddhist ordination is a voluntary act and need not be undertaken for life. *Monks and *nuns are free to disrobe and return to lay life at any time if they wish, and in certain countries it has become the custom for males to spend a short time in a monastery (*see* TEMPORARY ORDINATION). In the early days of the *Buddha's teaching ministry those who wanted to follow him were admitted simply with the words 'Come, monk' (ehi bhikkhu) but a more formal ceremony was soon established. Although there is now much regional variation, the normal pattern in *Theravāda countries is for the aspirant to be admitted first as a novice (*śrāmaṇera), and then later as a fully fledged monk (*bhikṣu) or nun (*bhikṣunī). The former is known as the lower ordination (*pravrajyā) and the latter as the higher ordination (*upasampadā). In the former, the novice repeats three times the formula of the Three Refuges (*triśaraṇa) and undertakes the Ten Precepts (*daśa-śīla). He/she is then assigned an instructor (*ācārya) and a preceptor (upādhyāya). The head is shaved and the novice is presented with three robes (*cīvara) and a *begging-bowl (piṇḍa-pātra). At the higher ordination the novice become a full member of the *Saṃgha and is obliged to follow the rules of the monastic code (*Prātimokṣa). Both forms of ordination require a quorum of five ordained monks or nuns with a minimum of ten years in the Order. In *Mahāyāna countries there is sometimes a third ordination known as the 'Bodhisattva ordination' in the course of which the Bodhisattva vow (*pranidhāna) is additionally taken.

ordination certificates. Official government documents issued in *China and *Japan from time to time certifying a person's eligibility to enter the monastic Order (*Saṃgha). At times, the purpose was to limit entrance into the order to prevent those who simply wished to evade taxes and corvée labour obligations from using *ordination to obtain these ends. At other times, such as periods of national emergency, the government sold great quantities of ordination certificates as a quick means of raising revenues. Such was the case in China when the An Lu-shan Rebellion broke out in 755.

original face. A term used in *Ch'an, *Zen, and *Sŏn *Buddhism to refer to an individual's true nature in the sense of the true identity, or 'face', which lies behind the ever-changing, evanescent procession of identities that one takes from life to life.

ö-sel (Tib., 'od-gsal; Skt., prabhāsvara). Often translated as 'radiant light' or 'clear light', this term refers to the intrinsic purity of the mind (prakṛti-prabhāsvara-citta) in contrast to the illusory, adventitious defilements which seem to obscure it. Though the concept was known from the earliest times in *Buddhism, it gained prominence particularly in the *Tathāgata-garbha teachings and later *tantric derivatives. According to this view, the mind has two complementary aspects—emptiness and radiance—which both need to be realized and united for enlightenment (*bodhi). Practices associated with this concept also form part of the *Six Yogas of *Nāropa.

Oxhead school. One of the earliest identifiable divisions of the *Ch'an school in *China during the first half of the *T'ang dynasty (618–907). This school was founded by *Fa-jung (594–657), a *monk whose first affiliation was with the *San-lun school, which emphasized the study of Perfection of Insight literature (*see* PRAJÑĀ-PĀRAMITĀ SŪTRAS). He is also reported to have been a disciple of the fourth *patriarch of Ch'an after *Bodhidharma, *Tao-hsin (580–651), but this cannot be historically verified. The school derives its name from Fa-jung's temple, located on Oxhead Mountain (Chin., Niu-t'ou shan) south of Nanking. During the controversy between the *Northern School and the *Southern School (*see* NORTHERN–SOUTHERN

SCHOOL CONTROVERSY), the Oxhead school represented a third way, and sought to find a middle path between the extreme position each of the other schools had taken while the debate was at its height. It joined the Southern School in its insistence that meditative practice be joined to the realization of perfect wisdom, but, with the Northern School, did not insist on the abandonment of all other practices and Buddhist scriptures in favour of an exclusive reliance on *meditation. The Oxhead school appears to have died out after eight generations, and the last name given in its patriarchal line is that of Ching-shan Tao-ch'in (714–92).

Oxherding pictures. A series of ten pictures that developed within the *Ch'an tradition of *China as a way of presenting a model of the path of *meditation and attainment of enlightenment (*bodhi) using an artistic metaphor. 'Herding an ox' as a literary metaphor for learning to control the wanderings of the mind dates back to the *T'ang dynasty (618–907) and came to be quite popular within Ch'an circles. Sequences of pictures developed showing the practitioner as a herdsman training an ox which became gradually whiter in each subsequent picture in the series, until by the end it had disappeared completely, making the point that to tame the mind was to eliminate it as a separate object of clinging. Such sequences could have from five to eight pictures. In the 12th century, the master Kuo-an Shih-yüan created a set of ten pictures that has become the standard version. In order, the pictures are as follows: (1) searching for the ox; (2) seeing the traces; (3) first glimpse of the ox; (4) catching the ox; (5) taming the ox; (6) riding the ox home; (7) ox forgotten, self alone; (8) both ox and self forgotten (depicting a blank circle); (9) return to the origin; (10) returning to the city with gift-bestowing hands. These pictures have served as both teaching aids and objects of meditation for Ch'an and *Zen practitioners since Kuo-an's time.

P

paccantajanapada (Pāli, outlying territory). General term for those geographical regions lying outside the 'central region' (*majjhimadesa) in north-east *India where *Buddhism was established.

paccaya (Pāli, condition; Skt., pratyaya). A condition, or that on which something depends. The *Abhidharma arrived at a comprehensive list of 24 kinds of conditions. These are described in the **Paṭṭhāna*, the last book of the *Theravāda Abhidharma. The analysis is thought to encompass all conceivable relationships between phenomena, whether mental or physical.

padma (Skt.). A white lotus (*Nymphaea alba*), one of the major symbols used in *Buddhism, iconographically as well as in literary works, to represent purity. The lotus is distinctive in that though its roots lie within the mud of a pool, its flower blooms above the water in untainted beauty.

Padmasambhava. The great 8th century CE *yogin, often known as *Guru Rinpoche, who was instrumental in introducing *Buddhism into *Tibet during the reign of King Trisong Detsen (Tib., Khri srong lde brtsan). He is especially venerated by the *Nyingma school who view him as a 'second *Buddha'. He is said to have been born in *Oḍḍiyāna and travelled widely throughout *India prior to visiting Tibet. His name means 'Lotus-born' and derives from a legend that he was born in a *lotus blossom on the river Indus. During his relatively brief stay in Tibet, it was his task to subdue the native gods and spirits who were hostile to the introduction of Buddhism and the construction of the monastery at *Samyé (*c.*767). In this role, Padmasambhava became especially associated with the teachings and practices of *Vajrakīla. Many legends have been handed down about the events of his life such as his involvement with the Indian princess *Mandarāva and the Tibetan noble woman *Yeshé Tshogyel who became his chief Tibetan disciple. The twelve most important events of his life are remembered and celebrated in turn on the tenth day of each month by followers of the Nyingma school. He is also supposed to have buried secret treatises (*terma) in the earth which are periodically rediscovered from time to time.

Pagān. Ancient capital city of *Burma situated at the centre of the country, along the Irrawaddy river, best known for the some 13,000 temples and other religious structures that once covered its region, only about 2,000 of which are still standing. Although inhabited since the beginning of the Christian era, it entered its golden age in the 11th century with the conversion to *Theravāda *Buddhism of King *Anawrahtā, who initiated a great programme of building monuments. This was continued by his successors until the 13th century when the city started to decline rapidly, possibly as a consequence of Kublai Khan's invasion of the region (*see* MONGOLIA).

pagoda. In east Asia, a funerary monument for the interment of ashes after the *cremation of a deceased *monk. The pagoda form evolved from the *stūpas of *India.

Pāhārpur Vihāra. *See* SOMAPURI MAHĀVIHĀRA.

Pai-chang-ch'ing-kuei. Chinese work whose name means 'The Pure Rule of Pai-chang'. The title denotes a set of monastic regulations for *Ch'an monasteries, and can refer to one of two works. The first is a set of rules first devised by the *T'ang-dynasty Ch'an *monk *Pai-chang Huai-hai (749–814), that formalized what had previously been a set of *ad hoc* regulations put into effect by Ch'an communities whose size necessitated formal structures, rules, and procedures. Pai-chang's original '*Pure Rules' are no longer extant. The second is a work published in 1338 under the direction of the emperor. Separated from Pai-chang by some five centuries, it is doubtful that the contents of this rule, found in the *Taishō *canon as document 2025, reflect those of the original.

Pai-chang Huai-hai (749–814). A mid-*T'ang dynasty Chinese *Ch'an *monk who attained enlightenment (*bodhi) as a disciple of the famous master *Ma-tsu Tao-i (709–88). He is primarily known for formulating a rule called the '*Pure Rules of Pai-chang' (Chin., Pai-chang ch'ing-kuei) that regularized and systematized the accumulated 'house rules' of previous Ch'an communities, creating a formal tradition out of what had been a set of *ad hoc* regulations. Pai-chang's original rule is no longer extant, but other '*Pure Rules' arose based upon it, and in 1338 the Yüan-dynasty emperor ordered the publication of a new revision of Pai-chang's rule.

Pai-i Kuan-yin (Chin.). The 'White-Robed Kuan-yin'. An iconographic depiction of the *Bodhisattva *Kuan-yin (Skt., Avalokiteśvara) wearing a white garment. In Chinese *esoteric *Buddhism this is the sixth of the 33 forms in which the Bodhisattva is visualized. This form has also been very popular in Chinese and Japanese ink painting, in which the Bodhisattva is usually depicted seated on a stone overlooking the sea.

Pai-lien tsung (Chin.). The 'White Lotus Sect' of folk *Buddhism in *China. The sect originated with the layman Mao Tzu-yüan in the 12th century. After a period of time studying *T'ien-t'ai doctrines, Mao fashioned his own teachings centring on the union of *Ch'an *meditation and *Pure Land nien-fo practice. According to him, leaving home and family to join the monastic order were not necessary, since *Amitābha *Buddha was merely a manifestation of one's own mind and the Pure Land was located within one's heart. He called his organization the 'White Lotus Sect' out of respect for the 'White Lotus Society' first organized in the 4th-5th centuries by the Pure Land figure *Lu-shan Hui-yüan (334–416). His followers observed strict vegetarianism and undertook the Five Precepts for laymen (*see* PAÑCA-ŚĪLA), but carried out their activities and observances without the oversight of the monastic establishment.

After Mao's death, a disciple in his lineage named Hsiao Mao (or 'little Mao') began mixing other elements into the teaching. The lack of centralized leadership and control in addition to contacts with, and influences from, other lay religious groups led to a fragmenting of the group and the appearances of many splinter groups with all kinds of doctrines. Most notable among these was a belief in the imminent appearance of the future Buddha *Maitreya, along with *Taoist practices aimed at longevity and the creation of amulets that would render their bearers invulnerable to weapons. During the later Sung dynasty and throughout the Yüan, Ming, and Ch'ing dynasties (*see* CHINA), 'White Lotus' groups came under constant government suspicion and surveillance. They were continually accused of holding secret meetings at night in which men and women met together, conjuring up images of orgies and sedition in the eyes of both the government and the monastic Buddhist establishment. In addition, during times of popular unrest, White Lotus groups did indeed prove a fertile ground for the formation of rebel garrisons. The proliferation of groups bearing the name 'White Lotus Sect', 'White Lotus Society' (Chin., Pai-lien hui), or 'White Lotus Teaching' (Chin., Pai-lien chiao), as well as the movement of individual leaders from one group to another, has made this strain of folk Buddhism extremely difficult to document.

Pai-ma Ssu. 'White Horse Temple'. A Chinese Buddhist temple located in Chiang-nan Province near the old capital city of Loyang. Historical records set its founding during the reign of the Emperor *Ming-ti of the Eastern *Han dynasty, around the year 75, making it the oldest Chinese Buddhist temple. *See also* CHINA.

Pakudha Kaccāyana. One of the *Six Sectarian Teachers mentioned in the *Pāli Canon as contemporary with the *Buddha. Pakudha taught a doctrine of seven eternal and unchangeable principles, consisting of the four elements plus pleasure, pain, and the soul (*ātman). According to him these principles act without aim or conscious direction: for example, if someone's head is split with a sharp sword there is no guilt because all that has happened is that certain atoms have been rearranged. His teachings therefore belong to those which deny the reality of moral choice (*akiriya-vāda), and for this reason were condemned by the Buddha.

Pāla dynasty. The last major dynasty (8th-12th century CE) of classical *India, centred on the area covered by present-day Bihar and West Bengal and noteworthy for its range of brilliant intellectual and artistic achievements. During this period *Mahāyāna *Buddhism reached its zenith of sophistication, while *tantric Buddhism flourished throughout India and surrounding lands. This was also a key period for the consolidation of the epistemological-logical (*pramāṇa) school of Buddhist philosophy. Apart from the many foreign pilgrims who came to India at this time, especially from *China and *Tibet, there was a smaller but important flow of Indian pandits who made their way to Tibet and inaugurated the organized transmission of the *Dharma.

Pāli. The language of the texts of *Theravāda *Buddhism. The Pāli language is the product of the homogenization of the dialects in which the teachings of the *Buddha were orally recorded and transmitted. The term Pāli originally referred to a canonical text or passage rather than to a language. No script was ever developed for Pāli and scribes used the scripts of their native languages to transcribe the texts. Tradition states that the language of the *canon is Māgadhī (*see* MAGADHA), the language believed to be spoken by *Gautama Buddha.

Pāli Canon. *See* TRIPIṬAKA.

Pāli Text Society. Society founded in England 1881 by Thomas W. *Rhys Davids in order to promote the study of *Pāli texts. The early activities of the Society centred around making the books of the *Tripiṭaka available to scholars, as interest in *Buddhism grew throughout the West in the second half of the 18th century. The society publishes Pāli texts in roman characters, translations in English, and works including dictionaries, books for students of Pāli, as well as the *Journal of the Pāli Text Society*.

paṃsukūlikā (Pāli, rag wearers). An *ascetic sect of uncertain origin that flourished for a time in medieval *Sri Lanka before disappearing in the 12th century. The name derives from the practice of wearing only robes (*cīvara) that have been cast off as rags, and it is likely this was the distinguishing practice of the group.

pañca-jñāna (Skt., five awarenesses). The five facets of perfect enlightenment (*bodhi), especially according to *Yogācāra-based *Mahāyāna doctrines, ultimately derived from the Mahāyāna *Buddhabhūmi Sūtra*. The 'five awarenesses' are (1) the Awareness of *Suchness (tathatā-jñāna) or *Dharmadhātu Awareness, which is the bare non-conceptualizing awareness of emptiness (*śūnyatā) and acts as the basic ground unifying the other four; (2) Mirror-like Awareness (ādarśa-jñāna) which is devoid of all dualistic thought and ever united with its 'content' as a mirror is with its reflections; (3) Awareness of Sameness (samatā-jñāna) which perceives the identity of all phenomena (*dharma); (4) the Investigating Awareness (pratyavekṣaṇa-jñāna) which perceives the general and specific qualities of all phenomena; and (5) Awareness of Accomplishing Activities (kṛty-anuṣṭhāna-jñāna) which spontaneously carries out all that has to be done for the welfare of beings, manifesting itself in all directions. According to Yogācāra thought, these awarenesses emerge through a transformation (*parāvṛtti) of the eight consciousnesses at the moment of enlightenment. The concept of the five awarenesses later underwent considerable development with the rise of *tantric *Buddhism where they are said to be symbolized or embodied in the form of the five *Jinas, *Vairocana, *Akṣobhya, *Ratnasaṃbhava, *Amitābha, and *Amoghasiddhi.

Pañcāla. One of the major states of ancient *India lying to the east of its rival *Kuru, corresponding to territory the north and west of present-day Delhi. The country was often split into north and south Pañcāla, with hegemony over the northern part being in dispute with the Kurus. The *Buddha is not known to have visited this region during his lifetime although *Buddhism probably spread there during the reign of *Aśoka.

pañca-mārga (Skt.). The 'Five Paths', being a systematization of the stages of an *Arhat's or a *Bodhisattva's spiritual progress current in many pre-*Mahāyāna forms of *Buddhism, and also particularly emphasized in the *Yogācāra school. The five paths comprise: (1) the path of accumulation (*saṃbhāra-mārga) in which one gathers the requisite accumulation of merit and awareness (puṇya-jñāna-saṃbhāra); (2) the path of preparation (*prayoga-mārga) when one develops skill in *meditation; (3) the path of seeing (*darśana-mārga) when one attains a direct insight into the true nature of phenomena or emptiness (*śūnyatā) (4) the path of cultivation (*bhāvanā-mārga) when one broadens one's experience of emptiness and makes it a living experience; (5) and the path of 'no-more-learning' (*aśaikṣa-mārga) when all defilements (*kleśa) and perverse views about the knowable—such as a belief in an inherent, permanent self (ātman)—are overcome. It is at this point one either becomes enlightened as either an Arhat or a *Buddha.

pañca-śīla (Skt.; Pāli, pañca-sīla). The Five Precepts. A set of five moral rules, dating to the origins of *Buddhism and common to almost all schools. They are: (1) not to kill or injure living creatures; (2) not to take what has not been given; (3) to avoid misconduct in sensual matters; (4) to abstain from false speech; (5) not to take intoxicants. The Five Precepts are the cornerstones of Buddhist morality, particularly for the laity. *Monks and *nuns have additional codes of rules to follow (*see* PRĀTIMOKṢA; VINAYA).

pañcavaggiyā (Pāli). Name for the group of five *ascetics to whom the *Buddha preached his *first sermon in the *Deer Park at *Vārāṇasī. Their names were *Aññāta-Koṇdañña, Bhaddiya, Vappa, Mahānāma, and Assaji. They had previously been *ascetic companions of the Buddha but had abandoned him when he renounced the path of austerities and began to follow the Middle Way (*madhyamā-pratipad). When he approached them after having gained enlightenment (*bodhi) they were at first reluctant to hear him but were soon won over by his charisma. After hearing the sermon they asked to become disciples and were ordained the first Buddhist *monks (*see also* ORDINATION).

Panchen Lama (Tib., Paṇ-chen bla-ma). An honorific title first conferred upon Losang Chökyi Gyel-tshen (Tib., blo-bzang chod-kyi gyal-mtshan), 1570–1662, the teacher of the *Dalai Lama V. Since the *Dalai Lamas are considered to be incarnations of *Avalokiteśvara, the Panchen Lamas are considered to be incarnations of *Amitābha, as that *Buddha is Avalokiteśvara's spiritual father. Serving as the abbots of the *Gelukpa *Tashilhumpo monastery, the Panchen Lamas have the important role of authenticating the selected reincarnation of a Dalai Lama. There have been eleven Panchen Lama incarnations although the identity of the most recent one has been subject to dispute, with two different candidates recognized by the Dalai Lama and the Chinese authorities respectively. The current whereabouts in *China of the incarnation favoured by the Dalai Lama are unknown.

p'an-chiao (Chin.). Term denoting the systems developed within Chinese *Buddhism, primarily by the *T'ien-t'ai and *Huayen schools, for taking the often confusing and contradictory mass of Buddhist teachings and scriptures and classifying them into a hierarchical structure using principles of organization. These principles could include the period in the *Buddha's life during which he gave a particular teaching, or judgements about the extent to which a given school or doctrine presented the truth straightforwardly or adapted it for audiences of lower abilities.

P'ang Yün (d. 808). A famous lay practitioner of *Ch'an during the *T'ang dynasty (618–907), also known as 'Layman P'ang'. He studied with many of the eminent Ch'an masters of his day and attained several profound enlightenment experiences (*satori). He is known as the source of the saying, 'My supernatural powers? I carry water and chop firewood'.

Paññāsa Jātaka (Pāli). Collection of 50 birth-stories of the *Buddha also known with the Burmese name of *Zimmè Paññāsa. Although some of the stories are based upon those in the *Pāli *Jātaka, they are not regarded as canonical. This collection is believed to have been compiled, by an unknown author, around the 15th century, possibly in northern *Thailand. The name Zimmè Paññāsa in fact means 'Chieng May Fifty' in Burmese, and it is thought that these stories may have originated in that city in northern Thailand. Three recensions of these birth-stories, all from *south-east Asia, have survived to the present day.

pansil. An abbreviation of *pañca-śīla, or the Five Precepts observed by the laity.

pāpa (Skt.; Pāli, sin). That which is *evil or wrongful and leads to *suffering. Pāpa is the opposite of *puṇya (meritorious action) and whereas puṇya leads to a heavenly *rebirth, pāpa brings about rebirth in one of the three states of woe, namely as an animal, a hungry ghost (*preta), or in hell (*see* GATI). Pāpa arises from intentions and actions that are unwholesome (*akuśala), namely those motivated by greed, hatred, and delusion, the three roots of evil (*akuśala-mūla). Essentially, pāpa is that which leads one away from nirvāṇa, and is closer to the concept of error than an offence against divine authority or a condition innate in human nature such as original sin. In *Buddhism sins cannot be forgiven, but may be confessed (*see* PĀPA-DEŚANĀ).

pāpa-deśanā (Skt., the revealing of wrongdoing; Pāli, pāpa-desanā.). The practice of confession. In *Buddhism, confession is not a sacrament nor an appeal for absolution to a divine power. *Monks do not act as confessors or have the power to forgive sins. Instead, the confession of wrongdoing is seen as psychologically healthy and an aid to spiritual progress by allowing feelings of shame (hrī) and remorse (apatrāpya) to be acknowledged and discharged. A guilty conscience is viewed as a hindrance to religious progress, and it is believed that owning up to wrongful deeds inhibits their repetition. For monks there is an official occasion for confession at each *poṣadha (Pāli, uposatha), when the *Prātimokṣa is recited and monks are obliged to declare any infringements of the rules by themselves or others. There is no equivalent ceremony for lay Buddhists.

Papañcasūdanī. Commentary on the *Majjhima Nikāya, the second collection of the *Sūtra Piṭaka of the *Pāli Canon, compiled by *Buddhaghoṣa in the 5th century CE. The colophon states that it was written at the request of the *monk Buddhamitta of Mayūrapaṭṭana.

pārājika-dharma (Skt.). Group of four offences that are the first and most serious in the Buddhist monastic code of discipline (*Prāṭimokṣa). The penalty for any of the four offences is lifelong expulsion from the monastic order (*Saṃgha). The four offences are (1) sexual intercourse; (2) serious theft; (3) murder, and (4) falsely claiming to have attained supernatural powers. A *monk who commits a pārājika offence is compared to 'a person whose head is cut off, or a withered leaf dropped from the tree, or a stone slab split in two, or a Palm tree cut from the top'. Such a one has been 'defeated' (the traditional etymology of pārājika) and cannot be readmitted to the Order.

Parakkamabāhu I. King of *Sri Lanka, 1153–86. His violent life and times are recorded in the Sinhalese chronicle, the **Cūlavaṃsa*. After a turbulent period of political upheaval he suppressed a rebellion in Rohaṇa and became sole ruler. He sent forces to *India to do battle with the Coḷas but later turned to more peaceful objectives including becoming a generous patron of *Buddhism. He built many shrines and residencies for use by *monks and united the three rival Buddhist groups of the *Mahavihāra, the *Abhayagiri, and the *Jetavana.

paramāṇu (Skt.). An atom, being the smallest unit of matter posited in *Buddhism and defined as a speck of matter which is partless and indivisible. Standard *Abhidharma doctrines hold that each paramāṇu is a composite of various *dharmas or their 'seeds', but this view was criticized by *Mahāyāna followers of *Yogācāra and *Madhyamaka who maintained that such atoms were conceptual fictions as their existence was logically incoherent.

Paramārtha (499–569). Also known by his Chinese name, Chen-ti, he was an Indian scholar-*monk from the Avanti region of western *India. He arrived in *China by sea in 546 CE and took up residence in Chien-K'ang at the invitation of the Emperor Wu of Liang in the south of China. His prolific translation work has led to his being counted among the 'four great translators' in Chinese *Buddhism. Among the 64 works translated by him are a number of key Buddhist texts, especially *Yogācāra, works which include the **Abhidharma-kośa*, the **Suvarṇa-prabhāsottama Sūtra*, the **Mahayana-saṃgraha*, and the **Madhyānta-vibhāga-kārikā*. A translation of the *Awakening of Faith in the Mahāyāna* (**Mahāyāna-śraddhotpāda Śāstra*) is also attributed to him but some scholars doubt the authenticity of this text. The Chinese She-lun school was derived from his translation of the *Mahāyāna-saṃgraha*. His translations of Yogācāra works are often characterized by the inclusion of editorial comments interwoven with the original text that present his understanding of Yogācāra doctrines, though it is not certain whether this derives from the western *Valabhī school of Yogācāra or was unique to himself. It was concern with these innovations that partly prompted *Hsüan-tsang to travel to India to ascertain and later reject the validity of Paramārtha's rendering of Yogācāra.

paramārtha-satya (Skt.). Absolute truth or absolute reality. The ultimate level of truth or reality which denotes direct experience devoid of an overlay of conceptualization, and stands in contrast to 'relative truth' (*samvṛti-satya). Both terms are used epistemologically as well as ontologically in *Mahāyāna Buddhist thought. *See also* TWO TRUTHS.

Paramatthadīpanī. 'The Explanation of the Supreme Meaning', a *Pāli commentary by *Dhammapāla on the *Udāna*, *Itivuttaka*, *Vimānavatthu*, *Petavatthu*, *Theragāthā*, and *Therīgāthā*.

Paramatthajotikā. 'The Illuminator of the Supreme Meaning', a *Pāli commentary traditionally attributed to *Buddhaghoṣa on the *Khuddakapāṭha*, *Dhammapada*, *Sutta Nipāta*, and *Jātaka*.

Paramatthamañjūsā. 'The Casket of Supreme Meaning', a *Pāli commentary by *Dhammapāla on the *Visuddhimagga* of Buddhaghoṣa. The *Paramatthamañjūsā* is most commonly known as the *Mahāṭīkā* (Great Subcommentary).

pāramī (Pāli). One of ten virtuous qualities mentioned in *Pāli sources that are said to lead to Buddhahood. The ten qualities occur frequently in the *Jātakas, and are also found in the *Buddhavaṃsa* and *Cariyāpiṭaka*. The list of ten pāramīs is: (1) generosity (*dāna); (2) morality (sīla); (3) renunciation (nekhamma); (4) insight (paññā); (5) energy (viriya); (6) patience (khanti); (7) truthfulness (sacca); (8) resolution (adhiṭṭhāna); (9) loving-kindness (*metta); (10) equanimity (upekkhā).

pāramitā (Skt., crossed over). In *Mahāyāna *Buddhism a 'perfection' or virtuous quality practised by a *Bodhisattva in the course of his spiritual development. Apparently related to the ten *pāramīs of early Buddhism, an original list of six Mahāyāna perfections was eventually increased to ten to complement the ten stages or levels (*bhūmi) of a Bodhisattva's career. The full list of the ten Perfections is: (1) generosity (*dāna); (2) morality (*śīla); (3) patience (*kṣānti); (4) courage (*vīrya); (5) meditation (*samādhi), (6) intuitive insight (*prajñā); (7) skilful means (*upāya-kauśalya); (8) vow (*pranidhāna); (9) power (*bala); (10) knowledge (*jñāna). The sixth is the subject of the extensive corpus of Perfection of Insight literature (*see* Prajñā-pāramitā Sūtras).

paramparā (Skt., succession). A lineage of teachers collectively composing a channel for the transmission of religious knowledge from master to student.

paratantra (Skt.) The 'dependent' or 'relative' nature, one of the three natures (*tri-svabhāva) according to *Yogācāra philosophy. Paratantra denotes the conditioned stream of experience itself associated with *saṃsāra, through which a falsely imagined (*parikalpita) duality of a subject and objects is generated and projected onto reality by the activation of imprinted predispositions (*vāsanā) contained in the storehouse consciousness (*ālaya-vijñāna). *See also* GRĀHYA-GRĀHAKA; PARINIṢPANNA.

parāvṛtti. *See* ĀŚRAYA-PARĀVṚTTI.

parikalpita (Skt.) The 'imagined', one of the three natures (*tri-svabhāva) according to *Yogācāra philosophy. It denotes the unreal (*parikalpita) duality of a perceiving subject and perceived objects that has been projected onto reality by the dependent nature (*paratantra), resulting in the existence of an individual in *saṃsāra. *See also* GRĀHYA-GRĀHAKA; PARINIṢPANNA.

parinirvāṇa (Skt.). The 'final' or 'highest' *nirvāṇa, usually denoting the state of nirvāṇa that is entered at *death, in contrast to that attained during life. Also known as *nirupādhi-śeṣa-nirvāṇa. In the earliest sources nirvāṇa and parinirvāṇa are used interchangeably.

pariniṣpanna (Skt.). In *Yogācāra philosophy, the level of ultimate truth or perfection, the highest of the three levels of truth recognized by the school. This is the condition of the storehouse consciousness (*ālaya) when perceived non-dualistically in its natural unitary state. *See also* YOGĀCĀRA; THREE TRUTHS; PARIKALPITA; PARATANTRA.

paritta. *Pāli term meaning 'protection' and referring to various formulae which are recited for protection or blessing. The term also denotes the collection of such texts, as well as the ritual at which the collection of these texts or parts of them are recited. This ritual, performed by the followers of *Theravāda *Buddhism, is a complex religious rite with individual formulae appropriate for specific circumstances such as ill health, natural calamity, or the blessing of a new house. *Monks chant the texts while holding a ritual string in their hands. This string is tied to various ritual implements, including a pot of water, before finally reaching the assembled people to whom the blessings of the chanting is transmitted. At the end of the ceremony the ritually pure water is sprinkled and pieces of the thread are tied either round the neck or wrist for protection.

Parivāra (Pāli, appendix). The final of the three divisions of the *Vinaya Piṭaka. It consists of nineteen chapters and provides a résumé of the earlier parts of the text.

parivrājaka (Skt., wanderer; Pāli, paribbājaka). Class of Indian religious mendicants holding various beliefs who have travelled around *India from ancient times, including at the time of the *Buddha. These wandering teachers, who included *women in their number, engaged with one another in *debate on a range of topics. Special meeting places were set aside for them and the local inhabitants came to pay their respects. A representative sample of their views may be found in the **Brahmajāla Sutta* of the *Pāli Canon. Some Parivrājakas claimed their teachings were the same as those of the Buddha, but he rejected this assertion. Many converts to *Buddhism were made from the ranks of the Parivrājakas, the two most notable being *Śāriputra and *Mahāmaudgalyāyana.

pariyatti (Pāli) **1.** Skill or accomplishment, particularly in the study of the scriptures. **2.** The scriptural corpus itself and by extension the *Dharma or teachings of *Buddhism.

Pasenadi. King of the state of *Kosala and a devoted friend and follower of the *Buddha. The two were of a similar age, and Pasenadi visited the Buddha often for discussions on a range of topics. Early in his reign he sought to take a wife from the Buddha's clan in order to strengthen the bonds between their two families. However, the *Śākyans deceived him and sent him a slave girl by whom he had a son, Viḍūḍabha. When Viḍūḍabha later discovered the true status of the girl he invaded the Śākyan territories and killed large numbers of them. Pasenadi's sister was married to *Bimbisāra, the first king of *Magadha, and *Ajātaśatru was his nephew. Uncle and nephew waged war several times over the possession of a village.

Pāṭaliputra (Pāli, Pāṭaliputta). Modern-day Patna, originally built by *Ajātaśatru and later the capital of the ancient Indian state of *Magadha. Its key central location in north central *India led rulers of successive dynasties to base their administrative capital here, from the *Mauryans and the *Guptas down to the *Pālas. In the *Buddha's day it was a village known as Pāṭaligāma. He visited it shortly before his *death and prophesied it would be great but would face destruction either by fire, water, or civil war. Two important councils were held here, the first at the death of the Buddha and the second in the reign of *Aśoka (*see* COUNCIL OF PĀṬALIPUTRA I, II). The city prospered under the Mauryas and a Greek ambassador *Megasthenes resided there and left a detailed account of its splendour. The city also became a flourishing Buddhist centre boasting a number of important monasteries. Known to the Greeks as Pālibothra, it remained the capital throughout most of the *Gupta dynasty (4–6th centuries BCE). The city was largely in ruins when visited by *Hsüan Tsang, and suffered further damage at the hands of Muslim raiders in the 12th century. Though parts of the city have been excavated, much of it still lies buried beneath modern Patna.

path of accumulation. *See* SAṂBHĀRA-MĀRGA; PAÑCA-MĀRGA.

path of cultivation. *See* BHĀVANĀ-MĀRGA; PAÑCA-MĀRGA.

path of no more learning. *See* AŚAIKṢA-MĀRGA; PAÑCA-MĀRGA.

path of preparation. *See* PRAYOGA-MĀRGA; PAÑCA-MĀRGA.

path of seeing. *See* DARŚAṆA-MĀRGA; PAÑCA-MĀRGA.

patho. Burmese term for a square, enclosed, shrine hall containing *Buddha images.

pāṭihāriya (Pāli, miracle). A *miracle or marvel, particularly one performed to impress and gain converts. In the *Pāli Canon the power to perform three such marvels is ascribed to the *Buddha: the marvel of magic power (iddhi); the marvel of mind-reading (ādesanā); and the marvel of instruction (anusāsanī). The Buddha condemned the first two because they played on people's credulity and could also be performed by non-Buddhist *ascetics. The third he praised as 'noble and sublime' because it was not a form of exhibitionism but a means of teaching the *Dharma. *See also* ṚDDHI.

Paṭisambhidāmagga. 'The Way of Analysis', the twelfth book of the *Khuddaka Nikāya of the *Pāli Canon. Although forming part of the *Sūtra Piṭaka it is really a scholastic treatise in the *Abhidharma style, and provides a systematic exposition of certain points of doctrine. The text quotes extensively from the *Vinaya and Sutta Piṭakas.

patriarch. An office or institution in east Asian *Buddhism that replicates traditional kinship relations in order to legitimize a teaching lineage. In secular terms, a 'patriarch' (Chin., tsu) is the paterfamilias, the eldest male ascendant in an extended family. The line from him to his eldest son and then to his eldest son represents the main line of kinship, while other lines represent collateral lines. In Buddhism, a line that goes from one 'patriarch' to the next has, by association with the secular usage, the sense of a main line. This is especially true in schools such as *Ch'an and *esoteric Buddhism, where the link between master and disciple is especially important in determining one's teaching credentials. In other cases, such as the *Pure Land school, where direct contact between master and pupil is not so vital to the transmission of the teachings or practices, the patriarchate may consist simply of those masters who, at various times, have contributed to the advancement or reform of the school. In such cases, it is not necessary that they represent a continuous lineage, only that they form a series of milestones in the tradition's history.

Paṭṭhāna (Pāli, origin). The last book of the *Abhidharma Piṭaka of the *Pāli Canon. The book is divided into two parts, the *Tika-paṭṭhāna dealing with 'groups of three' and the *Duka-paṭṭhāna, dealing with 'groups of two'. The work can be described as the 'book of causes' in that it deals with the 24 modes of relations (*paccaya) between things, mental and material. It is a highly technical text, giving a minutely detailed analysis of the doctrine of conditionality or Dependent Origination (*pratītya-samutpāda). Its commentary was compiled by *Buddhaghoṣa in the 5th century.

Pāvā. The site of the *Buddha's last meal as served to him by *Cunda the blacksmith. From Pāvā the Buddha made his way to *Kuśinagara, which was to be his last resting-place.

paya. Burmese term meaning 'holy one'. The term can be applied to people, deities, and places associated with religion. When applied to religious monuments the word is translated as *stūpa.

peace pagoda. *See* NIPPONZAN MYŌHOJI.

Peltrül Rinpoche (1808–88) (Tib., dpal-sprul rin-po-che). A leading *Nyingma figure in the dissemination of the *Eclectic Movement who was famous for his modesty and ability to communicate profound teachings in a simple manner. This ability is exemplified in his *Instructions of the All-Good Teacher* (Tib., *Kun-bzang bla-ma zhal-lung*) which acts as a general introduction to the Nyingma version of the *preliminary practices.

perahera. Sinhalese term meaning 'parade' or 'procession'. The best known perahera is the *Esala Perahera held in *Kandy at the time of the full moon of the months of July/August. *See also* DURUTHU PERAHERA.

Petavatthu. The seventh book of the *Khuddaka Nikāya of the *Pāli Canon. It narrates the *evil destiny of those reborn as hungry ghosts (Skt., *preta; Pāli, peta) after a lifetime of wicked deeds. There is a commentary on the *Petavatthu* by *Dhammapāla.

pha. Lao term meaning 'holy image' and usually referring to an image of the *Buddha.

Phadampa Sangyé (d.1117) (Tib., Pha-dam-pa sangs-rgyas). The south Indian *yogin who introduced the *chöd teachings into *Tibet where he transmitted them to his chief disciple *Machig Lapgi Drönma. During his wanderings, he also visited *China and is considered by some Tibetans to be the same person as the *Ch'an *patriarch, *Bodhidharma.

Phags pa blo drö (1235–89) (Tib., 'Phags pa blo gros). Leading figure of the *Sakya (Tib., Sa skya) school of Tibetan *Buddhism and nephew of *Sakya Paṇḍita, the founder of the order. In 1244 he accompanied his uncle to the Mongol court and was kept at court after his uncle was sent back to *Tibet to rule as Mongol vassal. Phags pa impressed the court with his learning and *tantric skills and was appointed imperial tutor. He is said to have converted the Mongol emperor Kublai Khan (r. 1260–94) and his consort Chamui to Buddhism. There thus began what became known as the 'patron-priest' (Tib., *yon-mchod) relationship between *China and Tibet, by which the emperor protected Tibet and the *Sakyapas in return acted as spiritual preceptors and enactors of the sacred liturgies.

phala (Skt.; Pāli, fruit). Result or effect, particularly in the sense of the fruition of a course of action. It has two primary referents: (1) the fruition of the four *supermundane paths, namely those of the stream-winner (*śrotāpanna), once-returner (*sakṛdāgāmin), non-returner (*anāgāmin), and *Arhat; (2) the experienced effect or karmic maturation of prior deeds.

pho-ba. *See* PHOWA.

phongyi. Burmese term for a *bhikṣu or Buddhist *monk.

phowa (Tib., 'pho-ba). The technique popular in Tibetan *Buddhism of transferring ('pho-ba) one's consciousness (*vijñāna) at the time of *death directly to one of the *Pure Lands such as *Sukhāvatī. Though now practised by adherents of all Tibetan Buddhist schools, the teachings are said to have originally been transmitted to *Tibet as part of the *Six Yogas of *Nāropa by *Marpa.

phurba (Tib.; Skt., kīla). Term for a ritual implement used in *tantric *Buddhism to pin down and subdue demonic forces. Originally a simple peg, stake or even a large acacia thorn, the phurba in Tibetan Buddhism takes the form of a three-sided dagger surmounted with the head of a wrathful being usually viewed as *Vajrakīla.

pigu. Korean term for a *bhikṣu or Buddhist *monk.

pilgrimage. Undertaking religious pilgrimage is a seen as a meritorious practice since it focuses the mind on places associated with the *Buddha, saintly people, or holy objects. Those undertaking a pilgrimage are believed to accumulate good *karma as a result. Pilgrimages are undertaken for many reasons, including to gain merit (*puṇya), to ask for a boon, or as the result of a vow. The Buddha himself provides authority for the practice of pilgrimage in the **Mahāparinibbāna Sutta* of the *Pāli Canon where he recommends as suitable sites to visit the places of his birth, enlightenment (*bodhi), *first sermon, and death. He further instructs that his remains should be placed in a *stūpa, and states that anyone who pays reverence to a stūpa with a devout heart will reap benefit and happiness for a long time. Sites containing *relics of the Buddha, or places associated with his life, are therefore the most important centres of pilgrimage. Included among these are the Buddha's *tooth relic at *Kandy and his footprints at Mt. Siripāda (both in *Sri Lanka). Places where a cutting from the *Bodhi Tree is believed to flourish, as in *Bodhgayā, are also revered. In *China the 'Five Peaks' are popular pilgrimage centres, and in *Japan the main centres of pilgrimage are Saikōku, where there are 33 temples dedicated to *Kannon, and the island of Shikōku, where there are 88 temples associated with the life of *Kukai (774–835).

Piṇḍola-Bhāradvāja. An *Arhat. He joined the Order (*Saṃgha) out of greed and carried a large bowl, which he kept under his bed at night. In due course he conquered his appetites and became an Arhat. He was once rebuked by the *Buddha for performing a miracle in *Rājagṛha, in the course of which he ascended into the air to retrieve a sandalwood bowl that had been placed on top of a high pole.

pirit. Sinhalese term for *paritta.

piśāca. A class of flesh-eating demons, similar to the *rākṣasa and *yakṣa.

piṭaka. *Sankskrit and *Pāli word meaning 'basket', and used as a technical term for the three main divisions of the Buddhist canon, namely the *Sūtra Piṭaka, *Vinaya Piṭaka, and *Abhidharma Piṭaka. In early *Buddhism, the term came to be applied collectively to the *Pāli Canon, the first division of which was into *Sūtra (Pāli, Sutta) and Vinaya only: these comprised the stock paragraphs learnt by heart, and the monastic rules. Independently of this we find the designation '*Dharma' (Pāli, Dhamma) applied to the doctrinal portions from which developed the Abhidhamma Piṭaka. Knowledge of the three Piṭakas is a highly regarded accomplishment for members of the Order (*Saṃgha) and those who master them are known by the title of 'tepīṭaka', literally meaning 'one who knows the three Piṭakas'.

piṭha (Skt.). A 'seat' or place of *pilgrimage associated with the *Mother class of *anuttara-yoga-tantras, probably derived from a similar concept in Hindu Śaivite *tantra. A basic group of four is mentioned: Jālandhara, *Oḍḍiyāna, Pūrṅagiri, and Kāmarūpa, to which others are sometimes added. As well as being places with geographical locations in *India, they are also linked to an internal spiritual geography.

Platform Sūtra of the Sixth Patriarch (Chin., *Liu-tsu t'an ching*). An early Chinese *Ch'an classic containing the traditional biography and teachings of *Hui-neng (638–713), a figure revered as the sixth *patriarch of the Chinese Ch'an school. The autobiographical sections, though unreliable as historical witness, tell us much about ideological struggles within early Ch'an. Hui-neng is portrayed as an illiterate woodcutter who attains a sudden awakening upon hearing some passages from the **Diamond Sūtra* chanted aloud from within a Buddhist temple. He travels to the East Mountain monastery to study with the traditional fifth patriach of the Ch'an tradition, *Hung-jen (601–74). Hung-jen disparages him as an ignorant southerner, to which Hui-neng replies that 'in *enlightenment there is no north or south'. Hung-jen puts him to work pounding rice in the monastery kitchen, but does not ordain him. Later, when Hung-jen felt it was time to bestow the mantle of sixth patriarch upon one of his followers, he ordered all his disciples to compose a verse to demonstrate the depth of their understanding. All of the disciples decide to let *Shen-hsiu (606–706) present a verse without competition, which he does after much hesitation. Hung-jen, upon hearing the verse, publicly praises it and assigns all of the *monks to recite it, but in private tells Shen-hsiu it is short of perfect understanding. Later, Hui-neng hears an acolyte reciting the poem, and realizes immediately how to correct it. He asks about it, and the acolyte tells him of the contest. He then asks the acolyte to take him to a hallway where a wall had been cleared and whitewashed so that a painter could paint scenes from the **Laṅkāvatāra Sūtra* upon it, and dictates his own verse to the acolyte. Hung-jen, hearing the verse, publicly disparages it, but dismisses the painter so as to leave the verse on the wall. Later that night, he calls Hui-neng to his room and privately gives him the robe (*see* cīvara) and bowl (*see* begging-bowl) of *Bodhidharma as a sign that he is the sixth patriarch, and tells him to escape lest the monks of East Mountain, jealous of this unordained stranger, do him harm.

This story appears to involve at least two currents of debate within the nascent Ch'an school. First, prior to that time the school had been known as the 'Laṅkāvatāra School', denoting its emphasis on the study of that scripture. Hui-neng's awakening upon hearing passages from the *Diamond Sūtra* and the manner in which his poem pre-empts the painting of scenes from the *Laṅkāvatāra Sūtra* appear to be part of an attempt to shift the school's emphasis from the long, disorganized, and eclectic *Laṅkāvatāra Sūtra* to the brief and clearly focused *Diamond Sūtra*. Second, the story of the poetry contest pits Hui-neng against Shen-hsiu, two monks who probably did not live at the East Mountain monastery at the same time. Shen-hsiu later became very famous at the imperial court and the paterfamilias of a lineage that came to be known as the '*Northern School', while Hui-neng is traditionally identified as the progenitor of the '*Southern School', which vied with the Northern School for supremacy in the *Northern–Southern School controversy. The story of the contest puts Shen-hsiu in a very unflattering light and purports to show that, despite Hung-jen's public approval of his senior disciple, in private he named Hui-neng as the true inheritor of his teaching and enlightenment.

The sermons which follow the autobiographical section deal with issues of practice and enlightenment, much of which is common to all Ch'an lineages and indeed to Chinese *Buddhism as a whole. The distinctively 'Southern' teachings have to do with practice envisioned as 'no-thought' (Chin., wu-nien) and the transmission of the 'formless *precepts' (Chin., wu-hsiang chieh). 'No-thought' means that, while in seated *meditation, the practitioner simply allows the mind to work naturally, and does not attempt to suppress any thoughts that might arise. This is based in Perfection of Insight (*Prajñā-pāramitā) thought that undercuts any distinction between the ignorant mind and the enlightened mind; simply to observe the workings of the ordinary mind is to observe directly the *Buddha's mind. This method, which conflates practice and attainment into a single moment, is the basis for teachings of '*sudden enlightenment', that is, enlightenment seen as instantaneous because there is nothing to attain and no goal to reach. This is obviously much easier than traditional forms of meditation that took much practice and discipline to tame the mind. It is interesting that, in his sermons, the supposedly illiterate Hui-neng quotes scriptures several times.

The 'formless precepts' as given in this text do not refer to any efforts to amend one's behaviour, but to do everything within the realization that one is manifesting perfect Buddhahood already. Certain sections of the text depict Hui-neng as if he were actually transmitting these vows to an assembled crowd, and after he pronounces the vows, contains rubrics such as 'recite the above three times', which leads some scholars to believe that these sections might have actually been used as *ordination texts. The origins of this text are obscure. That the East Mountain master Hung-jen had a disciple named Hui-neng is not in doubt, but beyond the mere appearance of his name in lists of Hung-jen's pupils, no other details of his life and teachings are known. The 'autobiographical' sections are certainly fictitious, and many of the teachings in the sermons repeat almost verbatim records of sermons preached by Hui-neng's disciple Shen-hui (670–762), the instigator and chief polemicist in the Northern–Southern School controversy. In spite of this, it is probably not merely Shen-hui's fabrication, as it contains much other material, some of which is disparaging of Shen-hui. The fact that the earliest extant manuscripts are much shorter than later versions shows that the text underwent some development after its initial composition in the late 8th or early 9th centuries, and some scholars have theorized that the *Oxhead school, a group that existed independently of the Northern and Southern Schools, may have had a hand in its composition in an effort to quell hostilities by presenting a moderate interpretation. The text remains remarkable in bearing the title '*sūtra', despite the fact that it does not report sermons of the Buddha, and in the manner in which it transcended its own contentious origins to become a classic beloved and studied by the Ch'an tradition as a whole.

Pŏmnang (fl. 632–46). Korean *monk who studied *Sŏn (*Ch'an/*Zen) *Buddhism in *China under the fourth *patriarch of the sect, *Tao-hsin (580–651). Pŏmnang is credited with introducing the Sŏn form of Buddhism to *Korea and establishing a lineage in the Silla kingdom.

Popsong jong. A school of Buddhist thought indigenous to *Korea. The name means 'school of dharma-nature', and it concentrated its study on the ultimate nature of phenomena (*dharmas) rather than their individual, distinguishing characteristics. In this vein, it focused primarily on the doctrines of the embryonic *Buddha (*tathāgata-garbha) and the storehouse consciousness (*ālaya-vijñāna). Its initial formation is credited to the Korean Buddhist scholar *Wŏnhyo (617–86).

poṣadha. *Sanskrit form of the *Pāli term *uposatha.

Poson. Festival celebrated in *Sri Lanka on the full moon of June. It commemorates the first arrival of *Buddhism in the island following the conversion of King *Devānampiya Tissa by *Mahinda, the *monk son of Emperor *Aśoka. *Anurādhapura and *Mihintale, where Mahinda met and converted the Sinhalese king, are the main sites for this celebration. During the festival, thousands of white-clad pilgrims climb the stairs to the summit of Mihintale.

Potala. The former residential palace of the *Dalai Lamas in *Lhasa. The palace was constructed by *Dalai Lama V from 1645 onwards on the site of an older palace built by the early Tibetan *Dharma king, *Songtsen Gampo.

poya. Sinhala term for *uposatha. Every poya day is treated as a holiday in *Sri Lanka, especially if it falls on a Friday or Monday.

prabhākarī-bhūmi (Skt.). The third of the ten *Bodhisattva Levels (*bhūmi), whose name means 'the Illumintaing One', according to the **Daśabhūmika Sūtra*. At this level the Bodhisattva accepts the non-arising of phenomena and cultivates the Perfection of Patience (*kṣānti-pāramitā).

pradakṣina (Skt.). The practice of *circumambulating a holy object, person or place. Locating the encircled object at the centre symbolizes its centrality in the lives of those who walk around it. The activity also represents integrity and cosmic harmony in mirroring natural phenomena such as the clockwise course the sun was believed to follow over the surface of the earth (*see* COSMOLOGY).

pragoya-mārga (Skt.). The 'path of preparation', the second of the five paths to Buddhahood (*see* PAÑCA-MĀRGA), in which the adept develops skill in meditation.

Prajñā. Name of an important Indian *monk. Originally from north-west *India he was later resident in *China at *Ch'ang-an during the mid-9th century CE where he translated the **Gaṇḍavyūha Sūtra*. He is also known to have met and befriended *Kūkai, the founder of the Japanese *Shingon school.

prajñā (Skt.). Important concept in Buddhist epistemology, often translated as 'wisdom' but closer in meaning to insight, discriminating knowledge, or intuitive apprehension. It is the faculty which apprehends the truth of Buddhist teachings. In the *Abhidharma it is classified as one of the mental functions (*caitta), and is defined as the analytical discrimination of phenomena (dharma-pravicaya). Although all beings possess prajñā, it is usually underdeveloped and needs to be cultivated through the practice of insight meditation (*vipaśyanā) or similar forms of mental training.

prajñā-pāramitā (Skt.). The Perfection of Insight, the last of the Six Perfections (*ṣaḍ-pāramitā) that make up the central element of the *Mahāyāna path. The cultivation of insight results in the direct realization of emptiness (*śūnyatā) and is regarded by many Mahāyāna texts, such as the *Prajñā-pāramita Sūtra* corpus, as the culmination of the *Bodhisattva's practice, although it is only the sixth (known as *abhimukhī-bhūmi) of the ten *Bodhisattva Levels (daśa-bhūmi). In older literature the term is translated somewhat inaccurately as the 'Perfection of Wisdom'.

Prajñā-pāramitā Sūtras. The 'Perfection of Insight' (Prajñā-pāramitā) *sūtras were composed over a long period, with the nucleus of the material appearing from 100 BCE to 100 CE, with additions for perhaps two centuries later. There followed a period of summary and restatement in the form of short *sūtras such as the **Diamond* and **Heart Sūtras*, *c.*300–500 CE, followed by a period of *tantric influence extending from 600 to 1200 CE. The oldest text is the **Aṣṭa-sāhasrikā-prajñā-pāramitā Sūtra* (The Perfection of Insight in Eight Thousand Lines). The place of origin of the Prajñā-pāramitā is disputed: the traditionally accepted area is south *India but there is evidence of its presence also in the north-west.

The Prajñā-pāramitā literature was innovative in two principal ways. First of all it advocates the *Bodhisattva ideal as the highest form of the religious life, and secondly the 'insight' (*prajñā) it teaches is into the emptiness (*śūnyatā) and non-production of phenomena (*dharmas), rather than into their substantial (albeit impermanent) mode of being as previously assumed. The scholar who pioneered research in this field, Edward *Conze, summarizes as follows: 'The thousands of lines of the Prajñā-pāramitā can be summed up in the following two sentences. 1) One should become a Bodhisattva (or Buddha-to-be), i.e. one who is content with nothing less than all-knowledge attained through the perfection of insight for the sake of all beings. 2) There is no such thing as a Bodhisattva or as all-knowledge or as a being or as the Perfection of Insight or as an attainment. To accept both these contradictory facts is to be perfect' (*The Prajñā-pāramitā Literature* (1978), 7–8 Tokyo: the Reiyukai). Other interesting developments in the Perfection of Insight literature are the concept of skilful means (*upāya-kauśalya) and the practice of dedicating one's religious merit (*puṇya) to others so that they may gain enlightenment (*bodhi).

Prajñaptivāda. Name of a subschool that broke away from the *Mahāsaṃghikas and which maintained that there is a distinction between reality, and the manner it is experienced by ordinary beings. The latter, it was believed, superimpose false designations (prajñapti) upon reality through language and conceptual thought. This form of nominalism was later adopted by *Mahāyāna Buddhists, especially those affiliated to the *Madhyamaka school, and led to the elaboration of the theory of the '*Two Truths'.

Prajñāruci. An Indian *monk active in *China during the Wei period (220–65 CE), whose work includes the *Liberation Vinaya* of the *Kāśyapīya school.

Prakrit (Skt., prākṛta). A term that denotes the 'natural' or vernacular languages of medieval *India in contrast to *Sanskrit. These languages were the forerunners of many modern north Indian languages such as Bengali and Oriya.

pramāṇa (Skt.). The Indian science concerned with epistemology as well as logic and the methods of *debate. As Buddhist scholars encountered and entered into polemical discussions with other Indian religious groups, it became necessary for them to standardize the rules and methods of debate. From this developed a formal system of logic based on syllogisms which was acceptable to all parties in order to decide the outcome of such debates. The earliest sources within *Buddhism for such rules seem to be found in portions of *Asaṅga's **Yogācārabhūmi Śāstra* and a work extant only in Chinese attributed to *Vasubandhu. These early works were followed by the epoch-making **Pramāṇa-samuccaya* of *Dignāga and the **Pramāṇa-varttika* of *Dharmakīrti. According to Buddhist pramāṇa tenets, there are only two valid and authoritative means of veridical cognition: direct perception (*pratyakṣa) based on the senses; and inference (*anumāṇa) based on rationality and logic. These two topics form the major concerns of Buddhist pramāṇa literature. Buddhist pramāṇa made a major impact on all other Indian schools of religious philosophy and its influence continued to be felt even after the demise of Buddhism in *India in the early medieval period. Though introduced into *China, it did not achieve any great popularity there whereas it has continued to be studied with considerable fervour among Tibetan Buddhist circles, especially by the *Gelukpas.

Pramāṇa-samuccaya. The seminal work on Buddhist logic and epistemology (*pramāṇa) composed in verse by *Dignāga. It comprises six chapters: (1) Direct Perception (*pratyakṣa); (2) Inference for One's Own Benefit (svārtha-anumāṇa); (3) Inference for Another's Benefit (parārtha-anumāṇa); (4) Examination of Examples (dṛṣṭānta-parīkṣa); (5) Examination of Exclusion of the Other (anya-apoha-parīkṣā); (6) Examination of Universals (jāti-parīkṣā). This work was extremely influential throughout *India, both within the Buddhist world and beyond, and its contents set the agenda for philosophical *debate for many centuries after it was written. Unfortunately, only a few fragments survive of the original *Sanskrit although a complete translation is available in Tibetan. The text was widely studied in *Tibet until the translation of *Dharmakīrti's **Pramāṇa-vārttika* superseded it in influence, except perhaps among the *Nyingma school.

pramāṇa-vāda (Skt.). General term for the school of logic and epistemology founded by *Dignāga (*c.*480–540). Famous exponents of the tradition include Dignāga's student *Dharmakīrti (*c.*530–600), Prajñākaragupta (*c.*850), *Śāntarakṣita (*c.*8th century), *Kamalaśīla (*c.*8th century), and Ratnakīrti (*c.*11th century). For the doctrines of the school, *see* PRAMĀṆA.

Pramāṇa-vārttika. An important work on Buddhist logic and epistemology (*pramāṇa) written in verse by *Dharmakīrti. It comprises four chapters: (1) Inference for One's Own Benefit (svārtha-anumāṇa); (2) Establishment of Valid Cognition (pramāṇa-siddhi); (3) Direct Perception (*pratyakṣa); and (4) Inference for Another's Benefit (parārtha-anumāṇa). Although purportedly written as a kind of commentary to *Dignāga's

**Pramāṇa-samuccaya*, the work actually redefines some of Dignāga's concepts and innovates with new theories designed to counter shortcomings that had been exposed in Dignāga's pramāṇa theories. A copy in the original *Sanskrit is extant as well as a translation in Tibetan. The work also has many associated commentaries and subcommentaries both of Indian and Tibetan composition, the latter due to the immense popularity of pramāṇa studies with the *Sakya and *Geluk schools. *See also* INDIA; TIBET.

pramuditā-bhūmi (Skt.). The first of the ten *Bodhisattva Levels (*bhūmi) whose name means 'the Joyful One', according to the **Daśabhūmika Sūtra*. At this level, the *Bodhisattva joyfully engages in the Perfection of Generosity (*dāna-pāramitā) and also gathers other beings to the *Dharma through the four 'means of attraction' (*saṃgraha-vastu).

pranidhāna (Skt.). The aspiration or resolution undertaken by a *Bodhisattva at the outset of his spiritual career. This resolution includes a vow to liberate all beings before he himself enters *nirvāṇa and leaves the world.

prapañca (Skt.). Term meaning 'proliferation', in the sense of the multiplication of erroneous concepts, ideas, and ideologies which obscure the true nature of reality. In terms of *Yogācāra thought, it is a general term for the false dualistic concepts (*vikalpa) which involve the erroneous division into perceiving subject and perceived objects. In this sense it is largely synonymous with *mano-jalpa.

Prāsaṅgika (Tib., thal-gyur-pa). One of the major schools of *Madhyamaka *Buddhism whose main representatives were *Buddhapālita and *Candrakīrti. These authors use a *reductio ad absurdum* method of argumentation (prasaṅga) to derive undesired consequences from the premises of their opponents. Through the works of these philosophers, most other forms of Buddhism were subjected to extreme criticism, especially the rival *Svātantrika–Madhyamaka and the *Yogācāra schools. This form of Madhyamaka is the most influential in Tibetan Buddhism, especially among the *Geluk school. It should be noted that the term itself is not attested in Indian Buddhist texts but has been created by modern scholars on the basis of the Tibetan exegetical term.

prasat. *Khmer term for a temple complex or central shrine.

Prasenajit. Name in *Sanskrit of King *Pasenadi.

Prātimokṣa (Pāli, Pāṭimokkha). Also referred to as the *Prātimokṣa Sūtra* (Pāli, *Pāṭimokkha Sutta)*, being a set of rules observed by members of the Buddhist Order (*Saṃgha). The derivation of the term is uncertain, perhaps 'that which should be made binding', or 'that which causes one to be released (from *suffering)'. The rules are contained in the Sūtra Vibhaṅga, the first division of the *Vinaya Piṭaka. The number of the rules slightly varies in each version of the Vinaya, be it *Theravāda, *Mahāsāmghika, *Mahīśāsaka, *Dharmaguptaka, *Sarvāstivādin, or *Mūla-sarvāstivādin. In the Theravāda Vinaya the rules for *monks number 227. Across all schools the rules for monks vary from 218 to 263, and for *nuns from 279 to 380. The rules are not all ethical and deal mainly with the behaviour of the members of the order in respects of food, clothes, dwellings, furniture, etc. The rules are arranged in eight sections, in decreasing degree of punishment and therefore roughly corresponding to the degree of importance attached to their observance. These are (1) *pārājika-dharmas (sexual intercourse, stealing, taking human life, lying about superhuman powers), the penalty for which is lifelong expulsion; (2) saṃghāvaśeṣa dharmas, involving temporary exclusion and probation; (3) aniyata dharmas, undetermined cases relating to sexual matters; (4) naiḥsargika-pāyantika dharmas, requiring expiation and forfeiture; (5) pāyantika-dharmas, requiring only expiation; (6) pratideśanīya dharmas, miscellaneous matters requiring only confession; (*pāpadeśanā) (7) śaikṣa dharmas, concerning matters of etiquette and deportment; (8) adhikaraṇa-śamatha dharmas, legalistic procedures for settling disputes. Besides the Prātimokṣa, the Sūtra Vibhaṅga contains an old commentary explaining the rules and a new commentary containing further supplementary information concerning them. The rules are divided into two sections: one for the monks (Bhikṣu-prātimokṣa) and the other for the nuns (Bhikṣunī-prātimokṣa).

The rules are recited at the gatherings of members of the order in their respective districts on *poṣadha (Pāli, uposatha) days (the fifteenth day of the half moon). After reciting each section of the rules, the reciter asks the members of the order who are present if any one of them has infringed any of the rules, if they have not they remain silent. The ceremony thus ensures the collective purity of the assembly.

pratisaṃkhyā-nirodha (Skt.). Literally, 'the cessation (*nirodha) that arises as a result of reflection'. The achievement of this is viewed as synonymous with *nirvāṇa. Pratisaṃkhyā-nirodha is classed as an unconditioned *dharma (*asaṃskṛta-dharma) by the *Sarvāstivāda and *Yogācāra schools.

pratiṣṭhita-nirvāṇa (Skt.). Literally 'localized nirvāṇa', or that form of *nirvāṇa, according to the *Mahāyāna, in which a *Buddha or other liberated being remains utterly separated or isolated from the world. Such an individual was identified with the post-mortem form of nirvāṇa known as *nirupadhiśeṣa-nirvāṇa. According to the Mahāyāna this was the inferior goal advocated by the *Hīnayāna, in contrast to the Mahāyāna ideal of 'unlocalized nirvāṇa' (*apratiṣṭhita-nirvāṇa).

pratītya-samutpāda (Skt; Pāli, paṭicca-samuppāda). The doctrine of Dependent Origination, a fundamental Buddhist teaching on causation and the ontological status of phenomena. The doctrine teaches that all phenomena arise in dependence on causes and conditions and lack intrinsic being. The doctrine is expressed in its simplest form in the phrase 'idaṃ sati ayaṃ bhavati' (Skt., when this exists, that arises), which can be expressed in the logical form A → B (when condition A exists, effect B arises), or as its negation –A → –B (where condition A does not exist, effect B does not arise). The important corollary of this teaching is that there is nothing that comes into being through its own power or volition, and there are therefore no entities or metaphysical realities such as *God or a soul, (*ātman) that transcend the causal nexus. In this respect the doctrine dovetails with the teaching of no self (*anātman). Early sources indicate that the *Buddha became enlightened under the *Bodhi Tree when he fully realized the profound truth of Dependent Origination, namely that all phenomena are conditioned (*saṃskṛta) and arise and cease in a determinate series.

There are various formulations of the doctrine in early sources, but the most common one illustrates the soteriological implications of causality in a series of twelve stages or links (*nidāna) showing how the problem of suffering (*duḥkha) and entrapment in *saṃsāra arises due to craving (*tṛṣṇā) and ignorance (*avidyā). The twelve links in the process (often depicted around the rim of the 'wheel of life' or *bhavacakra) are: (1) Ignorance (*avidyā); (2) Compositional Factors (*saṃskāra); (3) Consciousness (*vijñāna); (4) Name and Form (*nāma-rūpa); (5) Six Sense Spheres (*ṣad-āyatana); (6) Contact (*sparśa); (7) Feelings (*vedanā); (8) Craving (tṛṣṇā); (9) Grasping (*upādāna); (10) Becoming (*bhava); (11) Birth (*jāti); (12) Old Age and Death (*jarā-maraṇa). The significance of the links is open to interpretation, but one popular understanding is that of *Buddhaghoṣa in terms of which the series extends over three lives. Thus (1)–(2) relate to the previous life, (3)–(7) to the conditioning of the present existence, (8)–(10) to the fruits of the present existence, and (11)–(12) to the life to come. Various later schools came to their own, sometimes radical, understanding of the doctrine. Chief among these is that of the *Madhyamaka, for whom Dependent Origination came to be synonymous with emptiness (*śūnyatā). According to *Nāgārjuna, the doctrine of Dependent Origination could only be coherent if phenomena were devoid of self-essence (*svabhāva). If they enjoyed a more permanent mode of being, he argued, it would be impossible for them to be originated and cease to be in the way the doctrine describes.

pratyakṣa (Skt.). Direct sensory perception. According to Buddhist logic and epistemology (*pramāṇa) this, together with inference (*anumāṇa), forms the sole valid and authoritative means of knowledge.

pratyātma-adhigama (Skt.). Personal or immediate realization, understood as the direct experience of reality wherein the cognizer, the content of cognition, and the cognition are identical due to the absence of any dualistic split into subject and objects.

Pratyekabuddha (Skt.; Pāli, Paccekabuddha). A 'private' or 'solitary' *Buddha, one who remainins in seclusion and does not teach the *Dharma to others. In this way the Pratyekabuddha differs from the 'perfectly enlightened Buddha' or *samyak-saṃbuddha. The latter is thought superior by virtue of the compassionate concern that motivates him to teach the path to liberation to others. *Mahāyāna sources distinguish the Vehicle of the Pratyekabuddhas (*Pratyekabuddhayāna) as one of three different paths to salvation. The other two are the Vehicle of the Hearers (*Śrāvakayāna) as followed by the *Arhats, and the Vehicle of the Bodhisattvas (*Bodhisattvayāna), which is regarded as the highest.

Pratyekabuddhayāna (Skt.). The path, way, or 'vehicle' of the solitary Buddha. *See* PRATYEKABUDDHA.

Pratyutpanna Sūtra. The short title of the early *Mahāyāna *sūtra whose full name is the *Pratyutpanna-buddha-saṃmukha-avasthita-sāmadhi Sūtra*. The work describes a trance (*samādhi) which, when perfected, leads to a direct encounter with the *Buddhas of the present. It shares an interest in the *Pure Land and *Amitābha cults with other early Mahāyāna sūtras but is more akin to the **Prajñā-pāramitā Sūtra* corpus in its stress on emptiness (*śūnyatā) than faith-orientated sūtras like the **Sukhāvatī-vyūha Sūtra*. Certain features of its meditative practice are also suggestive of later *Yogācāra. The text only survives in four Chinese translations, the earliest done in 179 CE by *Lokakṣema, and Tibetan and Mongolian versions. The appearance of the work in *China is said to mark the origins of Pure Land practice (*see* PURE LAND SCHOOL, CHINA).

pravrajyā (Skt., going forth; Pāli, pabbajjā). The act of leaving the world and adopting an *ascetic lifestyle. It is the lower *ordination and the preliminary of the two stages by which one becomes a Buddhist *monk.

prayer. Prayer in the Christian sense of the acknowledgement of God as the source of all goodness is not found in *Buddhism since it does not believe in a creator-God. In general terms, it is *meditation rather than prayer that is recommended as the main spiritual practice of Buddhism. However, there are in Buddhism many religious practices which parallel those in theistic traditions, particularly at more popular levels of practice. Aspirational and petitional prayer is common, the latter particularly in *Mahāyāna Buddhism where it is directed towards *Buddhas and *Bodhisattvas. The recital of texts and *mantras is also an ancient and widespread practice, as is the counting of rosaries.

prayer flag. Associated with Tibetan *Buddhism (*see* TIBET), these are coloured squares of cloth printed with *mantras and images of Buddhist deities. They are attached to cords and hung up so that they may flutter in the wind. The movement is believed to 'activate' the power of the mantras and bestow protection and merit (*puṇya).

prayer wheel. Associated with Tibetan *Buddhism (*see* TIBET), this is a metal cylinder packed with printed sheets of *mantras that pivots on a spindle or handle. When rotated, it is believed that the power of the mantras is 'activated' and they bestow protection and merit (*puṇya). Prayer wheels are usually small hand-held objects, although larger wall-mounted ones are seen. Some prayer wheels in *Tibet were water-powered.

Fig 16 prayer wheel

precepts. *Buddhism has many sets of precepts, including the Five Precepts (*pañca-śīla), Eight Precepts (*aṣṭāṅga-śīla), Ten Precepts (*daśa-śīla), and Ten Good Deeds (*daśa-kuśala-karmapatha). Monastic precepts are set out in the *Prātimokṣa and *Vinaya. The precepts are understood not as commandments laid down by divine authority but injunctions derived from rational principles intended to promote human well-being.

preliminary practices (Tib., sngon-'gro). A set of preparatory practices undertaken by adherents of Tibetan *Buddhism to accumulate sufficient merit (*puṇya) to enable the practitioner to engage subsequently in *tantric practices. Though the set of practices is overall identical, each school of Buddhism in *Tibet follows its own specific tradition due to devotional and doctrinal differences. Typically, the preliminary practices comprise two parts, the ordinary and the extraordinary practices. The former includes *meditations on the precious human existence, impermanence (*anitya), the defects of *saṃsāra, the workings of *karma and the need for a spiritual guide or *guru. The extraordinary practices are suffused with a tantric approach and include the taking of refuge (*see* TRIŚARAṆA), generation of the aspiration to enlightenment (*bodhi), recitation of the *Vajrasattva *mantra, the offering of *maṇḍalas, and *guru *yoga. The extraordinary practices are done, usually in sequence, for a minimum of 100,000 times each.

preta (Skt.; Pāli, peta). 'Hungry ghosts', one of the miserable modes of existence in *saṃsāra. Various kinds of these spirits exist but all are subject to *suffering in the form of insatiable and unsatisfiable appetites as a punishment for greed and avarice in previous lives. *See also* BHAVACAKRA; GATI.

Protestant Buddhism. Term introduced by the scholar Gananath Obeyesekere referring to a phenomenon in Sinhalese *Buddhism having its roots in the latter half of the 19th century and caused by two sets of historical conditions: the activities of the Protestant missionaries and the close contact with the modern knowledge and technologies of the West. In 1815 the British become the first colonial power to win control over the whole of *Sri Lanka and signed the Kandyan convention declaring the Buddhist religion practised by the locals to be inviolable. This article was attacked by Protestant evangelicals in England and the British government felt obliged to dissociate itself from Buddhism. The traditional bond between Buddhism and the government of the Sinhala people had effectively dissolved while official policy favoured the activities of Protestant missionaries and the conversion to Christianity had become almost essential for those who wished to join the ruling élite. Leader of the movement that started as a result of these conditions was *Anagārika Dharmapāla. The movement can be seen both as a protest against the attacks on Buddhism by foreign missionaries and the adoption in the local Buddhism of features characteristic of Protestantism. In essence, Protestant Buddhism is a form of Buddhist revival which denies that only through the *Saṃgha can one seek or find salvation. Religion, as a consequence, is internalized. The layman is supposed to permeate his life with his religion and strive to make Buddhism permeate his whole society. Through printing laymen had, for the first time, access to Buddhist texts and could teach themselves *meditation. Accordingly, it was felt they could and should try to reach *nirvāṇa. As a consequence lay Buddhists became critical both of the traditional norms and of the monastic role.

pṛthagjana (Skt., ordinary person; Pāli, puthujjana). The man in the street; a 'worldling' or ordinary person, who may be a believer or non-believer. Defined doctrinally as one with worldly aspirations still bound by the ten fetters (*saṃyojana), in contrast to the Noble Persons (*ārya-pudgala) who have attained one of the *supermundane paths. In terms of the scheme of the five paths to Buddhahood (*pañca-mārga), a pṛthagjana is one who has not attained the third of the five paths, the 'path of seeing' (*darśaṇa-mārga).

Pubbārāma (Pāli). A park often mentioned in the *Pāli Canon as a place where the *Buddha often resided and spent his afternoons resting. It was located outside the eastern gate of the town of *Śrāvastī.

Pubbavideha (Pāli). One of the mythical four continents of ancient Buddhist *cosmology. It was said to be 7,000 leagues in extent and located to the east.

pudgala (Skt., person; Pāli, puggala). **1.** A person, in the everyday sense of an individual. **2.** The concept of personhood, particularly in the philosophical sense of an enduring self similar to (but not quite the same as) the eternal soul (*ātman), which *Buddhism denies. *See* PUDGALA-VĀDA.

pudgala-vāda (Skt., the doctrine of personhood). The heretical view that beings are endowed with a real 'self' (*pudgala). Although normative *Buddhism denies the reality of the eternal soul (*ātman), various groups in early Indian Buddhism, such as the *Vātsīputrīyas, felt the need to posit the existence of some kind of subsisting identity to act as the basis for *karma and *rebirth. The notion of the pudgala was evolved to fulfil this function. In terms of the standard Buddhist theory of personal identity set out in the doctrine of the five 'aggregates' (*skandha), the pudgala was said to be neither identical to the five skandhas nor different from them. The relationship between them was compared to that between fire (the pudgala) and its fuel (the skandhas). Although the pudgala-vāda position was eventually rejected, the question of karmic continuity was to persist throughout the centuries in *India and other solutions were suggested, among which the storehouse consciousness (*ālaya-vijñāna) and the embryonic *Buddha (*tathāgata-garbha) may be noted. Other schools which accepted the doctrine of the pudgala include the *Saṃmitīyas, Dharmottarīyas, Ṣaṇṇagarikas, and Bhadrāyanīyas.

Puggalapaññatti. 'The Designation of Persons', the fourth of the seven books of the *Abhidharma Piṭaka of the *Pāli Canon. As its name suggests, the work is concerned with the classification of human individuals whom it groups into types according to how many of between one and ten qualities they possess.

P'u Hua (d. 860). A *monk in the line of *Ma-tsu Tao-i (709–88) who is mentioned in the biography of *Lin-chi I-hsüan (d. 866) as one who helped the latter establish himself when he had just arrived at the Lin-chi Temple. He is remembered for his highly eccentric behaviour and lack of any fixed abode. The *Fuke school, founded in *Japan by Shinchi *Kakushin (1207–98), claimed to derive from P'u Hua ('Fuke' being the Japanese pronunciation of his name), and its adherents imitated the Chinese monk's peripatetic lifestyle, but any actual connection to P'u Hua is doubtful.

pūjā. A ritual of worship, offering or reverence. Many forms are known in Buddhist countries, ranging from a simple offering of flowers, incense, and chanting in *Theravādin countries to complex lengthy ceremonies in Tibetan forms of *Buddhism. The different kinds of pūjā may be performed in public or privately both by individuals and groups.

Pulatthinagara. Capital of *Sri Lanka during the medieval period. Also known as Pulatthi-pura, the city flourished between the 7th to the 14th centuries, and was captured at different times by Tamil and Cola forces from *India. It was recaptured by *Vijayabāhu I around 1070 who renamed it Vijayarājapura and constructed the temple of the *tooth relic to house a tooth believed to belong to the *Buddha. The city was looted around 1215 by forces from south India and was largely in decline from then on, with occasional periods of renaissance.

pulgyŏ. Korean term for *Buddhism. *See* KOREA.

punarbhava. *Pāli term meaning 'renewed becoming' which refers to the process of *rebirth or continued existence from one life to another and is thus synonymous with *saṃsāra. This process can only be ended by attaining *nirvāṇa.

puṇḍarīka (Skt.). A white lotus (*Nelumbo nucifera*), one of the major symbols used in *Buddhism. The lotus blossom is used widely iconographically as well as in literary works as a symbol of purity, for though its roots lie within the mud of a pool, its flower blooms above the water in untainted beauty. This particular species of lotus was also used medicinally in *India and has large edible roots. *See also* LOTUS.

puṇya (Skt.; Pāli, puñña). Term meaning 'merit', meritorious action', or 'virtue'. Sometimes also used to refer to the results or potential results of good *karma such as a heavenly *rebirth and a future blissful existence, the enjoyment and duration of which depends of the amount of merit accumulated in a previous life. *Pāli sources mention three factors known as puñña-kiriya-vatthūni (grounds of meritorious action) which produce merit: these are *dāna (generosity), sīla (Skt., *śīla, good conduct), and *bhāvanā (contemplation). *See also* PUṆYA-JÑĀNA-SAṂBHĀRA; PUṆYA-KṢETRA.

puṇya-jñāna-saṃbhāra (Skt.). The accumulation of merit and awareness. According to *Mahāyāna teachings, a being needs to accumulate sufficient stores of merit and awareness to progress along the path. Merit (*puṇya) is necessary to overcome defilements (*kleśa), and knowledge or awareness (*jñāna) to overcome ignorance (*avidyā). According to some interpretations of the Mahāyāna doctrine of the *Buddha's three bodies (*trikāya), it is merit that results in the *nirmāna-kāya and *saṃbhoga-kāya of a Buddha, while awareness results in the *dharma-kāya.

puṇya-kṣetra (Skt.; Pāli, puñña-khetta). A 'field of merit', being an individual or group that is a particularly worthy recipient of a gift. After a *Buddha, the greatest field of merit is said to be the monastic order (*Saṃgha), and gifts or donations made to monks, for example by providing food or offering cloth for *robes (*see* KAṬHINA), are believed to produce greater merit (*puṇya) than gifts to other recipients.

Pūraṇa Kassapa. One of the *Six Sectarian Teachers who was contemporary with the *Buddha. He held to the doctrine of akiriya-vāda, namely that good and bad actions have no consequences for the agent, a view that the Buddha strongly condemned as counter to the belief in *karma.

pure abodes. *See* SUDDHĀVĀSA.

Pure Land. The term 'Pure Land' is a Chinese invention, but it refers to a concept long known in *Buddhism under other names such as Buddha-land or Buddha-field (Skt., *Buddha-kṣetra). The idea arose in *India with the development of *Mahāyāna Buddhism, among whose innovations was the teaching that beings do not simply go into extinction upon the attainment of Buddhahood, but remain in the world to help others. Since they continue to exist, they must exist in a place, and since they are completely purified, their dwelling must also be completely pure. In some scriptures, such as the **Vimalakīrti-nirdeśa Sūtra*, this did not imply the existence of a separate realm distinct from that in which unenlightened beings dwelt, but was this very world of *suffering. Its purity derived from the fact that the *Buddhas saw its true nature, which was pure, whereas other beings saw it through the lens of their delusion, which rendered it impure. However, another strain of thought did assign different realms to different Buddhas, and in time several of the more prominent Buddhas received Pure Lands with names and definite locations: to the west, the Buddha *Amitābha dwelt in the land of *Sukhāvatī, while to the east, the Buddha *Akṣobhya presided over *Abhirati. Within the esoteric tradition (*see* ESOTERIC BUDDHISM), these lands and their directions became part of maps of the cosmos known as *maṇḍalas. Despite the specificity of their locations and features, however, these lands were seen as outside of *saṃsāra, and were thus not to be confused with the '*heavens', the realms of the popular gods (*deva) derived from Hindu mythology.

In India, the composition of the classic 'Pure Land Scriptures' (such as the *Longer* and *Shorter *Sukhāvatī-vyūha Sūtras*) helped to popularize the idea that the Buddhas who dwelt in these Pure Lands could bring unenlightened beings into them for teaching without compromising the purity of the environs. In *China, the rise of the *Pure Land school popularized this idea, and spurred many centuries of theoretical accounts of the nature of the Pure Lands, and the genesis of typologies that sought to classify the various types of Pure Lands. For example, the thinker *Ching-ying Hui-yüan (523–92) identified three different types of Pure Land, depending upon the beings that dwell in them or attain their vision: (1) the phenomenal Pure Land where unenlightened beings go which, while purified by the Buddha's presence, still presents itself to their minds according to their desires; (2) the Pure Land with characteristics, which accommodates those who achieved enlightenment (*bodhi) following the *Hīnayāna path and Mahāyāna followers in the early stages of practice; and (3) the true Pure Land, achieved by accomplished *Bodhisattvas on the Mahāyāna path. This latter type had further subdivisions into lands of Bodhisattvas and lands of Buddhas, with the latter further categorized into two aspects: the land as it appears to the Buddha residing in it, and the way he manifests it to other beings.

The *T'ien-t'ai school of China established a four fold typology of both pure and impure lands. (1) 'Lands where the holy ones and ordinary beings dwell together' indicated impure lands where Buddhas appear in order to teach. (2) 'Lands of skilful means with remainder' pointed to lands inhabited by Hīnayāna adepts who had taken the path of skilful means in which teachings were adapted to their capacities rather than expressed directly. They had escaped saṃsāra, and so this realm is outside the ordinary realms of *rebirth and represents a true liberation, but the inhabitants still have more to learn. (3) 'Lands of true recompense without obstruction' are attained by those Mahāyāna Bodhisattvas who have achieved a direct vision of the truth. (4) Finally, the 'Land of eternally quiescent light' is the destination of perfected Buddhas and is free of all defining characteristics and dualisms, and so manifests only quiescence and peace, with nothing to fix the mind upon.

Within the Pure Land movement in China, another issue was whether the particular manner in which Sukhāvatī, the Pure Land of the Buddha Amitābha, manifests is due to the *karma of the Buddha or of the unenlightened beings whom he draws into his land after their death. In part, the answer to this question depended upon correlating the Pure Land with one of the three bodies (*trikāya) of a Buddha. Early Pure Land masters regarded Sukhāvatī as corresponding to a Buddha's Emanation Body (*nirmāṇa-kāya), which meant that the Buddha emanated it as a teaching device for the worldlings who entered it; its appearance did not reflect the enlightened vision of its Buddha. Breaking with this view, the master *Tao-ch'o (562–645) held that it was a 'reward-land' corresponding to the Buddha's Enjoyment Body (*saṃbhoga-kāya), which implied that the appearance of the land did indeed correspond to the Buddha's own level of realization, and was not adapted to the inferior capacities of worldlings. Logically, the third body, the Truth Body (*dharma-kāya), would have corresponded to something like the land of eternally quiescent light referred to above, but Tao-ch'o denied that such a thing existed: being a complete vision of the final nature of all reality, it could not be separated from impure phenomena or localized in any way, and so such a land could not be identified anywhere. The above is a sampling of some of the reflections of Chinese masters on the nature of Pure Lands in general, and Sukhāvatī in particular. There were other issues upon which various writers disagreed, such as whether or not Pure Lands exist within the 'Triple World', and how to think of Pure Lands using the dyadic notions of 'principle' (Chin., li) and 'phenomena' (Chin., shih) that became popular later. All of these issues yielded a richly textured body of literature explaining the nature of Pure Lands.

Pure Land school, China. Strictly speaking, there is no Pure Land 'school' in *China. Although one may speak of specific teaching lineages and social or religious movements at various points in Chinese history, there has never existed a unified school with a geographically located headquarters (such as *T'ien-t'ai), a set of standard scriptures and commentaries (such as *San-lun), or single, continuous lineage of masters and disciples (such as *Ch'an or *esoteric *Buddhism). The two main sources for positing any unity to this mode of belief and practice are (1) the belief that a *Buddha named *Amitābha vowed prior to his attainment of Buddhahood that, as a condition of his achievement of perfect enlightenment (*saṃbodhi), he would create a Pure Land to which unenlightened beings could come for instruction, practice, and enlightenment; and (2) a line of thirteen *patriarchs (Chin., tsu) who, at various times, reinvigorated or provided a credible apologia for the tradition. However, unlike Ch'an and *esoteric lineages, this line does not consist of masters and disciples, nor are its members contiguous in time or region of activity; rather the list itself is the result of a later reconstitution of the tradition, and it omits several significant Pure Land thinkers. In China, this school is sometimes also referred to as the 'Lotus School' (Chin., Lien tsung).

Recent scholarship has shown that, even in *India during the early years of the development of *Mahāyāna *Buddhism, the idea took root that Buddhas, rather than simply going into extinction, remained active in the world to help beings still trapped in suffering. This being the case, it followed that the environments in which they dwelt must reflect the purity of their own wisdom, and thus the idea of the 'Buddha-land' or 'Buddha-field (Skt., *Buddha-kṣetra) came into being. Somewhat later, one particular Buddha, Amitābha, came to predominate in popular consciousness, and his Buddha-land, called *Sukhāvatī, the 'Land of Bliss', became a destination to which even ordinary beings could aspire. According to the *Longer* and *Shorter* **Sukhāvatī-vyūha Sūtras*, this Buddha, while still a *Bodhisattva, made a series of vows including one which said that he would not enter into final Buddhahood unless he brought into being a 'Pure Land' to which all could come if they but heard and recollected his name. With the popularization of these texts, devotees came to believe that, through faith (*śraddhā) in Amitābha's vow, they could come into his Pure Land without first becoming pure and enlightened themselves, and, once there, they would have a perfect instructor in the person of the Buddha, and ideal conditions for study, practice, and enlightenment. Several significant Indian Buddhist thinkers, such as *Nāgārjuna, *Vasubandhu, and *Aśvaghoṣa, contributed to the systematization of this mythologem into theological form.

The first appearance of Amitābha-centred thought and practice in China came in 179, when *Lokakṣema produced a translation of the **Pratyutpanna Sūtra*, a work that extolled the value of a type of *meditation which would cause all the Buddhas to appear before the practitioner. In one brief passage, this work states that the practitioner should be aware that Amitābha dwells in the land of Sukhāvatī many millions of Buddha-lands off to the west, and that, by simply calling him to mind, the practitioner can attain a vision of him and all the Buddhas of the present cosmos. Although Amitābha practice receives only this brief mention, and although the goal of the practice is a vision of the Buddha in this life rather than *rebirth in Sukhāvatī after death, the appearance of this work is counted as the first appearance of Pure Land belief in China, and provided the textual basis for the first instance of organized Pure Land practice.

Based on this text, in the year 402 the *monk *Lu-shan Hui-yüan (334–416) gathered together a group of 123 clergy and local literati in the Tung Lin Temple (in modern Chiang-hsi Province) where he resided, where they all practised this *visualization of Amitābha together, with the intention of gaining rebirth in Sukhāvatī. The emphasis of their practice was very much on visualization, not on oral repetition of the Buddha's name, and Hui-yüan corresponded with the Kuchean monk and translator *Kumārajīva (343–413) on a number of points, including the nature of the image of the Amitābha seen in one's dreams. The group that Hui-yüan formed came in later centuries to be known as the White Lotus Society (Chin., Pai-lien she), and Hui-yüan himself was later placed first on the list of Pure Land patriarchs.

Subsequent developments took place in the north central part of China, around the imperial capitals of *Ch'ang-an and *Lo-yang. The appearance of translations of the scriptures that were to become known as the three Pure Land sūtras (the *Longer* and *Shorter Sukhāvatī-vyūha Sūtras* and the *Meditation Sūtra*) provided a fuller recounting of the Pure Land mythos of Amitābha Buddha, his Pure Land, and his vows, providing the basis for new accountings of Pure Land theology and practice. The master *T'an-luan (476–542), frightened by a serious illness, left behind the conventional life of the monk-scholar and devoted himself to the oral invocation of Amitābha's name as a means of gaining rebirth, based upon the record of the 48 vows of the Buddha as recorded in the *Longer Sukhāvatī-vyūha Sūtra*. He also devoted himself to teaching others to follow this practice, and so became one of the first popularizers of the method of Nien-fo (Buddha-recitation). Another master, *Tao-ch'o (562–645), discouraged by the turmoil of the *Northern and Southern dynasties period, counselled people to recite the Buddha's name as much as possible as a way of purifying the mind, and instructed them to use beans as counters. He wrote a commentary on the *Meditation Sūtra* called the *An-lo chi* (Collection of Ease and Bliss) that included an anthology of scriptural passages supporting the efficacy of the practice and defending it against its detractors. His disciple *Shan-tao (613–81) also wrote in support of the oral recitation of the Buddha's name and composed a number of liturgical works for societies formed to practise together, but he devoted his intellectual energy to composing a commentary on the *Meditation*

Sūtra, a work which teaches a complex set of difficult visualizations as a means of attaining a vision of Amitābha in this life, and advocated 'auxiliary practices' to be done in combination with the 'true practice' of chanting the name. These three masters and their successors formed the leadership for a Pure Land movement concentrated in the north that devoted itself more or less exclusively to Pure Land practice.

There were other streams of Pure Land thought outside of this movement as masters identified with other schools sought to incorporate Pure Land practice and the Pure Land mythos into a wider set of doctrinal and practical options. For example, *Chih-i (538–97), the founder of the *T'ien-t'ai school, included meditative practices aimed at the visualization of Amitābha in this life and rebirth in the Pure Land in the afterlife within his encyclopedia of meditation, the *Mo-ho chih-kuan* (Great Calming and Insight). In this work, Pure Land practice was very demanding and exhausting: the practitioner, after initial purifications and consecration, was to repair to a specially assembled room with an image of Amitābha in the centre, and was to circumambulate it for 90 days without stopping, sitting, or sleeping. Other masters outside of the Pure Land 'school' wrote commentaries on the three Pure Land sūtras as part of their overall scholarly programme: Chih-i, the San-lun master *Chi-tsang (549–623), and *Ching-ying Hui-yüan (523–92; not to be confused with Lu-shan Hui-yüan), among others, also composed commentaries on the *Meditation Sūtra* that often differed significantly with commentaries written within the movement (such as that of *Shan-tao) on many important points: whether the appearance of the Pure Land was an expedient means devised by Amitābha for the benefit of impure beings or whether it reflected his own enlightened nature; whether the Amitābha seen in visualization was a manifestation of his Emanation Body (*nirmāṇa-kāya) or his Enjoyment Body (*saṃbhoga-kāya); whether the activity of visualization was phenomenal (Chin., shih) or noumenal (Chin., li); and so on.

Many Pure Land thinkers in China devoted themselves to the task of apologetics. The central claim of Pure Land thought—that beings could escape from saṃsāra and dwell in a purified Buddha-land without becoming either pure or enlightened themselves—offended the sensibilities of many Buddhists. Many critics argued, following the **Platform Sūtra* and the **Vimalakīrti-nirdeśa Sūtra*, that to posit a Pure Land over against the present, impure world, and a Buddha who literally existed outside of the practitioner's own mind, constituted an impermissible dualism when seen in light of the teaching of emptiness (*śūnyatā). They argued that the Pure Land is nothing more than the present world of suffering seen correctly, and the Buddha was only the practitioner's own mind free of all misconceptions. Later controversial literature labelled this position 'Mind-Only Pure Land' (Chin., wei hsin ching-t'u).

To this, many Pure Land apologists, ranging from Tao-ch'o and *Tz'u-min Hui-jih (680–748) in the early period to later figures such as (*Yün-ch'i) Chu-hung (1535–1615), *Yüan Hung-tao (1568–1610), Ch'o-wu (1741–1810), and *Yin-kuang (1861–1940) replied that such a critique was circular. To criticize unenlightened beings for not having an enlightened view of the world only castigated them for not being enlightened before achieving enlightenment (*bodhi), a criticism that was self-contradictory. They explained that Pure Land teachings were compassionately given by the Buddha for people in this world of suffering who did not have the time, inclination, or talent for the strenuous and uncertain path to the attainment of enlightenment in this world. Once reborn in the Pure Land, they would have perfect conditions for the attainment of enlightenment, at which point they would come to the realization that the Pure Land really was only the world of suffering seen correctly. For the time being, however, they needed expedient teachings that, though admittedly dualistic, would nevertheless lead them skilfully to the goal. This position, which left room for a literal reading of the Pure Land myth as the way things really are, came to be characterized as 'Western Direction Pure Land' (Chin., hsi fang ching-t'u).

As scholars have long observed, after the persecution of 845, only a few schools of Buddhism remained viable in China: *Ch'an and Pure Land because of their portability and independence from economic and political centres of power, and T'ien-t'ai because of its ongoing identification with a central headquarters. During the Sung dynasty (960–1279) some new developments took place in Pure Land thought and practice. In terms of social movements, one sees the first appearance of large-scale Buddha-recitation societies boasting thousands of members, most of which were formed under the auspices of T'ien-t'ai masters working along the southeastern seaboard of Kiangsu and Chekiang provinces. Other developments took place in the interaction of Pure Land and other styles of cultivation. The master Yüng-ming Yen-shou (904–75) attempted to harmonize Pure Land with other Buddhist schools of thought such as Ch'an into a system in which both could be cultivated without contradiction; this came to be known as the 'joint practice of Ch'an and Pure Land' (Chin., ch'an-ching shuang-hsiu). The main manifestation of this 'joint practice' was the so-called Nien-fo kung-an (Jap., *Nembutsu *kōan), advocated by Chung-fang Ming-pen (1262–1323), T'ien-ju Wei-tse (14th century), and Chu-hung. The practitioner, while reciting Amitābha's name, would periodically stop and consider the kōan, 'Who is this who is reciting the Buddha's name?'

Other masters, however, resisted this syncretism, insisting on maintaining the integrity of Pure Land practice. *Yin-kuang, for example, decried any 'psychological' reading of Pure Land thought and forcefully defended the literal existence of the Pure Land and the self-sufficiency of Pure Land practice done without resort to kōan practice or any other extraneous method. While all defenders of Pure Land practice in China have accepted its characterization as an 'easy path' opposed to the 'difficult path' of conventional Buddhist practices, one must understand that the practice as envisaged by these Chinese masters was far from easy. In contrast to the Pure Land school in *Japan, which at its extreme held that a single utterance of Amitābha's name sufficed to assure rebirth in the Pure Land, the Chinese tradition always saw it as a constant striving for a purity of mind and an attunement with the Pure Land and its Buddha. As Ch'o-wu wrote, speaking for the tradition as a whole, Pure Land practice, whether seen as a complex practice of meditative visualization or simple repetition of the Buddha's name, has purification of the mind as its goal. However, the mind is constantly changing: an instant of verbal repetition of the name purifies the mind completely in that instant, but a return to worldly thought in the next instant defiles it once again. The point of Tao-ch'o's use of beans as counters and the later use of rosaries was to encourage practitioners to constancy of repetition in order to keep the mind pure at all times. In addition, visualization and repetition both served to harmonize the practitioner's mind with that of the Buddha in order to create karmic links with Sukhāvatī so as to strengthen the likelihood of achieving rebirth there. The ultimate goal was to have the mind focused on Amitābha and the Pure Land at the critical moment of death; distraction at that instant could nullify the results of years of faithful recitation of the name and cause one to veer back into saṃsāra. Thus, constant practice was necessary in order to make it more and more likely that one's mind, fortified by habituation, would be unshakably attuned to the Pure Land right at the point of death.

Since the Sung dynasty, Pure Land practice has not been the province of any single Pure Land school, despite the acknowledgement of a central line of patriarchs. With very few exceptions, Chinese Buddhists accept that the chances of attaining enlightenment so complete that it guarantees one an exit from saṃsāra at the end of this life through the unaided strength of one's own practice are very slim, and that one must have Pure Land practice and the hope of rebirth in Sukhāvatī as a kind of insurance policy, regardless of what other practices or studies one does. Thus, Pure Land thought and practice pervades all of Chinese Buddhism as foundation and guarantor of the path one treads towards Buddhahood.

Pure Land school, Japan. This term refers to a number of sects of *Buddhism rather than a single school, of which the most important are the *Jōdo Shū founded by *Hōnen (1133–1212), the *Jōdo Shinshū founded by *Shinran (1173–1262), the *Jishū founded by *Ippen (1239–89), and the *Yūzū-nembutsu school founded by *Ryōnin (1072–1132). While all of these schools established themselves as independent organizations during the *Kamakura period and after, the general complex of *Pure Land thought and practice had actually existed in *Japan for some centuries already. The *monk *Saichō (767–822) founded the *Tendai school after travelling to *China with the express intention of bringing the teachings and practices of the Chinese *T'ien-t'ai school home. The T'ien-t'ai school was a repository and transmitter of a great number of meditative techniques, among which were some directed towards *Amitābha and his Pure Land *Sukhāvatī. Because of this, Pure Land writings and practices derived from the Chinese T'ien-t'ai school came into Japan and during the early 9th century and were preserved and studied within that school thereafter. A further advance in the Tendai tradition of Pure Land practice came with the publication of the **Ōjōyōshū* by the monk *Genshin (942–1017). The dissemination of this work had two important effects. First, it represents the introduction into Tendai Pure Land thought of the formulations of the Chinese master *Shan-tao (613–81), who popularized oral invocation of the *Buddha Amitābha's name among the masses with the intention of gaining *rebirth in the Pure Land after *death. Second, the book consisted of all known passages relating to this Buddha and his Pure Land in Sinitic Buddhist scriptures and treatises, and so helped to make the study and defence of Pure Land thought much more convenient than it might otherwise have been. In this second respect, its influence cannot be overestimated: not only has it remained a popular book for the study of Pure Land in Japan down to modern times, it was also one of the few Japanese Buddhist works to be exported back to China and achieve influential status. In Genshin's time, its appearance raised the visibility of Pure Land within the Tendai school, and inspired even clerics of other schools to adopt Pure Land practice. Besides Genshin, one other pre-Kamakura Pure Land figure deserves mention. The monk *Kūya (903–72) was one of the first to spread Pure Land practices among the common people, and is widely recognized as the first of the Pure Land *hijiri, or wandering holy men. Born into an aristocratic family (or the imperial family itself, according to some legends), he left household life in his youth and received the novice's *ordination at the Owari Provincial temple at the age of 20. After a period of study, he took to the road, chanting Amitābha's name ceaselessly while beating a gong, and preaching the virtues of orally invoking the Buddha's name to all and sundry. He distributed the alms he collected among the poor, preached in prisons, smoothed roads, buried abandoned corpses, dug wells, and built bridges as well. Because of his devotion to Pure Land practice, his itinerant lifestyle, and his dedication to the common people, he because the model for later *Amida hijiri. He took full ordination in the Tendai school later in life, but retained his novice name of Kūya and continued his activities for the remainder of his life.

As can be seen, the Tendai school was the incubator for Pure Land thought and practice, both scholastically oriented and popularizing. It is little wonder, then, that the figures mentioned at the beginning of this entry came out of the Tendai school to establish their own schools of Pure Land Buddhism. However, during this early phase, Pure Land did not stand alone. Genshin composed many other works and commentaries on non-Pure Land topics, and, as seen above, Kūya engaged in other practices besides the invocation of Amitābha. For these men, Pure Land was simply an emphasis, not an independent practice. During the early Kamakura, many movements arose that sought to simplify Buddhism to a single practice and to spread it among the masses: *Zen, *Nichiren, and Pure Land. The great difference between the founders of the Pure Land schools and these early Pure Land figures lies in the great pessimism that the founders had with regard to the human capacity to achieve enlightenment (*bodhi) and bring an end to *suffering. Seeing the times as too corrupt and human frailty as too great to hold any hope of liberation, they settled on *nembutsu, or oral invocation of Amitābha's name, as the only practice by which one might have a realistic chance of ending suffering, and on this basis they established groups dedicated to the exclusive practice of the nembutsu, groups which evolved into the main Pure Land schools listed above. For the theology and subsequent history of these schools, the reader is referred to the individual entries. Since the founding of these schools, Pure Land has gone on to become the dominant mode of Buddhist practice in Japan among both lay and clerical devotees, and the Jōdo Shinshū has become the largest and most economically powerful of the Buddhist schools.

Pure Rules. A genre of *Ch'an and *Zen literature, rendered 'ch'ing-kuei' in Chinese and 'shingi' in Japanese. Drawing on a work (no longer extant) called *Pai-chang ch'ing-kuei*, or 'Pure Rules of Pai-chang', a work attributed to the *T'ang dynasty Ch'an master *Pai-chang Huai-hai (749–814), this class of literature sets forth the 'house rules' of individual Ch'an and Zen temples. Such literature was usually composed by the founding abbot of a monastery, and encapsulated his vision for the life of the *monks residing therein. As such, this literature could be quite heterogeneous: in some instances it takes the form of a breviary, giving the liturgies for various annual services, and in others, it sets up procedures for the monks' daily routine; in others it establishes the number and kind of administrative officers and specifies their duties; in still others (such as *Dōgen's *Eihei shingi*) it consists also of essays intended to exhort the monks to vigorous practice. While this genre has been seen as a characteristic form of Ch'an or Zen literature in the past, recent scholarship has shown that extant examples from the earliest period drew heavily not only from the traditional Indian *Vinaya, but also from rules of Chinese *T'ien-t'ai monasteries, casting some doubt on its uniquely 'Ch'an' character.

Pu-tai (10th c.). A *Ch'an *monk of the Five Dynasties period (907–60) of whom very little is known but whose image has become very famous. His name means 'cloth bag', and derives from the cloth bundle that he carried on the end of his staff. Traditional sources describe him as very fat and of unrefined and free speech. One story relates that he kept small pastries and sweets in his bag, which he would give to children; as his supply gave out, he would beg money in order to buy more. Later Chinese tradition identified him as a manifestation of the *Bodhisattva *Maitreya, the future *Buddha. His image—fat, jolly, with robe hanging open exposing his considerable bulk—has become widely recognized as the 'laughing Buddha' seen in many homes and businesses. It is popularly believed that rubbing his stomach brings good fortune. *See also* HŌTEI.

P'u-t'i-ta-mo. The Chinese rendering of the name of the first *patriarch of *Ch'an, the Indian *monk *Bodhidharma. *See also* DARUMA.

P'u-t'o, Mt. *See* P'U-T'O-SHAN.

P'u-t'o-shan. A mountainous island of approximately 48 square miles situated over 62 miles east of the coast of Chekiang province that has long been popular as a *pilgrimage site for Chinese Buddhists, and is traditionally counted as part of the list of either three or four great mountains of the Chinese Buddhist landscape. Its success as a centre for the worship (*pūjā) of the *Bodhisattva *Kuan-yin arose from its geography. In the **Hua-yen ching*, as the youth Sudhana travels from one site to another seeking teachings from great masters, he calls on the Bodhisattva at his residence on Mt. Potalaka, a mountainous island rising alone from the 'end of the sea'. P'u-t'o-shan, similarly situated, offered an earthly analogue, and became a site where many visitors sought and received visions of the Bodhisattva. In the course of the *T'ang (618–907) and Sung (960–1279) dynasties, the island's originally *Taoist identification gradually gave way to a new Buddhist identity, and economic expansion in the area of Ningpo, the nearest coastal seaport, supported an ever-larger body of pilgrims willing to make the five-day voyage to see it. In time, it became the pre-eminent site for Kuan-yin devotion in *China. The island houses several Buddhist monasteries and natural formations connected with Buddhist legends, all of which have undergone periods of popularity, destruction, and rebuilding.

Q

question and answer. *See* MONDO.

Questions of King Milinda. *See* *MILINDA-PAÑHA.*

R

raft parable. Often-cited parable that occurs in the *Discourse on the Parable of the Water Snake* (*Alagaddūpama Sutta*) in the *Majjhima Nikāya of the *Pāli Canon. The parable relates to a traveller who fords a stream by paddling across using a coracle or raft, and the *Buddha asks whether it would be appropriate or not for the man to carry the raft with him once he had crossed. The parable is often thought to mean that the body of Buddhist teachings and moral *precepts have only provisional utility as a means to gaining enlightenment (*bodhi) and can thereafter be discarded. A more careful reading of the passage shows, however, that its meaning is not that the teachings themselves are to abandoned en bloc but simply that certain teachings may on occasion be misunderstood or abused.

rāga. Craving or strong *desire, the first of the three roots of evil (*akuśala-mūla). *See also* TṚṢṆĀ; LOBHA.

Rāhula. The only child of the *Buddha, born shortly before the Buddha took his decision to renounce the world. The boy was named Rāhula, which means 'fetter', because the Buddha perceived his son's birth as a tie that could bind him to family life and, according to some sources, therefore left home on the very same day. After his enlightenment (*bodhi), the Buddha returned to his home town of *Kapilavastu and on departing was followed by Rāhula, who had been sent by his mother to 'ask for his inheritance'. At the request of the Buddha, Rāhula was then admitted to the *Saṃgha by *Śāriputra. Following a protest by the boy's grandfather *Śuddhodana, the Buddha agreed to the introduction of a rule thereafter requiring parental consent to the *ordination of novices (*śrāmaṇera). The Buddha preached several sermons to his son, and after hearing one of these, the *Cūla-Rāhulovāda Sutta*, he became an *Arhat.

Rāhulabhadra. The legendary sixteenth *patriarch of *Ch'an *Buddhism.

Rāhulamātā (Pāli, mother of Rāhula). Name generally used in the *Pāli Canon for the mother of *Rāhula and wife of the *Buddha. There appears to be a confusion of names in the sources, and the later ones refer to her as Bhaddakaccā, *Yasodharā, Bimbādevī, or Bimbāsundarī. According to the *Jātakas, she married the Buddha when they were both aged 16. Their son, Rāhula, was born when the Buddha was 29 years old, and the Buddha left home that very day. When he returned to *Kapilavastu after his awakening, he learnt from his father that his wife had adopted the same yellow robes (*cīvara) and lifestyle of an *ascetic.

Rājagṛha (Skt.; Pāli, Rājagaha). The capital of *Magadha until the end of the *Haryaṅka dynasty. Built by King *Bimbisāra, the town was in a valley, surrounded by seven hills, the most famous of which is *Vulture's Peak (Gṛdhrakūṭa). The town was visited on numerous occasions by the *Buddha, who formed a lifelong friendship with Bimbisāra. The king donated the adjacent parkland of *Veluvana to the Order (*Saṃgha). While staying in Rājagṛha, the Buddha recruited a number of his foremost disciples, including *Śāriputra and *Mahākāśyapa. With the transference of the Magadhan capital to *Pāṭaliputra, the importance of Rājagṛha faded and it was in virtual ruins by the 7th century when it was visited by the Chinese pilgrim *Hsüan-tsang.

rakṣasa (Skt.). In Buddhist mythology, a class of evil flesh-eating demons who also cause sickness and misfortune.

Rāmañña. *Pāli name for the *Mon territories on the southern coast of present-day *Burma.

rang-dong. *See* INTRINSIC EMPTINESS.

rasanā (Skt.). In *tantric mystical physiology, the channel (*nāḍī) to the left of the *avadhūti or central channel, which starts in the left-hand nostril and terminates at the genitals. It is visualized as a fine white tube and the energy (*vāyu) flowing through it is thought to generate the objective aspect of cognition. Like the *lalanā, the right-hand channel, it is believed to coil around the avadhūti and form knots at the mystic centres (*cakras) of the navel, heart, throat, and the crown of the head.

Ratnagiri. A major Buddhist monastic centre located in the Asia Hills near Cuttack in present-day Orissa. The centre dates from the 5th century CE and formed part of a complex of monastic settlements with Udayagiri and Lalitagiri. A number of great *Mahāyāna and *tantric masters are associated with Ratnagiri such as *Dignāga and *Nāropa. It also seems to have survived longer than the other great Buddhist centres such as *Nālandā and thus was a last refuge for many Buddhist scholars after the 12th century. Excavation of the extensive ruins have also yielded a wealth of sculptural treasures which indicate that Ratnagiri and its neighbouring establishments were important centres for the development and practice of tantric *Buddhism.

Ratna-gotra-vibhāga. A key text in five chapters associated with *Tathāgata-garbha (embryonic *Buddha) thought, also known as the *Uttara-tantra*, comprising verses and a prose commentary which includes substantial quotations from Tathāgata-garbha orientated *sūtras. As well as an extant *Sanskrit original, versions also exist in Chinese and Tibetan. The text is attributed to a *Sthiramati or Sāramati in the earlier Chinese tradition, while the Tibetan tradition considers the verse portion to have been composed by *Maitreyanātha and the prose commentary by *Asaṅga. Apart from the small group of so-called Tathāgata-garbha sūtras, this work is the cornerstone of the Tathāgata-garbha trend of thought in *Mahāyāna *Buddhism.

Ratnākaraśānti (11–12th c.). Also known as Śānti, a philosopher in the *pramāṇa-vāda tradition of logic and epistemology who attempted to systematize various strands of *Madhyamaka and late medieval Indian Buddhist thought. He was a pupil of Ratnakīrti and wrote commentaries on the **Prajñā-pāramitā Sūtras* in 8,000 and 25,000 lines, as well as on the **Hevajra Tantra*, and on the works of *Śāntarakṣita.

Ratnakūṭa (Skt., heap of jewels). A compilation of early *Mahāyāna *sūtras. The work comprises 49 sūtras, some of particular importance such as the *Kāśyapa-parivarta*, the *Akṣobhya-vyūha*, the **Sukhāvatī-vyūha*, the *Śrī-mālā-devi-siṃhanāda*, and the *Raṣṭrapāla-paripṛcchā*. Though the entire corpus is only available in Chinese and Tibetan translation, copies of the *Sanskrit original texts do survive for some items.

Ratnasaṃbhava (Skt.). 'The Jewel-born One', one of the five *Jinas. Normally depicted iconographically as a yellow *saṃbhoga-kāya *Buddha associated with the southern quarter. He is also viewed as the embodiment of the 'Sameness Awareness', one of the five awarenesses (*pañca-jñāna) and as the lord of the Jewel Family (*see* FIVE BUDDHA FAMILIES). He is said to have a *Pure Land, but this attracted little devotional interest in *India or elsewhere.

ratna-traya. *See* TRIRATNA.

Ratnāvalī. 'A Garland of Jewels', being a didactic work in *Sanskrit by *Nāgārjuna comprising 500 verses arranged in five chapters. Although it includes teachings typical of other works by Nāgārjuna on emptiness (*śūnyatā), much of the contents are of a practical nature and deal with the daily conduct of lay-persons, especially rulers. The fourth chapter is of particular interest for its programme of humanitarian activities which Nāgārjuna suggests are incumbent upon Buddhist rulers. The work partially survives in *Sanskrit as well as versions in Tibetan and Chinese.

Raṭṭhapāla. An *Arhat, said to be chief among those who renounce the world through faith (Pāli, saddhāpabbajita). He came from a wealthy family and his parents refused permission for him to become a *monk until he threatened to starve himself to death. They reluctantly agreed, on condition that he return after being ordained. He soon attained arhatship and returned to his parents but was unrecognized and reviled. When his identity was revealed his father tried to tempt him back to lay life with a lavish display of wealth, and his beautiful wives were paraded before him. Raṭṭhapāla, remaining steadfast, preached a sermon on the futility of wealth and the snares of beauty before leaving.

ṛddhi (Skt.; Pāli, iddhi). A stock group of psychic powers which it is believed can be gained through *meditation at the fourth level of trance (*dhyāna). According to *Pāli sources, these are the product of one of the six kinds of higher knowledge (abhiññā; Skt., abhijñā), and there are said to be eight such powers, namely: (1) to project replicas of oneself; (2) to become invisible; (3) to pass through solid objects; (4) to sink into solid ground; (5) to walk on water; (6) to fly; (7) to touch the sun and moon with one's hand; (8) to ascend to the world of the god *Brahmā. The *Buddha and many of his disciples were said to possess these powers, as were many non-Buddhist *ascetics. However, their use was frowned upon by the Buddha and he prohibited any display of them before layfolk. The *Mahāyāna adopts a different attitude and sees the display of magic power by a *Bodhisattva as a legitimate means of gaining converts. *See also* MIRACLES; PĀṬIHĀRIYA.

rebirth. The belief that one is reborn after *death. The idea is pre-Buddhist and is first encountered in the early Upaniṣads (*c.*800 BCE). The notion is widespread in Indian religions, which believe in a continuity of the individual from one life to the next. Belief in rebirth is a corollary of the doctrine of *karma, which holds that a person experiences the good or bad fruits of moral action at a later date. According to *Buddhism, there are six possible realms of rebirth (*see* BHAVA-CAKRA; GATI). Rebirth is one of the 'givens' of Buddhist thought and since its truth is universally assumed it is rarely asserted or defended as a dogma. The authorities claim that the fact of rebirth is open to empirical verification by advanced *yogins (such as the *Buddha) who it is said can recall in great detail the circumstances of countless previous lives. Some contemporary Buddhists have suggested that belief in rebirth is not an essential part of Buddhist teachings, but the notion is deeply engrained in the tradition and the ancient texts. *See also* REINCARNATION.

Red Hats. A Chinese term used indiscriminately for the three non-*Geluk schools of Tibetan *Buddhism, on account of their ceremonial red caps, in contrast to those of the *Gelukpas which are yellow. Neither term is used by the Tibetans who only apply 'Red Hat' to the leader and adherents of one branch of the *Karma-kagyü school.

refuge tree. A pictorial representation in tree form of the Three Jewels (*triratna) and the *guru, used in Tibetan *Buddhism as an object of veneration when taking refuge (*see* TRIŚARAṆA). Each school has its own distinctive form in which the various lineage-holders and favoured protectors (*dharmapāla) are represented.

Reiiki. *See* *NIHON RYOIKI.*

reincarnation. Term generally avoided by writers on *Buddhism since it implies the existence of an immortal soul (*ātman) that is periodically incarnated in a fleshly host, a notion more proper to *Hinduism. By contrast, Buddhism denies the existence of an immortal soul and does not accept the dualistic opposition between spirit and matter it presupposes. Accordingly, the English term preferred by Buddhist writers to designate the dynamic and constantly changing continuity of the individual from one life to the next is '*rebirth'. Neither this term nor 'reincarnation' has a direct *Sanskrit equivalent, and Indian sources speak instead of 'rebecoming' (Skt., *punarbhava) or 'repeated death' (Skt., punarmṛtyu).

Reiyūkai Kyōdan. One of the 'new religions' of *Japan that derives its primary teachings and practices from the matrix of *Buddhism. Kotani Kimi (1901–71) and Kubo Kakutarō (1892–1944) founded this group sometime between 1919 and 1925, and its name means 'Association of Friends of the Spirits'. As with other Buddhist-derived new religions in Japan, it is entirely a lay organization, is devoted to the **Lotus Sūtra*, and practises faith-healing. It derives its name from its emphasis on the proper and assiduous worship (*pūjā) of ancestors. When Kotani succeeded Kimi after the Second World War, her leadership gave the organization more appeal to *women at the grass-roots level. The group teaches that *karma is inherited from ancestors, and that religious cultivation done in this life not only benefits the practitioner, but also works backwards to help one's ancestors grow closer to Buddhahood. The aim of practice is the achievement of kokoro naoshi, or the 'straightening of the heart/mind'.

release of the burning mouths. *See* FANG YEN-K'OU.

relics (Skt.; Pāli, dhātu). Relics, understood as

the material remains of a holy person or a sacred object, have been revered in *Buddhism since ancient times. The most sacred relics are those of the *Buddha, and on his *death his bodily remains were divided into eight parts and distributed among the local communities. These bodily relics (śarīra-dhātu) were enshrined in funeral mounds (*stūpa) and became centres of *pilgrimage. The most important surviving bodily relic believed to belong to the Buddha is a tooth housed in the *Temple of the Tooth in *Kandy, *Sri Lanka. The bodily remains of other revered teachers are preserved throughout the Buddhist world. Among sacred objects, anything associated with the Buddha or influential religious masters, can be revered as a relic. Examples include cuttings from the *Bodhi Tree, robes (*see* CĪVARA), bowls (*see* BEGGING-BOWL), statues, and religious texts.

Rennyo (1415–99). An eighth-generation grandson of *Shinran (1173–1262), the founder of the Japanese *Pure Land school of *Jōdo Shinshū. Rennyo is widely credited with the revival of the school and the establishment of the *Honganji, a temple built around Shinran's mausoleum, as the undisputed head temple of the school. Although the eldest son of his father Zonnyo, Rennyo was actually illegitimate, and at first it appeared that the first son of Zonnyo's wife would succeed him as head of the Honganji. However, influential leaders within the school, recognizing Rennyo's talent, persuaded the school to accept Rennyo as the temple head. Rennyo then went on preaching tours to make converts and consolidate temple devotees in various areas, a task made difficult by the violent opposition of the *Tendai headquarters at Mt. *Hiei to the Honganji's growth. When this opposition eventuated in open, armed conflict, Rennyo chose to move the Honganji to safer grounds away from Mt. Hiei.

Rennyo was very successful in building up the Jōdo Shinshū membership because of his skill as a speaker, letter-writer, and diplomat. He spoke persuasively of the need for people in his troubled age to put their faith in the saving power of the *Buddha *Amitābha, and he wrote letters prolifically to local congregations resolving doubts, settling internal conflicts, and inspiring followers to greater faith. These letters, or ofumi, were written in very accessible vernacular and illustrated their points with memorable stories; they have been conserved and are still treasured as Shinshū classics to this day. Furthermore, when the peasant rebellions, called *ikkō ikki broke out, he became a trusted mediator; the aristocrats appreciated his willingness to counsel non-violence (*see* AHIṂSĀ) and to expel those who advocated armed conflict from the Shinshū rolls, and the peasants felt he represented their grievances fairly to the landowning classes. At the time of his birth, the Jōdo Shinshū was a fragmented, struggling sect, and the Honganji was a dilapidated temple with no real influence or authority. By the time of his death, the school had achieved unity with the Honganji at its apex. These developments are widely credited to Rennyo, and the school thus acclaims him as its 'second founder'.

Reōiki. *See* *NIHON RYOIKI.*

Revata. Senior *monk who presided over the second council (*see* COUNCIL OF VAIŚĀLĪ). A native of Soreyya, he was consulted over the legitimacy of the 'ten points' of monastic practice adopted by the *Vṛjiputraka (Pāli, Vajjiputtaka) monks and condemned them as illegitimate. His verdict was confirmed by a jury of eight monks (himself included) made up from four belonging to either side of the dispute. A recital of the *Dharma was held to conclude the preceedings. *See also* YASA.

Rgyel Tshab. *See* GYEL-TSHAP.

rhinoceros horn. *See* *KHAGGAVISĀNA SUTTA.*

Rhys Davids, Caroline Augusta Foley (1858–1942). British *Pāli scholar and wife of T. W. *Rhys Davids, she taught at the School of Oriental and African Studies in London and edited and translated numerous Pāli texts for the *Pāli Text Society. She was also the author of numerous secondary works on *Buddhism.

Rhys Davids, Thomas William (1843–1922). Pioneering British scholar of *Pāli and husband of C. A. F. *Rhys Davids, whom he married in 1894. After training as a solicitor Rhys Davids studied *Sanskrit and went on to join the Ceylon Civil Service, which brought him into first-hand contact with *Theravāda *Buddhism. He resigned from the Civil Service in 1872 and returned to England intending to practise law, but instead began to translate texts from the *Pāli Canon. In 1881 he founded the *Pāli Text Society and in 1882 took up the post of Professor of Pāli at University College, London. He wrote many secondary works on early Buddhism and his contribution to Pāli studies remains unrivalled.

Rimé. *See* ECLECTIC MOVEMENT.

Rinchen Sangpo (958–1055). (Tib., Rin-chen bzang-po). One of the greatest Tibetan translators whose activities heralded the beginning of the *Second Propagation or *New School period in *Tibet. Based in western Tibet, he made three visits to *India where he spent over seventeen years in study. He is also credited with important cultural activities such as the dissemination of texts and the foundation of many temples and monasteries in western Tibet. In his later years he met *Atiśa who praised his scholarly acumen, though the two scholars seem to have treated each other with reserve.

rinpoche. A Tibetan title of respect usually reserved for *tülkus. The term means 'precious guru'.

Rinzai (Jap., Rinzaishū). One of the schools of Japanese *Zen *Buddhism, founded in the early *Kamakura period by the *monk *Eisai (or Yōsai, 1141–1215). Eisai, a *Tendai monk, made two excursions to *China during his life, and on the second trip, he received training and certification in the Huang-lung lineage of *Lin-chi Ch'an ('Rinzai Zen' is the Japanese pronunciation of 'Lin-chi Ch'an'). Even though he is revered as the 'founder' of the Rinzai school in *Japan, recent scholars have pointed out that he never explicitly set out to establish a new school that would practise only Zen techniques or propagate only Zen literature and teachings. Rather, he seems to have wanted to revive Zen within the overall framework of Tendai's multifaceted programme of religious training, called 'enmitsuzenkai' (perfect teachings [of the **Lotus Sūtra*]), esoteric ritual (*see* ESOTERIC BUDDHISM), Zen meditation, and monastic *precepts). Nevertheless, he did set in motion the chain of events that would eventuate in the establishment of Rinzai as an independent school of Buddhism.

Eisai's immediate disciples carried on their master's mixed practice, and some went in almost entirely for performing esoteric rituals. A purer tradition of Rinzai Zen appeared under the leadership of Eisai's third-generation disciple *Enni Ben'en (1202–80). After studying with two of Eisai's disciples, though without any certification of enlightenment, Enni set out for China in 1235 and had a certified enlightenment experience under a Lin-chi master. However, this master was from the Yang-ch'i line, the primary rival to the Huang-lung line in China. Thus, since Enni never received recognition as a Zen master from his own teachers within Eisai's lineage, and since the *inka (certification) he received in China came via a different lineage than Eisai's, we may say that Enni represents a second transmission of the Rinzai teachings to Japan. After some setbacks upon his return, Enni established the Tōfuku-ji in *Kyoto, and in his leadership of this temple he departed from Eisai's practice and brought Zen to the forefront. At first he encountered some resistance from both the established schools of Buddhism who resented his encroachments into their membership base, and also from *Dōgen (1200–53), who, in a nearby temple, was attempting to develop support for his own fledgeling *Sōtō Zen school. Despite this hostility, Enni's diplomatic skills carried the day, and he was able to make peace with his rivals and maintain a viable school that taught a purer practice of Zen than that of his predecessors. However, it must be noted that Enni's training merely emphasized Zen, and he did not exclude other practices in principle.

During the period when Buddhism appealed primarily to the aristocracy, Buddhist monks were compelled to perform the services demanded if they wished to receive support. Aristocrats and rulers demanded the performance of esoteric rituals for various this-worldly ends, and so it remained impractical for monks to give all of their time and energy to a purely Zen practice. The Sōtō school's insistence on unadulterated Zen practice kept it marginalized for a time, but in the mid-to-late 13th century, two interlocking developments helped change the situation of the Rinzai school. First, the warrior classes began to discover the practical effects of Rinzai's results- oriented style of practice in the pursuit of their martial duties. Rinzai made use of *kōans in the pursuit of enlightenment (*satori), and warriors who engaged in this training found it helped them concentrate on the present moment in the pitch of battle, assisted them in letting go of clinging to life and victory, and the fear of death and defeat, as well as helping to improve their reflexes and concentration. Thus, they were more willing than their aristocratic masters to support Zen for its own sake and not demand any admixture with esoteric ritualism. Second, the Rinzai school became active in inviting Chinese *Ch'an masters to come to Japan to train disciples. These Chinese masters, such as Lan-chi Tao-lung (Jap., Rankei Dōryū (1213–78), Wu-an P'u-ning (Jap., Gottan Funei 1197–1276) among others, had not learned the esoteric arts in China and did not care to learn them to accommodate the Japanese aristocrats. They taught only Zen, and their activities helped to further purify the Rinzai school of extraneous elements. However, it must be noted that the mixed practice of esoterism and *meditation continued through such masters as *Musō Soseki (1275–1351).

The next generation of Rinzai masters found themselves under closer government scrutiny, partly because of the influence they wielded among the warrior class, and partly because of the ruling Ashikaga family's interest in Zen even prior to their rise to power. When the Ashikaga shōgunate came to power and set up their government in Kyoto, they asserted more direct supervision over Rinzai monasteries by organizing them into ranks, with the five most distinguished temples, called the 'Five Mountains' (Jap., gozan) after an earlier Chinese Lin-chi Ch'an institution, at the top. (*See* FIVE MOUNTAINS AND TEN TEMPLES.) The actual temples included in the gozan changed with the ruler's favour, and at various times there might even be more than five temples in the 'Five Mountains' rank.

In the course of the Muromachi period (1392–1568), the favour shown by the Ashikaga shōguns to Rinzai Zen led to monks becoming heavily involved in affairs of state, and the corruption that usually accompanies membership in a religious group when it serves as a conduit of upward social mobility. Not all monks were happy with this state of affairs, and *Ikkyū Sōjun (1394–1481) protested by boycotting life in a conventional Rinzai monastery and living an itinerant life, composing verses, and behaving outrageously. Others, such as Battai Tokushō (1327–87), simply removed themselves from temples within the gozan system and lived in the provinces under the patronage of local worthies. These monks grew close to the families that would become the great estate-holders (Jap., daimyō) upon whom power would devolve at the end of the Muromachi period, and so, even with the loss of the Ashikaga government and the erection of the Tokugawa shōgunate, Rinzai, with its appeal to the *samurai, remained popular. During the Tokugawa period (1615–1868), Rinzai Zen practice continued to function as a training device for the samurai, and contributed to the formation of the warrior's ethic of *bushidō. The Tokugawa rulers made use of this close connection with Zen in requiring all local families to register with a local Zen temple, thus turning the Rinzai school into a de facto census bureau. Involvement with the warrior class and government record-keeping led, in the minds of many, to an unhappy secularization of the school, but there were still many signs of vitality, as witnessed in the careers of masters such as *Bankei Eitaku (1622–92) and *Hakuin Zenji (1685–1768). Such men could still inspire reverence for their learning and accomplishments in religious practice. Hakuin in particular was a great reformer and revitalizer of the Rinzai tradition; he took the vast body of kōans then in use, systematized them into a kind of graded curriculum, and classified them according to the kind of experience they evoked.

Sōtō and Rinzai are the two primary schools of Zen Buddhism in Japan, and their difference is generally characterized in this way: whereas Sōtō emphasizes the practice of 'just-sitting' in the conviction that human beings are already possessed of an enlightened nature that needs only to be realized, Rinzai actively pursues the goal of enlightenment through the use of tools such as kōans and strenuous practice. It is this more active and goal-oriented approach that made Rinzai popular among the samurai, and still draws practitioners today.

Rinzairoku. The Japanese title of the Chinese work *Lin-chi lu*, or 'record of Lin-chi', a work containing biographical material and recorded sayings of the Chinese *Ch'an master *Lin-chi I-hsün (d. 866).

rishi. Thai term for an *ascetic hermit.

Risshō Kōseikai. One of the Buddhist-derived new religions of *Japan, whose name means 'Society for Success in Establishing the Right'. This religion was established in 1938 when Mrs Naganuma Myōkō and *Niwano Nikkyō (1906–99), two members of *Reiyūkai, another such new religion, left to form their own group based on devotion to the **Lotus Sūtra*. After Naganuma's death in 1957, Niwano became sole president, holding office until 1991, when he retired and was succeeded by Niwano Nichiko (1938–). Risshō Kōseikai is a lay organization, having no *monks, *nuns, or ordained clergy of any sort. Although its success has enabled it to grow to great numbers, at its core is the small group that meets for 'group counselling' (Jap., hōza). This provides an intimate setting in which members, often feeling at a loss for companionship and support after a move into a new city, can find friends and assistance. The group's religious practice is based upon the *Nichiren Buddhist teaching of the supremacy of the *Lotus Sūtra* as the preeminent Buddhist scripture, and the efficacy of simply chanting its title (Jap., *daimoku) as a means to salvation. It runs many business and social-welfare concerns in Japan and abroad, and has been very involved in world peace movements and inter-religious dialogue. As of the year 2000, the organization estimated its membership at 6.15 million individuals.

Risshū. *See* RITSU SCHOOL.

Ritsu school. One of the *Six Schools of Nara *Buddhism that flourished during the earliest period of the religion's transplantation to *Japan. 'Ritsu' means '*Vinaya', or the set of regulations and procedures that governs the lives of *monks and *nuns and the institutions in which they reside, and the Ritsu school saw itself as the Japanese successors of the Chinese Lü school, which specialized in Vinaya study. Because of its specialized knowledge, the school also administered *ordinations for all monastics in Japan until *Saichō (767–822) received permission from the court in the year of his death to conduct ordinations for his nascent *Tendai school without Ritsu control.

The early history of the school is unclear. When *Buddhism first arrived in Japan in the 6th century, the procedures and conditions for valid *ordinations were unknown, and Japanese who wished to seek ordination either ordained themselves unofficially or went abroad. Within the first few decades, cleric-scholars studied imported Vinaya texts and commentaries, and began to conduct ordinations at several temples, while private and foreign ordinations continued. Two hundred years later, in the 8th century, there still existed sufficient doubt as to the validity of these procedures that the emperor sent an embassy to *China in 732 to find a Vinaya master willing to travel to Japan to train students in Vinaya and oversee ordinations. After discovering that, according to Chinese Buddhist standards, their own ordinations were invalid, the Japanese clerics stayed in China to receive the *precepts in an orthodox ceremony, and persuaded several Chinese clergy, notably Tao-hsüan (Jap., Dōsen, 702–60) and Chien-chen (Jap., *Ganjin, 688–763), to make the journey. Chien-chen, a widely renowned Vinaya master, made many attempts to cross the straits to Japan and finally arrived in 754. The arrival of the Chinese masters caused some tension at first, since the Ritsu school had already been in place for over a century and had settled into its own pattern. After some initial successes, Chien-chen retired from public life and settled in his own temple, where he could train students and conduct ordinations in his own way. Nevertheless, the fresh infusion of scholarship and orthodox practice gave the Japanese clergy the assurance that their ordinations were valid and acceptable within the Buddhist world at large. *See also* LÜ-TSUNG.

robes. *See* CĪVARA.

Rokkakudō. A temple of the *Tendai school in *Kyoto. Although its proper name is Chōbō-ji, it received the popular name Rokkakudō ('Hall of six corners') after its hexagonal shape.

rokusō (Jap.; Chin., liu hsiang). In *Hua-Yen (Jap., *Kegon) thought, the 'six characteristics' or features that all phenomena are thought to exhibit: (1) universality, meaning the sum of all characteristics proper to a phenomenon (as when all persons have both eyes and ears); (2) particularity, meaning those characteristics that distinguish it from other phenomena (as the eyes and ears of individual persons remain distinct); (3) sameness, referring to those characteristics that it shares in common with other phenomena (eyes and ears both mediate sense data to the mind); (4) difference, meaning that all the parts of a single phenomenon differ from one another; (5) integration, as when eyes and ears come together to contribute to the formation of the single person; and (6) disintegration, which means that eyes and ears still have their own paths to follow even in integration, and will break apart eventually. As can be seen, these six characteristics are arranged in three pairs in which the first emphasizes commonalities, the second differences.

roots of evil. *See* AKUŚALA-MŪLA.

rōshi (Jap.). In *Zen, an honorific meaning 'venerable master'. The term is also used in other schools as a respectful way of addressing or speaking to elders. It is a contraction of rōdai shūshi, or 'venerable great master of the school'.

Royal Asiatic Society (RAS). An organization founded in 1823 by a group led by the *Sanskrit scholar Henry Colebrooke. He had worked in south Asia and wished to pursue the objectives set out in the Society's Royal Charter of 1824, namely 'the investigation of subjects connected with, and for the encouragement of, science, literature and the arts in relation to Asia'. During the 19th century the RAS was the main centre in *Britain for scholarly work on Asia and had many distinguished Fellows including the Duke of Wellington, Rabindranath Tagore, Sir Henry Rawlinson, and Sir Richard Burton. The Society has some 700 members, half of whom are based outside Britain. The Society is run by a Council of around twenty elected Fellows. It currently has a staff of seven, some of whom work part time. Over the years a number of societies with similar purposes and programmes have been established in South Asia, Hong Kong, *Japan, *Korea, Malaysia, and *Thailand, and have been recognized as associates of the Royal Asiatic Society. Members of these societies are entitled to attend lectures and use the library while in London temporarily, and to join as subscribing Fellows without other sponsorship. The Society lists its main activities as: publishing the *Journal of the Royal Asiatic Society;* providing access to the Society's extensive collection of books, historic documents, paintings and artefacts, and promoting research into its holdings; arranging a programme of lectures and seminars; publishing books and monographs on Asian subjects; organizing conferences and exhibitions; and making awards to recognize achievements in the field.

rūpa (Skt.; Pāli, matter). Matter or form, that which has shape and manifests itself to the senses as substance. It is the first of the five aggregates (*skandha) and in that context stands for the material component or body of the human individual. In the compound 'name and form' (*nāma-rūpa), which designates the psycho-physical totality of the individual subject, rūpa again denotes the body while nāma signifies the four psychological or immaterial aggregates of feeling (*vedanā), perceptions (*saṃjñā), volitional impulses (*saṃskāra), and consciousness (*vijñāna).

rūpa-dhātu (Skt.; Pāli). The Form Realm, being the second of the Three Realms in Buddhist *cosmology and *meditation theory. The Form Realm comprises seventeen *heavens, subdivided into four groups which parallel the four levels of trance (*dhyāna), where the faculties of smell and taste, sexual organs, physical suffering, and certain unwholesome mental factors are absent. The highest of these heavens is *Akaniṣṭha. These states can also be reached through meditation, hence their association with the four trances (dhyāna).

Ryōbu-Shintō (Jap.). Also known as Ryōbu Shūgō Shintō, this was a form of *Shintō that took in elements of Buddhist esoteric practice (*see* ESOTERIC BUDDHISM) from the *Shingon school. It came to identify the Inner and Outer Ise Shrines with the two *maṇḍalas of the Shingon school, and also identified the *kami enshrined within these shrines with the *Buddhas of these maṇḍalas. These developments occurred in the larger context of *honji-suijaku thought, in which kami were seen as local, provisional manifestations of eternal and universal Buddhas.

Ryōgen (912–85). Japanese *monk and reviver of the *Tendai tradition. A lifelong member of the Tendai school, he was elevated to the position of head priest in 966, and spent nearly 20 years restoring buildings damaged by fire, building new temples and monasteries on other precincts of Mt. *Hiei, encouraging scholarship in doctrinal studies, and publishing original works.

Ryōkan (1758–1831). A Japanese *monk of the *Sōtō school of *Zen during the Edo period. After receiving a Confucian education (*see* CONFUCIANISM) in his youth, he turned aside from the path of governmental work laid out by his father and entered the Sōtō order at 18. This was a period in which, under the influence of Chinese *Ts'ao-tung *monks, the Sōtō school was undergoing a wave of reform, and many were advocating strict regimens of meditation and the study of Sōtō founder *Dōgen's works. Ryōkan fell in with this reformist programme, and studied with several strict and uncompromising masters. In 1792, he received word that his father had travelled to *Kyoto to present a work to the government denouncing political intrigue and corruption, and had then committed *suicide, apparently to call attention to his protest. Ryōkan arranged the funeral and subsequent memorial services, and then set out on religious *pilgrimage for several years. Only in 1804 did he settle down on Mt. Kugami, where he stayed for twelve years. He is remembered for the depth of his *enlightenment that manifested in the spirit of acceptance and equality that he showed to all, from officials to prostitutes. He played with children, composed poetry in praise of nature, was renowned for his calligraphy, lived in extreme simplicity, and showed love for all living things to the extent of placing lice under his robes (*see* CĪVARA) to keep them warm, allowing thieves to take freely from his possessions, and letting one leg protrude from his mosquito net at night to give the mosquitos food.

Ryōnin (1072–1132). Japanese *Tendai *monk and founder of the *yūzū-nembutsu, a form of *Pure Land practice based on *Hua-yen (Jap., *Kegon) metaphysics. He is also noted for his revival of the practice of musical chanting within the Tendai school and his mastery of esoteric rituals (*see* ESOTERIC BUDDHISM). A native of Owari Province, he spent most of his monastic career in the Ōhara district north of *Kyoto, an area known as a gathering place for itinerent practitioners of the *nembutsu. He had a vision of *Amitābha *Buddha in 1117, in which the Buddha taught him the interpenetration of all persons and all practices. He spent the rest of his life founding temples and teaching people this practice, even presenting himself before the emperor in 1124.

S

saala long tham. Lao term for an open-sided shelter where *monks and lay-people listen to Buddhist teachings.

Sacred Books of the Buddhists. A series of English translations of important early scriptures. The series was begun by Max *Müller and continued by C. A. F. *Rhys Davids.

sadā. In *Burma, a horoscope cast shortly after birth and regularly consulted throughout life, especially when any major changes in normal routines have occurred or are imminent. Known in northern *Thailand as cata, the horoscope charts the configuration of the fixed cosmic elements (the heavenly bodies, the cardinal points, the topography of the land, and so forth) whose juxtaposition is thought to influence the evolution of a person's life. Although canonical *Buddhism discourages belief in *astrology, many Buddhists see no contradiction between the concept of fate, as something that can be known through horosocopes, and *karma, or one's future as determined by moral acts. Fate is regarded as a force that exerts influence over the vicissitudes of daily life, whereas karma is believed to determine the more fundamental aspects of human destiny, such as the circumstances of death and rebirth.

ṣad-āyatana (Skt.; Pāli, salāyatana). The 'six sense spheres', or the objects of the six senses, namely the objects of sight, hearing, touch, taste, smell, and thought. *See also* āyatana.

Saddharma-puṇḍarīka Sūtra. *See* LOTUS *SŪTRA*.

Saddhātissa. Younger brother of *Duṭṭhagāmaṇi and king of *Sri Lanka from 77 to 59 BCE. On the death of their father he seized the throne and the brothers went to war over the inheritance. Saddhātissa was defeated but the brothers were eventually reconciled.

sādhana (Skt.). A key form of *tantric *meditation through which a practitioner aims to achieve union or identity with a particular divine being through a process of *visualization and subsequent dissolution of subject and object into emptiness (*śūnyatā). Each practice is based on one of the countless descriptive and liturgical texts that have been composed through the ages. Though chiefly associated with tantric *Buddhism in *Tibet, similar texts and their practices are also known in *China and *Japan.

sādhumatī-bhūmi (Skt.). The ninth of the *Bodhisattva Levels (*bhūmi), 'the One with Good Discrimination', according to the **Daśabhūmika Sūtra*. On this level the Bodhisattva cultivates the Perfection of Strength (bala-pāramitā). *See also* PĀRAMITĀ.

ṣaḍ-pāramitā (Skt.). The 'Six Perfections' which are practised and brought to perfection by *Bodhisattvas in the course of their training. These are: the perfection of generosity (*dāna-pāramitā), of morality (*śīla-pāramitā), of patience (*kṣānti-pāramitā), of effort (*vīrya-pāramitā), of meditation (*dhyāna-pāramitā), and of insight (*prajñā-pāramitā). *See also* PĀRAMITĀ

sahaja (Skt.). Literally 'innate', a term denoting the natural presence of enlightenment (*bodhi) or purity in contrast to the adventitious nature of obscurations that conceal it. *See also* SAHAJAYĀNA.

Sahajayāna. A late antinomian offshoot of *tantric *Buddhism associated with some of the 'great adepts' (*mahā-siddhas) such as *Saraha that later gained popularity in *Tibet especially in the *Kagyü school. Although usually viewed as a form of tantric Buddhism, the practice of Sahajayāna makes little use of the complex rites and visualizations normally associated with tantric practice. *See also* SAHAJA.

Sahampati. A god from the *heaven of the 'Pure Abodes' (*suddhāvāsa). Sahampati appears on several occasions in the *Pāli Canon, but his most famous intervention is shortly after the *Buddha's awakening when the Buddha was hesitating about whether or not to preach the *Dharma. Sahampati appeared and pleaded with him to do so in order that those 'with just a little dust before their eyes' might achieve salvation.

Sahor. Also known as Zahor in Tibetan sources. A small kingdom in early medieval *India, mentioned in some *tantric sources as one of the places where Buddhist tantras were first revealed or compiled. The precise location of this country is debatable and some conflation with *Oḍḍiyāna seems to have occurred as both countries are said to have been ruled by a King Indrabhūti. It may have been located somewhere in present-day West Bengal or Orissa. According to Tibetan sources, *Atiśa came from Sahor, and elsewhere West Bengal is given, which strengthens the identification between the two regions.

Saichō (767–822). Japanese *monk and founder of the *Tendai school. Saichō was born in 767 into a family of devout Buddhists, after his father climbed up Mt. *Hiei to pray to the local gods (*kami) for a son. He first entered the order at the age of 12, was ordained as a novice at 14, and as a full monk at the canonical age of 19. Three months after his full *ordination, he took the unusual step of going into a mountain hermitage on Mt. Hiei for an extended solitary retreat. In 788, he set up a permanent temple on top of Mt. Hiei. At this point Saichō's fortunes took a radical upturn. He came to the court's notice through his acquaintance with one of the official court priests. Through his mediation, Saichō gained an appointment himself as a court monk in 797. In 802, a meeting was arranged at court for some lectures on the **Lotus Sūtra*, and Saichō was invited to appear as the main speaker; it was at this meeting that he came to the personal attention of Emperor Kammu. The capital city moved to Heian in 794. This site is located at the foot of Mt. Hiei, putting Saichō right in the seat of imperial power.

Saichō took advantage of the emperor's acquaintance in 804 to arrange a trip to *China to get *T'ien-t'ai literature. Once he arrived there, he headed straight for Mt. T'ien-t'ai. Saichō was fortunate to be at Mt. T'ien-t'ai directly after the T'ien-t'ai school had undergone a significant reformation and revitalization. He stayed in China for nine and a half months, actually six weeks longer than he originally had permission to stay. The extra time was highly significant for subsequent developements. During the six weeks he had to wait for transportation back to *Japan, he made the acquaintance of a Chinese esoteric master (*see* ESOTERIC BUDDHISM) named Shun-hsiao. After a brief period of study Shun-hsiao initiated Saichō into esoterism. Saichō returned in 805 to find the Emperor Kammu dying. Of all the teachings that Saichō brought back from China, the emperor was most interested in the esoteric rituals and practices. Saichō complied with the emperor's request that he perform an esoteric ritual for him, in return for which he received imperial permission to establish his new Tendai sect and to ordain two disciples each year—one for doctrinal study and one for esoteric initiation (*abhiṣekha).

Saichō's fortunes went into a permanent decline after Emperor Kammu's death in the days following Saichō's return. One of the major reasons for this decline was *Kūkai's return from China in 806 with significantly greater credentials as an esoteric teacher and ritualist. The two men maintained friendly relations for a while, and in 812 Saichō even received initiation into two esoteric traditions from Kūkai. But as time went on, Kūkai came into his own and no longer needed Saichō's help to get ahead at court. Saichō's esoteric monks began deserting to Kūkai, including Saichō's own chosen successor; a bitter blow to him. Their relations broke when Saichō contacted Kūkai about granting him a higher initiation certifying him as an esoteric master. Kūkai curtly wrote back to say that Saichō would need to study with him for three years first. The following year Kūkai refused to lend Saichō an esoteric text, and the relationship collapsed for good. By this time, Saichō's organization was in a shambles, and in 817 he left Mt. Hiei and retreated to the Kanto area to regroup. One of the first things he did at this time was compose the *Ehyō Tendaishū*, or 'Basics of the Tendai school', which circulated around the capital and came to the attention of a *Hossō monk named Tokuitsu. Tokuitsu wrote a refutation of it, and the *debate was joined that would establish Tendai permanently. It was not only Tokuitsu's arguments, but his political position that drew Saichō out. The

Hossō school was in charge of the Bureau of Monks at that time, and so in a position to block Saichō's writings from reaching the court. In frustration, the normally reticent and humble Saichō became more extreme in his positions, until finally the noise reached the court in spite of the Bureau's attempts to cut him off. From an initial position advocating some minor changes in the ordination process, Saichō came to request that Mt. Hiei be declared a solely *Mahāyāna temple exempt from having to use the *Hīnayāna ordination *precepts of the *Ritsu, or *Vinaya school. He proposed that, instead, they take their ordination from a Mahāyāna scripture, the **Fan wang ching*, or 'Sūtra of Brahma's Net'. These precepts are referred to as the Bodhisattva precepts, and had always functioned as a complement to the traditional monastic precepts; they were never designed to replace them. Thus, the establishment found Saichō's position entirely inadmissible.

In Saichō's view, the old Hīnayāna precepts, given at the time when the *Buddha first began preaching his message, were aimed at a group of people who were beginners in the Buddhist path, people who had not had time to study and meditate on the path, and who needed special moral restraints and special teachings in order to develop gradually. However, the Japan of Saichō's day was different in his view. *Buddhism had been around for a long time, the Mahāyāna path was well established and people no longer needed the simple Hīnayāna teachings and practices. Japan was a nation of people whose religious capabilities were perfectly matured, and so it was appropriate to dispense with taking the Hīnayāna monastic vows, taking the *Bodhisattva precepts in their stead as a more efficient path to liberation, or in Saichō's terminology, the 'direct path'. Fate intervened, however. The strain of this controversy took its toll on Saichō's health, and he died in 822 before it could be resolved. He was 56. Possibly stirred by his death, the court granted his request for Tendai monks to receive independent ordinations seven days after his death.

Sāketa. An ancient Indian town, identified by some with *Ayodhyā or nearby Sujankot, in the ancient state of *Kośala. Though an apparently unimportant place politically, the *Buddha chose to spend a number of the annual rainy season retreats here during the latter part of his life.

Śakra (Pāli, Sakka). The king or chief of the gods (*deva). Śakra rules over the *heaven of the 33 gods (Skt., *trāyastriṃśa; Pāli, tāvatiṃsa) which is the lowest of the heavens and thus the closest to the human world. He makes frequent appearances in Buddhist literature and is regarded as a devotee of the *Buddha and protector of the faith. He is regarded as noble, kindly, and just and a guardian of the moral law, but still subject to many frailties. The figure of Śakra bears some relation to the Vedic god *Indra.

sakṛdāgāmin (Skt.; Pāli, sakadāgāmin). A 'once-returner', one of the four *Noble Persons (*ārya-pudgala). Having reached the second stage of the *supermundane path (*ārya-mārga) he will have only one more *rebirth in the human world before gaining enlightenment (*bodhi).

Sakya (Tib., Sa-skya). One of the four main schools of Tibetan *Buddhism, taking its name from its original monastic centre at Sakya ('grey earth') in southern *Tibet. It was founded in 1073 by members of the Khon family who, though laymen, have traditionally acted as the heads of the school. While the Sakya school preserves the *lamdre ('path and result') teachings transmitted by Virūpa, it is is also renowned for a keen interest in Buddhist logic (*pramāṇa) and epistemology which derives from the seminal work of *Sakya Paṇḍita (1182–1251). The Sakya school was politically influential during the 13th and 14th centuries, especially through their dealings with the neighbouring Mongols (*see* MONGOLIA). The head of the school is known as the Sakya Trindzin or 'throne holder' (Tib., Sa skya khri 'dzin), and the present head now resides in *India at Sakya College, after fleeing Tibet following the Chinese invasion.

Śākya. Name of the clan or tribe into which the *Buddha was born. Like other tribes resident in the foothills of the *Himālayas and northern Bihar who were tributary to the great kingdoms but exercised internal autonomy, the Śākyas most likely practised a republican form of government. Though in later legend the Buddha's father, *Śuddhodhana, is depicted as a king, he was most probably a tribal chief, depending on the support of an assembly of householders who gathered regularly to discuss tribal politics in a meeting-hall. If it is assumed the Śākyas were like other kṣatriya tribes of north-east India or elsewhere (as described in the sources of the *Mauryan period or later, such as the Artha-śāstra), then each adult noble would have had the title rāja or 'prince', but would not be a ruler unless consecrated as such (mūrdhābhi-ṣikta). At certain periods some at least of such tribes would have had an oligarchic constitution, but at other times a monarchic one. There are no non-Buddhist sources extant on the Śākyas which could shed light on their political constitution.

Sakyadhita. An organization founded in 1987 whose name means 'Daughters of the *Buddha'. As the name suggests, the organization exists to improve the status of Buddhist *women, which it does through the medium of conferences, seminars, and discussion groups. It also publishes the *Sakyadhita Newsletter*. Membership is open to both laywomen and *nuns from all over the world. Since many of the *ordination lineages for nuns died out at various points in history, the organization is keen to develop alternative forms of ordination which will allow greater participation by women. The objectives of Sakyadhita, as expressed at its founding meeting in 1987 in *Bodhgayā, India, are: (1) to promote world peace through the practice of the Buddha's teachings; (2) to create a network of communications for Buddhist women throughout the world; (3) to promote harmony and understanding among the various Buddhist traditions; (4) to encourage and help educate women as teachers of *Buddha-dharma; (5) to provide improved facilities for women to study and practise the teachings; (6) to help establish the *bhikṣunī *Saṃgha (community of fully ordained nuns) where it does not currently exist.

Śākyamuni. Literally 'the Śākyan sage'. A title of the *Buddha, found particularly in *Mahāyāna sources where it distinguishes him from the numerous other Buddhas mentioned in the *sūtras. *See also* ŚĀKYA.

Sakyapa. Any person or thing associated with the *Sakya school of Tibetan *Buddhism.

Sakya Paṇḍita (1182–1251). The honorific title of Kön-ga gyel-tshan (Tib., Kun-dga' rgyal-mtshan). A member of the Khon family, he was the most outstanding scholar of the *Sakya school who also achieved considerable political influence in his dealings with the Mongols. In 1244 he was invited to the Mongol court, where the ruler Godan Khan was so impressed by his learning that he converted to *Buddhism. This event marked the origin of the 'patron-priest' (*yon-mchod) relationship in which Sakyapa *lamas served as religious preceptors to the Mongol court. Sakya Paṇḍita was able to read *Sanskrit fluently, and is noted for his profound understanding of Buddhist logic (*pramāna) through his short but influential set of essays, the *Knowledge Treasure of Valid Cognition* (Tib., *tshad-ma rig-gter*). These texts are commentaries on the treatises on logic by the great Indian philosophers *Dignāga and *Dharmakīrti.

samādhi (Skt.). **1.** A state of deep trance. In Buddhist teachings this is defined as 'one-pointed' concentration or composure of mind (*citta-ekāgratā) and is the result of meditative focus on a single wholesome object. Later *Mahāyāna sources mention a vast number of different samādhis by name and their attainment is said to lead to the ability to manifest certain specific *miracles through the associated development of higher knowledge (*abhijñā). **2.** The second of the three divisions of the *Eightfold Path, comprising the factors of Right Effort (samyag-vāyāma), Right Mindfulness (samyak-smṛti), and Right Meditation (samyak-samādhi).

Sāmaññaphala Sutta. The second discourse in the Collection of Long Discourses (*Dīgha Nikāya) of the *Pāli Canon. Its title may be translated as 'The Discourse on the Fruits of the Religious Life', and its theme is the benefit that accrues to one who follows the path of a *śramaṇa (Pāli, samaṇa) or religious mendicant. The occasion for the sermon is a visit by King *Ajātaśatru to the *Buddha. The king asks about the point of the religious life, and reveals he has previously put this question to six other religious teachers without receiving a satisfactory answer (*see* SIX SECTARIAN TEACHERS). In reply the Buddha explains how the religious life as taught by him leads step by step upwards towards the higher knowledge (*abhijñā) of the *Arhat. The king applauds this teaching and becomes a lay convert, expressing regret for the murder of his father. When he has gone, the Buddha observes that, were it not for this crime, the king would have attained the first stage of the Noble Path (*ārya-mārga).

Samantabhadra (Skt.). 'The All-good One'. **1.** A *Mahāyāna mythical or *celestial *Bodhisattva who is said to protect the *Dharma. He is often depicted holding a wish-fulfilling gem and a *lotus or book of the Dharma while riding on a white six-tusked elephant. **2.** Drawing from earlier antecedents in Indian *tantric works such as the **Sarva-tathāgata-tattva-saṃgraha*, in the *Nyingma form of tantric *Buddhism, Samantabhadra is the primordial Buddha (*ādi-Buddha) who is the embodiment of enlightenment (*bodhi) or ultimate reality (*dharma-kāya). Iconcographically, he is depicted as a dark-blue nude figure embracing his white consort Samantabhadrī.

Samantabhadra's Resolution (Skt., Samantabhadra-praṇidhāna). The ten resolutions and practices of the *Bodhisattva *Samantabhadra described in detail in chapter 56 of the **Gaṇḍavyūha Sūtra*. These are: homage, praise, and offerings to all *Buddhas, the confession (*pāpa-deśanā) and repentance of all one's wrongdoing, joy at the attainments of others, the request to the *Buddha to teach the *Dharma and to remain in the world, application to the Buddha's teachings at all times, the benefiting of all beings in ways suitable to their needs, and the transference of one's merit (*puṇya) to all beings.

Samantapāsādikā. Commentary on the *Vinaya Piṭaka of the *Pāli Canon compiled by *Buddhaghoṣa in the 5th century at the request of Buddhasirī. It is prefixed by an introduction, the *Bāhira-nidāna, relating the history of *Buddhism up to the establishment of the Vinaya Piṭaka in *Sri Lanka. It is based on the *Mahāpaccarī* and the **Kurundī-aṭṭhakathā*, two older commentaries.

sāmānya-lakṣaṇa (Skt.). A general attribute or universal characteristic, for example the property of extension or hardness. The term is found in the *Pāli commentaries from the time of *Buddhaghoṣa onwards, as well as in the schools of Buddhist logic (*pramāṇa) and related systems. In contrast to 'specific attributes' (*sva-lakṣaṇa), sāmānya-lakṣaṇa are purely nominal constructions generated by the mind and superimposed upon objects, without any reality in themselves. *See also* LAKṢAṆA.

samāpatti (Skt.; Pāli). Attainment or equipoise; a state where the body and mind abide in a state of tranquil composure. Often, samāpatti refers to the four trances (*dhyānas), the four levels of the Formless Realm (*arūpya-dhātu), and the state of cessation (*nirodha-samāpatti). It is also used as an equivalent to *samādhi.

śamatha (Skt.; Pāli, samatha; calming). One of the two main types of meditational technique taught in *Buddhism, the other being *vipaśyanā or insight meditation. It is normally recommended that the two techniques be developed in tandem since they complement one another. The primary aim of śamatha is to achieve the state of mental absorption known as 'one-pointedness of mind' (*citta-ekāgratā), in which state the mind remains focused unwaveringly on its meditation subject. When the mind is calm and focused in this way it can successively attain the eight *dhyānas (Pāli, jhānas) or trances. By contrast, vipaśyanā meditation leads to the intellectual understanding of doctrine and depends upon the mind being in a state of conscious awareness. The primary technique used in śamatha is to concentrate on the breath as it enters and leaves the body, perhaps counting the in and out breaths up to a certain number and then resuming again at zero. The aim is to monitor the breath with bare attention rather than trying to control it. Other methods include focusing on an external object, known in *Pāli sources as a *kasiṇa, or by concentrating on any of the 40 traditional meditation subjects. These practices lead to physiological changes in the body and an altered state of consciousness which is amenable to spiritual development. The practice of śamatha frees the mind from distractions and removes mental impurities such as the five hindrances (*nīvaraṇa), which are left behind on the attainment of the first dhyāna.

samaya (Skt.). **1.** A given system of teaching or doctrines. **2.** The conduct required of a *tantric practitioner, often as a set of vows or commitments. **3.** The realization (*abhisamaya) of Buddhahood. **4.** In tantric *Buddhism, union with the *body, speech, and mind of the *Buddha.

samaya-mudrā (Skt.) Seal of Symbols; one of the four meditation seals (*mudrā) according to *yoga-tantra. It refers to the process of imaging the *Buddhas in transformational *meditation practice by way of symbolic emblems which correlate to their mind aspect (*see* BODY, SPEECH, MIND).

samaya-sattva (Skt.). 'Symbolic being'. In the course of *tantric *sādhanas, the practitioner generates an image of the focal deity—either as himself or in front—which is understood as a representation of that deity as a model for worship (*pūjā) or personal transformation. The image is contrast to the actual presence of the deity, the *jñāna-sattva.

saṃbhāra-mārga (Skt.). The 'path of accumulation', the first of the five paths to Buddhahood (*see* PAÑCA-MĀRGA) in which one gathers the requisite accumulation of merit and awareness (puṇya-jñāna-saṃbhāra).

saṃbhoga-kāya (Skt.). The Enjoyment Body of a *Buddha, the second of a Buddha's three bodies, according to the *Mahāyāna *trikāya doctrine. The saṃbhoga-kāya is thought to be a more subtle mode of embodiment than the Emanation Body (*nirmāṇa-kāya) and thus only visible to *Bodhisattvas. Arising from the Truth Body (*dharma-kāya), saṃbhoga-kāyas take on the appearance of the many different Buddhas mentioned in Mahāyāna *sūtras, such as *Amitābha, *Akṣobhya, or *Vairocana, each one thought to reside in their own particular *Pure Land. There, adorned with the 32 major and 80 secondary marks of perfection (*see* DVĀTRIṂŚADVARA-LAKṢAṆA; ANUVYAÑJANA) they communicate the *Dharma to select audiences of Bodhisattvas and gods. In later *tantric *Buddhism, the saṃbhoga-kāya is considered to be the equivalent of the speech vector of a Buddha's activities.

sambō. The Japanese term for the 'Three Jewels' (*triratna) of *Buddhism: the *Buddha, his teachings or *Dharma, and the community (*Saṃgha) that maintains them.

saṃbodhi (Skt.). The 'perfect *enlightenment' attained by a *Buddha. The earliest sources make no distinction between the quality of the awakening (*bodhi) of the *Arhat, Buddha, and *Pratyekabuddha, although the enlightenment of a Buddha is often termed 'sammā-sambodhi' (Pāli, 'full and perfect enlightenment) largely as a mark of respect. Later non-canonical *Pāli sources distinguish three classifications of enlightenment in accordance with the resolve of the aspirant to become either an Arhat, Paccekabuddha (Skt., Pratyekabuddha), or Buddha. *Mahāyāna sources regard the awakening of a Buddha as profounder than that of the other two. *See also* SATORI, KENSHŌ.

Saṃgha (Skt.; Pāli, group or collection). The Buddhist community, especially those who have been ordained as monks (*bhikṣu) and nuns (*bhikṣunī) but originally referring to the 'fourfold saṃgha' of monks, nuns, laymen (*upāsaka), and laywomen (*upāsikā). The minimal requirements for admission to the Saṃgha are faith in the 'three jewels' (*triratna) of the *Buddha, the *Dharma, and the *Saṃgha (in this context meaning the *ārya-saṃgha), usually demonstrated in the act of 'taking refuge' (*see* TRIŚARAṆA). Laymen are expected to keep the Five Precepts (*pañca-śīla) while monks and nuns follow the *Prātimokṣa code of over 200 rules.

Saṃgha Administration Act. A legal measure popularly known as the 'Saṃgha Law', drafted and enacted in *Thailand in 1902 by Prince Wachirayān (Vajirañāṇavarorasa), a son of King *Mongkut and brother of King Chulalongkorn. The law sought to integrate the *Saṃgha throughout Thailand and provide a central administration and single ecclesiastical authority. It provided for a nationally organized system of education so that monastic teaching and procedures relating to ordination could be standardized. Abbots of monasteries were henceforth to be appointed by government officials, or the king. The implementation of the law took many years but was well under way by Prince Wachirayān's death in 1921. As a consequence of these reforms Thailand emerged from the colonial period with a strong and unified national Saṃgha. The model was emulated in Laos and Cambodia, although adapted to the colonial context of those countries.

Saṃghabhadra (5th c. CE). A learned doctor of the *Vaibhāṣika school of north *India who developed a theory of temporality to explain the school's doctrine that phenomena (*dharmas) exist simultaneously in the past, present, and future. He was critical of the views of *Vasubandhu, of whom he was a junior contemporary.

Saṃghavarman. A early Indian translator active in *China who translated a number of *Mahāyāna works including the **Amitābha Sūtra*.

saṃgraha-vastu (Skt.). The four 'means of attraction', comprising one aspect of a *Bodhisattva's training in relationship to other beings. A Bodhisattva uses the means of attraction to draw beings to the *Dharma by means of generosity (*dāna), kind words (priya-vadyatā), beneficial acts (*artha-kriyā), and sympathy (samānārtha).

Sāmindavisaya. *Pāli name for *Thailand (formerly Siam).

saṃjñā (Skt.; Pāli, saññā). The third of the five aggregates (*skandha), saṃjñā is the psychological faculty of perception or discernment. Saṃjñā is said to recognize the distinctive characteristics of things, for example, by identifying different colours. It is sixfold, with respect to perception of the objects of the five senses plus the ideas perceived by the mind. Sometimes the term is used simply in the sense of 'idea' or 'concept', especially in lists of meditation topics (for example, anitya-saṃjñā as the concept of impermanence; *see* ANITYA).

Saṃmitīya. One of the major groups within the *Eighteen Schools of Early Buddhism. It emerged around the late 1st century BCE as a subschool of the parent *Vātsīputrīyas, who in their turn were an off-shoot of the early *Sthavira school. Like their parent group, the Sammitīyas advocated a form of *pudgala-vāda, a belief in the substantial (though temporary) reality of the individual.

Sammohavinodanī. Buddhaghoṣa's commentary on the **Vibhaṅga*, the second book of the *Abhidharma Piṭaka.

saṃsāra (Skt.; Pāli, flowing on). The cycle of repeated birth and death that individuals undergo until they attain *nirvāṇa. The cycle, like the universe, is believed to have no beginning or end and individuals transmigrate from one existence to the next in accordance with their *karma or moral conduct. Blinded by the three roots of evil (*akuśala-mūla), namely greed, hatred, and delusion, beings are said to wander in saṃsāra until such time as they are fortunate enough to hear the *Dharma and put it into practice. The way this process of continuous *rebirth occurs is explained step by step in the doctrine of Dependent Origination (*pratītya-samutpāda). Although not mentioned by name, saṃsāra is the situation that is characterized as suffering (*duḥkha) in the first of the *Four Noble Truths (āryasatya).The word saṃsāra does not appear in the *Vedas, but the notion of cyclic birth and death is an ancient one and dates to around 800 BCE. It is common to all mainstream Indian religions.

saṃskāra (Skt, formation; Pāli, saṅkhāra). The constructing activities that form, shape or condition the moral and spiritual development of the individual. The saṃskāra-skandha is the fourth of the five aggregates (*skandha) that constitute the human person, and also the second link (*nidāna) in the twelvefold scheme of Dependent Origination (*pratītya-samutpāda). The term refers in particular to volitions and intentions (which may be morally good, bad, or neutral) and the way that these contribute to the formation of individual patterns of behaviour or traits of character. Repetition imprints a particular saṃskāra on the psyche and the imprint is carried over into the next life. The aim of Buddhist practice is to replace negative imprints with positive ones.

saṃskṛta (Skt., conditioned; Pāli, saṅkhata). Things that are conditioned or brought into being by contributory causes. This applies to anything that bears the characteristics (*lakṣaṇa) of arising (utpāda), duration (sthiti), and disappearance (vyaya). The class of conditioned phenomena is contrasted with the 'unconditioned' (*asaṃskṛta), a synonym for *nirvāṇa. Nirvāṇa is regarded as transcendent and not subject to the laws of temporality or causation (*pratītya-samutpāda) that affect all phenomena in the conditioned realm of *saṃsāra.

samurai. Member of the Japanese warrior class that developed alongside the late medieval system of land ownership by feudal lords known as 'shōen'. Due to the weakness of the central government in the medieval period, local nobles were able to recruit their own fighting forces, and the founding of the Kamakura Shōgunate in 1192 (*see* KAMAKURA PERIOD) ushered in an era of military rule that lasted until the *Meiji Restoration of 1868. The relationship between the samurai warrior and his lord was governed by a code of conduct known as *bushidō, which emphasized honour, glory, heroism, and loyalty. Many samurai found Buddhist religious teachings, particularly those of *Zen, helpful in remaining mentally concentrated in battle and in developing an attitude of calm detachment in the face of death. *See also* MARTIAL ARTS.

saṃvṛti-satya (Skt.). 'Relative truth'. In early *Buddhism and some forms of *Mahāyāna, relative truth was used as an epistemological term to denote the conventional view of the world as constructed by the mind and projected onto ultimate reality (*paramārtha-satya). In other forms of Mahāyāna, especially *Madhyamaka, it came to be seen in ontological terms as a delusive or deficient dimension of reality. A soteriological problem then arose since this view seemed to suggest that there could be no possible grounds for an unenlightened person to gain access to or achieve enlightenment (*bodhi). Various solutions to this problem were suggested, such as the *Yogācāra theory of three ontological levels (*tri-svabhāva) and the notion of the embryonic *Buddha (*tathāgata-garbha). *See also* TWO TRUTHS.

samyak-prahāṇa (Skt.; Pāli, sammappadhāna). The four right efforts related to the sixth stage of the *Eightfold Path (right effort). They are the efforts (1) to avoid; (2) to overcome; (3) to cultivate; (4) to foster. The first two items are aimed at avoiding and overcoming what is *akuśala or unwholesome, and the third and fourth are aimed at cultivating and fostering what is *kuśala or wholesome.

samyak-sambuddha (Skt.). 'Completely and perfectly awakened'. A term used to emphasize the superiority of Buddhahood when contrasted with the achievement of the other two classes of enlightened persons, namely *Arhats and *Pratyekabuddhas. Although all attain essentially the same awakening (*bodhi), the status of Buddhahood became regarded, particularly in *Mahāyāna *Buddhism, as much superior by virtue of the compassionate concern for others manifested in the *Buddhas' teaching mission. Apart from the fact of discovering the truth for themselves, Buddhas were said to be superior by virtue of their omniscience (sarvajñātā) and their ten special powers (*daśa-bala). *See also* SAṂBODHI.

Samyé (Tib., bsam-yas). The oldest monastic establishment and translation centre in *Tibet, constructed in 767 CE during the reign of King Trisong Detsen. When it was being built, *Padmasambhava took responsibility for pacifying the hostile local deities while the design was drawn up by *Śāntarakṣita based on the layout of the Indian monastery (*vihāra) of *Odantapurī. It was here that the famous *debate took place between *Kamalaśīla and *Hvashang Mahāyāna known as the *Council of *Lhasa. The buildings were severely damaged and desecrated by the Chinese during the Cultural Revolution, though restoration work has been carried out in recent years.

Samyé debate. *See* COUNCIL OF LHASA.

Samyé Ling. A Tibetan Buddhist centre, located in Dumfriesshire, Scotland, affiliated to the *Kagyü lineage and founded in the late 1960s by Ānanda Bodhi and then given to Chogyam *Trungpa Rinpoche. After Chogyam Trungpa left the UK, Akong Rinpoche took over as abbot and director of the centre and under his guidance a Tibetan-style monastery building (*gompa) was contructed. The centre provides accommodation for retreats and teaching as well as fostering traditional Tibetan crafts. More recently, Holy Island (Strathclyde) was purchased to provide a suitable environment for long-term retreats and inter-faith communion.

saṃyojana (Skt.; Pāli, binding). A restriction or limitation, usually translated as a 'fetter', in the sense of something that binds one to *saṃsāra or the cycle of *rebirth. There are said to be ten: (1) belief in a permanent self (*satkāya-dṛṣṭi); (2) sceptical doubt (*vicikitsā); (3) obsession with rules and rituals (*śīlavrata-parāmārśa); (4) sensous craving (kāma-rāga); (5) hatred (vyāpāda); (6) craving (*rāga) for the Form Realm (*rūpa-dhātu); (7) craving for the Formless Realm (*ārūpya-dhātu); (8) conceit (*asmi-māna); (9) restlessness (uddhatya); (10) ignorance (*avidyā). The first five are known as 'lower fetters' since they bind one to rebirth in the Desire Realm (*kāma-dhātu); the second five are known as 'higher fetters' since they bind one to rebirth in the Form and Formless Realms. The four noble persons (*ārya-pudgala) have freed themselves of a different number of fetters: the stream-winner (*śrotāpanna) is free of the first three; the once-returner (*sakṛdāgāmin) is also free of the grosser forms of four and five; the non-returner (*anāgāmin) is completely free of the first five, and the *Arhat is free of all ten.

Samyukta Āgama (Skt.). The 'Connected Discourses', being one of the major sections of the *Sūtra Piṭaka comprising around 3,000 *sūtras and corresponding to the *Saṃyutta Nikāya of the *Pāli Canon. Many of the major *Eighteen Schools of Early *Buddhism had their own versions of these texts, although for the most part these have not survived. As well as recent discoveries of small portions of the *Sarvāstivāda Saṃyukta Āgama in *Sanskrit and several sūtras from that tradition in Tibetan translation, a complete version from the Sarvāstivādin school and an incomplete version from the *Kāśyapīya school exists in Chinese. A comparison of the different versions that survive shows overall a high degree of consistency of content although each recension contains texts not found in the others. *See also* ĀGAMA.

Saṃyutta Nikāya (Pāli). The 'Connected Discourses', the third of the five divisions (*Nikāya) of the *Sūtra Piṭaka of the *Pāli Canon. It consists of 7,762 *suttas arranged thematically in 56 groups, called saṃyuttas. It is the equivalent of the *Sanskrit *Saṃyukta Āgama.

san-chiao. A Chinese term referring to the 'Three Teachings' of *China, namely *Buddhism, *Taoism, and *Confucianism.

San-chiao school. A school of Chinese religion that coalesced around the Ming dynasty thinker Lin Chao-en (1517–98), which ostensibly placed the 'Three Teachings' of *Buddhism, *Taoism, and *Confucianism on an equal footing as three aspects of the path. In fact, Lin's teaching favoured Confucianism over the other two, and reinterpreted them within a Confucian framework.

San-chieh-chiao. A school of Chinese *Buddhism established during the Sui dynasty by the *monk *Hsin-hsing (540–94). This school took as its basic theory the idea that the history of Buddhism, and indeed of the present world, was divided into three periods: the period of the True *Dharma, of the Counterfeit Dharma, and of the Final Dharma. At this period of Chinese Buddhist history, many thinkers put forward ideas about the meaning of the three stages, and how Buddhist teaching would develop in each. According to Hsin-hsing, based on his reading of the **Lotus Sūtra*, the first period witnessed the teaching of the One Vehicle, the second the teaching of the Three Vehicles (or separate teachings and practices for *Śrāvakas, *Pratyekabuddhas, and *Bodhisattvas), while the third, which had begun in the mid-6th century, was to be dominated by his own teachings. Because of the loss of the true teaching and the absence of any teacher in the world, his followers did not live in traditional monasteries or study scriptures and perform devotions before images as had been usual, but lived in courtyards and outbuildings and circulated among the people. However, they did maintain a strict discipline in an attempt to purify themselves. They also believed in the presence of *Buddha-nature in all things, giving the world a pervasive sanctity along with its pervasive degeneracy. As a sign of this universality of Buddha-nature, they would prostrate before all people and other beings to honour them as *Buddhas. During the 7th century, their advocacy of almsgiving (*dāna) led to the establishment of the Inexhaustible Treasury at the Hua-tu Temple in *Ch'ang-an. This treasury functioned in some ways as a lending institution, and as alms came in and loans were repaid, its wealth grew until the size of the treasury made it a potential source of economic power that alarmed the imperial court. This, plus its claims regarding the depravity of the age and the illegitimacy of the ruling authorities, finally induced the court to dissolve the sect and seize its assets in 713.

Sāñcī. Ancient religious centre in present-day Madhya Pradesh near the city of Bhopal in central *India. It is the site of important architectural remains dating from the 3rd-1st centuries BCE. The most famous is the Great *Stūpa, the oldest part of which may date from the time of *Aśoka and which was enlarged and altered continuously down to the beginning of the Christian era. It is 53 feet high and is approached through one of four large stone gateways (toraṇa) lavishly carved with scenes from the life of the *Buddha, *animals, plants, and female deities (yakṣī, *see* YAKṢA). There are two other stūpas on the site, the oldest dating from the Śuṅga period (185–72 BCE).

Fig 17 Sāñcī, the Great Stūpa

Sandhi-nirmocana Sūtra. The 'Elucidation of the Intention', an important *Mahāyāna *sūtra in ten chapters which contains the earliest presentation of the essentials of *Yogācāra *Buddhism. Dating from around the late 2nd century, it is a highly philosophical work which may be viewed as a corrective to certain misguided interpretations of the earlier *Prajnā-pāramitā Sūtra corpus. The sūtra is evidently a composite of three separate sections placed together during the course of the 2nd century CE, and reaching its final form early in the 3rd century. The work introduces the key concepts of the 'storehouse consciouness' (*ālaya-vijñāna), the 'three natures' (*trisvabhāva) and the '*Three Turnings of the Wheel' (the last notion originating in the *Buddha's *first sermon). Although no *Sanskrit version survives, there are five Chinese translations and one in Tibetan.

sanei gyo-daing. Burmese term meaning literally 'planetary post'. It consist of a small shrine near the base of a *zedi containing a *Buddha image to which worshippers make offerings according to the day of the week they were born. There are usually eight posts, one for each day of the Burmese week, in which Wednesday is divided into two days. *See also* BURMA.

Saṅghamittā (*c.* 280–221 BCE). *Nun, daughter of emperor *Aśoka, and sister of the *monk *Mahinda, she was ordained at the age of 18 together with her brother Mahinda, and, like him, is said to have attained Arhatship on that day (*see* ARHAT). At the request of King *Devānampiya Tissa of *Sri Lanka she went to that country with eleven other nuns so that a tradition of ordaining nuns could be started there. On the same journey she brought with her a branch of the original *Bodhi Tree. Saṅghamittā lived in Sri Lanka until her death, at the age of 59. After her *cremation a *stūpa was erected over her ashes.

Sañjaya Belaṭṭhiputta. One of the *Six Sectarian Teachers contemporary with the *Buddha. Sañjaya is satirized in Buddhist accounts as a sceptic who would offer no firm opinion on any matter. His beliefs are similar to another group known as 'eel-wrigglers' (*amarāvikkhepika) mentioned in the early sources. It appears that Sañjaya was formerly the teacher of *Śāriputra and *Mahāmaudgalyāyana before they abandoned him and followed the Buddha.

San-lun (Chin.). An early school of *Buddhism in *China. The name means 'Three Treatises', and refers to the school's focus on three works devoted to *Madhyamaka philosophy that had recently been translated by *Kumārajīva (343–413): the *Chung-lun* (Treatise on the Middle [Way]) and the *Po-lun* (Treatise in One Hundred [Verses]), both by the Indian master *Nāgārjuna (2nd century CE), and the *Shih-erh men lun* (Treatise on the Twelve Gates) by his disciple *Āryadeva. After the death of Kumārajīva, the main Chinese proponent of the school was his disciple *Seng-chao (374–414), although the latter did not outlive his master by more than one year. Seng-chao digested the complex and foreign thought of the Indian three treatises into a more native idiom in his brief works *The Immutability of Things*, *The Emptiness of the Unreal*, and *Prajñā is Not Knowledge*. In these works he criticized commonly held ideas about the way in which things exist, the sequence of events (particularly causes and effects) in time, and conventional knowledge as lacking in profound wisdom.

After Seng-chao, the main transmission of the San-lun teachings passed through a line of disciples that included the Korean *monk Seng-lang, Seng-ch'üan, and *Fa-lang (507–81). The school, never large, found it difficult to gain acceptance for its critique of reality, which appeared overly negative to the Chinese. Towards the end of Fa-lang's life, *Chih-i (538–97) was having success in propagating his new *T'ien-t'ai teachings which, among other things, analysed the final nature of reality not as a static 'emptiness' (*śūnyatā), but as a dynamic construct that he designated 'Middle-way Buddha-nature'. Under this name, Chih-i could speak of truth as a dynamic power in the world revealing the marvellous nature of things to all beings. Because of this competition, the last great San-lun master, *Chi-tsang (549–643), brought innovative new ideas into the school's teaching, which analysed the traditional '*Two Truths' of Indian Madhyamaka thought into three levels. Where there was orignally the Worldly Truth of Being countered by the Absolute Truth of non-being or emptiness, Chi-tsang took two further steps. Where a Worldly version of the Two Truths could then affirm either being or non-being, the next level of Absolute Truth denied both being and non-being as artificial human constructs. Finally, where a Worldly Truth might affirm both being and non-being, Absolute Truth would neither affirm nor deny either being or non-being. Thus, the Two Truths constantly led the believer into ever-greater depths of realization in a dynamic process that might have rivalled that of the T'ien-t'ai system. However, in the end, T'ien-t'ai won out, and the San-lun school slipped into oblivion.

saññā-vedayita-nirodha (Pāli, the cessation of ideation and feeling). A deep state of meditative trance in which the vital bodily functions are suspended, in a manner similar to hibernation. Also used as a synonym for *nirodha-samāpatti.

Sanron (Jap.). One of the *Six Schools of *Nara *Buddhism during the early history of Buddhism in *Japan. The word is a Japanese pronunciation of the Chinese '*San-lun', and represented an effort to import the texts and teachings of the Chinese school into Japan. It is said to have been transmitted to Japan by the Korean *monk Hyegwan (Jap., Ekan) in 625. Perhaps as many as three other transmissions occurred over the next century, leading to various streams of Sanron thought based in different temples. However, the school, which limited itself to academic study and practice by a handful of clergy, never reached out to the masses of people, and so never became a major force outside the realm of theory and doctrine. The various streams died out one by one, and the last actual Sanron master passed away in 1149.

Sanskrit. The primary language of classical Indian literature, philosophy, and scripture. Its origins are uncertain since the earliest extant inscriptions are rather late. Though it has some links to the language of the *Vedas, some scholars believe Sanskrit is an artificial language as the name suggests ('perfected', 'completed') compiled from various dialects and languages current in *India during the 4th to 3rd centuries BCE. Commanding an enormous prestige and authority, it possesses a complex grammatical structure and a vast vocabulary suited to expressing subtle philosophical and religious concepts. Not used originally by Buddhists, it was adopted first by the *Sarvāstivāda school and then later became the standard language for most *Mahāyāna literature. A variant form, known to scholars as *Buddhist Hybrid Sanskrit, was often used in Mahāyāna *sūtras. This is (like *Pāli) a form of Middle Indian with a relatively high level of Sanskritization.

Śāntarakṣita. A son of the king of *Sahor, he received his monastic vows from Jñānagarbha at *Nālandā and became a recognized expert of the *Svātantrika form of *Madhyamaka. He composed several important works such as the *Ornament of the Madhyamaka* (Skt., *Madhyamaka-alaṃkāra*) and the *Compendium of Truths* (Skt., *Tattva-saṃgraha*). During the reign of Trisong Detsen, he went to *Tibet in the later part of the 8th century CE where he lived for thirteen years until his death. He designed and supervised the construction of *Samyé Monastery, introduced the monastic community to Tibet, and began the major task of translating Buddhist scriptures into Tibetan.

Santi Asok. Radical sectarian movement in *Thailand founded by Phra Bodhirak, a former television entertainer who was ordained into the *Thammayut order in 1970 after a sudden conversion experience. He attracted a following in Bangkok which became known as the 'Asoka group', and established a centre called 'Asoka's Land' (Dan Asok) some 30 miles from Bangkok. Because of his increasingly unorthodox activities he was forced to leave the Thammayut order and join the Mahānikai sect in 1973. In due course he fell out with this group too, and he and his followers eventually severed all ties with the national Thai *Saṃgha. Santi Asok monks live in communities in simple thatched huts and follow a moderately ascetic regime in the *Theravāda forest-dwelling tradition. The movement is critical of what it sees as the laxity of the Thai Saṃgha, the immorality in Thai society, and corruption in the government. Phra Bodhirak's outspoken manner and his strident critique of the establishment and disregard for ecclesiastical law led to the Supreme Saṃgha Council taking punitive measures against the movement in 1989. Bodhirak and 79 of his followers were arrested but no charges were brought.

Śāntideva (685–763). Buddhist *monk, poet, scholar, and adherent of the *Prāsaṅgika branch of the *Madhyamaka school. Little is know with certainty about his life, although there are many legendary accounts. According to these he was born a prince but (like the *Buddha) renounced his social position to follow the religious life. He was particularly devoted to *Mañjuśrī, the *Bodhisattva of wisdom, who instructed Śāntideva through dreams and visions. He became adviser to a king and subsequently a Buddhist monk. In later life he was based at *Nālandā university where he wrote on and taught basic *Mahāyāna doctrines from a Madhyamaka viewpoint. As a monk he was revered for his modesty although possessing great learning and magic powers. Nothing is recorded about his death and many Buddhists believe he remains active in the world doing good in the manner of a true *Bodhisattva. Two of his works survive in *Sanskrit, the *Compendium of Discipline* (Skt., **Śīkṣā-samuccaya*) and *Entering the Path of Enlightenment* (Skt., **Bodhicāryāvatāra*).

Saraha. A *tantric adept (*mahā-siddha), possibly from the region of present-day Orissa. The dates of his life are obscured by hagiographical fictions although he seems to have been active during the 9th century CE. He is a representative of *Sahajayāna, an antinomian form of *Buddhism, and transmitted his teachings in a characteristic style of song known as a *doha, several of which survive in his name in the *Apabhraṃśa language.

Sāratthappakāsinī. 'The Revealer of the Essential Meaning,' being the title of *Buddhaghoṣa's commentary on the *Saṃyutta Nikāya.

Śāriputra (Pāli, Sāriputta). The chief disciple of the *Buddha. A lifelong friend of *Mahāmaudgalyāna, the two renounced the world on the same day and first became disciples of the sceptic *Sañjaya Belaṭṭhiputta. Thereafter both converted to *Buddhism, and on the day of their *ordination the Buddha declared them to be his two chief disciples. Both soon became *Arhats. The Buddha declared Śāriputra to be a perfect disciple and second only to himself in transcendent knowledge (*prajñā). Śāriputra frequently preached with the Buddha's approval, and for his contribution to the propagation of the faith was rewarded with the title 'General of the *Dharma' (Pāli, Dhammasenāpati). He had special expertise in analytical philosophy and is regarded as the originator of the *Abhidharma tradition. Śāriputra was renowned for his exemplary qualities of compassion, (*karuṇā), patience, and humility. He was older than the Buddha and when he died a few months before him, the Buddha pronounced a eulogy.

śarīra (Skt., body). The *relics of a *Buddha or saint, normally enshrined in a *stūpa.

Sārnāth. An important Indian Buddhist centre located some 6 miles north of present-day *Vārāṇasī. It is famed as the location of the *Deer Park, the site of the first discourse taught by the *Buddha after his enlightenment (*bodhi). Visited again by the Buddha on an number of occasions later in his life, Sārnāth became an important Buddhist centre until the 12th century CE. Modern excavations have revealed extensive remains of *vihāras and *stūpas, including the great

Dhamekh and Dharmarājika Stūpas, as well as numerous statues of the Buddha.

sarva-jña (Skt.). Term literally meaning 'awareness of all' and denoting a form of omniscience or awareness. This awareness, whether possessed by an *Arhat or a *Buddha, knows all the general attributes of phenomena.

sarva-jña-jñāna (Skt.). 'All-knowing Awareness'. The all-encompassing awareness unique to a *Buddha. According to later *Mahāyāna exegesis, this comprises the Mirror-like Awareness (adarśa-jñana), Investigating Awareness (pratyavekṣaṇa- jñāna) and the Awareness that Accomplishes Activities (kṛty-anuṣṭhāna-jñāna) that arise in the instant after enlightenment (*bodhi) is attained.

Sarva-maṇḍala-sāmānya-vidhi-guhya Tantra. 'The Secret Tantra concerning the General Rituals for all Maṇḍalas', an important early *tantric work, later classed as a *kriyā-tantra, which describes the basic procedures for creating and using *maṇḍalas for initiation (*abhiṣeka). No Sanskrit version survives although a Tibetan and Chinese translation exists.

Sarvāstivāda (Skt.; Pāli, sabbatthivāda). Important school of Indian *Buddhism that separated from the main body of the Elders (*Sthaviras) around the mid 3rd century BCE. Its name—'the school that holds that everything exists'—derives from its philosophical views concerning the nature of phenomena. Like other early schools its ontology was pluralist and realist, and the Sarvāstivādins believed (not unlike the ancient Greek atomists) that that reality could be analysed into a collection of discrete entities, known as *dharmas. In the Sarvāstivāda taxonomy there are 75 dharmas, 72 conditioned (*saṃskṛta), and three unconditioned (*asaṃskṛta). While agreeing with other schools that conditioned dharmas are momentary (kṣanika), they nevertheless maintained that they also enjoy real existence in both the past and future. Four theories were proposed to explain this, one being that these dharmas exist from beginningless time and simply undergo a change of mode from latent to manifest. Time itself, it was suggested, was simply the change of mode undergone by dharmas (*see* VASUMITRA). Although the Sarvāstivādins were apparently expelled at the council of *Pāṭaliputra (*see* COUNCIL OF PĀṬALIPUTRA II), they went on to become extremely influential particularly in the north-west of *India in *Kashmir and *Gandhāra, where they surivived until Buddhism disappeared from the subcontinent. The school possessed its own *canon, much of which survives today, and is renowned for its *Abhidharma texts, notably the **Abhidharma-kośa* of *Vasubandhu, and the **Mahāvibhāṣā*. The Kashmiri branch of the school is alternatively known as the *Vaibhāṣika, from the name of this text, while the Gandhāri branch became known as the Mūla-Sarvāstivāda or *Sautrāntika.

Sarva-tathāgata-tattva-saṃgraha. An extensive work in five parts. Composed during the late decades of the 7th century CE, it forms the root text of *yoga-tantra. Though it had some popularity in early Tibetan *Buddhism, it was more important in Sino-Japanese forms of *tantric Buddhism where attention was focused upon its first section, the Mahā-maṇḍala, which circulated separately under the title of the *Vajra-śekhara Sūtra*.

Sarvodaya. *Sri Lanka based reform movement that emphasizes a return to traditional village life based on Buddhist principles as the cure for the corruption and materialism of modern urban societies. It is often known by the name Sarvodaya Shramadana. Sarvodaya means 'the welfare of all', and shramadana means 'donation of work', in the sense of mutual collaboration and assistance with practical projects. Typical projects include digging wells, building roads, founding schools, providing medical facilities, and teaching new techniques of farming and animal husbandry to villagers. A lay Buddhist movement in which *monks may participate, Sarvodaya was founded by A. T. Ariyaratne in 1958. Although centred on Sri Lanka it has been influential in promoting *Engaged Buddhism in both the developed and developing world. Around one-third of Sri Lankan villages (some 8,000 or so) are affiliated, but the movement has remained decentralized working through Village Awakening Councils (samhiti) which take their own financial and policy decisions. The movement is a response to the charge that Buddhism lacks a 'social gospel', and marks a return to the traditional symbiotic relationship between the village and the monastery (*vihāra) in which the secular and religious domains go hand in hand.

śāsana (Skt.; Pāli, sāsana). A term used by Buddhists to refer to their religion. It has a range of possible translations, including teaching, doctrine, and as 'Buddha-śāsana', 'the teachings of the *Buddha', especially in the context of their historical continuity as religious tradition. Various predictions are made about the duration of the teachings. In the *Pāli Canon it is said that the Buddha's decision to admit *women reduced the lifespan of the śāsana from 1,000 to 500 years. Later sources predict various durations ranging from 1,000 to 5,000 years, usually passing through phases of continual decline until the teachings disappear altogether from the world (*see* MAPPŌ). It is thought that in due course a new Buddha will arise and the teachings will be proclaimed anew. *See also* BUDDHISM.

Sāsanavaṃsa. Literally 'chronicle of the doctrine'. An ecclesiastical chronicle in two parts compiled by Paññasāmi of *Burma, in 1861. The first part of the work, which begins with the birth of the *Buddha, and brings the history up to the Third Council (*see* COUNCIL OF PĀṬALIPUTRA II) and the sending of missionaries to nine different countries, concludes with an account of the religions of these countries. The second part is entirely devoted to Burma.

śāstra (Skt., rule). Genre of literature opposed to the category of *sūtra. The designation 'sūtra' is reserved for texts that are regarded as the word of the *Buddha, whereas 'śāstras' are works composed by other authors. These consist of treatises on all matter of learned topics as well as commentaries on other works. The *Pāli equivalent of the term is sattha, but is rarely found.

śāśvata-vāda (Skt.; Pāli, sassatavāda). Eternalism, one of the two 'extreme views' condemned by the *Buddha, the other being Annihilationism (*uccheda-vāda). Eternalism postulates the existence of a self (*ātman) that is eternal and unchanging, while the latter postulates the existence of a self that is cut off and utterly destroyed at death. According to the Buddha, both of these two extremes misrepresent the reality of the situation and the truth of the matter is to be found by reference to the principle of the 'Middle Way' (*madhyamā-pratipad). Thus the self is neither eternal nor is it cut off at death: rather there is a dynamic continuity of the individual from one life to the next.

Satipaṭṭhāna Sutta. Important *Pāli discourse concerned with meditational practice that has provided the foundation for Buddhist meditational techniques down the ages. The discourse occurs in two places in the *Pāli Canon: in the *Dīgha Nikāya (where it is known as the *Mahāsatipaṭṭhāna Sutta*), and in the *Majjhima Nikāya, in a slighter shorter version. Its name means 'the setting up of mindfulness' (*smṛti), and it describes a fourfold meditational exercise involving the body, feelings, the mind, and mental objects (concepts related to Buddhist doctrine). The meditator takes one of these as his *meditation subject and by focusing on it calms the body and mind and enters the trances (*dhyāna). Although the distinction is not made in the discourse, this phase of the practice came to be known as 'calming' (*śamatha). The next phase is the analytical examination of the meditation subject in the light of Buddhist doctrine in order to directly experience the object as endowed with the three marks (*trilakṣaṇa) of impermanence (*anitya), *suffering, and absence of self. This phase became known as 'insight meditation' (*vipaśyanā).

satkāya-dṛṣṭi. (Pāli, sakkāya-diṭṭhi). Term meaning 'personality belief', and referring to doctrines which postulate the existence of a permanent self or *ātman. In Buddhist teachings, this view is the result of a basic misconception concerning the nature of personal identity in relation to the five aggregates (*skandhas). There are twenty possible permutations of this wrong view. 1–5: that one's self is identical with any one of the five aggregates; 6–10: that it is contained in them; 11–15: that it is independent of them; and 16–20: that it is the owner of them. Satkāya-dṛṣṭi is the first of the Ten Fetters (*saṃyojana) and is only abandoned when one becomes a stream-winner (*śrotāpanna).

satori (Jap.). In Japanese *Zen *Buddhism, an

intuitive apprehension of the nature of reality that transcends conceptual thought and cannot be expressed through 'words and letters'. There are various degrees of satori and students work to deepen the experience by constant training. *See also* KENSHŌ.

satya (Skt.; Pāli, sacca). General term meaning 'truth'. On the *Madhyamaka notion of the 'Two Truths' (satya-dvaya), *see* PARAMĀRTHA-SATYA; SAṂVṚTI-SATYA. *See also* FOUR NOBLE TRUTHS.

Satyasiddhi Śāstra. The 'Establishment of Truth', being an *Abhidharma-style work by *Harivarman presenting the theories of the *Sautrāntika school, according to some scholars. The work contains a number of *Mahāyāna-like teachings such as the doctrine of emptiness (*śūnyatā) which suggests it is either proto-Mahāyāna or was itself influenced by early Mahāyāna thought, although the concept of emptiness (Pāli, suññatā) is an Abhidharma notion not a Mahāyāna one. On the basis of a mistaken belief that it was actually a fully-fledged Mahāyāna work, it was uniquely preserved and studied in east Asia in its Chinese translation. Recent scholars have suggested that the title should correctly be restored as the *Tattvasiddhi Śāstra* rather than *Satyasiddhi Śāstra*.

Sautrāntika. An early school whose origins and tenets are obscure. *Vasumitra mentions a school called the Saṃkrāntikas, ascribing to it specific teachings concerning rebirth (saṃkrānti) and no other teachings. Unfortunately, *Hsüang-tsang mistakenly translated this as Sautrāntika, although the Tibetan translation and the other two Chinese translations all render it correctly. Other Chinese references to the Sautrāntikas are probably the result of the same error. Apart from this, no *Sarvāstivādin source prior to the 6th century CE ever lists the Sautrāntikas as a school (*nikāya). One explanation of the origins of the name Sautrāntika may lie in the fact that certain Sarvāstivādin monasteries that had accepted Mahāyāna *sūtras and teachings developed their own Abhidharma system, which was referred to as Dārṣṭāntika or Sautrāntika. They can thus be regarded as Mahāyānists 'doing Abhidharma'. Later, after the Mahāyāna had developed its own Abhidharma, the Sautrāntika system became redundant and the earlier situation was no longer understood. It thus would appear, on this account, that the Sautrāntikas were never a separate school and should not be counted among the *Eighteen Schools of Early Buddhism. According to other authorities however, a cross-textual study of surviving *Āgamas and *Vinayas shows that the Sautrāntika Mūla-Sarvāstivāda and Gandhāri Sarvāstivāda are identical, and the Dārṣṭāntika is an earlier alternative name.

Sayadaw. Burmese term meaning the chief abbot of a *monastery.

schism. Schism appeared early in the history of *Buddhism due in part to the *Buddha's refusal to appoint a successor as leader of the monastic order (*Saṃgha) and his reluctance to impose a rigid discipline in matters of monastic practice. He counselled his followers to be 'lamps unto themselves' and Buddhism has never recognized a supreme source of authority in matters of doctrine or practice. Technically, a schism (saṃgha-bheda) is defined as occurring when nine fully ordained monks leave a community together as a result of dissent and perform their own ecclesiatical services. If the number is less than nine there is 'dissent' rather than schism. To cause a schism maliciously or from selfish motives is considered a grave offence and one destined for swift retribution (*ānantarya-karma). On the effects of schism in Buddhism *see* EIGHTEEN SCHOOLS OF EARLY BUDDHISM.

School of the Three Stages. *See* SAN-CHIEH-CHIAO.

Second Propagation (Tib., phyi-dar). The second period of the organized dissemination of Buddhist teachings and texts in *Tibet during the 11th century. This period followed the hiatus brought about after the *First Propagation ended with the suppression of *Buddhism by *Lang Darma. The Indian scholar-*monk *Atiśa and the Tibetan translator *Rinchen Sangpo were important figures in this process of the dissemination of Buddhism.

Secret Instruction Category (Tib., man-ngag-sde). The third of three subdivisions of the *Nyingma *atiyoga class of teachings in which intrinsic reality or awareness is allowed to manifest spontaneously without any artificial efforts or selective choices.

self-generation. A form of meditative visualization used in *tantric Buddhism in which the deity is invoked and then merged with the pratitioner as a means of self- transformation. This is as opposed to the method of '*front generation'. Self-generation is considered more advanced and accompanied by a degree of spiritual risk from the powers (*siddhi) it may rapidly unleash.

selflessness. *See* ANĀTMAN.

sems-sde. *See* MIND CATEGORY.

Sengai Gibon (1751–1837). A Japanese *Rinzai *Zen *monk of the Edo period who contributed to a revival of Zen calligraphy and ink painting.

Seng-chao (374–414). A second-generation master of the *San-lun school in early Chinese *Buddhism. He was one of the most gifted disciples of the great translator *Kumārajīva, and expounded the complex Indian-based thought of the *Madhyamaka school in a Chinese idiom in works such as *The Immutability of Things*, *The Emptiness of the Unreal*, and *Prajñā is Not Knowledge*. In these works he criticized commonly held ideas about the way in which things exist, the sequence of events (particularly causes and effects) in time, and conventional knowledge as lacking in profound wisdom.

Seng-ts'an (d. 606). A Chinese *Ch'an *monk held to be the third *patriarch of Ch'an after *Bodhidharma (d. 532) and *Hui-k'o (487–593). Historical records list him as a fairly minor disciple of the latter, having only studied with him for six years before being parted from him in the year 574 because of the general persecution of *Buddhism. Otherwise, little is known about him for certain.

sensei. A Japanese honorific meaning 'teacher' that is sometimes used in religious as well as secular settings.

seppuku. *See* HARA- KIRI.

Sera. One of the three great *Gelukpa monasteries of central *Tibet, founded in 1419 by Jamchen Chöjé Śākya Yeshé, (Tib., Byams chen chos rjes śākya ye shes).

sesshin (Jap.). In *Zen *Buddhism, this refers to a period of especially intensive Zen practice.

setsuwa bungaku. A Japanese Buddhist term referring to a type of literature that is narrative, rather than scholarly, scriptural, or didactic, in nature. The earliest and best-known example is the *Nihonkoku genpō zen'aku ryōiki* (Miraculous Stories of the Retribution of Good and Evil in the Country of *Japan) by the *monk Kyōkai in 822. This work, like others in the genre, presents stories of good and evil deeds and the manner in which the doers receive their karmic recompense (*see* KARMA), as a way of exhorting moral behaviour.

Shambhala. A mythical kingdom, especially associated with the **Kālacakra Tantra*, whose precise geographical location is uncertain but popularly thought to be located somewhere to the north of *Tibet, though there is some evidence that would place the land that was the source of the myth in western Orissa. With the rise of Islam in *India, it was thought that the kingdom of Shambhala became invisible and will remain so until a future king leads forth his armies to vanquish the Muslims and inaugurate a new golden age.

Shangri-la. A Western idea of a hidden paradise on earth, based on the Tibetan legends of *Shambhala, popularized in James Hilton's novel *Lost Horizon* (1933).

Shan-tao (613–81). A Chinese *monk who pioneered *Pure Land thought and practice in the area around the northern capitals during the *T'ang dynasty. He entered the order of monks as a young boy, under a master with probable connections to the *San-lun school. He entered into doctrinal and scriptural studies, at which he proved adept enough, but which did not suit his temperament, which tended to be more aesthetic and mystical. His conversion to Pure Land practice came about either as a result of viewing a painting of *Sukhāvatī (the Land of Bliss), or through discovering the *Sūtra on the Contemplation of the Buddha of Immeasurable Life* (**Amitāyurdhyāna Sūtra*). After this, he rejected philosophical study in favour of a contemplative practice centring on invocation of the name of *Amitābha and *visualization of the splendour of the Pure Land and its inhabitants. During this time, he sought out *Tao-ch'o (562–645) for inspiration and training in Pure Land practice. Tao-ch'o was renowned at that time both for his zeal in

Pure Land practice and his masterful lectures on the very *sūtra that had initially caught Shan-tao's attention. After Tao-ch'o's death, Shan-tao remained in the Chung-nan mountains for a few more years, and afterward went to the capital city of *Ch'ang-an. Once established there, he began proselytizing vigorously, and had enormous success in converting people to Pure Land practice. Later sources even report that perhaps a hundred or more of his followers committed *suicide in order to hasten their arrival in the Pure Land, and tradition had Shan-tao himself sacrificing himself in this manner. However, a critical examination of the sources has cast doubt upon both these assertions, and it seems closer to the truth to say that one of his followers took his own life, and the story eventually became attached to the master's name. In addition to Pure Land teaching and practice, Shan-tao is known for his artistic accomplishments, and supervised the casting of large Buddhist images. Although Shan-tao has been credited with popularizing Pure Land practice among the masses, his actual method of practice was much more complicated than simply reciting the *Buddha *Amitābha's name. He himself lived a rigorously *ascetic life and observed the monastic *precepts faithfully. He demanded of his followers absolute sincerity and faith in their practice, and taught them both oral invocation of the name and the complex visualization practices of the *Kuan wu-liang-shou fo ching*. Consequently, it is not surprising that actual records of his outreach activities do not show him reaching out to the masses with a simple, easily mastered practice. Instead, he appealed to the monastic community and the upper, educated strata of lay society, giving them a practice that required real talent and work. It is also not surprising that many of his lay students joined the monastic community, and that his major work was a commentary on the *Kuan wu-liang-shou fo ching*.

Shao-k'ang (d. 805). A Chinese *monk of the *T'ang dynasty who is commonly regarded as the fifth *patriarch (Chin., tsu) of the *Pure Land tradition. He joined the monastic order (*Saṃgha) as a young boy, and studied the literature of Chinese *Buddhism before moving to the capital city of *Lo-yang, where he continued *Shan-tao's (613–81) activities of preaching and converting people to Pure Land practice. He is famous for taking the money he received during his begging rounds and giving it out to young children in the street for reciting the name of the *Buddha *Amitābha just once. He later established a temple dedicated to Pure Land practice, and left behind one short work of poems of praise.

Shao-Lin monastery. A Buddhist monastery in Honan province founded in 496 CE under the auspices of the Emperor Hsiao Wen of the Northern Wei dynasty. It is famed as the site where the first *patriarch of the *Ch'an school, *Bodhidharma (d. 532) practised 'wall-contemplation' for nine years and where he received his disciple, the second patriarch *Hui-k'o (487–593). It is also noted as a centre for the practice of *martial arts. Legend has it that, when Bodhidharma first arrived there, he found the monks tired and listless due to lack of exercise, and so devised a system of physical training to complement their spiritual endeavours. Over the course of time his system evolved into the Shao-lin style of martial arts. *See also* CHINA.

Sheaf of Garlands of the Epochs of the Conqueror, The. *See* *JINAKĀLAMĀLĪPAKARAṆA*.

Shen-hsiu (605–706). In traditional histories of Chinese *Ch'an *Buddhism, Shen-hsiu is accounted the founder and first *patriarch of the short-lived (and somewhat heretical) *Northern School of Ch'an. Recent critical studies of early Ch'an sources, however, have revealed a different picture of the man and his religious practices. As a youth, Shen-hsiu is reputed to have been a very bright and adept student, reading widely in the classics of *Taoism and *Confucianism as well as Buddhism. The uncertainty of the years leading up to the establishment of the *T'ang dynasty impelled him into monastic life, and it is possible he was ordained a *monk in the very year of the first T'ang emperor's accession, 618. After this, there is no record of any of his activities until his meeting with the fifth patriarch of the Ch'an school, *Hung-jen (601–74), in the year 656. Even though the latter was only a few years Shen-hsiu's senior, Shen-hsiu took him for his master and studied with him for six years, reading the

**Laṅkāvatāra Sūtra*, Hung-jen's favoured scripture, and finally attaining the master's seal of authentic enlightenment (*inka). Upon receiving this recognition, he left the East Mountain (Chin., Tung Shan) community and withdrew into solitude. In contradiction to traditional accounts that depict Shen-hsiu vying unsuccessfully for recognition as the sixth patriarch in a poetry contest with *Hui-neng (638–713), Shen-hsiu's departure can be dated to 661, some ten years before Hui-neng's arrival at East Mountain.

Very little information exists on the next fifteen years of his life. He comes back into view in the year 676, already over 70 years of age. He may have reverted to lay life during this fallow period, eventually returning to the monastic fold and enrolling in the Yü-ch'üan Temple in Hupei province. Wishing to practise in solitude, he built a hermitage about $1\frac{1}{2}$ miles from the temple. Ten years later, he began taking in some students, but almost as soon as he began teaching, his reputation spread and many came to practise under his guidance. Interestingly, among those who studied with him was one *Shen-hui (684–758), the man who would eventually denounce Shen-hsiu's path as 'gradualist' and advocate its abandonment in favour of the 'subitist' (or sudden enlightenment) position (*see* SUBITISM) of the so-called '*Southern School'. Shen-hsiu's fame eventually reached the imperial court, where the Empress Wu Tse-t'ien, who had usurped imperial authority and was ruling in her own name, had been using Buddhism and eminent Buddhist clergy to bolster her claims to legitimacy. He was invited to the court in *Lo-yang in 700, when he was already well over 90, and when he arrived, the empress breached all protocol by prostrating to him. Both she and her successors honoured the master with titles such as *National Teacher (Chin., kuo shih), and kept him at court despite his wish to return to his home temple. He finally died in 706, over 100 years old. He was buried with state honours, and he is one of only three Buddhist monks to receive a biographical notice in the official histories of the T'ang dynasty. In spite of, or perhaps because of, the unwanted eminence that was thrust upon him, envy and hostility grew against him in some quarters after his death. In 732, his former disciple, Shen-hui, denounced him for having sold out to court life and abandoned the true teachings of Ch'an, exchanging the practice of sudden enlightenment for a gradual practice. Because the rhetoric of 'sudden enlightenment' eventually became normative as a result of the *Northern–Southern School controversy, the charges stuck, and Shen-hsiu's reputation faded over time.

However, the actual content of Shen-hsiu's teaching and practice is different from the caricature that emerged from the polemical writings of his critics. It is true that he never rejected textual and scriptural study, and for this the later Ch'an tradition, rejecting such pursuits and calling itself a 'special transmission outside of words and letters', was deficient in his eyes. He inherited a preference for the *Laṅkāvatāra Sūtra* from his master Hung-jen, and is known to have composed a lengthy commentary on the **Avataṃsaka Sūtra* (Chin., **Hua-yen ching*). In reality, however, the criticism is misplaced: Shen-hsiu never saw himself as the founder of a school of Ch'an, and so was unaware and unconcerned with the polemics of later times. He was a well-rounded Buddhist monk, accomplished in *meditation and study, and, in a non-partisan spirit, willing to learn from a multitude of sources. Modern scholarship is now drawing attention to his connections with and influence from both *T'ien-t'ai and *Hua-yen thought. In addition, his practice is not so easily boiled down to a strictly gradual approach. In fact, he and his followers recommended approaches both sudden and gradual, depending upon the abilities and previous experience of the trainee. For these reasons, Shen-hsiu's true accomplishments and contributions to the history of Buddhism in *China have been overshadowed for centuries by the polemics of earlier controversies, and it was only in the 20th century that scholarship has began to recover a more balanced picture.

Shen-hui. *See* HO-TSE SHEN-HUI.

Shen-rap Mi-wo (Tib., gshen-rab mi-bo). The legendary founder or systematizer of *Bön in which he occupies a position equivalent to *Śākyamuni. Shen-rap is said to have been a native of Tazik (stag-zig), possibly to be identified as eastern Persia.

shen-tong. *See* EXTRINSIC EMPTINESS.

shiguzeigan (Jap.; Chin., ssu hung shih yuan). Term for the 'four great vows' of the *Bodhisattva: (1) although sentient beings are numberless, I vow to save them all; (2) although defilements are measureless, I vow to cut them all off; (3) although the Dharma-gates are inexhaustible, I vow to study them all; (4) although the Buddha-way is unsurpassed, I vow to attain it. In east Asia, these vows are generally taken in rituals conferring the Bodhisattva *precepts, or in other rites of passage.

shikan-taza (Jap.). A term used by the Japanese *Sōtō school of *Zen, which means 'just sitting' or 'sitting-only' (literally, 'only attending to sitting in *meditation'). This refers to the Sōtō practice, which followed upon the teachings of the founder *Dōgen (1200–53), that sitting in meditation is not for the purpose of 'attaining' Buddhahood, for all beings already possess *Buddha-nature and have no need to seek its attainment. Rather, he taught that sitting in meditation is its own end and purpose, for by doing so practitioners manifest the Buddhahood that they already possess, in much the same way that a pianist manifests his or her ability to play by sitting and playing.

shiko (Jap.). Term literally meaning 'four witherings', and based on the legend that when the *Buddha passed into extinction there were twin trees at the four cardinal directions surrounding his pallet. Of each pair, one withered and one thrived, and this provided the image for the 'four witherings' and 'four glories' in Buddhist teachings. The four witherings represented by the dead trees indicated the four misapprehensions of Buddhist practitioners in the two vehicles of the Śrāvakas (*Śrāvakayāna) and *Pratyekabuddhas: that the Truth Body (*dharma-kāya) abides forever, that the purity of *nirvāṇa is blissful, that *Buddha-nature is the true self, and the purity of the *Tathāgata's body is great. This sets up an over-reified view of the rewards of practice, which, while perhaps useful in inspiring some to practise, is not ultimately correct.

Shin Arahan. A Burmese monk belonging to the *Mon people and a native of the Thaton region who was responsible for the conversion of King *Anawrahta to *Theravāda Buddhism shortly after the latter ascended the throne in 1044.

According to Burmese tradition, Shin Arahan arrived in the vicinity of Pagān and was discovered in his forest dwelling by a hunter. The hunter, who had never before seen such a strange creature with a shaven head and a yellow robe, thought he was some kind of spirit and took him to the king. Shin Arahan naturally sat down on the throne, as it was the highest seat, and the king thought: 'This man is peaceful, in this man there is the essential thing. He is sitting down on the best seat, surely he must be the best being.' The king asked the visitor to tell him where he came from and was told that he came from the place where the Order lived and that the Buddha was his teacher. Then Shin Arahan gave the king the teaching on mindfulness (*apramāda). Shin Arahan then told the monarch that the *Buddha had passed into *parinirvāṇa, but that his teaching, the *Dharma, enshrined in the *Tripiṭaka and the *Saṃgha, remained. The **Sāsanavaṃsa* gives an alternate version of Anawratha's conversion according to which Shin Arahan had originally come from Sri Lanka to study the Dhamma in Dvāravatī and Thaton and was on his way to Śrī Kṣetra in search of a text when he was taken to Anawrahtā by a hunter.

shinbutsu bunri (Jap.). Term meaning 'the separation of *kami and *Buddhas'. This was the name of a movement that was instituted as official policy after the accession of the *Meiji emperor in 1868 (*see* MEIJI RESTORATION), in which the government, in an effort to limit *Buddhism's influence in the spheres of politics, religion, and culture, decreed that Buddhism and *Shintō were to be separated both ideologically and institutionally. Thus, such syncretic creeds as *honji-suijaku (the theory that Buddhas and kami were different manifestations of the same beings) and institutions such as the jingūji (combined shrine-temple) came to their end. *See also* JAPAN.

shinbutsu shūgō (Jap.). Term meaning 'the unity of the [*Shintō] gods and *Buddhas'. This indicates a component in the Japanization of *Buddhism that is documented from the late 7th century that used various schemes to relate the indigenous gods of *Japan to the newly imported Buddhas and *Bodhisattvas of Buddhism. Three basic relationships emerged. First, the gods were suffering sentient beings in as much need of Buddhist teaching and practice as any other being. Second, the gods assumed the role of guardians of the new religion. Third, the gods came to be seen as local, provisional manifestations of Buddhas and Bodhisattvas in a theory called *honji-suijaku (fundamental ground-provisional traces). For example, the sun goddess Amaterasu, patron of the imperial family, came to be identified with *Vairocana, the Sun-Buddha. In practical terms, all of these theories led to the development of jingūji, or 'shrine-temples' that combined Buddhist and Shintō practice.

Shingon school. The 'esoteric' school of Japanese *Buddhism (*see* ESOTERIC BUDDHISM) founded by *Kūkai (774–834). Kūkai had become convinced that esoteric practice, which bypassed the necessity of strenuous exertions in religious practice by providing students a means for experiencing directly their own inherent Buddhahood, was the highest form of Buddhism. Thus, the practices of this school centred exclusively on an esoteric curriculum and the student took a particular master as his *guru. This master oversaw the *abhiṣeka, or initiation ritual, in which the student stood over a *maṇḍala, a sacred map of the cosmos that associated various *Buddhas and *Bodhisattvas with certain quarters and directions. By dropping a flower onto the maṇḍala, the student associated himself with and received the protection and empowerment (abhiṣeka) of a particular *Buddha or Bodhisattva. After this, the student would engage in ritual visualizations of this Buddha or Bodhisattva, constructing an eidetic mental image of the Buddha in as much detail as possible, realizing that this represented a manifestation of the inherent Buddhahood of his own mind. Such rituals involved the whole person, an ideal reinforced by its use of acts of *body, speech, mind (i.e. *mūdras or hand gestures, and proper posture; *mantras or magical utterances; and the *visualization itself). This was considered superior to 'exoteric' or conventional practices because, rather than involving the student in a long, slow ascent towards purification and enlightenment (*bodhi), it allowed the student to 'try on' the role of enlightened being from the outset, thus making possible the attainment, or rather the manifestation, of Buddhahood in a single lifetime. In addition to practices such as those described above, which were directly intended for the student's own enlightenment, esoteric Buddhism from its inception in *India also held out the promise of this-worldly benefits for practitioners: invulnerability to weapons, immunity from accidents, ability to heal and make rain, and the like. The *Shingon school, even during Kūkai's lifetime, attracted patronage by deploying rituals for these purposes on behalf of paying clients from the royal family and aristocracy. At times, the school concentrated almost exclusively on such lucrative rituals; such periods are generally accounted as times of decline for the school.

Shingon was never the only school of esoteric Buddhism in *Japan. From the outset, it competed with the *Tendai school, whose form of esoteric practice came to be known as taimitsu, and had its own rituals, scriptures, and was balanced with a complete programme of exoteric teaching and practice that tended to keep it more grounded in Buddhist goals and values. The Shingon form of esoteric practice, called tōmitsu, distinguishes itself by its reliance on two difference maṇḍalas, which, while different, are both affirmed as representing the sacred cosmos. However, Shingon has never enjoyed a great deal of institutional or ritual unity. At the time of Kūkai's death, three different temples all had credible claims to leadership in the school, and disputes over preeminence became quite heated. Also, over the years, Shingon practice has subdivided as styles (Jap., ryū) developed. Eventually, there were more than 36 such styles, generally associated with a particular temple or lineage of masters and students. *See also* CHEN-YEN TSUNG.

shinpyu. Burmese term meaning *temporary *ordination.

Shinran (1173–1262). The founder of the *Jōdo Shinshū (True Pure Land school), the largest of *Japan's schools of *Buddhism. Shinran was the son of a minor government bureaucrat. It seems that his family had fallen out of favour with the government due to some doings of his grandfather's, and so his own chances for a good career appeared slight. For this and possibly other reasons, he joined the monastic order at the age of 9.

Shortly after *ordination, he went to Mt. Hiei, and became a dōsō, a *monk who practises the perpetual *nembutsu, a practice whereby one undertook strenuous 90-day retreat periods in which one circumambulated an image of *Amitābha while reciting the nembutsu without respite. He kept this up until he was 29 years old, and then left Mt. Hiei to join *Hōnen's movement in 1201 and remained with him until both were exiled from the capital to different areas in 1207. The two men never met again, and throughout the remainder of his life Shinran claimed he was merely transmitting his master's teachings without innovation. Shinran's exile proved to be a decisive moment for the formation of his teachings. He was 35 years old at the time, and from the age of 9 had known no other life than that of a monk. Now defrocked, he was free from government monastic regulations and duties, and yet he had not freely chosen the lay life for himself. He felt like he was neither here nor there, and called his lifestyle 'hisō hizoku', 'neither *monk nor layman'. He also married during this time, another act which was to have profound consequences for the future of his movement. The school to which he gave rise is the only one whose authority centres on a direct blood line from its founder.

Shinran was pardoned in 1211, and in 1214 moved to the Kantō area where he had a major religious experience. He had taken a vow to chant the three *sūtras of the *Pure Land school 1,000 times for the benefit of sentient beings. But after only four or five days of this, he gave up. It had suddenly struck him how presumptuous it was of him to think that he could do anything at all to help sentient beings in their *suffering. He came to realize that one single recitation of the nembutsu was enough, if it was done in faith. While still living in the Kantō region, he began to work out his theology in a more systematic manner, which led to the completion of his major statement in 1224, a book called the *Kyōgyōshinshō*, or 'Teaching, Practice, Faith, and Attainment'. This was mostly a compendium of passages from earlier Buddhist literature arranged topically for reference, and sometimes Shinran added his own comments to them. He worked on this for 30 years, constantly adding to it and refining it. With new confidence now, he moved among the masses, teaching them to put their trust in *Amida *Buddha for their salvation, reciting the nembutsu with the three states of mind listed in the *Longer *Sukhāvatī-vyūha Sūtra*: sincerity, faith, and the aspiration for *rebirth in the Pure Land. He propagated his teaching by establishing local congregations in private homes known as 'nembutsu dōjō', or 'Buddha-recitation halls'. He never formally took any followers, and indeed did not claim any special knowledge or privilege not shared by any other believer. By repudiating any of the traditional honours normally accorded by disciples to their master, he set up one of the most egalitarian movements in east Asian Buddhist history. Eventually, this method of organization began to work against Shinran, especially when he left the Kantō region and returned to *Kyoto. Since each congregation was autonomous, and there was no centralized authority to maintain control and standards, the only thing holding the movement together was Shinran's own personality. Since he was now far away from his congregations in Kantō, problems developed as some local leaders became authoritarian, or began mis-spending funds, or propagating doctrines of their own, or simply fell into the common trap of believing that the saving grace of Amitābha made conventional morality superfluous (a heresy called 'licensed evil'). He wrote letters and essays deploring these abuses, which were later collected into an anthology called the **Tannishō* (Lamenting the Deviations). In one of the most painful experiences of his life, Shinran was even forced to disown his own son, Zenran. He had dispatched Zenran to Kantō to settle some of these disputes, but while there, Zenran began proclaiming that his father had given him secret teachings, and tried to set himself up in the very master-disciple relationships with them that Shinran himself had rejected. After much correspondence back and forth, it soon became obvious that he had to take the drastic step of disowning Zenran in order to bring the misunderstandings to a definitive conclusion. Shinran died at the age of 90 not long afterwards.

Shintō. The indigenous religion of *Japan. This is not so much an organized, unified religion as a cultural complex of religious myths and rituals carried out originally by clan and village groups and centring on tutelary deities called *kami. These kami can be thought of as deities with names and life-stories attached to them, as in the case of the sun goddess Amaterasu; as personifications of forces of nature; or as the spirit animating awe-inspiring natural features such as waterfalls, stones, mountains, or large and ancient trees. Later in Japanese recorded history, with the successful claim of the Yamato family to rule all of Japan, state-sponsored temples and cults arose to honour and petition kami that transcended familial and local concerns, and imperial/national rituals added a new layer to Shintō practice. The Yamato family was in the process of consolidating their power in the 6th century when *Buddhism arrived in Japan. Thereafter, various proposals were made and decisions taken on the question of how to relate the foreign religion to the native one, or how *Buddhas and *Bodhisattvas were to relate to kami. The *shinbutsu shūgō movement, beginning in the late 7th century, proposed that the kami were to be the guardians of the new religion, or, alternatively, that the kami, while powerful enough to answer certain petitions, were themselves caught in the cycle of *suffering and in need of Buddhist teaching. Finally, the *honji-suijaku theory identified the kami with the Buddhas and Bodhisattvas, claiming them as particularized, local manifestations of their original and universal natures. Such theories paved the way for the combination of Shintō and Buddhism at the institutional level with the founding of jingūji, or 'shrine-temples' where both Shintō priests and Buddhist *monks worked side by side, although with the Shintō functionaries generally in the subordinate position.

Buddhism also stimulated more philosophical reflection among Shintō priestly families. For example, Yoshida Shintō, founded in the 15th century by Urabe Kanetomo (1435–1511), proposed a *cosmology according to which a great Shintō deity created the universe and all that was in it, including Buddhas and Bodhisattvas. Later, in the Edo period (1603–1867), Shintō thinkers made use of new Neo-Confucian (*see* CONFUCIANISM) ideas from *China to bolster a philosophical system sophisticated enough to compete with Buddhism. Shintō also provided the rallying point for restoration of the imperial family to political power, since Amaterasu was both the kami of the nation and the tutelary god of the Yamato clan, and since the ruling warlords (Jap., shōgun) had made much use of Buddhist temples in their administration. Within this situation, it became easy to associate Shintō with the emperor and Buddhism with the warlords. When the Meiji emperor came to power in 1868 (*see* MEIJI RESTORATION), he declared a policy of sundering the connection between Shintō and Buddhism (this split is called *shinbutsu bunri in Japanese). This put an end to syncretism between Shintō and Buddhism, although many of the new religions that have appeared in Japan since the early 1800s, while ostensibly basing themselves on either Buddhism or Shintō, have in fact mixed elements of the two in a new synthesis.

shōbō. 1. The Japanese pronunciation of the Chinese term cheng fa, or 'orthodox *Dharma', a term that means the true teachings of *Buddhism as opposed to other religious teachings or intra-Buddhist heresies. **2.** In the 'three stages' scheme of Buddhist historiography, this refers to the first period, the period of the 'true Dharma', which lasted for the first 500 years after the death of *Śākyamuni *Buddha, and was followed by the periods of the 'counterfeit Dharma' and the 'decline of the Dharma'. *See* THREE PERIODS OF THE TEACHINGS.

Shōbō-genzō (Treasury of the True Dharma Eye). An anthology of 92 essays of varying length and on various topics composed by *Dōgen (1200–53), the founder of the *Sōtō school of Japanese *Zen. This work is important for a number of reasons. It is the first piece of literature to be written in the Japanese vernacular, rather than in the classical Chinese style. It is of high literary quality, showing the master's great skill at phrasing subtle ideas and word-play. Finally, it contains philosophical ideas of such quality as to command the attention of serious thinkers across centuries and cultures. The author's stated goal was to lead the reader to see everything, from the simple quotidian rituals of Zen monastic life to the most abstract philosophical vision, as a *Buddha would. To give an example, the essay 'Uji' (Being Time) plays on a standard classical Chinese compound of two characters that generally means 'at a certain time' or 'there was a time when', and reinterprets the two characters as parallel nouns, i.e. 'Being/Time'. With this play on words as the starting point, Dōgen expounds a view of time as inseparable from existence, where impermanence and change, both functions of time, also define the being or existence of things. As impermanence is the ultimate nature of things, then things are not objects that perdure through time; they are time.

Dōgen originally intended the *Shōbō-genzō* to extend to 100 books, but ill health cut his life short, and the project remained incomplete. Of the 92 essays in the standard edition, only twelve went through Dōgen's final revision, and so most are still initial drafts. However, the affinities of Dōgen's thought as contained in this book with currents of 20th-century Western philosophy, particularly that of Heidegger, has sparked a renaissance of Dōgen studies, both in *Japan and the West.

Shōbō-genzō Zuimonki (Treasury of the True Dharma Eye, Record of What Was Heard). A record of notes taken during Dharma-talks by the Japanese *Sōtō *Zen founder *Dōgen (1200–53), edited by his disciple Koun Ejō (1198–1280). These notes circulated in manuscript form until they were finally published in 1651.

shōdō (Jap.). Written with various Chinese characters, this can mean different things. (1) The abbot's quarters in a *Zen *monastery; (2) the true or orthodox path of practice; (3) an abbreviation for the *Noble Eightfold Path; (4) to 'sing the path', or preach the *Buddha or *Bodhisattva Path; (5) also meaning 'to sing the path', a Zen term for followers of non-Zen schools; (6) in the *Pure Land schools, the 'path of the sages', entailing *ascetic practice to attain the goals of *enlightenment and liberation in this world, as opposed to the 'path of purity' (or the Pure Land) (Jap., *jōdo) of reliance upon the grace of *Amida for liberation; (7) obstacles on the path of practice.

Shōmu Tennō (r. 724–49). The emperor of *Japan who constructed the Great *Buddha of Nara, a colossal image of *Vairocana *Buddha, $53\frac{1}{2}$ feet tall and weighing 452 tons, and installed it in a temple that he renamed the *Tōdaiji. This temple was made the head temple in a system of state-sponsored temples placed in each province and known collectively as kokubunji. Shōmu is also the first emperor to identify himself officially as 'a servant of the *Three Jewels' (*triratna). *See also* NARA PERIOD.

Shōtoku Taishi (572–621). The second son of Emperor Yōmei, Prince Shōtoku was broadly educated in *Confucian classics, Buddhist scriptures, and secular studies such as history, astronomy, and geography. In 592, five years after his father's death, he was named regent for his mother, the Empress, and ruled *Japan in this capacity until his death. He proved an enlightened ruler, and is sometimes credited with drafting Japan's first real constitution in seventeen articles and importing many ideas from *China such as city planning and political arts. In terms of Buddhist history in Japan, Shōtoku is regarded as the first Japanese aristocrat to understand basic Buddhist doctrines and to distinguish it clearly from native Japanese cults of *kami. Three of the earliest scriptural commentaries composed in Japan are attributed to him, and based on stylistic considerations and the fact that these works refer only to other *sūtras known in Japan at that time, some scholars find these attributions credible. He is also credited with building many of the early great temples in Japan, such as the Hōryūji and the Shitennōji. Whether or not he was personally responsible for their construction, he certainly provided the patronage and helped create an atmosphere conducive to such building projects. Finally, he sent many missions across the sea to China to bring the fruits of Chinese civilization to Japan, and these missions included many Buddhist *monks who worked actively to bring scriptures, treatises, and learned Chinese monks back to Japan. Even if scholars dispute some of the activities attributed to him, it is undeniable that Prince Shōtoku gave an enormous impetus to the early development and dissemination of *Buddhism in Japan.

shō-zō-matsu (Jap,; Chin., cheng-hsiang-mo). The names of the Three Periods of the Teachings in east Asian Buddhist thought. 'Shō' means 'true' or 'orthodox', and is short for shōbō, or the 'orthodox *Dharma'. This refers to the first period, which lasted for 500 years after the *Buddha's passing into *nirvāṇa, and represents a golden age in which practitioners are of high capacity and the teachings are transmitted intact, so that many achieve the goal. The next term is short for zōbō, or the 'semblance of the Dharma', and refers to the next period of either 500 or 1,000 years, during which time practitioners' capacities would be lower, their lifespans shorter, and the teachings transmitted imperfectly, with the result that attainment of the goal would be rarer. Finally, matsubō (usually shortened to mappō) means 'final Dharma' or 'the end of the Dharma', and is taken to characterize the age we now live in. During this time, the Dharma cannot be transmitted correctly, practitioners are of low capacity, and the world is beset by so many troubles as to make practice impossible. In east Asian thought, however, this typically was not a cause for despair, because this scheme was accompanied by teachings that the Buddha, having foreseen the coming of this dark age, had provided beforehand, and which were suitable for the time.

shugendō (Jap.). A style of esoteric *ascetic practice (*see* ESOTERIC BUDDHISM) in Japanese *Buddhism that can be found within both the *Tendai and *Shingon schools. The term literally means 'the way of cultivating experience', and is traced back to the *Heian period when privately ordained *monks went to the mountains, partly out of the native Japanese reverence for nature and mountains in particular, and partly to escape the government's increasingly intrusive regulation of monastic life. Such people, called *yamabushi (those who lie down in the mountains) practised austerities such as long and arduous hikes through the mountains, seen as *pilgrimages through sacred landscapes; fasting; long periods of scripture chanting without food and drink, and so on. While originally independent, they later became subsects within the Tendai and Shingon traditions, the two with the greatest emphasis on esoteric practice. The goal of practice is both personal transformation and liberation, and the acquisition of supernatural power.

Shūhō Myōchō (1282–1337). Also known as Daitō Kokushi (or *National Teacher Daitō), he was an eminent *Rinzai *Zen *monk in *Kamakura-era *Japan. He is known for his frequent and often innovative use of the 'capping phrase', which normally is a short utterance that 'caps', or completes, the solution to a Zen riddle (*kōan). Myōchō first entered the *Tendai school at the Enkyō-ji on Mt. Shosha at the age of 10. For the next nine years he received a characteristically wide-ranging Tendai education that included scripture study, monastic regulations, *meditation, and other topics. This is unusual; most Zen masters of the Kamakura period spent their entire careers within the Zen school. Myōchō's own writings attest that, beginning at about age 16, he became dissatisfied with the Tendai curriculum, seeing it as concentrating on peripherals and ignoring the essential event of *enlightenment and personal transformation. After some travel, he presented himself to the master Kōhō Kennichi (1241–1316) in the city of Kamakura.

After a year or two with Kōhō, Myōchō had a major awakening upon hearing someone recite a poem from the next room while in meditation. Kōhō joyfully confirmed his realization. Nevertheless, Myōchō left soon afterward to study in *Kyoto with Nampo Jōmyō (1235–1308). Some sources say that he was dissatisfied with the overly 'Japanized' form of Zen taught by Kōhō and was attracted by Nampo's emphasis on a more purely Chinese style of practice. After further enlightenment experience under his master Nampo Jōmyō in 1307, he went into 20 years of secluded practice (according to some sources, he lived as a beggar under a bridge during this period). After this, he went to Kyoto and founded a temple, the *Daitoku-ji, hard by Mt. *Hiei, and from there participated in the rapid expansion of Zen into western Japan, where the older schools still resisted its establishment. He was one of two monks to defend Zen at the imperially sponsored Shōchū Debate in 1325, responding to opponents (and allegedly converting one of them) with enigmatic Zen words and actions. The emperor awarded the victory to the Zen side, marking the end of the older schools' dominance in the area. Although his descendants suffered some reversals in the century after his death, in time both the Daitoku-ji that he founded, and the Myōshin-ji in which his disciple *Kanzan Egen (1277–1360) served as first abbot, became major temples within the Rinzai system.

Shwedagon Pagoda. The most sacred of all Buddhist sites of *Burma, the Shwedagon

*Pagoda or *Paya consists of a great golden *stūpa rising 321 feet above its base and standing on the 190 feet high Singuttara Hill in the middle of Rangoon, covering an area of some 14 acres. Around the stūpa is a great variety of smaller *zedis, statues, temples, shrines, images, and pavilions. The main stūpa rises from its platform in a fairly standard pattern. First there is the 21 feet high plinth immediately setting the Shwedagon Paya above the lesser structures. Smaller stūpas sit on this raised platform level—four large ones mark the four cardinal directions, four medium-sized ones mark the four corners of the square platform, and 60 small ones run around the perimeter. From this base the stūpa rises in terraces of changing shapes from square to octagonal and finally circular, topped by characteristic architectonic elements: a bell, an inverted bowl, mouldings, *lotus petals, banana bud, and *htī. According to legend, this structure goes back to the time of the *Buddha. However, on the basis of archaeological evidence it is suggested that the original stūpa was built by the *Mon people sometime between the 6th and the 10th centuries. Since then it has been rebuilt several times and its current form dates back to 1769. At one time the shrine terrace was decorated with images of the 37 *nats, but these have now been rehoused in an adjacent shrine. According to legend, two merchant brothers met the Buddha who gave them eight of his hairs to take back to be enshrined in Burma. The two brothers and their king, with the help of a number of spirits, also discovered the hill where *relics of the previous Buddha had been enshrined. Once the relics were safely enshrined, a golden slab was laid on their chamber and a golden stūpa was built on it. Over this a silver stūpa was built, then a tin stūpa, a copper stūpa, a marble stūpa, and finally an iron-brick stūpa, thus completing the Shwedagon Paya. Still according to legend, in subsequent times the stūpa fell into disuse and it is said that Emperor *Aśoka on a visit to Burma had great difficulty finding the site, which he subsequently had repaired. In the 15th century the tradition of gilding the stūpa began. Queen Shinsawbu provided her own weight in gold, which was beaten into gold leaf and used to gild the structure. Her son-in-law, Dhammazedi, offered instead four times his own weight and that of his wife in gold. In the following centuries the stūpa suffered a number of earthquakes and was raided several times. During the last century the complex was the centre of much political activity linked with the Burmese independence movement.

Shwegyin. One of the two main sects (*gaing) or monastic divisions (*nikāya) in the Burmese *Saṃgha founded during the reign of King Mindon (1852–77). In 1980, 7.1 per cent of all monks in Burma belonged to the Shwegyin. The sect takes its name from the village of its founder, U Jagara, and emphasizes stricter adherence to the monastic regulations than its much larger counterpart, the *Thudhamma. The distinction between the two groups parallels that between the Mahanikai (Pāli, Mahānikāya) and the *Thammayut (Pāli, Dhammayuttika) in *Thailand, Laos, and Cambodia. Stricter orders such as the Shwegyin carry their *begging-bowls in their hands rather than in a sling, receive all kinds of food in the same container, eat only once per day, and observe the regulations about handling money and visiting entertainments more strictly. They also tend to spend more time on study and *meditation and less on social affairs and community welfare programmes.

siddha (Skt., accomplished one). An enlightened master or *guru, particularly in the *tantric tradition. The siddha tradition arose in Indian tantric *Buddhism and had a great influence on the development of Buddhism in *Tibet. The term signifies a *yogin who has attained magical powers and has the ability to work miracles. Tibetan Buddhism recognizes a lineage of 84 such siddhas, including *Padmasambhava, *Naropa, and others.

Siddhartha Gautama (*c*.485–405 BCE) (Skt.; Pāli, Siddhattha Gotama). Name of the historical *Buddha. Siddhartha (meaning 'one whose aim is accomplished') was his personal name, and Gautama his clan or family name. His dates are still uncertain, but recent scholarship inclines to the dates shown as opposed to the more conventional ones of 563–486 BCE (*see* DATE OF THE BUDDHA). He was born into a noble family of the *Śākya clan, and for this reason came to be known also as *Śākyamuni (the sage of the Śākyas). His father was *Śuddhodana and his mother *Māyā. According to Buddhist sources his father was king of the city of *Kapilavastu, which was located just inside the southern border of present-day *Nepal. Siddhartha's *birth was preceded by a dream in which his mother saw a white elephant entering her womb. From this the soothsayers foretold that the child would be either a Buddha or a Universal Ruler (*cakravartin). Seven days after giving birth Queen Māyā died. Siddhartha was married to *Yaśodharā (or *Rāhulamātā) and a son, *Rāhula, was born when the Buddha was either 16 or 29. Tradition recalls that the Buddha's father shielded his son from the harsh realities of life until the young prince ventured outside the palace and was confronted by the sight of 'fours signs': an old man, a sick man, a corpse, and a renunciate. These experiences brought home to him the reality of *suffering and the nature of the human predicament, and turning his back on family life he renounced the world and became a religious mendicant. He studied with two teachers, *Udraka Rāmaputra and *Āḷāra Kālāma, but after six years of unproductive *ascetic exercises renounced the path of austerities and embarked on a more moderate spiritual path which he characterized as the 'Middle Way' (*madhyamā-pratipad). By following this he gained enlightenment (*bodhi) at *Bodhgayā at the age of 35 and became a Buddha. After his spiritual awakening he attracted a band of followers and instituted a monastic order (*Saṃgha). He travelled throughout north-east *India as an itinerant teacher for the remaining 45 years of his life. He died at age 80 after being in ill health for some months and having eating a meal of contaminated pork (*see* CUNDA; *MAHĀPARINIBBĀNA SUTTA*; SŪKARA-MADDAVA).

siddhi (Skt.). The extraordinary attainments achieved as the goal of *tantric practice. These comprise two categories: the mundane (*laukika) and the *supermundane. The first category usually comprises clairvoyance, clairaudience, flying in the sky, invisibility, everlasting youth, and other marvels. The supermundane category is enlightenment (*bodhi) itself.

Sigālovāda Sutta (also *Sigālaka Sutta*). The 31st discourse of the *Dīgha Nikāya of the *Pāli Canon, often refererred to as the 'householder's *Vinaya' since it contains practical moral advice for the laity. It is one of the few discourses to address the topic of lay *ethics. The *Buddha encounters Sigāla, a young *Brahmin householder of *Rājagṛha, making offerings to the six directions (the four cardinal points, zenith, and nadir). The Buddha teaches him instead a symbolic interpretation of the ritual according to which parents are the east, teachers the south, wife and children the west, friends and companions the north, servants and workpeople the nadir, and religious teachers and Brahmins the zenith. The Buddha explains in turn the responsibilities owed to each group, and the reciprocal duties they owe to one another. He also gives general homilectic advice concerning six vices in conduct, four motives for evil actions (*desire, hatred, fear, and delusion), the six ways in which wealth is squandered, and the characteristics of good and bad friends.

sikkhamat. The 'training mothers', being the name for Thai Buddhist *women who although not ordained as *nuns embrace elements of the monastic lifestyle, such as *celibacy. They have counterparts in other *Theravāda countries, such as the *dasa silmātā of *Sri Lanka and the *thilashin of *Burma.

Sikkim. A small *Himalayan state, once an independent Tibetan kingdom, which was integrated with *India by popular vote in 1975. Though *Hinduism is now followed by over two-thirds of the population, the influence of Tibetan *Buddhism remains strong. According to tradition, Buddhism was introduced here in the 8th century CE by *Padmasambhava.

śikṣāpada (Skt., training step; Pāli, sikkhāpada). General terms for a *precept or rule of training such as the Five Precepts (*pañca-śīla), the Eight Precepts (*aṣṭāṅga-śīla), or the Ten Precepts (*daśa-śīla).

Śīkṣā-samuccaya. A large compilation of quotations from *Mahāyāna *sūtras arranged by *Śāntideva (685–763 CE) around a small core of 27 verses to illustrate the practices and ideals of Mahāyāna. This work survives in *Sanskrit and provides scholars with important fragments of many Mahāyāna sūtras otherwise not extant in that language.

śīla (Skt.; Pāli, sīla). **1.** Morality, or a moral precept, for example, as in the Five Precepts (*pañca-śīla) and other formulations of normative moral rules. The purpose of śīla is to guide behaviour and cultivate virtue. The *precepts are not commandments and are not enforced by any religious authority. Śīla thus differs from the monastic code (*Vinaya) which is primarily a set of regulations for the harmonious conduct of the communal religious life and as such embodies externally enforceable penalties and sanctions. The śīlas are derived from the conduct of the *Buddha, and are essentially a condensation of the moral behaviour of the enlightened. They list those things an enlightened person will not do, hence their negative form. **2.** Name of the first of the three divisions of the Noble *Eightfold Path, that which includes steps 3–5, namely (3) Right Speech (samyag-vāc), (4) Right Action (samyak-karmānta), (5) Right Livelihood (samyag-ājīva). In Mahāyāna *Buddhism, śīla is the second of the Six Perfections (*ṣaḍ-pāramitā).

Śīlabhadra (529–645 CE). A renowned Indian master of the *Yogācāra school, originally from *Magadha. He was later based at *Nālandā where he became the intellectual successor of *Dharmapāla and his interpretation of Yogācāra doctrines. Śīlabhadra also taught the great Chinese scholar-*monk, *Hsüan-tsang from 636 while the latter resided at Nālandā.

śīla-pāramitā (Skt.). 'The Perfection of Morality', the second of the Six Perfections (*ṣaḍ-pāramitā) that make up the central element of the *Bodhisattva Path. The cultivation of morality involves the elimination of immoral and unethical behaviour through adhering to a code of discipline, while simultaneously cultivating positive moral attitudes that are beneficial to oneself and others.

śīlavrata-parāmārśa (Skt.; Pāli, sīlabbata-parāmāsa). Obsession with the mechanical performance of rules, rites, and rituals, in the mistaken belief that such practices in themselves will lead to salvation. This is a hindrance on the religious path and is listed as the third of the ten fetters (*saṃyojana) and one of the four kinds of clinging (*upādāna). The *Buddha viewed the sacrificial rites of the *Brahmins as falling into this category and as being inefficacious, like many of the severe austerities practiced by ascetics (*śramaṇas). While raising no objection to wholesome rites and rituals and the observance of moral precepts, he emphasized that these must be supplemented by meditative practice and the cultivation of insight and understanding.

silence of the Buddha. *See* AVYĀKṚTA-VASTU.

Silk Road. A trade route that passed from the eastern borders of *Europe through north *India, then through the oasis kingdoms at the borders of the *Himalaya mountain range and the Taklamakan desert, terminating in the desert regions of *Tun-huang in western *China. This route served as the primary path of commerce for the states along its way until it was cut off by the rise of Islamic empires after the 15th century. Its significance for *Buddhism is that it was the principal path for the early transmission of Buddhism from India to China, and later for Chinese pilgrims travelling from China to India in search of teachings and scriptures.

sim. Lao equivalent of the *Pāli term *sīmā.

sīmā (Pāli, boundary, limit). The boundary formally drawn around monastic territory.

sin. *Buddhism does not accept the existence of an omnipotent deity and has no concept of sin as the offence against such a being by the contravention of his will as expressed through revelation or deduced by reason. It does, however, in the doctrine of *karma, distinguish clearly between good and *evil deeds.

Sineru. *See* MERU.

Sinhalese Sect. *See* CHAPATA.

Sivaraksa, Sulak (1933–). Thai activist and leading figure in the *Engaged Buddhism movement, along with Thich *Nhat Hanh and others. Sivaraksa's critical views of the policies of the ruling monarchy have often brought him into conflict with the Thai authorities, and he was arrested in 1984 but subsequently released after a popular campaign. Sivaraksa has supported causes such as the promotion of world peace, the protection of the environment, and an end to economic exploitation, particularly in the developing world. He believes these ends can be achieved by returning to a simpler form of life modelled on the social and political constitution of the Buddhist *Saṃgha. To further these aims he founded the *International Network of Engaged Buddhists (INEB) in 1989.

Six Perfections. *See* ṢAḌ-PĀRAMITĀ.

six realms of rebirth (Skt., ṣaḍ-gati). The six levels that make up the possible range of existence within *saṃsāra. These are the realms of the gods (*deva), the demi-gods (*asura), humans (manuṣa), *animals (tiryak), hungry ghosts (*preta) and *hell denizens (naraka). Generally *Buddhism tends to teach that these levels are real modes of existence although some forms of Buddhism, especially within *Mahāyāna, emphasize that they are rather more like symbolic of states of mind or modes of experience. According to Mahāyāna teachings, *rebirth in each of these modes of existence is brought about by a predominance of a particular spiritual defilement (*kleśa): as a god through pride, a demi-god through jealousy, human through lust, animal through stupidity, hungry ghost through greed and hell-denizen through hatred. These six levels are depicted in the popular Tibetan Wheel of Life (*bhavacakra) paintings.

Six Schools of Nara Buddhism. Six Buddhist schools which developed in *Japan during the *Nara period. (1) The *Sanron school focused on *San-lun teachings; (2) the *Kegon school took up *Hua-yen studies; (3) the *Ritsu school concentrated on monastic *precepts and *ordinations; (4) the *Jōjitsu school studied *Satyasiddhi* doctrines (*see* SATYASIDDHI ŚĀSTRA); (5) the *Hossō school dealt with *Fa-hsiang teachings; and (6) the *Kusha school read the **Abhidharmakośa*, a *Hīnayāna work attributed to the Indian philosopher *Vasubandhu.

Six Sectarian Teachers. Six teachers who were contemporaries of the *Buddha and who were criticized by him for their false teachings, principally because of their denial of the doctrine of *karma. The six are often discussed as a group, and the fullest exposition of their views is to be found in an early discourse entitled *The Fruits of the Religious Life* (**Sāmaññaphala Sutta*), the second discourse of the *Dīgha Nikāya of the *Pāli Canon. The text relates how the king of *Magadha, *Ajātaśatru, went to visit the six teachers and questioned them concerning the fruit of the religious life. After receiving unsatisfactory responses he eventually visited the Buddha and was 'pleased and delighted' at the Buddha's account of the religious life and its culmination in *nirvāṇa.

The views of the six briefly were as follows. *Pūraṇa Kassapa denied that the religious life had any purpose whatsoever, good and evil deeds being equally devoid of religious significance. *Makkhali Gosāla was a determinist who taught that a person's destiny was preordained by fate, while *Ajīta Kesakambala held a materialist view according to which man is utterly annihilated at *death. *Pakudha Kaccāyana espoused a doctrine of fatalistic pluralism, according to which human beings are a compound of elemental substances which disperse at death. All of the above four were ethical nihilists and denied the existence of moral causation. *Sañjāya Belaṭṭhaputta was described as an 'eel wriggler' because he refused to take a stand on any position, and the Jain (*see* JAINISM) leader *Nigaṇṭha Nātaputta, while accepting the doctrine of moral retribution (*kiriya-vāda) reduced the religious life to physical discipline and self-mortification. In view of their failure to appreciate the true purpose of the religious life and its goal all six teachers were roundly condemned by the Buddha. *Sārvāstivāda sources assign the views of the six teachers differently, and with slight variations in the accounts of the views. Since the names of the six teachers and the lists of the various views are found separately elsewhere, it is possible that originally the views were not correlated with a particular teacher.

sixteen Arhats. A tradition exists that when the *Buddha was about to enter final *nirvāṇa he entrusted the care of his teachings to a group of sixteen great *Arhats and their disciples. The Buddha asked these forest-dwelling saints (*see also* ĀRAṆYA-VĀSĪ) to make themselves available to the laity as recipients of offerings so that the donors might gain religious merit (*puṇya). The tradition maintains that in order to comply with the Buddha's request, the sixteen Arhats have extended their lives indefinitely through magical powers and are still accessible to those in need. This tradition is preserved in a number of Indian texts translated into Chinese, notably the *Nandimitrāvadāna*, which was translated by *Hsüan-tsang in the 7th century. The sixteen arhats are Piṇḍolabhāradvāja, Kanakavatsa, Kanakaparidhvaja, Subinda, Nakula, Bhadra, Kālika, Vajraputra, Śvapāka, Panthaka, Rāhula, Nāgasena, Iṅgada, Vanavāsi, Ajita, and Cūlapanthaka.

Six Yogas of Nāropa (Tib., nāro chos drug). Common term for six *dharmas or doctrines transmitted by the *tantric adept *Nāropa to the founder of the *Kagyü school, *Marpa. The Six Yogas have remained an important part of the teachings of the school since its foundation and are standard practice in the three-year, three-month, and three-day retreat undergone by trainee Kagyü *lamas. They consist of: (1) Tummo (gtum mo) or 'heat *yoga', a technique of heating the body by visualizing fire and the sun in the meditator's body; (2) Gyulü (sgyu lus), an illusory or subtle body endowed with the qualities of a *Buddha, including the Six Perfections (*ṣaḍpāramitā); (3) Milam (rmi lam) or 'dream yoga', in which the meditator learns to maintain conscious awareness in the dream state; (4) Osal ('od gsal) or 'clear light', by which the natural luminosity of emptiness (*śūnyatā) is apprehended; (5) *Bar-do or 'intermediate state yoga' which trains the meditator to withstand the disorienting experiences of the intermediate state between *death and *rebirth; (6) *Phowa ('pho ba) or transference of consciouness, in which the ability to separate the *consciousness from the body is attained. Sometimes a seventh yoga is mentioned known as 'transference' (grong 'jug), by means of which a meditator can transfer his consciousness into a recently deceased body in the event of premature death. This enables him to continue his meditational practice without the interruption caused by being reborn as a baby.

skandha (Skt., heap; Pāli, khandha). One of the five 'aggregates' or components which collectively constitute the human individual. According to *Buddhism, the human subject can be deconstructed into these five categories without remainder, and since the five make no reference to an eternal soul Buddhism is said to teach a doctrine of 'no self' (*anātman). According to this, the common but falacious belief in an eternal soul is a case of mistaken identity whereby one or more of the skandhas is mistaken for a soul. The five skandhas are (i) form (*rūpa); (ii) feelings (*vedanā); (iii) perception (*saṃjñā); (iv) volitional factors (*saṃskāra); (v) consciousness (*vijñāna). The five are known as the 'aggregates of attachement' (upādāna-skandha) because as the means to pleasurable experiences they are objects of *desire or craving (*tṛṣṇā). Each of the skandhas, like all compounded phenomena, bears the three marks (*trilakṣaṇa) of impermanence (*anitya), suffering (*duḥkha), and no self (anātman). Enlightenment (*bodhi) consists in realizing that the individual is in reality a process whereby the skandhas interact without any underlying soul or self.

Skandhaka (Skt.; Pāli, Khandhaka). Second of the three divisions of the *Vinaya. This portion of the canonical text deals with the collective rules for the operation of the *Saṃgha as a social and religious institution. It is divided into roughly 20 chapters dealing with topics such as how *ordinations are to be performed, how retreats should be organized, how *schisms should be dealt with, and many other matters of relevance to the daily life of a monastic community.

skilful means. *See* UPĀYA- KAUŚALYA.

śloka (Skt.). A stanza of verse in *Sanskrit comprising 32 syllables. Also used as a unit of measurement for the length of prose texts, possibly to enable scribes to charge their clients their fee for copying texts.

smṛti (Skt.; Pāli, sati). Mindfulness or awareness. An alert state of mind that should be cultivated constantly as the foundation for understanding and insight (*prajñā). Many meditational practices exist to help develop mindfulness, notably the four Foundations of Mindfulness (*smṛti-upasthāna). Smṛti features in many formulations of virtues: it is the third of the Five Powers (*bala), the first of the Factors of Awakening (*bodhyaṅga), and the seventh of the eight factors of the *Eightfold Path.

smṛti-upasthāna (Skt.; Pāli, satipaṭṭhāna). 'The establishment of mindfulness'. One of the most ancient and fundamental schemes of meditational practice. As taught in the *Pāli Canon, the practice consists of attending mindfully to four things in turn:

the body (kāya), feelings (*vedanā), mind (*citta) and mental concepts (dhammā). The meditator focuses on the four with 'clear comprehension' (sampajañña) paying attention to the various physical and mental processes that are taking place. Through observing the rising and passing away of physical, emotional, and mental phenomena the meditator comes to understand that there is no eternal self or soul (*ātman) and that his identity is composed of temporary configurations of impermanent elements.

Soga clan. A prominent family during the 6th century in *Japan, the period when the Yamato clan was consolidating its claim to the imperial throne. At the time of the introduction of *Buddhism into Japan via a diplomatic mission from the Korean kingdom of Paekche, the Yamato emperor was undecided as to whether or not to accept the new religion. Two other powerful clans, the Nakatomi and Mononobe, opposed it, insisting that the divine descent of the Yamato family be accepted as legitimizing their claim to the throne, a claim that would be threatened by the importation of a rival religion. The Soga clan, on the other hand, were managers of imperial estates whose job entailed much contact with foreigners, including the Koreans and Chinese. Seeing that Japan had much to gain from cultural imports, they argued for Buddhism's acceptance. The emperor, as a compromise, allowed the Soga to adopt Buddhism, while not insisting that other clans (including the Yamato) take a position. Thus, the Soga were the earliest 'converts' and patrons of Buddhism in Japan, and it took root under their auspices. *See also* KOREA; CHINA.

sōhei (Jap.). During the period of the *Tendai school's ascendancy from the 10th to the early 17th centuries, it had extensive landholdings and influence with the aristocratic classes. In order to protect these interests, the school's headquarters on Mt. *Hiei maintained a corps of men who, while ostensibly ordained as clergy, actually formed a small private army. At times the sōhei formed the largest fighting force in the capital, and the Tendai school deployed them to intimidate potential rival schools and teachers. The sōhei threat was a factor in the lives, strategies, and fortunes of virtually all of the new schools of *Buddhism that broke off from Tendai during the *Kamakura period.

Sōhō Myōchō. *See* SHŪHŌ MYŌCHŌ.

Sōjiji. One of the two main temples of the *Sōtō school of *Zen in *Japan, second only to *Eiheiji in importance. This temple was founded by *Keizan Jōkin (1268–1325), who had followed Tettsū Gikai (1219–1309) to the Daijō-ji after Tettsū lost a succession dispute at the Eiheiji. Keizan took over a former *Vinaya temple at Sagami (Kanazawa prefecture) and converted it to a Zen temple, giving it the name Sōjiji. Much of the temple's subsequent influence can be attributed to the next abbot, Gasan Jōseki (1275–1365), whose brilliance and energy attracted a corps of distinguished disciples, many of whom spread out to the countryside throughout Japan, establishing branches and forging solid connections with local aristocrats. In this way, the breakaway line of Sōtō, while having lost the succession dispute at the headquarters temple of Eiheiji, eventually came to dominate the Sōtō line as a result of its involvement in the life and needs of Japanese society, while the Eiheiji faction remained cloistered.

Sōka Gakkai International. One of the most successful of the new Buddhist sects, the Sōka Gakkai (Value Creation Society) is an offshoot of *Nichiren *Buddhism. The organization was first formed in 1937 by *Makiguchi Tsunesaburō (1871–1944) and Toda Josei (1900–58), two men who had known each other since 1920 and had joined the *Nichiren Shoshū together in 1928. They called their new group the Sōka Kyōiku Gakkai (Value Creation Education Society). Their original goal was to organize educators and promote a value-based educational system in place of the rote-learning emphasized at that time. They found a suitable religious framework in Nichiren Buddhism, with its emphasis at that time on human life and peace. However, their activities and conviction put them at variance with the militarist stance of the government going into the Second World War, and both were imprisoned in 1943. On 18 November 1944, Makiguchi died at the age of 73 in the Tokyo Detention House. Toda survived, and was released from prison in 1945. He set out to rebuild the organization, which had suffered a decline with the imprisonment of its leadership. He renamed it Sōka Gakkai, and sought to expand its mission outside of the field of education to reach society as a whole. He changed the direction of the group's teaching and activities. Whereas Makiguchi had stressed his theory of value and the responsibility of the individual to learn how to evaluate, or create value, properly, Toda turned the organization in a more religious direction, stressing the pursuit of happiness and the efficacy of the **Lotus Sūtra*, and in particular the chanting of its title as per Nichiren's teachings, as the key to its attainment. His energy and dedication paid off: the Sōka Gakkai grew rapidly under his leadership, to more than 750,000 households by the time of his death in 1958. The presidency of the organization was assumed in 1960 by Daisaku *Ikeda (1928–), who had joined several years before at the age of 19.

Ikeda undertook many initiatives to expand the Sōka Gakkai's membership still further, and also established many other educational, cultural, and political ventures. In January 1975 the Sōka Gakkai International was created, with Ikeda as its first president, and in April 1979 he stepped down as the Sōka Gakkai president, becoming honorary president, in order to further concentrate on the needs of the world-wide membership. In 1992, he officially separated the SGI from its parent group, the Nichiren Shoshū. At that time the group was estimated to have 8 million members. (The Nichiren Shoshū, for its part, excommunicated Ikeda and the SGI for arrogance and deviations from correct doctrine.) The SGI has been controversial for several reasons. Following Nichiren's own example, they practised a very aggressive form of proselytization called 'shakubuku' during the 1960s and 1970s, which contributed to their rapid growth, but alienated many in Japanese society who decried such confrontational methods. They also entered the field of politics in 1955, when a member was elected to the Tokyo prefectural assembly. The SGI responded by forming the Komeikai, or 'clean government association', in 1962 to promote *ethics in office, changing the title to Komeitō, or 'clean government party' in 1964. This party, which claims to be above bribery and corruption and to encourage resistance to militarism, is the third largest party in *Japan, and has suffered some criticism for its blending of politics and religion. Many of these practices (and thus the criticism that they draw) have ameliorated since the 1990s, and in contemporary Japan the SGI is a mainstream lay Buddhist organization with a large international presence.

sokushin jōbutsu (Jap.). A term used by *Kūkai (774–835), founder of the Japanese *Shingon school of *Buddhism, to indicate the attainment of Buddhahood by practitioners in their present lifetime, which pointed to his claim that *esoteric Buddhist practices and rituals constituted a shortcut to this goal. He opposed this to the gradual path of the exoteric schools, through which practitioners might take many lifetimes to achieve the same goal.

Somapuri Mahāvihāra. 'The great *monastery of Somapuri', also known as Pāhārpur Vihāra, is the most impressive of the Buddhist buildings of *Bangladesh. It is generally believed that the temple was built between the end of the 8th and the beginning of the 9th century CE by Emperor Dharmapāla. Somapuri comprises several buildings, surrounded by ramparts on its four sides. The main building contained 177 cells for the *monks, arranged on four floors, together with other halls and rooms. It is therefore thought that Somapuri Vihāra hosted at any time several hundred Buddhist monks. An unusual feature of Somapuri is not just the fine sculptures and terracotta plaques that used to decorate the buildings, but the architectural style of the main temple which stood in the middle of the compound. This brick temple had an unusual base in the shape of a cross, rising from the ground in three stepped terraces which contained several chambers.

Sŏn. The Korean rendering of the Chinese term *Ch'an (pronounced *Zen in Japanese). The Chinese Ch'an school, itself still very young, began filtering into *Korea during the late Silla period, beginning around 780 CE. The earliest transmission of Ch'an to Korea is credited to the *monk *Pŏmnang (fl. 632–46), who had travelled to *China and studied with *Tao-hsin (580–651), the traditional fourth *patriarch of Ch'an. He was closely followed by many other Korean students, who, upon returning to the Korean peninsula, were instrumental in establishing the so-called 'nine mountains' (Kor., kusan), or nine prominent temples that served as the bases of nine branches of masters and disciples. One especially important figure in the development of the Sŏn school is the monk *Chinul (1158–1210), who founded the Sŏngwang Temple on Mt. Chogye, helped to reform the monastic order, and put Sŏn practice on a philosophical foundation of *Hua-yen thought. The 'Chogye school' that emanates from him survives to the present, and the dominant school of Korean Sŏn is the *Chogye Order. Other masters, such as *T'aego Pou (1301–82) and Kihwa (1376–1433), also helped to advance the doctrines, practices, and fortunes of the school.

Korean Sŏn is characterized by its attention to scriptural, doctrinal, ritual, and philosophical matters as well as to the practice of *meditation, Dharma-talks by recognized masters, dialogues, and *kōan study. In its later history it, like the rest of Korean *Buddhism, was affected by the persecutions of the Confucian (*see* CONFUCIANISM) *Ch'osŏn rulers (1392–1910). The colonization of Korea by *Japan in the early 20th century created a new, more tolerant atmosphere for Buddhism, since Japan saw the religion as a cultural link that could be exploited to gain the support of their new subjects, but this new openness carried a price. The Japanese introduced a new degree of laxity into monastic practice, recognizing the right of monks to marry (*see* MARRIAGE), and ignoring restrictions on alcohol and meat (*see* DIET). Thus, after the end of the Pacific War in 1945, factional confrontations broke out within Sŏn between the monks who had followed the Japanese model, and the Chogye Order, who did not recognize the Japanese-influenced monks as monks at all, and wanted them evicted from temple properties, which would be handed into their care. After protracted legal battles and confrontations that extended even into the national legislature, the Chogye Order prevailed, and is today the largest and most powerful faction of Sŏn. *See also* DHYĀNA.

Songs of the Sixth Dalai Lama. The popular short collection of secular poem-songs composed by the controversial and tragic *Dalai Lama VI, Tshangyang Gyatsho (Tib., Tshang-dbyangs rgya-mtsho, 1683–1706). Though the theme of many of these songs is of a romantic nature, some believe they conceal a profounder significance.

Songtsen Gampo (*c.*609–50) (Tib., Srong-bstan sgam-po). One of the three great religious kings of *Tibet. He was a formidable warrior and politician who unified much of Tibet into a single state and opened successful diplomatic relations with the *T'ang Chinese and other countries. It was during his reign that *Buddhism made its first tentative inroads into Tibet with the construction of the *Jokhang. Noteworthy also is the introduction during his reign of a writing system based on a north Indian model.

Sōniryō. A governmental body that regulated the lives and activities of Buddhist *monks and *nuns in *Japan. In 624, the Empress Suiko set up its precursor, the sōgōsei (Bureau of Priests), which was later expanded into the Sōniryō. This body had several responsibilities, including registering the names and locations of all monks and nuns, recording deaths, adjudicating lawsuits against clergy, defrocking errant clergy, and so on.

sopādhiśeṣa-nirvāṇa (Skt.; Pāli, sa-upadhi-sesa-nibbāna). 'Nirvāṇa with the substratum of life remaining'. The condition or state of being awakened in this life (as was the *Buddha) through the destruction of the impurities (*āśrava) and defilements (*kleśa). Also known in *Pāli sources as the extinction of the defilements (kilesa-parinibbāna). In such a person the five aggregates (*skandha) that constitute individuality remain, and he is still exposed to the possibility of *suffering and the effect of previous *karma. Only at *death when final nirvāṇa (*parinirvāṇa) is attained is suffering completely at an end. *See also* NIRUPĀDHIŚEṢA-NIRVĀṆA.

Sŏsan Taesa (1520–1604). Respectful title of the *Ch'osŏn period Korean *Sŏn *monk Hyujŏng, one of the most historically important monks in Korean history. Initially educated in the Neo-Confucian (*see* CONFUCIANISM) orthodoxy of the period, he eventually became dissatisfied and went on a tour of Buddhist temples throughout the country. He joined the monastic order and distinguished himself by his *enlightenment and teaching in the Sŏn (*Zen) tradition, to the extent that

Queen Munjŏng appointed him the chief judge of the order. He soon repudiated the post and returned to the itinerant lifestyle. He taught in all monasteries in *Korea, and worked to achieve a higher integration of Sŏn practice with Buddhist doctrine. He left behind over 70 monastic disciples, both *monks and *nuns, and over 1,000 lay followers. The book entitled *Sŏnga Kwigam* he composed on Sŏn practice is still studied by present-day practitioners. Interestingly, he is also remembered for the army of monks he raised and trained that proved instrumental in turning back a Japanese invasion of the Korean peninsula by the armies of Hideyoshi Toyotomi.

Sōtō (Sōtō-shū). One of the two major schools of *Zen in Japanese *Buddhism. The school (Jap., shū) was founded by *Dōgen (1200–53), who saw it as a transmission of the *Ts'ao-tung school of Chinese *Ch'an; hence, the name Sōtō, which is the Japanese pronunciation of the characters 'Ts'ao-tung'. Dōgen established a style of Zen that made no distinction between practice and attainment; for him, the object of sitting was not to attain Buddhahood, but to manifest one's innate *Buddha-nature through the act of sitting itself. Thus, unlike the *Rinzai school that used riddles (*kōans) to spur practitioners to enlightenment (*bodhi; *satori), Dōgen downplayed the goal-oriented nature of *meditation and aimed instead at the realization of a reality that was always already present to those who would notice it. At the time of Dōgen's death, the Sōtō-shū consisted of a small group of disciples headquartered in the remote mountain Eihei Temple in Echizen prefecture. As it was so small, and as Dōgen himself rejected the concept of 'school' (Jap., shū) entirely, it is difficult to speak of the group he left behind as the Sōtō-shū. The development from small band of followers to one of the largest schools of Japanese Buddhism really stems from the activities of later generations of his disciples. After Dōgen's death, his chief disciple Koun Ejō (1198–1280) succeeded him as abbot of the Eihei Temple. Ejō himself picked a younger *monk named Tettsū Gikai (1219–1309), a man who had already been marked for leadership by Dōgen himself, to nurture as his own successor. However, Ejō's tenure as abbot was marked by a routine and unbending adherence to Dōgen's teachings and practices, but without Dōgen's vision and leadership, and the temple fell into decline. Differences between Ejō and Gikai appeared from the beginning, but Ejō, out of deference to Dōgen's wishes, did his best to train his younger colleague to take responsibility for the community.

Gikai travelled in *China from 1259 to 1262, and when he returned with sophisticated architectural drawings and plans, Ejō put him in charge of temple construction. Five years later, Ejō stepped down as abbot and handed the leadership over to Gikai. Almost immediately the monks broke into pro- and anti-Gikai factions. Those who opposed him thought he was abandoning the simplicity and focus of Dōgen's ideal monastic life, squandering time and resources on new buildings and external decor. Gikai even went so far as to introduce *Shingon liturgies into the life of Eiheiji, contaminating the 'pure' Zen of Dōgen. Finally, in 1272, the monks petitioned Ejō to resume the abbacy, which he did, and during his final years he successfully held dissension to a minimum. This set the stage for the division of Sōtō into two competing factions. After Ejō died in 1280, Gikai felt he should resume the abbacy, based on his previous experience and upon Dōgen's Dharma-transmission to him. Others within the community, uncomfortable with his progressiveness and (to their mind) over-accommodation with worldly concerns, wanted another of Ejō's prominent disciples, Gien (d. 1314) to succeed as abbot. The faction supporting Gikai prevailed, and he took up a second term as abbot of the Eihei Temple. However, the second wave of Mongol invasions (*see* MONGOLIA) in 1281 increased public demand for esoteric rituals for the protection of the nation, and Gikai was willing to make room in Eiheiji's regimen to meet this demand. His actions brought the simmering conflict to a head: open fighting broke out within the compound, and Gikai was forced to flee, leaving the office of abbot open to Gien. The Sōtō school was split. The Eihei temple, factionalized and concerned with maintaining the purity of its tradition, languished for a time, while the faction that went with Gikai out of the temple flourished. Gikai's careful cultivation of contacts with wealthy patrons and of good relations with other Buddhist groups, and his concern that his religious practice meet the needs of the times, paid off in terms of support, and he was able to found several monastic communities. Thus, for a time, the branch of Sōtō that dominated was precisely the one that did not follow Dōgen's single-minded Zen practice, but a mixture of meditation, esoteric ritual (*see* ESOTERIC BUDDHISM), and public service.

Gikai's disciple *Keizan Jōkin (1268–1325) helped to heal the divisions. Keizan brought together into a harmonious whole the affirmation of Dōgen's vision of Zen as the normative practice of the school as well as the outreach activities of the Gikai branch. One of his temples, the *Sōjiji, gained imperial recognition and patronage and became the head temple of the Sōtō order, despite which it managed under Keizan and his successor Gasan Jōseki (1275–1365) to come to terms with the former head temple Eiheiji. This combination of serious meditative practice emphasizing realization of an already-inherent *Buddha-nature, willingness to provide esoteric rituals for aristocratic clients, and engagement with the common people in such areas as road repair and free clinics, proved successful. Although there was further filiation of the Sōtō line, it managed to maintain a unified focus and went on to become the largest of the Zen schools in *Japan.

soul. *See* ĀTMAN.

south-east Asia. South-east Asian *Buddhism is the product of a highly complex system of intertwining historical, geographic, political, and cultural circumstances. The form of Buddhism that predominates in the region is *Theravāda, deriving historically from the *Sthavira group of schools that emerged in 3rd century BC *Sri Lanka. From Sri Lanka *monks carried the teachings of the *Buddha to *Burma, *Thailand, Laos, and *Cambodia, where, compounded with the previous religious practices of the people of those countries, it has produced the now existing local variations of Theravāda Buddhism. Despite these variations, and the fact that the early history of the religion in south-east Asia is even more piecemeal than the foregoing suggests, there are some common features. For example, among the factors that facilitated the spread of Buddhism in the area is the fact that it was adopted by the rulers of the region. These modelled their notion of the Buddhist king or ideal ruler (*cakravartin) on the Indian emperor *Aśoka, who had greatly promoted the spread of Buddhism. The close association between *Saṃgha and state in south-east Asia meant that the kings of this region took upon themselves the duty of overseeing the Saṃgha of their country to ensure that it conformed to the norms laid down in the *Vinaya Piṭaka. This interest of the king in the orthodoxy and orthopraxy of his national Saṃgha is due to the particular link between Saṃgha and kingship that developed in this region. On the one hand, the Saṃgha justified the authority of the king, legitimizing the symbols on which his power rested. This was done in several ways, most noticeably through the compilation of historic literary works. On the other hand, the king, who since the lifetime of the *Buddha had been the principal sponsor of the Saṃgha, not only acquired great merit (*puṇya), but by giving his favour to one or the other monastic group (*nikāya) made sure that none of them became so powerful as to threaten his control.

With the arrival of the colonial powers, the nature of the relationship between political and religious power in the region altered (most notably in Burma) and resulted in the birth of a modern Saṃgha, a greater involvement of the laity in religious matters and a strong correlation of religious and national identity. The modern centralised Saṃgha is largely a result of the development of the modern nation-state and the consequential centralisation of political power. The greater involvement of the laity in all religious matters is due to the fact that the Saṃgha had lost in the king its major sponsor and because with the advent of printed texts and increased literacy the teachings of Buddhism had become more accessible. The involvement of the laity in religious affairs has been mirrored by the social work the monks of this region have been involved in in more recent times. During the last decades of the 20th century various temples have pioneered development programmes geared primarily to the needs of the rural poor. These activities have been at the centre of much public debate, raising, again, the issue of what is appropriate behaviour for a monk.

The greater interest of the laity in Buddhism has generated a sense of national identity, especially in those countries that came to be under the rule of colonial powers. In Burma, for example, the Saṃgha used to be very much under the control of the king. There, a large administrative body headed by a Saṃgharāja, appointed by each king in turn, ruled over the Saṃgha. When the British annexed Burma this system collapsed and as a consequence new groups and movements originated within the Burmese Saṃgha and communities of lay supporters, which in turn became closely linked to the independence movements. Thailand also saw in the 19th century the revival of Buddhism in association with the introduction of social and political reforms. This country, however, had not been colonized. In this case it was the ruling Buddhist dynasty, that of the Chakri kings, that sponsored the revival and the social reforms. The Thai kings practically held divine status, but faced with the modernization movement that threatened to make their own existence obsolete, decided to use their traditional role to lead the movement by means of social reform. The more independent modern south-east Asian Saṃgha has also become more openly involved in all sorts of social and political matters. This remains true throughout the region, despite the fact that in more recent times in Laos and Cambodia the political events of the 1970s have severely curtailed the activities of Buddhist monks. In Burma, the monks have alternatively given and denied their support to the various post-war governments.

Two other important characteristics of south-east Asian Buddhism are the phenomenon of *temporary ordination and the lack of ordained *nuns. The virtual absence in this region of fully ordained nuns is due to the fact that their *ordination tradition has died out in Theravādin countries, and this feature is not only peculiar to this region. Provisions exist for *women to ordain to a level which is intermediate between the Five Precepts (*pañca-śīla) for a lay Buddhist, and the ten undertaken by the novice (*śrāmaṇera). These women, who wear robes, are known in Thailand as *sikkhamat or mae chii, in Sri Lanka as *dasa silmātā, and in Burma as *thilashin. Temporary ordination is a rite of passage into manhood practised exclusively in the Theravādin countries of south-east Asia. It requires that all men at some point in their life, before their *marriage, take ordination and spend some time in a monastery (*vihāra). This custom was not practised during the lifetime of the *Buddha and it is not known when it was introduced in south-east Asia.

Southern School. A school of *Ch'an *Buddhism in *T'ang-dynasty *China that traced its origins to the sixth Ch'an *patriarch Hui-neng (638–713) and embraced the position of '*sudden enlightenment'. *See* NORTHERN-SOUTHERN SCHOOL CONTROVERSY.

sparśa (Skt.; Pāli, phassa; contact). Technical term in Buddhist psychology referring to the contact between an organ of sense, such as the eye, and its corresponding object, such as a visible form. In an intact organism, the contact between the two gives rise to a particular kind of consciousness (*vijñāna), for example, eye-consciousness or the experience of seeing (cakṣu-vijñāna), ear consciousness or the experience of hearing (śrota-vijñāna), etc. Sparśa thus denotes the moment when the mind makes contact with the external world. This experience can trigger off a chain of either wholesome or unwholesome mental states (for example, the perception of a pleasant form may lead to *desire and craving (*tṛṣṇā) for the object perceived. Buddhist psychology emphasizes the need for constant mindfulness (*smṛti) in order to monitor—and when necessary interrupt—negative chains of consciousness which may follow an initial sensory contact. The function of sparśa is illustrated by its position in the twelvefold scheme of Dependent Origination (*pratītya-samutpāda): as the sixth link, it arises in dependence on the six sense-bases (*ṣad-āyatana) and conditions feeling (*vedanā). Sparśa is also one of the four nutriments (*āhāra).

spatial category (Tib., klong-sde). The second of three subdivisions of the *Nyingma *atiyoga class. Its teachings aim to establish that all phenomena arise as adornments of the infinite expanse of primordial awareness beyond all duality. *See also* DZOGCHEN.

śraddhā (Skt,; Pāli, saddhā). An attitude of

faith, trust, or confidence, especially in the *Buddha and his teachings. Faith is a prerequisite for embarking on the *Eightfold Path, but it must be tempered by critical reflection and tested against one's own experience. In general, there is no doctrine of 'salvation by faith' in *Buddhism, and blind faith is not regarded as a virtue: instead each person must cultivate insight and understanding (*prajñā) into the *Four Noble Truths. Some forms of *Pure Land Buddhism, however, do teach that *rebirth in a Pure Land (or *heaven) can be obtained through faith alone.

śraddhā-anusārin (Skt,; Pāli, saddhā-anusārin). 'One who follows in faith'. According to the early teachings, the Noble Path (*ārya-marga) may be entered and its fruit attained in a variety of ways. The śraddhā-anusārin is the first in a sevenfold list of noble persons (*ārya-pudgala) who enter the Noble Path through a range of dispositions. The śraddhā-anusārin is distinguished by the fact that he attains the path through the basis of the faculty of faith (*śraddhā), in contrast to the Dhammānusārī (Skt., *Dharmānusārin), who attains it through intellectual understanding of the *Dharma. For the complete list of seven noble persons, *see* ĀRYA-PUDGALA.

śramaṇa (Skt., striver; Pāli, samaṇa). One who exerts himself in the quest for religious knowledge, typically as a mendicant or homeless wanderer. Somewhat before the time of the *Buddha such individuals constituted a movement of religious seekers who rejected the orthodox teachings of *Brahmanism and typically formed themselves into small groups around a particular teacher or leader. It is out of this amorphous community that groups like the Jains (*see* JAINISM), *Ājivakas, and Buddhists subsequently emerged. In the *Pāli Canon the Buddha is frequently referred to as 'the samaṇa Gotama' and the Indian religious community is summed up in the phrase 'Samaṇas and Brāhmaṇas', referring to unorthodox and the orthodox religious practitioners respectively.

śrāmaṇera (Skt.; Pāli, sāmaṇera). A novice *monk, someone who has taken *pravrajyā, or lower *ordination, but not *upasaṃpadā, or higher ordination. Because the *Prātimokṣa rules do not apply to them, they do not take part in the recital of the Prātimokṣa on *Posadha (Pāli, uposatha) days. A female novice is known as a śrāmaṇerī (Pāli, sāmaṇerī).

śrāmaṇerī. *See* ŚRĀMAṆERA.

Śrāvaka. *See* ŚRĀVAKAYĀNA.

Śrāvakayāna (Skt., vehicle of the hearers). Name given by the *Mahāyāna to the early disciples who 'heard' the teachings of the *Buddha and by practising them sought to become *Arhats. Like *Hīnayāna, the term has a derogatory flavour (although in this case less pronounced) since the hearers are seen by the Mahāyāna as interested only in their personal salvation in contrast to the more altruistic path of the *Bodhisattvayāna which aims at universal liberation. The term frequently occurs in the threefold classification of Śrāvakas, *Pratyekabuddhas, and *Bodhisattvas, which represent the three main types of religious aspirant.

Śrāvastī (Skt.; Pāli, Sāvatthi). The capital of the ancient Indian state of *Kośala, which was located at present-day Sāheṭh-Māheṭh by the river Rapti in Uttar Pradesh. Its location on important trade routes ensured its prosperity and political importance. The *Buddha spent much of his later life in this city at the *Jetavana park donated by the rich merchant *Anāthapiṇḍika, and the Pūrvārāma which was constructed by the patroness *Viśākhā. By the 7th century, when it was visited by Chinese pilgrims such as *Hsūan-tsang, it was largely in ruins and its many *vihāras deserted, although a small Buddhist presence seems to have been maintained there until the 12th century. The site was discovered and excavated in 1908.

srid pa'i 'khor-lo. Tibetan term for the 'wheel of life'. *See* BHAVACAKRA.

Śrī Kṣetra Pyu Golden Pāli Text. One of the earliest known surviving *Pāli texts. It consist of 20 leaves of gold, bound as a palm-leaf manuscript and containing eight excerpts of canonical Buddhist texts. Dated around the mid- or late 5th century, it was compiled by several authors in what is now *Burma.

Sri Lanka. Modern state established on the

island off the southern tip of *India known in *Pāli sources as *Tambapaṇṇi-dīpa (copper leaf island). This was the first region outside of India to be converted to *Buddhism. It was brought to the island around 240 BCE by the *monk *Mahinda, son of Emperor *Aśoka. A monastery known as the *Mahāvihāra was built near the capital *Anurādhapura, and from there Buddhism spread throughout the island. An order of *nuns was established at the same time by Mahinda's sister, the *nun *Sanghamittā, who brought with her a cutting of the *Bodhi Tree that was planted at the Mahāvihāra. The early political history of the island was turbulent, and punctuated by frequent invasions by the Damiḷas (Tamils) from India. Out of fear that the *Buddha's teachings might be lost, the *Pāli Canon was committed to writing during the reign of King Vaṭṭagāmaṇi (r. 29–17 BCE). Around the same time, the king founded the *Abhayagiri monastery, which became a rival to the Mahāvihāra. Around the 4th or 5th century the island became home to the great scholar and commentator *Buddhaghoṣa, who composed many important works including the encyclopedic *Path of Purification* (**Visuddhimagga*), a compendium of *Theravāda teachings structured according to the three divisions of the *Eightfold Path, namely morality (*śīla), meditation (*samādhi), and insight (*prajñā). *Mahāyāna schools also enjoyed popularity at this time, but the Theravāda eventually reasserted itself as the dominant tradition. Due to a combination of political problems and doctrinal disputes, however, the *Saṃgha fell into decline, and the *ordination lineages of both monks and nuns died out. Monks were sent for from the *Mon region of present-day *Burma, and the male lineage was restored. There was further political turmoil in the early modern period when the island was ruled in turn by the Portuguese, the Dutch, and the British. Once again the ordination lineage died out and monks had to be sent from *Thailand to restart it. Sri Lanka gained independence from the British in 1948, but in modern times has continued to be plagued by political problems and intermittent civil war between the Sinhalese Buddhist majority (numbering over 70 per cent) and the minority Tamil population in the north. At times Buddhist monks have fanned the flames by likening the dispute to a holy war and campaigning for discriminatory constitutional reform. This reached an extreme in 1959 when the Prime Minister S. W. R. D. Bandaranaike was assassinated by a Buddhist monk who felt his position towards the Tamils was too conciliatory. At the time of writing the political problems show no sign of early resolution.

Śrīmālā-devi-siṃhanāda Sūtra. 'The Sūtra of Queen Śrīmālā', a middle-period *Mahāyāna *sūtra important for its teachings related to the 'embryonic *Buddha' (*tathāgata-garbha) theory, the 'one-vehicle' (*Ekayāna) doctrine, and its valorization of the female in the form of Queen Śrīmālā, the chief character of this text. It is predicted in the text that Queen Śrīmālā will become a *Buddha and preside over her own Buddha-field (*Buddha-kṣetra). The text survives in recently discovered *Sanskrit fragments as well as Chinese and Tibetan translations.

śrīvatsa (Skt.). A curl of hair or a mark in the shape of a *swastika on the *Buddha's chest.

śrotāpanna (Skt.; Pāli, sotāpanna). A 'stream-winner', one who has entered the *supermundane path (*ārya-mārga) at the lowest of the four levels and become one of the four 'noble persons' (*ārya-pudgala). Such a person is securely established on the path to *nirvāṇa and has eliminated the first three of the ten fetters (*saṃyojana) but still has defilements (*kleśa) remaining. A śrotāpanna will undergo a maximum of seven more *rebirths in the three higher realms of rebirth (*see also* GATI; SIX REALMS OF REBIRTH).

Stcherbatsky, Fedor Ippolitovich (1866–1942). Russian scholar who became famous for his pioneering work on Buddhist logic (*pramāṇa). Born in Poland to aristocratic parents he studied philology, *Sanskrit, and Indian philosophy before embarking on a number of trips to *Mongolia where he studied under Buriat lamas. His most influential works are *The Central Conception of Buddhism* (1923), *The Conception of Buddhist Nirvana* (1927), and *Buddhist Logic* (2 vols., 1932).

stem cell research. Based on recent breakthroughs in genetics, scientists see great potential for the use of human stem cells in the treatment of many medical conditions, ranging from Parkinson's and Alzheimer's diseases to diabetes, spinal cord injuries, and degenerative heart conditions. The pluripotent nature of these cells means that they can develop into any kind of bodily tissue. Given the emphasis that *Buddhism places on the central virtues of knowledge (*prajñā) and compassion (*karuṇā), and its long tradition of practising *medicine in the monasteries, the recent advances in scientific understanding and the prospect of the development of cures and treatments which alleviate human suffering are to be welcomed. At the same time, however, *Buddhism places great importance on the principle of **ahiṃsā*, or non-harming, and therefore has grave reservations about any scientific technique or procedure that involves the destruction of life, whether human or animal. Such actions are prohibited by the First Precept (*see* PAÑCA-ŚĪLA), which prohibits causing death or injury to living creatures.

Buddhism has no central authority competent to pronounce on ethical dilemmas, and different sects and groups will typically discuss and resolve such matters at a local level. In terms of general principles, however, it seems that in accordance with other world religions Buddhism would hold that: (*a*) there is no ethical problem in principle with the therapeutic use of adult stem cells; and (*b*) research which involves the intentional destruction of human life, such as harvesting embryonic stem cells from embryos, is morally impermissible. Buddhism teaches that individual human life begins at conception. By virtue of its distinctive belief in *rebirth, moreover, it regards the new conceptus as the bearer of the karmic identify (*see* KARMA) of a recently deceased individual, and therefore as entitled to the same moral respect as an adult human being. For this reason Buddhism sees the moral issues raised by stem cell research as not in principle different from those raised by IVF treatment where this involves the destruction of spare embryos, and a fortiori *abortion. The above holds true regardless of the benevolent intentions of those conducting the research or the eventual good consequences that may flow from it. It follows that it would be immoral to use as a source of stem cells for research purposes either surplus unwanted or frozen embryos created for IVF treatment (whether or not these would eventually be destroyed in any case), or cloned human embryos (*see* CLONING) specifically created for research purposes. Regarding the use of stem cells taken from aborted foetuses, there is scope for different views. Some would regard it as permissible, since in this case the central objection that a living being was harmed through the harvesting of the cells would not apply as the donor is already deceased. Where a legally valid consent has been obtained from the next of kin for the use of the cells the situation can be seen as analogous to the donation of cadaver organs for transplantation. The criterion here is similar to that employed by President Bush in his decision in 2001 to allow US government-sponsored research to utilize a list of 60 existing embryonic stem cell lines, but not to use or develop new ones. The alternative position takes a stricter view on the question of complicity and holds that the cells obtained through abortion would be tainted by the immorality of the abortion itself and should therefore not be used. The analogy of organ donation would be challenged by pointing out that in this case, unlike that of most cadaver transplants, the person providing the consent (usually the mother) will be the same person who has direct responsibility for the death of the donor. A closer analogy, it might be suggested, is with using money stolen in a bank robbery for charitable purposes, something which would still be wrong regardless of the good achieved. There is thus scope for legitimate disagreement on this particular point, although perhaps the majority of Buddhists would incline towards the former position.

Sthavira (Skt, elder; Pāli, thera). One of the two main sectarian groups in early Indian *Buddhism, the other being the Universal Assembly (*Mahāsaṃghikas). The two groups went their separate ways at the Council of Pāṭaliputra (*see* COUNCIL OF PĀṬALIPUTRA I). The Sthaviras claimed to represent older more orthodox teachings that could be traced directly back to the *Buddha, and they branded their opponents as heretics, although the Mahāsaṃghikas appeared to have been the more populous body. The *Theravāda school claims direct descent from the Sthaviras but, although they share the same name (Thera and Sthavira being the *Pāli and *Sanskrit forms of the same word meaning 'elder'), there is no historical evidence that the Theravāda school arose until around two centuries after the Great Schism which occurred at the Council of Pāṭaliputra.

Sthiramati. A 6th-century Indian scholar-*monk, based primarily in Valābhi (present-day Gujarat), although he is thought to have spent some time at *Nālandā. He was renowned for his numerous and detailed commentaries on *Yogācāra and *Abhidharma works by *Vasubandhu and others, as well as a commentary on the **Kaśyāpa-parivarta*.

storehouse consciousness. *See* ĀLAYA-VIJÑĀNA.

stūpa (Skt.; Pāli, thūpa). A religious monument which evolved from the prehistoric tumulus or burial mound into a dome-shaped structure such as the early Indian stūpas at *Sāñcī. To this shape a spire was subsequently added, and the final phase of development was the *pagoda style of tower found throughout east Asia. Stūpas were built originally to commemorate a *Buddha or other enlightened person, a practice validated by the *Buddha in the **Mahāparinibbāna Sutta* where he leaves instructions that a stūpa is to be constructed over his *relics. As well as relics, stūpas often contain sacred objects, such as texts. A small replica of a stūpa is often used as a reliquary.

Subāhu-paripṛcchā. An early key *kriyā-tantra in eleven chapters which describes the basic rituals and equipment needed for tantric practice. The text survives only in Tibetan, Chinese, and Mongolian translations.

Śubhākarasiṃha (637–735). An Indian scholar-*monk. Born into a royal family of Orissa, he inherited the throne at age 13 but renounced it when his brothers began a violent struggle over the succession. Later, after becoming a monk at *Nālandā, he travelled to *China at the behest of his master Dharmagupta and arrived in 716. He was particularly instrumental in popularizing early forms of *tantric *Buddhism in *China, through his translation, in collaboration with Yi-hsing, of the **Mahā-vairocana-abhisambodhi Tantra* and other key works such as the **Susiddhikāra Tantra* and the **Subāhu-paripṛcchā*. He is also counted as one of the *patriarchs of Japanese *Shingon Buddhism.

Subhūti. An *Arhat. A minor figure in the early tradition, declared to be the chief among the disciples who dwell in remote places (araṇavihārin). He becomes much more important in *Mahāyāna *Buddhism where he appears as chief interlocutor in many *sūtras, particularly in the early Perfection of Insight (*Prajñā-pāramitā) literature. There he is depicted as a wise *Bodhisattva who confounds the early disciples with his profound understanding of the doctrine of emptiness (*śūnyatā).

subitism. The name given in *Ch'an and *Zen thought to the position that enlightenment (*bodhi; *satori) must be instantaneous, and not attained through practice over a period of time, however short. *See* SUDDEN ENLIGHTENMENT; NORTHERN-SOUTHERN SCHOOLS CONTROVERSY.

suchness. *See* TATHATĀ.

sudden enlightenment. The position on *enlightenment supposedly taken by the '*Southern School' of Chinese *Ch'an in the *Northern–Southern Schools Controversy of the 8th century. This position is generally opposed to that of '*gradual enlightenment'. Based on an extreme philosophical non-dualism that denies any inherent or substantial difference (though without positing an identity) between dyadic pairs such as practice and attainment, ignorance (*avidyā) and wisdom, *saṃsāra and *nirvāṇa, and cause and effect, this position asserts that enlightenment comes suddenly, or more accurately instantaneously. This is so because the lack of difference between path and goal means that there is literally nowhere to go and nothing to attain; the goal is already in hand and needs only be known. In contrast, the gradualist position holds that one must go through a process, however short or long, to purify the mind and rectify conduct, thereby moving along a path toward the goal. The 'subitists' (*see* SUBITISM), or those who held to the position of sudden enlightenment, criticized such a vision of Buddhist practice and attainment as philosophically untenable, since it artificially differentiated the paired terms given above. In the aftermath of the controversy, the language of sudden enlightenment became normative, and even though historically the Ch'an school in *China and its derivatives in *Japan, *Korea, and *Vietnam taught paths of practice, they were always careful to explain the efficacy of these practices in terms of the philosophy of sudden enlightenment.

suddhāvāsa (Pāli, pure abode). Name of a group of five *heavens, being the five highest in the Form Realm (*rūpa-dhātu). It is here that 'non-returners' (*anāgāmins) are born, and where they attain *arhatship.

Śuddhodana. The father of *Siddhartha Gautama, the *Buddha. According to Buddhist sources he was a king (rāja) of the *Śākya people, although historically the Śākyas may have had a republican constitution. Śuddhodana ruled from his capital at *Kapilavastu, which today would lie inside the southern borders of *Nepal. He belonged to the noble or warrior (*kṣatriya) *caste and is depicted as wealthy and indulgent towards his son. On hearing a prediction that his son would renounce the world and become a religious teacher, he used every means to keep him inside the palace, providing luxuries and distractions of all kinds. *Māyā, the mother of the Buddha, was his chief consort, and after her death he married her sister *Mahāprajāpatī, by whom he had a son, *Nanda. When the Buddha ordained both Nanda and his grandson *Rāhula, Śuddhodana was distressed and obtained the Buddha's agreement that *monks should not be ordained in future without parental consent. *See also* SIDDHARTHA GAUTAMA.

sudurjayā-bhūmi (Skt.). The fifth of the *Bodhisattva Levels (*bhūmi), 'the One Difficult to Conquer', according to the **Daśabhūmika Sūtra*. The level bears this name because at this stage the Bodhisattva engages in the Perfection of Meditative Concentration (*samādhi-pāramitā) which is very difficult for demons to overcome.

suffering. Common English translation of the *Sanskrit word *duḥkha (Pāli, dukkha) which embraces a range of meanings from 'suffering' to 'unsatisfactoriness'. It characterizes the defective nature of life in *saṃsāra. Duḥkha is the subject of the first of the *Four Noble Truths.

Suhṛllekha. 'Letter to a Friend', a didactic letter in 123 verses by the 2nd century philosopher *Nāgārjuna, thought to have been composed for the benefit of Gautamīputra Śatakarṇī of the south Indian Śātavahāna dynasty. The work provides a succinct overview of the *Mahāyāna path for the general reader.

suicide. Suicide is seen by *Buddhism as a futile act that will not provide a solution to suffering (*duḥkha). By virtue of its belief in *rebirth, Buddhism teaches that that suicide does not offer a permanent release from life's problems but merely postpones them to be faced at a later time. Moreover, the taking of any life (including one's own) is prohibited by the first of the Five Precepts (*pañca-śīla). This means that suicide produces evil *karma that will simply aggravate the difficulties rather than diminish them. Buddhism teaches that what it calls 'a precious human rebirth' is extremely difficult to attain, and that to cut it short is to waste an invaluable opportunity for spiritual development. It also deprives others of the benefits one might bring to them as a *Bodhisattva, apart from the grief it brings to friends and relatives. There are two particular circumstances that have been thought to be exceptions to the above general rule. The first concerns suicide by *Arhats, and some scholars have concluded that Buddhism regards this as morally permissible. This popular but doctrinally dubious notion has gained currency by being linked to the idea that the enlightened pass beyond conventional moral norms, a view that no longer commands wide respect. The second case is the practice of ritual suicide in *Japan (*hara kiri). This is a striking feature of Japanese culture that has no precedent in Indian Buddhism and is not sanctioned by mainstream Buddhist *ethics. *See also* EUTHANASIA; VAKKALI.

sūkara-maddava (Pāli). The name of the dish served to the *Buddha shortly before he died, as recorded in the **Mahāparinibbāna Sutta*. The term sūkara-maddava literally means 'soft pork'. However, the understanding that this was a meat dish has been rejected by many *Mahāyāna Buddhists who insist that the Buddha was vegetarian. It was also rejected by some very early sources who were probably not vegetarian themselves, not least because the natural expression for 'pork' in *Pāli would be not sūkara-maddava but sūkara-maṃsa. The meal could therefore have been either some particular form of pork or something otherwise associated with pigs, such as a kind of food they enjoy. The name therefore may have only a tangential connection to the content of the meal itself, as in the case of a 'hot-dog', which does not contain dog meat. *See also* DIET.

Sukhāvatī (Skt.). 'Land of Bliss', the western paradise or *Pure Land of the *Buddha *Amitābha. This heavenly realm, one of many mentioned in *Mahāyāna *sūtras, was created by Amitābha through the power of his merit (*puṇya) as a utopia where beings who invoke his name with faith (*śraddhā) and devotion may be reborn. Once there, they dwell in bliss and may reach *nirvāṇa easily. The goal of *rebirth in such a place became the object of the '*Pure Land' schools (Chin., *Ch'ing- T'u; Jap. Jōdo) that flourished in east Asia. The delights of Sukhāvatī are described in texts such as the *Longer* and *Shorter* **Sukhāvatī-vyūha Sūtras* and the **Amitāyurdhyāna Sūtra*.

Sukhāvatī-vyūha Sūtra. A scripture that is central to the *Pure Land schools of *China and *Japan, as well as other parts of east Asia. This scripture exists in two versions, called the *Longer* and *Shorter Sukhāvatī-vyūha Sūtras*. Both describe the merits of the Pure Land (Sukhāvatī, or Land of Bliss) that exists an unimaginable distance to the west of the present world of *suffering and was created by the *karma generated by the practices of the *Buddha *Amitābha ('Boundless Light', or sometimes *Amitāyus, 'Boundless Life'). The longer version contains the story of how the *monk Dharmākara, at the instigation of a previous Buddha, meditatively inspected all the Pure Lands of other Buddhas, and then made a series of 48 vows (the number varies in different recensions) whereby he determined the features that his Pure Land would exhibit upon his attainment of Buddhahood, and without which he would not enter into Buddhahood. Significant for the development of Pure Land practices, he also specified (in the eighteenth vow) that any being could gain access to his land simply by calling out his name or thinking on him only ten times. Even though unenlightened at the time of their death, beings could gain *rebirth in the Land of Bliss and there find perfect conditions for practice as well as a Buddha and highly evolved Bodhisattvas to guide them to Buddhahood. The shorter version omits the story of Dharmākara and his vows, and simply has the Buddha *Śākyamuni teaching about that land, praising its qualities, and exhorting his disciples to make a vow to seek rebirth there. In fact, it is so short that, in its Chinese translation, it is memorized by Chinese *monks and *nuns and recited daily as part of morning devotions.

Both sūtras have extant versions in *Sanskrit and Chinese, and a Tibetan version of the *Shorter Sūtra* still exists. In Chinese, there are five different translations of the *Longer Sūtra* still available (*Taishō 362, 361, 360, 310, and 363), and two of the *Shorter Sūtra* (Taishō 366 and 367). Of these, the translation of the *Longer Sūtra* by *Saṃghavarman (Taishō 360) and that of the *Shorter Sūtra* by *Kumārajīva (Taishō 366), are considered the standard texts in east Asia. These two texts, together with the **Amitāyurdhyāna Sūtra*, form the 'Three Pure Land Sūtras' in east Asian *Buddhism.

Sule Paya. *Stūpa complex located in the centre of Rangoon, Burma. The golden *zedi, 150 feet high, is unusual in that its octagonal shaped terraces do not change into circular ones before being topped by the other characteristic elements. According to legend, it was erected over 2,000 years ago. However, the original buildings were possibly built by the *Mon people and the present complex is the result of much rebuilding and repair. The central stūpa, as suggested by its Mon name 'Kyaik Athok' meaning 'the stūpa where a Sacred Hair Relic is enshrined', is said to contain a hair of the *Buddha. *See also* RELICS; BURMA.

Sumaṅgalavilāsinī. 'Radiating good fortune', being the title of *Buddhaghoṣa's commentary on the *Dīgha Nikāya of the *Pāli Canon.

Sumedha. The name of the *Buddha when he was a *Bodhisattva in the time of the Buddha *Dīpaṅkara. It was at this point that he first resolved to become a Buddha and his religious career commenced. According to the legend recorded in the *Jātakas, Dīpaṅkara looked into the future and prophesied that Sumedha would in future attain enlightenment (*bodhi) as *Siddhartha Gautama.

Sumeru. *See* MERU.

Sundo. The Korean pronunciation of the name of the Chinese *monk Shun-tao, who was dispatched by the king of the Former Ch'in dynasty to take Buddhist scriptures and images to the Korean kingdom of Koguryŏ. His arrival there in the year 372 is regarded as the official inception of *Buddhism to the Korean peninsula. *See also* KOREA.

Sun Wu-k'ung. *See* MONKEY.

śūnyatā (Skt.; Pāli, suññattā). Emptiness or nothingness, a concept mainly, but not exclusively, associated with the *Mahāyāna. It has various particular nuances in the different Mahāyāna schools: according to the *Madhyamaka, it is equivalent to Dependent Origination (*pratītya-samutpāda), while for the *Yogācāra it is the direct realization of the non-existence of a perceiving subject and perceived objects, said to be the natural state of the mind. In the philosophical doctrine of śūnyavāda ('the way of emptiness') it not to be equated with nihilism since the term is equivalent in meaning to suchness (*tathatā) and ultimate reality or ultimate truth (*dharma-dhātu). What is sometimes referred to as 'Great Emptiness' (mahā-śūnyatā) is the abandonment of even the notion of emptiness.

Śūnyatā-saptati. A text in 73 verses by *Nāgārjuna, establishing the nature of emptiness (*śūnyatā) and refuting the reification of various *Abhidharma categories such as the five aggregates (*skandhas).

supermundane (Skt., lokottara). Term denoting matters relating to the *Noble Path (*ārya-marga) and its fruits, and thus connected with, or conducive to, liberation. In other words, any activity or practice not associated with the mundane (*laukika) world of unenlightened beings (*pṛthagjana).

Śūraṅgama-samādhi Sūtra. 'The Sūtra of the Concentration of Heroic Progress'. An early *Mahāyāna *sūtra, of which only a few fragments of the *Sanskrit original survive. The work is preserved in an early 4th-century Chinese translation by *Kumārajīva, and a Tibetan translation dating from the beginning of the 9th century. The content is related to that of the **Vimalakīrti-nirdeśa Sūtra*, and the concentration (*samādhi) referred to in the title is a state of mind fixed on one point (*citta-ekāgratā) which is said to be unlimited and unimpeded, like the free movement (gama) of a hero (śūra).

Susiddhikara Tantra. An early *kriyā-tantra of great importance in approximately 38 chapters, describing in great detail the preparations and methods to be used by a *mantra-practitioner to guarantee the successful attainment of accomplishments (*siddhi). Knowledge of the information given in this text was widely assumed in *tantric Buddhist practice in *Tibet and among the esoteric schools (*see* ESOTERIC BUDDHISM) of *China and *Japan. Though no *Sanskrit text survives, translations are currently available in both Chinese and Tibetan.

Śuśunāga (Pāli, Susunāga). An early Indian dynasty which ruled the state of *Magadha for 68 years from *c.*414–*c.*346 BCE. The Śuśunāgas were successors to the *Haryaṅkas.

sūtra (Skt; Pāli, sutta, a thread). A discourse of the *Buddha. In the *Pāli Canon these texts are grouped together in the second of the three 'baskets' (*piṭaka) or divisions of the teachings, namely the *Sūtra Piṭaka. This in turn is divided into five collections known as *Nikāyas (*Āgamas in *Sanskrit), in which the *suttas are grouped in order of length. These early discourses are all attributed to the historical Buddha,*Siddhartha Gautama. The *Mahāyāna canonical collection of sūtras is more extensive and includes many lengthy independent works. While the historical Buddha is plainly not the author of these works, they are regarded by followers of the Mahāyānas as of no less, and perhaps greater importance, than the earlier texts. Many, such as the **Lotus Sūtra* and the **Laṅkāvatāra Sūtra*, became the foundational scriptures of new schools of *Buddhism. The tradition of composing sūtras continued for many centuries during the medieval period. Most of these were composed in Sanskrit but many now survive only in Tibetan or Chinese translation. Sometimes independent works were amalgamated into more extensive ones known as *vaipūlya sūtras.

Sūtra in Forty-Two Sections. A scripture in the Chinese Buddhist *canon (*Taishō 784) that purports to date from the mid-*Han dynasty. According to legend, Chinese envoys sent to Scythia in search of *Buddhism after the Emperor Ming had a dream (around 67 CE) brought the text back to *China (*see* MING-TI). In other versions, Indian *monks residing in China translated it. It appears to be a compendium of essential passages from various *Hīnayāna scriptures, intended as an introduction to Buddhism for Chinese inquirers. Although there is some question that the version presently preserved in the *Taishō canon may not be the same as the version originally circulated during the Han, it is fairly certain that a scripture by that name, and of the nature of a *summa*, did exist at that time.

Sūtra of Perfect Enlightenment. *See YUAN-CHÜEH CHING.*

Sūtra Piṭaka (Skt; Pāli, Sutta Piṭaka). The collection or 'basket' of the discourses delivered or purported to have been delivered by the *Buddha. An overall division into two types of Sūtra Piṭaka may be distinguished: the various collections of discourse that formed closed canons for pre-*Mahāyāna schools, and the looser open *canon of later Mahāyāna sūtras. In the case of the pre-Buddhist schools, the Sūtra Piṭaka forms a part of the teachings of the Buddha, originally transmitted orally, known variously as *Āgamas or *Nikāyas. The number of individual sūtras contained therein are approximately 5,000, although the precise number of discourses included and the manner of grouping them varied. Most commonly four divisions were recognized: the *Dīrgha (Pāli, *Dīgha) or 'long' collection; the *Madhyama (Pāli, *Majjhima) or 'medium' collection; the *Saṃyukta (Pāli, *Saṃyutta) or 'linked' collection; and the *Ekottara (Pāli, *Aṅguttara) or 'incremental' collection. To these four, the *Theravādin school adds a fifth, namely the *Khuddaka or 'minor' collection. The most complete recension readily available is that transmitted in *Pāli by the Theravādin tradition, although Chinese versions affiliated with other schools such as the *Sarvāstivāda, *Dharmaguptaka, and others have survived, as well as a number of fragments extant in *Sanskrit belonging to the Sarvāstivāda school. Scholars believe that many of the discourses contained in the Sūtra Piṭaka are compositions post-dating the death of the Buddha and that, despite its popularity, the Pāli recension may be no more an authoritative guide to the teachings of the Buddha than any of the other *Hīnayāna recensions. The Mahāyāna sūtra collection may be viewed as an extension to the basic Āgama collection of sūtras; being an open canon, it was possible for Mahāyāna adherents to compose new texts or compile older fragments of teachings that had been available as a pool of oral tradition to propagate certain innovative ideas and practices.

sutta. *Pāli term meaning a discourse of the *Buddha. *See also* SŪTRA.

Sutta-nipāta. The fifth book of the *Khuddaka Nikāya of the *Sūtra Piṭaka of the *Pāli Canon. It mainly consists of verses, apparently compiled from a number of sources, divided into five sections: Uraga, Cūla, Mahā, Aṭṭhaka, and Pārāyaṇa. Some of the poems of the *Sutta-nipāta* are found in other books of the *canon, indicating that they probably existed separately, as popular poems, before being incorporated in this text. The commentary to the *Sutta-nipāta*, compiled by *Buddhaghoṣa, is part of the **Paramatthajotikā*.

Suvaṇṇabhūmi (Pāli). Name of a country, variously identified with the region of Lower *Burma around *Pagān, a locality in Bengal, and part of Thailand and Sumatra. Most probably it refers to the *Mon coastal lands stretching from the frontier with Arakan to parts of present-day Malaya. After the *Third Council (*see* COUNCIL OF PĀṬALIPUTRA II), the elders Soṇa and Uttara visited the region in order to convert it to *Buddhism.

Suvarna-prabhāsottama Sūtra. 'The Sutra of Golden Light'. An important *Mahāyāna sūtra that emphasizes the cosmic aspect of the *Buddha's nature and describes him as omnipresent in all phenomena. The text contains the famous story of how the Buddha out of compassion (*karuṇā) once sacrificed his body to a hungry tigress. The sūtra was influential in *Japan, particularly during the *Nara period, due to the political implications of its teaching that the *Dharma transcends the division between church and state.

Suzuki, D. T. (1870–1966). Daisetsu (usually rendered Daisetz) Teitarō Suzuki, a Japanese scholar of *Zen *Buddhism who was instrumental in bringing Zen to *Europe and *America in the first half of the 20th century. He was born in Kanazawa, and his father died while he was 6, leaving his mother to raise him in very difficult circumstances. He entered the Tokyo Semmon Gakkō at the age of 21, but left there to undertake Zen training at the Engaku Temple (*Engakuji) under Imakita Kōsen. When the latter died in 1892, Suzuki continued study under his successor, Shaku Sōen (1859–1919). He undertook five years of training, and is said to have attained an awakening in 1895. At the same time, he was studying as a non-degree student at Tokyo Imperial University on the recommendation of his friend, the Kyoto school Zen philosopher *Nishida Kitarō (1870–1945). Also during this time, he made the acquaintance of Paul Carus, editor of Open Court Press in Chicago. He went with Carus to the USA, and lived in his basement for eleven years, polishing his English and producing translations of various east Asian religious works. At the age of 41, he married Beatrice Lane. He went to work in academia, first as an English professor at the Gakushūin in Tokyo, and, after 1919, as professor of Buddhist philosophy at Ōtani University in *Kyoto. In this position, he began to publish extensively, both in English and Japanese, on Zen and *Pure Land thought. He also founded the English journal *Eastern Buddhist* during this period. In his publications he remained concerned with Zen philosophy (in which he was greatly influenced by the work of his friend Nishida), and the interaction of Zen and Japanese culture. He explored other areas as well, such as scriptural studies, and he produced translations and studies of the **Laṅkāvatāra Sūtra* and other classic works.

Suzuki's academic career in *Japan was quite successful, but he suffered some criticism after the Second World War on two counts. First, some cited his limited vision of Buddhism in Japanese culture, in particular, the complete omission of *Nichiren Buddhism from his account of the interaction of Buddhism with Japanese spirituality. Second, after the war, he recanted some of the things he had written prior to and during the war that, implicitly at least, defended Japanese militarism. Many young men had taken his books as their inspiration into battle; his post-war disavowal of his previous writings, and his claim that he had always known Japan would lose but feared that his works would be banned if he spoke his mind, dismayed those young men, and provoked a backlash against him. His influence in the English-speaking world which knew nothing of these criticisms was unaffected. His fluency in English, his willingness to speak of Zen enlightenment (*satori) in theoretical terms, and his deep familiarity with the wide scope of Zen traditions, made him a primary channel for the West to learn about Zen. He served as Shaku Sōen's translator when the latter came to America, and his three volumes of *Essays in Zen Buddhism*, published by Rider, secured his reputation in England. He became a media presence in both England and America, with profiles in the *New Yorker* and *Vogue*, and many sought his company, from Thomas Merton to Christmas *Humphreys and Alan *Watts. He went to work at Columbia University until his retirement in 1957. His longevity (he died at age 95) and prolific scholarship (over 100 books, many in an informal and accessible style suited to the general reader) made him a major force in the dissemination of Zen to the West.

Suzuki Shōsan (1579–1655). A *Zen master who grew up in the atmosphere of the 'Warring States' (Jap., sengoku) period of Japanese history and who subsequently became identified with a form of Zen that drew heavily upon martial imagery. Born into the warrior class, he had served as a retainer in the army of Tokugawa Ieyasu (1541–1616), one of the military rulers of *Japan. He saw many battles, but took time during his military service to visit Zen temples and talk with Zen masters. He showed a talent for cutting directly to the heart of the matter in all these discussions, and he wrote a pamphlet asserting the superiority of *Buddhism over *Confucianism while still on active duty. He ordained himself in 1620 and went to study with Daigu Sōchiku. The latter said that Suzuki was already well-known as a Buddhist teacher and did not need a new religious name, and so he continued on under his secular name. It was not until he studied with a *Vinaya master in Nara that he took proper *ordination as a novice and learnt fundamental Buddhist doctrine. He was very active in spreading Buddhism after that, and boldly petitioned the military government to cease its practice of executing female members of the families of condemned criminals to save the nation from bad *karma. His desire was to have a non- (or supra-) sectarian Buddhism declared the faith of the nation, and, at a time when Jesuit missionaries were active in the land, he felt compelled to resist their efforts at proselytization. To this end, he composed the work *Ha Kirishitan* (Against the Christians). Suzuki Shōsan's form of Buddhism was intended for all people, and so was designed to be suited to secular as well as clerical life. He stressed energetic engagement, and counselled his followers to keep the prospect of *death before them at all times as a means of focusing, and to take the example of the Niō, or two kings, as their inspiration (these are images of two fierce-looking guardian deities that adorn the main doors of Buddhist temples).

Suzuki Shunryū (1905–71). A Japanese *Zen *monk of the *Sōtō school who came to the United States in 1958. Intending only a short stay at first, he decided to settle permanently in the San Francisco area where he founded the Zen Centre, which became a major force in the maturation of American Zen. In his teaching (collected in the short book *Zen Mind, Beginner's Mind*), Suzuki stressed ordinary life as the vehicle for expressing one's innate *Buddha-nature, and did not emphasize (or even mention) enlightenment (*bodhi; *satori) as a goal.

svabhāva (Skt.). Intrinsic nature, self-being or own-being; a technical term found in early sources but used mainly in later *Buddhism to denote the concept of an *ātman or a permanent and unchanging identity or substratum. In contrast to some pre-*Mahāyāna schools such as the *Sarvāstivāda, all Mahāyāna schools reject the existence of any such intrinsic nature and maintain that all phenomena are devoid or empty (*see* ŚŪNYATĀ) of any kind of svabhāva. According to the *Abhidharma, the svabhāva was the unique and inalienable 'mark' or characteristic (*lakṣaṇa or *sva-lakṣana) by means of which entities could be differentiated and classified. By identifying the svabhāva of an entity a taxonomy of real existents could be produced. For example, the svabhāva of fire was identified as heat, and the svabhāva of water was defined as fluidity. Thus the schools of the *Hīnayāna, while denying a self of persons (pudgala-nairātmya) nevertheless accepted the substantial reality of those elements (*dharmas) which composed the world at large, including five *skandhas of the individual subject. Beginning with *Nāgārjuna, the *Mādhyamaka undercut this teaching by denying the substantial reality not just of the self (*ātman) but of all phenomena, a view known as dharma-nairātmya. All entities were therefore seen as alike in lacking a discrete mode of being or self-essence (svabhāva), and in sharing instead the common attribute or 'mark' of emptiness (śūnyatā).

svābhāvika-kāya (Skt.). The 'embodiment of Buddhahood in its essence', a term first attested in the **Abhisamaya-alaṃkāra*. The precise nature of this embodiment became a source of controversy in *Mahāyāna *Buddhism as a result of *Haribhadra's textual exegesis which deemed it to be an additional unitary aspect of Buddhahood underlying the standard 'three bodies' (*tri-kāya). This was in contrast to the majority view that the term is merely a synonym for absolute reality or the *dharma-kāya.

sva-lakṣaṇa (Skt., own mark). The specific attribute or characteristic of a thing. The term is used especially in Buddhist epistemology (*pramāṇa) to denote the true aspect of any object as it presents itself in bare experience prior to the superimposition of concepts that give rise to the manifestation of its so-called 'universal attributes' (*sāmanya-lakṣaṇa). According to the *Abhidharma, only objects with specific attributes are capable of causal efficacy (*artha-kriyā).

Svātantrika-Madhyamaka (Skt.; Tib., rang-rgyud-pa). One of the two main schools of *Madhyamaka *Buddhism, whose main representatives were *Bhāvaviveka and the later *Śāntarakṣita. The school was defined by its use of a syllogism-based (svatantra) method that aimed to establish true and valid propositions, in contrast to the *reductio ad absurdum* dialectic of the *Prāsaṅgikas (identified with *Nāgārjuna, *Buddhapālita, and *Candrakīrti) that sought only to reveal the contradictions in the postulates of their opponents. According to *Tsongkhapa, the difference between the two groups is that the Svātantrikas accept inherent existence (*svabhāva) in the conventional sense (*see* SAṂVṚTI-SATYA), whereas the Prāsaṅgikas deny it both at the levels of conventional and absolute truth (*see* PARAMĀRTHA-SATYA). It should be noted that the term Svātantrika-Madhyamaka itself is not attested in Indian Buddhist texts and has been created by modern scholars on the basis of the Tibetan exegetical tradition.

swastika (Skt., svastika). An ancient sign said to be of solar origin and signifying good luck. The sign may be Neolithic and is found world-wide. Its Indian name comes from *Sanskrit 'sv-asti' meaning good fortune, luck, or success. The swastika is a cross with the extremities of each arm bent at right angles. It is used as an auspicious mark on images or structures, and is often found on the chest, palms, or soles of the feet of *Buddhas and *Jinas. It is also used in the earliest Buddhist art which does not represent the *Buddha in human form.

Swayambunāth. A large Buddhist temple and *stūpa sited near Kathmandu in *Nepal.

T

Tachikawa-ryū. A subsect of the esoteric *Shingon school of Japanese *Buddhism that is generally considered heterodox. The school formed in the early 12th century by combining Taoist yin-yang thought with Shingon ritual practice. It is so named because it was in the town of Tachikawa that the Shingon priest Ninkan is said to have transmitted esoteric teachings to a Taoist master, who then combined the two methods into a single school. Because of its actual use of ritual sex and accusations of involvement in black magic, the school was frowned upon and its leaders frequently sent into exile. The *monk Yūkai (1345–1416) is generally credited with extirpating the Tachikawa school from Shingon. *See also* TAOISM.

Ta-chu Hui-hai. A *T'ang dynasty Chinese *Ch'an *monk. Very little is known of him, including the dates of his life, other than that he was a disciple of the famous monk *Ma-tsu Tao-i (709–88), and that he wrote the influential treatise *Essential Gate for Entry Into Sudden Enlightenment* (Chin., *Tun-wu ju dao yao-men*), which is still extant.

T'aego Pou (1301–82). A Buddhist figure of the *Koryŏ period credited with the introduction of the *Lin-chi line of *Ch'an *Buddhism into *Korea, where it became known as Imje. Ordained at the age of 12, he spent many years meditating on riddles (Chin., kung-an; Jap., *kōan) until he had two major *enlightenment experiences at the ages of 32 and 37. Afterwards, he travelled throughout the north and south of Yüan-dynasty *China between 1346 and 1348, during which time his experience was confirmed within the Lin-chi line. Returning to *Korea, he divided his time between his agricultural temple in the south and the royal court of Koryŏ, where he was recognized as a *National Teacher and arbitrated over the Buddhist establishment. In this position he attempted to unify all of the Ch'an sects in Korea, with limited success. By 1368 intrigues at court worked against him, and he returned once again to south China. While abroad, his detractors turned the king against him, and he was exiled, but the king relented and restored his honours and titles. After returning in 1369, T'aego was given control over a newly constructed temple in the capital, and was later given charge of another temple. He returned home to south Korea in 1381, and died the following year. He left behind a body of *Dharma-talks, poems, prefaces, and stele inscriptions that show him to be a vigorous and demanding teacher who pushed his students in kung-an (Jap., *kōan) practice and scriptural study.

Ta-hui Tsung-kao (1089–1163). One of a pair of Chinese *Ch'an monks of the Sung dynasty period who defined the difference in the practices of the *Ts'ao-tung and *Lin-chi schools. The other, *Hung-chih Cheng-chüeh (1091–1157), argued that *meditation was a self-fulfilling activity rather than a goal-oriented one, and counseled students to just sit and in so doing to manifest their innate *Buddha- nature. Ta-hui, in contrast, belittled this as 'silent illumination Ch'an' (Chin., '*mo chao Ch'an', a term that ironically came to be used as a proper designation rather than a derogatory term), and promoted a more active style of Ch'an wherein the practitioner strove after *enlightenment with all his energy, primarily through the use of riddles (Chin., kung-an; Jap., *kōan). He used the kōan to generate a great doubt in the student's mind so as to induce a crisis that could only be overcome through awakening. His teachings, and his controversy with Hung-chih, helped to identify the Lin-chi school as the more active and goal-oriented, and the Ts'ao-tung as the more passive and philosophical.

T'ai-hsü (1890–1947). A Republican-era Chinese Buddhist *monk known for his efforts at reforming and modernizing Buddhist life and practice. As with other monastics in *China at the beginning of the 20th century, T'ai-hsü was dismayed at the state of *Buddhism—

the clergy's neglect of education and practice, and their over-reliance on the performance of funerals and other rituals for paying clients bothered him especially. The disunity of the monastic order also vexed him. To his mind, a comprehensive, rational structure was needed to provide the way for the implementation of the reform measures he envisioned. He also faulted the clergy for their unwillingness to engage with the present world, preferring to counsel people to seek *rebirth in the *Pure Land rather than work to improve their present situation. T'ai-hsü's efforts to redress these weaknesses produced patchy results. His efforts to organize the *Saṃgha never succeeded, as one projected Buddhist association after another died in the planning stages. His educational enterprises, on the other hand, produced more positive results. He founded several seminaries designed to take Buddhist education into the modern era, eschewing the traditional methods of lecturing exclusively on scriptures, *meditation, and monastic regulations and adding to the curriculum modern science, English language study, and secular literature. He founded the magazine *Hai Ch'ao Yin* (Sound of Ocean Tides), and through this vehicle propagated his ideas of a new *Buddhism he referred to as 'Buddhism for Human Life' (Chin., jen sheng fo-chiao), a phrase that pointed to a move away from funeral performances and a focus on the next life to serious engagement with present human concerns and social problems. He also worked to create connections between Buddhists around the world and between Buddhism and other religions. During the 1920s he began a series of meetings of the World Buddhist Federation, an organization that existed primarily on paper. Later in the decade, he helped organize the East Asian Buddhist Conference of 1925, which attracted participants from *Japan (including its colonial possession Taiwan) and China. In 1928, he convinced the Nationalist Government of China to send him abroad as a representative of Chinese culture, and embarked on a nine-month tour of *Europe and *America, during which the press, through some misunderstanding of his actual status within the Chinese Saṃgha, referred to him frequently as 'the Buddhist Pope'. This tour failed to impress many Westerners, due to his lack of preparation and failure to secure competent translators, but it established his reputation at home as an international figure. Other initiatives followed. In the 1930s he attempted to establish an exchange programme with the *Theravāda Buddhists of *Sri Lanka, and later in the decade the Nationalist Government sent him abroad again, this time to drum up support for China in its war of resistance against *Japan. Perhaps the greatest result of these contacts came about after his death: during a tour of *Sri Lanka, he met Dr G. P. Malalasekera to discuss the need for an international Buddhist organization, but agreed that it should wait until the end of the Second World War. In 1950, Malalasekera set up the *World Fellowship of Buddhists, which endured and thrived.

Although many of T'ai-hsü's efforts and initiatives came to very little (primarily because he spread himself too thinly over too many grandiose plans), his influence endured through the efforts of his disciples. Many of his followers, such as Yin-shun (1902–), Li Tzu-k'uan (1882–1973), as well as modern masters such as Sheng-yen (1930–) and Hsing Yun (1927–) have carried out the work of fitting Buddhism to the demands of the modern world while acknowledging their debt to the vision of T'ai-hsü.

Taishō Canon. Short name of the *Taishō Shinshū Daizokyō*, being a collection of east Asian Buddhist scriptures and other canonical writings. Its name means 'the great treasury of scriptures newly edited in the Taishō reign-period'. Commonly referred to simply as 'Taishō', this collection of 2,920 texts in 85 volumes was compiled and redacted between 1924 and 1932 by the Editorial Committee of the Japanese *Tripiṭaka under the direction of Takakusu Junjirō. This edition of Chinese-language scriptures from *China, *Japan, and *Korea was based on critical readings of several earlier canons, and is the most complete collection of east Asian scriptures available. It has become the standard reference for scholars of east Asian *Buddhism, and citations from works included within this collection will generally give the document number and/or volume number, with the prefix 'T.', followed by the page number, register, and line in order to give the exact location of the passage. Thus, a reference that reads 'T. 2016,

48: 524c13' would point the reader to a passage from Yung-ming Yen-shou's *Tsung ching lu*, which is document number 2016 in the Taishō *canon, which would be found in volume 48, page 524, the third register, beginning at line 13. Though other old editions of the Chinese canon have recently become available, this edition is still regarded as the standard among scholars and its ease of use has recently been enhanced by the publication of a CD-ROM version. Additionally a large multivolume concordance was compiled by the publishers during the 1970s and 1980s. *See also* CHINESE TRIPIṬAKA.

Takuan Sōhō (1573–1645). An influential *Rinzai Zen master in *Japan during the transition from the Ashikaga to the Tokugawa regimes. When he was 9 years old, political adversity induced his father to place him in a Buddhist temple. He began his monastic career in a *Pure Land temple, but soon transferred to a *Zen temple for training. After practising under different masters, some of whom he found worldly and overly concerned with political success, he achieved *enlightenment in 1604, and quickly gained such eminence that the imperial household named him abbot of the Daitoku Temple by Mt. *Hiei near *Kyoto. This was one of the highest honours to which a *monk might aspire, but Takuan resigned the post three days after his investiture, wishing to avoid worldly concerns. In 1611, however, he consented to take the abbotship of a subtemple of the *Daitoku-ji, called the Daisen-in. At this time, the Tokugawa government was promulgating a series of new temple regulations. Takuan, along with two other monks, co-signed a petition to the shōgunate pointing out that the new regulations were unworkable and asking for their repeal. For this, he was tried in 1629 and sent into exile. His exile lasted three years, during which time he was comfortably housed. After release, he was called back to Edo by the new shōgun. From disfavour with the previous shōgun, Takuan now moved to a position of extraordinary intimacy and trust with the new shōgun, Tokugawa Iemitsu. The shōgun built a temple in Edo, the Tōkai-ji, for his use, and he lived out his days chafing under the irony that he, who had shunned fame and desired only a simple and pure Zen practice, had ascended to the very position that the most crafty and worldly monks could have desired. On his deathbed, asked by disciples to inscribe a last testament, he took a writing brush and wrote the single word 'dream' on a sheet of paper, threw down the brush, and died.

takuhatsu (Jap.). A term for the *monk's alms-begging round, or, in a *Zen temple, the time when monks bring their bowls (*see* BEGGING-BOWL) to the refectory.

Tambapaṇṇi-dīpa (Pāli, copper-coloured leaf island). Ancient name in Buddhist literature for the island of *Sri Lanka.

T'ang dynasty. A period of Chinese history spanning the years 618 to 907 when the T'ang ruling house held imperial power. This period, which followed upon the reunification of the empire by the short-lived Sui dynasty (581–618), is regarded as one of the 'golden ages' of Chinese history, when the nation enjoyed a prolonged period of unity and prosperity. It is also frequently referred to as the 'golden age' of Chinese *Buddhism, for it was a period of unprecedented creativity that saw the establishment and/or consolidation of virtually all the major schools of the religion: *Ch'an, *T'ien-t'ai, *Hua-yen, and *Fa-hsiang, all of which, at various times, enjoyed lavish imperial and aristocratic patronage.

However, this picture must be tempered somewhat by a realization that the T'ang period also saw many calamities and hardships, both for the empire and for Buddhism. The dynasty itself suffered the usurpation of the throne by the infamous Empress Wu Tze-t'ien (whose enthusiasm for Buddhism made her reign a particularly prosperous one from the religious perspective) and the An Lu-shan rebellion of 755, the large scale of which required the expenditure of vast amounts of imperial resources to quell it, and from which the dynasty never completely recovered. On the Buddhist side, in addition to lavish patronage and intellectual ferment, the period also saw the disastrous suppression of Buddhism in 845, in which scores of major monasteries and centres of learning were razed along with their libraries and objects of art, and thousands of *monks and *nuns forcibly laicized or killed, and event that altered the character of Buddhism in *China thereafter.

Tangut. A central Asian people related to the Tibetans, who founded a vibrant though short-lived multinational kingdom (1032–1227 CE). Due to their proximity to *Tibet, they were strongly influenced by Tibetan forms of *Buddhism and iconography although their translation of the Buddhist *canon, using their unique script, was based on the Chinese verion.

T'an-luan (476–542). Early Chinese *Pure Land thinker and popularizer. He began his monastic career as a scholar, and was in the middle of composing a massive commentary on the **Mahāsaṃnipāta Sūtra* (Chin., *Ta-chi ching*) when he came down with a serious illness. He left his monastery and sought out a renowned Taoist alchemist to receive the teachings on immortality. After receiving from him ten scrolls of Taoist scripture, he set out for home. However, on his way back he reportedly ran into the Indian *monk *Bodhiruci. T'an-luan asked him if there were any Indian Buddhist *sūtras better than Taoist works on immortality. At this Bodhiruci is said to have become very angry and spat on the ground, saying that one cannot find the secret of immortality in any Chinese book. *Taoism may prolong your life for a while, but by means of its teaching one cannot escape *death. Bodhiruci then taught T'an-luan the practice of reciting the name of *Amitābha, here significantly called by his other name *Amitāyus, which means 'infinite life'. T'an-luan believed, and threw away his magic formulae and set himself to the practice of reciting Amitābha's name. T'an-luan is then said to have thrown away his books and adopted Bodhiruci's teaching wholeheartedly, but there is some doubt about this, as ancient bibliographies list works on Taoist topics under his name and some scholars continue to identify Taoist themes even in his later Buddhist works.

What is historically significant for the development of Pure Land *Buddhism is: (1) the single-minded way T'an-luan set about Pure Land practices; (2) his reliance on the 'other-power' of Amitābha to bring him to the Pure Land; and (3) the fact that he turned his devotion into a mass movement. In terms of the first point, whereas before his illness he had been a fairly typical, well-rounded monk, engaging in scholarship and cultivating different meditations, after his 'conversion' he came to rely solely on Pure Land practices, reflecting a growing pessimism about the suitability of this world as a place to practise. This was a significant development. Second, after his illness he clearly grew despondent about his own power to affect his destiny, and so he responded to the teaching that the power of Amitābha's vow was sufficient to bring him to a better world. Now one begins to see what will become a dominant theme in Pure Land Buddhism, especially in *Japan: the opposition between the 'self-power' (*jiriki) of the practitioner and the 'other-power' (*tariki) of Amitābha. This was related to two historical factors: the almost constant state of war that existed in north *China at the time, and the growing acceptance of the division of Buddhist history into three periods, each marked by the decreasing efficacy of traditional Buddhist practices. Feeling that the third and worst period (*mappō) was either imminent or already present, many came to believe that individual initiative and power were either useless or of sharply reduced efficacy, and sought help from other powers outside themselves.

T'an-luan advocated five related practices in his *Commentary on [Vasubandhu's] Upadeśa on the Sūtra of Immeasurable Life* (*Taishō 1819), which Bodhiruci had translated earlier: (1) worshipping Amitābha; (2) praising his name; (3) vowing constantly to be reborn in the Pure Land; (4) meditating on the Pure Land, probably through visualizing it; and (5) transferring the merit (*puṇya) one attains through this practice to helping all sentient beings. However, he placed the greatest emphasis on the first practice, worshipping or reciting Amitābha's name. Through this, even one who has committed the five great offences (with the exception of slandering the teachings) can be reborn in the western Pure Land. The purpose of *rebirth in the Pure Land, he taught, is to return to this earth in order to save others. T'an-luan stands as one who took Pure Land practice out of the matrix of Buddhist religious practices and popularized it as a self-standing expedient for those who, in this troubled time, cannot engage in the rigours of *meditation and monastic life.

Tannishō. A classic text of the *Jōdo Shinshū, or 'True Pure Land school' of Japanese *Buddhism. The title means 'Notes Lamenting Deviations', and its contents are said to go back to Jōdo Shinshū founder *Shinran (1173–1262), although it is not held to have been composed by him directly. Traditionally, it was compiled by Shinran's great-grandson *Kakunyo (1270–1351) from notes taken at Shinran's talks, but internal evidence points to Yuienbō (date unknown), one of Shinran's direct disciples in the Hitachi area. It is thought he may have composed or compiled the work out of concern over misinterpretations of Shinran's teachings. The work is very short, consisting of two parts: ten of Shinran's aphorisms with short commentaries, and eight brief chapters dealing with various misapprehensions of Shinshū doctrine and practice. It is famous as the *locus classicus* of Shinran's dictum, 'Even the good person is reborn into *Amida's Pure Land; how much more the evil person', indicating that Amida's grace is directed at the salvation of the more depraved individual. In other passages, Shinran disavows any claims on the part of others that he took personal disciples, and asserts that the *nembutsu is itself recited under the grace of Amida *Buddha, and cannot be manipulated by the practitioner for worldly or other-worldly gains.

tantra. *See* TANTRIC BUDDHISM.

tantric Buddhism. A special path which arose within *Mahāyāna *Buddhism based on treatises known as tantras and, while generally embracing the same aims, claimed to provide a rapid means to accomplish the goal of enlightenment (*bodhi) by means of its distinctive techniques. Certain key features can be identified which serve to distinguish it from other forms of Indian Buddhism. It offers an alternative path to enlightenment; its teachings are aimed at lay practitioners in particular, rather than *monks and *nuns; it recognizes mundane (*laukika) aims and attainments, and often deals with practices which are more magical in character than spiritual; it teaches special types of meditation (*sādhana) as the path to realization, aimed at transforming the individual into an embodiment of the divine in this lifetime or after a short span of time; such kinds of meditation make extensive use of various kinds of *maṇḍalas, *mudrās, *mantras, and *dhāraṇīs as concrete expressions of the nature of reality; the formation of images of the various deities during meditation by means of creative imagination plays a key role in the process of realization; there is a proliferation in the number and types of *Buddhas and other deities; great stress is laid upon the importance of the *guru and the necessity of receiving the instructions and appropriate initiations for the sādhanas from him; a spiritual physiology is taught as part of the process of transformation; it stresses the importance of the feminine and utilizes various forms of sexual *yoga.

The origins of this movement within Buddhism is shrouded in mystery but a consensus of modern scholars place the emergence of tantric Buddhism as a distinct path around the 7th century CE among circles of adepts based in the regions corresponding to present-day Orissa, Bengal, Gujarat, and *Kashmir. Many elements that make up its doctrines, meditational practices, and rituals can be found considerably earlier both within Buddhism and without—meditative *visualization was known from texts such as the **Pratyutpanna Sūtra* and the **Sukhāvatī-vyūha Sūtra*; maṇḍalas can be seen as idealized *stūpas, *dhāraṇī texts were in use before the 1st century CE, the ritual of fire-offerings (*homa) derives from *Vedic practice. These various elements were gradually combined over the centuries until the emergence of recognizable tantric texts such as the **Mahā-vairocana-abhisaṃbodhi* in the mid-7th century, which included all the hallmarks of tantric Buddhism listed above with the exception of sexual yoga. By the end of the 7th century, the **Sarva-tathāgata-tattva-saṃgraha* and other texts had been composed, now utilizing the *Five Buddha Family system in contrast to the earlier *three Buddha family system. Within a few decades, the **Guhyasamāja Tantra* was next composed, the first tantra known to contain explicit sexual imagery. This was followed by an explosion in the number of tantric texts appearing in *India, both along the lines of the *Guhyasamāja* and texts like the **Hevajra Tantra* which make greater use of sexual yoga, an internal spiritual physiology, and emphasize the role of the feminine to a greater extent. This period also saw the rise of the *mahā-siddhas and the antinomian practices associated with *Sahajayāna. With the emerging diversity of tantric texts, various schemes were used to classify them. Initially, tantric Buddhism was seen as an alternative path within Mahāyāna and was termed the mantra method (mantra-naya) in contrast to the Perfection method (pāramitā-naya). This mantra method was subdivided into two groups—*kriyā-tantra, emphasizing rituals, and *yoga-tantra emphasizing meditative practices—the former group including texts such as the **Subāhu-paripṛcchā* and the **Susiddhikāra*, while the latter included the *Sarva-tathāgata-tattva-saṃgraha* and the *Guhya-samāja*. The *Mahā-vairocana-abhisaṃbodhi* was deemed to share features of both groups and thus was placed in a special dual (ubhaya) category. At a later date, this system was revised into the now standard fourfold division of kriyā-tantra, *caryā-tantra, yoga-tantra and *anuttara-yoga-tantra. Anuttara-yoga itself was further subdivided into three categories: *Father Tantra, *Mother Tantra, and *Non-dual Tantra, although it seems that other naming systems were used such as *mahāyoga, *anuyoga, and *atiyoga still utilized by Tibetans in *Nyingma circles.

Although tantric Buddhism seems likely to have originated outside monastic circles among unorthdox *yogins, it was soon introduced into the various great centres of Buddhist such as *Nālandā, *Vikramaśīla, and *Ratnagiri. Many of the greatest scholar-monks in *India from the 8th century onwards were also renowned as adepts who produced a considerable volume of commentarial literature and independent treatises. Through their influence, tantric Buddhism became widespread throughout India and neighbouring countries. However, although it is known to have been transmitted to *Sri Lanka, *Burma, *Thailand, and Indonesia, outside of India tantric Buddhism achieved its greatest success in Tibet and *China, with *Shingon as a secondary offshoot in *Japan.

Tao. A Chinese word meaning 'the way' that occurs in all the religions of *China. Within Buddhist circles, it became synonymous with the path of practice and the goal towards which one strove. To 'attain the Way' (Chin., te tao) became a term indicating the achievement of *nirvāṇa. *See also* TAOISM.

Tao-an (312–85). An early Chinese Buddhist *monk and literary scholar renowned for textual-critical work that helped to sort genuine from spurious scriptures, identify textual variants and translations, and produce the earliest bibliography of Buddhist works in *China. He also wrote commentaries on existing scriptures and helped to set new guidelines and standards for translating Buddhist texts from Indian languages into Chinese.

Tao-ch'o (562–645). An early Chinese *Pure Land thinker and theoretician. Tao-ch'o lived through the persecution of *Buddhism in the north in 574, and from this experience he concluded that he was indeed living in the third age of the *Dharma (*see* MAPPŌ), in which the situation and capacities of people to hear the teachings of Buddhism and put them into practice were too degenerate for any to succeed under their own power. The proper response, therefore, was to forget about any kind of religious practice and concentrate on calling upon *Amitābha's name so that by his power one may be reborn in a place more conducive to attaining liberation. Thus, Tao-ch'o went further than his master *T'an-luan (476–542) in reducing Buddhism to the single practice of reciting Amitābha's name. T'an-luan had four other auxiliary practices which Tao-ch'o, out of pessimism for the times, seems not to have emphasized, although it is certainly not clear that he rejected them either. He concentrated on getting his followers and disciples to recite Amitābha's name as many times as possible, using dried beans as a way to keep track of their progress. They would literally fill whole bushel baskets every day in their zeal for the practice. He himself recited the name 70,000 times daily. In his only surviving work, the *An Lo Chi*, ostensibly a commentary on the **Amitāyurdhyāna Sūtra* but really a wide-ranging exposition of Pure Land thought, Tao-ch'o attempted mainly to answer criticisms of Pure Land thought and practice, primarily from the *Ch'an camp. For example, the critics asked how simply reciting Amitābha's name could possibly have such powerful effects. The answer to this was simple: there is no power inherent either in the reciter or in the words recited. The power was with Amitābha alone, and his was certainly sufficient to bring the devotee to the Pure Land.

Tao-hsin (580–651). A Chinese *Ch'an *monk traditionally regarded as the fourth *patriarch of the school. He left home at an early age and studied with Ch'an's third patriarch *Seng-ts'an (d. 606), attaining *enlightenment and receiving his master's robe and bowl as a token of his transmission of the *Dharma. In 617, he is reputed to have saved a town from siege, creating the illusion of soldiers along the ramparts by having all the town's inhabitants recite the word '*prajñā-pāramitā' ('great insight'). He eventually settled on Shuangfeng ('twin peak') mountain in Huang-mei in modern Hupei province, where he gathered a community of practitioners, including the next patriarch *Hung-jen (601–74), who continued the line that is traditionally considered the main trunk of the Ch'an lineage, although it should not be forgotten that one of his other disciples, *Fa-jung (594–657) became the head of the *Oxhead school. Tao-hsin is also supposed to have left behind a work called *The Five Gates of Tao-hsin*, extracts of which appear in other works. It seems to indicate that he received much exposure to and was influenced by *T'ien-t'ai teachings, particularly in his use of the term 'single-practice *samādhi' (Chin., i-hsing san-mei) and his two-pronged practice of seated *meditation and mindfulness in every sphere of activity. He also lived at a time when Ch'an was in an institutional transition from isolated monks or very small communities of itinerant practitioners to large settled communities; his own community on Shuangfeng mountain was said to number around 500. Thus, his spiritual attainments, energy and charisma, and organizational abilities all seem to have set the agenda for further developments in Ch'an history.

Tao-hsüan (596–667). The founder of the *Lü (Disciplinary) school (Chin., Lü-tsung) in Chinese *Buddhism, a school that specialized in commenting on the monastic rules and procedures that governed life in temples and monasteries. Tao-hsüan's first contribution was to select the version of the monastic rules that would be employed in governing monastic life; among the various *Vinayas that had been translated into Chinese by his day, he chose the Vinaya of the Indian *Dharmaguptaka school, called the 'Vinaya in Four Divisions' (Chin., szu fen lü) as the most consistent and easy to apply, and he provided a commentary to guide others in its application. He is also renowned as the author of the *Continued Biographies of Eminent Monks* (Chin., *Hsü kao seng chuan*, *Taishō 2060), a major source for biographical information on early Buddhist *monks.

Taoism. One of the indigenous religions of *China that played a role in the sinification of *Buddhism after its transmission to China. The legendary founder of Taoism is the sage *Lao-tsu (*c.*6th century BCE), to whom is attributed the authorship of the classic work the *Tao-te-ching* (The Book of the Way and its Power), although this probably dates to the 4th-3rd centuries BCE. The *Tao or 'Way', is the all-embracing matrix of the patterns by which things happen in the world, and it is from this concept that the school derives its name. Taoists generally hold to the ideal of coming to a knowledge or vision of this matrix for a variety of purposes: to see the intricate interconnectedness of all things, to attain long life, to achieve spontaneity in thoughts and actions, to gain supernatural powers, and so on. Such achievements involve finding a balance between the two opposing energies of yin and yang, from whose interaction all phenomena and change arise. These are seen as two complementary facets of the infinite Tao, represented in the yin–yang symbol of a circle with two dots in each half, indicating that yin and yang both contain the seed of their opposite. All opposition and duality can be expressed in terms of yin and yang; for example, yin stands for what is feminine, soft, and receptive and yang for what is masculine, hard, and dynamic. Taoists seek to harmonize these cosmic energies within themselves by observing and emulating the rhythms of nature, and it is an existential as opposed to an intellectual understanding that they seek. One text in particular, the *Chuang-tzu* (*c.*4th to 2nd centuries BCE), presents a thorough critique of language as a means of communicating truth and discursive thought as a mode of knowledge, and counsels direct observation of nature, both in the world and within oneself. This will lead to a calm acceptance of the circumstances of one's life and the inevitability of one's death, and a joyous spontaneity from day to day. Many scholars believe that this text was a formative influence in the genesis of *Ch'an Buddhism. Much of the cross-fertilization of Taoism and Buddhism took place after the fall of the *Han dynasty and the flight of many Chinese gentry and literati to the south, beginning in the 3rd century CE. The destabilization of the empire and the difficulties of life during this turbulent period led many to question the hegemony of a now-discredited *Confucianism, and to look for other ways to think about the problems of life. Many took to a newly revitalized Taoism and its close relative, the so-called 'Dark Learning' (Chin., hsüan hsüeh), sometimes also called 'Neo-Taoism'. Buddhism made its first inroads into the upper echelons of Chinese society at this time, and many scholars met to discuss and compare the ideas of these two religions.

Tao-sheng (355/60–434). An early Chinese *monk and literary scholar. A disciple of *Lu-shan Hui-yüan (334–416) on Mt. Lu, he later moved to the capital of *Ch'ang-an. In both places he studied Buddhist philosophy and participated in the translation activities of Indian or central Asian masters; in Ch'ang-an he worked with *Kumārajīva (343–413). He was instrumental in helping turn Chinese *Buddhism from the essentially negative way of the Perfection of Insight (*Prajñā-pāramitā) texts received from Indian Buddhism to a more positive analysis of reality and the beings within it in their 'Suchness' (*tathatā). In a famous episode, he disagreed with a newly translated scripture called the *Nirvāṇa Sūtra* which seemed to assert the doctrine of *icchantikas, beings who lack the nature to achieve *Buddhahood. He stated that this was wrong, that every being had '*Buddha- nature', and that all therefore had the possibility of attaining Buddhahood. For this, he was forced out of the office he held in his temple in Chien-k'ang and he returned to Mt. Lu. Later, when a newer translation of the same scripture appeared which contained a passage supporting his position, he was vindicated and returned to office, universally admired for his foresight and ability to see the truth behind the text. For the rest of his life, he stressed the teaching that, once the application of Perfection of Insight thought had served to clear away all misconceptions about beings and phenomena, then the result would not be unqualified negation (which Indian *Madhyamaka thought seemed to indicate), but the pure, subtle, and characterless truth of the phenomena would instead become apparent. This led to a more positive assessment of phenomenal reality within Chinese Buddhism.

Tapussa (or Tapassu). One of the first lay converts to *Buddhism. With his friend Bhalluka, he met the *Buddha in the eighth week after his enlightenment (*bodhi). They made an offering of food to the Buddha and became the first lay disciples.

Tārā. An important female deity in Tibetan *Buddhism. Tārā is a *Sanskrit word the precise meaning of which is uncertain (perhaps 'star'), but is understood by Tibetans to mean 'saviouress'. She is regarded with great affection and devotion by Tibetans, and her cult occupies a status similar to that of the Virgin Mary in Christianity. She is closely associated with *Avalokiteśvara (Tib., *Chenrezi), the *Bodhisattva of compassion (*karuṇā), of whom she is said to be an emanation. According to one account, she sprang from the tears of Chenrezi as he was about to enter final *nirvāṇa. When he looked back and saw the suffering beings who still remained to be saved he wept and decided to remain until all beings had reached salvation. Tārā embodies and expresses the compassionate nature of this Bodhisattva. Many sources regard her as a *Buddha and speak of her as the 'mother of all the Buddhas'. The cult of Tārā became widespread in *Tibet with the arrival of *Atiśa in 1042, who was a lifelong devotee. In iconography, Tārās of various colours are encountered, the two most common being white and green. The former was the earlier and the latter has a closer association with *tantric sources. In all,

Fig 18 Tārā

21 Tārās are recognized in Tibetan Buddhism. These are referred to in the main liturgical text associated with her cult, *Homage to the Twenty-One Tārās*, brought from *India by Dharmadra in the 11th century. Each Tārā has a different function (curing illnesses, averting disasters, etc.) and each has its own distinct iconographical gestures (*mudrās), and sacred syllables (*mantras). The main Tibetan schools revere different forms of Tārā, but her *mantra om tāre tuttāre ture svāhā (meaning roughly 'Praise to Tārā, Hail!) is one of the most popular invocations for all Tibetans.

Tārānātha (1575–1634). The honorary title of Künga Nyingpo (Tib., Kun-dga' snying-po), a leading teacher of the *Jonangpa school. He is best known for his important *Doctrinal History of India* (Tib., rgya-gar chos-'byung) as well as the many treatises he composed expounding Jonangpa tenets. Apart from his teaching and literary activities in *Tibet, he also spent 20 years propagating *Buddhism among the Khalkha Mongols (*see* MONGOLIA).

tariki. A Japanese *Pure Land term derived from the Chinese term t'a li meaning 'other-power'. This refers to the power of *Amitābha *Buddha that supports and empowers the *Pure Land devotee's practice. In Japanese Pure Land thought, tariki came to be seen as the only effective power that could save the practitioner; 'self-power' (*jiriki) was seen as arrogant and useless.

Tashilhumpo (Tib., bkra-shis lhun-po). An important *Gelukpa monastery in the town of Shigatse in southern *Tibet. It was founded in 1447 by *Dalai Lama I and has been the residence of successive *Panchen Lamas. It managed to escape the wholesale destruction of religious sites that took place following the Chinese invasions of the 1950s and the Cultural Revolution.

tathāgata (Skt.; Pāli). A title or epithet of the *Buddha. The term can mean either 'one who has thus come' or 'one who has thus gone'. The Buddha used the term to refer to himself after he had attained enlightenment (*bodhi), and it became one of the stock epithets of a Buddha. Other honorific titles include *Bhagavan (lord), *Jina (conqueror), *Arhat (worthy one), and *Samyak-saṃbuddha (perfectly enlightened Buddha). The historical Buddha *Siddhartha Gautama was also known as *Śākyamuni or 'the sage of the Śākyas', and is commonly referred to this way in the *Mahāyāna tradition.

tathāgata-garbha (Skt.). The 'embryonic *Buddha'. A *Mahāyāna concept which holds that all beings inherently possess the potential to become a *Buddha. According to this view, the negative elements that bind an individual to *saṃsāra are adventitious (*āgantuka-kleśa) and merely conceal or veil the underlying pure *Buddha-nature. The Tathāgata-garbha doctrine is based on a set of ten *sūtras that teach this concept, such as the **Tathāgata-garbha Sūtra*, the **Śrīmālā-devi-siṃhanāda*, and the **Nirvāṇa Sūtra*, as well as the treatise attributed to *Sthiramati or *Maitreyanātha, the **Ratna-gotra-vibhāga*, though it has a historical antecedent in the early Buddhist concept of the intrinsically *luminous mind. According to the position adopted by these sūtras, the Tathāgata-garbha is a real and eternally existing essence that is primordially replete with all the qualities of a Buddha. The concept was understood slightly differently in the Tibetan and the Chinese traditions where the term is translated as 'Tathāgata embryo' and 'Tathāgata womb' respectively. The term is also used synonymously with *ātman and *gotra in a number of these texts and was additionally influential in the formation of the Tibetan zhen-tong concept (*extrinsic emptiness) linked with the *Jonangpas.

Tathāgata-garbha-sūtra. 'The Sūtra of the Embryonic Buddha', the foundational source for the *tathāgata-garbha theory. It is a short text which demonstrates the existence of an inherent potentiality for enlightenment (*bodhi) in all beings through a series of similes showing how this potentiality or *Buddha-nature lies concealed within each individual. Apart from some *Sanskrit fragments, the text only survives in Tibetan and Chinese translations.

tathatā (Skt.). Term meaning 'suchness', and denoting the way things are in truth or actuality, and used especially in *Mahāyāna *Buddhism to denote the essential nature of reality and the quiddity or true mode of being of phenomena which is beyond the range of conceptual thought (*vikalpa). The term is one of a range of synonyms for the absolute, which include emptiness (*śūnyatā), thusness (*tattva), the limit of reality (*bhūta-koṭi), and true suchness (*bhūta-tathatā).

tattva (Skt.). Philosophical term with a range of meanings, including truth, reality, actuality, and fundamental principle.

Tattvasiddhi Śāstra *See* SATYASIDDHI ŚĀSTRA.

Taxila. The ancient capital of the *Gandhāra region, known in *Sanskrit, as 'Takṣaśilā' and in *Pāli as 'Takkasilā'. It is described in Buddhist sources as a great centre of commerce and learning, visited by merchants and scholars from all around. At the university there students were taught the *Vedas and the eighteen traditional Indian arts and sciences, including archery and swordsmanship.

tazaung. Burmese term meaning a shrine building of the kind usually found around a *zedi.

tea ceremony. Japanese practice involving a highly ritualized gathering of people to prepare and drink tea. It has had a long association with the *Zen school and represents an extension of Zen practice into a wider, secular culture. The association of Zen and tea goes back to *Eisai (1141–1215), the founder of the *Rinzai school of Zen who brought tea plants back with him from *China and recommended the drinking of tea to combat drowsiness while meditating. Tea found its way into aristocratic circles, where it was drunk in elegant surroundings. The artist Nōami (1397–1471) created the innovation of having tea in a separate small chamber, using a portable table and simple utensils, and restricting the conversation to aesthetic matters. His student Murata Shukō (1423–1502), who had studied Zen with *Ikkyū Sojun (1394–1481), gave the preparation and drinking of tea its Zen connection, seeing it as a way to practise the mindfulness in daily affairs that Ikkyū emphasized. Murata sought to incorporate tea into the Japanese lifestyle outside of the monastery and formulated the four principles of tea: harmony, purity, tranquillity, and reverence. Finally, Sen no Rikyū (1521–91) moved the ceremony from a residential setting to a hermit's hut. He is credited with bringing the art of tea (Jap., cha no yu) to its highest expression of simplicity and refinement.

teacher's fist. *See* ĀCARIYAMUṬṬHI.

telakhon (Karen, fruit of wisdom). Religious movement among the Karen people of *Burma inspired by Buddhist millennialism and aiming at political liberation, initially from the British and now from the present military regime. The movement was founded in the mid-19th century by Con Yu, and its millennial expectations revolve around a golden book that bestows knowledge and power. In the 1960s American missionaries shipped large numbers of Bibles to the Karen but the Bible was rejected as not being the authentic golden book of which the legends speak.

Temple of the Tooth. Series of *Sri Lankan temples in different towns in which, at different times, the *tooth relic has been housed. The temple in which the relic is now preserved is the *Dalada Maligawa.

temporary ordination. Rite of passage into manhood practised in certain *Theravādin countries of *south-east Asia. It requires that all men at some point in their life, before their *marriage, take *ordination and spend some time in a monastery (*vihāra). Besides its social function temporary ordination is taken as a way of acquiring and transmitting *puṇya (merit). In some countries, like *Thailand, it is customary for the temporary *monks to spend at least one rainy season in the monastery, while in others, like *Burma, this is rarely the case, probably because of the younger age of the temporarily ordained. Temporary ordination was not practised during the lifetime of the *Buddha and it is not known when this practice was introduced in Theravāda *Buddhism. A recent attempt to introduce temporary ordination in *Sri Lanka did not meet with success.

Tendai. One of the two major schools of Japanese *Buddhism that arose during the early *Heian period (794–1185). This school was founded by the *monk *Saichō (767–822), and, because of the circumstances of the founder's life, became a broadly eclectic school encompassing both esoteric rituals (*see* ESOTERIC BUDDHISM) and exoteric studies in doctrine and scripture, as well as early forms of *Pure Land and *Zen. Its headquarters were on Mt. *Hiei, next to the capital city of Heian (modern *Kyoto), and after a shaky start during the founder's lifetime, went on to become a very wealthy and powerful school. The school that Saichō founded was in a state of disarray after his death. Since he had gone to *China specifically looking for *T'ien-t'ai teachings (Tendai is simply the Japanese pronunciation of T'ien-t'ai), it officially adhered to T'ien-t'ai teachings and practices, in particular its classification of doctrine which held the **Lotus Sūtra* to be the highest expression of the *Buddha's teaching. However, since he had also embraced esoteric rituals, and indeed this became the school's most popular feature, a problem arose, since the T'ien-t'ai classification of teachings had been formulated in China prior to the rise of esoteric practice there, and so did not include it. *Annen (d. 889–98) solved this problem by adding esoteric teachings as a new and separate category that transcended all the others and so existed on a different plane than the traditional four classifications of T'ien-t'ai. Mt. Hiei and the *Tendai school quickly became favourite objects of patronage on the part of the imperial and aristocratic families, which led inevitably to a concentration of wealth and power on the mountain. This led to a moral decline as high office within the school became politicized, and people sought to rise through the ranks in order to gain power and influence rather than pursue religious goals. There was a revival of the original spirit of the school under the abbot *Ryōgen (912–85), but the situation quickly deteriorated once again after his death.

Tendai's broad range of teaching (compared to the very narrow interests of its main rival at the time, the *Shingon school), combined with its spiritual decay, made it the breeding grounds for the new reform movements that arose during the *Kamakura period (1185–1392): Zen, Pure Land, and *Nichiren Buddhism were all founded by former Tendai *monks who had learnt of the teachings of the schools they founded within the Tendai school. Their activities were hampered by Tendai's power and intolerance of competition; frequently, those who began new movements found themselves the victims of Mt. Hiei's notorious *sōhei, or warrior-monks. These were little more than bands of thugs in priestly robes who would descend with clubs and torches to destroy new temples and try to stamp out rivals. Many Kamakura-era reformers found themselves fleeing before the sōhei at various times. The wealth of Mt. Hiei, as well as the military power it exercised through its sōhei, turned it from an object of patronage by those in power to a direct military and political threat, and it was destroyed in 1571 by the warlord Oda Nobunaga. All of the temple complexes were demolished and over 3,000 priests and laymen died in this assault. Although devastated by this blow, Tendai survived. Mt. Hiei was reconstructed after Oda's assassination, and Tendai branch temples in other places continued to thrive. Nevertheless, as time went on, Tendai was eclipsed by the massive popularity of the newer schools of Zen, Pure Land, and Nichiren, and remains today a minor part of Japanese Buddhism.

ten good actions. *See* DAŚA-KUŚALA-KARMA-PATHA.

ten great disciples. A group of ten of the *Buddha's most famous disciples whose names are constantly mentioned in *Mahāyāna *sūtras. The ten are: (1) *Mahākāśyapa, (2) *Ānanda, (3) *Śāriputra, (4) *Subhūti, (5) Pūrna, (6) *Mahāmaudgalyāyana, (7) *Mahākatyāyana, (8) Aniruddha, (9) *Upāli, (10) *Rāhula. The first two are regarded by the *Ch'an tradition as its first two Indian *patriarchs.

Tenjur (Tib., bstan-gyur). The second main division of the Tibetan canon (*see* KANJUR) of religious works mainly translated from Indic languages, it comprises around 225 volumes of commentarial and independent treatises written by the great masters of Indian *Buddhism. It is subdivided into a number of classificatory sections and additionally includes secular works on grammar, *medicine, and crafts.

ten kings. In Chinese folklore, these figures were ten judges that the souls of the newly deceased encountered at various times after their death. These kings would judge their sins and guilt and assign appropriate punishments, and many of the standard postmortem rituals conducted on the deceased's behalf were aimed at influencing their decisions in the dead person's favour. Belief in the ten kings appears to have arisen in *China during the *T'ang dynasty, and was carried in both Buddhist and *Taoist circles.

Ten Precepts. *See* DAŚA-ŚĪLA.

Tenzin Gyatso. *See* DALAI LAMA XIV.

terma (Tib., gter-ma). Literally 'hidden treasure', termas are believed to be texts hidden in *Tibet during the *First Propagation period by *Padmasambhava and others to be later discovered and disseminated by 'treasure revealers'. These texts are venerated as authentic revelations of the *Dharma by adherents of the *Nyingma school and include such works as the 'Tibetan Book of the Dead' (**Bar-do thos-grol*). There are Indian antecedents for this belief in hidden literary treasures as many *Mahāyāna scriptures are said to have come to light in *India in a similar manner.

Tertön. *See* GTER-STON.

Te-shan Hsüan-chien (782–865). One of the Chinese *Ch'an monks of the late *T'ang dynasty who explored the teaching methods now known as 'shock Ch'an'. He originally set out from northern *China to combat the Ch'an tendency to deprecate scriptural and doctrinal study, but was converted to Ch'an methods instead and burnt his scriptures and commentaries. He used a short staff in his teaching and rained blows on his disciples to spur them on. He is credited with teaching, 'If you can say anything, thirty blows! If you cannot say anything, thirty blows!'

thabeik. Burmese term for (1) a *monk's *begging-bowl and (2) traditional element of *stūpa architecture.

Thailand. Formerly known as Siam, Thailand became a constitutional democracy in 1932. *Buddhism (almost entirely of the *Theravāda form) plays a leading role in all aspects of national life, and since the *Saṃgha Administration Act of 1902 has enjoyed constitutional status as the official religion. Under this measure a religious hierarchy was created presided over by a supreme *patriarch (saṃgha-rāja) who is appointed by the king. Because of this link between Buddhism and nationalism, it is traditional for all young men to spend a short period of time as *monks, usually during the three-month rainy-season retreat. Most parents would consider it a great honour should their son wish to prolong his stay and take up the religious life on a permanent basis, but for most it is a kind of 'national service' forming a step on the way to an alternative professional career.

The *Pāli chronicles refer to Thailand as *Sāmindavisaya, and speak of a close relationship between it and *Sri Lanka dating back to the Middle Ages. Monks were sent from Thailand to restore the *ordination lineage in Sri Lanka when Buddhism had fallen into decline there. The original inhabitants of the region were the Mons, who may have been introduced to Theravāda Buddhism in the early centuries CE by missionaries sent from *India by *Aśoka. It became firmly established in those areas of the *Mon kingdom known as Haripuñjaya and Dvāravatī. From the 5th to the 15th century, an important power in the area was the *Khmer Empire, in which various forms of *Hinduism and *Mahāyāna Buddhism were also popular. In the 11th century, missionaries were sent from *Burma, and the Thai people arrived in the region having been displaced from *China by the Mongols. They found the Theravāda form of Buddhism congenial and it began to displace Mahāyāna forms. Around 1260 the kingdom of Sukhothai became independent from the Khmers and King Rama Khamheng (1275–1317) declared Theravāda the state religion. Sukhothai fell in 1492 and was replaced by the kingdom of Ayudhya, which ruled until 1767. During this time an edition of the *Pāli Canon was produced by King Songdharm (r. 1610–28) and relations between the *Saṃgha and the crown became closer. Ayudhya was overthrown by Rama I (1782–1809) who founded the Chakri dynasty and devoted himself to the purification of the Saṃgha. One of his successors, *Mongkut (Rama IV, r. 1851–78) was himself a *monk for 27 years before becoming king. Having been a member of the strict *Thammayut order (which he himself founded) he decreed on becoming king that all monks, including those of the majority Mahānikai (Pāli, Mahānikāya) should henceforth observe the stricter disciplinary practices. Although monks are the main source of religious authority, lay groups have also been established in recent times, and many Thais are pressing for a more modern outlook on the part of the clergy and an updating of the ancient teachings to make them more relevant to the problems of contemporary life.

Thammayut (Pāli, Dhammayuttika). A reform movement in the Thai *Saṃgha founded around 1833 by *Mongkut, ruler of *Thailand, 1851–68. The movement, whose name means 'those holding to the Law', advocated stricter compliance with the *Vinaya in contrast to the mainstream Mahānikai (Pāli, Mahānikāya) order. As abbot of Wat Bovoranives, which became the centre of the Thammayut sect, Mongkut laid down strict rules governing ordination, wearing of the monastic robe (over both shoulders instead of just one), and for the conduct of the *kaṭhina or robe-giving ceremony. He was also concerned to purge Buddhism of its superstitious elements and emphasize its rational aspects so as to make it compatible with science and modern attitudes. The Thammayut movement was instituted in southern Laos around 1850 and Cambodia in 1864 by monks trained in Thailand. It now enjoys the status of official orthodoxy in contemporary Thai Buddhism.

thang-ka (Tib.). A Tibetan scroll-painting which generally uses gouache on a cotton canvas and depicts various religious topics such as the *Buddha, episodes from his lives, *tantric deities, *maṇḍalas, Buddhist scholars, and saints. The paintings are normally framed with three bands of fine silk brocade and can be rolled up for transport. Exceptionally valuable thang-kas use a background of gold (Tib., gser-thang) upon which a central deity is painted in colour, surrounded by rows of smaller duplicate figures in outline. Art historians recognize a number of distinct styles, reflecting the main painting traditions of *Tibet.

Thangtong Gyelpo (Tib., Thang-song rgyal-po). A 15th-century Tibetan *yogin and teacher, famed for his construction of many iron-chain suspension bridges as well as being a revealer of *terma texts.

that. Thai term for a *stūpa.

thein. Burmese term for a *sīma.

Theosophical Society. An organization founded in New York in 1875 by the Russian mystic Helena Petrovna *Blavatsky (1831–91) and Henry Steel *Olcott (1832–1907), an American psychic investigator who became its first president. Through the study of comparative religion the Society sought to uncover the truths which it believed to constitute the core of all religions. Its main beliefs, which include many Indian doctrines such as *karma, *reincarnation, and belief in astral bodies, are explained in Blavatsky's books *Isis Unveiled* (1877) and *The Secret Doctrine* (1888). Other influential figures include Annie Besant and C. W. Leadbetter. Leading members of the society visited *India and other parts of Asia to study mystical teachings and seek out occult phenomena. Although Buddhist ideas are represented to some degree, the primary Indian influence on theosophy came from *Hinduism.

thep. Thai transliteration of the term *deva, meaning a god or divinity.

thera. *Pāli honorific term meaning 'old' or 'venerable', and used with reference to the senior *monks of the Buddhist monastic order (*Saṃgha). The seniority of a *monk is determined not by age but by the time elapsed since *ordination. Normally ten years' standing is required for a monk to be considered as a thera.

Theragāthā. Literally 'verses of the elders'. The eighth book of the *Khuddaka Nikāya of the *Sūtra Piṭaka of the *Pāli Canon. The work consists of a collection of verses, most of which are believed to have been composed by elder monks (*thera) during the lifetime of the *Buddha. Most of the verses are accounts of religious experiences and some are of a high poetic standard. Others contain accounts of the life histories of the elder monks. The commentary to the *Theragāthā*, compiled by *Dhammapāla around the 6th century, is part of the **Paramatthadīpanī*.

Theravāda. (Pāli, way of the elders). The only one of the early Buddhist schools of the *Hīnayāna or 'Small Vehicle' to have survived down to modern times. Today, the Theravāda is the dominant tradition of *Buddhism throughout most of *south-east Asia, particularly *Sri Lanka, *Burma, *Thailand, Laos, and *Cambodia. According to tradition, the school spread initially as the result of missionary activity after being brought to Sri Lanka by *Mahinda, the son of *Aśoka. The school claims its origins go back to the ancient body of the Elders (*sthaviras) before the separation from the *Mahāsaṃghikas, but there is no historical evidence to support this. There are close similarities, however, between the

Theravāda and the ancient *Vibhajyavādins who were declared by Aśoka to be the orthodox party at the *Council of Pāṭaliputra II. The school is characterized by fidelity to the texts of the *Pāli Canon, the earliest complete set of Buddhist scriptures preserved intact in a single canonical language. Its attitude to doctrine and its outlook on social issues is generally conservative, although in modern times *monks have come forward to challenge traditional attitudes. *See also* EIGHTEEN SCHOOLS OF EARLY BUDDHISM.

Therīgāthā. Literally 'verses of the elder nuns'. The ninth book of the *Khuddaka Nikāya of the *Sūtra Piṭaka of the *Pāli Canon. It consists of a collection of verses, most of which are believed to have been composed by elder *nuns. Most of the verses are accounts of religious experiences and some are of a high poetic standard. Others contain accounts of the life histories of the elder nuns. It corresponds to the **Theragāthā*, a collection of verses compiled by elder monks. The commentary to the *Therīgāthā*, compiled by *Dhammapāla around the 6th century, is part of the **Paramatthadīpanī*.

Theriya school. *See* ABHAYAGIRI.

Thich Quang Duc. A Vietnamese Buddhist *monk who, on 11 June 1963, publicly immolated himself at a busy intersection in Saigon to protest about the war in *Vietnam and the incarceration of Buddhist monks by the government.

thilashin. Name for Burmese *women who live according to the *precepts of a novice *nun (*śrāmaṇerī). In many respects their lifestyle resembles that of a nun, even to the extent of making a daily alms-round, but they cannot obtain full *ordination since the lineage died out in Burma and elsewhere in *south-east Asia many centuries ago. In certain respects they resemble the *dasa- silmātā of *Sri Lanka, and the *sikkhamat of *Thailand, although with a somewhat higher social status.

thögal (Tib., thod-rgal). Literally 'direct crossing', this is one of the two main techniques used in advanced *Dzogchen practice. Its aim is to bring about the spontaneous accomplishment of primordial awareness. *See also* THREKCHÖ.

thought of enlightenment. *See* BODHICITTA.

three bodies. *See* TRIKĀYA.

three Buddha families. An early classification of *Buddhas and *Bodhisattvas with their associated qualities. These were comprised of three groups or families known as the Tathāgata, Vajra, and Lotus Families, epitomized by *Śākyamuni, *Vajrapāṇi, and *Avalokiteśvara. This classification is also related to the *body, speech, mind aspects of the Buddhas as well as to their 'three bodies' (*trikāya), namely *dharma-kāya, *saṃbhoga-kāya and *nirmāṇa-kāya. In the later *tantras from the **Tattva- saṃgraha* onwards, this set is supplanted by the system of *five Buddha families formed by the addition of the Ratna (Jewel) and Karma families.

three jewels. *See* TRIRATNA.

three liberations. *See* VIMOKṢA.

three marks. *See* TRILAKṢAṆA.

three periods of the teachings. A way of schematizing Buddhist history that arose in *China during the period of disunity following the fall of the *Han dynasty in the early 3rd century CE. According to this teaching, the history of *Buddhism divides into three periods. First is the Age of the True *Dharma, which lasts 500 or 1,000 years, depending on the source. This is the age right after the death of a *Buddha, when the teaching is vigorous, people are capable of comprehending it and putting it into practice, and many attain enlightenment (*bodhi) under their own power. Second is the Age of the Counterfeit Dharma, in which the true teachings become obscured and only a semblance of it exists. At this time, which again lasts for 500 or 1,000 years depending on the source, only a few people of great intelligence are able to grasp the doctrine correctly and attain enlightenment. Third was the Age of the Final Dharma (Chin., mo-fa; Jap., *mappō), in which people's capacities were feeble and the teachings were lost. Many Buddhists in east Asia during the medieval period felt that this age was either imminent or had already arrived. The resulting loss of faith in traditional practices and teachings as means of gaining liberation led to the popularization of new modes of practice that relied more on the power of an already-enlightened Buddha (in the case of *Pure Land Buddhism) or a text (in *Nichiren Buddhism) for liberation.

Three Pillars of Zen. 1. The three constituent elements of teaching, practice, and *enlightenment. **2.** Title of a book by Rōshi Philip Kapleau (1912–) that has been highly influential in *Zen's transmission to and subsequent development in the West.

three realms (Skt., tridhātu). The hierarchical structure of a universe or 'world-system' according to Buddhist *cosmology, comprising the Desire Realm (*kāma-dhātu), the Form Realm (*rūpa-dhātu), and the Formless Realm (*ārūpya-dhātu). Also known by the alternative designation of the 'three worlds' (*tri-loka).

three refuges. *See* TRIŚARAṆA.

three roots of evil. *See* AKUŚALA-MŪLA.

Three Stages, Teaching of. *See* SAN-CHIEH-CHIAO.

three times (Skt., tri-kāla). The past, present, and future.

Three Truths. A doctrine developed by *Chih-i as a result of dissatisfaction with the essentially negative metaphysical analysis of the *Madhyamaka teachings. The problem, as he saw it, was that the '*Two Truths' of Madhyamaka presented the Ultimate Truth as simple negation: it said what things were not, without making any positive statement of what they were. Thus, Chih-i proposed the Three Truths: the truths of emptiness (*śūnyatā), provisionality, and the middle. The first broke down all illusions about things, denying their permanence and the existence of any essence within them. The second affirmed their existence as impermanent objects that arose, abided, decayed, and ceased according to the laws of cause and effect. Thus, these first two truths corresponded to the Ultimate (*paramārtha-satya) and Conventional (*saṃvṛti-satya) Truths of Madhyamaka. The third truth, that of the middle, synthesized these into a positive statement about the nature of reality. The impermanence (*anitya) and interdependence of all phenomena was the ultimate truth about them. In this way, Chih-i denied that emptiness and provisionality were two different and unrelated aspects of things, or that emptiness negated provisionality, but stated that the contingency of things was in itself the ultimate truth about them. *T'ien-t'ai doctrine, as developed by Chih-i, thus embodies a view of an immanent transcendent. That is to say, it does not look for a pure, undefiled realm that is above and beyond the present, defiled world. Rather, by positing the threefold truth, it affirms that the absolute abides in and through the contingent, not outside or beyond it. This found expression in one of the characteristic doctrines of the school—that of the non-obstruction of phenomena with the absolute (Chin., li shih wu ai).

three turnings of the wheel (Skt., tri-dharma-cakra-pravartana). **1.** Notion arising from the *Buddha's first sermon where each of the *Four Noble Truths is viewed from three perspectives: as a noble truth, as a truth to be realized, and as a truth that has been realized. **2.** A *Yogācāra theory first taught in the **Sandhi-nirmocana Sūtra* which classifies the *Buddha's teachings into three levels. These are the First Turning which taught the basic *Dharma for Śrāvakas (*see* ŚRĀVAKAYĀNA); the Second Turning which taught the provisional doctrine of emptiness (*śūnyatā) through such *sūtras as the *Prajñā-pāramitā Sūtra* corpus; and the Third Turning which taught a definitive presentation of the true nature of reality by way of the 'three natures' (*tri-svabhāva) theory. The content of the Second Turning is implicitly linked to the *Madhyamaka school while the Third Turning should be identified with the Yogācāra school, an interpretation naturally not shared by Madhyamaka adherents.

three uncountable kalpas (Skt., try-asaṃkhyeya-kalpa). The period of time necessary for a *Bodhisattva to arrive at enlightenment (*bodhi), according to the *Mahāyāna. The precise duration of one 'uncountable' (asaṃkhyeya) *kalpa or aeon varies but values sometimes given are 10^{51}, 10^{59}, or 10^{63} years. Other sources describe these in terms of spans of time of inconceivable duration.

three vows (Tib., sdom-gsum). A Tibetan term for the three levels of moral restraints and *ethics, comprising the *Vinaya code of discipline, the *Bodhisattva vows, and the *tantric commitments (*samaya). The precise relationship and hierarchy of these three kinds of vows, apparently contradictory in certain respects, gave rise to much debate in Tibetan religious circles.

threk-chö (Tib., mkhregs-chod). Literally, 'cutting through'. One of the two main techniques used in advanced *Dzogchen practice. The aim is to help the practitioner cut through the stream of delusive appearances and thoughts by a direct revelation of intrinsic awareness (rig-pa).

Thudhamma. Name of the largest monastic order or *gaing in *Burma, comprising 88.6 per cent of all monks in 1980. The group comprises those who remained under the control of the Thudhamma Assembly (or Council) after the *Shwegyin gaing was established around 1860. The Thudhamma outnumbers the Shwegyin by a ratio exceeding 12:1.

Thūpārāma. Name of a monastery (*vihāra) erected by *Devānampiya Tissa (247–207 BCE) in his capital *Anurādhapura. According to legend, the spot was consecrated by the *Buddha who sat there in *meditation like former Buddhas had done. The *stūpa (Pāli. thūpa), enshrining the Buddha's collar bone, was the first of its kind in *Sri Lanka and the monastery, which was built later, took its name from it.

Thūpavaṃsa. 'Chronicle of the Thūpas' (Skt., *stūpa), a *Pāli poem in sixteen chapters often attributed to Vācissara (12th century), but the authorship of which is uncertain. The last eight chapters of the work contain a description of the construction of the *Mahā-thūpa by *Duṭṭhagāmaṇi at *Anurādhapura.

Tibet. Although Tibet is geographically closer to India, *Buddhism reached that country many centuries after its arrival in east Asia. This is due to a combination of geographical and economic reasons. Tibet is the highest country in the world located on a vast plateau occupying over 1.5 million square miles surrounded by high mountains. For a country the size of western Europe, it has a tiny population, estimated at some 6 million in the present century. Isolated between the economically and culturally advanced civilizations of *India and *China, Tibet had few readily accessible natural resources and only a subsistence economy, so there were few trade missions or caravans for *monks to attach themselves to. It was thus not until the 7th century CE that Buddhism made an appearance. Traditional chronicles speak of three 'diffusions' of Buddhism, the first of which begins with Songtsen Gampo (Tib., Srong bstan sgam po, ca. 618–50), the first of the three 'religious kings'. This king had a Nepalese and a Chinese wife, both of whom brought Buddhist artefacts with them to Tibet. The second 'religious king' was Trisong Detsen (Tib., Khri srong lde brtsan), who invited the scholar-*monk *Śāntarakṣita from India to promulgate Buddhist teachings. The latter made little progress, and withdrew in favour of *Padmasambhava, a *tantric *guru and popular Tibetan folk hero. It is said that through his magical powers Padmasambhava was able to overcome the demons who were obstructing Buddhism's progress in Tibet. These 'demons' can, perhaps, be identified with practitioners of the indigenous *Bön religion, a form of central Asian shamanism which imprinted something of its distinctive character, including an interest in rites, rituals, and magical practices surrounding death, on Buddhism. With the 'demons' subdued and the way clear, Śāntarakṣita returned to Tibet, and with Padmasambhava co-founded the first *monastery at *Samyé (bsam yas) *c.*767 CE. Another important missionary to arrive in this period was *Kamalaśīla, who played a decisive role in ensuring that Tibetan Buddhism developed along Indian rather than Chinese lines. The third 'religious king', Relpa Chen (Tib., Ral pa can, r. 815–36), continued the construction of temples and monasteries and as a result of royal patronage the ranks of the *Saṃgha began to swell. This led to a backlash against Buddhism and Relpa Chen was assassinated in 836 and succeeded by *Lang Darma (Tib., glang dar ma), a king less favourably disposed to Buddhism, who was himself subsequently assassinated by a Buddhist monk. The arrival of *Atiśa (982–1054) from India in 1042 marks the start of the second diffusion. Atiśa laid emphasis on the conventional monastic curriculum, but his disciples also included more colourful individuals who became known as Mahāsiddhas or 'great adepts'. Chief among these tantric gurus are *Marpa (1012–97), *Milarepa (Tib., Mi la ras pa, 1040–1123), and

*Gampopa (Tib., sgam po pa, 1079–1153). Gampopa established this lineage as a monastic order known as the *Kagyüpa (Tib., bka' brygud pa). Two further orders were established during the high medieval period, the *Sakyapa (Tib., Sa skya pa) and the *Gelukpa (Tib., dge lugs pa). The latter, a reform movement founded by *Tsongkhapa (Tib., Tsong kha pa, 1357–1419), went on to become the most influential in both the spiritual and temporal spheres, effectively ruling Tibet from the 17th century through the office of the *Dalai Lama. Together with the *Nyingma pa (Tib., rnying ma pa), who trace their origins to Padmasambhava, these constitute the four main orders of Tibetan Buddhism.

After many centuries of relative isolation, the 20th century was turbulent. The country was invaded by China in 1959, leading the Dalai Lama to flee into exile in Dharamsala in India. The Communist Chinese authorities have suppressed Buddhism and persecuted monks and *nuns in an effort to purge the country of 'superstition' and what it regards as a medieval feudal social system. According to Tibetan authorities, 1.2 million people were killed during the Chinese invasion and its aftermath, and some 150,000 have since sought refugee status in India and the West to escape the ongoing repression. Large tracts of Tibetan territory have been annexed, and the reduced political entity that remains, called by the Chinese the 'Tibetan Autonomous Region', has a population of only 2 million. Although the excesses of the Cultural Revolution have now subsided, Buddhism is still strictly controlled. Most of the 6,000 monasteries that existed in Tibet were destroyed. The few that have been restored are today inhabited by only a handful of monks instead of the thousands they were home to formerly.

Tibetan Book of the Dead. *See BAR-DO THOS-GROL.*

T'ien-t'ai. A school of Chinese *Buddhism that dates from the late 6th and early 7th centuries, and which takes its name from the site of its head temple, Mt. T'ien-t'ai in Chekiang Province on *China's eastern seaboard. The *de facto* founder is the *monk *Chih-i (538–97), but tradition regards him as the third *patriarch of the school, the first two being *Hui-wen (fl. *c.*550), and Chih-i's teacher, the *meditation master *Hui-ssu (515–77). T'ien-t'ai is known for three innovative features: its system of doctrinal classification (Chin., p'an-chiao), its highly articulated system of meditation, and its doctrine of the *Three Truths.

Doctrinal Classification

One of the problems with which Chih-i dealt was that of making sense of the disorderly mass of Buddhists texts that had been translated into Chinese by the end of the 6th century. Buddhism had entered *China at a time when the *Mahāyāna teachings were just coming into prominence in *India, and both doctrines and scriptures continued to develop, while older texts of the *Hīnayāna variety also circulated. It was difficult to understand how these heterogeneous and often contradictory scriptures, all purporting to be the word of the *Buddha, formed any sort of unified teaching. Although attempts at doctrinal systematization had been attempted before, these had largely been based on judging the degree to which a text accurately gave the Buddha's teaching. Chih-i created a set of criteria that contextualized scriptures according to three standards: the period of the Buddha's life in which a scripture was preached, the audience to whom it was preached, and the teaching method the Buddha employed to convey his message. The first criterion yielded the scheme of 'Five Periods'. (1) The Avataṃsaka period (three weeks) immediately followed the Buddha's enlightenment (*bodhi), and was preached while he was still in an ecstatic state to convey the entire content of his vision. However, beings were unable to grasp the totality of the message, so the Buddha quickly changed his teaching. (2) In the *Āgama period (twelve years) the Buddha preached the Hīnayāna scriptures in order to provide an easy introduction to the teachings. (3) In the Vaipulya period (eight years) the Buddha began slowly introducing Mahāyāna themes and undercutting the teachings of the previous period so as to clear the way for a fuller understanding. (4) In the *Prajñā-pāramitā period (22 years) the Buddha taught the full Mahāyāna doctrine of universal emptiness (*śūnyatā). (5) During the period of the *Lotus* and **Nirvāṇa Sūtras* (eight years) the Buddha switched from the negative language of the *Prajñā-pāramitā Sūtras to the positive language of the *Lotus Sūtra*, which affirmed the *Buddha-nature of all beings and the identity and common goal of the so-called 'three vehicles' of Buddhism. Because the Buddha at this time returned to teaching the full content of his enlightenment, the *Lotus Sūtra* is considered the highest of all scriptures and most directly expressive of the Buddha's meaning by the T'ien-t'ai school. The criterion of intended audience produced four divisions in scripture: (1) the Piṭaka teachings were given for the two vehicles of the Śrāvakas (*Śrāvakayana) and *Pratyekabuddhas; (2) the common teachings were intended for the above two groups, and also for lower-level *Bodhisattvas just starting out on the Mahāyāna path; (3) the Distinct teachings were for Bodhisattvas on the Mahāyāna path only; and (4) the 'Round' (or Perfect) teachings gave a complete account of the totality of reality for the highest Bodhisattvas. Finally, the criterion of teaching method gave another four categories: (1) the Abrupt teaching was intended to jolt practitioners into a sudden realization of the complete truth; (2) the Gradual teaching took a step-by-step approach to teaching and led practitioners systematically to a realization of the truth; (3) the Secret teaching is one in which the Buddha spoke to a large crowd, but veiled his message so that only a specific person or persons would catch his meaning—it also indicates a situation in which not all members of the audience are aware of each other, as when in several Mahāyāna scriptures it is revealed that gods and Bodhisattvas have been listening to the Buddha's discourse undetected by the less spiritually advanced members—and (4) the Indeterminate teachings, in which the members of the audience are aware of each others' presence, but the Buddha speaks to each one individually while appearing to address the crowd at once.

Meditation

Chih-i and his teacher Hui-ssu were both masters of meditation, and two of Chih-i's works, the *Mo-ho chih-kuan* (Great Calming and Contemplation) and *Hsiao chih-kuan* (Small Calming and Contemplation) take a great number of methods of meditation and systematize them. While a complete exposition of these methods is beyond the scope of this work, it should be noted that this comprehensive classification of techniques fed into other traditions that would arise alongside of or later than T'ien-t'ai. For example, it included methods of exercising mindfulness in everyday activities and of perceiving the ultimate truth through the contemplation of phenomenal reality, which would directly influence the development of Ch'an. It also included methods of invoking the name of and visualizing the form of *Amitābha Buddha, which would give new impetus to the already-existing Pure Land tradition. (Many of the organizers of large-scale Pure Land devotional societies in the Sung dynasty were T'ien-t'ai monks.)

The *Three Truths

Chih-i felt some dissatisfaction with the essentially negative metaphysical analysis of the *Madhyamaka teachings (as seen by the fact that, in the 'Five periods' portion of his doctrinal classification scheme, the *Prajñā-pāramitā period is not the final period). Thus, Chih-i proposed the Three Truths: the truths of emptiness (*śūnyatā), provisionality, and the middle. Chih-i also turned this middle truth from a statement about ontology to one that affirmed agency operating within the universe. Whereas Madhyamaka teachings of emptiness asserted how things existed in a dry and static way, saying merely that they lacked any inherent essence or self-nature, Chih-i characterized the final nature of things as consciousness (*vijñāna), coining the term 'Middle-Way Buddha-Nature' (Chin., chung-tao fo-hsing). The omniscient mind of the Buddha took in all phenomenal reality, and so everything in the world was part of the Buddha's consciousness. This absolute mind thus operated through all things to work compassionately for the liberation of all beings. The fact that this mind took in defiled phenomena as well as pure phenomena led T'ien-t'ai to embrace a unique teaching: that the absolute mind had defiled as well as pure aspects; in other words, that immoral and impure things in the world served as the vehicle for the saving activity of the Buddha mind just as much as things that were pure did. T'ien-t'ai is the only school of Chinese Buddhism that attributes impure aspects to the Buddha-mind. For T'ien-t'ai, however, this was simply the logical outcome of attributing omniscience to the Buddha's mind—that it would perceive everything and thus incorporate everything, whether defiled or pure, into itself and make use of it to reach all beings.

History after Chih-i

T'ien-t'ai is the only one of the schools of Chinese Buddhism that derives its name from its geographical center (Mt. T'ien-t'ai) rather than from a central text (as the *Hua-yen school does) or its method of practice (as Ch'an or Pure Land). This gave it a measure of stability and continuity, as those who resided on Mt. T'ien-t'ai felt the need to keep the vision and practices of the school alive. This allowed it to survive even the great persecution of Buddhism in 845 that destroyed all the other schools save the highly decentralized Ch'an and Pure Land. Chih-i was succeeded by his disciple of 20 years, Kuan-ting (561–632), who composed commentaries on the *Nirvāṇa Sūtra* after Chih-i's style. The sixth patriarch, *Chan-jan (711–82) was instrumental in revitalizing T'ien-t'ai after it had lost some ground to the newly arisen Hua-yen, Ch'an, and esoteric schools (*see* ESOTERIC BUDDHISM). He composed commentaries on scriptures and the works of Chih-i, and is also credited with an interesting doctrinal development. Building on Chih-i's doctrine of the pervasion of absolute mind through all phenomena and his term 'Middle-way Buddha-nature', Chan-jan asserted that all things, both animate and inanimate, possess Buddha-nature, and can thus attain enlightenment (*bodhi). The school flourished greatly under his leadership. Two generations later, however, the *Hui-ch'ang persecution of 845 broke out, and the temple complex on Mt. T'ien-t'ai was destroyed along with its library and manuscripts, and its clergy scattered. The school went into a steep decline after this, but did not die out. Korean disciples responded to invitations to bring the texts and teachings of the school back to the mountain, and it slowly began to rebuild. During the Sung dynasty, two eminent T'ien-t'ai monks, Ssu-ming Chih-li (960–1028) and Tsun-shih (964–1032) were very active not only in propagating T'ien-t'ai teachings, but in establishing large-scale Pure Land societies among clergy and educated laypeople.

Ssu-ming Chih-li also initiated a controversy that split the T'ien-t'ai school into two factions for the next several centuries. Beginning in the year 1000, this became known as the Shan-chia ('mountain house', i.e. orthodox) versus Shan-wai ('off the mountain', i.e. heterodox) controversy, and it touched on at least four separate issues regarding the authenticity of a particular version of one of Chih-i's works, the placement of a particular doctrine of Dependent Origination (*pratītya-samutpāda) within either the 'Distinct Teaching' or elsewhere within the p'an-chiao framework, the relationship between the evil inherent in the absolute principle and the evil within particular beings, and the nature of the Pure Land. The Shan-chia/Shan-wai controversy provided fodder for a steady stream of treatises and letters well into the Ming dynasty. After this time, the school settled into a quiet existence, and by the end of the Ming dynasty, was less a self-standing school than a set of texts and doctrines in which some scholars might choose to specialize (although certain clergy still claimed to be part of the T'ien-t'ai school). Also, starting in the 9th century, with the visit of *Saichō to China in search of Mt. T'ien-t'ai, the school came to *Japan, where it became known as the *Tendai school, one of the major traditions of Japanese Buddhism.

ṭīkā. A *Sanskrit and *Pāli term for a sub-commentary on a text.

Tika-paṭṭhāna. *Pāli term meaning literally 'origins of triads'. First part of the *Paṭṭhāna*, the final book of the *Abhidharma Piṭaka of the *Pāli Canon. It is a highly technical text, consisting of a minutely detailed analysis of the doctrine of conditionality (*pratītya-samutpāda). Its commentary was composed by *Buddhaghoṣa in the 5th century.

Tilopa (989–1069). One of the famous Indian *mahā-siddhas or great *tantric adepts, his name derives from the tradition that he was a manufacturer of sesame-seed oil. Believed to have been the first teacher who expounded the *mahāmudrā (Great Seal) doctrines and practices, he passed these and other tantric teachings to his disciple *Nāropa who in turn passed them on to *Marpa.

Ti-lun. The conventional short form of the title of a Buddhist scripture in Chinese translation. The full title is *Shih-ti ching lun* (Treatise on the Scripture of the Ten Stages, *Taishō 1522), a commentary by the Indian Buddhist scholar *Vasubandhu. This commentary aroused considerable interest among Chinese Buddhist scholars, and called attention to *Buddhabhadra's translation of the *Avataṃsaka Sūtra* (Chin., *Hua-yen ching) completed around 418, since the eighth fascicle of this work was the *locus classicus* for the ten stages (*bhūmi) through which a *Bodhisattva passes on the way to full Buddhahood. Thus, Ti-lun scholars generally were familiar with the *Avataṃsaka* as well. During the *T'ang dynasty, when the *Hua-yen school was established on the basis of the *Avataṃsaka Sūtra*, it quickly absorbed Ti-lun scholars into its fold.

tīrthika (Skt.). Term meaning a 'ford-maker' used in Buddhist sources as a general designation for all those philosophical schools and traditions that are non-Buddhist. The sense of the term is obscure, but connotes the idea of teachings promulgated with the aim of fording the stream of cyclic existence (*saṃsāra).

Tissa. *See* DEVĀNAMPIYA TISSA.

Ti-tsang. The Chinese name of the *Bodhisattva *Kṣitigarbha. *See also* JIZŌ BOSATSU.

Tōdaiji. A temple in the ancient Japanese city of Nara that served as the headquarters for the six sects of *Nara period *Buddhism, and also served as the centre for the governmental agencies that dealt with monastic affairs. Originally known as the Konshōji, it was rededicated as the *Tōdaiji in 757 by the Emperor *Shōmu Tennō, and consecrated as the site of the colossal Buddha-image that he had commissioned, known today as the Great Buddha of Nara. The name means Great Eastern Temple and it was the counterpart to the Saidaiji, or Great Western Temple. This was done to follow the Chinese model of city planning, which divided cities into eastern and western districts, each with a major temple.

Tōji. A temple begun in the year 793 by the Emperor Sammu when the Japanese government moved from Nara to Heian. The name means 'Eastern Temple', and it was the counterpart to the Saiji, or 'Western Temple'. As with its predecessor in the former capital city of Nara, the *Tōdaiji, this was to follow the Chinese model of city planning, which divided cities into eastern and western districts, each with a major temple. Construction did not go smoothly, however, and 30 years later the temple was still not finished, and so the Emperor Junna called *Kūkai (774–835), the founder of the *Shingon school, to oversee completion, with the promise that the temple would subsequently belong to the Shingon school. Thus, it became both an official imperial temple and one of the headquarters temples of Shingon.

tong-len (Tib., btang-len). A practice in Tibetan *Buddhism of meditatively 'sending' (btang) one's good fortune and happiness out to others and 'receiving' (len) any misfortune and negativity others may be experiencing.

tongyō (Jap, sudden enlightenment). In *Zen *Buddhism, the attainment of enlightenment (*satori) as a sudden event, as taught by the *Southern School of *Ch'an Buddhism (Chin., Nan-tsung-ch'an). This is in contrast to the slower path of gradual training (*zengyō) taught by the *Northern School (Chin., Pei-tsung).

tooth relic. Sacred relic of *Gautama *Buddha preserved in *Kandy, *Sri Lanka. According to legend it was brought to the island in the 4th century CE hidden in the hair of a princess. At first it was preserved in *Anurādhapura and then in a number of different locations. For a short period in 1283 it was carried back to *India by an invading army but was brought back again to Sri Lanka by King Parakkamabāhu III. In the 16th century the Portuguese captured what they claimed was the tooth and burnt it in Goa. The real tooth was, however, safe in *Sri Lanka, and the temple where it is now kept (*see* DALADA MALIGAWA; TEMPLE OF THE TOOTH) was built in 1592. It is regarded as a symbol of faith (*śraddhā) and sovereignty and its possession conferred on a king the legitimate right to the throne of the island. This belief seems to have become established at the beginning of the 12th century and continued even after the capture of the Kandyan kingdom and the tooth relic by the British in 1815.

torma (Tib., gtor-ma). Literally 'a cast-out thing', a torma is a sculpted offering made of coloured barley flour and butter used in *tantric rituals as an offering or propitiation to various spiritual beings.

transformation texts (Chin., pien-wen). Vernacular texts used for evangelical purposes in medieval Chinese *Buddhism. Unlike the scriptures, which were in a very high literary style and used much technical vocabulary, these texts were cast in a popular form, and were mostly narrations of marvellous events adapted from Buddhist canonical literature. They were intended to be read aloud to temple visitors during *festivals. They are significant on a literary level as they contain features that would become prominent later in Chinese novels, and are among the first examples of vernacular literature in Chinese history.

trāyastriṃśa (Skt.; Pāli, tāvatiṃsa). A heavenly realm located, according to traditional *cosmology, on top of Mt. *Meru above the realm of the four great kings (*caturmahārāja; *lokapāla) who guard the cardinal points. *Śakra (Pāli, Sakka) is the king of both these worlds. Occasionally sages visit this realm and according to tradition the *Buddha spent some months there teaching the *Abhidharma to his mother when she was reborn in this heavenly realm. *Mahāmaudgalyāyana was also a frequent visitor. The name 'thirty-three' derives from the fact that this world is the residence of the 33 gods of *Hinduism, an ancient mythological notion originating in *Vedic times.

Tridharma (Skt., three teachings). Eclectic Indonesian group that bases its beliefs on a combination of the teachings of the *Buddha, Confucius (*see* CONFUCIANISM), and *Lao-tze. It was founded by the Chinese writer Kwee Tekhoay in Jakarta in 1938 and its membership comprises not more than a few thousand.

trikāya (Skt.). A doctrine that came to prominence in *Mahāyāna *Buddhism according to which the *Buddha manifests himself in three bodies (trikāya), modes, or dimensions. Even in early Buddhism the precise nature of the *Buddha had been ambiguous: on the one hand he was born and lived as a human being and on the other hand he transcended human nature through his enlightenment (*bodhi), by virtue of which he participated in the *supermundane condition attained by all Buddhas past and future. Having realized the *Dharma meant that he had become transformed in accordance with it and to a large extent identified with it. The Buddha himself had stated 'He who sees the Buddha sees the Dharma, and he who sees the Dharma sees the Buddha.' In addition to the transcendent aspect of his nature, on the one hand, and his earthly physical form and activity on the other, the Buddha as a great *yogin possessed supernatural powers by means of which he could travel at will through the *heavens and manifest himself in the form of a magical body to preach the doctrine to the gods.

Several centuries after his *death these three facets of the Buddha's nature became hypostasized in the form of a doctrine developed initially by the *Sarvāstivāda school of the *Hīnayana but taken up and elaborated on by the Mahāyāna. According to this development in Buddhology, the Buddha (and all Buddhas) are in their essential nature identical with the ultimate truth or absolute reality known as the Truth Body (*dharma-kāya). This is their first 'body'. At the same time, Buddhas have the power to manifest themselves in a sublime celestial form in splendid paradises where they teach the doctrine surrounded by hosts of *Bodhisattvas and supernatural beings. This is their second body, known as the Enjoyment Body (*saṃbhoga-kāya). Furthermore, motivated by boundless compassion (mahā-karuṇā), they project themselves into the world of suffering beings (e.g. the human world) disguised in an appropriate manner through the use of 'skilful means' (*upāya-kauśalya) so as not to frighten and alarm but instead to provide that which is most necessary and useful. This is their third body, known as the Emanation Body (*nirmāṇa-kāya). The doctrine of the three bodies appears to be unknown as such in early Mahāyāna, where reference is usually to the 'physical body' (rūpakāya), not conceived docetically, or to the second body, known as the 'mind-made body' (manomayakāya). Such ideas were generally accepted by all schools, not just the Mahāyāna. The developed doctrine has played a central role in Mahāyāna Buddhist thought but has not had much influence in *Theravāda Buddhist countries, where the Buddha continues to be regarded for the most part as simply a remarkable human being who, through his attainment of *nirvāṇa, has forever gone beyond the possibilty of involvement in human affairs.

trilakṣaṇa (Skt.; Pāli, tilakkhaṇa). The three characteristics or marks of all conditioned phenomena. They are impermance (*anitya), suffering (*duḥkha), and absence of self (*anātman). Although separate, they are also interrelated: it is because things are impermanent that they involve suffering, and it is a corollary of their impermanence that they have no enduring self or core. The implications of the three marks are set out in the first two of the *Four Noble Truths.

triloka (Skt.; Pāli, three worlds). The 'triple world' of *saṃsāra or *rebirth. Buddhist *cosmology adopts an ancient *Āryan conception of the world having three strata or layers (earth, atmosphere, and sky) and renames these as the Desire Realm (kāma-loka), the Form Realm (rūpa-loka), and the Formless Realm (ārūpya-loka). Human beings live in the Desire Realm, the lowest of the three, and they (along with other denizens of the *six realms of rebirth) are reborn here because they are still subject to *desire. In the Form Realm there is no desire but corporeality remains, and in the Formless realm there is neither desire nor corporeality. Access from one world to another is by two methods: by being reborn there in accordance with one's *karma, or through the meditational practice of the *dhyānas. These worlds are alternatively known as realms (*dhātu) or spheres (avacara), thus *kāma-dhātu, kāma-avacara, etc. *See also* THREE REALMS.

Triṃśikā. The 'Thirty Verses', a key *Yogācāra work by *Vasubandhu which can be viewed as a companion to his **Viṃśatikā*. The work briefly discusses the manner in which the duality of experience arises, the nature of mind and its operations, the three natures (*tri-svabhāva), and the process by which delusive duality (*vikalpa) may be eliminated through an understanding that all experience is no more than an illusory construct of cognition (*vijñapti-mātra). Interpretation of the text is controversial since it may be understood in an ontological sense that denies external reality, thus implying idealism, or else in an epistemological sense which explains the manner in which cognitive experience is fabricated by the mind. The text survives in *Sanskrit as well as a Tibetan and two Chinese translations. The Chinese translation by *Hsüan-tsang formed the basis for his commentorial compilation, the *Cheng-wei-shi-lun (Skt., Vijñapti-mātratā Siddhi).*

Tripiṭaka (Skt.; Pāli, Tipiṭaka). 'Three baskets'. Collective name for the Buddhist canon, which consists of a threefold collection of sacred texts, namely: (1) the *Sūtra Piṭaka (Pāli, Sutta Piṭaka) or 'Basket of Discourses'; (2) the *Vinaya Piṭaka or 'Basket of Monastic Discipline'; and (3) the *Abhidharma Piṭaka (Pāli, Abhidhamma Piṭaka) or 'Basket of Higher Teachings'. According to tradition, the composition of the Tripiṭaka was determined at the *Council of Rājagṛha in the year of the *Buddha's *death, although some schools (notably the *Theravāda) maintain that only the first two divisions were established at this time. The tradition that the canon was fixed at this early date is unlikely to be correct since there is internal evidence of evolution and change within the three collections. The third in particular shows the greatest variation, suggesting that it is the latest of the three. Each of the early schools (*see* EIGHTEEN SCHOOLS OF EARLY BUDDHISM) preserved its own version of the Tripiṭaka, and the only one that survives intact is the canon of the Theravāda school in the *Pāli language. By the end of the 1st century CE all the different versions had been committed to writing in a variety of Indian languages and dialects. Only fragments of these originals remain, although longer extracts have survived in Chinese translations. While the early schools regarded the canon as closed, the *Mahāyāna believed that it was still open and continued to incorporate new literature for over a thousand years after the death of the Buddha. New *sūtras, *śāstras, and finally *tantric compositions were incorporated and given canonical status, with the result that in the Chinese and Tibetan Tripiṭakas the threefold structure breaks down. The Tibetan canon, for example, reflects essentially a twofold structure being divided into the *Kanjur (Tib., bka'-'gyur), or word of the *Buddha (over 100 volumes), and the *Tenjur (bstan-'gyur), or commentarial literature (over 200 volumes). *See also* CHINESE TRIPIṬAKA; TAISHŌ; TRIPIṬAKA KOREANA.

Tripiṭaka Koreana. A Korean version of the Chinese Buddhist canon containing over 1,500 scriptures. The scriptures are carved on more than 81,000, wood blocks housed in the library of *Haein Temple on Mt. Kaya near Taegu. The Tripiṭaka Koreana (Kor., Koryŏ Taejangkyong) dates to the 13th century and is based on earlier versions produced in the preceding centuries.

triratna (Skt.; Pāli, tiratna). Also ratna-traya. The 'three jewels' or 'triple gem' revered by all Buddhists and constituting the nucleus of the faith, namely the *Buddha, the *Dharma (the teachings), and the *Saṃgha (the monastic community). The three jewels are also referred to as the 'three refuges' (*triśaraṇa).

triśaraṇa (Skt.; Pāli, tisaraṇa). The 'three refuges', namely the *Buddha, *Dharma, and *Saṃgha, particularly when used as a profession of faith. The formal procedure by which a layman becomes a Buddhist is by 'taking refuge', which involves repeating three times the formula 'I take refuge in the Buddha, I take refuge in the Dharma, I take refuge in the Saṃgha' (in *Pāli, Buddhaṃ saraṇam gacchāmi, Dhammaṃ saraṇam gacchāmi, Saṃghaṃ saraṇam gacchāmi). The utterance of this formula is followed by recital of the Five Precepts (*pañca- śīla). In addition to the three refuges Tibetan forms of *Buddhism, influenced by *tantric Buddhism, have added the *guru as an additional refuge to the formula, since access to the other three refuges is considered to be dependent upon the kindness of a teacher. The three refuges are also referred to as the 'three jewels' (*triratna). *See also* REFUGE TREE.

tri-svabhāva (Skt.) The 'three natures'—the dependent (*paratantra), the imagined (*parikalpita) and the consummate (*pariniṣpanna). A key *Yogācāra theory first mentioned in the **Sandhi-nirmocana Sūtra*, the concept of the three natures serves to explain the relationship between the experiences of *saṃsāra and *nirvāṇa. The theory may have arisen as a means to counter perceived shortcomings in the *Madhyamaka theory of the *Two Truths, which seems to create an unbridgeable hiatus between enlightenment (*bodhi) and everyday experience. According to the tri-svabhāva theory, parikalpita corresponds to the mundane *saṃvṛti-satya and pariniṣpanna to the supramundane *paramārtha-satya, but the two are linked by paratantra, the conditioned process of experience itself, which acts as a common pivotal factor between those two. Though the three natures theory has sometimes been viewed as an ontological statement, it should more properly be understood as a model of the epistemological process—itself a major concern of the Yogācāra school. *See also* GRĀHYA-GRĀHAKA.

Tri-svabhāva-nirdeśa. 'The Treatise on the Three Natures', a key *Yogācāra work in 38 verses by *Vasubandhu, thought by some to have been his last work. It covers similar ground to his **Triṃśikā* but deals with his interpretation of the 'three natures' (*tri-svabhāva) theory at greater length. The work is important since it clearly demonstrates through the analogy of a magically created elephant that early Yogācāra is not an idealistic system but rather deals with epistemological matters. The text survives in *Sanskrit and a Tibetan translation but curiously no Chinese version is known.

triyāna (Skt, three vehicles). In *Mahāyāna literature, a name used for the three ways to salvation. These are: (1) the *Śrāvakayāna or 'vehicle of the hearers' (also known as the *Hīnayāna); (2) the *Pratyekabuddhayāna or 'vehicle of the Solitary *Buddhas'; and (3) the *Bodhisattvayāna or 'vehicle of the *Bodhisattvas'. Different 'vehicles' are said to have been taught by the Buddhas at different times as appropriate for different individuals. According to the Mahāyāna, however, the highest and greatest is the last.

tṛṣṇā (Skt., thirst; Pāli, taṇhā). Craving or excessive or inappropriate *desire. Tṛṣṇā is described in the second of the *Four Noble Truths as the cause of the arising of suffering (*duḥkha). It is subdivided into three forms: (1) sensual craving (kāma-tṛṣṇā); (2) craving for existing (bhava-tṛṣṇā); (3) craving for non-existence (vibhava-tṛṣṇā). In the doctrine of Dependent Origination (*pratītya-samutpāda), tṛṣṇā occurs as the eighth link in the chain of twelve, where it is preceded by sensation (*vedanā) and followed by grasping (*upādāna). In relation to the senses, six forms of craving are distinguished: craving for sights, sounds, odours, tastes, contact, and mental impressions. Craving is also said to be threefold as directed towards the goal of *rebirth in one of the three realms (*triloka; *dhātu).

Trungpa, Chogyam (1940–87). An important though somewhat controversial modern master of the *Kagyü and *Nyingma schools who was especially instrumental in popularizing Tibetan *Buddhism in the West. Born in *Tibet, he fled the country in 1959 and was initially resident in the United Kingdom where he studied at Oxford University and founded the *Samyé Ling centre in Scotland. Subsequently he moved to the USA in 1970 where he founded the *Vajradhatu Foundation in 1973. With the founding of *Naropa University in 1974, he realized his vision of creating a university that would combine contemplative studies with traditional Western scholastic and artistic disciplines. In 1977 he founded Shambhala Training, an international network of centers offering secular *meditation programmes designed for the general public. After his death in 1987, Trungpa Rinpoche left a legacy of teachings and writings. Among his many publications are *Born in Tibet, Cutting through Spiritual Materialism, The Myth of Freedom,* and *Shambhala: The Sacred Path of the Warrior.*

Ts'ao-shan Pen-chi (840–901). One of the two founders of the *Ts'ao-tung school of Chinese *Ch'an *Buddhism. A quiet man of studious temperament, he received a basic education in the Confucian (*see* CONFUCIANISM) classics in his youth, and continued Confucian studies even after joining the Buddhist monastic order at the age of 16. He studied briefly with *Tung-shan Liang-chieh, the other founder of Ts'ao-tung, and received from him the dialectical teaching of the *Five Ranks. He was not inclined to travel, and spent 30 years living on Mt. Ts'ao (hence his title 'Ts'ao- shan'). Although his own line of disciples died out in four generations, his systematization of the Five Ranks became his lasting legacy to the development of Ts'ao-tung thought and practice.

Ts'ao-tung school. One of the major schools of *Ch'an *Buddhism in *China that arose during the late *T'ang dynasty (618–907). The name derives from the first character in the names of the two founding figures, *Ts'ao-shan Pen-chi (840–901) and *Tung-shan Liang-chieh (807–69), the former being the student of the latter. Although the school takes its name from these two figures, the line of disciples emanating from Ts'ao-shan actually died out after four generations; it was the line of Tung-shan's other distinguished student, Yün- chü Tao-ying (d. 902), that thrived and carried on. Perhaps because of this, others say that the 'Ts'ao' actually derives from the Ts'ao-hsi Temple where the sixth *patriarch of Ch'an, *Hui-neng (638–713), made his home; this might also account for the fact that the 'Ts'ao' comes first in the name.

The main achievement of Tung-shan and Ts'ao-shan was to systematize the teaching of the *Five Ranks, a scheme which mapped out five stages of ever-deeper realization of the interrelationship between absolute and phenomenal reality (in Chinese, li, principle, and shih, phenomena). While the generations immediately following Tung-shan and Ts'ao-shan showed little interest in this teaching, it became the basis for a revival of the school during the Sung dynasty (960–1279). At this time, a controversy broke out between two monks that helped define the Ts'ao-tung vision of practice and attainment over against that of the other dominant school of Ch'an, *Lin-chi. A Lin-chi *monk named *Ta-hui Tsung-kao (1089–1163) wrote letters and tracts asserting that the practice of *meditation ought to be energetic and goal-oriented. He stressed *kōan (Chin., kung-an) practice as a quick and efficient way to overcome ignorance and attain the goal of *enlightenment. *Hung- chih Cheng-chüeh (1091–1157) of the Ts'ao-tung school argued that practice was not to be so goal-directed, as this implied an artificial distinction between ignorance and enlightenment, ordinary beings and *Buddhas, and practice and attainment. Instead, he articulated the view that came to be known as 'silent illumination Ch'an' (Chin., *mo-chao Ch'an), in which no such dualities are propounded, and, consequently, meditation becomes a self-fulfilling rather than a goal-directed activity. One sits just to sit, and the sitting itself manifests the *Buddha-nature that is already inherent in every being. Ironically, the term 'silent illumination Ch'an' began as a term of disparagement given by the Lin-chi side, but it stuck. In the

13th century, the Japanese *monk *Dōgen (1200–53) came to *China to study Ch'an, and brought the philosophy and practice of the Ts'ao-tung school back to *Japan, where he established it under the Japanese pronunciation of the two Chinese characters: *Sōtō (*see* SŌTŌ-SHŪ).

tsha-tsha (Tib., tshva-tshva). Small bas-relief images of *Buddhas and other holy beings stamped on to clay that sometimes has been mixed with the *cremation ashes of a deceased person.

Tsongkhapa (1357–1419) (Tib., Tsong kha pa losang drakpa). The founder of the *Geluk school of Tibetan *Buddhism. Tsongkhapa was born in Amdo at a place known as 'Onion Valley' from where he derives his popular name. In his youth he studied under masters of the *Sakya, *Kagyü, and *Kadampa schools. Dissatisfied with the way in which Buddhism was taught and practised in *Tibet at that time, he established a following of like-minded students who became known as the 'Virtuous Ones' (*Gelukpa) and set up the reformed school of Buddhism of that name. He had an encyclopedic knowledge of Buddhism and attempted to systematize what he believed were the authentic teachings of Indian Buddhism through his many important literary works such as the *Great Stages of the Path* (*Lam-rim Chen-mo*) and the *Stages of Mantra* (*sngags-rim*).

Fig 19 Tsongkhapa

Tsung-mi (780–841). The fifth and last recognized *patriarch of the *Hua-yen school in *China, as well as a widely admired *Ch'an master. He received a standard Confucian (*see* CONFUCIANISM) education as a youth and was about to take the civil service examinations when he encountered the Ch'an *monk Tao-yüan in 807. He was so impressed by him that he abandoned his career in order to join him. After a year of Ch'an study he read a commentary on the *Hua-yen ching* by *Ch'eng-kuan (738–820), and switched his focus to Hua-yen studies. He travelled to the capital city of Lo-yang, where he studied with Ch'eng-kuan until the latter's death. His fame spread, and he was invited to lecture in the imperial palace and was subsequently given many honorific titles by the throne. His wide-ranging studies, coupled with his meditative experience, led him to criticize Ch'an's rejection of scriptures and oral teachings. As an alternative, he proposed that doctrinal study and Ch'an *meditation mutually supported and reinforced each other, a theory called 'doctrine and meditation leading to the same goal' (chiao ch'an yi chih).

Aside from his Hua-yen lectures and writings, Tsung-mi wrote commentaries on other *Mahāyāna scriptures as well as some original works. Perhaps most significantly, he proposed a theoretical framework to settle the lingering controversy over *sudden and *gradual enlightenment within the Ch'an school. He set forth a typology of cultivation and enlightenment that recognized the possibility of either suddenness or gradualness in both. This led him to postulate an ideal course of Ch'an practice as one marked by an initial experience of *sudden enlightenment which was subsequently deepened by gradual cultivation; he criticized the *Northern School for reversing these stages, which he thought left one's gradual cultivation without any foundation in an experiential realization of the nature of reality. However, he also criticized the heirs of the *Southern School for having neglected the aspect of cultivation in favour of an all-sufficient experience of sudden enlightenment.

Tucci, Giuseppe (1894–1984). A pioneering Italian Buddhist scholar who specialized in studies of Tibetan *Buddhism, history, and culture. He was one of the first Western scholars to travel extensively in *Tibet where he collected many unique texts and artefacts. However, later in his life, a shadow was cast over his undoubted achievements when his activities in Tibet were subjected to hostile scrutiny, as it became known that his expeditions had been financed by the Italian Fascist government of the 1930s and that he was somewhat unscrupulous in his methods of obtaining materials from their Tibetan custodians.

tülku (Tib., sprul-sku). Literally, 'Emanation Body', the term is descriptive of certain teachers in *Tibet who are thought to reincarnate over a number of generations. Though known in principle in *India, the tülku system was first formally developed and adopted in Tibet by members of the *Karmakagyü lineage and then spread to the other schools of *Buddhism.

tummo (Tib., gtum-mo; Skt., caṇḍalī). The energy channel that is thought to extend upwards from the heart centre in some forms of *tantric practice. The term is also used derivatively for the yogic practice of the *completion-phase which results in the generation of inner heat as practised by *Milarepa.

Tung-shan Liang-chieh (807–69). One of the two founders of the *Ts'ao-tung school of *Ch'an *Buddhism. A native and lifelong resident of southern *China, he left the household life at the age of 10 and wandered long and far, studying with many masters before becoming a disciple of Yün-yen T'an-sheng (780–841). He made his permanent home on Mt. Tung (hence the title 'Tung-shan') at the age of 52, and took in many disciples, among whom was the other founding figure of Ts'ao-tung, *Ts'ao-shan Pen-chi (840–901). He was known for his gift of seeing all things, including the inanimate, as manifestations of the *Buddha's mind, allowing him to hear all things preaching to him. He was also fond of poetry, and among his literary *relics one finds a poetic exposition of the Ts'ao-tung teaching of the *Five Ranks.

Tun-huang. A settlement in the desert area of north-western *China that formed the terminal point for the *Silk Road. A former Buddhist centre located on the borders of China, it flourished as a cosmopolitan frontier town between the 6th and 12th centuries CE and used much of its wealth to excavate the famed cave-temples, known as the Caves of the Thousand Buddhas, and decorate them with stunning murals and statues. As well as Chinese *Buddhism, Tibetan Buddhism was also influential here during the 8th century when the region was under Tibetan rule. It was in one of the caves that the French scholar Paul Pelliot discovered a huge cache of manuscripts in many languages including Chinese, Tibetan and *Uighur that had been concealed in the 9th century for safety during a period of civil unrest and then left undisturbed for centuries after. This priceless collection of manuscripts, which has thrown light on many aspects of contemporary central Asian and Chinese history and culture, was removed from Tun-huang by Pelliot and Sir Aurel Stein and divided between the British Library in London and the Bibliothèque Nationale in Paris, with smaller holdings in Beijing and Copenhagen. The earliest examples of Chinese movable-type printing, as well as the earliest versions of many Buddhist texts, emerged from this find, making it an invaluable source for the history of Buddhism in China, *India, and *Tibet.

Tu-shun (557–640). An early master of the *Hua-yen school of Chinese *Buddhism, commonly regarded as the first '*patriarch' of the school. A native of the area now covered by Shaan-hsi Province, he served in the military briefly, becoming a *monk at age 18. He mastered meditation, and developed a deep and penetrating philosophical mind. He steeped himself in the teachings of the **Avataṃsaka Sūtra* (Chin., **Hua-yen ching*), and became well-known as a master of this scripture. Students of the *Ti-lun school, who already concentrated their studies on one chapter of this scripture, came to him. However, it should be noted that he also put forth works extolling *Amitābha *Buddha and his *Pure Land, and advised some students to contemplate the *Buddha as their main practice. He was renowned for his practice, learning, and virtue, and was honoured by emperor Wen of the Sui Dynasty.

Tuṣita (Skt., contented; Pāli, Tusita). A *heaven, home to the 'contented gods'. A day in this world is said to be equal to 400 years of human life. This particular heaven is distinguished by being the one in which *Bodhisattvas are reborn before they attain enlightenment (*bodhi) in their next life as a human being. Graced by the presence of the Bodhisattva, the Tuṣita heaven is the most beautiful of all the celestial worlds. It is now said to be the residence of the *Buddha-to-be, *Maitreya. In *Mahāyāna cultures, those of more humble aspiration would seek *rebirth not in Tuṣita but in the *Pure Land of *Amitābha.

twin miracle. *See* YAMAKA-PĀṬIHĀRIYA.

Two Truths (Skt., satya-dvaya). The two levels of truth or reality in *Madhyamaka philosophy, known as relative truth (*saṃvṛti-satya) and absolute truth (*paramārtha-satya). In many forms of *Buddhism, the concept of two levels of truth concerned the validity of epistemological experience but in some forms of *Mahāyāna it was also applied to matters of ontology. This is especially so in later Madhyamaka where saṃvṛti-satya applies to the mundane reality of *saṃsāra and paramārtha-satya to the transcendental reality of *enlightenment and *nirvāṇa. The apparent hiatus between these two levels of reality or truth led to serious soteriological difficulties which generated much *debate in later Mahāyāna concerning the relationship between these two forms of truth or reality. The relation between the two is discussed in treatises such as Jñānagarbha's *Satyadvaya-vibhāga*, where there is a tendency to identify them as two facets of the same phenomenon, neither identical nor different.

Tz'u-min Hui-jih (680–748). An early thinker and apologist for the *Pure Land movement in North *China, known mainly for his defence of Pure Land thought and practice against *Ch'an attacks. Originally from Shantung Province, he entered the monastic order at a young age, and had the opportunity to meet the *monk *I-ching (635–713) after the latter's return from *India. He was deeply impressed by I-ching, and resolved to study in India and *Sri Lanka himself, which he did between 702 and 719. While there, he found many erudite masters who praised the merits of *rebirth in the Pure Land; he also had a vision of the *Bodhisattva *Avalokiteśvara as he prayed for seven days before his image, and the Bodhisattva instructed him in Pure Land thought and practice in this vision. Upon his return to China bearing many Indian texts, he was distressed to find Ch'an school critics attacking the Pure Land path, and decided to devote himself to rebutting their aspersions. However, because the style of Pure Land philosophy and practice he sets forth in his apologetic works differs significantly from the practices of *Lu-shan Hui-yüan (334–416) and from the founders of the 'main line' of Pure Land thought—identified with *T'an-luan (476–542) and his followers—scholars of Chinese Pure Land history have spoken of a separate 'Hui-jih line' of Pure Land.

U

ubhato-bhāga-vimutta (Pāli, one who is liberated in both ways). A person who achieves liberation in two ways, namely by liberation of mind through the trances (ceto-vimutti) and liberation through insight (paññā-vimutti). It is possible to attain liberation by insight alone, but to perfect both methods is superior. The *Buddha was one 'liberated in both ways'. *See also* VIMUTTI.

ubosaku. The Japanese transliteration of the *Sanskrit term *upāsaka, meaning a Buddhist layman.

ubosoth. Thai term equivalent to *sīmā, meaning a monastic boundary.

uccheda-vāda (Skt., the teaching of cutting off). Also known as uccheda-dṛṣṭi, 'the doctrine of Annihilationism', one of the 'two extremes' condemned by the *Buddha. This is the view that there is no *rebirth or fruition of *karma, and that the individual is utterly annihilated at *death. It is considered especially pernicious since it encourages moral irresponsibility and hedonism. The Buddha raised two objections to this notion: that it is disproved by recollection of past lives, and it implies the existence of a self (*ātman) that is destroyed at death. The other extreme view is Eternalism (*śāśvatavāda).

Udāna. Literally 'breathing out, exulting', the term has come to indicate an utterance, mostly in metrical form, inspired by a particularly intense emotion. The book by this name is the third division of the *Khuddaka *Nikāya of the *Pāli Canon. This is a short collection of 80 stories, in eight sections, containing solemn utterances of the *Buddha, made on particular occasions. The core of the book, comprising the utterances of the Buddha, is mostly in verse and it is accompanied by a prose account of the circumstances in which these were uttered. The term also refers to one of the sections of the Pāli Canon when arranged according to matter. Eighty-two suttas (Skt., *sūtras), all containing verses uttered in a state of great emotion, belong to this category. The commentary of the *Udāna* is contained in *Dhammapāla's **Paramatthadīpanī*.

Udaya I–IV. Kings of *Sri Lanka who ruled on the island between the 8th and the 10th centuries.

Udraka Rāmaputra (Pāli, Uddaka Rāmaputta). One of the *Buddha's first two teachers, the other being *Āḷāra Kālāma. Udraka taught the Buddha a meditational practice leading to a state of trance known as 'neither-perception-nor-non-perception,' a condition of pure awareness devoid of any perceptual experience. When the Buddha mastered this technique, Udraka offered to become his student, but the Buddha declined and left the group. Udraka's teaching were rejected by the Buddha since they lead to only a temporary release from *suffering and not to the permanent liberation of *nirvāṇa. However, the state of trance attained through his teachings later became incorporated into the Buddhist scheme of *meditation as the last of the eight *dhyānas (Pāli, jhāna).

Ŭich'ŏn (1055–1101). A Korean Buddhist *monk of the *Koryŏ period. The fourth son of a king, he received a thorough grounding in Confucian studies (*see* CONFUCIANISM) before leaving the household life. After joining the monastic order (*Saṃgha), he began the study of Hwaŏm (Chin., *Hua-yen) *Buddhism. Later, in 1085, he travelled to *China, where he studied widely under over 50 masters, covering *T'ien-t'ai, *Ch'an, Hua-yen, and *Vinaya studies. Upon his return to *Korea, he attempted to lay the foundations for a synthesis of *Ch'an and doctrinal/textual studies in order to help ameliorate the rivalry between them. However, his own bias in favour of doctrinal studies hindered acceptance of his theories, and he died at too young an age to have had much impact. Nevertheless, he is remembered for his wide learning and his literary output, and for his efforts in preserving Buddhist texts that had been lost in China after the persecutions of the mid-*T'ang.

Uighur. A Turkic people who ruled a central Asian empire in the medieval period, first in the Turfan-Kucha region and later in the *Tun-huang area. Though its early rulers were keen Manicheans, many of the general population were Buddhist, and Buddhist texts were translated into Uighur as early as the 7th century CE. Later the rulers also became Buddhists and with their support several flourishing centres of Buddhist learning were established. The Uighurs often functioned as traders and scribes and thus were instrumental in transmitting *Buddhism to other people in the area. Their script, itself derived from an earlier Sogdian model, served as the basis for the standard script that was adopted by the Mongols. *See also* MONGOLIA.

Ŭisang (625–702). The founder of Hwaŏm (Chin., *Hua-yen) *Buddhism in *Korea. Ŭisang travelled to *China, settling in the capital of the *T'ang dynasty, *Ch'ang-an. There he studied with the second Hua-yen *patriarch *Chih-yen (600–68), and held seniority over the third patriarch *Fa-tsang (643–712). After 20 years, he returned to Korea and founded Hwaŏm studies. The integrative vision of Hwaŏm, which stresses the mutual and unobstructed interpenetration of all phenomena, both with ultimate reality and with each other, fits well with the 't'ong pulgyŏ' or 'unitive Buddhism' of his friend and colleague *Wŏnhyo. Ŭisang is also credited with overseeing the construction of numerous temples, contributing to the high achievements of Buddhism in Korea during the first part of the Unified Silla period (668–918).

UK Association for Buddhist Studies (UKABS). An organization founded on 8 July 1996 by Peter Harvey and Ian Harris to act as a focus for Buddhist Studies in the UK. Membership is open to academics, postgraduates, and unaffiliated Buddhist scholars or interested Buddhist practitioners. The association's constitution states: 'The object of the Association shall be the academic study of *Buddhism through the national and international collaboration of all scholars whose research has a bearing on the subject'. The association aims to hold an annual conference and to help inform people of the ongoing work of others, and of any relevant conferences, visiting scholars, seminar series, and so forth. It seeks to foster communication between those working in various fields: Buddhism in south, south-east, central, and east Asia; historical and contemporary aspects (including developments in 'Western' Buddhism); theoretical, practical, and methodological issues; textual, linguistic, archaeological, and art-historical studies. The association's journal is *Buddhist Studies Review*.

Ullambana. Festival of the *pretas or 'hungry ghosts', traditionally celebrated on the fifteenth day of the seventh month when offerings of food, money, and clothing are made to departed spirits. The ritual derives from the *Ullambana Sūtra* and the practice is said to have originated with offerings made by the *Arhat *Mahāmaudgalyāyana when he realized through his magical powers that his mother had been reborn as a hungry ghost. The festival has been particularly important in Chinese *Buddhism from the *T'ang dynasty, and was first celebrated in 538 CE.

Ummon school. *See* YÜN-MEN WEN-YEN.

unanswered questions. *See* AVYĀKṚTA-VASTU.

unsui (Jap.). Literally meaning 'clouds and water', this term describes *Ch'an or *Zen *monks who, having achieved enlightenment (*satori) after an initial period of training under their first master, take to the road in search of other masters. This is done in order to either test their awakening against them or deepen it with them. The term refers to their lack of a fixed abode during this period. Present-day usage also refers to simple beginner-monks.

U Nu. The first Prime Minister of the newly independent Union of *Burma, U Nu took office in January 1948 and attempted to govern through a political ideology based on a blend of Buddhism and socialism. He sought to forge a national community in which individuals would overcome self-interest and desire for material goods, and a society in which property and class distinctions would be transcended. Drawing inspiration from the classical model of the *Cakravartin or righteous king, his goal was to develop a welfare state under the benevolent rule of a wise leader. In 1950 he created the Buddha Sāsana Council and appointed a minister of religious affairs to supervise and regulate the monasteries. He also convened a council and produced a new edition of the *Pāli Canon. Critics of U Nu suggested he was overly concerned with religious affairs to the point of neglecting the political, economic, and social problems that the country faced in adapting to the modern world. U Nu's government faced an insurrection only six months into office, but survived this and was ultimately overthrown in a military coup led by General Ne Win in 1962 who, in a move away from the Buddhist values of U Nu, sought to establish a secular, socialist state.

upacāra-samādhi. *Pāli term denoting a stage of mental concentration which is passed through prior to entering any of the levels of trance (*dhyāna).

upādāna (Skt.; Pāli). Clinging or grasping, an intensified form of craving (*tṛṣṇā). It is said to have four forms: (1) clinging to pleasurable sensual experiences (*kāma); (2) clinging to views and theories (*dṛṣṭi); (3) clinging to rules and rituals (*śīlavrata-parāmarśa); clinging to belief in a soul or self (ātma-vāda). In the series of twelve links in the doctrine of Dependent Origination (*pratītya-samutpāda), upādāna is preceded by craving (tṛṣṇā) and succeeded by becoming (*bhava), illustrating the connection between *desire and *rebirth. The same point is made in references to the five aggregates as objects of grasping when they are referred to as the 'aggregates of attachment' (*upādāna-skandha).

upādāna-skandha (Skt.). The 'aggregates of attachment', or the five aggregates (*skandha) seen as the source or the object of grasping (upādāna). The final part of the first Noble Truth (*see* FOUR NOBLE TRUTHS) states that 'the five aggregates of attachment are suffering' (*duḥkha). This means both that suffering is intrinsic to embodied existence, and that such existence itself leads to grasping after pleasurable sensations, generating an endless cycle of suffering in *saṃsāra.

Upagupta. An important saint (*Arhat) who resided in the region of *Mathurā sometime between the 3rd century BCE and the 1st century CE. Upagupta is not mentioned in the *Pāli Canon, and although featuring in non-canonical Pāli literature does not become prominent in *Theravāda countries until around the 12th century as a result of his importance in the *Sanskrit sources. In the *Sarvāstivāda tradition he is the fifth *patriarch after Mahākāśyapa, *Ānanda, Madhyāntika, and Śāṇakavāsin, and in the *Ch'an tradition he is regarded as the fourth. He features prominently in the *avadāna literature (chapters 21 and 27 of the *Divyāvadāna* contain the fullest account of his life), and he is said to have lived during the time of *Aśoka, who held him in high esteem.

Upāli. An eminent disciple of the *Buddha famed for his knowledge of monastic law and discipline (*Vinaya). A member of the barber clan in the Buddha's home town of *Kapilavastu, Upāli sought *ordination when the Buddha first returned to see his family after gaining enlightenment (*bodhi). As a *monk he devoted himself to the study of the monastic rules and held numerous discussions with the Buddha over problematic cases. These questions and answers are recorded in the *Parivāra section of the *Vinaya Piṭaka. In the *First Council held at *Rājagṛha, Upāli was called upon to recite the Vinaya, which, according to tradition (almost certainly erroneously), was fixed at that time.

upāsaka (Skt.). A Buddhist layman. One of the four divisions of the Buddhist community consisting of monks (*bhikṣu), nuns (*bhikṣunī), laymen (upāsaka), and laywomen (*upāsikā). In the early tradition layfolk became Buddhists by 'taking refuge' in the *Buddha, *Dharma and *Saṃgha through recitation of the three refuge formula (*triśaraṇa). They were also required to adopt the Five Precepts (*pañca-śīla). Lay practice centres on moral conduct and providing material support for the Saṃgha through offerings of food and robes (*see* CĪVARA; KAṬHINA). Through the performance of good deeds of this kind it is hoped that merit (*puṇya) will be gained which will secure improved material conditions in this life and the next, with the hope that at a more remote future time the opportunity will arise to renounce the world and become a monk. In *Mahāyāna *Buddhism, the role of the laity is more prominent, and the division between laity and monks is subsumed in the ideal of the

*Bodhisattva. The most famous lay Bodhisattva of the Mahāyāna is *Vimalakīrti.

upasampadā (Skt.; Pāli). The higher *ordination that confers full admission as a member of the *Saṃgha.

upāsikā. A female lay Buddhist. *See* UPĀSAKA.

Upatissa. *See VIMUTTIMAGGA.*

upāya-kauśalya (Skt.). The concept of 'skilful means' is of considerable importance in *Mahāyāna *Buddhism and is expounded at an early date in texts such as the *Upāya-kauśalya Sūtra,* the **Lotus Sūtra,* and the *Teachings of Vimalakīrti Sūtra* (**Vimalakīrti-nirdeśa Sūtra*). In chapter two of the *Lotus Sūtra* the *Buddha introduces the doctrine of skilful means and demonstrates through the use of parables throughout the text why it is necessary for him to make use of stratagems and devices. The text depicts him as a wise man or kindly father whose words his foolish children refuse to heed. To encourage them to follow his advice he has recourse to 'skilful means', realizing that this is the only way to bring the ignorant and deluded into the path to liberation. Although this involves a certain degree of duplicity, such as telling lies, the Buddha is exonerated from all blame since his only motivation is compassionate concern for all beings.

At the root of the idea is the notion that the Buddha's teaching is essentially a provisional means to bring beings to enlightenment (*bodhi) and that the teachings which he gives may vary: what may be appropriate at one time may not be so at another. The concept is used by the Mahāyāna to justify innovations in doctrine, and to portray the Buddha's early teachings as limited and restricted by the lesser spiritual potential of his early followers. In the Mahāyāna, skilful means comes to be a legitimate method to be employed by Buddhas and *Bodhisattvas whenever the benefit of beings warrants it. Spurred on by their great compassion (mahākaruṇā), Bodhisattvas are seen in some sources (such as the *Upāya-kauśalya Sūtra*) breaking the *precepts and committing actions that would otherwise attract moral censure. The assumption underlying the doctrine is that all teachings are in any case provisional and that once liberation is attained it will be seen that Buddhism as a body of philosophical doctrines and moral precepts was only of use as a means to reach the final goal and that its teachings do not have ultimate validity. The equivalent term in *Pāli sources (upāya-kosalla) is relatively rare and simply denotes the Buddha's skill in expounding the *Dharma.

upekṣā (Skt., looking on; Pāli, upekkhā). Equanimity, or impartiality. The emotionally detached state of one who witnesses without becoming emotionally involved. It is a virtue, and an attitude to be cultivated as opposed to simple indifference or lack of interest. Upekṣā is the fourth of the Divine Abidings (*Brahma-vihāra) and seventh of the 'limbs of enlightenment' (*bodhyaṅga).

uposatha. *Pāli equivalent of the *Sanskrit term *poṣadha, indicating the day preceding the four stages of the moon's waxing, that is the 1st, 8th, 15th, and 23rd nights of the lunar month. Long before the advent of *Buddhism these were considered sacred days in *India. In particular, these days were utilized by the pre-Buddhist reforming communities for the expounding of their views, a practice that early Buddhists adopted. Buddhists also utilize one or other of these uposatha days for the recitation of the *Prātimokṣa, the set of monastic rules which are contained in the *Sūtra Vibhaṅga of the *Vinaya Piṭaka. On uposatha days laymen take upon themselves the Eight Precepts (*aṣṭāṅga-śīla), known on that occasion as uposatha vows.

Uppalavaṇṇā. A female elder (Therī) and the second of the two chief female disciples of the *Buddha (the first being *Khemā). Her name means 'colour of the *lotus', and she was so called because her complexion resembled the hue of the blue lotus. Famed for her beauty she nevertheless renounced the world and quickly became an *Arhat. She was renowned for her psychic abilities and the Buddha declared her to be chief among *women who have mastered the supernatural powers (*ṛddhi).

ūrṇā (Skt.). In iconography, a circle of hair between a *Buddha's eyebrows, being one of the 32 marks (*dvātriṃśadvara-lakṣaṇa) of a 'superman' (*mahāpuruṣa). This individual feature is itself sometimes also personified as a goddess in later *Mahāyāna and *tantric *Buddhism.

Uruvelā. Name of a place on the banks of the *Nairañjanā river in the vicinity of *Bodhgayā. It was here that the *Buddha spent six years practising austerities after taking leave of his first two teachers, *Āḷāra Kālāma and *Udraka Rāmaputra in order to seek his own spiritual path. During his residence at Uruvelā he was in the company of five *ascetics, later known as the *pañcavaggiyā *monks, who later abandoned him when he renounced the practice of harsh austerities in favour of the Middle Way (*madhyamā-pratipad). It was at Uruvelā that the Buddha was assailed several times by *Māra. The first was on the night of his enlightenment (*bodhi) under the *Bodhi Tree, and on three further occasions he attempted to divert the Buddha from his ministry without success.

Uruvela-Kassapa. An *ascetic who dwelt on the banks of the *Nairañjanā river who was converted by the *Buddha at *Uruvelā (from whence his name) shortly after the Buddha attained enlightenment (*bodhi). He was one of three brothers who between them had many hundred followers. The Buddha resided with Uruvela-Kassapa for a time and performed many feats of magical power, including defeating a fire-breathing demon (*nāga). Impressed by these powers, the *ascetic sought *ordination along with his brothers and their followers. They all became *Arhats when the Buddha preached the Fire Sermon to them. The scene of Uruvela-Kassapa's conversion is recorded at *Sāñcī.

uṣṇīṣa (Skt.). In iconography, the swelling of flesh or the top-knot of hair on a *Buddha's head, one of the 32 marks (*dvātriṃśadvara-lakṣaṇa) of a 'superman' (*mahāpuruṣa), sometimes personified as a goddess such *Uṣṇīṣa-vijaya.

Uṣṇīṣa-vijaya. 'Victorious Uṣṇīṣa'; a popular female *tantric deity who is considered to be a manifestation of *Vairocana. She is depicted white in colour with three faces and eight hands.

utpala (Skt.). The blue lotus (*Nymphaea caerula Linn.*).

Uttaramūla Nikāya. Name of a *Sri Lankan *Nikāya, or group of *monks, being an offshoot of the *Abhayagiri Nikāya. Their headquarters were probably at the Uttaroḷa *monastery, which was built by King Mānavamma and given to the monks of the Abhayagiri monastery. Several monks famous for their literary achievements belonged to this Nikāya.

uttarāpatha. A region described in the early sources as lying in the northern part of the continent of *Jambudvīpa. The boundaries of the region are not clearly specified. Frequent references to trade, however, suggest that the name may in fact designate a trade route, or network of trade routes, that traversed north *India from *Gandhāra to the east coast.

Uttarārāma. An image-house carved out of rock constructed by *Parakkamabāhu I to the north of his capital city of Pulatthipura (modern Polonnaruva, *Sri Lanka). The complex marks the high point of Sinhalese rock carving. *See also* GAL VIHĀRA.

Uttaravihāra. *See* ABHAYAGIRI.

Utturakuru. 1. An alternative name for the ancient Indian state of *Kuru. **2.** The continent lying to the north of Mt. *Meru according to ancient Indian *cosmology. With its two subsidiary islands, it was thought to be square in shape. Its inhabitants were thought to lead long, happy, and virtuous lives of a 1,000 years duration.

V

Vacchagotta. An *ascetic (*parivrājaka) whose conversations with the *Buddha are mentioned several times in the *Pāli Canon. It was he who posed the famous 'undetermined' questions (Skt., *avyākṛta-vastu) in the *Aggi-Vacchagotta Sutta* of the *Majjhima Nikāya to which the Buddha responded with silence. The questions related to matters such as whether or not the world was eternal and whether the *Tathāgata existed after *death. Vacchagotta eventually sought *ordination from the Buddha at *Rājagṛha and became an *Arhat.

Vaibhāṣika. An influential Buddhist school of the Small Vehicle (*Hīnayāna), closely related to the *Sarvāstivāda, which flourished in north-west *India principally in *Gandhāra and *Kashmir. Their name derives from a great treatise known as the **Mahāvibhāṣā* (Great Book of Alternatives) which summarizes their views.

vaipulya sūtra (Skt., extensive discourse). Term referring to the longer *sūtra compositions in *Mahāyāna *Buddhism that have a broader and more inclusive philosophical basis. They contrast with shorter works that put forward a single or more limited teaching. Many vaipūlya sūtras are in fact collections of shorter independent works. Sūtras falling into the vaipūlya category include the **Prajñā-pāramitā Sūtra*, the **Avataṃsaka Sūtra*, the **Ratnakūṭa* collection of sūtras, and the Chinese **Nirvāna Sūtra*. These are works whose themes spread across a wide range of teachings. Mahāyāna sources list vaipūlya as the eleventh of a twelvefold classification of Buddhist literature.

Vairocana (Skt.). 'Illuminator', one of the five *Jinas. Normally depicted iconographically as a white *saṃbhoga-kāya *Buddha associated with the centre or sometimes the eastern quarter. He is also viewed as the embodiment of the 'Awareness of the Continuum of Reality', one of the five awarenesses, and as the lord of the *Tathāgata Family. In the *Hua-yen school in *China (*Kegon in Japanese) and *esoteric *Buddhism in east Asia, Vairocana is the *Buddha who occupies the central position in almost all *maṇḍalas, or sacred diagrams of the cosmos. Several prominent Buddhist scriptures, such as the **Avataṃsaka Sūtra* (Chin., *Hua-yen ching) and the *Mahāvairocana Sūtra* depict him not only as one enlightened being among many, but as the central figure from whom all other Buddhas emanate as a skilful means (*see* UPĀYA-KAUŚALYA) to reach all suffering beings. In certain later forms of Buddhism, both in *Tibet and China, Vairocana came to be viewed as the personification of the *dharma-kāya and, as such, as the primordial Buddha, in which case he is often called Mahāvairocana. As esoteric thought developed, he came to be known not only for projecting all other Buddhas and *Bodhisattvas from his own being, but also for emanating all of reality and in this way he became a kind of urgrund or ground of being, and this fact endowed nature itself with a kind of intelligence and ability to communicate as an expression of Vairocana's teaching. The Japanese *Shingon master *Kūkai (774–635) referred to Vairocana to explain how the world itself preaches the *Dharma. His primary symbol was the sun, which is above everything in the world while at the same time is intimately involved with everything in the world as its rays reach everywhere and stimulate growth.

Vaiśālī (Pāli, Vesālī). The capital of the *Licchavi republic at the time of the *Buddha, it was famed as a city of great beauty. It was frequently visited by the Buddha on his travels and a number of his discourses were delivered there. It was also the site of the Second Council (*see* COUNCIL OF VAIŚĀLĪ) held about 100 years after the Buddha's passing. Even by the 8th century, most of the city lay in ruins. Modern excavations have revealed that Vaiśālī was located about 25 miles north-east of Patna, at Besarh.

vaiśāradya (Skt.). Confidence, fearlessness,

or proficiency. *Buddhas (and according to *Mahāyāna, also *Bodhisattvas) are endowed with four types of unshakable confidence known as the 'Four Fearlessneses'. These are (1) his perfect enlightenment (*bodhi) is irreversible; (2) all the impurities (*āśrava) have been destroyed; (3) all obstacles have been overcome; (4) the means to overcoming *rebirth (*saṃsāra) has been proclaimed.

Vajjī (Pāli; Skt., Vṛji). In the time of the *Buddha, one of the sixteen early Indian states (*mahājanapada). The chief inhabitants of Vajjī were the *Licchavi and *Videhā clans with their capitals at *Vaiśālī and *Mithilā, respectively. The Buddha was a frequent visitor to Vajjī and the inhabitants are described as a happy and prosperous people with a republican political structure supported by seven practices that the Buddha approved of, namely: (1) they held frequent public meetings; (2) they met together to take collective decisions and acted in concord; (3) they respected their customs and traditions; (4) they respected and supported their elders; (5) they did not allow the abduction of womenfolk; (6) they respected their places of worship; (7) they supported and protected the saints (*Arhats) among them. After the Buddha's death the fortunes of the state declined and it was conquered by *Ajātaśatru. It was ten lax practices of a group of *monks from Vajjī, known as the Vajjiputtaka (Skt., *Vṛjiputraka), that led to the convening of the *Council of Vaiśālī some 100 years after the Buddha's death.

vajra (Skt.; Tib., rdo-rje). Originally, the thunderbolt weapon of the *Vedic god *Indra in early Indian religion, the term later also denoted a diamond. The Buddhist use of the term combines these two meanings to connote the indivisible and imperishable nature of enlightenment (*bodhi). While maintaining this significance in its literature, a vajra in *tantric *Buddhism also refers to the double-headed ritual implement, usually made of metal, with one, three, five, or nine prongs at each end. When paired with the ritual bell (ghaṇṭā) in Tibetan Buddhism, the vajra symbolizes skilful means (*upāya-kauśalya) in contrast to insight (*prajñā). In Japanese *Shingon, the vajra is associated with the concept of the Vajra Realm which is derived from the **Sarva-tathāgata-tattva-saṃgraha*.

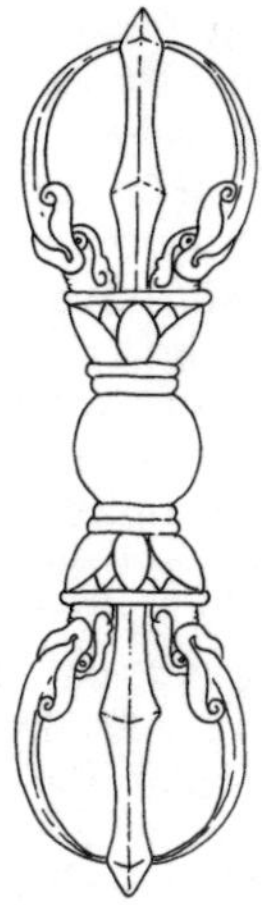

Fig 20 vajra

Vajrabhairava. A *tantric tutelary deity (*yi-dam), thought to be the wrathful aspect of *Mañjughoṣa or *Yamāntaka. Meditational practices and rituals associated with Vajrabhairava are expounded in the *Vajrabhairava Tantra* and related texts introduced from *Oḍḍiyāna by Lalitavajra. Vajrabhairava is especially venerated in the *Geluk school, both in *Tibet and *Mongolia.

Vajrabodhi (671–741). An Indian *monk, possibly of south Indian origin, who was later active as a translator and ritual master in *China. After a thorough training in *Yogācāra doctrines, he is said to have received initiation into the **Sarva-tathāgata-tattva-saṃgraha* system of *tantric *Buddhism in 702 from Nāgabodhi. Later, acting on a vision, he set sail for China and eventually arrived at Canton in 720 CE. Unfortunately, he lost all the texts he was carrying with him in a shipwreck en route and was only able to translate a portion from memory when he settled in *Lo-yang in 723. In the subsequent years of his residence in China, he translated and composed a substantial amount of other texts concerned with tantric Buddhism as well as gaining the attention of the emperor to whom he gave tantric initiations. Together with his disciple, *Amoghvajra, he is counted among the eight *patriarchs in the Japanese *Shingon lineage.

Vajracchedika Sūtra. A short text from the corpus of the 'Perfection of Insight' (*Prajñāpāramitā) literature which compresses the essential teachings into a few short stanzas. Composed around 300 CE it was translated into Tibetan and Chinese many times, and has remained immensely popular as a summary of the doctrine of 'emptiness' or 'voidness' (*śūnyatā) which lies at the heart of the Perfection of Insight writings. The full title of the text is *The Diamond-cutter Perfection of Insight Sūtra (Vajracchedika-prajñāpāramitā Sūtra)*.

Vajradhara (Skt., wielder of the thunderbolt). **1.** One of the Five *Jinas, he is identified with the Absolute or primordial reality (*dharma-kāya). In iconography he is portrayed holding a thunderbolt (*vajra) in his right hand symbolizing the power of compassion (*karuṇā) and skilful means (*upāya-kauśalya), and a bell (*ghaṇṭā) in his left symbolizing the pure clear sound of transcendental insight (*prajñā) which penetrates everywhere without obstruction. Dark blue in colour, he is anomalously depicted in the regal attire of a *saṃbhoga-kāya *Buddha. **2.** A *tantric term for a fully accomplished adept (*siddha).

Vajradhatu Foundation. One of the largest Buddhist organizations in the West, founded by Chogyam *Trungpa in 1973 and based in Halifax, Nova Scotia. The organization has over 100 centres and a membership of over 5,000.

Vajrakīla (Skt,; Tib., rdo-rje phur-ba). A wrathful tantic tutelary deity (*yi-dam), being a personification of the three-sided ritual dagger that is his emblem. He is especially associated with the *Nyingma school, and the teachings and practices associated with Vajrakīla were first introduced into *Tibet by *Padmasambhava.

Vajrapāṇi. One of the eight great *Bodhisattvas, especially associated with the transmission of *tantric teachings. His name derives from the thunderbolt (*vajra) which he holds in his hand (pāṇi) as his emblem. Iconographically, he is encountered in a yellow peaceful form or a dark blue wrathful forms.

Vajrasattva (Skt., adamantine being). A *Buddha in the Tibetan *tantric tradition associated with spiritual purification and the overcoming of negative mental tendencies. He is depicted as white in colour and holding a thunderbolt (*vajra) in his right hand, symbolizing his indestructible purity, and a bell (*ghaṇṭā) in his left, signifying *compassion. His 100-syllable *mantra is well known and commonly recited in all schools of Tibetan *Buddhism.

Vajra-śekhara Tantra. **1.** The 'Diamond Pinnacle Tantra', a supplementary text, surviving only in Tibetan translation, to the **Sarva-tathāgata-tattva-saṃgraha*. The supplementary text elucidates a series of questions arising from the root *tantra. **2.** The title generally given in its Chinese equivalent to those portions of the *Sarva-tathāgata-tattva-saṃgraha* which were translated into Chinese by *Vajrabodhi, *Śubhakarasiṃha, and *Amoghavajra during the *T'ang dynasty.

Vajrayāna (Skt., diamond vehicle). A late Indian term used to designate the path (*yāna) of *tantric *Buddhism. The name is derived from the image of the thunderbolt (*vajra) which was used to symbolize the imperishable nature of enlightenment (*bodhi), the indivisibility of appearances and emptiness (*śūnyatā) or of compassion (*karuṇā) and insight (*prajñā).

Vajrayoginī. An enlightened deity (*ḍākinī) or yogic adept (*yoginī). She is the chief female tutelary deity (*yi-dam) of the *Mother Tantras.

Vakkali. A *monk who was fascinated by the physical appearance of the *Buddha and who followed him around in admiration. It was to Vakkali that the Buddha uttered the famous statement 'who sees the *Dharma sees me, who sees me sees the Dharma'. This was said with the intention of helping the monk go beyond his obsession with physical appearance. In the end, however, the Buddha had to order Vakkali to leave his presence. On another occasion, according to the *Saṃyutta Nikāya, Vakkali fell ill while on his way to visit the Buddha at *Rājagṛha, and in great pain committed *suicide by cutting his throat. The Buddha went to see his body and declared that he had attained *nirvāṇa, and that *Māra would be unable to find his departed consciousness (*vijñāna). On the basis of this and a few similar cases of suicide (notably those of Godhika and *Channa) it has been thought by some Western scholars that *Buddhism does not regard suicide as immoral for the enlightened, but this conclusion is not supported by the *Theravāda commentaries and tradition nor by a close reading of the canonical passages in question.

Valabhī. An important centre of *Buddhism located on the Kāthiāwar Peninsula in present-day Gujarat, *India. Although inroads had been made earlier, Buddhism became predominant in the region around the 5th century CE and was renowned as a centre of learning throughout *India with royal patronage. It was the site of many important monasteries associated with the *Saṃmitīya school in addition to those connected with other *Hīnayāna and *Mahāyāna groups. In the 7th century, the Chinese pilgrim *Hsüan-tsang noted the existence of over 100 monasteries which housed some 6,000 monks. A religious university existed in Valabhī which rivalled *Nālandā in fame and authority; it was there that *Vasubandhu's disciples *Sthiramati and Guṇamati taught, while *Paramārtha also studied there. Valabhī was an important centre for *Yogācāra studies—it is believed that Valabhī favoured a more epistemological approach in contrast to the idealist interpretation then current at Nālandā under the aegis of *Dharmapāla. Valabhī declined in importance through the disruptions caused by the Arab invasions of the 8th century CE.

Vallée Poussin. *See* DE LA VALLÉE POUSSIN, LOUIS.

Vārāṇasī (Pāli, Bārāṇasī). The Indian holy city and capital of the ancient state of *Kāśī on the Ganges, formerly known in English as Benares. Its proximity to the Buddhist centre of *Sārnāth would have attracted many Buddhist pilgrims (*see* PILGRIMAGE). Despite its cultural importance in *India, the *Buddha does not seem to have had a strong connection with this city, although several discourses were given there.

vāsanā (Skt.). Habitual tendencies or dispositions, a term, often used synonymously with *bīja ('seed'). It is found in *Pāli and early *Sanskrit sources but comes to prominence with the *Yogācāra, for whom it denotes the latent energy resulting from actions which are thought to become 'imprinted' in the subject's storehouse-consciousness (*ālaya-vijñāna). The accumulation of these habitual tendencies is believed to predispose one to particular patterns of behaviour in the future.

vassa (Skt., varṣya). The annual rain-retreat undertaken by Buddhist *monks for a three-month period during the monsoon season, which normally lasts from June to October. The custom of remaining in one place was instituted by the *Buddha, and arose due partly to the practical difficulties of travel in that season, but also to ethical concerns about causing injury to the tiny creatures that become abundant after the rains. Monks returned year after year to the same retreats, like the *Jetavana at *Śrāvastī, leading to the foundation of semi-permanent residences and ultimately the establishment of monasteries (*vihāra).

Vasubandhu. The half-brother of *Asaṅga, he was probably born during the late 4th century CE in north-west *India where he initially studied *Sarvāstivādin *Abhidharma as presented in the **Mahāvibhāṣā*. Dissatified with those teachings, he wrote an important summary and critique of the *Mahāvibhāṣā* from the *Sautrāntrika viewpoint. Later in his life he is said to have converted to *Mahāyāna and become one of the most influential founders of the *Yogācāra school. He wrote two key works summarizing *Yogācāra doctrines, the **Viṃśatikā* and the **Triṃśikā* as well as several major commentaries on works by *Asaṅga and *Maitreyanātha. Some modern scholars, notably Frauwallner, have sought to distinguish two Vasubandhus, one the Yogācārin and the other the Sautrāntika, but this view should probably be rejected now on the basis of the anonymous **Abhidharma-dīpa* which clearly identifies Vasubandhu as the sole author of both groups of writings.

Vasumitra. Doctor of the *Sarvāstivāda school of *Buddhism who flourished in the 2nd century CE. A native of *Gandhāra, he presided over the *Council of Kaniṣka. Vasumitra put forward a thesis to defend the basic tenet of the *Sarvāstivāda school that entities (*dharma) exist in the past and future as well as in the present. According to him, dharmas exist in a noumenal or latent condition in the future until they attain their moment of causal efficacy (karitra) in the present. This marks their entry into a functional relationship with other phenomena. When this moment is past, they once again enter into a noumenal mode which is now described as 'past'. Vasumitra's theory of temporality was accepted by the school in preference to the contending views of three other philosophers, Dharmatrāta, Ghoṣaka, and Buddhadeva.

Vātsīputrīya. A school of early *Buddhism, founded by Vātsīputra, that separated from the *Sthāviras around the 3rd century BCE and which was later condemned as heretical on account of their espousal of the 'personhood theory' (*pudgala-vāda). This posited the existence of an indescribable something which was 'neither the same as nor different to' the five aggregages (*skandha) and that acted as a basis for *rebirth and *karma. It was rejected by more orthodox schools as too similar to the non-Buddhist heretical *ātman concept.

Vaṭṭagāmaṇi Abhaya. King of *Sri Lanka, he lost his kingdom to the Indian Tamils in 43 BCE, the first year of his reign, but was later restored to the throne from 29 to 17 BCE. Upon his restoration he founded the *Abhayagiri *monastery (an act ascribed in some sources to one of his predecessors) in the capital of *Anurādhapura, which he donated to an individual *monk. Such an act, the first gift of a monastery to an individual, caused a split within the ranks of the monks on the island. According to tradition, during his reign the *Pāli Canon and its commentaries were committed to writing for the first time. Later generations have regarded Vaṭṭagāmaṇi as a great protector of the Buddhist religion.

vāyu (Skt.). 'Wind', a general term in *tantric physiology used to describe the psychic energy, differentiated according to its function, which pervades the body and enables it to perform its various physiological and motor functions. The significance of this energy is that it may be manipulated for transformational purposes during the *completion-phase *meditation of *anuttara-yoga-tantra. It is thought that one form of vāyu 'leaks' from the central channel (*avadhūti) into the left (*lalanā) and right channels (*rasanā), thus generating the dualistic world of unenlightened experience. The aim of the completion-phase meditation is, in part, to reverse this process.

Veda. A collection of religious literature in *Sanskrit dating from approximately 1200 BCE and forming the foundation of the orthodox scriptures of *Hinduism. The term 'Veda' derives from the Sanskrit root vid-, 'to know', and the texts are believed to be the repository of ultimate truth as revealed by the gods (*deva) to the ancient seers. The Vedic scriptures are divided into four collections: the *Ṛg Veda*, the *Yajur Veda*, the *Sāma Veda*, and the *Atharva Veda*. Originally the Vedas were divided into two parts: *mantras (verses or hymns of praise), and *Brāhmaṇas (priestly commentaries on the ritual use of the texts). In the course of time appendages were added so that each of the Vedas in turn came to comprise four sections, namely Saṃhitā (the mantras organized into various categories), *Brāhmaṇas (texts concerned with sacrificial ritual), Āraṇyakas ('forest texts' or esoteric teachings), and Upaniṣads (mystical treatises). Vedic religion believed in a plurality of gods (traditionally 33) to whom sacrifice should be offered, in return for which the gods bestow their favour and protection. *Buddhism rejected the supremacy of the gods, teaching that sacrifice was ineffectual and that salvation could not be attained by divine intercession but only by following the *Eightfold Path. It also rejected the practice of *animal sacrifice and the *caste system, both of which are legitimated by the Vedas.

vedanā (Skt., Pāli; feeling). The psycho-physiological faculty of experiencing sensations. Vedanā is the faculty that is said to 'taste' or 'relish' experiences, and these experiences are classified into three kinds, as pleasant, unpleasant, or neutral. Again, there are said to be six classes of feelings, corresponding to each of the six sense-organs (eye, ear, nose, tongue, body and mind). Vedanā is the second of the five aggregates (*skandha), and embraces all phenomena relating to the affective dimension of human experience. It is also the seventh link in the chain of Dependent Origination (*pratītya-samputpāda) where it follows the sixth link, the contact between the senses and their object (*sparśa) and gives rise to craving (*tṛṣṇā), the eighth link.

vegetarianism. *See* DIET.

Veḷuvana (Pāli, bamboo grove). A park near *Rājagṛha, so-called because it was surrounded by a wall of bamboo (veḷu). The park was chosen for the the *Buddha by

King *Bimbisāra since it was a quiet spot suitable for *meditation as well as being in a convenient location not too far outside the town. The Buddha spent the second, third and fourth rain-retreats (*vassa) at Veḷuvana, and after the *First Council in the year of the Buddha's death the *monks who had taken part retired there to rest. Many early discourses were preached at this site.

Vesak. *See* WESAK.

Vessantara Jātaka. A story in the *Jātaka collection extolling the virtue of generosity (*dāna). The story is one of the most widely known in the Buddhist world and tells of the great generosity of Prince Vessantara. The prince, son and heir of King Sañjaya, lives in the capital city with his wife Maddī and their small children. His generosity is unrivalled, but when he gives away the magic elephant which ensures adequate rainfall to his country his citizens become enraged, and force Sañjaya to banish him. His wife chooses to share his exile with the children. After giving away all his possessions, Vessantara and his family make a long journey through mountains and forests until they reach a valley, where they settle down. While his wife is away, Vessantara gives his children to a *brahmin who wants them as slaves and it is only through the intervention of the king of the gods that Vessantara is prevented from giving her away as well. Finding his grandchildren working as servants, Sañjaya ransoms them and full of remorse he invites Vessantara and Maddī to return. Once the family is reunited, Vessantara becomes king and all live happily ever after.

Vibhajjavāda (Pāli). 'The Distinctionists'. A school of early *Buddhism belonging to the Elder (*Sthavīra) tradition, which at the Council of Pāṭaliputra in *c.*250 CE (*see* COUNCIL OF PĀṬALIPUTRA II), was adjudged to embody the orthodox teachings of the *Buddha. It is unclear, however, whether the Vibhajjavādins comprised one sect or a group of sects, and the precise nature of the movement and its doctrines and duration remain obscure. Since the Buddha is sometimes referred to in *Pāli sources as a 'Distinctionist' (vibhajjavādī), the appellation may be an alternative designation for the *Theravāda school. The 'distinction' in question may refer to the Buddha's basic methodological practice of making a 'distinction' between extremes and emphasizing the Middle Way (*madhyamā-pratipad), but this interpretation of the origin of the term is conjectural.

Vibhaṅga (or *Vibhaṅgappakaraṇa*). The second of the seven books of the *Abhidharma Piṭaka (Skt., Abhidharma Piṭaka) of the *Pāli Canon. It deals in a general way with different topics central to the *Buddha's teaching by means of technical analysis, though different methods of treatment are used. The book is divided into eighteen chapters, each of which is called a vibhaṅga, or 'division'. Each chapter has three portions: Suttantabhājaniya, Abhidhammabhājaniya, and Pañhāpucchaka, the last title literally meaning 'list of questions'. There is a commentary to the *Vibhaṅga*, by the title of **Sammohavinodanī*, attributed to *Buddhaghoṣa.

vicāra (Skt.). Discursive thought and examination; one of the mental functions (*caitta), classed as morally neutral, it is the mental process which picks out the details of any object presented to the mind. The term is used at times in *Mahāyāna as a neutral synonym for *vikalpa.

vicikitsā (Skt.; Pāli, vicikicchā). A form of neurotic doubt or uncertainty that hinders resolution and action. It denotes undue scepticism and a wavering and indecisive attitude. It is the last of the five hindrances (*nīvaraṇa) and in this context relates to doubts concerning the *Buddha, the *Dharma, the *Saṃgha, to whether certain things are good, bad, right, or wrong, and other matters. It is also the second of the ten fetters (*samyojana), where it impedes the attainment of the stage of stream-winner (*śrotāpanna), the first of the stages of the Noble Path (*ārya-mārga).

Videha. One of the two main centres within the confederacy of *Vajjī having its capital at *Mithilā. The territory was bordered by the Ganges, on the other side of which was the state of *Magadha. Videha was a prosperous trading centre and merchants came from *Śrāvasti and *Vārāṇasī, and possibly also as far away as *Gandhāra, by means of the *uttarāpatha or northern trade route. In the *Buddha's day Videha was a republic, although earlier it had been ruled by kings.

Viḍūḍabha. Son of King *Pasenadi of

*Kosala. After his father's *death, Viḍūḍabha set out with a large army to attack the *Śākya clan, that to which the *Buddha belonged. This was to avenge an insult to his father on an earlier occasion when the Śākyans had sent a low-class woman to be his bride. On three occasions the Buddha stood in the way of the army and Viḍūḍabha retreated. On the fourth the Buddha realized the fate of his people was sealed and made no attempt to prevent the ensuing slaughter.

vidyā (Skt.). **1.** General term for 'knowledge' in an everyday sense. **2.** Science or art, in the technical sense of applied skills or crafts, and in particular the occult arts. **3.** In *tantric *Buddhism, the term connotes any manifestation of enlightenment (*bodhi) in the form of spells (*mantras) and gestures (*mudrās), as well as various embodiments of its qualities, usually in female form.

vidyādhara (Skt.). 'Knowledge-holders'. **1.** A class of powerful beings thought to live in the snowy mountains of north *India and have various supernatural powers derived from their mastery of magical powers (*vidyā) such as longevity, the ability to fly or to change shape. According to some sources, they were thought to have been guardians of *tantric lore, hence the early tantric corpus of texts was called the Vidyādhara Piṭaka in contrast to the *Sūtra and *Vinaya Piṭakas. **2.** By extension, vidyādhara is used as a title for people who have completed the tantric training and who are believed to be endowed with various magical powers.

vidyā-sthāna (Skt.). The bases of knowledge or science in ancient *India. These comprised: grammar, logic (*pramāna), religion, *medicine, and technology. A further group of five minor sciences were often appended to these: poetry, synonymy, composition, drama, and *astrology.

Vietnam. By virtue of its geographical location, Vietnam has been exposed to two main forms of *Buddhism. The *Mahāyāna form predominates in the north, where Chinese influence is strongest, and the *Theravāda school is pre-eminent in parts of the south, which has stronger links to the Buddhism of *south-east Asia. Historically, Buddhism reached different regions at different times, and its evolution has been eclectic, often mingling with *Taoism and *Confucianism. The history of Buddhism in the territory now covered by the country of Vietnam dates back at least to the 2nd century CE, when it was transmitted southward from *China to the area then known as Chiao-chou. This territory remained under Chinese hegemony through to the 10th century, and while Buddhism certainly existed and probably thrived during that time, later historians tended to discount it as 'Chinese' Buddhism, and concentrated their efforts on the period of independence. Thus, materials relating the history of Buddhism during the period of Chinese dominance are scarce. Stories dating from this period show the presence of monastic Buddhism, and present tales of scripture-chanting, the erection of images, and the miraculous intervention of monks with little comment, which indicates that such things were common enough for the reader to need no explanation. Early records also indicate that the late *Han-dynasty governor of Chiao-chou, Shih Hsieh (Si Nhiep) had a large number of Chinese and central Asian monks in his entourage. Official Chinese court records speak of eminent and accomplished *monks from Chiao-chou who made their way to the northern capitals, showing that there were sufficient resources there for them to receive detailed training in doctrine, scripture, and *meditation, and we also have records of foreign monks who settled in Chiao-chou to carry out translation activities. *I-ching (635–713), a monk who journeyed to *India and later wrote an account of other monks who had done the same, mentions that several of them, having taken the southern maritime route either coming or going, stopped off in Chiao-chou. In other words, in some respects Buddhism in Vietnam during this period was simply an extension of Chinese Buddhism, and much of what transpired there reflected developments elsewhere in the empire.

However, there was another strain of Buddhism active in the area at this time. Waves of Indian cultural export had made their way across south-east Asia, penetrating as far as Indonesia, and Theravāda forms of Buddhism were among these. Many people in the southern part of Vietnam were more influenced by this form of Buddhism than by Chinese Mahāyāna Buddhism, and so Vietnam came to be the meeting place for the two streams: Mahāyāna going north from India along the *Silk Road, down into China, then into Vietnam; and Theravāda going south along the seacoasts through *Thailand, Laos, and *Cambodia and into Vietnam. Vietnamese Buddhism, as a result, is a unique mixture of Mahāyāna and Theravāda forms.

By the time Vietnam achieved independence from China in the 10th century, Buddhism had been an integral part of the cultural landscape for over 800 years. The first emperor of independent Vietnam, Dinh Bo Linh, put together a system of hierarchical ranks for government officials, Buddhist monks, and Taoist priests after ascending to power in 968. Thereafter, Buddhist monks were part of the national administration, serving the ruler as advisers, rallying the people in times of crisis, and attending to the spiritual needs of the masses. The Lý dynasty (1010–1225) was more stable and long-lived than the Dinh and Lê dynasties that preceded it. This dynasty was willing to take in many elements in its task of constructing a national culture and identity, and so many elements of Chinese, Indian, and Cham culture were included, and many schools of Buddhism were able to exist side by side and compete in an open religious marketplace, further facilitating the intermingling of Mahāyāna and Theravāda forms. Archeological evidence also indicates that *tantric Buddhism had also made its way into Vietnam during this time (stelae with *mantras incribed on them have been discovered). During this time, Buddhism also became more widely disseminated among the common people, as monks came into villages and 'converted' local deities, ancestors, and culture heroes to the religion and declared them now 'protectors of the *Dharma'. This move worked to unify the disparate local cults under the Buddhist umbrella, and aided in the unification of the country. In return, the Lý kings supported Buddhism lavishly: giving stipends to eminent monks, erecting and refurbishing temples, and sending envoys to China in search of scriptures. In this way, new developments in Chinese Buddhism were noted in Vietnam, particularly with the importation of *Ch'an 'transmission of the lamp' genre works. This created a dichotomy between an older form of Buddhism that was highly syncretistic and incorporated many elements and practices under its umbrella, and a newer Buddhism that inclined to a purer Chinese nature, centred mostly on Ch'an.

Ch'an study and practice became more entrenched under the Tran dynasty (1225–1400), although the older forms also remained vital. A kind of division of labour arose, with Confucianism adjudicating worldly affairs and Buddhism providing the metaphysical and soteriological framework for human life. Many Tran emperors abdicated and retired to Mt. Yan Tu to practise Buddhism full-time after a Confucian career as national ruler. Tran rulers also sponsored the establishment of the first actual 'schools' of Buddhism in Vietnam, beginning with the Truc Lam (Bamboo Grove) Ch'an school founded by the third Tran king. Missionary monks also arrived continuously from China, bringing both the *Lin-chi and *Ts'ao-tung schools into Vietnam, and they found a ready audience among the Tran aristocracy. Unfortunately, the surviving literature tends to give only lists of lineages and temples, making it difficult to determine the actual content of teaching and practice. The works that remain show many features reminiscent of the 'Ch'an of the *patriarchs' found in China: encounter dialogues, enlightenment verses, direct transmission of the mind of enlightenment, and so on.

In the 15th century, the Vietnamese began to conquer and absorb parts of Cambodia, bringing the religion of the *Khmer people into the Vietnamese fold. This strengthened the coexistence between the Vietnamese Ch'an of the élites alongside the Theravāda teachings and practices of the Cambodians. The country took its current shape during the 18th century, and the country's unique blend of schools of Buddhism was fixed from that time. The occupation of the area by the French, in giving the different ethnic groupings of the land a common tongue, facilitated interchange between different forms of Buddhism. In the early 20th century, Vietnamese culture, like other cultures in east and southeast Asia, had to deal with modern trends of science, Western thought, and Marxism. During this time, many educated Vietnamese began abandoning Mahāyāna and Ch'an Buddhism, which seemed superstitious with all its deities, magical rituals, and practices for gaining *rebirth in the Pure Land. They came to favour Theravāda Buddhism, which seemed more pragmatic and this-worldly in comparison. An instrumental figure in this evolution was Le Van Giang, who studied Theravāda meditation with a Cambodian teacher, took the name Ho-Tong, and came back to Vietnam to build the first formally Theravāda temple near Saigon. From this headquarters he began actively disseminating Theravāda Buddhism in the local language, and produced translations of the *Pāli scriptures into Vietnamese. The Vietnamese Theravāda Buddhist Saṃgha Congregation was formally established in 1957, making what had formerly been an element dispersed throughout Vietnamese Buddhism in a diffuse manner into a formal school to rival the Chinese-style Ch'an schools. By 1997, this Congregation had 64 temples scattered throughout the country. Buddhist organizations founded in the 1960s include the Unified Buddhist Church of Vietnam, the United Buddhist Association, and the School of Youth for Social Services. Under the leadership of the monk Thich *Nhat Hanh, well known in the West as a leading exponent of *Engaged *Buddhism, the latter has become a crusading volunteer organization dedicated to improving the lot of rural communities. During the Vietnam War, Buddhist monks were active in efforts to bring hostilities to a close, and many of them immolated themselves publicly to protest the war (*see* THICH GUANG DUC). Others, including Thich Nhat Hanh, went abroad to propagate Vietnamese Ch'an. The Lam-te lineage of *Rinzai *Zen introduced in the 17th century is today the largest Buddhist order.

Vigraha-vyāvartanī. The 'Deflection of Disputes', a key work by *Nāgārjuna in 70 verses in which he defends his thesis that all phenomena are empty (*śūnya), using standard debating procedures. The text is extant in *Sanskrit as well as Tibetan and Chinese translations.

vihāra (Skt.; Pāli). Term meaning literally 'dwelling', but associated particularly with a Buddhist monastery. Originally, when *monks and *nuns used to wander through the countryside, settling down only during the rainy season, the term was used to designate an individual hut within the rainy season retreat. Later, with the establishment of permanent dwellings for the monks, the term came to indicate an entire monastery. For this reason, it is customary to refer to monasteries by this generic term, although in some countries, such as *Thailand, it is reserved for a shrinehall. In the early period, monks of differing doctrinal affiliations lived side by side in the same vihāra. This would typically comprise individual cells arranged around a central courtyard very often enclosing a railed *Bodhi Tree, a shrine room, and an ambulatory. As times changed, and the needs of the *Saṃgha began to reflect growing institutionalization, some vihāras became enormously large, complex, and wealthy units with elaborate administrative hierarchies. Some, like *Nālandā and *Somapuri, developed into universities with many thousands of resident students. The modern Indian state of Bihar takes its name from the fact that Buddhist monasteries were abundant in the region.

viharn. Thai term for a *vihāra or temple assembly hall for the laity. The hall usually houses the principal *Buddha image.

Vijayabāhu. Name taken by six *Sri Lankan kings from the 11th to the 15th centuries. The greatest of these was Vijayabāhu I (1059–1114), who later took the name Sirisaṅghabodhi. In the early part of his reign he conquered and united a number of provinces, including *Anurādhapura, as well as defeating the Indian Coḷa forces. When peace had been established he sent messengers to the *Mon king in order to bring *monks from that country to assist in the restoration of the *Saṃgha in Sri Lanka. He became a great patron of *Buddhism, having many copies of the *Tripiṭaka made, and constructing many *vihāras for monks. He also had the **Dhammasaṅgaṇī*, the first book of the *Abhidharma, translated into Sinhalese, but the translation has since been lost. *See also* BHUVANEKABĀHU; PULATTHINAGARA.

vijñāna (Skt.; Pāli, viññāna). Consciousness or awareness, in both its active, discriminative form of knowing, and its subliminal or unconscious bodily and psychic functions. It is important to realize that vijñāna means more than the stream of mental awareness, which the English word 'consciousness' primarily denotes. For example, from the earliest times Buddhist sources have distinguished six forms of vijñāna corresponding to the six senses, thus eye-consciousness, ear-consciousness, nose-consciousness, taste-consciousness, touch-consciousness, bodily consciousness, and mental consciousness. Vijñāna thus encompasses both the Western terms 'conscious' and 'unconscious' and for that reason is difficult to translate by any single term. It is an important element in the Buddhist analysis of human nature as the last of the five aggregates (*skandhas). In the scheme of Dependent Origination (*pratītya-samutpāda) it forms the third link in the twelvefold series.

Vijñānavāda (Skt.). 'The Way of Consciousness', an alternative name for the *Yogācāra school. The title Vijñānavāda emphasizes the interest of that school in the workings of consciousness (*vijñāna) and its role in creating the experience of *saṃsāra.

vijñapti (Skt.). Representation; a *Yogācāra term which denotes the mentally generated projections of subject and object that are falsely believed to exist. In reality, according to Yogācāra teachings, they are merely superimposed by unenlightened beings upon actuality. The aim of Yogācāra practice is to realize the false and illusory nature of these projections and attain non-dual awareness (*nirvikalpa-jñāna).

vijñapti-mātra (Skt.). 'Mere representation'; the *Yogācāra theory that the contents of everyday, unenlightened experience are merely a false superimposition upon actuality of dualistic concepts generated by the mind that prevent direct experience of reality as it truly is (yathā-bhūta). Some later forms of Yogācāra lend themselves to an idealistic interpretation of this theory but such a view is absent from the works of the early Yogācārins such as *Asaṅga and *Vasubandhu.

Vijñapti-mātratā Siddhi (Chin., Cheng-wei-shi lun). 'The Establishment of the State of Mere Representation'. Title of a work in Chinese by *Hsüan-tsang which presents a synthetic commentary on *Vasubandhu's **Triṃsikā*. The work is based on ten Indian commentaries but emphasizes the views of *Śīlabhadra and *Dharmapāla.

vikalpa (Skt.). **1.** 'Imagining', an intellectual process which leads to the formation of concepts, judgements, views, and opinions. In Buddhist thought, the term usually signifies deluded or erroneous thinking which is tainted with emotions and *desires and fails to grasp the true nature of things as they are. In this sense it is synonymous with the term *prapañca, meaning 'mental proliferation', an activity of the deluded and unenlightened mind. **2.** The process, according to *Yogācāra, which sets up a false dualistic split that is imposed upon reality, and involves belief in the existence of a perceiving subject and perceived objects. Some sources consider both 'subjectivity' (grāhaka) and 'objectivity' (grāhya) to be the result of vikalpa (*see* GRĀHYA-GRĀHAKA).

Vikramaśīla. One of the great Buddhist monastic universities of ancient *India, located about 150 miles east of *Nālandā near the present-day city of Bhagalpur on the Ganges. Tibetan sources provide most of the known details about this university since a number of masters from Vikramaśīla were active in *Tibet during the *Second Transmission period. It was founded in the early 9th century through the inspiration of *Haribhadra and the patronage of the *Pāla King Dharmapāla. *Tantric Buddhist studies particularly flourished here under the guidance of such masters as Buddhaśrījñāna and *Nāropa, although a number of celebrated masters of Buddhist logic (*pramāṇa) also taught here such as Jñānaśrīmitra. Like the other nearby Buddhist universities of *Nālandā and *Odantapurī, Vikramaśīla was plundered and destroyed by invading Muslim raiders in the 12th century CE.

vimalā-bhūmi (Skt.). The second of the ten Bodhisattva Levels (*bhūmi). According to the **Daśabhūmika Sūtra* it is known as 'the Stainless One', because at this level the *Bodhisattva engages in the Perfection of Morality (*śīla-pāramitā).

Vimalakīrti-nirdeśa Sūtra. A Buddhist scripture that has been highly influential in east Asia. The *Sanskrit title means 'The Teaching of Vimalakīrti', and indeed the principal character and speaker throughout the work is not the *Buddha or any high *Bodhisattva, but the layman Vimalakīrti. The Sanskrit original was lost long ago, although fragments of it are preserved as quotations in other works, and recently the discovery of a Sanskrit manuscript in the Potala palace in

*Lhasa was announced in *Japan. The work's many qualities—such as its eloquence, orderliness of exposition, and even humour—have made it a very popular text throughout the world of *Mahāyāna *Buddhism. According to its translator, Étienne *Lamotte, the *sūtra 'is perhaps the crowning jewel of the Buddhist literature of the *Great Vehicle'. He describes it as 'vibrating with life and full of humour', avoiding the prolixity of other Mahāyāna works while equalling them in the profundity of its teachings.

The *sūtra was translated into Chinese as early as 185 CE, (although this translation has been lost), and was translated six more times after that. The translation made by *Kumārajīva around 406 (*Taishō 475) is considered the standard among the three still extant. A Tibetan translation also exists, as do other translations (or retranslations from the Chinese or Tibetan) in other languages of central Asia. The primary topic of this sūtra is the perfection of insight (*Prajñā-pāramitā) teachings of *Mahāyāna Buddhism. It also concerns itself to refute *Hīnayāna doctrine, as represented by the ten major disciples of the Buddha who are consistently reproved by Vimalakīrti for their faulty understanding. One of the strengths of the sūtra is that it teaches by action as well as by word. For example, while it teaches that the concepts of time and space are mere conventions, it also demonstrates this by several miraculous events: the great throng who call on Vimalakīrti in his narrow room somehow all fit comfortably inside it; an entire Buddha-field (*Buddha-kṣetra) with all its inhabitants is shrunk so that it fits into the palm of the hand. The distinctions between monastic follower and lay follower and between Buddha and ordinary being are called into question by the person of Vimalakīrti, a layman and ordinary man of the world who nevertheless rivals the Bodhisattva *Mañjuśrī himself in understanding. The scripture also shows a mystical turn in its presentation of the Mahāyāna teaching of emptiness (*śūnyatā). In one of the most famous scenes, called the 'thunderous silence of Vimalakīrti', a *debate ensued over the proper manner in which to teach this doctrine. After many participants—culminating with Mañjuśrī—give their understanding, all turn to Vimalakīrti to give the final word, at which point he keeps silent, eloquently demonstrating the ultimate failure of language to produce a proper understanding of reality. All of these features, along with the wry humour of many of the episodes (particularly those that produce the discomfiture of the Buddha's disciples) have made this sūtra a favourite in east Asia, especially within the *Ch'an and *Zen schools.

Vimalamitra. Born in western *India in the 8th century CE, Vimalamitra became a notable scholar-*monk whose learning encompassed the *Vinaya, *Abhidharma, *Mahāyāna *sūtras, and the *tantras. Later in his life, he is said to have travelled to *China where he received *atiyoga teachings from Śrīsiṃha. He was later invited to *Tibet during the reign of Trisong Detsen where he resided for thirteen years and taught both exoteric Mahāyāna and *Dzogchen. Thereafter he is said to have travelled on to China.

Vimānavatthu (Pāli, tales of the mansions). The sixth book of the *Khuddaka Nikāya of the *Pāli Canon. It describes the spendour of the various celestial mansions of the gods and sets out in 83 stories an account of the good moral deeds which led to the gods being reborn in a heavenly paradise. There is a commentary on the work by *Dhammapāla, forming part of the **Paramatthadīpanī*.

vimokṣa (Skt., liberation; Pāli, vimokkha). **1.** The three 'liberations', or 'gateways to deliverance', said to be three 'doors' (mukha) through which *nirvāṇa can be approached. In *Pāli sources they are known as the empty (suññato), the signless (animitto) and the wishless (appaṇihito). These three emphasize the transcendent nature of *nirvāṇa. It is empty of self in that it has no essence; it is without any of the 'signs' or marks (*lakṣaṇa) characteristic of *saṃsāra (such as arising and passing away); and it is without *desire, since one who has attained it seeks nothing more. *See also* VIMUKTI. **2.** Pāli sources also contain a list of eight vimokkhas (Skt., vimokṣa) or stages of liberation, which are concerned with proficiency in the attainement of the levels of trance (*dhyāna). The last five consist of the four higher trances together with the 'attainment of cessation' (*saññā-vedayita-nirodha).

Viṃśatikā. The 'Twenty Verses', a key *Yogācāra work by *Vasubandhu which can be viewed as a companion to his **Triṃśikā*. The treatise discusses the nature of perceptual objects but interpretation of the text is controversial since it may be understood either as an ontologically orientated refutation of the existence of all external objects, or else in an epistemological sense which suggests that objects as they appear to the mind are merely contructs superimposed upon an indeterminate external reality. The work survives in *Sanskrit as well as a Tibetan and two Chinese translations.

vimukti (Skt.; Pāli, vimutti). Liberation; the release from *suffering and *rebirth (*saṃsāra) attained through a realization of the *Four Noble Truths. In the *Mahāyāna, there are three so-called 'gates' to liberation which are said to facilitate release: emptiness (*śūnyatā), signlessness, or the absence of perceptual forms (*animitta); and wishlessness, or the absence of purpose or desires (apraṇidhāna). To these a fourth item is sometimes added, namely intrinsic luminosity (prakṛti-prabhāsvara). In *Pāli sources, two kinds of 'gates to liberation' (vimokkha-mukha) are distinguished, namely freedom through understanding (paññā-vimutti) and freedom through mind (ceto-vimutti). The former is intellectual in nature and cultivated through the practice of insight meditation (*vipaśyanā), while the latter involves transic states of consciouness and is cultivated through calming meditation (*śamatha). The ideal is to be one who is 'freed in both ways' (*ubhato-bhāga-vimutto), as the *Buddha was understood to be, but it is thought to be possible to attain liberation through insight alone (paññā-vimutti): such a one is then known as 'dry-eyed' or 'dry visioned' (sukkha-vipassaka).

Vimuttimagga (Pāli). 'The Path to Liberation', a treatise expounding the various aspects of the path to awakening (*bodhi) as understood within the *Theravāda tradition. The author of the work is Upatissa, who may have lived in the 3rd century CE. This work is generally thought to to have provided the inspiration for *Buddhaghoṣa's later and more comprehensive compendium 'The Path of Purification' (**Visuddhimagga*).

Vinaya. General term referring to monastic discipline, law, custom, and practice, the regulations concerning which are set out in the *Vinaya Piṭaka.

Vinaya Piṭaka. One of the three divisions of the *Pāli Canon, being the 'basket' (*piṭaka) or collection of monastic law. The purpose of these scriptures is to regulate in all detail the life within the community of *monks and *nuns as well as their relationship with the laity. The collection, which is attributed to the *Buddha himself, deals with the rules relating to individual conduct and with the legal procedures and formulae used by the community as a whole. It is divided into three sections, the first of which contains the set of rules for monks and nuns known as the *Prātimokṣa (Pāli, Pāṭimokkha). This, according to some Buddhist schools, is an independent text. The Vinaya Piṭaka also contains a large number of stories and biographical material relating to the Buddha, as well as a certain amount of historical matter regarding the Order (*Saṃgha). An old commentary, incorporated into the *Pāli version of the text, gives accounts of the occasions on which the rules were formulated. The Pāli version of the Vinaya Piṭaka is the only one that has survived in its original language. Beside that of the *Theravādins, other schools have produced versions of the Vinaya which have been preserved in Chinese translation. These are: the *Mahāsaṃghika, the *Mahīśāsaka, the *Dharmaguptaka, the *Sarvāstivādin, and *Mūla-sarvāstivāda. Of the last there is a Tibetan version as well as some parts of the *Sanskrit text. The Vinaya Piṭaka consists of the Sūtravibhaṅga, the Skandhaka, and the *Parivāra (an appendix). The first is divided into Pārājikā and Pācittiya and the second into *Mahāvagga and *Cullavagga. The commentary to the Vinaya Piṭaka, compiled by *Buddhaghoṣa in the 5th century, is known by the title of **Samantapāsādikā*.

Vinaya school. A school of Chinese *Buddhism that specialized in study of all aspects of the *Vinaya, or rules of conduct for clergy and laity. Established by the *monk *Tao-hsüan (596–667), this school began by establishing which of the several redactions of the monastic regulations that had been translated into Chinese would become the standard. Tao-hsüan chose the Vinaya of the *Dharmaguptaka school in *India, in Chinese called the 'Vinaya in Four Divisions' (Chin.,

Ssu fen lü), as the standard. After this had been settled, the school went on to function as a sort of *canon law department for Chinese Buddhism, producing commentaries on the Vinaya, establishing procedures for handling difficult cases, defining what constituted an infraction of a rule and setting up sanctions and mitigating circumstances, and so on. They also dealt with matters of clerical status, setting criteria for valid *ordinations and expulsion. The school was never large, but because of this 'gatekeeping' function, had extraordinary influence over the character of the Chinese *Saṃgha. *See also* RITSU; LÜ-TSUNG.

vipāka (Skt.). Maturation, coming to fruition; one of the five kinds of results (*phala). Used generally in connection with the arising of the results of *karma but also found in *Mahāyāna to connote the salvific activities of a *Buddha or *Bodhisattva as they cause beings to mature spiritually.

viparyāsa (Skt.). Inversion or cognitive distortion in relation to four things. By virtue of this misapprehension, beings treat the impermanent (*anitya) as permanent (nitya), suffering (*duḥkha) as happiness (sukha), non-self (*anātman) as self (*ātman) and the impure (aśubha) as pure (śubha).

vipaśyanā (Skt., insight; Pāli, vipassanā). One of the two main types of meditational technique taught in *Buddhism, the other being *śamatha, or calming meditation. The technique leads to the direct personal apprehension and verification of the truth of Buddhist teachings, such as the cognition that all formations (*saṃskāra) bear the 'three marks' (*trilakṣana), namely that they are impermanent (*anitya), without self-essence (*anātman), and sorrowful (*duḥkha). This insight leads to entry into the *supermundane paths and to *nirvāṇa. Vipaśyanā thus leads to an intellectual understanding of doctrine, in contrast to śamatha which leads to a transic state of rapt absorption. It is normally recommended, however, that the two techniques be developed in tandem, since insight is hard to attain if the mind is distracted.

vīrya (Pāli, viriya). Vigour, energy, or effort directed towards religious goals. It is one of the five powers (*bala), and the seven factors of enlightenment (*bodhyaṅga). *See also* VĪRYA-PĀRAMITĀ.

vīrya-pāramitā (Skt.). The Perfection of Strenuousness, the fourth of the Six Perfections (*ṣaḍ-pāramitā) that make up the central element of the *Bodhisattva Path in *Mahāyāna *Buddhism. The cultivation of this virtue involves unselfish application and effort to benefit others, as well as self-development, often at considerable personal expense. *See also* VĪRYA.

viṣaya (Skt.). The 'spheres' of the six senses and their objects, comprising colour-form, sounds, smells, tastes, tactile sensations, and additionally thoughts and feelings.

visualization. A form of *meditation where an image of a *Buddha or some other divine being is creatively imagined for purposes of devotion or spiritual transformation. Pre-*Mahāyāna Buddhist forms of visualization include the use of *kasinas and other inanimate objects, while in early *Mahāyāna such methods are taught in texts such as the **Sukhāvatī-vyūha Sūtra* and the **Pratyutpanna Sūtra* in connection with evoking the presence of an idealized form of a Buddha and his dwelling place. Visualization was further developed to form the cornerstone of *tantric practice (*sādhana) in which an individual creates an image of a divine being for the purposes of self-identification and transformation.

Visuddhajanavilāsinī. *Pāli commentary on the **Apadāna* by an unknown author.

Visuddhimagga. The 'Path of Purification', one of the most influential *Pāli commentarial texts. This compendium of Buddhist doctrine and metaphysics was written by *Buddhaghoṣa (5th century CE) at the request of Saṅghapāla *Thera. It is the most important book written by this author, providing a systematic exposition of Buddhist teaching besides being a detailed manual for *meditation. The structure of the work follows the three divisions of the *Eightfold Path into morality (*śīla), meditation (*samadhi) and insight (*prajñā). The commentary to the *Visuddhimagga* was compiled by *Dhammapāla and is known as the *Paramattamañjūsā* or *Mahā-ṭikā*. According to tradition, the two stanzas quoted at the beginning of the book were given to Buddhaghoṣa as a test by the monks of the *Mahāvihāra when he asked permission to translate the Sinhalese commentaries into Pāli. The *Visuddhimagga* seems to have been inspired by the earlier **Vimuttimagga* of Upatissa.

vitarka (Skt., thought conception; Pāli, vitakka). In Buddhist psychology the initial application of the mind to its object. It is defined as the mind laying hold of the object of thought and directing attention towards it. Closely associated with vitarka, and usually following it, is *vicāra or 'discursive thought'. The relationship between the two is said to be like taking hold of a bowl in one hand and scrubbing it with the other, to the striking of a bell and its resounding, or to the fixed point of a compass and the revolving point which moves around it. Both vitarka and vicāra are eliminated from the mind in the early stages of transic meditation (*dhyāna).

Vṛji. *See* VAJJĪ; VṚJIPUTRAKA.

Vṛjiputraka (Skt,; Pāli, Vajjiputtaka). Name given to a body of monks resident at *Vaiśālī and belonging to the *Vṛji (Pāli, Vajji) clan. The Vṛjiputraka were condemned at the second council, the *Council of Vaiśālī, for ten unorthodox practices. According to the Sinhalese chronicles, this group then formed a separate sect known as the *Mahāsaṃghikas, numbering 10,000 monks. *See also* VAJJĪ.

Vulture's Peak (Skt., Gṛdhrakūṭa; Pāli, Gijjhakūṭa). A hill in Bihar, so-named because its peak was shaped like a vulture's beak or because many of the birds lived there. One of a group of five hills surrounding the ancient city of *Rājagṛha it was in a remote area popular with *ascetics. The location is frequently mentioned in both early and late sources (for example, the **Lotus Sūtra*) as the site of teachings given by the *Buddha.

vyākaraṇa (Skt.). **1.** Explanation, elucidation, or analysis, particularly with reference to points of doctrine. **2.** The science of grammar. **3.** A prediction or prophecy, used especially in *Mahāyāna *sūtras with reference to the prediction given by a *Buddha to a *Bodhisattva who has just embarked on the path. The prediction often details the Bodhisattva's future deeds, his achievement of enlightenment (*bodhi) and his eventual name as a Buddha.

vyavahāra (Skt.). **1.** In general terms, the domain of secular or worldly life as opposed to sphere of religion. **2.** In relation to language, a designation or manner of speech of a mundane (*laukika) kind that the Buddhas may make use of in order to communicate with unenlightened beings. It is opposed to the terminology of Buddhist philosophy which is thought to accurately decribe without redundancy the true nature of things. **3.** Especially in *Madhyamaka thought, a term used to connote relative or conventional truth (*saṃvṛti-satya) as opposed to ultimate truth (*paramārtha-satya).

W

waka. A form of Japanese poetry written in 31 syllables, and composed in Japanese rather than in imitation of a classical Chinese form. Several Japanese Buddhist clerics were known for their abilities in composing waka, such as *Ryōkan (1758–1831).

Wang Jih-hsiu (d. 1173). A Chinese Buddhist layman of the Sung dynasty (960–1279) who helped to revitalize the *Pure Land tradition. A native of Shu-ch'eng in Anhwei Province, his Buddhist name was layman Lung-shu. He obtained the chin-shih degree during the reign of the Sung Emperor Kao-tsung (r. 1127–63), and evidently wrote many essays on *Confucianism, but never held office. However, he abandoned this and dedicated his life completely to Pure Land practice, charitable donations, and performing a thousand prostrations per day. In 1160 he began the project of re-editing and publishing a critical edition of the *Larger *Sukhāvatī-vyūha Sūtra*, which he completed three years later (*Taishō 364). Accounts of his life recount the prayers and vows he used to make daily and some stories of miraculous healings attributed to him. His greatest achievement was the composition and subsequent popularization of an anthology called the *Lung-shu ching-t'u wen*, or 'Lung-shu's Pure Land Anthology'. This was a collection of excerpts from other works with Wang's commentary arranged topically in order to arouse faith in the Pure Land, give instruction in methods of practice, and tell edifying stories of others' successes with Pure Land practices as attested by stories of those who attained *rebirth or experienced miraculous occurrences in their lives as a result of the practice. *See also* CHINA.

Warren, Henry Clarke (1854–99). American scholar who overcame severe physical injuries in a childhood accident to do pioneering research on *Sanskrit and *Pāli texts. He graduated from Harvard in 1879 and then studied Sanskrit with Charles Lanman at Johns Hopkins University. With Lanman he founded the Harvard Oriental Series of publications, to which he contributed two volumes. Volume 3, *Buddhism in Translations*, remains a perennially popular anthology of early literature, while volume 41 is an edition of the **Visuddhimagga* of *Buddhaghoṣa.

warrior monks. *See* SŌHEI.

wat. Thai, Khmer, and Lao term for a *vihāra.

Wat Dhammakāya. The fastest-growing Buddhist organization in *Thailand, enjoying the support of the royal family, the military, and political leaders. Officially registered in 1978 the Dhammakāya movement was begun in the 1970s by two monks, Phra Dhammajayo and Phra Dattijīvo. Both held advanced degrees in business administration and marketing and sought to work for the renewal of Buddhism in Thailand and throughout the world. The movement founded a 1,000 acre centre at Pattum Thani, near Bangkok and there are plans to extend the site further to cater for the thousands of supporters who visit at weekends and for festivals. The movement has become the dominant voice in the Buddhist associations of most Thai universities, and also has a network of *Dharma practice centres throughout the country. Critics of Wat Dhammakāya claim its recruitment and promotional campaigns are too evangelical and commercial, and that it is overly influenced by the ruling élite.

Wat Phra Keo. The Temple of the Emerald Buddha. It is the most sacred of all Buddhist sites of *Thailand. This compound is part of the Grand Palace complex in Bangkok and it takes its name from the *Buddha image it houses in its *ubosoth. Carved from a single piece of jade, the 30 inch high figure is one of the most venerated images of the Buddha in the world. Its origin is unknown, but history places it in Chian Rai, in north-east Thailand in 1464. From there it travelled first to Chiang Mai, then to Lamphun, and finally back to Chiang Mai, from where the Laotians took it to their country. Eventually, the Thais again took possession of it. The statue was then moved to the present complex, purposely built by King Rama I. There the statue is displayed high above an altar and visitors can see it only from afar. Behind the altar and above the window frames are murals depicting the life of the Buddha. The ubosoth is covered by a gilded three-tiered roof and royal griffins stand guard outside it. The *wat is extremely ornate and embellished with murals, statues, and glittering gold. The compound is guarded by a number of 20 feet tall helmeted and tile-encrusted statues in traditional Thai battle attire. The inner walls of the complex are decorated with murals depicting the whole *Ramakien* (the Thai version of the Hindu epic the *Rāmāyana*) and gold *stūpas stand in the grounds.

Watts, Alan (1915–73). Eclectic British thinker and writer who relocated to California and played a central part in the counterculture of the 1960s. Watts became a leading light in the Human Potential Movement and was affiliated to the Esalen Institute. Although he had no academic background in eastern religions and no knowledge of oriental languages, his elegant writings caught the popular imagination and enjoyed considerable success. His books *The Way of Zen* (1957) and *Psychotherapy East and West* (1961) offered a way of personal growth based on Eastern psychology as an alternative to what many regard as the egocentric hedonism of Western culture.

wei-shih. A Chinese term meaning 'consciousness-only' that also serves as another name for the *Fa-hsiang school.

Wei-t'o. A guardian deity popular in east Asian *Buddhism. He was originally a Hindu deity named Kārttikeya or Skandha, the son of Śiva born with six heads. With the advent of Buddhism, he was 'converted' and adopted into the Buddhist pantheon as a protector of the teachings, and found his place as the chief of the 32 generals under the command of the four great kings (*lokapāla, *caturmahārāja). From about the *T'ang dynasty onwards in *China, he has been regarded as a guardian of temples and practitioners, as well as a symbol of fierce determination in spiritual exercises. His image is frequently found at the front of temples to one side of the main Buddha shrine.

Wen-shu (also Wen-shu-shih-li). The Chinese form of the name of the Indian *Bodhisattva *Mañjuśrī.

Wesak. Name of the month corresponding to the Western April–May. The name has come to indicate the festival celebrated by *Theravāda Buddhists on the full-moon day of the same month commemorating the *Buddha's birth, renunciation, enlightenment (*bodhi), and death.

western paradise. *See* SUKHĀVATĪ; PURE LAND.

wheel of life. *See* BHAVACAKRA.

wheel of the law. *See* DHARMA-CAKRA.

White Lotus Society. *See* PAI-LIEN TSUNG.

wihaan. Lao term for a *vihāra.

women. The *Buddha's attitude towards women was not radically different from that of his contemporaries. For male renunciates pursuing the religious life, women were seen as a temptation and a snare. The Buddha frequently cautioned *monks to be on their guard when dealing with women lest they be overcome by lust and craving (*tṛṣṇā). The following interchange between the Buddha and *Ānanda from the **Mahā-parinibbāna Sutta* illustrates this attitude:
—Lord, how should we conduct ourselves with regard to women?
—Don't see them, Ānanda.
—But if we should see them?
—Don't talk to them.
—But if they should talk to us?
—Keep wide awake, Ānanda.
(It should be noted that similar warnings were given to women about the dangers of men.) It was following the intervention of Ānanda that the Buddha was reluctantly persuaded to allow women to join the *Saṃgha as *nuns (*bhikṣunī). In the context of the time, this was something of a radical step, since only one other group in *India, the Jains (*see* JAINISM), appears to have allowed women to become nuns. In contrast to the role of women in the religious life, in the context of lay society the role of woman as wife and mother was seen as crucial to the stability of the social order. Regarding the role of women in lay life, the Buddha upheld the traditional values of his time, describing the relationship between husband and wife in the following terms:

'In five ways should a wife . . . be ministered to by her husband: by respect, by courtesy, by faithfulness, by handing over authority to her, by providing her with adornments. In these five ways does the wife ministered to by her husband . . . love him: her duties are well performed; by hospitality to the kin of both; by faithfulness; by watching over the goods he brings; and by skill and industry in discharging all her business' (**Sigālovāda Sutta*). In modern times the *Sakyadhita organization has been founded to further the participation of women in the religious life. *See also* DASA-SILMĀTĀ; SIKKHAMAT; THILASHIN.

Wŏn Buddhism. A modern branch of Korean *Buddhism founded in 1924 by Pak Chungbin (1891–1943) as a reform movement outside of clerical supervision. Pak studied the tenets of Buddhism, Protestantism, and Catholicism and concluded that all religions pointed to the same reality, represented by the *dharma-kāya, or formless Truth Body of the *Buddha. The formlessness and ineffability of the *Buddha are represented by a circle (Kor., wŏn), giving the sect its name and primary symbol. While its doctrines draw primarily from Buddhism, its forms of worship (*pūjā), self-improvement, and social involvement derive mainly from Protestantism.

Wŏnch'uk (631–96). A Korean *monk who studied consciousness-only (*vijñapti-mātra) philosophy in *China under the famous scholar-translator *Hsüan-tsang (596–664). Wŏnch'uk's commentary on the **Sandhinirmocana Sūtra*, a foundational consciousness-only scripture, was recognized as authoritative not only in *Korea, but also in China and *Tibet, where it became known as the 'great Korean commentary'.

Wŏnhyo (617–86). One of the most eminent scholar-monks in Korean history, and an influential figure in the development of the east Asian Buddhist intellectual and commentarial tradition. His extensive literary output runs to over 80 works in 240 fascicles, and some of his commentaries, such as those on the **Nirvāṇa Sūtra* and the *Awakening of Faith* (**Mahāyana-śraddhotpāda Śāstra*), became classics revered throughout *China and *Japan as well as *Korea. In fact, his commentary on the *Awakening of Faith* helped to make it one of the most influential and intensively studied texts in the east Asian *Mahāyāna tradition.

Wŏnhyo lived at a time of social and religious ferment and upheaval. His life extends over the period when the three kingdoms of the Korean peninsula were united under Silla in 668, and when Buddhists were coming out of a period of focused study of individual texts and beginning to address questions of *Buddhism's doctrinal coherence. By temperament, Wŏnhyo was a systematizer and integrater, and he broadly surveyed the literature and doctrines of all of the various schools of thought that had entered Korea: *San-lun, *Satyasiddhi (Ch'eng-shih), *T'ien-t'ai, *Hua-yen, *Pure Land, and *Ch'an. He set their various teachings into an overall framework so that each could be seen as a part of the larger tapestry of Buddhist wisdom and practice, and he is credited with the foundation of the first fully indigenous school of Korean Buddhist thought, *Pŏpsŏng ('dharma-nature'), which sought to account for the ultimate nature of all phenomena that bound them together in spite of their apparent diversity. Wŏnhyo's own integrative vision of Buddhism came to be called 't'ong pulgyŏ', or 'unitive Buddhism'. In addition to his scholarly activity, Wŏnhyo is credited as one of the men who took Buddhist study out of the aristocracy and spread it among the common people, a development that followed his resignation from the monastic order (*Saṃgha) and subsequent *marriage. It was through his endeavours among the people that the Pure Land practice of reciting the Buddha's name became widespread.

World Fellowship of Buddhists. Organization founded by G. P. Malalasekera with the aim of propagating the teachings of *Buddhism and reconciling different traditions. The group has its headquarters in Bangkok and holds periodic world conferences, the first of which coincided with its founding in 1950.

world protectors. *See* LOKAPĀLA.

worship. *See* PŪJĀ.

wrathful deities. In *tantric *Buddhism, certain deities are depicted in a ferocious and terrifying form. These forms have various layers of symbolic meaning. Most simply, they represent the vice of hatred (*dveṣa), which is one of the three roots of evil (*akuśala-mūla), and all the other negative emotions associated with it, such as anger. On another level they are a reminder that when properly channelled through the use of tantric practices, the misdirected psychic energy of negative emotions can be transformed into a more spiritually productive form and turned against the hatred itself in order to obliterate it. Each of the five *Jinas has a wrathful (krodha) form, and these symbolize their victory over the various passions and desires. Known collectively as the 'five kings of knowledge' (vidyārāja), they are Acalanātha, Trailokavijaya, Kuṇḍalī, *Yamāntaka, and Vajrayakṣa. In iconographic depictions such as *maṇḍalas, Acalanātha appears in the centre, and the others to the east, south, west, and north in the order mentioned.

wu. 1. A Chinese term corresponding to the *Sanskrit *bodhi, meaning '*enlightenment' or 'awakening'. The same character forms the root of the Japanese term *satori. **2.** A Chinese term meaning 'non-being' or 'to lack'. In the earliest attempts by Chinese Buddhists to understand Indian Buddhist thought and translate texts, wu was used to mean 'emptiness' (*śūnyatā), but was later supplanted by the word *k'ung. The word wu has been retained to denote the absence of all distinguishing characteristics that would separate phenomena from each other in an ultimate way; as such, it is the negation of all dualities. In this regard, it appears in the compound pen wu, or 'original nonbeing', in contraposition to miao yu, or 'marvellous being', which complements it by affirming the real existence of separate things within the matrix of Dependent Origination (*pratītya-samutpāda). In the famous riddle (*kōan) 'Chao-chou's dog', a *monk asked *Chao-chou Ts'ung-shen whether or not a dog had *Buddha-nature, to which the master replied, 'wu', meaning it has not. This word 'wu', then, became the 'critical phrase' (Chin., hua-t'ou), and the object of *meditation when working with this kōan.

Wu-liang-shou fo. A traditional Chinese rendering of the name of *Amitāyus *Buddha (an alternative name for *Amitābha) that translates the literal meaning of the name, 'the Buddha of immeasurable life'.

Wu-men Hui-k'ai (1183–1260). A Sung-dynasty Chinese *Ch'an *monk best known for compiling the *kōan collection known by his name, the *Wu-men kuan* meaning 'Gate of Wu-men' or, more literally, the '*Gateless Gate'.

Wu-men kuan. *See* GATELESS GATE; WU-MEN HUI-K'AI.

Wu-t'ai-shan. One of the 'Four Famous Mountains' known as major *pilgrimage sites in Chinese *Buddhism. Located in Shansi Province along the northern tier of provinces adjoining *Mongolia, the site is actually a series of five gentle peaks covering over 100 square miles which give it its name ('Five-terraced mountain'). Its highest peak rises more than 10,000 feet above sea level. It lies a little way from the Great Wall, and so symbolized a spiritual frontier between *China and the barbarians, just as the Great Wall marked the political boundary. This liminal quality made it a sacred place even before the advent of Buddhism in China. Buddhist temples appeared on the site in the 5th or 6th century CE, and became known as a site sacred to the *Bodhisattva *Mañjuśrī, who embodies wisdom.

Wu-tsung. An emperor of the *T'ang dynasty in *China who ruled from 841 to 846, and was the instigator of the persecution of *Buddhism in 845 that did serious damage to the religion for a long time afterwards.

wu-wei. 1. A Chinese term borrowed from *Taoism in order to indicate Buddhist concepts. It generally means 'unconditioned', and is used to translate the *Sanskrit term *asaṃskṛta. **2.** Using a different Chinese character to write the second word, a Buddhist term meaning 'fearless', as in the 'four fearlessnesses' (*see* VAIŚĀRADYA).

Y

yab-yum. Literally 'father and mother', a Tibetan term for the sexual union of male and female *Buddhas associated with *anuttara-yoga-tantra. Various interpretations of the symbolism exist, but most commonly the male figure is linked to compassion (*karuṇā) and skilful means (*upāya-kauśalya) while the female partner is linked to insight (*prajñā).

yakṣa (Skt.). Generally thought to be malevolent flesh-eating demons in later *Buddhism, the yakṣa and their female counterparts, the yakṣinī, were originally more or less benevolent local nature divinities who if correctly propitiated would protect the community. If not treated with due respect they wreaked their vengeance upon the populace in the form of sickness and natural catastrophes. They were also believed to have many magical powers, especially that of shape-shifting. Yakṣinīs were particularly associated with trees, and are frequently depicted in Indian art as sinuous young *women with great sexual grace, though with an undertone of menace.

Yama (Skt., restraint). The god of *death and lord of the underworld (*naraka). Yama is a *Hindu god who first appears in the *Ṛg Veda* (*see* VEDA), and in later mythology rules the underworld as judge and punisher of the dead. In *Buddhism, he loses these two functions since according to Buddhist teachings *karma alone determines one's fate in the afterlife, and the intervention of a supernatural judge is therefore not required. To a certain degree, Yama is also eclipsed by *Māra, and it is the latter who appears with greater frequency and clarity in Buddhist literature as the personification of moral evil. Nevertheless, the older conceptions are not entirely lost, and in the *Pāli Canon Yama is depicted as a kind of superintendent of the karmic process of post-mortem retribution that takes place in purgatory. He rules over this realm together with his eight generals and a retinue of 80,000 servants. The souls of the dead are led before him and he reminds them that they themselves are the authors of their fate and are alone responsible for the expiatory punishment they are about to undergo. His messengers are old age, sickness, and death, and he dispatches them into the human world as an omen and warning about the brevity of life. In *Pāli sources sometimes two or four Yamas are mentioned. In *tantric Buddhism, Yama is depicted as a terrifying figure adorned with human skulls and surrounded by flames. In his left hand he holds the mirror of karma that reflects the good and evil deeds an individual has performed, and in his right hand the sword of insight (*prajñā).

yamabushi. Japanese term meaning 'those who lie down in the mountains'. It refers to practitioners of *shugendō in Japanese *Buddhism: these are mountain *ascetics who practise severe austerities in search of personal transformation and supernatural power.

yamaka-pāṭihāriya (Pāli, twin miracle). A miracle said to have been performed by the *Buddha at *Śrāvastī in the course of which he caused fire and water to issue from opposite sides of his body. First of all flames came from the upper part and water from the lower, then they were reversed, and then they were emitted from opposite sides of his body. The spectacle was accompanied by other supernatural phenomena, such as rays of light of six different colours that streamed from each pore of his skin. When the miracle was concluded it is reported that the Buddha ascended in three strides to the *heaven of the 33 gods and instructed his mother (who had been reborn there) in the teachings of the *Abhidharma. *See also* PĀṬIHĀRIYA; MIRACLES; ṚDDHI.

Yamamoto Gempo (1866–1961). A Japanese *Rinzai *Zen priest who was the teacher of *Nakagawa Soen (1907–84), one of the chief transmitters of Zen to the United States (*see* AMERICA) during the first half of the 20th century.

Yamāntaka. The 'Destroyer of *Yama', the wrathful manifestation of the *Bodhisattva *Mañjuśrī. He is depicted as a black or red, multi-armed, multi-legged, and nine-headed being with a central face of a bull enveloped in flames. Sometimes he stands alone or else with his consort, Vajra-veṭalī. It was this form that the Bodhisattva assumed to overcome *Yama, the embodiment of *death. Yamāntaka is also the protector deity linked most closely to the Tibetan *Geluk lineage.

yāna (Skt.). A way or a vehicle. The term came into use with the advent of the *Mahāyāna, and denotes the various paths taught by the *Buddha according to the spiritual acumen of the audience. Typically, Mahāyāna posits the existence of three ways: *Śrāvakayāna, or the Vehicle of the Hearers; *Pratyekabuddhayāna, or the Vehicle of the Solitary Buddhas; and *Bodhisattvayāna, or the Vehicle of the Bodhisattvas. *See also* EKAYĀNA; VAJRAYĀNA.

Yang-shan Hui-chi (840–916). A Chinese *Ch'an *monk of the *T'ang dynasty who belonged to the House of Kuei-yang among the *Five Houses. Originally from Kuangtung province, he left his family at the age of 9; at 17, he showed his determination to achieve *enlightenment by shaving his head and cutting off two fingers. Interestingly, he did not receive the full monastic *precepts until after he had received the *inka, or certification of the authenticity of his enlightenment, from *Kuei-shan Ling-yu (771–853). After receiving the precepts and conducting a study of the *Vinaya, he returned to Kuei-shan and served his master for another fifteen years, and many of their dialogues during this time have been preserved and passed down. In 879, he moved to Ta Yang Shan (Great Yang Mountain) in Kiangsi Province, which explains that part of his name.

yantra (Skt.). **1.** Diagrams composed of interlocking geometrical shapes, most typically triangles, used as symbols of various aspects of the divine. They are not used in earlier Buddhist practice but are common in south-east Asian esoteric Buddhist traditions. They are used for magical purposes throughout the Buddhist world. **2.** General term for a machine or mechanical device.

Yasa. A disciple of *Ānanda who played an important part in the *Council of Vaiśālī. It was Yasa who discovered and brought to light the ten illicit practices (Pāli, dasavatthu) of the *Vajjian *monks, such as handling gold and silver (meaning accepting donations of money). Largely due to his efforts, a committee of eight venerable monks was formed (on which he served) to investigate the disputed practices. After due consideration all ten were declared to be illegal and the *Vinaya was recited by 700 monks. This recital is referred to as the 'recital of the Elder Yasa' (yasatherasaṅgīti) in recognition of the role he played in the proceedings.

Yaśodharā. Name of the wife of the *Buddha. *See also* RĀHULAMĀTĀ.

yathā-bhūta (Skt.). The way things are in actuality; a term used to designate the true nature of phenomena or direct experience unmediated by the superimposition of false concepts such as the idea of an inherent and permanent identity or self (*ātman). As such, the term is used in *Mahāyāna synonymously with emptiness (*śūnyatā), actuality (*tattva), suchness (*tathatā), and so forth.

Yavana (also Yona, Yonaka). *Pāli name for the region, and the inhabitants of the region, extending from north-west *India into Afghanistan. The word itself is probably a corruption of 'Ionian', a term used to refer to the Greeks resident in the province of Bactria. *Buddhism spread to the region some time after the *Council of Pāṭaliputra II (*c.* 250 BCE).

Yellow Hats. A Chinese term used to denote the *Geluk school of Tibetan *Buddhism, on account of the yellow ceremonial caps they wear. In contrast the three earlier schools used red caps. *See also* RED HATS.

Yeshé Tshogyel (757–817). (Tib., Ye-shes mtsho-rgyal). The renowned Tibetan consort of *Padmasambhava, she was born into a noble family and later resided at the court of Trisong Detsen. She met the Indian scholar-*monk *Śāntarakṣita and the *yogin Padmasambhava while there. Her actual contact with Padmasambhava seems to have been relatively brief but during that time he transmitted to her many important teachings especially those connected to the tutelary deity (*yi-dam) *Vajrakīla. As well as writing a biography of Padmasambhava, she is said to have recorded many of his teachings which were concealed as *terma for later discovery. After Padmasambhava left *Tibet, she propagated the *Dharma in the eastern regions of the country.

yi-dam (Tib.). A tutelary deity associated with *tantric *Buddhism. The image and attributes of the deity are appropriated and used during personal meditation (*sādhana) for the purpose of transformation through self-identification. Examples of yi-dams include *Cakra-saṃvara, *Hayagrīva, *Heruka, *Mahākāla, *Vajrabhairava, and *Vajrayoginī, all of whom have a distinctive iconography and are the object of cultic practices such as rites of propitiation.

Yin-kuang (1861–1940). A Chinese Republican-era *monk and reformer of the *Pure Land tradition widely recognized as the thirteenth *patriarch of Pure Land. A native of Shansi Province, he left his family early in life to join the monastic order (*Saṃgha). Once, his family tricked him into returning home, but they were unable to keep him there, and he ran away again and severed all contact. During his early training, he struggled with conjunctivitis, and was cured by vigorous recitation of *Amitābha *Buddha's name. He had been a good student as a child, and his literary abilities induced the abbots of the various temples where he resided during his early monastic career to ask him to take charge of the monastic library. This involved periodic 'sunning of the scriptures', laying the volumes out in the sun to dry them and prevent mildew. During these times, he was able to peruse Buddhist literature freely, and he felt particularly drawn to the works of the twelfth Pure Land patriarch Chi-hsing Ch'o-wu (1741–1810) while residing at the Tzu-fu Temple where Ch'o-wu himself had lived. He was particularly impressed that Ch'o-wu, an acknowledged *Ch'an master who had experienced full *enlightenment, late in life abandoned the path of Ch'an as too rigorous and uncertain for the majority of people and devoted himself to Pure Land practice. These experiences fixed his loyalty in the Pure Land path from the start.

Wishing for solitude, Yin-kuang spent 30 years on P'u-t'uo Island under an assumed name, and underwent two consecutive three-year periods of sealed confinement. Even though he kept well hidden from the public eye, he still answered letters that came his way inquiring about teachings and practices. His literary skill and genuine sincerity and piety showed through in these exchanges, and in 1917 his correspondents began collecting and publishing his letters. He himself oversaw the republication of classics of Pure Land literature such as *Chih-hsü's *Ten Essentials of the Pure Land* and *The Recorded Sayings of Ch'an Master Ch'o-wu*, along with essays of his own denigrating Ch'an and endorsing Pure Land practice, included in his *Treatise Resolving Doubts About the Pure Land* (Chin., *Ching-t'u chüeh-i lun*). These publications caught the heart of the Buddhist reading public, and Yin-kuang became quite well-known in spite of himself. In 1930, he agreed to take over as abbot of the Pao-kuo Temple in Soochow, and became involved in the life of the nearby Ling-yen Shan Temple as well. In 1937, he moved to the latter in the face of the Japanese invasion of *China, and in the three years remaining to him he produced a new breviary for monastic daily liturgies and rituals that turned away from the Ch'an emphasis of previous breviaries and included more Pure Land practice. This breviary became the basis for the one most commonly used in Taiwan today. At the same time, he remained cloistered, but faithfully counselled the stream of people who came to his wicket to exchange words with him. After his death in 1940, he was popularly acclaimed the thirteenth patriarch of the Pure Land tradition in China.

yin-yang. *See* TAOISM.

yoga (Skt., yoking, joining). Any form of spiritual discipline aimed at gaining control over the mind with the ultimate aim of attaining liberation from *rebirth. Yogic practices such as bodily postures and breath control are common to many Indian religions, although such practices were only termed 'yoga' a little before the time of the *Buddha. The Buddha used such techniques primarily as aids to *meditation, whereas other teachers emphasized the physical exercises and bodily postures that became known as Haṭha yoga. The process of systematization of these techniques was carried out by the Yoga school, one of the six systems (*darśana) of Indian philosophy, and its teachings are codified in the *Yoga Sūtra* (2nd–3rd century CE) of Patañjali. According to this text, the goal of yoga is 'the cessation of mental fluctuation' (cittavṛtti nirodha), and the practical methods it uses to attain this are very similar to early Buddhist techniques of meditation based on breath control.

Yogācāra. (Skt.) The 'practice of *yoga', a major *Mahāyāna school that emerged in the 4th century CE, viewed by its founders as a corrective to epistemological and soteriological difficulties inherent in later *Madhyamaka. The school is also known as *Vijñānavāda ('the Way of Consciousness'), alluding to its epistemological interests. The term *citta-mātra ('mere mind') is also sometimes incorrectly applied to it through the influence of Tibetan doxological traditions.

The origins of the Yogācāra school are shrouded in mystery though recent research suggests that it had definite links with the Gandhāra school of the *Sarvāstivāda—also known as *Sautrāntika or *Mūla-sarvāstivāda—which did not accept the authority and theories of the **Vibhāṣā* literature produced by the Kashmiri branch of the Sarvāstivāda. The founders of the school were *Maitreyanātha, *Asaṅga and *Vasubandhu, each contributing innovative nuances, with important additions from later commentators such as *Sthiramati and *Dharmapāla. Yogācāra flourished in India until the 8th century CE when it gradually merged with a modified form of *Svātantrika-Madhyamaka, thus combining the best elements of the two schools. Other later members of the Yogācāra school, such as *Dignāga and *Dharmakīrti, also made seminal contributions to the development of Buddhist logic (*pramāṇa). Yogācāra was transmitted to China through the efforts of *Paramārtha and *Hsüan-tsang, the latter being responsible for the introduction of Dharmapāla's idealistic and ontological interpretation through his teacher *Śīlabhadra. Yogācāra was also introduced and widely studied in Tibet but its accurate understanding there has been seriously compromised by the predominant Madhyamaka bias reflected in Tibetan traditional doxology.

The key scriptural basis for Yogācāra theories is the **Sandhi-nirmocana Sūtra* with earlier adumbrations in the **Daśabhūmika Sūtra* and the **Avataṃsaka Sūtra*. Sometimes the **Laṅkāvatāra Sūtra* is erroneously cited as a Yogācāra work but this late syncretic text, which combines *tathāgata-garbha concepts with elements of Yogācāra theory, was unknown to the founders of Yogācāra and thus should not be counted among the school's authentic works. Works variously attributed to Maitreyanātha, Asaṅga and Vasubandhu include the **Abhidharma-samuccaya*, the **Dharma-dharmatā-vibhāga*, the **Madhyānta-vibhāga-kārikā*, the **Mahāyāna-saṃgraha*, the **Mahāyāna-sūtrālaṃkāra*, the **Tri-svabhāva-nirdeśa*, the **Triṃśikā*, the **Viṃśatikā* and the encyclopaedic **Yogācārabhūmi Śāstra*.

Yogācāra thought arguably represents the most complex and sophisticated philosophy developed by Indian Buddhism but this richness has led to considerable difficulties in accurately evaluating its doctrines. Through a neglect of research based on the authentic Yogācāra texts combined with the distortions found in east Asian and Tibetan secondary literature, itself largely based on late Yogācāra trends, it was common to see Yogācāra as a Buddhist form of idealism but this understanding is gradually being revealed as misleading and inadequate by a new generation of scholars who suggest that early Yogācāra is actually an epistemological rather than ontological system.

As its name suggests, the central Yogācāra doctrines and theories derive particularly from meditational experiences and concern two key interconnected themes: the nature of the mind and the nature of experience. To account for all aspects and functions of the mind, eight aspects or modes of consciousness were distinguished—the *ālaya- vijñāna, the afflicted mind (kliṣṭa-manas) and the traditional six perceptual consciousnesses of sight, hearing, smell, taste, touch and thought. As long as unenlightened beings undergo rebirth in *saṃsāra, a stream of imprints (*bīja or *vāsanā) derived from experiences and actions are implanted in their minds, lying dormant until suitable circumstances occur for them to manifest their content in the form of the delusory dualism of the experiencing subject and experienced objects.

The aspect of the mind involved in this process is the substratum or storehouse consciousness (ālaya- vijñāna) which, through the effects of these imprints, also gives rise sequentially to further modes of subjective consciousness as well as their perceived contents. These are the afflicted mind (kliṣṭa-manas) which generates the idea of a self (*ātman) through its indistinct awareness of the ālaya-vijñāna and taints the remaining six consciousness with cognitive and emotional distortions that predispose a being to the creation of further imprints. In this way, all unenlightened experience is fabricated by the various aspects of the mind as it generates a false self and projects delusory objects onto reality. The ontological nature of reality is not discussed although it is clear from early Yogācāra texts that the bare objects (vastu-mātra) which comprise reality were thought to exist independently of the individual, though they are never directly experienced by the dualistic minds of the unenlightened. The manner in which beings experience the world is further described in detail by means of the innovative Yogācāra doctrine of the 'three natures' (*tri- svabhāva) the imagined (*parikalpita), the dependent (*paratantra) and the consummate natures (*pariniṣpanna).

When all the implanted unwholesome predispositions have been eliminated from an individual's ālaya-vijñāna and the false dualism of a perceiving self and perceived objects utterly abandoned at the moment of enlightenment or *nirvāṇa, a radical transformation occurs in which various aspects of the mind change into the Buddha Awarenesses (buddha-jñāna)—the ālaya-vijñāna becomes the Mirror-like Awareness, the afflicted mind becomes the Awareness of Sameness, thought consciousness (mano-vijñāna) become Investigating Awareness and the remaining perceptual consciousnesses become the Accomplishing Activity Awareness. Each of these Awarenesses is a facet of enlightenment and, unlike the ordinary consciousnesses, are non-conceptualizing and non-dual, able to experience reality directly and authentically.

The Yogācāra school also made major contributions to Buddhology by refining the theories concerning the 'three bodies' (*trikāya) and the Five Awarenesses; to soteriology through the Five Stage Path (*see* MĀRGA); and to hermeneutics through the doctrine of *three turnings of the wheel.

Yogācārabhūmi Śāstra. A huge encyclopedic *Yogācāra work, attributed variously to *Maitreya or *Asaṅga but in all probability the work of several writers who compiled it around the 5th century CE. The complete work comprises five major sections embracing seventeen levels (bāhu-bhūmi), which covers the entire range of mental and spiritual levels in *Buddhism according to the *Mahāyāna. The five divisions are (1) the compendium of definitions (viniścaya-saṃgrahaṇī); (2) the compendium of exegesis (vivaraṇa-saṃgrahaṇī); (3) the compendium of synonyms (paryāya-saṃgrahaṇī); (4) the compendium of bases (vastu-saṃgrahaṇī); and (5) the compendium of the *Vinaya (vinaya-saṃgrahaṇī). Most of the bāhu-bhūmi section—which includes such seminal works as the **Bodhisattvabhūmi* and the *Śrāvakabhūmi*—survives in *Sanskrit but little survives from the other parts, although the entire work is available both in Chinese and Tibetan translation.

yoga-tantra (Skt.). The third class of *tantra according to the late standardized classificatory scheme, although during the 8th century CE, tantras later categorized as *anuttara-yoga-tantra were also included in this class. In contrast to *kriyā-tantra type of practice, yoga-tantra is traditionally said to emphasize internal meditational and yogic practices. Few tantras belonging to this class have survived but most noteworthy is the large **Sarva-tathāgata-tattva-saṃgraha* which is regarded as the root tantra of the yoga-tantra class.

yogin (Skt.). A practitioner of *yoga, a female practitioner being known as a *yoginī. The term is commonly applied to practitioners of *tantric *Buddhism who engage in intensive meditational and ritual practice for long periods of time in caves or other isolated sites. The *Six Yogas of *Nāropa provide an example of these practices.

yoginī. A female practitioner of *yoga. *See also* YOGIN.

yon-mchod. A Tibetan term for the 'patron–priest' relationship which developed between rulers and the Buddhist *Saṃgha.

Yōsai. *See* EISAI.

Yuan-chüeh ching. A *Mahāyāna Buddhist scripture whose short Chinese title translates as 'The Sūtra of Perfect Enlightenment'. This scripture probably originated in *China itself around the beginning of the 8th century. In concise language, this scripture conveys philosophical and practical concerns rooted in the Chinese Buddhist currents of the day: *Ch'an, *T'ien-t'ai, and *Hua-yen thought, along with instructions in *meditation, monastic ritual, and confession (*pāpa-deśanā). In the aftermath of the sudden–gradual controversy that had shaken the Ch'an establishment not long before the *sūtra's composition, the text attempts a nuanced adjudication of the two positions. Speaking from within a deep state of trance, the *Buddha, in response to questions put to him by advanced *Bodhisattvas, takes a strict *subitist position early in the work, but by the end has introduced gradualist teachings to correct an overly zealous attachment to subitist doctrine. This brief, one-fascicle text is document 842 in the *Taishō collection.

Yüan Hung-tao (1568–1610). A Chinese lay Buddhist of the Ming dynasty who is revered as one of the great systematizers of the *Pure Land tradition. One of three brothers renowned for their abilities as essayists and *Confucian literati (*see* CONFUCIANISM), he earned the highest degree in the examination system in 1592. Although not desiring official position, he did accept a turn as magistrate of Wu-hsien in Soochow in 1595, but left after a year to pursue literary and philosophical interests. He studied *Ch'an *meditation and teaching for ten years with one Li Chih. However, the death of his brother in 1600 shook him, and he left worldly pursuits again for a time (he had been working as an instructor in the imperial schools of the capital) and applied himself again to Buddhist teaching, this time turning to Pure Land doctrine. He is remembered in Chinese culture as a thinker, essayist, and poet of no mean ability, but his main fame in Buddhist circles derives from his ten-volume work, *Hsi fang ho lun* (*Colloquy on the Western* [*Pure Land*], *Taishō 1976). This is a lengthy catechetical and apologetic work that both explains the Pure Land school's teachings and practices and defends it against criticisms made of it.

Yüan-wu K'o-ch'in (1063–1135). A Chinese *Ch'an *monk known mainly as the editor of the *Blue Cliff Records* (Chin., *Pi-yen lu*; Jap., *Hekigan-roku*), a collection of *kōans first compiled by *Hsüeh-tou Ch'ung-hsien (980–1052). Hsüeh-tou had compiled the 100 cases comprising the work and added his own verse to them, while Yüan-wu added an introduction and commentaries to the case and Hsüeh-tou's verse to each case.

Yukti-ṣaṣtikā. 'Sixty [Verses] of Reasoning', a work by *Nāgārjuna discussing the relationship between absolute truth (*paramārtha-satya) and relative truth (*saṃvṛti-satya) in terms of the doctrine of Dependent Origination (*pratītya-samutpāda).

Yün-ch'i Chu-hung (1532–1612). A defender and reformer of Chinese *Buddhism in the Ming dynasty. In addition to the above dates the alternative dates of 1535–1615 are also found for his life. He originally led a householder's life, marrying twice (remarrying after the death of his first wife), but left to become a *monk at the age of 32 upon the death of his mother. He studied Buddhist literature and doctrine, but after arriving in Hang-chou decided to restore a dilapidated temple on Mt. Yün-ch'i where he resided for the remainder of his life. His efforts on behalf of Buddhism went in many directions. First, he defended Buddhism against the attacks of Jesuit missionaries, and launched a counter-critique of Christian beliefs and practices in a book called *Four Chapters on the Explanations of Heaven* (Chin., *T'ien shuo ssu p'ien*). Second, he fought against the popular perception of Buddhism as corrupt and the clergy as lax and overly commercial by insisting on a detailed study of and adherence to the traditional *Vinaya rules in his temple. The strict reputation of his monastery attracted hundreds of serious disciples. In addition, he conferred *precepts on the laity and insisted on compassionate practice and moral repentance. For the first, he was a leader in performing the Release of the Burning Mouths ceremony (*see* FANK YEN-K'OU) to feed hungry ghosts (*preta) and the Release of Living Beings ceremony to set free captive *animals. For the second, he recommended keeping a 'Record of Merits and Demerits', a kind of diary of one's good and bad deeds for each day as an aid to self-examination. Third, he attempted to unify Chinese Buddhism by showing the basic congruence between *Ch'an *meditation, *Pure Land practice, and doctrinal study. In this regard, he is noted as one of the propagators (but not the inventor) of the so-called 'Pure Land *kōan', in which the practitioner, while reciting the name of the Buddha *Amitābha, reflects 'Who is this who recites the Buddha's name' as a way of discovering their 'true face'. This practice is found among the quotations in Chu-hung's *Spur for Advancement through the Gate of Ch'an* (Chin., *Ch'an-kuan ts'e chin*). It is debatable whether or not he enjoyed much success in this endeavour, as many in the Ch'an camp regarded him as more of a Pure Land partisan and doubted the authenticity of his *enlightenment. Within Pure Land, he wrote a very influential commentary on the *Shorter *Sukhāvatī-vyūha Sūtra*, which provided a philosophical understanding of Pure Land doctrines regarding the nature of Amitābha Buddha, his relationship to the practitioner, the nature of the Pure Land, its relationship to the present defiled world, and how Pure Land practice works to save devotees and lead them to *rebirth in the Pure Land after death. For these accomplishments, he is listed as one of the *patriarchs of the Pure Land school in *China.

Yung-chia Hsüan-chüeh (665–713). An early *T'ang dynasty Chinese *Ch'an *monk and a direct disciple of the sixth *patriarch *Hui-neng (638–713). Almost nothing is known about him, and a work reformulating the ideas of the **Platform Sūtra of the Sixth Patriarch* is attributed to him, although his authorship is not certain.

Yün-kang caves. A site in north *China near the ancient capital city of Ta-t'ung (modern Shansi Province) where a number of images were carved in rock representing *Buddhas and *Bodhisattvas. Work began shortly after 460, as part of a revitalization of *Buddhism after the persecution in North China of 446. Work continued even after the Northern Wei rulers moved the capital to *Lo-yang in 493.

Yün-men Wen-yen (864–949). An eminent *Ch'an figure in China who lent his name to one of the '*Five Houses' of Ch'an in the late *T'ang period, and who appears in many *kōans in the collections **Gateless Gate* and **Blue Cliff Records*. He left the householder's life at an early age, and spent time in conventional monastic life before taking to the road in the search for a higher level of truth. He studied with various masters, but attained *enlightenment with one Mu-chou Tao-tsung, an eccentric disciple of the famed Ch'an master *Huang-po Hsi-yün who practised an extremely *ascetic life in the harsh mountain terrain of North China. Yün-men attained enlightenment under him when the teacher, responding to his request for teaching, threw him through the front gate and slammed it on his leg hard enough to break it. After this, he travelled south, taking up residence under the auspices of a local ruler on Mt. Yün-men near the city of Shao-chou in Kuang-tung Province; both he and the monastery that the rulers built for him took their names from this mountain. There, he taught many disciples using methods reminiscent of his own training–sharp blows, loud shouts, and paradoxical, one-word answers to questions. Using these methods, he tried to push students to see the nature of all aspects of reality and to transcend all dualities of pure and impure, enlightened and ignorant. He is perhaps most famous for answering the question 'What is the *Buddha?' with a word that indicated a stick used to clean the anus after defecation, again showing that human concepts of 'pure' and 'impure' were mere constructs not reflecting the highest truth about things.

Yūzū-nembutsu school. One of the earliest schools of *Pure Land *Buddhism in *Japan. The school was founded by *Ryōnin (1072–1132), a *monk of the *Tendai school. He tried a variety of practices, including the *nembutsu or contemplation of the *Buddha *Amitābha, but in the year 1117 he had a vision of Amitābha, who appeared before him and explained the philosophy of the yūzū-nembutsu, or 'nembutsu of perfect interpenetration' to him. The Buddha also revealed a *maṇḍala to him that was to be his object of *visualization. For several years, he kept this practice as his own, but in 1124 the deity Bishamonten appeared to him and implored him to teach this method of practice to the world. Thus, he left his quiet hermitage and went about, gathering followers and enlisting them in the practice.

The practice of the yūzū-nembutsu is based on *Kegon (Chin., *Hua-yen) philosophy, which holds that all individual phenomena in the universe are interconnected and affect each other constantly. On this basis, Ryōnin asserted that a single person's recitation of the Buddha's name affected all other beings, rather than being a practice that aided only the practitioner. When two people recited the Buddha's name, then their efforts were interconnected, and the power to affect others multiplied. This concept had two effects in terms of the practice. First, it alleviated the need for the kind of strenuous, constant practice that was often given as the norm. If many people chanted the name, then the power of their practice combined and all benefited from the sum of their combined practice; this was opposed to the need for each individual to put forth heroic effort on their own behalf. Followers of Ryōnin could take on the burden of as few as 100 recitations of the name per day, rather than the 70,000 or more for which prior Chinese and Japanese masters were noted. Second, it gave a new twist to the idea of *tariki, or 'other-power', which had previously been understood as the power of the Buddha Amitābha to bring about the *rebirth of the individual. Under the yūzū-nembutsu, 'other-power' also included the cumulative power of all practitioners in addition to the power of the Buddha's vows.

Ryōnin was quite successful in enrolling members in a register, and possession of this book became the prerogative of the leader after his death. However, succession to the leadership lapsed after six generations, and the school went into a decline. The last abbot, Ryōchin, died in 1182 without a successor, and asked that the register be entrusted to the *kami Hachiman, who would select the next leader. One hundred and forty years later, in 1321, Hachiman appeared to a prominent member named Hōmyō (1279–1349) in a dream, and named him the new leader. When Hōmyō reported this dream the next morning to the priests of the Hachiman shrine, they surrendered the register to him and he became the seventh abbot. Since Hōmyō had once been a *Shingon monk, he was able to establish a special relationship between his school and the Shingon headquarters on Mt. *Kōya, which led to the incorporation of the yūzū-nembutsu into Shingon practice. The school went into another decline after Hōmyō, especially because of the popularity of the newer Pure Land schools, the *Jōdo Shū and the *Jōdo Shinshū. It experienced another revival under the leadership of Daitsū (1649–1716). The school, though always small compared to other Japanese Pure Land schools, remains viable today.

Z

zabuton (Jap.). A square mat, about a yard or metre square, used for seated *meditation in east Asian Buddhist practice. The zabuton provides cushioning for the knees, while the *zafu placed upon it provides a cushion for the buttocks.

zafu (Jap.). A small, round, or crescent-shaped cushion used in seated *meditation, usually placed on top of a mat known as a *zabuton.

Zahor. *See* SAHOR.

zazen. Japanese term meaning literally, 'to sit in *Zen'. In Japanese Zen, this refers to the practice of seated *meditation.

zedi (Burm.). A solid, bell-shaped, *paya.

Zen. The Japanese pronunciation of the Chinese word '*Ch'an', meaning '*meditation'. This word stands not only for a particular religious technique, but is an umbrella term for the various schools of *Zen in *Japan: *Rinzai, *Sōtō, *Ōbaku, and *Fuke. Besides specific reference to the above-named Japanese schools (and their American and European derivatives), the term is also used to cover the entire tradition from which Japanese Zen arose in *China, and all of the other derivatives of Ch'an in other countries such as *Sŏn in *Korea.

zendō (Jap.). A hall in a *Zen monastery for the practice of *zazen, or seated *meditation.

zengyō (Jap.). This term can have several meanings, depending upon the Chinese characters with which it is written. **1.** 'Gradual teachings' in several different classificatory schemes, such as 'sudden teaching' versus 'gradual teaching', or as the 'gradual method' in the *T'ien-t'ai/*Tendai schema of doctrinal classification (Chin., p'an-chiao). **2.** 'Zen practice', or the practice of *meditation and *kōan study in the *Zen school. **3.** 'Good opportunity'; as a contraction of 'zengyō hōben', it indicates a good opportunity for the practice of skilful means (*upāya-kauśalya), a chance to present Buddhist teaching to someone or to spur their practice according to their capacities and inclinations.

Zenrin-kushū. A text of Japanese *Zen, the title of which means 'Anthology of Passages from the Forests of Zen'. This two-fascicle work was first assembled in the medieval period by the *Rinzai *monk Tōyō Eichi (1428–1504), but did not see publication until the 1680s. It consists of a collection of quotations from Buddhist scriptures, Zen literature such as recorded sayings of past masters, Confucian (*see* CONFUCIANISM), Taoist (*see* TAOISM), and other sources. Altogether, it contains some 5,000 passages, and was probably used as a study aid.

zhen-tong. *See* EXTRINSIC EMPTINESS.

Zimmè Paññāsa. Burmese term meaning 'Chiengmai Fifty'. *See* PAÑÑĀSA JĀTAKA.

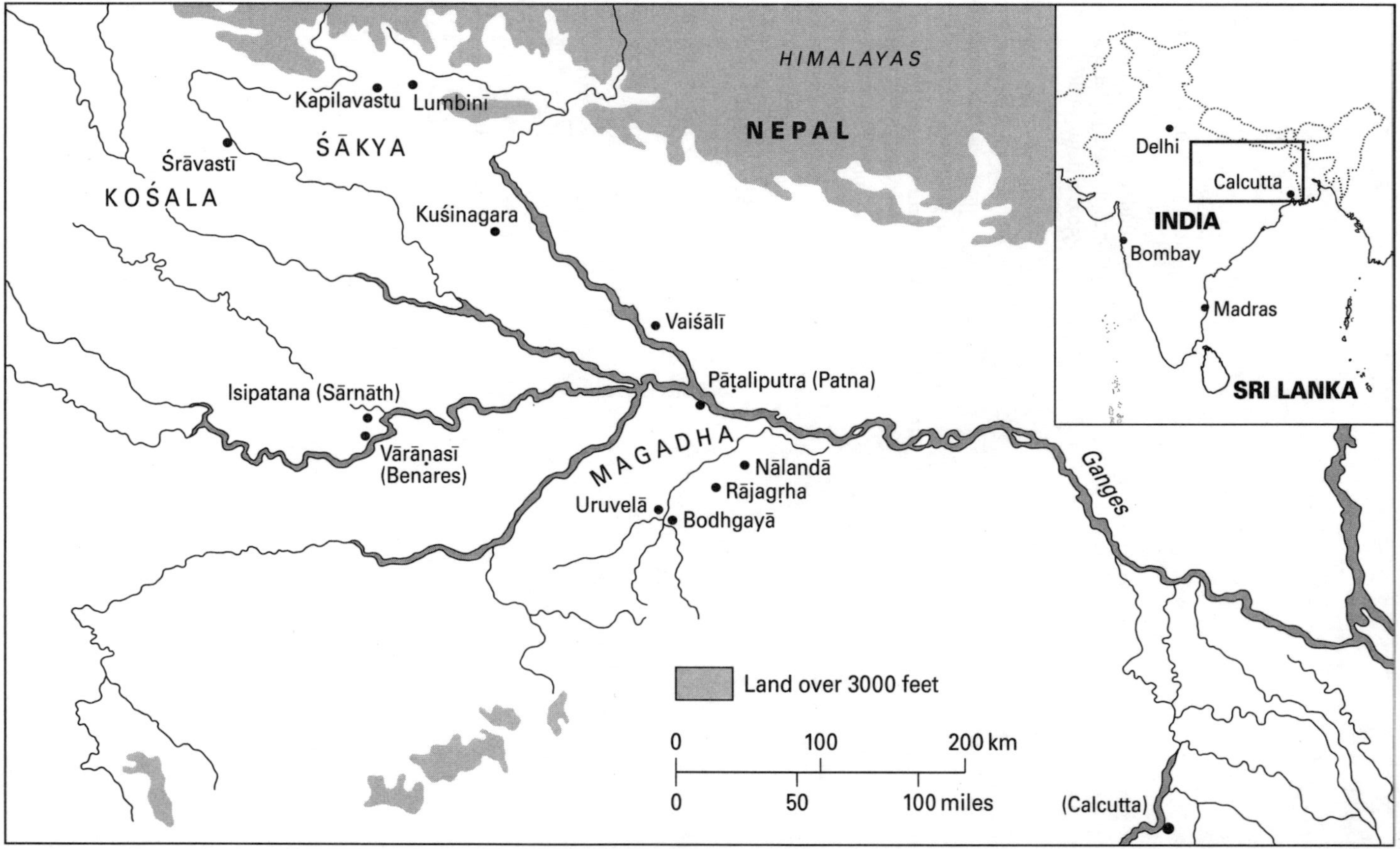

Appendix I: Map of India and the region where the Buddha taught and lived

Appendix II: Map showing Theravāda Buddhism in Asia

Appendix III: Map showing Mahāyāna Buddhism in Asia

Appendix IV: Pronunciation Guide

In the course of its long history Buddhism has spread to every part of Asia. One result of this is that Buddhist concepts have come to be expressed in languages as diverse as Sanskrit, Pāli, Tibetan, Chinese, Mongolian, Japanese, Korean, Thai, Sinhala, Vietnamese and many more. Since this dictionary is intended to reflect the cultural diversity of Buddhism it contains terms drawn from all the major Buddhist languages. Following the scholarly convention, however, the primary language used is Sanskrit. Sanskrit served as the *lingua franca* of ancient India, just as Latin did in medieval Europe, and most of the translations made into other Asian languages were based on Sanskrit originals. The most important scriptures of Mahāyāna Buddhism were composed in a variant of Sanskrit known as Buddhist Hybrid Sanskrit, while the earliest Buddhist scriptures are preserved in Pāli, a literary language derived from Sanskrit.

One feature of Asian languages like Sanskrit is that their alphabets are larger than those of Western languages. In order to represent the additional characters diacritical marks have to be added to the Roman letters. These typically take the form of symbols such as dots and dashes placed above or below certain characters. These symbols do not affect the alphabetical order of entries in the present work, but do affect pronunciation in various ways. As far as Sanskrit is concerned, the most important of these is that a macron above a vowel serves to lengthen it, roughly doubling the length of the sound. Thus the character 'ā' is pronounced as in 'far' rather than 'fat'. With respect to consonants, an underdot (ṭ ḍ etc) indicates that the tongue touches the roof of the mouth when pronouncing these letters, giving the characteristic sound of English when spoken with an Indian accent. For the most part the other marks do not affect pronunciation enough to be of any special concern. A summary of the most important points in connection with the pronunciation of Sanskrit and Pāli terms is shown below:

ā	pronounced as in far
ī	pronounced as in seek
ū	pronounced as in brute
ṛ	pronounced as in risk
ñ	pronounced as in Spanish mañana
ś or ṣ	pronounced sh, as in shoe
ṅ/ṃ	pronounced with a nasal sound as in ring
c	pronounced ch, as in church

More detailed guidance on the pronunciation of Sankrit can be found in chapter 1 of Michael Coulson *Sanskrit: An Introduction to the Classical Language* (Teach Yourself Books, 1992).

Chinese

The transcription and pronunciation of Chinese poses special problems due to the fact that there are two systems in use for transcribing it, namely Wade-Giles and Pinyin. The latter was introduced in 1979 by the People's Republic of China as its official system, but the earlier Wade-Giles method of transcription is still in widespread use, and is the form used in the present work. Pinyin has gained acceptance among specialists, but students are more likely to encounter Wade-Giles in introductory and popular literature. A helpful guide on converting from Wade-Giles to Pinyin can be found in A. C. Graham, *Disputers of the Tao* (La Salle, Ill.: Open Court, 1989) 441–4. Neither Pinyin or Wade-Giles, however, provides a way of representing the sounds of spoken Chinese with any accuracy since the same characters in Chinese may be pronounced in one of four different tones.

Japanese

The transcription of Japanese is relatively unproblematic, and this book uses the widely adopted Hepburn system. The characters used correspond closely to their Roman equivalents, with the exception of the long vowels ō and ū. As in the transliteration of Sanskrit, the macron over the letter indicates that the sound of the vowel is lengthened, thus kōan is pronounced 'koh-an', with the emphasis on the first syllable.

Tibetan

In contrast to Japanese, Tibetan orthography and pronunciation poses many complex problems. This is despite the fact that a standard system of transliteration exists that does not rely on diacritics, namely the system devised by Turrell Wylie and explained in his article 'A Standard System of Tibetan Transcription' (*Harvard Journal of Asiatic Studies*, 22 (1959), 261–7). The present work adopts this method of transliteration, but difficulties still remain. Not least among these is the fact that Tibetan words frequently contain letters that are not pronounced (this is also a feature of English, as in words such as 'through', 'ought', and so forth). Even more problematic from the point of view of alphabetization is that in Tibetan these redundant letters are often found at the start of a word: thus the term for a senior monk—lama—is in fact spelt 'blama'. A problem therefore arises as to whether the entry for 'lama' belongs under B or L. Since this dictionary is intended primarily for a general readership, the policy of using a simplified phonetic form for the spelling of Tibetan headwords has been adopted. The headword is accordingly shown in a simplified phonetic form with the correct transliteration from Tibetan given in brackets, thus: lama (Tib., blama).

Korean

The Korean system of writing is known as Hangŭl, and the present work uses the standard conventions for transcription into English. This method uses the standard Roman alphabet pronounced for the most part as in English, with the exception of the two vowels ŏ (pronounced as in cot) and ŭ (pronounced as in burn).

Appendix V: Guide to Buddhist Scriptures*

There are three main collections of canonical scriptures preserved in different languages. These are the Pāli Canon, the Tibetan Canon, and the Chinese Canon.

The Pāli Canon

Preserved in the Pāli language, this is the canon of the Theravāda school, the only sect of the Hīnayāna to survive down to modern times. Although other early schools had their own canons, the Pāli Canon is unique in being the only set of scriptures to be preserved in its entirety. The Pāli Canon is also known as the Tipiṭaka ('three baskets') because of its three divisions into Vinaya (monastic law), Sutta (the Buddha's discourses), and Abhidhamma (scholastic treatises).

I. Vinaya Piṭaka

- A. Suttavibhaṅga. The rules of the Saṃgha or monastic code (Pāṭimokkha)
  1. Mahāvibhaṅga. 227 rules for monks
  2. Bhikkhunīvibhaṅga. 311 rules for nuns
- B. Khandhaka. Matters concerning the organization of the Saṃgha.
  1. Mahāvagga. Regulations for ordination, retreats, clothing, food, etc.
  2. Cullavagga. Procedural matters and the history of the first two councils.
- C. The Parivāra. An appendix summarizing the rules.

II. Sutta Piṭaka

- A. Dīgha Nikāya. 34 long discourses.
- B. Majjhima Nikāya. 154 medium length discourses.
- C. Saṃyutta Nikāya. 56 groups of discourses arranged by subject matter.
- D. Aṅguttara Nikāya. Discourses grouped by incremental lists of subjects.
- E. Khuddaka Nikāya. A collection of fifteen minor texts.
  1. *Khuddakapāṭha*. Short suttas.
  2. *Dhammapada*. Popular collection of 423 verses on ethics.
  3. *Udāna*. 80 solemn utterances of the Buddha.
  4. *Itivuttaka*. 112 short suttas.
  5. *Sutta-nipāta*. 70 suttas in verse.
  6. *Vimānavatthu*. Accounts of the heavenly rebirths of the virtuous.
  7. *Petavatthu*. 51 poems about rebirth as a hungry ghost.
  8. *Theragāthā*. Verses by 264 male Elders.
  9. *Therīgāthā*. Verses by around 100 female Elders.
  10. *Jātaka*. 547 stories about the Buddha's previous lives.
  11. *Niddesa*. Commentary on portions of the *Sutta-nipāta*.
  12. *Paṭisambhidāmagga*. Abhidharma-style analysis of points of doctrine.
  13. *Apadāna*. Verse stories about the present and former lives of monks and nuns.
  14. *Buddhavaṃsa*. An acount of the 24 previous Buddhas.
  15. *Cariyāpiṭaka*. Jātaka stories about the virtues of Bodhisattvas.

III. Abhidhamma Piṭaka

- A. *Dhammasaṅganī*. Psychological analysis of ethics.
- B. *Vibhaṅga*. Analysis of various doctrinal categories.
- C. *Dhātukathā*. Classification of points of doctrine.
- D. *Puggalapaññatti*. Classification of human types.
- E. *Kathāvatthu*. Doctrinal disputes among the sects.
- F. *Yamaka*. Pairs of questions about basic categories of teachings.
- G. *Paṭṭhāna*. Causation analysed into 24 groups.

*Adapted from Charles S. Prebish, *Historical Dictionary of Buddhism* (Scarecrow Press, 1993).

The Chinese Canon

Various editions of the Chinese Canon have been produced. The first complete edition was printed in 983 CE and the standard modern edition known as the Taishō Shinshū Daizōkyō was published in Tokyo between 1924 and 1929. The latter consists of 55 volumes containing 2,184 texts, together with 45 supplementary volumes.

I. Āgama section: volumes 1–2, 151 texts. Equivalent to the first four Pāli Nikāyas and part of the fifth.

II. Story Section: volumes 3–4, 68 Jātaka texts.

III. Prajñā-pāramitā section: volumes 5–8, 42 texts of Perfection of Insight literature.

IV. Saddharmapuṇḍarīka section: volume 9, 16 texts relating to the *Lotus Sūtra*.

V. Avataṃsaka section. Volume 9–10, 31 texts relating to the *Avataṃsaka Sūtra*.

VI. Ratnakūṭa section. Volumes 11–12, 64 early Mahāyāna texts.

VII. Mahāparinirvāṇa section. Volume 12, 23 texts concerning the *Nirvāṇa Sūtra*.

VIII. Great Assembly section. Volume 13, 28 texts containing early sūtras, beginning with the *Great Assembly Sūtra*.

IX. Sūtra-Collection Section: Volumes 14–17, 423 texts. Collection of miscellaneous (primarily Mahāyāna) sūtras.

X. Tantra Section: Volumes 18–21, 572 texts. Contains Vajrayāna Sūtras and tantric materials.

XI. Vinaya Section: Volumes 22–4, 86 texts. Contain the disciplinary texts of a variety of Hīnayāna schools as well as texts on Bodhisattva discipline.

XII. Commentaries on Sūtras: Volumes 24–6, 31 texts. Commentaries by Indian authors on the Āgamas and Mahāyāna Sūtras.

XIII. Abhidharma Section: Volumes 26–9, 28 texts. Translations of Sarvāstivādin, Dharmaguptaka, and Sautrāntika Abhidharma texts.

XIV. Madhyamaka Section: Volume 30, 15 texts. Texts on Madhyamaka thought.

XV. Yogācāra Section: Volumes 30–1, 49 texts. Texts on Yogācāra thought.

XVI. Collection of Treatises: Volume 32, 65 texts. Miscellaneous works on logic and other matters.

XVII. Commentaries on the Sūtras: Volumes 33–39. Commentaries by Chinese authors.

XVIII. Commentaries on the Vinaya: Volume 40. Commentaries by Chinese authors.

XIX. Commentaries on the Śāstras: Volumes 40–4. Commentaries by Chinese authors.

XX. Chinese Sectarian Writings: Volumes 44–8.

XXI. History and Biography: Volumes 49–52, 95 texts.

XXII. Encyclopedias and Dictionaries: Volumes 53–4, 16 texts.

XXIII. Non-Buddhist Doctrines: Volumes 54, 8 texts. Contains materials on Hinduism, Manichean, and Nestorian Christian writing.

XXIV. Catalogues: Volume 55, 40 texts. Catalogues of the Chinese Canon, starting with that of Seng-yu (published 515 CE).

The Tibetan Canon

The Tibetan Canon consists of two parts: (1) the Kanjur (Tib., bstan 'gyur) being the Word of the Buddha, and (2) the Tenjur (Tib., bstan-'gyur) or Commentaries. Because this latter collection contains work attributed to individuals other than the Buddha, it is considered only semi-canonical. The first printing of the Kanjur took place in Peking, being completed in 1411. The first native Tibetan edition of the canon was at Narthang, (Tib., snarthang) with the Kanjur appearing in 1731 and the Tenjur in 1742.

I. **Kanjur:** The Word of the Buddha; 98 volumes according to the Narthang edition.
   A. Vinaya: 13 volumes.
   B. Prajñā-pāramitā: 21 volumes.
   C. Avataṃsaka: 6 volumes.
   D. Ratnakūṭa: 6 volumes.
   E. Sūtra: 30 volumes. 270 texts, some three-quarters are Mahāyāna, one quarter Hīnayāna.
   F. Tantra: 22 volumes. Contains more than 300 texts.

II. **Tenjur:** The Commentaries; 224 volumes (3,626 texts) according to the Peking edition.
   A. Stotras (hymns of praise): 1 volume; 64 texts.
   B. Commentaries on the Tantras: 86 volumes; 3,055 texts.
   C. Commentaries on the Sūtras: 137 volumes; 567 texts.
      1. Prajñā-pāramitā Commentaries, 16 volumes.
      2. Madhyamaka Treatises, 17 volumes.
      3. Yogācāra Treatises, 29 volumes.
      4. Abhidharma, 8 volumes.
      5. Miscellaneous Texts, 4 volumes.
      6. Vinaya Commentaries, 16 volumes.
      7. Tales and Dramas, 4 volumes.
      8. Technical Treatises: 43 volumes.
         a. Logic: 21 volumes.
         b. Grammar: 1 volume.
         c. Lexicography and Poetics: 1 volume.
         d. Medicine: 5 volumes.
         e. Chemistry and Miscellaneous: 1 volume.
         f. Supplements: 14 volumes.

Appendix VI: Chronology

*c.*1500–1000 BCE	Vedic period in India
*c.*1000–800 BCE	Composition of Brāhmaṇas
*c.*800–500 BCE	Composition of major Upaniṣads
*c.*500 BCE	Life of Lao-tsu
552–479 BCE	Life of Confucius
*c.*485–405 BCE	Life of the Buddha (Śākyamuni)
*c.*465–413 BCE	Reign of Bimbisāra
*c.*405 BCE	Council of Rājagṛha
327–325 BCE	Alexander the Great in India
322–298 BCE	Reign of Candragupta Maurya
303 BCE	Megasthenese at court of Candragupta
*c.*300 BCE	Council of Vaiśālī
*c.*284 BCE	Council of Pāṭaliputra I
*c.*272–231 BCE	Reign of Aśoka
*c.*250 BCE	Council of Pāṭaliputra II
247 BCE	Mahinda introduces Buddhism to Sri Lanka
200 BCE	Beginnings of Mahāyāna Buddhism. Composition of Prajñā-pāramitā texts begins.
*c.*200–000 BCE	Stūpa construction at Sāñcī
148 BCE	An Shih-kao arrives in China and establishes first translation bureau
200 BCE–200 CE	Invasion of India by Śuṅgas and Yavanas (187–30 BCE), Śakas and Pahlavas (100–75 BCE), and Kuṣāṇas (1st–2nd century CE)
101–77 BCE	Reign of Duṭṭhagāmaṇi Abhaya in Sri Lanka; Buddhism becomes state religion
*c.*100–000 BCE	Abhayagiri monastery founded in Sri Lanka
29–17 BCE	Pāli Canon written down in Sri Lanka during reign of Vaṭṭagāmaṇi Abhaya
*c.*100–000 CE	Buddhism enters central Asia and China. Composition of *Lotus Sūtra* and other early Mahāyāna texts
*c.*100–200 CE	Founding of Nālandā
*c.*100–200 CE	Council of Kaniṣka
150–250 CE	Life of Nāgārjuna
*c.*200 CE	Buddhism transmitted to Burma, Cambodia, Laos, Indonesia
*c.*200–300 CE	Buddhism arrives in Vietnam
*c.*300 CE	Life of Asaṅga and Vasubandhu
334–416 CE	Life of Hui-yüan
343–413 CE	Life of Kumārajīva
350–650 CE	Gupta dynasty in India, Buddhist philosophy and art flourish
372 CE	Buddhism transmitted to Korea
399–414 CE	Fa-hsien travels to India
*c.*400–500 CE	Life of Buddhaghoṣa
499–569 CE	Life of Paramārtha
*c.*500–600 CE	Composition of tantric texts in India
*c.*500 CE	Development of Hua-yen, T'ien-t'ai, Ch'an, and Pure Land schools in China
520 CE	Bodhidharma arrives in China
538–97 CE	Life of Chih-i; development of T'ien-t'ai school
552 CE	Buddhism enters Japan from Korea
572–621 CE	Prince Shotoku sponsors Buddhism in Japan
581–618 CE	Chinese Sui dynasty
*c.*600 CE	first diffusion of Buddhism in Tibet
*c.*600 CE	Life of Dharmakīrti; flourishing of logic and epistemology
617–86 CE	Life of Wŏnhyo; foundation of 'unitive Buddhism' in Korea
618–50 CE	Life of Songtsen Gampo; establishment of Buddhism in Tibet.
618–907 CE	Chinese T'ang dynasty; golden age of Buddhism in China

625–702 CE	Life of Ŭisang; introduction of Hwaŏm (Hua-yen) into Korea
629–45 CE	Hsüan-tsang travels to India
638–713 CE	Life of Hui-neng; Northern–Southern schools controversy
643–712 CE	Life of Fa-tsang; consolidation of Hua-yen school
650–950 CE	Pala dynasty in India
668–918 CE	Unified Silla Period in Korea; Buddhism flourishes
671–95 CE	I-ching travels to India
*c.*700 CE	Life of Padmasambhava
*c.*700 CE	Northern–Southern Schools controversy in Japan
*c.*700 CE	Esoteric school (Chen-yen tsung) develops in China
*c.*700–800 CE	Construction of Borobudur
*c.*700–1100 CE	Pala dynasty; Mahāyāna and tantric Buddhism flourish; consolidation of school of logic and epistemology (pramāṇa)
710–94 CE	Nara period in Japan; Six Schools of Nara Buddhism
742 CE	Council of Lhasa
767 CE	Construction of Samyé monastery in Tibet
767–822 CE	Life of Saichō; founding of Tendai school
774–835 CE	Life of Kūkai; founding of Shingon school
794–1185 CE	Heian period in Japan
*c.*800 CE	Founding of Vikramaśīla monastery
836–42 CE	Reign of Lang Darma and suppression of Buddhism in Tibet
845 CE	Persecution of Buddhism in China
960–1279 CE	Sung dynasty in China
978–1392 CE	Koryŏ period in Korea
983 CE	First printing of Chinese Buddhist canon (Szechuan edition)
1012–97 CE	Life of Marpa and origins of Kagyü order
1016–1100 CE	Life of Nāropa
1040–77 CE	King Anawrahtā unifies Burma and gives allegiance to Theravāda Buddhism
1040–1123 CE	Life of Milarepa
1042 CE	Atīśa arrives in Tibet; beginning of second diffusion of Buddhism
1055–1101 CE	Life of Ŭich'ŏn
1073 CE	Sakya order of Tibetan Buddhism founded
1079–1153 CE	Life of Gampopa
*c.*1100 CE	Construction of Angkor Wat
1133–1212 CE	Life of Hōnen, founding of Jōdo-shu school
1141–1215 CE	Life of Eisai; transmission of Rinzai Zen to Japan
1158–1210 CE	Life of Chinul; Chogye order founded; development of Sŏn in Korea
1173–1262 CE	Life of Shinran; founding of Jōdo-shinshū in Japan
1185–1392 CE	Kamakura Period in Japan
1197 CE	Nālandā University sacked by Mahmud Ghorī
*c.*1200 CE	Buddhism disappears from north India. Traces linger in south.
*c.*1200 CE	Printing of Tripiṭaka Koreana
1200–53 CE	Life of Dōgen; Sōtō Zen established in Japan
1222–82 CE	Life of Nichiren
1239–89 CE	Life of Ippen; foundation of Jishū school
1244 CE	Sakya Paṇḍita converts Mongols to Buddhism
*c.*1260 CE	Theravāda declared state religion of kingdom of Sukhothai (Thailand)
1290–1364 CE	Life of Butön; compilation of Tibetan canon.
1357–1419 CE	Life of Tsongkhapa; Gelukpa order founded in Tibet
1360 CE	Theravāda becomes state religion of Thailand
1368–1644 CE	Ming dynasty in China
1392–1909 CE	Ch'osŏn period in Korea, Buddhism suppressed
1411 CE	Tibetan Kanjur printed in China
1578 CE	Office of Dalai Lama instituted by Mongols
1617–82 CE	Life of Dalai Lama V and beginning of rule of Tibet by Dalai Lamas
1644–94 CE	Life of Bashō; Buddhism influence on haiku and the arts in Japan

*c.*1700 CE	Beginning of colonial period and Western domination of south and south-east Asia
1749 CE	Mongolian Buddhist canon translated from Tibetan
*c.*1800 CE	Beginning of the academic study of Buddhism by Western scholars
1823 CE	Royal Asiatic Society founded
1851–1868 CE	Reign of Rama IV in Thailand; reform of Thai Saṃgha
1853 CE	First Buddhist temple founded in USA, in San Francisco.
1868–1912 CE	Meiji period in Japan; Buddhism suppressed in favour of Shintō
1870–1945 CE	Life of Nishida Kitarō, founder of Kyoto school
1875 CE	Theosophical Society founded
1879 CE	Publication of the *The Light of Asia* by Sir Edwin Arnold
1881 CE	Pali Text Society founded in England by T. W. Rhys Davids
1891 CE	Mahabodhi Society founded by Anagārika Dharmapāla
1891–1956 CE	Life of B. Ambedkar; conversion of former Untouchables in India
1899 CE	Buddhist Churches of America founded
1924 CE	The Buddhist Society founded in London
1924 CE	Wŏn Buddhism founded
1924–9 CE	Compilation of Chinese canon (*Taishō Shinshū Daizōkyō*) in Japan
1937 CE	Nichiren Shōshū Sōkagakkai formally established
1938 CE	Risshō Koseikai founded
1950 CE	People's Liberation Army enters Tibet
1950 CE	World Fellowship of Buddhists founded
1954–6 CE	Council of Rangoon
1959 CE	Dalai Lama XIV flees to India; persecution of Buddhism in Tibet by Chinese
1967 CE	Friends of the Western Buddhist Order founded
1970 CE	Development of Engaged Buddhism
1973 CE	Vajradhatu Foundation founded
1976 CE	International Association of Buddhist Studies founded
1989 CE	International Network of Engaged Buddhists founded
1995 CE	UK Association of Buddhist Studies (UKABS) founded
2001 CE	Destruction of standing Buddha statues at Bāmiyān by Taliban regime